THE OXFORD HANDBOOK OF

GENDER AND CONFLICT

THE OXFORD HANDBOOK OF

GENDER AND CONFLICT

Edited by

FIONNUALA NÍ AOLÁIN

NAOMI CAHN

DINA FRANCESCA HAYNES

and

NAHLA VALJI

OXFORD
UNIVERSITY PRESS

OXFORD
UNIVERSITY PRESS

Oxford University Press is a department of the University of Oxford. It furthers
the University's objective of excellence in research, scholarship, and education
by publishing worldwide. Oxford is a registered trade mark of Oxford University
Press in the UK and certain other countries.

Published in the United States of America by Oxford University Press
198 Madison Avenue, New York, NY 10016, United States of America.

CIP data is on file at the Library of Congress
ISBN 978–0–19–930098–3

1 3 5 7 9 8 6 4 2

Printed by Sheridan Books, Inc., United States of America

For Christine Hyland-Horrigan
FNíA

For those fighting for gender justice
NC

For Isabella Francesca Lecona and
in memory of Sheri Rosenberg
DFH

In memory of Shirin Valji and Kulsam Lakhani
NV

Collectively the editors would like to dedicate this book to the memory of Judy El-Bushra
who passed away during the final months of this project. Her contribution to this field has
shaped the thinking and work of so many, and will continue to do so for future generations.

CONTENTS

PART II. THE SECURITY COUNCIL'S WPS AGENDA/CONTEMPORARY SURVEY

PART III. LEGAL AND POLITICAL ELEMENTS

PART IV. CONFLICT AND POST-CONFLICT SPACE

PART V. CASE STUDIES

Foreword I

SEVENTEEN years after the United Nation's Security Council linked gender equality and the maintenance of international peace and security, men still overwhelmingly dominate the halls of politics, the composition of peace tables, the decision-making positions of governance institutions in most nations across the world, and even the staffing tables of regional and international organizations, including the United Nations itself. All forms of violence against women are still met with unacceptable levels of neglect and impunity. Funding for women's needs and priorities in the aftermath of conflict, and for the thankless work of community-based women's organizations that prevent violence and build peace and reconciliation, remains grossly inadequate.

Yet, the world has made progress in all those areas over the last few years. This progress can be maddeningly slow, and is often met with backlash and resistance, but it is undeniable. If women are able to organize effectively, it is unstoppable.

Progress is noticeable not just in the increasing numbers of women winning elections, but in the type of laws and policies they adopt. It is noticeable not just in the proliferation of political declarations made in the world's capitals, but in the change in cultural attitudes toward women's rights that is taking place in villages away from those centers. It is equally noticeable in the jurisprudence emerging from national and international tribunals, and in the programs servicing hundreds of thousands of survivors today that simply did not exist two decades ago.

This *Handbook* explores the gap between those two seemingly contradictory trends: both the unprecedented steps and measurable progress; and the distance remaining to our goals and the strength of the intervening forces. Most important, this *Handbook* shows that to understand the current wave of armed conflicts, or find a way to address it effectively, it is essential to pay close attention to the role of gender, both as a category of analysis and as tool for positive change and transformation in the twenty-first century.

We face today some of the most dire and complex challenges to security and sustainable peace in modern times. It is no coincidence that this occurs alongside a resurgence of nationalisms and a pushback on women's rights. This book provides critical insights into how our existing tools, analyses, and responses have been based on incomplete and partial thinking, with chapters contributed by many of the leading academics on gender and conflict from multiple disciplines, alongside practitioners and policymakers. It is only by addressing inherent inequalities, and understanding gender in relation to peace and conflict, that we will deliver the responses needed for the challenges we confront.

Phumzile Mlambo-Ngcuka
UN Under-Secretary-General and Executive Director, UN Women

FOREWORD II

A *Handbook of Gender and Conflict* is long overdue. As the Cold War was drawing to a close, women activists campaigned and lobbied for recognition of the gendered harms suffered by women in conflict and more broadly of the role that gender plays in people's experiences and understanding of armed conflict and its aftermath. This activism, alongside the publicity given to the widespread and systematic atrocities in Bosnia-Herzegovina, Somalia, Rwanda, and Haiti in the first years of the 1990s, generated greater awareness of the occurrence of gender-based and sexual violence in conflict. Significant changes in international institutional practice and procedures, both legal and political, followed. There has also been an exponential growth in cross-disciplinary work on the gendered nature of conflict, and its manifestations and consequences. However, this literature has until now remained largely disjointed, located in the academic scholarship of different disciplines, in NGO "gray literature," in UN documentation, and in policy briefs and guidelines. The editors thus had a wealth of information and material upon which they could draw in putting together the *Handbook*. In favoring inclusivity, they have brought together leading voices from across activism, international institutions, and academia with those from within conflict-affected areas to provide a holistic and critical account of the diverse ways in which gender constructs our knowledge of conflict and, correspondingly, how conflict disrupts and reconfigures gender.

The book encompasses multiple issues relating to gender and conflict, including but not limited to theory and practice; historical developments and contemporary (and future) challenges; "insider" and "outsider" case study accounts; seeking peace during conflict; post-conflict dilemmas; and the continued vital importance of weapons regulation. The chapters both recap well-rehearsed themes and arguments and introduce new ones. Although not always explicitly addressed, to me one theme especially emerges from the chapters: the importance of maintaining human rights guarantees throughout cycles of violence. The 2015 Global Study on one aspect of this story, the UN Security Council's Women, Peace and Security Agenda that commenced with resolution 1325 (2000), emphasized that this resolution was "conceived of and lobbied for as a human rights resolution that would promote the rights of women in conflict situations" and that as such it forms "part of the international tradition of human rights." This book makes clear how important gender analysis is in keeping to the forefront the human rights of all those caught up in various ways in conflict. It will undoubtedly and deservedly take its place on university reading lists, in practitioners' offices, and in the field. It will thus help to secure gender as an indispensable topic of conflict discourse. It is a magisterial achievement for which the editors are to be both congratulated and sincerely thanked.

Christine Chinkin
Professor of International Law and
Director of the Women Peace and
Security Centre at the London School of Economics

Acknowledgments

THIS book is the product of many long-standing collaborations, relationships, and friendships. All four editors have long worked on issues of gender and conflict; all have lived in conflicted and violent societies; all have witnessed the costs of conflict on lives, infrastructures, and futures. Each of us has long been committed to the advancement of women's rights, dignity, and inclusion in the most challenging circumstances, including armed conflict. And we are committed to recognizing that gender analysis, including but not limited to the role of men and masculinities in conflict settings, is critical to enabling a more fulsome discourse on the causes and resolution of conflict.

In bringing together the diverse group of scholars and practitioners for this *Handbook*, the editors sought to represent the diversity of voices writing across the globe on issues of conflict and gender. We were acutely aware of the challenges of those "outside" conflict writing for a *Handbook* about those "inside" the conflict. As much as possible, we sought to close that gap by inviting contributions from scholars and practitioners living in, or having deep connection to, conflict sites.

This *Handbook* has taken much longer for us to complete than we expected. The competing challenges of teaching, research, policy advancement, and lives lived in multiple countries has meant that the *Handbook* has accompanied us all for many years. We are grateful to our contributors, who have recognized that the value of deep and wide inclusion in the *Handbook* would inevitably bring some delays. We are grateful to the University of Minnesota Law School for hosting a conference on the theme of "Gendering Conflict and Post-Conflict Terrains: New Challenges and Opportunities" to bring many of our contributors together in May 2012. We also thank the Transitional Justice Institute in Belfast, Northern Ireland, which hosted another conference for *Handbook* participants in November 2013, enabling us to bring a large group of scholars together and encourage dialogue and synergy across contributions.

Naomi thanks Anne Goldstein and Susan Deller Ross for that first International Women's Rights course so long ago, and Martha Fineman, for hosting the conference that, somewhat circuitously, resulted in this collaboration. Thanks to my *amazing* co-editors, and, as always, gratitude to Tony, for so much, including all of our time at the bends in the river, to my children, and to my parents, all of whom teach me the importance of fighting for justice.

Dina thanks foremost her co-editors, Fionnuala, Naomi, and Nahla, who have been consistently wise and gracious collaborators; the contributors to this *Handbook*, from whom she has learned so much. She offers particular thanks to Bert Lockwood, who got her started; Janie Chuang, who helped bring this group together; and to the late Sheri

Rosenberg, for being her wise self. Finally, she thanks Bella and Ken for their constant love and support.

Fionnuala is grateful for the privilege of working again with Dina and Naomi, as well as being able to collaborate with Nahla on this *Handbook*. She would like to particularly thank her Deans at Minnesota and Ulster, respectively, David Wippman and Paul Carmichel. She owes debts to her colleagues at the Transitional Justice Institute, including Lisa Thompson, Rory O'Connell, Monica McWilliams, and Eilish Rooney, who provided consistent support and encouragement during the completion of this *Handbook*. She notes the funding provided by the UK's Department for International Development (DfID) through the Political Settlement Research Program in enabling completion of this project through the prism of the gender research work at the Transitional Justice Institute (Belfast). She thanks Oren, Aodhtan, Noa, and Malachi Gross for their support on the home front.

Nahla thanks first her co-editors, for having infinite patience with her over these past few years as she juggled the unanticipated, and her family, parents in particular, and husband for their support over the years; as well as the investment of a few incredible mentors she has been privileged to work with. And lastly, thanks to the Peace and Security team of UN Women, who in 2015 took on, in addition to their daily work, the Secretariat of the Global Study—the fifteen-year review of women, peace, and security—and made miracles happen through pure commitment.

We particularly want to thank the research assistants and administrative staff who have enabled the completion of this work. They include Anne Dutton (Minnesota Law School) for ongoing work over the past two years to help us get to the finish line, as well as Rebecca Cassler (Minnesota Law School), Victoria Jackson (Minnesota), Elaine McCoubrey (Ulster/TJI), and Alisha Malkani, Priom Ahmed, and Beverley Mbu at George Washington University. Our thanks to Dave McBride, for, so many years ago, asking us if we might be interested in writing this *Handbook* (little did we know!). And we thank each other for our long conversations and long-lasting commitment to the *Handbook* and its role in supporting the struggles of those for whom we write.

EDITORS AND CONTRIBUTORS

Naomi Cahn is the Harold H. Greene Professor at George Washington University Law School. Her research and writing focus on gender issues in both domestic and international law. She first co-taught a Women and International Law course in 1992, at Georgetown University Law Center. With Fionnuala Ní Aoláin and Dina Francesca Haynes, she is the co-author of *On the Frontlines: Gender, War, and the Post-Conflict Process* (Oxford University Press, 2011). She has written or co-written numerous other books and articles, including *Marriage Markets: How Inequality Is Remaking the American Family* (Oxford University Press, 2014, with Professor June Carbone).

Dina Francesca Haynes is Professor of Law at New England Law, Boston, where she teaches courses related to migration, refugees, and human rights, as well as human trafficking and constitutional law. She has published numerous books, chapters, and articles, including *Deconstructing the Reconstruction: Human Rights and the Rule of Law in Postwar BiH* (Ashgate, 2008), and *On the Frontlines* (Oxford University Press, 2011, with Fionnuala Ní Aoláin and Naomi Cahn). Prior to teaching law she served as Protection Officer with the UN High Commissioner of Refugees, Human Rights Officer with the UN High Commissioner for Human Rights, and Director General of the Human Rights Department of the Organization for Security and Cooperation in Europe.

Fionnuala Ní Aoláin holds the Regents University Professorship and Robina Chair in Law, Public Policy, and Society at the University of Minnesota Law School and is concurrently Professor of Law and Associate Director at Ulster University's Transitional Justice Institute (Belfast). Her book *Law in Times of Crisis*, with Oren Gross (Cambridge University Press, 2006) was awarded ASIL's Certificate of Merit for creative scholarship (2007). She is co-author of *On the Frontlines: Gender, War and the Post Conflict Process* with Naomi Chan and Dina Haynes (Oxford University Press, 2011). Ní Aoláin was appointed by the UN Secretary-General as Special Expert on promoting gender equality in times of conflict and peace-making (2003). She has served as Expert to the ICC Trust Fund for Victims (2015), and Consultant to UN Women and OHCHR on a Study on Reparations for Conflict Related Sexual Violence (2013). She was nominated twice by the Irish Government as Judge to the European Court of Human Rights (2004 and 2007). She is Board Chair of the Open Society's Women's Program, and serves on the Board of the Center for Victims of Torture and the Georgetown Institute for Women, Peace, and Security. She was appointed by the United Nations Human Rights Council to hold the mandate of UN Special Rapporteur on the Promotion and Protection of Human Rights while Countering Terrorism in August 2017.

Nahla Valji is the Senior Gender Adviser in the Executive Office of the UN Secretary General. She was formerly the acting Chief/Deputy Chief, Peace and Security, in UN Women's headquarters in New York, where she led at different points the organization's work on peacekeeping, peace negotiations, countering violent extremism, transitional justice, and rule of law, involving both global programming and policy work, particularly with regard to the Security Council. During this time, she headed the Secretariat for the Global Study on the implementation of Security Council resolution 1325, a comprehensive study requested by the Security Council for the fifteen-year review of women, peace, and security. Following the completion of the Global Study review, she headed the secretariats of the resulting Security Council mechanism, the Informal Expert Group on Women, Peace and Security (established by resolution 2242), and a new pooled funding mechanism on women's engagement in peace, security, and humanitarian assistance. Prior to joining the UN she worked in South Africa, where she founded and managed the *International Journal of Transitional Justice* and led the regional transitional justice work of the Centre for the Study of Violence and Reconciliation, including the African Transitional Justice Research Network and joint work with the African Union.

Jerusa Ali is a doctoral candidate in Law and Legal Studies at Carleton University, Ottawa, Canada. She holds a BSc in Foreign Service from Georgetown University, an MA in International Relations from Keele University, and an LLM in International Human Rights Law from the University of Nottingham. She completed the fieldwork component of her doctoral project on the crime of persecution in residence at the Department of Jurisprudence and International Law, University of Ilorin, Nigeria.

Anton Baaré has since 1990 worked as international development and conflict-resolution practitioner in East and West Africa, and Southeast Asia. More recently he has started working in South and Central Asia. His experience covers human security, community-driven recovery and development, and disarmament, demobilization, and reintegration (DDR) programming. His work in Uganda started in 1993 when he was Danida advisor to the Uganda Veterans Assistance Board (UVAB), where he worked on the demobilization of the National Resistance Army (now UPDF). He has since worked on numerous projects in Uganda, including the ongoing Northern Uganda Social Action Fund 2 (NUSAF 2). In 2000–2002 he was Danida advisor to the Uganda Human Rights Commission (UHRC) and manager of the Danish support Human Right and Democratisation Programme. Between 2006 and 2008 he was seconded to the GOSS mediation team on the LRA "Juba Peace Talks" and was involved in drafting the Cessation of Hostilities agreement of August 2006, training the Cessation of Hostilities Monitoring Team, and drafting the Disarmament, Demobilization, and Reintegrationprotocol of the Juba Peace Agreement.

Christine Bell is Professor of Constitutional Law, and Assistant Principal (Global Justice) of the University of Edinburgh. She is a Fellow and Council member of the British Academy, and a member of the International Board of International IDEA. She is a former Director of the Human Rights Centre, Queens University of Belfast, and of the Transitional Justice Institute, University of Ulster. She was also Chairperson of the

Committee on the Administration of Justice, and a member of the first Northern Ireland Human Rights Commission established under the Belfast Agreement, which had responsibility for drafting a bill of rights for Northern Ireland. Her research interests lie in the interface between constitutional and international law, gender and conflict, with a particular interest in peace processes and their agreements. She has participated in and given legal and constitutional advice to participants in a number of peace negotiations (Basque country, Northern Ireland, Sri Lanka, Ogaden-Ethiopia, Philippines, Myanmar, and Colombia).

Karima Bennoune is Professor of Law and Martin Luther King, Jr., Hall Research Scholar at the University of California, Davis School of Law. She is the author of "Your Fatwa Does Not Apply Here: Untold Stories from the Fight against Muslim Fundamentalism," which won the 2014 Dayton Literary Peace Prize. Bennoune has served as legal advisor for Amnesty International, and sits on the Board of the Network of Women Living Under Muslim Laws. She currently serves as Special Rapporteur in the field of cultural rights.

Theresa S. Betancourt, ScD, MA is a professor at the Boston College School of Social Work and Director of the Research Program on Children and Adversity (RPCA). Her central research interests include the developmental and psychosocial consequences of concentrated adversity on children, youth, and families; resilience and protective processes in child and adolescent mental health and child development; refugee families; and applied cross-cultural mental health research. She is Principal Investigator of a prospective longitudinal study of war-affected youth in Sierra Leone, which led to the development of group interventions for war-affected youth that are now being scaled up in Sierra Leone in collaboration with the World Bank and the Government of Sierra Leone. She has developed and evaluated the impact of a Family Strengthening Intervention for HIV-affected children and families and is also investigating the impact of a home-visiting early childhood development (ECD) intervention to promote enriched parent-child relationships and prevent violence in Rwanda. Domestically, she is engaged in community-based participatory research on family-based prevention of emotional and behavioral problems in refugee children and adolescents resettled in the United States. She has written extensively on mental health and resilience in children facing adversity, including recent articles in *Child Development, The Journal of the American Academy of Child and Adolescent Psychiatry, Social Science and Medicine, JAMA Psychiatry*, and *PLOS One*.

Tess Borden is the 2015–2017 Aryeh Neier Fellow at the American Civil Liberties Union and Human Rights Watch. She works on the intersection of drug policy and criminal justice and is author of the 196-page ACLU/Human Rights Watch report, "Every 25 Seconds: The Human Toll of Criminalizing Drug Use in the United States." Tess clerked for the Honorable George A. O'Toole, Jr., of the United States District Court for the District of Massachusetts, and was a researcher for the United Nations Special Rapporteur on extrajudicial, summary, or arbitrary executions. She received her bachelor's degree from Yale College, where she majored in French, and her law degree from Harvard Law School, where she was a member of the International Human Rights Clinic and an editor of the *Harvard Human Rights Journal*.

Pascha Bueno-Hansen is an Associate Professor of Women and Gender Studies at the University of Delaware and serves as the Coordinator of the Sexualities and Gender Studies Minor and the Academic Coordinator of the LGBTQ+ and Racial Justice Activism Living and Learning Community. She is the author of *Feminist and Human Rights Struggles in Peru: Decolonizing Transitional Justice* (University of Illinois Press, 2015) as well as journal articles and book chapters on sexual violence, feminicide, women of color feminisms, sexuality, race, transitional justice, internal armed conflict and social movements. Her next project examines the emerging issue of violence against gender and sexual minorities within transitional justice efforts in Latin America.

Doris Buss is Professor of Law at Carleton University, Ottawa, Canada, and teaches and researches in the areas of international law and human rights, women's rights, global social movements, and feminist theory. She is the author (with Didi Herman) of *Globalizing Family Values: The International Politics of the Christian Right* (University of Minnesota Press, 2003), co-editor (with Ambreena Manji) of *International Law: Modern Feminist Approaches* (Hart, 2005), and co-editor (with Joanne Lebert, Blair Rutherford, and Donna Sharkey) of *Sexual Violence in Conflict and Post-Conflict Societies: International Agendas and African Contexts* (Routledge, 2014).

Jo Butterfield is a Visiting Assistant Professor of History at the University of Iowa. Her research examines the history of modern human rights by exploring the intersections between policy, ideology, and activism. Her book manuscript (in progress), *Social Justice, Not Charity: International Women's Activism, Gender Politics and the Making of Modern Human Rights*, explores how feminist activists navigated international politics and ideas about gender in their efforts to promote a global "social revolution" for women in the aftermath of World War II. She co-authored "Eleanor Roosevelt: Negotiating the Universal Declaration of Human Rights" in *Junctures in Women's Leadership: Social Movements* (Rutgers University Press, 2016). She currently teaches courses on the World since 1945, the United States in World Affairs, the History of Human Rights, and Cold War America.

Pablo Castillo Díaz is a policy specialist at UN Women, focused on efforts to prevent and respond to sexual and gender-based violence in conflict, post-conflict, and emergency settings; mainstream gender equality in peacekeeping operations; and engaging with the Security Council on women, peace, and security. He has contributed to the negotiations and adoption of several new Security Council resolutions on women, peace, and security, monitoring and accountability frameworks for the UN system on resolution 1325, research on women's participation in peace talks, conflict prevention, peacekeeping operations, and programmatic initiatives on community-led protection and specialized trainings for peacekeepers. In 2015, he helped shape UN Women's contributions to the global study and high-level review of resolution 1325 and the high-level independent panel on peace operations. Before joining the United Nations in 2009, he spent several years teaching international politics at various universities in the United States. He grew up in the Canary Islands (Spain) and has a degree in Political Science and International

Relations from Universidad Complutense de Madrid and a Doctorate from Rutgers University for his work on international criminal justice and conflict resolution.

Naureen Chowdhury Fink is a Policy Specialist on gender and counterterrorism/CVE at UN Women, where she also works closely with the UN's counterterrorism bodies including the Counter-Terrorism Executive Directorate (CTED). She has spent over a decade focusing on the international and multilateral response to terrorism and the role of the United Nations and its partners, including governments, experts and civil society. Previously, she worked for the Global Center on Cooperative Security, leading on multilateral programs and CVE, and before that, the International Peace Institute, where she developed the counter-terrorism portfolio. She has published numerous reports and articles, has contributed to policy and program development at national and multilateral levels, and has been a frequent speaker at high level and expert conferences. She is a Senior Fellow at the Global Center on Cooperative Security and at Hedayah. She has also worked with the Middle East Programme in Chatham House, the World Intellectual Property Organization and World Trade Organization in Geneva. Ms. Fink holds a BA from the University of Pennsylvania, an MA from the Courtauld Institute of Art, and an MA in War Studies from King's College London.

Hanny Cueva Beteta is UN Women's Regional Governance and Security Advisor for Asia and the Pacific. Before taking this position, she was the coordinator of the Global Study on the Implementation of Security Council resolution 1325 (2000) and until October 2014 she served as the Gender Advisor to UNCT for the UN Women office in Peru. Previously, she was the Policy Advisor and Deputy to the Chief Advisor for the Peace and Security Section in UN Women HQ. Before joining the United Nations in 2006, Hanny worked as a researcher and lecturer at the Universidad del Pacifico in Lima, Peru, where she published extensively on issues of poverty and development economics. She is Peruvian and holds a BA in Economics (Universdad del Pacifico, Lima) and a MPhil in Development Studies (Institute of Development Studies, University of Sussex, UK).

Alison Davidian is currently a Programme Specialist on Women, Peace and Security with UN Women's regional office in Thailand. Previous to this, she worked with UN Women's Peace and Security Section in New York where her portfolio areas included transitional justice and countering violent extremism and with its office in Uganda as a Transitional Justice Specialist. She has worked for ten years on peace and security, access to justice and gender issues for organizations including the International Center for Transitional Justice in the Democratic Republic of Congo, Equality Now in Zambia, UNDP Somalia, and the Refugee Advice and Casework Service in Australia.

Chris Dolan is Director of the Refugee Law Project, Makerere University, Kampala, Uganda. Since 1992 he has worked extensively in South Africa, Mozambique, Democratic Republic of Congo, Rwanda, and Uganda, and has consulted for UNHCR, UNSRSG-SVC, IICI, and numerous NGOs. His research and writing are focused on conflict-related sexual violence against men, gender, sexuality, masculinities, dynamics of inclusion/exclusion in conflict, and forced migration settings, including humanitarian and transitional justice processes. He is the author of *Social Torture: The case of Northern Uganda 1986–2006* (Berghan, 2009) and, together with Moses Chrispus Okello, editor of *Where Law Meets Reality: Forging African Transitional Justice* (Pambazuka Press, 2012).

Judy El-Bushra was an independent researcher on issues of gender, conflict, development, and peace-building. Her main experience was gained with the development agency ACORD (1982 to 2002) and the peace-building organization International Alert (2006 to 2011). She coordinated a research project on the impact of conflict on gender relations in five African countries ("Cycles of Violence: Gender Relations and Armed Conflict") for ACORD, and helped develop International Alert's recent work on "Rethinking Gender in Conflict," which aimed to set out and expand the parameters of the topic. With Judith Gardner, she co-edited Somalia, The Untold Story: The War through the Eyes of Women, which they followed in 2016 with The Impact of War on Somali Men for the Rift Valley Institute. Her main work has been on the Horn of Africa, the Great Lakes, and Nigeria.

Karen Engle is the Minerva House Drysdale Regents Chair in Law and founder and co-director of the Bernard and Audre Rapoport Center for Human Rights and Justice at the University of Texas at Austin. She researches and writes on international human rights law and advocacy, particularly as they intersect with women's rights and indigenous rights movements. She is author of numerous scholarly articles and *The Elusive Promise of Indigenous Development: Rights, Culture, Strategy* (Duke University Press, 2010). She is also co-editor of *Anti-Impunity and the Human Rights Agenda* (Cambridge University Press, 2016).

Maria Eriksson Baaz is Professor in Peace and Development Research at the School of Global Studies, University of Gothenburg, Sweden. Her main research interests are in civil-military relations, gendered dynamics of conflict and violence, and post-colonial theory. She is the co-author (with Maria Stern) of *Sexual Violence as a Weapon of War? Perceptions, Prescriptions, Problems in the Congo and Beyond* (2013) and the author of *The Paternalism of Partnership: A Post-colonial Reading of Development Aid* (2005). Additionally, her articles have appeared in several leading international academic journals, such as International Studies Quarterly, African Affairs, Third World Quarterly and Armed Forces and Society.

Barbara A. Frey, J.D., directs the Human Rights Program in the College of Liberal Arts at the University of Minnesota. She is a Senior Lecturer in the Institute for Global Studies and co-director of graduate studies for the Master of Human Rights, a joint degree of the College of Liberal Arts and the Humphrey School of Public Affairs. From 2003 to 2006 she was special rapporteur for the UN Sub-Commission on the Promotion and Protection of Human Rights on the topic of preventing human rights abuses committed with small arms and light weapons. Frey co-founded the Advocates for Human Rights (formerly Minnesota Advocates for Human Rights), where she also served as the first full-time Executive Director (1985–1997).

Kathy L. Gaca is Associate Professor of Classics and an Associate Member of the Divinity School at Vanderbilt University. Her research explores aspects of social injustice rooted in antiquity that remain problematic in the modern day and that need a clearer ethical and historical understanding. She focuses mainly on ancient customs of sexual violence and repression and their ongoing relevance for comprehending current norms of injustice and violence against women and girls. She is the author of several publications, including *The Making of Fornication: Eros, Ethics, and Political Reform in Greek Philosophy and Early Christianity* (University of California Press, 2003, winner of the CAMWS 2006 Outstanding Publication Award), and is currently at work on her second book, provisionally titled, *Rape as Sexual Warfare against Girls and Women: Ancient Society and Religion, Modern Witness.* She received her PhD in Classics at the University of Toronto and held the Hannah Seeger Davis Postdoctoral Fellowship in Hellenic Studies at Princeton University.

Judith Gardam is Emeritus Professor at the Law School, University of Adelaide in South Australia, and a Fellow of both the Academy of Social Sciences in Australia and the Australian Academy of Law. She is an International Lawyer and a feminist scholar. Her particular areas of expertise are international humanitarian law and the international law rules that regulate the use of force between states. She is the author of "A New Frontline for Feminism and International Humanitarian Law" in *The Ashgate Research Companion to Feminist Legal Theory*, M. Davies and V. Munro (eds.) (Ashgate, 2013); "War, Law, Terror, Nothing New for Women," *Australian Feminist Law Journal* 32 (2010): 61–76; and of numerous other books and articles in her field.

Anne Marie Goetz is a Professor at New York University at the Center for Global Affairs. She was a Fellow of the Institute of Development Studies at the University of Sussex and was a senior advisor on Women, Peace and Security at UNIFEM/UN Women, where she developed policy on women and peace-building and combating sexual violence in conflict. Goetz is the author or co-author of seven books on women's rights, democratization, and accountability, including *No Shortcuts to Power: African Women in Politics and Policy-Making* (Zed Press, 2003), and *Governing Women: Women in Politics and Governance in Developing Countries* (Routlegde, 2009).

Lejla Hadzimesic is specialized in international human rights law. She has sixteen years of professional experience in capacity building, research, and analysis in the human rights field, both in the civil society sector and in international organizations, including the United Nations. She holds a Master's Degree in International Human Rights Law from the University of Oxford.

Gina Heathcote is a Reader in Gender Studies and International Law at SOAS University of London, where she teaches a portfolio of courses on Public International Law and Gender Studies, including Gender, Armed Conflict and International Law, and Feminist Legal Theory. Gina is the author of *The Law on the Use of Force: A Feminist Analysis* (Routledge, 2012) and co-editor (with Dianne Otto) of *Rethinking Peacekeeping, Gender Equality and Collective Security* (2014). Gina is also a member of the Feminist Review editorial collective.

Elizabeth Heineman is Professor of History and Gender, Women's, and Sexuality Studies at the University of Iowa, where she served as Acting Associate Director and member of the Executive Board of the Center for Human Rights. Her recent publications include *Sexual Violence in Conflict Zones: From the Ancient World to the Era of Human Rights* (ed., University of Pennsylvania Press, 2011).

Marsha Henry is Deputy Director of the Centre for Women, Peace and Security and Associate Professor in the Gender Institute, London School of Economics and Political Science. She has previously worked at the University of Bristol and the University of British Columbia. Dr. Henry's research interests focus on gender and militarization, peacekeeping, and qualitative methodologies. For the past twelve years she has been conducting research on the social, cultural, and gendered aspects of peacekeeping. She has co-authored *Insecure Spaces* with Zed Press in 2009, and her recent work on female peacekeepers from the Global South can be found in the journal *Globalizations*.

Christof Heyns is Professor of Human Rights Law and Director of the Institute for International and Comparative Law at the University of Pretoria and is a member of the UN Human Rights Committee. He was United Nations Special Rapporteur on extrajudicial, summary or arbitrary executions (2010–2016). During 2016 he chaired the UN Independent Investigation on Burundi.

Amelia Hoover Green is Assistant Professor in the Department of Politics at Drexel University, and a Field Consultant to the Human Rights Data Analysis Group. Her research primarily falls in two areas: the politics of quantification in human rights practice, and the role of armed group institutions in creating and controlling violence against civilians in wartime. As a consultant to HRDAG, she has aided prosecutions in both national and international courts. Her current book manuscript, *The Commander's Dilemma*, focuses on variation in repertoires of violence against civilians during civil war in El Salvador.

Lucy Hovil is the Senior Research Associate at the International Refugee Rights Initiative and the Managing Editor of the *International Journal of Transitional Justice* and a deployable civilian expert for the UK government's stabilization unit. She has seventeen years of experience in carrying out research in Africa's Great Lakes region, where she previously founded and led the Research and Advocacy Department at the Refugee Law Project, Faculty of Law, Makerere University, Uganda. She recently published *Refugees, Conflict and the Search for Belonging* (Palgrave Macmillan 2016), drawing on eight years of research in Africa's Great Lakes region.

Rob Jenkins is Professor of Political Science at Hunter College and the Graduate Center, City University of New York. Though his research focuses on the political economy of policy change and movement activism in India, Jenkins has also published widely on peace-building, including a monograph, *Peacebuilding: From Concept to Commission* (Routledge, 2013). As a consultant to the UN Peacebuilding Support Office, he was the lead author of the Report of the Secretary-General on Women's Participation in Peacebuilding (2010). His most recent book, *Politics and the Right to Work* (Oxford University Press, 2017), co-authored with James Manor, examines the political origins and implications of India's National Rural Employment Guarantee Act, one of the world's largest participatory anti-poverty programs.

Patricia Justino is a Professorial Fellow at the Institute of Development Studies in the United Kingdom. She is a development economist specializing in applied microeconomics. Her current research work focuses on the impact of violence and conflict on household welfare and local institutional structures, the micro-foundations of violent conflict, and the implications of violence for economic development. Patricia has led several research projects funded by the British Academy, DFID, the European Commission, the ESRC, FAO, the Leverhulme Trust, UNDP, UNESCO, UN Women, and the World Bank. She was the Director of MICROCON, and co-founder and co-director of the Households in Conflict Network. Since June 2010, Patricia convenes the Conflict and Violence cluster at IDS.

Kristin Kalla is a senior expert on the Gender-based Violence Surge Global Humanitarian Emergency Roster with the United Nations Populations Fund. She led the creation of the ICC Trust Fund for Victims from 2007–2015; and was responsible for overseeing the victims' assistance and reparations programs, including providing leadership toward gender-sensitive and inclusive programming for survivors of sexual and gender-based violence. Ms. Kalla led the development of the first reparations implementation plan in ICC Prosecutor v. Thomas Lubanga Dyilo. She is a public health anthropologist with over twenty-five years of experience managing humanitarian, human rights, and public health efforts in over twenty countries in conflict situations, primarily in Africa. In 2014, Ms. Kalla was inducted into the Alumni Hall of Fame at the UCLA Fielding School of Public Health.

Amrita Kapur is an independent consultant and the former Senior Associate in the Gender Justice Program at the International Center for Transitional Justice in New York, where she focused on the gender dimensions of measures such as truth-seeking, criminal prosecutions, reparations, and institutional reform. She lectures at New York University, and previously at the Faculty of Law at the University of New South Wales in Australia. Previously she worked on gender justice issues in Timor-Leste, Mozambique, Tanzania, Colombia, Guinea, Uganda, Democratic Republic of Congo, and Kenya; and has practiced domestic and international criminal law. Amrita holds psychology and law degrees, and an LL.M in International Legal Studies from New York University. She is completing a PhD on the ICC's potential to catalyze national prosecutions for international crimes of sexual violence, including field research in Colombia and Guinea.

Sabrina Karim (PhD, Emory University) is an Assistant Professor in Government at Cornell University. She is the co-author of *Equal Opportunity Peacekeeping* (Oxford University Press, 2017). The book was the winner of the Conflict Research Studies Best Book Prize for 2017. Her work has appeared in *International Organization*, the *British*

Journal of Political Science, The Journal of Peace Research, International Interactions, World Development, and *Conflict Management and Peace Science*. Her research focuses on conflict and peace processes, particularly state building in the aftermath of civil war. Specifically, she studies international involvement in security assistance to post-conflict states, gender reforms in peacekeeping and domestic security sectors, and the relationship between gender and violence. Much of her research has been in sub-Saharan Africa, where she has conducted field experiments, lab experiments, and surveys. Her research has been supported by the National Science Foundation, the Folke Bernadotte Academy, the International Growth Centre, and the British Research Council.

Avila Kilmurray is a practitioner in the area of peace-building and community-based action, drawing experience from developments in Northern Ireland through her work as Director of the Community Foundation for Northern Ireland (1994–2014) and as a founding member of the Northern Ireland Women's Coalition. Avila is a Board member of Conciliation Resources (UK) and a founding member of the Foundations for Peace Network, independent funders working in Sri Lanka, Serbia, Georgia, Palestine, Colombia, Nepal, India, and Bangladesh. Appointed an Hon. Visiting Professor at the University of Ulster's Transitional Justice Institute, Avila's recent publications include "Civil Society Actors and the End of Violence," in *The Ashgate Research Companion to Political Violence* (ed. M. Breen-Smyth, 2012); *Philanthropy and Peacebuilding in Conflict-Affected Environments: A Guide for Funders* (Social Change Initiative, 2016); and *Community Action in Contested Society: The Story of Northern Ireland* (Peter Lang, 2016).

Lisa Kindervater is a doctoral researcher at The University of the Witwatersrand in Johannesburg. She has a Master of Arts in International Development Studies (Dalhousie University) and a Bachelor of Arts (Honours) in Political Science. Using Liberia as a case study, her master's thesis examined women's political participation and gender equality outcomes in transitions to peace and democracy. Her research and teaching interests include the comparative politics of postcolonial African states and gender politics in transitional societies, particularly in African contexts. Lisa is living in Liberia, and working on gender inclusive elections and conducting her PhD fieldwork. This research focuses on multilevel governance in the area of women's political participation and representation, especially on the struggle for a legislative quota and gender and elections in the 2017 presidential and legislative elections.

Sari Kouvo is Adviser for Human Rights and Gender at the European External Action Service in Brussels. Sari's previous engagements include founder and co-director of the Afghanistan Analysts Network, Senior Associate at the International Centre for Transitional Justice, and Special Adviser to the European Union Special Adviser for Afghanistan. She has held visiting fellowships at the NATO Defense College, Australian National University, and Kent/Keele Universities. Sari holds a doctorate and an associate professor degree from Gothenburg University, and has published extensively on gender, international law, and Afghanistan.

Roxanne Krystalli is the Program Manager for the Humanitarian Evidence Program, a UK aid-funded partnership between Oxfam GB and the Feinstein International Center to synthesize evidence-based humanitarian research and improve its use in humanitarian policy and practice. Roxanne is a PhD Candidate at The Fletcher School of Law and Diplomacy, where she is exploring questions related to victim-centered justice.

Corey Levine is a human rights and peace-building policy expert, researcher, and writer with a specialization in gender. She has worked in conflict and post-conflict areas for more than twenty years. She has worked in Afghanistan at various periods between 2002 and 2014, and was the Gender Advisor for the UN Assistance Mission in Afghanistan (UNAMA) in 2004–2005.

Amina Mama, widely published and traveled Nigerian/British feminist activist, researcher, and scholar, has lived and worked in Nigeria, South Africa, Britain, the Netherlands, and the United States. She is Professor in the Department of Gender, Sexuality and Women's Studies at UC Davis. She spent ten years (1999–2009) leading the establishment of the University of Cape Town's African Gender Institute as a continental resource dedicated to developing transformative scholarship, bringing feminist theory and activism together. Founding editor of the continental journal of gender studies, *Feminist Africa*, her publications include *Beyond the Masks: Race, Gender and Subjectivity* (Routledge, 1995), *Women's Studies and Studies of Women in Africa* (CODESRIA, 1996), *Engendering African Social Sciences* (co-edited, CODESRIA, 1997) and numerous book chapters and journal articles. Committed to strengthening activism and activist research in African contexts, her research interests include culture and subjectivity, politics and policy, women's movements, and militarism. She and Yaba Badoe co-produced the fifty-minute documentary film *The Witches of Gambaga* (2010).

Dyan Mazurana, PhD, is Associate Research Professor at the Fletcher School of Law and Diplomacy, Tufts University, and Research Director at the Feinstein International Center, Tufts University. Her areas of focus include women, children, and armed conflict; documenting serious crimes committed during conflict and working with survivors; accountability, remedy, and reparation; and research methods in situations of armed conflict. Her latest book is *Research Methods in Conflict Settings: A View from Below* (Cambridge University Press, 2013) with Karen Jacobsen and Lacey Gale.

Monica McWilliams is Professor of Women's Studies and Research Fellow in the Transitional Justice Institute at Ulster University. Monica was involved in the multi-party peace talks leading to the 1998 Belfast/Good Friday Agreement and served as Chief Commissioner for the Northern Ireland Human Rights Commission. Her research and writing focus on the impact of political conflict on women's lives.

Donny Meertens is Associate Professor at Javeriana University (retired) in Bogota, Colombia, and formerly worked in the Gender Studies School at Colombia's National University, and for UNHCR and UNIFEM in Colombia. She was the Rapporteur of the Historical Memory Report on violent land dispossession of women and men in Colombia's armed conflict (published in Spanish as *La Tierra en Disputa*, 2010) and Fellow (2013–2014) at the Woodrow Wilson Center, Washington, DC. She has published numerous articles in English and Spanish on gender and conflict, forced displacement, transitional justice, and access to land.

Sheila Meintjes recently retired as Professor from the Department of Political Studies at the University of the Witwatersrand in Johannesburg, where she taught African politics and feminist theory and politics. She was involved in the anti-apartheid movement, and worked with rural social movements and women's movements in the 1980s and 1990s. She was a Commissioner in the South African Commission for Gender Equality from 2001 to 2004. She has sat on numerous NGO boards working for social justice and gender equality, and against gender violence. She has published on post-conflict and gender politics, co-editing *The Aftermath: Women in Post-conflict Transformation* (Zed Books, 2002), *One Woman, One Vote: The Gender Politics of Elections* (Electoral Institute of Southern Africa, 2003), *Women Writing Africa: The Southern Region* (The Feminist Press, CUNY, 1st edition, 2002), and *Women's Activism in South Africa: Working across Divides* (UKZN Press, 2009). Currently, she co-leads a research project on South Africa and Switzerland entitled "Safeguarding Democracy: Contests of Values and Interests."

Vasuki Nesiah is Associate Professor of Practice at New York University. Her main areas of research include the law and politics of international human rights and humanitarianism, international feminisms, and the history of colonialism in international law. Her most immediate projects includes a book on reparations for colonialism and slavery, a book on International Conflict Feminism and a co-edited volume (with Luis Eslava and Michael Fakhri) on *A Global History of Bandung and Critical Traditions in International Law* (Cambridge University Press, 2017). She is one of the founding members of Third World Approaches to International Law (TWAIL), continues as core faculty in Harvard Law School's Institute for Global Law and Policy (IGLP) and is a Senior Fellow at Melbourne Law School. Professor Nesiah's publications can be accessed at http://nyu. academia.edu/VasukiNesiah.

Lauren C. Ng is an Assistant Professor at Boston University School of Medicine and staff psychologist at Boston Medical Center. Her work focuses on the psychological impact of war, conflict, and daily hardships on children and families, risk and resilience factors in child and adolescent global mental health, and the development and assessment of culturally appropriate evidence-based interventions for trauma and its correlates.

Valerie Oosterveld is the Associate Dean (Research) and an Associate Professor at the University of Western Ontario Faculty of Law (Canada). She previously served as a Legal Officer with Canada's Department of Foreign Affairs, providing legal advice on international criminal law. Her research and writing focus on gendered forms of genocide, crimes against humanity, and war crimes, as well as on gender-sensitive international criminal prosecutions.

Dianne Otto is Professorial Fellow at Melbourne Law School, Australia. She held the Francine V. McNiff Chair in Human Rights Law 2013–2016 and was Director of the Institute for International Law and the Humanities (IILAH) 2012–2015. Her research covers a broad range of interests, including addressing gender, sexuality, and race inequalities in the context of international human rights law, the UN Security Council's peacekeeping work, the technologies of global "crisis governance," threats to economic, social, and cultural rights, and the transformative potential of people's tribunals and other NGO initiatives. Her recent publications include *Queering International Law: Possibilities, Alliances, Complicities, Risks* (editor, Routledge 2017), *Rethinking Peacekeeping, Gender Equality and Collective Security* (co-editor with Gina Heathcote, Palgrave-Macmillan, 2014), three edited volumes, *Gender Issues and Human Rights* (Edward Elgar, 2013).

Pramila Patten is the Special Representative of the Secretary General on Sexual Violence in Conflict since June 2017. She has been a member of the CEDAW Committee between 2003 and 2017. She was previously a member of the Advisory Panel for the African Women's Rights Observatory of the United Nations Economic Commission for Africa. She has served on the Governing Council and the Executive Committee of the African Centre for Democracy and Human Rights Studies (ACDHRS) and Women in Law and Development in Africa (WILDAF), both large Pan-African organizations. She was appointed Commissioner by the Secretary-General of the United Nations on the International Commission of Inquiry that investigated the massacre in Guinea Conakry on September 28, 2009. Ms. Patten chaired the Working Group on General Recommendation No. 30 on "Women in Conflict Prevention, Conflict and Post-Conflict Situations," adopted by the CEDAW Committee on October 18, 2013, and has provided technical assistance to several states parties to CEDAW, including Albania, Iraq, Pakistan, Afghanistan, Haiti, Timor Leste, Ukraine, Belarus, Azerbaijan, Turkmenistan, Kazakhstan, Turkey, India, Bangladesh, Philippines, Vietnam, Indonesia. In July 2014, Ms. Patten was appointed by UN Women to a High Level Expert Advisory Panel on the monitoring of implementation of Security Council resolution 1325. Ms. Patten was a consultant for several regional and international organizations. She has been a practicing lawyer in Mauritius since 1982 and is a member of Gray's Inn.

Patti Petesch, an independent researcher, specializes in qualitative field research on gender, poverty, conflict, and participatory development. She co-authored three World Bank global studies: *Voices of the Poor, Moving Out Poverty*, and *On Norms and Agency* (Oxford University Press [for the World Bank], 2000); and authored, for USAID, *Women's Empowerment Arising from Violent Conflict and Recovery: Life Stories from Four Middle-Income Countries*. She is currently advising on design and analysis for a twenty-six-country study with the CGIAR entitled "GENNOVATE: Enabling Gender Equality in Agricultural and Environmental Innovation."

Eilish Rooney teaches in the School for Applied Social and Policy Sciences and is a member of the Transitional Justice Institute at Ulster University. She uses intersectionality in her research on gender and women's lives in conflict and applies the theory to

practice in the Institute's Grassroots Toolkit program with Bridge of Hope, http://www.
transitionaljustice.ulster.ac.uk/TJToolkit.htm.

Ambika Satkunanathan was appointed a Commissioner of the Human Rights
Commission of Sri Lanka in October 2015. From February 1998 to March 2014, Ambika
functioned as Legal Consultant to the Office of the High Commissioner for Human
Rights attached to the Office of the UN-Resident Coordinator in Colombo. Her research
has focused on transitional justice, militarization, and gender and Tamil nationalism.
Her forthcoming publications include contributions to the *Routledge Handbook on
Human Rights in South Asia*, and *Contemporary South Asia*. Ambika is Chairperson of
the Neelan Tiruchelvam Trust, an indigenous grant-making organization. She is also
an Advisory Board Member of Suriya Women's Development Centre, Batticaloa in
the Eastern Province. Ambika has a Master of Laws (Human Rights) degree from the
University of Nottingham, where she was Chevening Scholar, and earned bachelor's
degrees (LL.B/BA) at Monash University, Australia.

Patricia Viseur Sellers is an international criminal lawyer and Special Advisor on
Gender to the Office of the Prosecutor of the International Court. As a Visiting Fellow at
Kellogg College of Oxford University, she lectures on international criminal law. From
1994 to 2007, Ms. Sellers was the Legal Advisor for Gender Related Crimes and Senior
Acting Trial Attorney in the Office of the Prosecutor for the International Criminal
Tribunals for the Former Yugoslavia and for Rwanda, where she advised and litigated
cases, such as *Prosecutor v. Furundzija, Prosecutor v. Akayesu*, and *Prosecutor v. Kunarac*.
She has been a Special Advisor to the Secretary-General's Special Representative for
Children in Armed Conflict, and, in 2000, was the Co-Prosecutor at the International
Women's Tribunal in a symbolic trial to redress crimes committed against the
Comfort Women. She is a recipient of the American Society of International Law's
Prominent Women in International Law Award. Her articles include "Wartime Female
Slavery: Enslavement?"; "Gender Strategy Is Not a Luxury"; "Rape and Sexual Violence,"
in *The 1949 Geneva Conventions, A Commentary* (ed. A. Clapham, P. Gaeta, M. Sassòli,
Oxford University Press, 2015), and "Issues of Sexual and Gender-Based Violence in
the Extraordinary Chambers in the Courts of Cambodia" with Valerie Oosterveld in
The Extraordinary Chambers in the Courts of Cambodia. International Criminal Justice
Series, vol. 6 (ed., S. Meisenberg, I. Stegmiller, T.M.C. Asser Press, 2016).

Nadera Shalhoub-Kevorkian is the Lawrence D. Biele Chair in Law at the Faculty of
Law-Institute of Criminology and the School of Social Work and Public Welfare at the
Hebrew University of Jerusalem. She is a longtime anti-violence, native Palestinian feminist activist and the director of the Gender Studies Program at Mada al-Carmel, the Arab
Center for Applied Social Research in Haifa. Her research focuses on law, society, and
crimes of abuse of power. She studies the crime of femicide and other forms of gendered
violence, crimes of abuse of power in settler colonial contexts, surveillance, securitization, and social control, and trauma and recovery in militarized and colonized zones.
Shalhoub-Kevorkian's recent works include *Militarization and Violence against Women
in Conflict Zones in the Middle East: The Palestinian Case Study* (Cambridge University

Press, 2010) and *Security Theology, Surveillance and the Politics of Fear* (Cambridge University Press, 2015). She has published articles in multi-disciplinary journals, including the *British Journal of Criminology, International Review of Victimology, Feminism and Psychology, Middle East Law and Governance, International Journal of Lifelong Education, American Behavioral Scientist Journal, Social Service Review, Violence Against Women, Journal of Feminist Family Therapy: An International Forum, Social Identities, Social Science and Medicine, Signs, Law & Society Review*, and more. As a resident of the old city of Jerusalem, Shalhoub-Kevorkian is a prominent local activist. She engages in direct actions and critical dialogue to end the inscription of power over Palestinian children's lives, spaces of death, and women's birthing bodies and lives.

Laura Sjoberg is Associate Professor of Political Science at the University of Florida. She holds a BA from the University of Chicago, a JD from Boston College, and PhD in International Relations from the University of Southern California. Dr. Sjoberg's work has been published in more than three dozen journals in Political Science, Law, International Relations, Gender Studies, and Geography. She is author or editor of ten books, including, most recently, *Gender, War, and Conflict* (Polity, 2014) and *Beyond Mothers, Monsters, Whores* (with Caron Gentry, Zed Books, 2015). Her current projects include an edited volume on quantitative methods in critical and constructivist IR, *Interpretive Quantification* (with J. Samuel Barkin, 2017, University of Michigan Press), and a book on women's perpetration of conflict sexual violence, *Women as Wartime Rapists* (New York University Press, 2016).

Maria Stern is Professor in Peace and Development Studies at the School of Global Studies, University of Gothenburg. Her research interests include feminist security studies, security-development, critical military studies, and the international political sociology of violence. She is the co-author (with Maria Eriksson Baaz) of *Sexual Violence as a Weapon of War? Perceptions, Prescriptions, Problems in the Congo and Beyond* (Zed Books, 2013), co-editor of *Studying the Agency of Being Governed*, (Routledge, 2014); *Feminist Methodologies for International Relations* (Cambridge University Press, 2006) and the author of *Naming Security – Constructing Identity* (Manchester University Press, 2005). Additionally, her articles have appeared in leading international academic journals. She is currently Associate Editor of *Security Dialogue*.

Kimberly Theidon, a medical anthropologist, is the Henry J. Leir Professor of International Humanitarian Studies at the Fletcher School of Law and Diplomacy. Her research interests include political violence, transitional justice, reconciliation, and the politics of postwar reparations. She is the author of many articles, and *Entre Prójimos: El conflicto armado interno y la política de la reconciliación en el Perú* (Instituto de Estudios Peruanos, 1st edition, 2004; 2nd edition, 2009) and *Intimate Enemies: Violence and Reconciliation in Peru* (University of Pennsylvania Press, 2012).

Aili Mari Tripp is the Wangari Maathai Professor of Political Science and Gender & Women's Studies at the University of Wisconsin-Madison. Tripp's research has focused on women and politics in Africa, women's movements in Africa, women and peace-building, transnational feminism, African politics (with particular reference to Uganda and Tanzania), and on the informal economy in Africa. She is author of several award-winning books, including *Women and Power in Postconflict Africa* (Cambridge Studies in Gender and Politics, Cambridge University Press, 2015), *Museveni's Uganda: Paradoxes of Power in a Hybrid Regime* (Lynne Rienner, 2010), *African Women's Movements: Transforming Political Landscapes* (Cambridge University Press, 2009) with Isabel Casimiro, Joy Kwesiga, and Alice Mungwa, and *Women and Politics in Uganda* (University of Wisconsin Press, 2000). She has co-edited (with Myra Marx Ferree and Christina Ewig) *Gender, Violence, and Human Security: Critical Feminist Perspectives* (New York University Press, 2013).

Martina E. Vandenberg is the founder and president of The Human Trafficking Pro Bono Legal Center (HT Pro Bono). Vandenberg established HT Pro Bono in 2012 with generous support from the Open Society Foundations (OSF) Fellowship Program. Prior to becoming an OSF Fellow, Vandenberg served as a partner at Jenner & Block LLP, where she focused on complex commercial litigation and internal investigations under the Foreign Corrupt Practices Act. Vandenberg has spent two decades fighting human trafficking, forced labor, rape as a war crime, and violence against women. A former Human Rights Watch researcher, Vandenberg spearheaded investigations into human rights violations in the Russian Federation, Bosnia and Herzegovina, Uzbekistan, Kosovo, Israel, and Ukraine. In 2013, she received the Harry S. Truman Scholarship Foundation's Stevens Award for outstanding service in public interest law. T'ruah presented Vandenberg with the Raphael Lemkin Human Rights Award in 2014. She received the Katharine and George Alexander Law Prize the following year. Vandenberg currently serves as a co-chair of the International Bar Association's Human Trafficking Task Force. A Rhodes Scholar and Truman Scholar, Vandenberg has taught as an adjunct faculty member at the American University Washington College of Law and at the Oxford University Human Rights Summer Program.

Dubravka Žarkov is Associate Professor of Gender, Conflict, Development at the International Institute of Social Studies/Erasmus University Rotterdam (The Netherlands). Her work addresses intersections of gender, sexuality, and ethnicity in (sexual) violence in war and their media representations, the nexus of neoliberal globalization and violent conflict, and ontological and epistemological questions in contemporary theorizing of war. Her recent publications include *Conflict, Peace, Security and Development. Theories and Methodologies* (Routledge, 2015, co-edited with Helen Hintjens), and *Narratives of Justice in and out of the Courtroom: Former Yugoslavia and Beyond* (Springer, 2014, co-edited with Marlies Glasius). She is co-editor of *European Journal of Women's Studies*.

INTRODUCTION

Mapping the Terrain: Gender and Conflict in Contemporary Perspective

EDITORS: FIONNUALA NÍ AOLÁIN, NAOMI CAHN, DINA FRANCESCA HAYNES, AND NAHLA VALJI

IN recent years, the differing and overlapping experiences of men and women in situations of armed conflict have garnered significant international attention. Such attention results from the confluence of multiple factors, including greater visibility of the violations experienced by women in times of war; an opportunistic focus on gendered violations by some states as a basis for justifying humanitarian and/or military interventions; greater exposure of the broader social, economic, and cultural effects on women of inter-state and intra-state armed conflict, and deepening awareness of the vulnerability of and costs for men of engaging in war. The growing visibility of women in conflict, enhanced by increased media attention, is also being reflected in institutional attention and policy reorientation. This cumulative political and legal movement has placed corresponding pressure on those involved in conflict-resolution processes to pay greater attention to the experience of women and to ensure their inclusion in peace negotiations and agreements. Consequently, how women fare in the aftermath of war has garnered greater scrutiny, with the transformative potential of conflict, as well as its detrimental effects on women's social, political, and economic security, now better understood.

This *Handbook* sets out to capture the contemporary state of the gender and conflict field. Our authors offer a range of views on difficult topics, and we have sought to capture a variety of perspectives on highly controversial issues. The *Handbook's* breadth of coverage shows how gender is everywhere in the practice of war and its aftermath. We have brought together a cacophony of voices and styles that reflect very differing views on gender and conflict, not all of whom we individually agree with or agree with one another, in totality, they reflect a wide spectrum of opinion in the gender and conflict landscape. We recognize that this is an interdisciplinary field and that the perspectives offered by a variety of viewpoints enrich and deepen our understanding of conflict, as well as reveal how gendered identities emerge, frame, and are transformed by the experience of collective violence. This *Handbook* endorses an intersectional approach, whereby we remain attuned to the variety of experiences, contexts, and factors that inform the lived realities of conflict in multiple configurations across geographies, time, and cultures. Profoundly engaging with the multiple forms of conflict as they manifest in different local contexts helps us disaggregate the phenomena of conflict, drill down to the granular manifestations of violence, and thus better understand the commonalities of conflict for women and men around the world, while simultaneously remaining attuned to the differences found in different places.

The word "gender" is often used interchangeably with the word "women," "conflating the two and leaving men as the unmarked, default category—the generic human against which others are compared and potentially deviate."[1] This *Handbook* takes a nuanced and multidimensional approach to the concept of "gender" and its many manifestations, developing a constructive critique of the entrenched practices and application of gender categorization. One of the cross-cutting themes involves analyzing the political consequences, positive and negative, of the unrelenting equation of gender and women that seems inherent in many of the international conventions and norms framing conflict and post-conflict regulation. The structure and content of this *Handbook* makes clear that gender, with its emphasis on gendered roles and outcomes, does not mean an exclusive focus on women. Instead, substantively addressing both gender and women's roles necessitates greater attention to the normative masculinities that are visible during war and the post-conflict resolution processes, as well as to particular cultural and social contexts that may provide a more formidable understanding of men's experience of war. This experience is now more fully understood as exposing the vulnerabilities of men to wartime violence, and the socially enforced roles that men are coerced and/or socialized into adopting in violent societies. Moreover, consideration of men's roles during and after conflict aids in understanding and responding to women's positionality, and both must therefore be considered when addressing the complex intersection of gender and war. Greater reflection on the interplay between masculinity theory and masculinities studies with feminist analysis of conflict and post-conflict settings provides an enriched terrain of knowledge and policy application.

Nonetheless, because there has been so little formal recognition of women's status and experiences during and after conflict, and indeed, because this exclusion is the factual reality that has driven recent attention to gender and war, the *Handbook* includes substantively more material addressing the extent to which women's needs and experiences are or are not attended to during and after conflict. Men and their concerns have dominated discussions of war throughout the ages, and a particular attention to women will track newly developing legal and political attention to women's concerns. The *Handbook* avoids duplicating existing exclusions and marginalization that suppose an even-handedness in conflict experiences for men and women.

The legal framework regulating armed conflict has been little concerned with women over the centuries. The law of armed conflict (IHL) is a deeply gendered set of legal norms, in large part structured to support and reflect the experiences and challenges of male combatants when engaged in structured hostilities with one another. From the early laws on armed conflict (e.g., the Geneva Law of the 1850s, the Lieber Code, the

Hague Regulations, the Geneva Conventions of 1949, and the Additional Protocols to the Geneva Conventions of 1977), the focus on women was minimal. Where women were viewed at all, it was primarily as victims of conflict, whose honor and dignity required protection, rather than as autonomous rights-bearing subjects. Rape has only recently been formally included as a breach of the laws of war, and the paucity of full legal recognition for the range of harms experienced by women in conflict has been only partly ameliorated by the agreement on the Statute of the International Criminal Court (Rome Statute) in 1998. Understanding the reach of these legal instruments and human rights norms and their lacunae is an essential part of mapping the gender and conflict intersection, and the *Handbook* underscores this significance.

The 1990s and the first decade of the 2000s saw a multitude of conflicts, most intra-state, each of which also impacted women in myriad horrific ways, and in which the United Nations and the international community were involved under various legal justifications and political agreements: Rwanda, Liberia, Sierra Leone, Croatia, Bosnia and Herzegovina, Kosovo, East Timor, Iraq, Afghanistan, Darfur, and the Democratic Republic of Congo. These wars starkly illustrated the limitations of the existing normative framework for the legal regulation of armed conflict and its capacity to adequately protect women in conflict, as well as to "capture" the harms they experience for the purposes of post-conflict accountability.

In fact, a gendered experience of conflict can be traced back through the ages. Historical analysis has revealed that women have been distinctly targeted in times of violence, ranging from ancient Greece to medieval England, from the American Revolution to pre-colonial warfare in Tanzania, and from the Bangladeshi war to World War II. Despite the long historical record, little official and systematic attention was paid to the functionality of gender targets and gender patterns in times of war. Thus, while rape as the most visible harm for women under war has had a long history of prohibition, it has an even longer history of impunity.

It was not until the 1990s, significantly as a result of lobbying by a mobilized transnational women's rights movement, that human rights groups even became more sensitive to gender-based harm and the gendered aspects of war. The armed conflict in the Former Yugoslavia and genocide in Rwanda revealed the widespread and systematic nature of sex-based violence to a watching international audience. While systematic violence to women was not a new facet of war, the media saturation resulting from sustained coverage of the disintegration of the Former Yugoslavia and post-genocide attention to mass migration from Rwanda meant that violence against women found Western media space and attention. Media capture gave rise to sustained transnational feminist advocacy on the inclusion of gender-based harms when the Security Council moved to create ad hoc International Criminal Tribunals to pursue justice and accountability, and promote deterrence in the Former Yugoslavia. Attention to conflict-related sexual violence has now, as a result, become recognized in the international legal and policy framework—in laws, jurisprudence, and normative frameworks such as Security Council resolutions advancing the Women, Peace, and Security (WPS) Agenda.

Since the passage of the landmark UN Security Council resolution 1325 (2000), the WPS Agenda has become the dominant discourse framing women's engagement in international affairs over the past seventeen years. The engagement of the Security Council, through a series of high-profile resolutions from 1325 onward, has delivered a visible presence for women in the war and peace terrain. The resolutions have produced a political vocabulary of requirement and benchmarking, resulting in greater attention being paid to women's harms during conflict management and conflict regulation. Yet as the WPS Agenda has emerged, so too has a critique that its subsequent direction for too many years was one of preoccupation with protection, and within that, specifically protection from sexual harms. This focus is felt by some as having resulted in a corresponding failure to adequately explore other gendered harms that accrue during and after war, or to sufficiently address and implement the original drive for resolution 1325—a focus on prevention of conflict, gender equality, and women's participation in all spheres of peace and security decision-making.

Notwithstanding this critique, the WPS Agenda has continued to augment and expand. Although women have been invisible during and after conflict in multiple ways, the "official" end of women's relative invisibility after conflict came even later than recognition of women's experience during conflict. Recognition only followed after considerable lobbying and advocacy efforts by women's organizations and key states. UN Security Council resolution 1325 specified that women should be "mainstreamed" into all peacekeeping and peace-building processes. To help ensure enforcement and oversight, the United Nations has enacted a series of subsequent resolutions: 1820 (2008), 1888 (2009), 1960 (2010), 2106 (2013), 2122 (2013), and 2242 (2015); international organizations have created benchmarks; and states have been encouraged to develop national action plans addressing gender in the context of the WPS Agenda. As these new resolutions and related initiatives emphasized, women's inclusion in post-conflict processes is crucial: this is the phase in which laws, institutions, and political, economic, and legal systems are created or restructured. Nevertheless, the potential capacity of these efforts to bridge the implementation gap remains largely theoretical.

An important contribution to understanding the progress and trajectory of the WPS Agenda was the publication of the Global Study on the implementation of resolution 1325 on the fifteen-year anniversary of its passage. The Study resulted in a clear evidence base that gender equality and women's meaningful participation are critical to the success of peace and security efforts, and formally recommitted states to resolution 1325 and subsequent resolutions to this end. The handover of the Study to the Security Council in October 2015 was marked by the largest Security Council debate in the history of the United Nations, highlighting that an agenda that had been born from the efforts of international women's civil society, combined with that of a handful of supportive states, and largely marginalized for many years by the Council, had become an agenda with significant mobilization behind it. With the passage of resolution 2242 on that day, the Security Council committed states to engaging women and girls in addressing the challenges of terrorism, counterterrorism, and preventing violent extremism, layering women's security into the fulcrum of the new wars and new security challenges of the United Nations.

Women directly experience numerous impacts during conflict, many related to sexual violence, including unwanted pregnancies, sexually transmitted diseases, and community stigma. There is increasing recognition that gendered harms are insufficiently captured by the narrow rubric of sexual harm and encompass a range of economic, social, and political dimensions. Moreover, the gendered impact of wartime violence is also not limited to sexual violence against women (rather, it includes men, girls, and boys). Increasingly, as this *Handbook* notes, we are aware of the extent to which men experience sexual violence and harm in conflict, underscoring the complexity of the harm terrain when communal violence is ignited. Even as we acknowledge these multidimensional facets, those on the ground working in the conflict environment have noted that as a country's infrastructure disintegrates, women are the first to be affected in multiple ways, as economic infrastructures disintegrate, as migration and exile become the only perceived choices to ensure safety from harm, and as violent extremism in many new conflict settings target women and non-conformists first.

After conflict, violence against women may continue or even increase as a direct result of the lack of security and the perception of impunity associated with war crimes. Violence against women in communities, homes, and private spaces may play out as a continuation of, or may be aggravated by, the violence of the formal conflict. Of course, in many post-conflict settings, the opportunities to report violence may increase, thereby making visible the layers of violence and harm that women experience in both conflict and post-conflict settings. And additional forms of gender discrimination appear during the post-conflict period. Women are poorly represented in the formal peace processes designed to end conflict, although women contribute in many informal ways to conflict-ending and post-conflict processes. Ongoing formal and informal discrimination and inequitable laws can prevent women from accessing education, employment, land, or inheritance, from becoming financially independent, and from participating in governance and peace-building.

Although much of the focus of work on gender and conflict has been organized around women as victims, there is an increasing amount of research highlighting that women are actors as well as victims in conflict and post-conflict reconstruction. In parallel, more consideration has been paid to the experiences of men and the masculinities that emerge and dominate in conflict and post-conflict settings. Scrutiny of the militarization and consequent demilitarization processes, for example, has begun to develop awareness of how conflict exacerbates stereotypically masculine behavior. The analysis of the gender and conflict intersection now includes a more nuanced understanding of the motives of perpetrators, who are often, but not always, male. Men are, to be sure, perpetrators, but they must also be recognized and understood as victims. Studies of masculinity practices and the construction of the "man" in militarized settings have given a greater understanding of the pressures and choices faced by male combatants, male civilians, and child soldiers in situations of armed conflict. Some aspects of the United Nations' WPS Agenda have attempted to move the dialogue forward from "women as victims" and "men as perpetrators" stereotyping, and there is increasing evidence that women can also be perpetrators of crimes in general, and sexual violence in particular. We recognize that this book is coming together at a particular moment in history, with centrifugal forces competing over women's rights and gender equality. The rise of nationalisms and global conservative forces are leading a backlash on women's rights. Alongside this, however, we see new norms, policies, and influential champions in the international sphere, including the articulation of some feminist values at the forefront of foreign policy in Sweden, and a new UN Secretary-General who has made gender equality and the implementation of the WPS Agenda cornerstones of his new term. The working out of these competing influences will do much to shape how the issues encompassed in this book evolve in the coming decade.

While we have tried to ensure that the *Handbook* is as comprehensive as possible in its approach, there are nevertheless areas that we were unable to cover due to the constraints of timing, but equally of the difficulties of capturing at any one moment a rapidly evolving field. Two areas deserve specific mention in this regard—the first is the intersection of gender and LGBTQI experiences of conflict. This is an area where fascinating work is being done, looking not only at the intersections of identity in relation to conflict, but also at how legal frameworks can be expanded to address these experiences. For example, new thinking is emerging on using international law to capture persecution on the basis of gender non-conformity—which would allow law to protect not just those persecuted on the basis of sexual orientation and gender identity, but equally those perceived as being part of that group, and women and men who do not conform to perceived gender roles. The second key area where we would have liked to have had a dedicated chapter is youth. It is clear that when we talk of gender, we often do so in an age-blind way. The international community is now playing catch-up—with the passage of the first Security Council resolution on youth, peace, and security—resolution 2250—passed in 2015 and intended to mirror resolution 1325. In a context where many conflict-affected countries have populations that are 60–70 percent under the age of thirty-five, and where any attention to youth has either been simply shorthand for young men as potential perpetrators and spoilers or a lumping of "women and youth" as vulnerable populations, specific attention to the roles and experiences of young women and a greater understanding of young men and masculinities are crucial to addressing the conflicts of today. These and other issues are at the forefront of new experiences, practice, and writing and will continue to shape and inform the field of gender and conflict as it grows.

Part I of this *Handbook* will provide background and context, addressing contemporary and historical perspectives in gender conflict research. This section addresses theoretical and contextual approaches to gender and conflict, drawing on methodologies from the areas of international relations, international law, peace and conflict studies, feminist theories, and masculinities studies. In Chapter 1, Laura Sjoberg sets out the broad terrain of conflict theory from a political science perspective, enabling a textured understanding of how conflict takes form and functions. Chapter 2, by Dubravka Žarkov, sets forth a timeline for the creation of the term "gender," and addresses the multiple meanings and usages of the term as it operates in conflict and post-conflict settings. Chapter 3, Judith Gardam's contribution, surveys the regulatory framework of international humanitarian law, and its gendered dimensions exploring the regulatory gaps in the law of armed conflict for women experiencing war. Judy El-Bushra's Chapter 4 examines how failures to inquire into gender dynamics might partially explain the recurrence of violent conflict. Chapter 5, by Jo Butterfield and Elizabeth Heineman, gives valuable historical context to the analysis, including a close review of citizenship status and soldiering. Chapter 6, by Patricia Justino, engages the development and conflict nexus to survey the relationship between conflict and economic development (and regression) for women. Chapter 7, provided by Chris Dolan, concludes this section by foregrounding men's experiences of vulnerability and sexual violence in war, and addressing the marginalization of male harms in contemporary discourses addressing conflict.

Part II tackles the contemporary with concentrated attention to the Women, Peace and Security Agenda. In Chapter 8, Dianne Otto provides a nuanced understanding of the development of women's transnational advocacy in the arena of peace and conflict, reclaiming the history of women's peace activism in the inter-state arena. Anne Marie Goetz and Rob Jenkins offer a thorough institutional analysis of the political and institutional engagement with women's security through the UN system in Chapter 9. In Chapter 10, Karen Engle provides contemporary analysis of the emergence of sexual violence as the primary motif of gendered engagement with conflict settings in the post–Cold War era. In Chapter 11, anthropologist Kimberly Theidon addresses two sizable gaps in the sexual violence literature on conflict, namely the harms experienced by men and boys, and the prevalence and complexity of the lives of children who were born of wartime rape. Underscoring the shifting nature of gender and conflict preoccupations, Naureen Chowdhury Fink and Alison Davidian explore the emerging terrain of counterterrorism, conflict, and its interface with the WPS Agenda in Chapter 12. Chapter 13, by Pramila Patten, offers an important study of the interface of the international human rights system through the CEDAW Committee with women's experiences of conflict. Chapter 14, by Pablo Castillo Díaz and Hanny Cueva Beteta, concludes this section with forensic attention to the kinds of benchmarks and indicators that have emerged to measures the success (or failure) of women's integration into the peace and security arena.

Part III tackles the legal and political architecture of conflict regulation. In Gina Heathcote's contribution (Chapter 15), she illuminates the gender dynamics of humanitarian intervention. Analysis of the jurisprudential and legal dimensions of gender justice is provided by Patricia Viseur Sellers in Chapter 16, as she addresses the jurisprudence of the ad hoc criminal tribunals of the Former Yugoslavia, Rwanda, and Sierra Leone. The subsequent Chapter 17, by Amrita Kapur, delves further into the synergies of gender justice in international criminal law with a thorough review of the complimentary regime of the International Criminal Court and its capacity to effect gender justice both nationally and internationally. In Chapter 18, Valerie Oosterveld concentrates on one particular gendered crime, namely the crime of forced marriage, and explores the scale and consequence of this crime for women in conflict sites. Kristin Kalla follows by rounding out the criminal and transitional justice analysis with a compelling analysis of emerging reparations practice in international law (Chapter 19). In concluding this section, three meta themes are further advanced. In Chapter 20, Amina Mama returns us to foundational questions about the relationships of colonial harms and experiences with the contemporary conflict challenges we experience today. Here the challenge of colonialism is not only its relationship with the present; the more vexing question of legal accountability for colonial harms in the present is interrogated as well. Chapter 21, by Lucy Hovil, addresses the parallel application of international human rights law with refugee and asylum law in situations of conflict. Finally, in Chapter 22, Vasuki Nesiah addresses the relevance of international conflict feminism (ICF), arguing that too often ICF defines the notion of conflict victims and the landscape of "women, peace, and security" (WPS) in ways that empower globally hegemonic structures and ideas.

Section IV addresses conflict and post-conflict spaces, including not only geographical locals but sub-fields and institutions of legal, political, and social interface for women with war and its consequences. In Chapter 23, by Kathy Gaca, we revisit historical space and are given insight into the longevity of sexual violence as a wartime pastime and the relationship between antiquity and modernity in the practices of sexual violence and conquest. An emphasis on methodology and data analysis showcased in the work of Amelia Hoover Green (Chapter 24) concentrates on the importance and challenges of data collection and data quality for assessing gendered experiences of conflict. Intersectionality and its centrality to any form of gendered conflict analysis is established by Eilish Rooney in Chapter 25. In Chapter 26, Patti Petesch asserts the importance of economic development and opportunity in situations of conflict, exploring the paradox of the opportunities available for women to exert (albeit limited in some cases, and short-lived in others) agency for economic entrepreneurship and some economic mobility. The contribution by public health experts Lauren Ng and Theresa Betancourt (Chapter 27) affirms both the risks and resilience exposed during conflict for men and women. In Chapter 28, the centrality of weaponry is detailed, as Barbara Frey exposes the gender implications of the small and light arms trade in conflicted sites. The weaponry theme is followed through in Chapter 29, as Christof Heyns and Tess Borden discuss the development of unarmed weaponry and the gendered effects of their deployment and usage. Their chapter exposes the challenges of new technologies to a gendered experience of armed conflict, and the overlap and consequences of an increasingly complex international administrative structure to regulate armed conflict and its aftermath. The *Handbook* then turns to address peacekeeping. Sabrina Karim and Marsha Henry in Chapter 30 set forth the impacts of gendered hiring and practices on peacekeeping forces. Exposing the relationship between peacekeeping and the physical and sexual exploitation of women in Chapter 31, Martina Vandenberg details the imperative of developing accountability to end impunity. In sequence, we turn to address the role of gender in peacemaking, as Christine Bell delves deeply into the gendered structures, opportunities, and limitations of peace agreements and peace processes for women (Chapter 32). Thereafter, Aili Tripp turns to address the role and capabilities of women's organizations and their role in centralizing and mobilizing peace initiatives

(Chapter 33). Issues of demobilization, disarmament, and reintegration are addressed in Chapter 34 by Mazurana, Krystalli, and Baaré. The section concludes with a thoughtful reflection in Chapter 35 by Pascha Bueno-Hansen on the relationship between decolonial politics in Latin America and the impunity cycles that remain in place today following authoritarian and military transitions, followed by a meticulous overview of the interface between gender and governance in post-conflict and democratizing settings by Lisa Kindervater and Sheila Meintjes (Chapter 36).

Finally, Part V provides specific case studies grounded in the experiences of several countries, exploring different gendered experiences of conflict in various regions. The country-specific case studies will pull out key themes of the *Handbook*, including but not limited to truth recovery processes, amnesty, violent extremism, restitution, political representation, and militarization. These contributions address some unique challenges in the post-conflict setting, particularly in identifying the differing roles of multiple national and international actors, and assessing their positive roles in securing peace and developing the post-conflict state. *Inter alia*, this section documents the highly variable influences and complexities of the influx of international actors in the unstable post-conflict environment. These the creation of false economies, the promise and (non) delivery of secure governance, the global-local arms trade nexus, as well as the positive impact of international presence and the potential for modeling expanded gender roles through that interaction. Sari Kouvo and Corey Levine discuss women's rights in post-conflict Afghanistan and question those decisions and processes in Chapter 37. In Chapter 38, Karima Bennoune decries the elimination of women's voices and the crimes committed against them in the documentation of mass atrocities in Algeria during the 1980s. Lejla Hadzimesic offers Chapter 39 as a reflection on the failures of reparations provided to women victims of violence in post-conflict Bosnia and Herzegovina. Chapter 40 looks at a different kind of reparation, with Donny Meertens detailing the land-restitution process in Columbia and its gendered omissions. In Chapter 41, Maria Eriksson Baaz and Maria Stern offer personal reflections on their research in the Democratic Republic of Congo, questioning how, or even whether, we understand gender in the context of conflict. Monica McWilliams and Avila Kilmurray, in Chapter 42, set forth a detailed discussion of the impact that the grassroots women's movement had on the resolution of violence in Northern Ireland. In Chapter 43, Nadera Shalhoub-Kevorkian offers the perspective of women living under occupation, with particular attention to the "politics of birth." Doris Buss and Jerusa Ali, in Chapter 44, identify key components of women's political participation to post-conflict Rwanda, and finally, Ambika Satkunanathan, in Chapter 45, details the impacts of militarization on women in Sri Lanka.

While women are increasingly becoming visible in the study of war, and we are developing better understandings of the role of gender beginning in the pre-war environment and ending with the post-conflict process, there has been little integration of the entire timeline of gendered experiences. This *Handbook* takes a holistic approach addressing pre-war experience, and continuing with the examination of the conflict itself, during peace negotiations, throughout the post-conflict reconstruction phase, and into long-term post-conflict development. Its goal is to help policymakers, UN staff, peacekeepers, activists, and scholars pull the gender and conflict terrain together into a coherent whole.

NOTE

1. Catherine MacKinnon, *Feminism Unmodified* (Cambridge MA: Harvard University Press, 1987).

PART I

BACKGROUND AND CONTEXT

CHAPTER 1

....

THEORIES OF WAR

....

LAURA SJOBERG

A significant amount of research in international relations (IR) has been inspired by inquiry into the meaning, causes, and consequences of the phenomenon of war—both in contemporary global politics and throughout history. That inquiry has produced many contributions to thinking about "the war puzzle" in global politics, but no single or consensus theory of war (Vasquez 2009). In fact, the multiple causes of war make it too complicated for any single theory to cover (Suganami 1997). The complexity of the "war puzzle" has led to a significant amount of theorizing from diverse perspectives. This chapter will discuss many of those theories, and will show the ways in which they individually and collectively neglect gender. I argue that this neglect is problematic because war gender analysis is necessary to fully understand war. This chapter makes that argument first, by outlining a number of traditional approaches to war, and then by discussing the ways in which gender is key to understanding war—conceptually, empirically, and normatively.

DEFINING WAR

....

Many scholars suggest that the varying definitions of war have several common elements (Levy and Thompson 2010). One element of war is that it is *violent*, involving "the use of force to kill and injure people and destroy military and economic resources" (Levy and Thompson 2010, 5). Second, war is between two or more political groups—where "between" requires two or more parties actually fighting, and "political groups" include states, substate actors, and international organizations. Third, war is *sustained*—war is often (though not always) distinguished from lesser political violence by the degree of intensity and the length of the conflict. Scholars looking to understand trends in wars see several of them: in recent years, intra-state wars are increasing, "great power" wars are decreasing, war is increasingly asymmetric, and illicit economies are increasingly involved in war and conflict (Goldstein 2011; Kaldor 2006; Levy and Thompson 2011; Paul 1994).

Work in critical IR theorizing has questioned the traditional great-power focus of war theorizing (Booth 2007). Marxist-inspired critical theorists are interested in understanding war for the purpose of freeing ourselves from it (Booth 2007, 65). Human security theorists suggest that a myopic focus on war neglects the major threats to most people's security, including economic, environmental, health, food, personal, and political insecurities (Axworthy 2001). The Copenhagen school of thought focuses on how things come to be classified as "security" and "war" in state policy discourses, and what forms of violence are left out of those classifications (Buzan, Waever, and de Wilde 1998). Postmodern or poststructural critical theorizing pays attention to the politics of constructing knowledge about war, in global politics and in the study of global politics (George 1994).

All of this work contributes (if in very different ways) to fitting important pieces of the "war puzzle" into identifying what war is. At the same time, the overwhelming majority of this work neglects the potentially important tool of gender analysis. This chapter highlights and maps those conceptual gaps and addresses some of the consequences that follow from these gendered lacunae.

Feminists asking where women are in war and war theorizing show that wars start long before traditional theorists see them beginning and that their "end" is unclear—in Enloe's words, these are the "gender histories" of wars—histories of wars made longer and more complicated when women are made visible (Enloe 2010). Judith Gardam's work, represented in Chapter 3 in this book, shows how the laws of war use gendered constructs to define who fights in wars (Gardam 1993). Wars are fought in the gendered feminine private sphere of the "home front" as much as they are fought on the gendered masculine public sphere of the "battlefront" (see Ng and Betancourt, Chapter 27 in this volume; Horn 2010). Wars are both military and economic, and the economies of wars are gendered (see Justino, Chapter 6 in this volume; Raven-Roberts 2012). Feminists have shown that looking at war through gender lenses requires looking carefully at what is traditionally understood as "after" war but constitutes and is constituted by that war—including peacekeeping (Vandenberg, Chapter 31 in this volume), peace agreements (Bell, Chapter 32), disarmament processes (Mazurana et al., Chapter 34), transitional justice including international criminal justice (Bueno-Hansen, Chapter 35; Oosterveld, Chapter 18; Sellers, Chapter 16), and reconstruction (Kindervater and Meintjes, Chapter 36)—and they have led the charge to expand war theorizing to include these elements.

While some feminist scholarship has some commonalities with other critical war theorizing, feminist scholars argue that gender analysis provides a unique view on what constitutes war. Feminist analyses of war ask how the dynamics of masculinities and femininities shape how war is constructed (Tickner 2001), experienced (Enloe 2010), sensed (Sylvester 2013), continued (Cohn 2012; Cuomo 1996), and defined as multilocational (Cockburn 2010), embodied (Wilcox 2014), and always gendered in meaning, performance, and interpretation (Sjoberg 2013). The importance of gender analysis to thinking about *what war is* has motivated feminists to suggest that it is also key to thinking about *the causes of war*, discussed next.

THE CAUSES OF WAR

Often, war theorists distinguish their approaches to war on the basis of what "level" they focus on: the international system, the state, or the individual (Waltz 1959). Scholars using gender analysis have questioned the utility of this analytic scheme for two major reasons. First, they have expressed concern that the very attempt to distinguish "levels" makes it look like the "levels" can be disaggregated, when they are really interdependent (True 1996). Second, they have suggested that the concepts used to shape the levels, including the international system (Tickner 2001), the state (Peterson 1992a), the autonomous individual (Hirschmann 2003), and human nature (Jagger 1983), are gendered. Often, marginalized people (see Rooney, Chapter 25 in this volume), non-traditional actors (Tripp, Chapter 33), and ethical issues (Žarkov, Chapter 2) are neglected in causal accounts of wars that focus around the international system, the state, or individual leaders. Gender analysis has offered critiques and reconstructions of causal theorizing of wars across these levels of analysis as well, as discussed later in the chapter.

Scholars using gender analysis often have questioned the methods used by most IR scholars investigating the causes of war. Feminist work recognizing the interdependence of the personal and the political has critiqued the notion that the causes of war are even capable of being identified and objectively knowable. If knowledge is perspectival and experiential, as feminist research suggests, then scholarship *about war* is subjective, as are the decisions of policymakers who *make* and *fight* wars. Such an approach has impacts for both how war is thought about and how war scholarship is thought about—where feminist scholarship suggests focusing on sense (Sylvester 2013), narrative (Wibben 2011), and performance (Shepherd 2008), as discussed in the following section (see also Žarkov, Chapter 2 in this volume). This chapter argues that the directions that feminist scholarship has been pursuing are productive directions for war theorizing.

System-level war theorizing

This section reviews various traditional theories addressing the causes of war and feminist challenges to them. Most system-level war theorizing comes from political realism, which has dominated both the theoretical landscape of IR and the influence that IR scholars have had in the policy world since the end of World War II (Morgenthau 1948; Waltz 1979). Waltz and other structural realists characterize the international system as "decentralized and anarchic," a situation that leaves states without outside authorities to moderate behavior or provide protection from other states' bad behavior (Waltz 1979, 18). In this view of the world, "there is a constant possibility of war in a world in which there are two or more states seeking to pursue a set of interests and having no agency above them on which they can rely for protection," and they therefore act to "ensure their survival," often violently (Waltz 1959, 227; 1979, 94). This is why states make war, in the view of structural realists.

While political realism is dominant, a number of other system-level theories merit mention. System-level war theorists from the liberal tradition in IR think about the ways that states as firms (like companies) manufacture security and can effect changes in and of the international system (Lake 1996). By contrast, world-systems theorists focus on structural factors inspired by Marxist principles, considering the relationship between the core (the "inside," or great powers) and the periphery (states with less power and/or resources) in the international system (Wallerstein 1984). Long-cycle theories of war are focused on understanding global wars as lengthy periods of crisis and conflict, typically spanning two to three decades (Rasler and Thompson 1984).

Engagement with third-image (focused on the international system level) theorizing on the causes of wars shows some commonalities with feminist theorizing, including a long view of conflict and an understanding of war as pervasive. Still, feminist critiques of system-level war theorizing have pointed out normative and empirical problems inherent in its understandings of the ways that the world works. Feminist work has problematized structural theorists' tendency to focus on the government-level actions of most powerful states in the international system at the expense of the political margins within these states, as well as within less powerful states (Brown 1988). Feminist scholars have suggested that structural war theorizing has been partial, based "on knowledge about men" and how they interact (Tickner 2001). As such, it not only tells just part of the story, but also neglects the part of wars that feminist scholars have focused most on: "low" politics, everyday violences, and people's lives (Peterson 1992b; Tickner 2001). Through a gender lens, looking at the ways goods are distributed *within* the household in conflict zones is as important as looking at the ways that militaries station troops in order to understand what war is and how it works. As a result, a significant amount of feminist work on war has focused on how people are positioned vis-à-vis war and conflict, on the basis of not only gender, but also race, nationality, class, and religion.

Research using gender as a category of analysis has also drawn links between the individual level and the system level, rather than focusing solely on the latter (see Žarkov, Chapter 2 in this volume; Sjoberg and Peet 2011). Recently, feminist analysis has also begun to suggest the productivity of studying gender hierarchy in/of the international system (Sjoberg 2013). Building on work that has characterized gender as constitutive of global politics (Scott 1986), it has argued that there are strong empirical and normative reasons for "seeing gender hierarchy as a/the permissive cause of war," which has the potential to "account for (as structural realism claims to) war's existence (in a permissive sense) but also (as structural realism cannot) variation in the occurrence of specific wars" (Sjoberg 2013, 99, 103). Seeing gender hierarchy as a permissive cause of war means understanding the ways in which any attempt by states to seek gender dominance consequently *genders* dominance relations and creates a possibility for war and conflict as they currently function in global politics. In this view, it is key to pay attention to the structural ways in which gendered expectations, stereotypes, and competitions play out in the production of conflict in the global political arena.

State-level war theorizing

Much of the accounting for the occurrence of specific wars in traditional war theorizing happens at the state level, focused on states in the international arena and/or interactions between them. This section discusses that second-image theorizing, dividing it into two major categories: dyad-level war theorizing (focused on relationships between two states) and monad-level war theorizing (focused on the behaviors of individual states).

Dyad-level theories identify a number of different patterns that might influence the likelihood that two states will make war. They suggest that the majority of the world's wars are repetitive conflicts between sets of states identified as rivals (Diehl and Goertz 2000). Among dyad-level research programs, "steps to war" theorists focus on the different issues that states fight wars about, and how those issues become disputes and ultimately wars (Senese and Vasquez 2008). Among the issues these theorists study are private information (Senese and Vasquez 2008., 66), commitment problems (where states cannot commit to a cooperative relationship out of fear the other will renege; Powell 2006), indivisible issues (things that cannot be divided among parties; Fearon 1995), and the absence of bargaining outcomes that states prefer to war (Odell and Crump 2008). Rather than focusing on issues, many liberal theorists interested in the dyadic causes of war trace path dependence to traits that states do (or do not) have in common, like trade interdependence (Oneal and Russett 1999), regime type (largely focused on democracy; Doyle 1983; Russett 1993), or capitalism (Gartzke 2007). The most popular of these theories, the democratic peace, suggests a number of different reasons that democratic commonality might bring peace, including common culture, the slowness of democratic processes, and the incentive structure of democratic governance (Maoz and Russett 1993). Scholars focusing on alternate causal mechanisms explain the dyadic peace using other mechanisms, including collective security (Cederman 2001), liberal alliances (Cederman and Rao 2001), great power status (Lake 1992), established state security (Layne 1994), American exceptionalism (Rosato 2003), selectorate behavior (Bueno de Mesquita et al. 2005), and territorial stability (Gibler 2007).

Rather than focus on inter-state dynamics, single-state theories of war focus on what states do or what happens within states to cause conflicts, analyzing relationships between branches of government (Snyder 1991), coalitions among domestic interest groups (Olson 1971), the phenomenon of states making wars to divert attention from domestic political conflicts (Tir 2010), and domestic cultural factors that make states more aggressive (Huntington 1993). Single-state war theorizing has explored the ways that conflicts over ideology (English 2000), religion (Little 1996), cultures of national security (Katzenstein 1996), and other similar variables influence whether and how conflicts are made. These approaches, often associated with IR constructivism, suggest that social factors contribute to states' likelihood to start wars (Katzenstein 1996).

Feminists have suggested that analyses of between-state and intra-state security that do not take account of gender are incomplete representations of how wars are made. Feminist scholarship has recognized that there are various ways that traditional methods for making states "secure" make the women in them *less secure*—through increased domestic violence, increased physical and health vulnerability, decreased economic opportunity, or the increased salience of the gendered values and expectations associated with militarism(s) (Tickner 2001). This means that state-level theories that emphasize democracy or trade *for security* have gendered implications, and are often complicit in the development and perpetuation of gendered militaristic, nationalistic cultures (McClintock 1993). In policy terms, then, it is important to pay attention to the gendered impacts of securitizing particular issues both *within* and among states. Traditional paths toward state security often have negative impacts on women *in addition to* the gendered distribution of goods under traditionally valued regimes like capitalism and democracy, and war theories analyzing and/or endorsing them are often silent on these implications.

As a result, a number of feminist scholars have emphasized the importance of paying attention to the *relational* dynamics of *relationships* among states in looking at the causes of war between them (Allison 2001). Critical readings of relationships debunk theories that suggest that simple commonalities decrease the likelihood of conflict in favor of more complicated analyses of how *relating* takes place (Sjoberg 2013). For example, gender analysis has suggested that state-based theories of war emphasize coercive power while ignoring the importance of collaborative power, at the expense of potential explanatory leverage (Allen 2000). Feminist theorizing suggests that collaborative power plays a role in motivating soldiers, in forming alliances, and in constituting the nationalisms that fuel conflicts. Studying collaborative power might not only help us to understand how wars come to be, but also provide powerful tools for understanding how to end them.

As a corrective, gender analysis has suggested that "gendered war narratives" within and between states are a key condition of the possibility of war at the state level, and often are repeated by war theorists (Wibben 2011). "Gendered war narratives" reference gender (explicitly or implicitly). In these narratives, gender stereotypes serve to justify and perpetuate state violence. The subject matter of gendered war narratives ranges from "defending women" in Iraq or Afghanistan (see Kouvo and Levine, Chapter 37 in this volume) to encouraging strategic interference with reproduction in Bosnia or Rwanda (Kouvo and Levine, Chapter 37; Sjoberg 2006). Looking at the role that gender plays in how states justify war suggests that relationships among states are influenced by the gendered nature of the state, gendered nationalisms, gendered narratives, gendered strategic cultures, and gendered interactions. States' understandings of their interests, of their needs, and of their responses in crisis politics are often dictated by states' self-perceived (or desired) positions on gender hierarchies among states. For these reasons, feminist work has contended that state-level war theorizing cannot be done well without attention to gender (Sjoberg 2013). Still, most state-level war theorizing has yet to pay significant attention to issues of gender.

Substate-level war theorizing

Most substate-level war theorizing also has yet to pay significant attention to issues of gender. There are two sorts of substate-level war theorizing: those that focus on the behavior of individual people, and those that focus, more broadly, on the elements of "human nature" that might cause violence in global politics. Individual-level war theories argue that people can impact the course of conflict within or between states with their behavior and decision-making (Byman and Pollack 2001). Accordingly, these theories focus on how individual beliefs (Holsti 1967), leadership styles (Hermann 2001), misperceptions (Jarvis 1976), and risk propensity (Levy 1992) interfere with rational behavior patterns that might avoid war and violence in global politics. Recently, first-image IR theorizing has been paying attention to social movement theorizing to understand the root causes of collective violence in international politics (Zimmerman 2013), drawing on political psychology to understand the foundations of group violence (Bar-Tal 2007). Theories of war based on "human nature" draw most seriously on evolutionary biology (Thayer 2000), emphasizing processes like egoism, domination, and the search for females to mate with (Thayer 2000), or adaptability and natural selection (Cederman and Gleditsch 2004).

Gender analysis has provided a number of engagements with substate war theorizing. Feminists have argued that the work paying attention to individuals in war-making often prizes masculine characteristics over feminine characteristics (Sapiro 2003), and men over women (Sjoberg 2013). Gender analysis has demonstrated that militarized femininities as well as masculinities incentivize individual violence and serve as a condition of possibility for war-making (Goldstein 2001). Feminist scholars have shown that the relationship between the personal and the international is much more complicated than mainstream war theorizing has portrayed (Enloe 2010; Sjoberg and Gentry 2007), and feminist research has demonstrated that there is a bi-directional relationship between normal people's lives and war. This is especially clear as individual women's lives impact international conflicts, and international conflicts impact individual women's lives (Moon 1997). This serves as a corrective to theories that treat women as the *object* rather than the *subject* of international politics generally, and war specifically.

As a result, there has been an increasing focus on how people at the margins of global politics experience war and are instrumentalized in war discourses in order to account for the possibility of war. Particularly, feminists have argued that expectations about *what women are* both motivate wars and serve to support them (Sjoberg 2013). For example, calls for men to fight wars often invoke a perceived responsibility to protect "women and children" in their countries, and perceptions that enemies threaten (presumed innocent) women either "at home" or "abroad" can call for a violent response. Feminist work recognizes that women are agents *even when* they are victims in war and conflict, and pays attention to where women are, what women do, and what women experience. This work engages, and critiques, first-image work that treats (elite, male) individuals as the only people significant in causing war. A number of the chapters in this book (e.g., Tripp, Chapter 33; McWilliams and Kilmurray, Chapter 42) show the importance of non-elite, gendered-feminine individuals in making war possible and making war end. This is true whether those women serve in a support capacity, a protest capacity, or even a capacity that involves them in committing significant conflict-related violence.

Gender analysis intervenes in evolutionary accounts of war-making a little bit differently than in the individually focused accounts. It is important to note that, unlike most causal theories of war and conflict, evolutionary biology accounts of human nature *do* explicitly discuss gender roles (Gat 2009; Fukuyama 1998). At the same time, they do so in a way that is both *gender-essentialist* (they assume fundamental characteristics of women and men that each "sex" has in common, and that differ from the other sex) and *heterosexist* (they assume that heterosexuality is the "natural" lifestyle that humans live), when there is evidence that both of those assumptions are problematic (Butler 2000; Peterson 1999). The underlying assumptions of evolutionary theories of human nature and war are both empirically unrepresentative of human experience and normatively problematic for gender subordination in global politics. In the alternative, a queer theory understanding of war might suggest that the "both/and" presence of the "good guy" and "bad guy" logics on both sides of any war or conflict hints at a liminality and queerness both to war and to theories of its making and fighting.

The Practice of War

War theorizing is not just limited to thinking about the causes of wars. A significant amount of war theorizing has paid attention to how wars are fought. These scholars analyze strategy, tactics, logistics, and experiences of war. Strategy can be thought of as macro-level war-fighting, or "the art of distributing and applying military means to fulfill the ends of policy" (Hart 1942, 321). Strategists, then, look to match the use of force to the military goals of war and to the policy ends that the states and/or other groups that they serve have. Scholars who study strategy are interested in which strategic approaches are chosen when, and their relative effectiveness (Gray 1991). Strategies can be classified as offensive and defensive (Posen 1992), or by the techniques that militaries use when deploying them (Reiter and Meerk 1999).

Tactics can be thought of as battlefield-level decisions about how wars are made and fought. While the distinction between strategy and tactics is increasingly blurry as war technologies evolve, theorizing about strategy and theorizing about tactics have been distinct for a long time. Theorizing about tactics has focused on available technology (Alexander 2002), the appropriateness of particular tactics to war situations (Pape 1996), and the moral implications of tactical decisions (Walzer 1977). Logistics is the science of how supplies, soldiers, and rations get to battle sites or are moved with standing armies (Van Crevald 2004). Theorists study the impact of more or less successful supply chains on military victory possibilities, as well as the impact of those supply chains on the civilian populations that they run through (Kane 2001).

The study of how war is fought typically lacks any significant gender analysis. Yet, gendered assumptions delineate the combatant/civilian distinction (Kinsella 2011), and sexual violence is a key strategy and tactic of war-fighting (Kirby 2013). Gendered militarisms produce gendered strategies (Peterson 2010); the development of war technologies are gendered (see Heyns and Borden, Chapter 29 in this volume; Wilcox 2009); war-fighting practice remains androcentric (Brown 2011; Sjoberg 2013); and gender stereotypes are often appropriated as weapons in war (see Fink and Davidian, Chapter 12 in this volume; Oliver 2007).

GENDER DYNAMICS, WAR, AND WAR THEORIZING

Most (though not all) feminist theorizing on war and conflict in IR suggests that the omission of thinking about gender dynamics poses a serious problem for the completeness, empirical accuracy, and normative value of IR theorizing. The remainder of the chapters in this book make a wide variety of different observations and arguments that show how gender *matters* to understanding what war is, how it happens, and how it is practiced in global politics. Accordingly, this chapter closes with a discussion of the factors that gender analysis looks for when attempting to understand the importance of gender in thinking about the meaning, causes, and practices of war and conflict.

First is one of the questions that inspired early gender analysis in IR: Where are women in global politics? Asking how men and women are differently positioned in conflict not only helps to understand what conflict is, how it comes to be, and how it is practiced; it also helps to understand how gender dynamics are constituted by conflict, much as conflict is constituted by gender dynamics. Asking how men and women are differently situated along the various axes, and at the different levels, of conflict, however, is only useful if that inquiry is paired with an exploration of how the power dynamics between masculinities and femininities work to construct and maintain those different positions.

Looking at the ways that power dynamics between masculinities and femininities position men and women differently in conflicts can open up a second major line of questioning—work that asks how associations with traits understood as masculine or traits understood as feminine affect competition between, positioning of, and conflict among political groups, states, and international organizations. This line of inquiry asks about the use of feminization as a tactic between belligerent states (Peterson 2010), the ways in which states compete using gendered war narratives (Wibben 2011), and the ways in which the gender significations of combatants influence their strategic effectiveness (Sjoberg and Gentry 2007).

Exploring the ways that gender dynamics impact how actors in the international arena are positioned and compete leads to a third set of questions about gender, war, and conflict—inquiries that deal with how the gendered dynamics of conflict are interconnected. For example, the gendered expectations of peacekeepers (Karim and Henry, Chapter 30 in this volume) and the gendered expectations of soldiers (Theidon, Chapter 11) are connected to perceptions of women as spoils of war (Gaca, Chapter 23). The gendered dynamics of inter-state relationships and the gendered experiences of marginalized actors (e.g., Rooney, Chapter 25) are different phenomena—as are the subjects of most of the chapters in this book—but they are interrelated. They are linked by the presence of gendered power, gendered social dynamics, gendered hierarchies, and gendered conflicts—and analyzing those links helps to understand *both* the nature of conflict and the nature of gender subordination.

This is true whether one is analyzing dynamics of conflict that traditionally receive a significant amount of attention from scholars and media outlets, such as the motivation that states have to intervene in other states' conflicts, or dynamics of conflict that are traditionally invisible in those sources, like the sensed experience of war. In the case of the former, gendered (chivalric) notions of (protector) masculine citizen-soldiering can be related to notions of responsibilities to protect and calls to intervene, laced with raced dynamics about who counts as a protector and who is in need of protection. Expectations of women's innocence and men's violence are prominent in everyday accounts of civilian immunity, and gendered expectations of both soldiers and civilians (mapped onto masculinities and femininities) pervade not only war theorizing but war practice. Gender lenses also call for an analysis, however, of the gendered dynamics of war that are traditionally neglected by war theorizing—such as the sensed experiences of war. What does war smell like? Taste like? Feel like? Sound like? Look like? And do those experiences change based on the (gendered) positions that one has in relationship to that war and conflict?

In this way, feminist theorizing suggests changes to both the *scope* and the *substance* of war theorizing as traditionally conceived. Feminist questions about who fights wars, why they are fought, and the gendered ways in which they are experienced can enrich understandings of *both* gender and war.

References

Alexander, Bevin. 2002. *How Great Generals Win*. New York: W. W. Norton.
Allen, Amy. 2000. *The Power of Feminist Theory*. Boulder, CO: Westview Press.
Allison, Juliann Emmons. 2001. "Peace among Friends: A Feminist Interpretation of the Democratic Peace." *Peace and Change* 26, no. 2: 204–222.

Axworthy, Lloyd. 2001. "Human Security and Global Governance: Putting People First." *Global Governance* 7, no. 1: 19–25.

Bar-Tal, Daniel. 2007. "Sociopsychological Foundations of Intractable Conflicts." *American Behavioral Scientist* 50, no. 11: 1430–1453.

Booth, Ken. 2007. *Theory of World Security*. Cambridge: Cambridge University Press.

Brown, Katherine E. 2011. "Blinded by the Explosion? Security and Resistance in Muslim Women's Suicide Terrorism." In *Women, Gender, and Terrorism*, edited by Laura Sjoberg and Caron Gentry, 194–226. Athens: University of Georgia Press.

Brown, Sarah. 1988. "Feminism, International Theory and International Relations of Gender inequality." *Millennium: Journal of International Studies* 17, no. 3: 461–475.

Bueno de Mesquita, Bruce, et al. 2005. *The Logic of Political Survival*. Cambridge, MA: MIT Press.

Butler, Judith. 2000. *Bodies That Matter*. London: Routledge.

Buzan, Barry, Ole Waever, and Jaap de Wilde. 1998. *Security: A New Framework for Analysis*. Boulder, CO: Lynne Rienner.

Byman, Daniel, and Kenneth Pollack. 2001. "Let Us Now Praise Great Men: Bringing the Statesman Back In." *International Security* 25, no. 4: 107–146.

Cockburn, Cynthia. 2010. "Gender Relations as Causal in Militarization and War." *International Feminist Journal of Politics* 12, no. 2: 139–157.

Cohn, Carol, ed. 2012. *Women and Wars*. London: Polity.

Cederman, Lars-Erik. 2001. "Modeling the Democratic Peace as a Kantian Selection Process." *Journal of Conflict Resolution* 45, no. 4: 470–502.

Cederman, Lars Erik, and Kristian Skrede Gleditsch. 2004. "Conquest and Regime Change: An Evolutionary Model of the Spread of Democracy and Peace." *International Studies Quarterly* 48, no. 3: 603–629.

Cederman, Lars-Erik, and Mohan Rao. 2001. "Exploring the Dynamic of the Democratic Peace." *Journal of Conflict Resolution* 45, no. 6: 818–833.

Cuomo, Chris. 1996. "War Is Not Just an Event: Reflections on the Significance of Everyday Violence." *Hypatia* 11, no. 4: 30–45.

Diehl, Paul, and Gary Goertz. 2000. *War and Peace in International Rivalry*. Ann Arbor: University of Michigan Press.

Doyle, Michael. 1983. "Kant, Liberal Legacies, and Foreign Affairs." *Philosophy and Public Affairs* 12, no. 4: 323–353.

English, Robert. 2000. *Russia and the Idea of the West: Gorbachev, Intellectuals, and the End of the Cold War*. New York: Columbia University Press.

Enloe, Cynthia. 2010. *Nimo's War, Emma's War: Making Feminist Sense of the Iraq War*. Berkeley: University of California Press.

Fearon, James. 1995. "Rationalist Explanations for War." *International Organization* 49, no. 3: 379–414.

Fukuyama, Francis. 1998. "Women and the Evolution of World Politics." *Foreign Affairs* 77, no. 5: 24–40.

Gardam, Judith. 1993. "The Law of Armed Conflict: A Feminist Perspective." In *Human Rights in the Twenty-First Century: A Global Challenge*, edited by Kathleen Mahoney, 419–436. The Hague: Martinus Nijhoff Publishers.

Gartzke, Erik. 2007. "The Capitalist Peace." *American Journal of Political Science* 51, no. 1: 161–191.

Gat, Azar. 2009. "So Why Do People Fight? Evolutionary Theory and the Causes of War." *European Journal of International Relations* 15, no. 4: 571–599.

George, Jim. 1994. *Discourses of Global Politics: A Critical Introduction to International Relations*. Boulder, CO: Lynne Rienner.

Gibler, Douglas M. 2007. "Bordering on Peace: Democracy, Territorial Issues, and Conflict." *International Studies Quarterly* 50, no. 3: 509–532.

Goldstein, Joshua. 2001. *War and Gender: How Gender Shapes the War System and Vice Versa*. Cambridge: Cambridge University Press.

Goldstein, Joshua. 2011. *Winning the War on War: The Decline of Armed Conflict Worldwide*. New York: Penguin.

Gray, Colin. 1991. *War, Peace, and Victory: Strategy and Statecraft for the Next Century*. New York: Simon & Schuster.

Hart, B. Liddell. 1942. *The Way to Win Wars*. New York: Faber and Faber.

Hermann, Margaret. 2001. "How Decision Units Shape Foreign Policy: A Theoretical Framework." *International Studies Review* 3, no. 2: 47–81.

Hirschmann, Nancy. 2003. *The Subject of Liberty: Toward a Feminist Theory of Freedom*. Princeton, NJ: Princeton University Press.

Holsti, Ole. 1967. "Cognitive Dynamics and Images of the Enemy." In *Image and Reality in World Politics*, edited by John Farrell and Asa Smith, 16–39. New York: Columbia University Press.

Horn, Denise. 2010. "Boots and Bedsheets: Constructing the Military Support System in a Time of War." In *Gender, War, and Militarism: Feminist Perspectives*, edited by Laura Sjoberg and Sandra Via, 57–68. Santa Barbara, CA: Praeger Security International.

Huntington, Samuel. 1993. "The Clash of Civilizations?" *Foreign Affairs* 72, no. 3: 22–29.

Jagger, Alison M. 1983. *Feminist Politics and Human Nature*. New York: Rowman and Littlefield.

Jarvis, Robert. 1976. *Perception and Misperception in International Politics*. Princeton, NJ: Princeton University Press.

Kaldor, Mary. 2006. *New and Old Wars: Organized Violence in Global Politics*. London: Polity.

Kane, Thomas. 2001. *Military Logistics and Strategic Performance*. London: Cass.

Katzenstein, Peter, ed. 1996. *Cultures of National Security*. Ithaca, NY: Cornell University Press.

Kinsella, Helen. 2011. *The Image before the Weapon: A Critical History of the Distinction between Combatant and Civilian*. Ithaca, NY: Cornell University Press.

Kirby, Paul. 2013. "How Is Rape a Weapon of War? Feminist International Relations, Modes of Critical Explanation, and the Study of Wartime Sexual Violence." *European Journal of International Relations* 19, no. 4: 797–821.

Lake, David. 1992. "Powerful Pacifists: Democratic States and War." *American Political Science Review* 86, no. 1: 24–38.

Lake, David. 1996. "Anarchy, Hierarchy, and Variety in International Relations." *International Organization* 50, no. 1: 1–33.

Layne, Christopher. 1994. "Kant or Can't: The Myth of the Democratic Peace." *International Security* 19, no. 2: 5–49.

Levy, Jack. 1992. "Prospect Theory and International Relations: Theoretical Applications and Analytical Problems." *Political Psychology* 13, no. 2: 283–310.

Levy, Jack, and William Thompson. 2010. *Causes of War*. Oxford: Blackwell.

Levy, Jack, and William Thompson. 2011. *Arc of War*. Chicago: University of Chicago Press.

Little, Richard. 1996. "Religious Militancy." In *Managing Global Chaos: Sources of and Responses to International Conflict*, edited by Chester Crocker, Fen Osler Hampson, and Pamela Aall. Washington, DC: US Institute of Peace Press.

Maoz, Zeev, and Bruce Russett. 1993. "Normative and Structural Causes of Democratic Peace, 1946–1986." *American Political Science Review* 87, no. 3: 624–638.

McClintock, Anne. 1993. "Family Feuds: Gender, Nationalism, and the Family." *Feminist Review* 44: 61–80.

Moon, Katherine. 1997. *Sex among Allies: Military Prostitution in U.S.-Korea Relations.* New York: Columbia University Press.

Morgenthau, Hans. 1948. *Politics among Nations.* New York: Alfred Knopf.

Odell, John, and Larry Crump. 2008. "Analyzing Complex U.S. Trade Negotiations." *Negotiation Journal* 24, no. 4: 355–369.

Oliver, Kelly. 2007. *Women as Weapons of War: Iraq, Sex, and the Media.* New York: Columbia University Press.

Olson, Mancur. 1971. *The Logic of Collective Action.* Cambridge, MA: Harvard University Press.

Oneal, John R., and Bruce Russett. 1999. "Assessing the Liberal Peace with Alternative Specifications: Trade Still Reduces Conflict." *Journal of Conflict Resolution* 36, no. 4: 423–442.

Pape, Robert. 1996. *Bombing to Win: Air Power and Coercion in War.* Ithaca, NY: Cornell University Press.

Paul, T. V. 1994. *Asymmetric Conflicts: War Initiation by Weaker Powers.* Cambridge: Cambridge University Press.

Peterson, V. Spike, ed. 1992a. *Gendered States: Feminist Re(Visions) of International Security.* Boulder, CO: Lynne Rienner.

Peterson, V. Spike. 1992b. "Transgressing Boundaries: Theories of Knowledge, Gender, and International Relations." *Millennium: Journal of International Studies* 21, no. 2: 183–206.

Peterson, V. Spike. 1999. "Sexing Political Identities/Nationalism as Heterosexism." *International Feminist Journal of Politics* 1, no. 1: 34–65.

Peterson, V. Spike. 2010. "Gendered Identities, Ideologies, and Practices in the Context of War and Militarism." In *Gender, War, and Militarism: Feminist Perspectives*, edited by Laura Sjoberg and Sandra Via, 17–30. Santa Barbara, CA: Praeger Security International.

Posen, Barry. 1992. "Nationalism, the Mass Army, and Military Power." *International Security* 18, no. 3: 80–124.

Powell, Robert. 2006. "War as a Commitment Problem." *International Organization* 69, no. 1: 169–204.

Rasler, Karen, and William Thompson. 1994. *The Great Powers and Global Struggle, 1490–1990.* Lexington: University of Kentucky Press.

Raven-Roberts, Angela. 2012. "Women and the Political Economy of Wars." In *Women and Wars*, edited by Carol Cohn, 36–53. London: Polity.

Reiter, Dan, and Curtis Meek. 1999. "Determinants of Military Strategy: A Quantitative Empirical Test." *International Studies Quarterly* 43, no. 2: 362–387.

Rosato, Sebastian. 2003. "The Flawed Logic of Democratic Peace Theory." *American Political Science Review* 97, no. 4: 585–602.

Russett, Bruce. 1993. *Grasping the Democratic Peace.* New Haven, CT: Yale University Press.

Sapiro, Virginia. 2003. "Theorizing Gender in Political Psychology Research." In *The Oxford Handbook of Political Psychology*, edited by David Sears, Leonie Huddie, and Robert Jervis, 601–634. New York: Oxford University Press.

Scott, Joan. 1986. "Gender: A Useful Category of Historical Analysis." *American Historical Review* 91, no. 4: 1053–1075.

Senese, Paul, and John Vasquez. 2008. *The Steps to War: An Empirical Study.* Princeton, NJ: Princeton University Press.

Shepherd, Laura J. 2008. *Gender, Violence, and Security.* London: Zed Books.

Sjoberg, Laura. 2006. *Gender, Justice, and the Wars in Iraq.* New York: Lexington Books.

Sjoberg, Laura. 2013. *Gendering Global Conflict: Toward a Feminist Theory of War.* New York: Columbia University Press.

Sjoberg, Laura, and Caron Gentry. 2007. *Mothers, Monsters, Whores: Women's Violence in Global Politics.* London: Zed Books.

Sjoberg, Laura, and Jessica Peet. 2011. "A(nother) Dark Side of the Protection Racket." *International Feminist Journal of Politics* 13, no. 2: 163–182.

Snyder, Jack. 1991. *Myths of Empire: Domestic Politics and International Ambitions.* Ithaca, NY: Cornell University Press.

Suganami, Hidemi. 1997. "Stories of War Origins: A Narrativist Theory of the Causes of War." *Review of International Studies* 23, no. 4: 401–418.

Sylvester, Christine. 2013. *War as Experience: Contributions from International Relations and Feminist Analysis.* New York: Routledge.

Thayer, Bradley A. 2000. "Bringing in Darwin: Evolutionary Theory, Realism, and International Politics." *International Security* 25, no. 2: 126–151.

Tickner, J. Ann. 2001. *Gendering World Politics: Issues and Approaches in a Post-Cold War Era.* New York: Columbia University Press.

Tir, Jaroslav. 2010. "Territorial Diversion: Diversionary Theory of War and Territorial Conflict." *Journal of Politics* 72, no. 3: 413–425.

True, Jacqui. 1996. "Feminism." In *Theories of International Relations*, edited by Scott Burchill and Andrew Linklater, 237–259. London: MacMillan.

Van Crevald, Martin. 2004. *Supplying War: Logistics from Wallenstein to Patton.* Cambridge: Cambridge University Press.

Vasquez, John. 2009. *The War Puzzle Revisited.* Cambridge: Cambridge University Press.

Wallerstein, Immanuel. 1984. "Three Instances of Hegemony and the History of the World Economy." *International Journal of Comparative Sociology* 24, no. 1: 100–108.

Waltz, Kenneth. 1959. *Man, The State, and War.* New York: Columbia University Press.

Waltz, Kenneth. 1979. *Theory of International Politics.* New York: McGraw Hill.

Walzer, Michael. 1977. *Just and Unjust Wars.* New York: Basic Books.

Wibben, Annick T. R. 2011. *Feminist Security Studies: A Narrative Approach.* New York: Routledge.

Wilcox, Lauren. 2009. "Gendering the Cult of the Offensive." *Security Studies* 18, no. 2: 214–240.

Wilcox, Lauren. 2014. *Bodies of Violence: Theorizing Embodied Subjects in International Relations.* Oxford: Oxford University Press.

Zimmerman, Ekkart. 2013. *Political Violence, Crises, and Revolutions.* London: Routledge Revivals.

CHAPTER 2

FROM WOMEN AND WAR TO GENDER AND CONFLICT?

Feminist Trajectories

DUBRAVKA ŽARKOV

THIS chapter addresses the following questions: What is "gender," and what does it mean in relation to wars and armed conflicts? Answering these questions requires venturing into a brief history of the concept, looking at what conceptual tools existed before "gender" and what came along after it. The chapter then specifically reflects on how the trajectories of feminist thinking about issues we today subsume under "gender" have been related to feminist theorizing of violent conflicts and wars. The chapter assesses trajectories of thinking about gender and war within specific streams of second wave Western feminist theorizing from the late 1960s to the second decade of the twenty-first century.

As a starting point, it is worth noting that feminist conceptualizations of women's and men's lives and feminist theorizing of violence, including war, have influenced each other quite substantially, and both have been influenced by a number of different feminist political projects. Thus, writing a brief genealogy of concepts and their trajectories necessarily tells us something about the social and political moments within which the concepts make sense. But looking back into the histories of concepts means reconstructing the past from the perspective of the present. Thus, this brief history is not impartial, complete, or exhaustive. Rather, like all histories, it is a view from a very particular present, here and now, from within which emphasis is placed on some feminist perspectives and analyses of women's lives in general and in relation to mass violence, because they are theoretically and politically pertinent for and beyond feminism.

Woman, Women: Asserting Global Sisterhood

Second wave feminism in the West emerged in the late 1960s with the tide of new social movements that included the anti-(Vietnam) war and civil rights movements, as well as anti-colonial movements in Africa and Asia. If the first wave of feminism (of the late nineteenth and early twentieth centuries) was characterized by the struggles for formal, political, and economic rights (such as voting and property rights), the second wave was marked by bringing the hitherto private into the public (particularly issues of sexuality and violence, be it as reproductive rights or as marital rape) and by pushing for anti-discrimination legislation in all social sectors, from labor protection to divorce laws.

From the start of the second wave, there were clear and often irreconcilable differences in feminist theorizing of social relations of power and the origins of women's oppression, and consequently, in their political projects. Indeed, radical feminism and liberal feminism are of particular relevance for feminist studies of war. Radical feminists believed that male dominance is rooted in male control over and exploitation of women's bodies and sexuality (Rubin 1975). This belief is linked to an (rather essentialist) assumption shared by many radical feminists that nature and biology matter, disadvantaging women physically, though potentially empowering them sexually and advantaging them ethically. Motherhood is seen as both central to women's enslavement by men within patriarchy and as a quintessential point of women's life-affirming ethics, thus as a ground for women's politics of nonviolence and peace (Ruddick 1980, 1989). Lesbian love is celebrated as a political, rather than just a sexual, choice (Rich 1976). In the vernacular of much radical feminism, men are often reduced to violent sexual predators, so male sexual violence against women and pornography become their main focus (Dworkin 1981).

Liberal feminism rejects nature and biology as having anything to do with women's oppression and points instead to male bias, ignorance, and prejudice. Taking liberal trust in free, rational individualism within the context of capitalism as its starting point, it is concerned with formal, legal equality between women and men, focusing its interventions on institutions such as the state, the law, and the market, which are assumed to be un-gendered, impartial guarantors of equality. It sees its task as re-educating both women and men: the former to gain enough autonomy and empowerment to claim equal rights, the latter to gain enough insights to stop being obstacles to women's equality (Baehr 2004; Nussbaum and Glove 1995; West 1998). While radical feminism often called for women's separatism, liberal feminism called for the integration of women in all domains of social, economic, and political life, but without attention to the preexisting structures and practices of inequality.

Despite huge disagreements in explanations of the origins of women's oppression and the strategies for intervention, however, much of second wave feminism in the West shared a number of assumptions and concepts, in particular taking "patriarchy" and sexual difference between women and men as central to feminist analysis, starting from "woman" as a unified and fixed analytical category, embedded in the structures of patriarchy on the opposite power-end of the equally fixed and unified category of "man." Probably the most important assumption—in terms of theoretical and political implications—was that of global sisterhood: that all women are oppressed; that all are oppressed in the same way; and that all women are oppressed by all men. This implies that all women also adhere to the same political struggle and, ultimately, that all women understand and support each other.

This simplified oppositional imagination was challenged within and outside the West throughout the 1970s and 1980s, especially by black, lesbian, and Third World feminists. They problematized the universality of white, upper-class, heterosexual women's experience and brought in race, nationality, citizenship, class, heterosexuality, and religion as crucial analytical categories and power relations, stressing the importance of particular social, cultural, and political histories within which these categories and power relations were produced. Third World feminist critiques (DAWN 1987; Moya 1997) noted that histories of colonialism, slavery, orientalism, and imperialism also mark Western feminist (i.e., not just mainstream) theoretical and political perspectives, and that women of the Third World invariably appear in Western feminist scholarship as a fixed, homogenous category defined through multiple victimizations (Mohanty 1984; Sen and Grown 1987). Postcolonial feminism throughout the 1990s continued with similar critiques of ethnocentrism and persistent representations of the Third World woman's subjectivity through victimhood (Alexander and Mohanty 1997; Rajan 1993). Black and (black-) lesbian feminists rejected unconditional sisterhood, postulating that differences between women are as important as those between women and men. They argued that not all women are oppressed, certainly not in the same way, and certainly not only, or primarily, by men, stressing that women often partake in and benefit from the oppressive systems—through racism, heteronormativity, and colonialism—even when they are not the direct oppressors of other women and men (hooks 1981).

Importantly, this criticism implied that not all women share the same political struggle, nor do they automatically understand and support each other; female solidarity must be built, not assumed. While this argument meant that women are not natural allies, it also meant that men are not women's natural enemies. Black, working-class, colonized, and marginalized men—those feminists argued—are closer to sharing the lives and struggles of black, working-class women and women from peripheries than are the rich women from the Western metropolis. Those views opened up possibilities for the subsequent development of "rainbow politics" and "transversal feminism," transnational and decolonial feminist alliances that reach beyond particular identity politics to address intersecting structures and histories of oppression, spread across geopolitical spaces and different social justice movements, and offer broad platforms for resistance and mobilization (Alexander and Mohanty 1997; Yuval-Davis 1999). Equally significant, men's lives and masculinities became an important focus of feminist research (see Dolan, Chapter 7 in this volume).

GENDER AND INTERSECTIONALITY: REFLECTING ON DIFFERENCES THAT MATTER

Parallel with and following those criticisms, several important theoretical developments arose among Western feminists in the late 1980s: Joan W. Scott (1986) gave the concept of gender new analytical strength; Kimberlé Crenshaw (1989) deployed the concept of intersectionality; and debates in feminist epistemology brought up questions about sexual difference, identity politics, and women's experience. In a broader field of social science, and especially within the various streams of social justice movements and their theorizing, constructivism gained power, opening further theoretical and political horizons in feminism. Joan W. Scott's groundbreaking work criticized the feminist focus on patriarchy for relying upon binary opposition (women/men), focusing on sexual difference, and seeing it as fixed and ahistorical. She also criticized mainstream feminism for ignoring other systems of social organization such as race, class, and sexuality; Marxist feminism for ignoring non-material aspects of social exclusion such as psyche, identity formation, symbolic systems, and sexual politics; and poststructuralist feminists for staying too much within the microcosm of interpersonal and family relationships, ignoring political and economic structures. But her lasting legacy is in establishing the concept of gender as a crucial feminist analytical category. Three specific aspects of Scott's concept of gender are worth mentioning here.

First, while Scott is not the first to use this concept, she elaborated its theoretical strengths, when compared to the concept of "women." She distinguished between gender as a social relation of power (i.e., an organizing principle of social life) and gender as an analytical category. As an organizing principle of social life, gender operates on several interrelated levels: from individual and group identities to normative/ideological, institutional, and symbolic meanings. As an analytical category, gender allows feminists to look beyond individual women—and, Scott argued, to include men! Gender asks how ideas about manhood and womanhood influence identities, norms, institutions, and symbols. Turning the noun into the verb allows us to see how each of these are gendered (i.e., informed by specific notions and practices of femininities and masculinities). In establishing a distinction between "women" and "gender" as analytical tools, Scott argued that the latter can do what the former cannot: offer insight into the processes of production and institutionalization of social relations of power, thereby exposing their material underpinnings and implications, as well as ideological and symbolic systems through which those processes are legitimized, maintained, or opposed.

Second, Scott argued that gender does not operate in a social vacuum, but in and through other social relations of power, such as race, class, religion, and sexuality. Even if, for feminists, gender remains a primary analytical tool, Scott argued, its working cannot be understood without understanding other power relationships within, through, or against which gender works. Finally, she insisted on historically and socially contextualized analyses of gender, stressing that gendered actors and relationships are always time and place specific. This attention to the context and the manifold power through which gender operates has also been central to Kimberlé Crenshaw's (1989) concept of intersectionality (see Rooney, Chapter 25 in this volume).

Scott's and Crenshaw's interventions questioned the very basics of feminism as an epistemological project. "If we are not justified in taking women as a category, then what political grounding does feminism have?" asked Elizabeth Grosz (1990, 341). If there is no uniform "women's reality" and "women's experience," can there be "women's subject position," "women's perspective," and "women's knowledge?" If being a woman does not bring epistemic privilege, what does? Those questions are simultaneously theoretical and political, and their implications for feminism are impossible to overstate. Gender and intersectionality, as feminist conceptual tools that stress politics of location, plurality, partiality, and the situatedness of feminist knowledge, rather than sexual difference and identity, demanded radically different worldviews and political strategies.

But, by the end of the 1990s and the start of the new millennium, both gender and intersectionality as concepts were criticized for exactly the opposite: for depoliticizing feminist theoretical and political struggles. Ironically, the failure of those concepts to generate social and theoretical transformations seems to have resulted from feminist successes in the late 1970s and through the 1980s. The 1980s was a decade of "femocrats," the time of feminist entry into various—including the highest—national and international bureaucracies. As a result of global feminist struggles, anti-discrimination laws and women's rights—from sexual and reproductive rights to rights to development—were put on agendas, not just in the West, but all over the world. The term "gender" spread beyond feminism and academia into national and supranational institutions such as the European Commission and the United Nations (Braidotti 2002), where a distinct field of "gender policies" was created. National governments around the world were opening ministries for women; the United Nations produced a series of conventions and resolutions, funds, conferences, and organizations specifically for women's issues and proclaimed the first decade of the woman (1976–1985). The World Bank followed suit with funding and projects for women only. In addition, from modest starts, universities in the United States and Western Europe started creating complete women's and gender studies departments and research centers with budgets and institutional support. Latin America, Asia, and Africa followed suit from the mid- to late 1980s, with Eastern European universities joining in the 1990s (Chen 2004). However, the entry of "gender" into these domains does not mean it has entered on the same footing with other concerns of those entities. Women's and gender studies, for example, remain to a large extent "specific" fields of knowledge, deemed inconsequential to the presumably universal knowledge of mainstream science. In this, they share the fate of black studies, indigenous studies, ethnic studies, or any other knowledge field that grew out of the new social movements in the 1960s and the desire of hitherto marginalized social groups to produce knowledge about, for, and by themselves.

Moreover, some argue that the result of the institutionalization and integration of women and gender issues into academia and national and supranational governing bodies was isolation, a loss of radical edge, the creation of technical "gender expertise" without feminist politics, and in the worst case, co-option (Crawford and Fox 2007; Stratigaki 2004). So, for example, "gender mainstreaming," once acclaimed as a feminist tool that would transform discriminatory government practices against women, has been critiqued as "gender away-streaming"—a tool that enabled the integration of women into the existing unequal power relationships and thus contributed to women's renewed marginalization and invisibility (Mukhopadhyay 2004). Some authors argue that "intersectionality" has became a depoliticized, whitened, neoliberalized academic concept that has nothing to do any longer with radical social critique and the feminist activism of its beginnings in the 1980s (Ferree 2011; Tomlinson 2013).

Those theoretical and geopolitical dynamics have left their mark on feminist studies of war, especially from the 1980s onward. Thus, the following questions emerge: What do the concepts of women, gender, and intersectionality, and their trajectories, mean for Western feminist theorizing of war and violent conflict? How have they been used, and what are the theoretical and political implications of this usage for feminist scholarship in the second decade of twenty-first century?

WOMEN AND WAR:
AGENCY, EMANCIPATION, EQUALITY

In 1987, Elshtain published *Women and War*. The book appeared at the time of the rise in power of neoliberalism and conservativism in the West. Within Western feminism, the 1980s were the time of femocracy and the ascension of liberal feminism.

Women's agency and emancipation and women's/gender equality have been major conceptual tools and political goals of much of second wave feminism and to liberal feminism in the West. Through the 1980s, women's equality—in its liberal feminist interpretation—became a dominant analytical and political project, resulting in some acceptance of women's integration into the world of politics and war, and in the marginalization of the radical US feminist politics of separatism and the standpoint of women's essential difference, peacefulness, and higher ethical standards. The hope of (liberal) feminist scholarship and struggle for equality of the time was (still) that, once women entered masculine institutions and social domains, they would transform them. Thus, the concepts of equality and women's agency had an explicitly liberatory and emancipatory cloak.

As an analytical tool, the concepts of equality and agency have inspired feminist studies on women's soldiering, arguing that women all over the world not only are capable of fighting, but also are motivated by the same political projects of nationalism, social justice, independence, and freedom (Peries 1998; Sklevicky 1987). As a political project, equality and agency have resulted, among other things, in women's actual entry into the Western states' armies, although generally not in combat roles (with a few specific exceptions, such as in Israel and since recently the United States). Militarism and militarization have since then become major issues in feminist theoretical work and activism (from the early work of Cynthia Enloe in 1983 to the recent work of Cynthia Cockburn in 2012), for both those who support and those who oppose idea that women's participation in wars and state armies is part and parcel of gender equality.

Seen from the perspective of that time and those debates, Elshtain's book is significant for several reasons. First, it is a comprehensive analysis of women's—and men's—engagements in and against war and violence, as well as of dominant social ideologies that inspire those engagements. While gender was not the substantive analytical tool Elshtain used, she analyzed social practices and ideas through which a majority of women are continuously positioned as peaceful and life affirming, and men as soldiers. But she also paid attention to those few men who engage against war and those few women who join the violence or instigate it. Second, Elshtain's work can be seen as both continuity of and a departure from the existing feminist scholarship on war at that time—especially the classical second wave Western feminist scholarship on World War I and II, anti-colonial wars, and the socialist revolutions of the 1960s and 1970s. In terms of continuity, that scholarship, using "woman/women" as the main analytical tool, addressed a vast variety of women's experiences, roles, and positions in violent conflicts, and engagements with war and violence, whether at the "home front" or in the fighting itself. It addressed everything from women's entry into the war industry and economy as replacements for men fighting on the frontlines, to women soldiering and nursing, to resistance and experiences of war violence, displacement, and losses (Greenwald 1990; Higonnet et al. 1987; Molyneux 1985; Molyneux and Halliday 1981; Reif 1986; Woollacott 1994).

However, Western feminist scholarship in (and since) the 1980s seldom addressed specific cases of women's participation in wars and violence that could not be characterized as liberatory or emancipatory struggles. Among the first, and valuable few, were works by Koontz (1987) on German women's engagement in Nazism and by Cock (1992, 1994) on women in the South African Defence Force. Stronger still, when women's participation in hegemonic or murderous political projects is addressed, those projects have long been characterized as essentially male, and the women within them seen as manipulated into joining (Seidel and Gunther 1988). It would take more than a decade for two other important collections on women, gender, and right-wing politics to appear (Bacchetta and Power 2002; Passmore 2003; recently, Malländer 2015, originally published in 2009 in German).

Elsewhere in the world, Western feminist blindness to women's will to power was criticized as expression of hegemony and privilege (Roy 1997). South Asian feminist studies of the Partition of India in 1947 and communal violence in the 1980s and 1990s, for example, have explicitly questioned the idea that women's emancipation and empowerment occur only within the social justice movements inspired by feminism. Rather than ignoring it, they have theorized women's violent agency within communal violence, and women's participation in the creation of radical, nationalist, violent ideologies and practices as an expression of women's empowerment (Butalia 2001; Jeffery and Basu 2001; Rajasingham-Senanayake 2001; Sarkar and Butalia 1995). Elshtain's attention to violence perpetrated by women therefore marks a departure from both essentialist notions of radical Western feminism that woman's agency is always and only an agency of peace, and from—surprisingly equally essentialist—notions of liberal Western feminism that women's participation in war and collective violence almost invariably means either brainwashing, or engagement in a struggle for social justice on the righteous side of the divide.

Gendering War: Practices, Processes, and Products

Toward the end of the 1980s, the concepts of gender and intersectionality, together with constructivist social science perspectives, opened up discursive possibilities for a different feminist scholarship. Thus, parallel with liberal feminist influence in the study of women and war, and the attention to women's experiences, roles, and agency, the new concepts and theoretical perspectives gave rise to another set of feminist arguments: that war and violence produce specific kinds of racialized and sexualized femininities and masculinities, rather than being the simple effects of (innate or learned) aggression by men. As a result, in the late 1980s and throughout the 1990s a number of feminists looked back again at the World War I and II, colonial and postcolonial violence, and in the United States at the Vietnam war, this time through a constructivist lens, using new analytical tools. A huge body of work followed: on culture, literature and media, the ways women and men have become symbols of—and not just actors in—specific war practices, and the ways in which those very practices are gendered (Cooper et al. 1989; Jeffords 1989, 1990; Macdonald 1987; Warner 1985). Equally important, this work displays significantly broader feminist attention to the ways our notions and practices of femininities and masculinities intersect with heteronormativity, race, and nationhood, among other elements (Cooke and Woollacott 1993; Melman 1998).

This stream of feminist scholarship has brought about a new set of inquiries, including how specific practices of war and violence produce subject positions and identities of women and men, foster specific kinds of femininities and masculinities, while marginalizing and delegitimizing others; and how race, sexuality, nationhood, and political ideologies become part and parcel of these violent processes.

Two wars in which the Western powers engaged in the 1980s and 1990s have made those questions both theoretically and politically pertinent for Western feminist thinking about violent conflicts. These were the Falklands/Malvinas war in 1982 and the First Gulf War in 1990–1991; the former was fought by Britain against Argentina, the latter fought by the United States and its Coalition against Iraq. During the British war with

Argentina, it was impossible to miss how gender, race, and nationhood became interwoven in British media representations of the war, and especially how British women became symbols of whiteness and nationhood (Seidel and Gunther 1988). During the First Gulf War, both British and US political leadership appropriated feminist language for war-mongering rhetoric. On the one hand, they used concepts of women's equality and emancipation to distinguish Western women (and especially women soldiers) from apparently multiple victimized (by religion, tradition, and men) women in Kuwait and Iraq (Forder 1995); on the other hand, they used radical feminist discourses on male sexual aggression, coupled with racism and Orientalism, to depict Iraqi men as rapists of Kuwaiti women and to distinguish them from US/Western men, who were represented as (potent/ial) saviors (Farmanfarmaian 1992).

The political importance of those two wars lies in the multiple and ambiguous positioning of women within contemporary Western hegemonic wars and militaries (Enloe 2000). Theoretically, they brought Western feminist scholarship on war and violence closer to other fields wherein feminists studied the ambiguous social position of white European women and men, such as in research on colonial projects (McClintock 1995; Sinha 1995; Stoler 1995, 2002). Furthermore, the use of gender and representation allowed for feminist attention to masculinities within which a man—including the male conscript and soldier—stops being reduced to "malevolent patriarch" or "killing machine" and becomes a socially produced subject whose willingness to die and kill in war was seen as requiring sustained material and symbolic investment (Bourke 1999; Cockburn and Žarkov 2002). Connell's (1995) concept of hegemonic masculinity contributed to feminist analysis of war and political and military institutions beyond the mere presence of men, as producers of identities, ideologies, and practices, and ultimately as constructive sites of social relations of power that structure not just relations between women and men, and those between men, but also other—intersecting, interlocking, and mutually constitutive—forms of domination and exploitation, from interpersonal to geopolitical (Cohn and Enloe 2014; Zalewski and Parpart 1997). This new stream of feminist scholarship on war reached its peak with yet another set of violent events at the dawn of the twenty-first century: the terrorist attacks on the United States in September 2001 and the consequent US war against Afghanistan; the Second Gulf War in 2003; and the media exposure of sexual violence against male Iraqi prisoners in Baghdad's Abu Ghraib prison, also in 2003.

If the Falkland and First Gulf wars brought up the questions of Western women's ambiguous positioning within Western hegemonies, the violence of the new millennium seems to have questioned the very Western feminist project and its theoretical tools as problematic (Hesford 2011). The "war on terror" and violence in Abu Ghraib in particular led to feminist analyses that recognize the significance of Orientalism, Islamophobia, racism, homophobia, and sexism, as practices and concepts, to the understanding of gender, war, and violence (Alexander and Hawkesworth 2008; Hunt and Rygiel 2006; Nguyen 2012). Feminists addressed the impacts of those wars and of their media, cultural, and political representations on the everyday lives of Muslim and

Arab communities within the West—and equally important—on the (re)construction
of the Western subject itself (Butler 2004, 2010; Puar 2007; Žarkov 2011).

Two aspects of the theoretical and political relevance of those studies should be
brought up. First, attention to sexual violence against men in Abu Ghraib destabilized,
to some extent, feminist attachments to women as exclusive victims of sexual violence, while the participation of women in sexual torture reinvigorated the feminist
self-examination of the question of women's participation in violence and entry into
Western militaries (Enloe 2004). Second, those studies further destabilized, to some
extent, the primacy of gender as an analytical tool in understanding war and violence.
While not all of those studies explicitly used intersectionality as a concept, they used
it as a theoretical perspective, stressing that there are social and geopolitical contexts
within which race, religion, and sexuality—rather than gender—become the primary
social relations of power that structure the position of social groups, and their male and
female members, within the contexts of violence (see especially Sexton and Lee 2006;
Gordon 2006; Žarkov 2011). However, while Western feminist research on wars waged
by their own societies across the globe during this period brought up all those important
theoretical and political insights into the gendered dynamics of violence, the early 1990s
saw two other violent conflicts that would result in very different feminist studies.

FEMINIST OTHERING:
GEOGRAPHIES OF THINKING

Between 1991 and 1995, the Socialist Federal Republic of Yugoslavia disintegrated
through a war that would become infamous for widespread patterns of sexual violence.
Between April and July 1994, genocide was conducted, systematically and thoroughly, in
Rwanda. In both cases, ethnic-based hatreds were quickly noted—by mainstream politicians and scholars both within and outside those countries—as the main cause of violence. In the case of Rwanda, there was an assumption (though not consistently followed
in scholarship) that ethnicities had been produced through colonial practices (Mamdani
2001). In the case of former Yugoslavia, however, ethnicities were taken—by scholars
and politicians outside of the country, as much as by nationalists inside the country—as
natural and essential characteristics of the population, rather than as socially produced
categories. With very few exceptions (such as Cockburn 1998; Copelon 1993; Seifert
1993, 1996), Western feminist scholarship on the war in former Yugoslavia did not differ
much from the mainstream scholarship, especially in the early years.

On the one hand, the war in former Yugoslavia, especially the patterns of sexual violence, has produced a huge body of feminist scholarship, from law to anthropology to
refugee studies, where intersections of gender and ethnicity have been crucial tools
of analysis. On the other hand, a strange mixture of unlikely bedfellow discourses has
made this body of knowledge highly problematic. First, the essentializing of ethnicity

has meant that feminists—just like the mainstream scholars—failed to ask how ethnicity became the privileged category of difference, by which social, economic, political, and symbolic processes has reality been reduced to ethnic identities, and how have people, places, and histories acquired this single signifier that erased all others? Second, old discourses of Balkanism returned, designating the region once again (as in the early twentieth century) as a place of violence and primitivism (Todorova 1997). These old narratives, together with the focus on ethnic identities, became enmeshed in a mixture of discourses on (post-)communism and people behind the "iron curtain" accustomed to autocratic leaders; on the "history of ethnic hatred" as a cause of the war by which socialist Yugoslavia disintegrated; and on the transition to capitalism. Together, these discourses created geographies of violence within which "the Balkans" became a new "symbolic continent" (Bakić-Hayden and Hayden 1992). Furthermore, those discourses easily lent themselves to the radical feminist discourses on gender and sexuality (Žarkov and Drezgić 2005). While, as already mentioned, radical US feminism was losing ground in the West throughout the 1980s, it came back with a vengeance to "the Balkans." Gender and intersectionality—marked here as a nexus of male sexual bestiality toward women and essentialized ethnic identities—produced clear-cut victims and villains, this time not divided only as male sexual violator and female rape victims, but assigned with local ethnic identities: Serb male rapist and Muslim female victim still stand as symbols of the war in former Yugoslavia. In addition, collective amnesia seems to have hit much of Western feminist scholarship, declaring the war rapes in Bosnia as the worst (or sometimes the only) known in history (see Stiglmayer 1993). This is not to deny the deliberate and widespread use of war rapes in Bosnia, nor the predominance of Bosnian Serb forces as perpetrators and Bosnian Muslim women as victims. Rather, this analysis points out that the way gender, sexuality, and ethnicity have been utilized through those discourses has created exclusive subject positions for specific groups of women and men in the region, through specific gendered understanding of sexual violence and ethnicity.

War rapes in former Yugoslavia have made feminists in the region (and elsewhere) engage in huge debates, leading to conflicts and splits of the feminist groups and movements (see from Benderly 1997 to Kajevska 2014). A variety of concepts for these rapes is still used, each with a particular political echo: rape as a weapon of war, rape as torture, genocidal rape, rape as a war crime, and so on. But, while Bosnia figures prominently and regularly in feminist debates about sexual violence against women in violent conflicts, Rwanda received much less attention from Western feminist scholarship (unlike in mainstream genocide studies, in which Rwandan genocide is minutely studied, but without attention to gender). This has prompted Patricia Sellers, also a contributor to this *Handbook*, who worked on cases of sexual violence in both Bosnia and Rwanda within the Prosecutor's Office of the International Criminal Tribunals for the Former Yugoslavia and Rwanda (ICTY/R), to note that European ethnocentrism has made the women of Bosnia much more important to Western feminist scholars than the women of Rwanda (see Sellers, Chapter 16 in this volume). However, as noted earlier, this attention to Bosnian women raped in the war was a double-edged sword: on the one hand, it put the rape of women on the international agenda, and created momentum that impacted international laws and legal practices on sexual violence in war. On the other hand, the overwhelming attention to war rape as women's ultimate war experience has drastically reduced the subjectivity of the Muslim women in Bosnia and Tutsi women in Rwanda to that of the "rape victim," and has equated their sexual vulnerability with their ontological position. Furthermore, as I discuss in the following, ever since the early 1990s, war rapes remain one of the most dominant topics in the Western study of war experiences of non-Western women, with grave theoretical and political consequences.

Toward Conclusion: On the Ramifications of Feminist Theorizing and Missing Pieces

Politically and in terms of global feminist organizing, the war in the former Yugoslavia and the genocide in Rwanda have generated huge feminist activism that has contributed significantly to international laws and legal structures; for example, UN war tribunals and international courts were established, and gender-based, sexual violence and the rape of women in wars was listed as a war crime in the Rome Statute. However, inadvertently, this also has elevated the crime of rape over all others, creating subject positions and hierarchies of victimhood. So, today, according to successive UN Security Council resolutions, the rape of a local woman by a local man, during a war, is a threat to international security. But demolishing her home, destroying her water source, stealing her land, and expelling her from her ancestral territory are not.

Not surprisingly, the elevation of war rape to the position of ultimate violence against women, as women's ultimate experience of war and an international security threat, has opened up a discursive space for the return of some old racist, colonial tales of (local) victims and savages, and (international/Western) saviors. The new humanitarianism and interventionism discourses (Jacoby 2015) have used these narratives of war rapes and local men's savagery to local women to their advantage, hijacking discourses of female victimization and human rights. And (as noted earlier) while those hijacking practices have been criticized by Western feminists in the cases of the "war on terror" in Afghanistan and Iraq, they have somehow passed with little notice in the cases of the former Yugoslavia and Rwanda.

At the same time, the ethnic and religious identity-based explanations for causes of "civil"/"local" wars were gaining prominence in the mainstream scholarship, with Kaldor's (1999) "new wars" theory as a crystallizer. And while those mainstream identity-based approaches to war do not actually use the concepts of gender and intersectionality, they utilize with great skill notions of female sexual vulnerability and a need of male protection, and combine it with racist notions of violent non-Western (Balkan and African) masculinities. There is currently little communication between feminist and mainstream theorizing of contemporary wars, so ideas about "new wars" remain largely unchallenged by feminists, or are even taken for granted (Peterson 2008). The task of feminist critics of such perspectives would be not just to refuse the hiearchization of rape as an ultimate crime against women, and the ontological construction of non-Western women through rapability and non-Western men through sexual aggression, but also to expose how those gendered and racist constructs inform practices and justifications of contemporary Western military interventions into non-Western countries, reconstruct the Western subject as peaceful, democratic, and justice-making (Žarkov 2014), and support exclusionary citizenship policies within the West (among other things).

There is yet another difference, and a missing piece, in the ways Western feminists analyzed wars in the 1980s and 1990s and those in the new millennium: attention to the economy. Global neoliberal economy and its nexus with militarism and their gendered effects at home and abroad became especially important subjects of US feminist research (Enloe 2010, 2013). This entry of economy into the study of militarism and US hegemony redresses to some extent the earlier criticism that feminists in the West have been so seduced by their own successes vis-à-vis the state and women's equality, and by identity politics, that they have forgotten about global economic inequalities, redistribution, and solidarity with the women of the South (Fraser 2009; Jaquette 2003; Mohanty 2002). This criticism could also be related to the fact that there is still no substantial feminist scholarship of war economies, the way it exists in critical mainstream war studies. In particular, there is little feminist critique of the dominant mainstream theoretical paradigms such as Collier's (2000) "greed and grievance," or engagement with those asserting the links between economic underdevelopment and war (Murshed 2002). Many of those economic and rational choice theories of the causes of contemporary wars were created in the 1990s and gained in popularity in the new millennium. Some support the argument that economic greed of local (in this case, African) warlords and male youth, in conjunction with failed states, produce wars. Such theorizing—which since the 1990s also informs the World Bank's conflict policies—uses intersections of gender, race, sexuality, ethnicity, and age as its essential ingredients and situates them within a geopolitically informed worldview that represents the Western model of capitalist, neoliberal economy as a "peace economy," disconnected from "war economies" elsewhere, and offers neoliberalism as a solution to wars (Žarkov 2015). The task of feminist critics would in this case be not only to analyze how women and men are affected by or engaged in war economies, but also (1) to analyze how war, violence, and militarism become intrinsic to the contemporary neoliberal economy; (2) how they become modes of both economic production and social reproduction; and (3) how racialized and sexualized gendered ideologies and practices, hierarchies, and inequalities become necessary for the sustenance and legitimization of the violent world order. Such feminist analysis would follow in the footsteps of the scholarship already noted here: one that is mercilessly self-critical of one's own position within the global society and one's own theoretical tools by which the world is explained.

REFERENCES

Alexander, M. Jacqui, and Chandra Talpade Mohanty, eds. 1997. *Feminist Genealogies, Colonial Legacies, Democratic Futures*. New York and London: Routledge.

Alexander, Karen, and Mary E. Hawkesworth, eds. 2008. *War and Terror: Feminist Perspectives*. Chicago: University of Chicago Press.

Bacchetta, Paola, and Margaret Power, eds. 2002. *Right-Wing Women: From Conservatives to Extremists around the World*. New York: Routledge.

Baehr, Amy R., ed. 2004. *Varieties of Feminist Liberalism*. Lanham, MD: Rowman & Littlefield.

Bakić-Hayden, Milica, and Robert M. Hayden. 1992. "Orientalist Variations on the Theme 'Balkans': Symbolic Geography in Recent Yugoslav Cultural Politics." *Slavic Review* 52, no. 1: 1–16.

Benderly, Jill. 1997. "Rape, Feminism, and Nationalism in the War in Yugoslav Successor States." In *Feminist Nationalism*, edited by Lois West, 59–72. New York: Routledge.

Bourke, Joanna. 1999. *An Intimate History of Killing: Face to Face Killing in 20th Century Warfare*. New York: Basic Books.

Braidotti, Rosi. 2002. "The Uses and Abuses of the Sex/Gender Distinction in European Feminist Practice." In *Thinking Differently, A Reader in European Women's Studies*, edited by Gabriele Griffin and Rosi Braidotti, 286–306. London: Zed Books.

Butalia, Urvashi. 2001. "Women and Communal Conflict: New Challenges for the Women's Movement in India." In *Victims, Perpetrators or Actors? Gender, Armed Conflict and Political Violence*, edited by C. Moser and F. Clark, 99–113. London: Zed Books.

Butler, Judith. 2004. *Precarious Life: The Powers of Mourning and Violence*. London and New York: Verso.

Butler, Judith. 2010. *Frames of War: When is Life Grievable?* London and New York: Verso.

Chen, Peiying. 2004. *Acting "Otherwise": The Institutionalization of Women's/Gender Studies in Taiwan's Universities*. New York: RoutledgeFalmer.

Cock, Jacklyn. 1992. *Women and War in South Africa*. London: Open Letters.

Cock, Jacklyn. 1994. "Women and the Military: Implications for Demilitarization in the 1990s in South Africa." *Gender & Society* 8, no. 2: 152–169.

Cockburn, Cynthia. 1998. *The Space between Us: Negotiating Gender and National Identities in Conflict*. London: Zed Books.

Cockburn, Cynthia. 2012. *Antimilitarism, Political and Gender Dynamics of Peace Movements*. Basingstoke, UK: Palgrave Macmillan.

Cockburn, Cynthia, and Dubravka Žarkov. 2002. *The Postwar Moment: Militaries, Masculinities and International Peacekeeping*. London: Lawrence & Wishart.

Cohn, Carol, and Cynthia Enloe. 2014. "A Conversation with Cynthia Enloe: Feminists Look at Masculinity and the Men Who Wage War." *Signs* 40, no. 1: 1188–1207.

Connell, R. W. 1995. *Masculinities*. Cambridge: Polity Press.

Collier, Paul, and Anke Hoeffler. 2000. "Greed and Grievance in Civil War." Policy Research Working Paper Series 2355. Washington, DC: The World Bank.

Cooke, Miriam G., and Angela Woollacott, eds. 1993. *Gendering War Talk*. Princeton, NJ: Princeton University Press.

Cooper, Helen M., Adrienne Auslander Munich, and Susan Merrill Squier, eds. 1989. *Arms and the Woman: War, Gender, and Literary Representation*. Chapel Hill: University of North Carolina Press.

Copelon, Rhonda. 1993. "Surfacing Gender: Reconceptualizing Crimes against Women in Time of War." In *Mass Rape: The War against Women in Bosnia-Herzegovina*, edited by A. Stiglmayer, 197–218. Lincoln: University of Nebraska Press.

Crawford, Mary, and Annie Fox. 2007. "IX. From Sex to Gender and Back Again: Co-optation of a Feminist." *Feminism & Psychology* 17, no. 4: 481–486.

Crenshaw, Kimberlé. 1989. "Demarginalizing the Intersection of Race and Sex: A Black Feminist Critique of Antidiscrimination Doctrine, Feminist Theory and Antiracist Politics." *University of Chicago Legal Forum* 140, 139–167. Reprinted in *The Politics of Law: A Progressive Critique*, 2nd ed., edited by David Kairys, 195–217. ed. New York: Pantheon, 1990.

Development Alternatives with Women for a New Era (DAWN). 1987. "Development, Crises and Alternative Visions: Third World Women's Perspective." Accessed November 16, 2015. http://www.dawnnet.org/.

Dworkin, Andrea. 1981. *Pornography: Men Possessing Women*. London: Women's Press.

Elshtain, Jean Bethke. 1987. *Women and War*. Chicago: University of Chicago Press.

Enloe, Cynthia. 1983. *Does Khaki Become You? The Militarization of Women's Lives*. Boston: South End Press.

Enloe, Cynthia. 2000. *Maneuvers: The International Politics of Militarizing Women's Lives*. Berkeley: University of California Press.

Enloe, Cynthia. 2004. "Wielding Masculinity Inside Abu Ghraib: Making Feminist Sense of an American Military Scandal." *Asian Journal for Women's Studies* 10, no. 3: 89–102.

Enloe, Cynthia. 2010. *Nimo's War, Emma's War: Making Feminist Sense of the Iraq War*. Berkeley: University of California Press.

Enloe, Cynthia. 2013. *Seriously! Investigating Crashes and Crises as if Women Mattered*. Berkeley: University of California Press

Farmanfarmaian, Abouali. 1992. "Sexuality in the Gulf War: Did You Measure Up?" *Genders* 13: 1–29.

Ferree, Myra M. 2011. "The Discursive Politics of Feminist Intersectionality." In *Framing Intersectionality: Debates on a Multi-Faceted Concept in Gender Studies*, edited by Helma Lutz, Maria Teresa Herrera Vivar, and Linda Supik, 55–65. Farnham, Surrey; Burlington, VT: Ashgate.

Forder, C. 1995. "'Women Warriors:' Representation of Women Soldiers in British Daily Newspaper Photographs of the Gulf War (January to March 1991)." In *(Hetero)sexual Politics*, edited by M. Maynard and J. Purvis, 108–123. London: Taylor & Francis.

Fraser, Nancy. 2009. "Feminism, Capitalism and the Cunning of History." *New Left Review* 57: 97–117.

Greenwald, Maria. 1990. *Women, War, and Work: The Impact of World War I on Women Workers in the United States*. London and Ithaca, NY: Cornell University Press.

Grosz, Elizabeth. 1990. "Conclusion—A Note on Essentialism and Difference." In *Feminist Knowledge: Critique and Construct*, edited by Sneya Gunew, 332–345. London: Routledge.

Gordon, Avery. 2006. "Abu Ghraib: Imprisonment and the War on Terror." *Race & Class* 48, no. 1: 42–59.

Hesford, Wendy. 2011. *Spectacular Rhetorics, Human Rights Visions, Recognitions, Feminisms*. Durham, NC: Duke University Press.

Higonnet, Margaret R., Jane Jenson, Sonya Michel, and Margaret Collins Weitz, eds. 1987. *Behind the Lines: Gender and the Two World Wars*. New Haven, CT: Yale University Press.

hooks, bell. 1981. *Ain't I a Woman? Black Women and Feminism*. Boston: South End Press.

Hunt, Krista, and Kim Rygiel. 2006. *(En)Gendering the War on Terror: War Stories and Camouflaged Politics*. Hampshire, UK: Ashgate.

Jacoby, Tim. 2015. "Humanitarian Assistance and New Humanitarianism: Some Old Questions." In *Conflict, Peace, Security and Development: Theories and Methodologies*, edited by Helen Hintjens and Dubravka Žarkov, 39–51. London: Routledge.

Jaquette, Jane. 2003. "Feminism and the Challenges of the 'Post-Cold War' World." *International Feminist Journal of Politics* 5, no. 3: 331–354.

Jeffery, Patricia, and Amrita Basu, eds. 2001. *Resisting the Sacred and the Secular: Women's Activism and Politicized Religion in South Asia*. New Delhi: Kali for Women.

Jeffords, Susan. 1989. *The Remasculinization of America: Gender and the Vietnam War*. Bloomington: Indiana University Press.

Jeffords, Susan. 1990. "Fathers: Gender and the Vietnam War." In *From Hanoi to Hollywood: The Vietnam War in American Film*, edited by Linda Dittmar and Gene Michaud, 202–215. New Brunswick, NJ: Rutgers University Press.

Kajevska, A. Miškovska. 2014. "Taking a Stand in Times of Violent Societal Changes: Belgrade and Zagreb Feminists' Positionings on the (post-)Yugoslav Wars and Each Other (1991–2000)." PhD diss., University of Amsterdam.

Kaldor, Mary. 1999. *New and Old Wars: Organized Violence in a Global Era*. Cambridge: Polity Press.

Koontz, Claudia. 1987. *Mothers of the Fatherland: Women, the Family and Nazi Politics*. New York: St. Martin's Press.

Macdonald, Sharon. 1987. "Drawing the Lines—Gender, Peace and War: An Introduction." In *Images of Women in Peace and War: Cross-Cultural and Historical Perspectives*, edited by Sharon Macdonald, Pat Holden, and Shirley Ardener, 1–26. Madison: University of Wisconsin Press.

Malländer, Elissa. 2015. *Female SS Guards and Workaday Violence: The Majdanek Concentration Camp, 1942–1944*. Translated by Patricia Szabor. Lansing: Michigan State University Press.

Mamdani, Mahmood. 2001. *When Victims Become Killers: Colonialism, Nativism and the Genocide in Rwanda*. Princeton, NJ: Princeton University Press.

McClintock, Anne. 1995. *Imperial Leather: Race, Gender, and Sexuality in the Colonial Contest*. London: Routledge.

Melman, Billie. ed. 1998. *Borderlines: Genders and Identities in War and Peace, 1870–1930*. New York: Routledge.

Mohanty, Chandra T. 1984. "'Under Western Eyes' Revisited: Feminist Scholarship and Colonial Discourses." *Boundary* 12, no. 3: 333–358.

Mohanty, Chandra T. 2002. "Under Western Eyes" Revisited: Feminist Solidarity Through Anticapitalist Struggles." *Signs* 28, no. 2: 499–535.

Molyneux, Maxine D. 1985. "Mobilization without Emancipation? Women's Interests, the State, and Revolution in Nicaragua." *Feminist Studies* 11, no. 2: 227–254.

Molyneux, Maxine D., and Fred Halliday. 1981. *Ethiopian Revolution*. New York: Verso Books.

Moya, Paula M. L. 1997. "Postmodernism, 'Realism,' and the Politics of Identity: Cherrie Moraga and Chicana Feminism." In *Feminist Genealogies, Colonial Legacies, Democratic Futures*, edited by M. Jacqui Alexander and Chandra Talpade Mohanty, 125–150. New York: Routledge.

Mukhopadhyay, Maitrayee. 2004. "Mainstreaming Gender or 'Streaming' Gender Away: Feminists Marooned in the Development Business." In *Repositioning Feminisms in*

Development, IDS Bulletin 35, edited by Andrea Cornwall, Elizabeth Harrison, and Ann Whitehead, 95–103. Brighton, UK: Institute of Development Studies.

Murshed, S. Mansoob. 2002. "Conflict, Civil War and Underdevelopment: An Introduction." *Journal of Peace Research* 39, no. 4: 387–393.

Nguyen, Mimi Thi. 2012. *The Gift of Freedom: War, Debt and Other Refugee Passages.* Durham, NC: Duke University Press.

Nussbaum, Martha, and Jonathan Glover. 1995. *Women, Culture, and Development: A Study of Human Capabilities.* Oxford: Oxford University Press.

Passmore, Kevin. 2003. *Women, Gender, and Fascism in Europe, 1919–45.* Manchester: Manchester University Press.

Peries, S. 1998. "Metamorphosis of the Tamil Woman in Nationalist War for Elam." Paper presented at the Women in Conflict Zone Network conference, York University, Toronto, Canada.

Peterson, V. Spike. 2008. "'New Wars' and Gendered Economies." *Feminist Review* 88: 7–20.

Puar, Jasbir. 2007. *Terrorist Assemblages: Homonationalism in Queer Times.* Durham, NC: Duke University Press.

Rajan, R. Sunder. 1993. *Real and Imagined Women: Gender, Culture and Postcolonialism.* London: Routledge.

Rajasingham-Senanayake, D. 2001. "Ambivalent Empowerment: Tragedy of Tamil Women in Conflict, in Women, War and Peace." In *South Asia: Beyond Victimhood to Agency*, edited by R. Manchanda, 102–130. London: Sage Publications.

Reif, Linda L. 1986. "Women in Latin American Guerrilla Movements: A Comparative Perspective." *Comparative Politics* 18, no. 2: 147–169.

Rich, Adrianne C. 1976. *Of Woman Born: Motherhood as Experience and Institution.* New York: W. W. Norton.

Roy, Anita. 1997. "Introduction: Cultural Studies, Violence and Femininity." *A Cultural Review* 8, no. 3: 259–263.

Rubin, Gayle. 1975. "The Traffic in Women: Notes on the 'Political Economy' of Sex." In *Toward an Anthropology of Women*, edited by Rayna R. Reiter, 157–210. New York: Monthly Review Press.

Ruddick, Sara. 1980. "Maternal Thinking." *Feminist Studies* 6: 342–367.

Ruddick, Sara. 1989. *Maternal Thinking: Toward a Politics of Peace.* New York: Ballantine Books.

Sarkar, Tanika, and Butalia Urvashi. 1995. *Women and Right-Wing Movements: Indian Experiences.* London: Zed Books.

Scott, Joan Wallach. 1986. "Gender as a Useful Category of Historical Analysis." *The American Historical Review* 91, no. 5: 1053–1075.

Seidel, Gill, and Renate Günther. 1988. "'Nation' and 'Family' in the British Media Reporting of the 'Falklands Conflict.'" In *The Nature of the Right: A Feminist Analysis of Order Patterns*, edited by Gill Seidel, 115–128. Amsterdam: John Benjamins.

Seifert, Ruth. 1993. "War and Rape: A Preliminary Analysis." In *Mass Rape: The War Against Women in Bosnia-Herzegovina*, edited by Alexandra Stiglmayer, 54–72. Lincoln: University of Nebrasca Press.

Seifert, Ruth. 1996. "The Second Front: The Logic of Sexual Violence in Wars." *Women's Studies International Forum* 19, no. 1–2: 35–43.

Sen, Gita, and Caren Grown. 1987. *Development, Crisis and Alternative Vision: Third World Women's Perspectives.* New York: Monthly Review Press.

Sexton, Jared, and Elizabeth Lee. 2006. "Figuring the Prison: Prerequisites of Torture at Abu Ghraib." *Antipode* 38, no. 5: 1005–1022.

Sinha, Mrinalini. 1995. *Colonial Masculinity: The "Manly Englishman" and the "Effeminate Bengali" in the Late Nineteenth Century*. New Delhi: Kali for Women.

Sklevicky, Lydia. 1987. "Konji, Zene, Ratovi: Problem utemeljenja historije zena u Jugoslaviji" [Horses, Women, War: the Problems in Establishing Women's History in Yugoslavia]. In *Zena i Drustvo: Kultiviranje Dijaloga [Woman and Society" Cultivation of a Dialogue]*, edited by Lydia Sklevicky, 51–61. Zagreb: Sociolosko Drustvo Hrvatske.

Stiglmayer, Alexandra. 1993. *Mass Rape: The War against Women in Bosnia-Herzegovina*, Lincoln: University of Nebraska Press.

Stoler, Ann L. 1995. *Race and the Education of Desire: Foucault's History of Sexuality and the Colonial Order of Things*. Durham, NC: Duke University Press.

Stoler, Ann. 2002. *Carnal Knowledge and Imperial Power: Race and the Intimate in Colonial Rule*. Berkeley: University of California Press.

Stratigaki, Maria. 2004. "The Cooptation of Gender Concepts in EU Policies: The Case of 'Reconciliation of Work and Family.'" *Social Politics* 11, no 1: 30–56.

Todorova, Maria. 1997. *Imagining the Balkans*. New York: Oxford University Press.

Tomlinson, Barbara. 2013. "Colonizing Intersectionality: Replicating Racial Hierarchy in Feminist Academic Arguments." *Social Identities* 19, no 2: 254–272.

Warner, Marina. 1985. *Monuments and Maidens: The Allegory of the Female Form*. New York: Atheneum.

West, Robin L. 1998. "Jurisprudence and Gender." *University of Chicago Law Review* 55, no. 1: 11–50.

Woollacott, Angela. 1994. *On Her Their Lives Depend: Munitions Workers in the Great War*. Berkeley: University of California Press.

Yuval-Davis, Nira. 1999. "What Is 'Transversal Politics'?" *Soundings* 12: 94–98.

Zalewski, Marysia, and Jane Parpart. 1997. *The "Man" Question In International Relations*. Boulder, CO: Westview Press.

Žarkov, Dubravka. 2011. "Exposures and Invisibilities: Media, Masculinities and the Narratives of Wars in an Intersectional Perspective." In *Framing Intersectionality. Debates on a Multi-Faceted Concept in Gender Studies*, edited by Helma Lutz, Maria Teresa Herrera Vivar, and Linda Supik, 105–120. Burlington, VT: Ashgate.

Žarkov, Dubravka. 2014. "Ontologies of International Humanitarian and Criminal Law: 'Locals' and 'Internationals' in Discourses and Practices of Justice." In *Narratives of Justice In and Out of the Courtroom: Former Yugoslavia and Beyond*, edited by Dubravska Žarkov and Marlies Glasius, 3–21. New York: Springer.

Žarkov, Dubravka. 2015. "Identity Politics of Wars: Theorizing, Policy and Intervention." In *Conflict, Peace, Security and Development: Theories and Methodologies*, edited by Hellen Hintjens and Dubravska Žarkov, 117–132. Abingdon, Oxon: Routledge.

Žarkov, Dubravka, and Rada Drezgić. 2005. "Feministicke nevolje sa Balkanom" [Feminist Troubles with the Balkans]. *Sociologija (Journal of Sociological Association of Serbia, Belgrade)* XLVII, no 4: 289–306.

CHAPTER 3

···

THE SILENCES IN THE RULES THAT REGULATE WOMEN DURING TIMES OF ARMED CONFLICT

···

JUDITH GARDAM

THE law of armed conflict (LOAC), as its name suggests, is that part of international law that regulates the conduct of armed conflict. Its aim is to protect persons who are not or are no longer directly participating in the hostilities and to restrict the means and methods of warfare available to the warring parties. On the whole, feminist international lawyers have sidestepped scrutinizing the adequacy of LOAC in its treatment of the situation of women caught up in armed conflict. The exception to this neglect is an intense—and some might say obsessive—focus on the criminalization and punishment of sexual violence against women during hostilities through international criminal law (ICL) (see Engle, Chapter 10 in this volume). This general disinterest in LOAC is in contrast to the vigorous, broad, and multifaceted debate that has characterized the topic of women and human rights law (HRL). Frequently, this latter debate has encompassed issues and situations involving women and armed conflict, and it is true that the distinction between the two regimes is becoming less rigid, with HRL assuming an increasing role during such times. Nevertheless, LOAC remains the *lex specialis* during periods of armed conflict and occupation, and it is a powerful and effective protective regime if an individual can fit into one of its categories.

It is not as if LOAC lacks challenges for feminists. It is a rich field in which to view the operation of gender on two distinct levels. As this chapter will detail, LOAC contains first the quintessential gender—male, the warrior—and his essential foil, the weak and powerless "feminine" civilian in need of protection (Gardam 1993). Second, the rules protecting both combatants and civilians assume a female subject that has certain "natural" characteristics, particularly modesty and weakness, that help to constitute her honor. All the provisions of LOAC dealing with this subject are based on these two characteristics, and the way the regime is interpreted, disseminated, and applied reinforces these limiting and destructive gender stereotypes. It is therefore disappointing, given the level of armed conflict experienced in today's world and its impact on women, that LOAC as a whole has not been subjected to broader scrutiny by feminists (but see Gardam and Jarvis 2001).

Against that background, this chapter is organized as follows. The discussion commences with a description of the nature of LOAC, its structure, its field of application, and its most important features. Second, it details the provisions of LOAC of relevance to women, with consideration given to the way in which the rules represent a gendered vision of women. The final section includes a reflection on feminist encounters with LOAC and the extent to which they have made inroads into the regime in terms of improving the protections of women against the impact of armed conflict and its aftermath, as well as some thoughts on the challenges that lie ahead.

What Is the Law of Armed Conflict?

The provisions of LOAC cover both international and non-international armed conflicts. This ancient, complex, and highly detailed set of rules deals with such diverse topics as air, sea, and land warfare, weapons, prisoners of war, civil defense, and the protection of civilians in occupied territories, to name just a few. Although LOAC is the most codified part of international law, the majority of its provisions also are reflected in customary modern-day international law (see Henckaerts and Doswald-Beck 2006). Such a status is significant for those conventional rules that do not enjoy widespread acceptance among states actively involved in armed conflict.

Two powerful and influential stakeholders have affected the development, implementation, and interpretation of LOAC: the military establishment of states and the International Committee of the Red Cross (ICRC). LOAC primarily governs the conduct of militaries that are, in the main, responsible for its implementation. The term "military" in this context refers to the traditional well-organized and well-equipped professional armed forces of primarily Western states, for which the LOAC regime was originally designed, a provenance that it still reflects today. In particular, LOAC has struggled to maintain its relevance in the era of armed hostilities involving non-state actors, as exemplified by the so-called war on terror (Gardam 2010). The Swiss-based association, the ICRC, is known as the promoter and guardian of LOAC. In this role it disseminates, monitors compliance with, and contributes to the development of LOAC. As such, the ICRC occupies a unique place in the international legal system, with its mandate recognized by states. The relationship between the military establishment of states and the ICRC is complex and multifaceted, but one thing is clear; without the support of both these entities, little can be achieved in terms of the improvement of the legal protections available to those caught up in armed conflict, a point I return to later.

The terminology in use today in this area of international law reflects the influence of both the military and the ICRC. Originally, LOAC was referred to as the laws and customs of war or the law of war. These terms are still in use today. Nowadays, however, with the advent of the 1945 United Nations Charter outlawing war and the adoption of the four 1949 Geneva Conventions, together with the growing emphasis on human rights, this area of law has become better known as either LOAC or international humanitarian law (IHL). LOAC is the preferred term of the military in recognition of the utilitarian nature of the regime and the fact that it serves the demands of military efficiency. IHL, with its emphasis on the humanitarian aspects of the rules, is the preferred term of the ICRC. Their choice of name is part of a deliberate strategy to expand the scope of the rules and to change the balance they incorporate between the demands of military necessity and considerations of humanity, in favor of the latter. The extent to which they have succeeded in achieving this aim is a matter of debate.

The distinction between the utilitarian and humanitarian basis of LOAC is not just a matter of terminology. It is reflected in the structure of the regime itself, where a distinction is often drawn between the Law of the Hague and the Law of Geneva. The former refers to the rules that govern the actual conduct of hostilities, for example, laws that determine the weapons which can legitimately be used in armed conflict and that define what constitutes a military target. The 1899 and 1907 Hague Convention IV Respecting the Laws and Custom of War on Land and their annexed Regulations are examples of these provisions. The Law of Geneva or humanitarian law proper, as it is often referred to, primarily deals with the victims of war, such as civilians in occupied territories and prisoners of war. The four 1949 Geneva Conventions and their two Additional Protocols adopted in 1977 (Protocol I dealing with international armed conflicts and Protocol II dealing with non-international armed conflicts) are the best known of the conventional documents in this area and are its major components. There has been a gradual breakdown in the distinction between Hague Law and Geneva Law that culminated in the adoption of Additional Protocol I, which deals with both the law of hostilities and humanitarian law. An illustration of this convergence is the provisions of the Additional Protocol that deal with the protection of the civilian population from the effects of hostilities, such as Article 51, which contains the requirement of proportionality in the conduct of attacks.

Traditionally, the law in relation to international armed conflicts, those between states, has been more developed than that in relation to non-international armed conflicts, those between a state and armed groups within the territory of a state or states. The major treaty rules of relevance to non-international armed conflicts are Common Article 3 to the four 1949 Geneva Conventions and Additional Protocol II, which provide limited protections for those caught up in these conflicts. State practice has moved beyond this treaty law, however, and there is now a considerable body of customary international law applicable to non-international armed conflicts. Consequently, there is growing convergence between the rules governing international and non-international armed conflicts so much so that there are calls for the abolition of the distinction. LOAC (along with HRL) is also one of the cornerstones of the body of ICL that governs armed conflict. For example, its provisions form a significant component of the jurisdiction of the two ad hoc international criminal law tribunals, the International Criminal Tribunal for the Former Yugoslavia and the 1994 International Criminal Tribunal for Rwanda, as well as that of the 1998 permanent International Criminal Court.

A final feature of LOAC in common with international law generally is that its development, implementation, and enforcement, until very recently, has taken place without any significant contribution from women, be it within the military establishment of states, the ICRC, or state delegations to the diplomatic meetings that have negotiated and adopted the treaty rules. This absence of women is perhaps even more marked in the case of LOAC than in international law generally in light of the intensely masculine nature of the activity it regulates and the participants therein.

Having described the nature and structure of LOAC, in the next section I provide, first, an overview of the provisions of LOAC of relevance to women. Second, I consider some of the ways in which gender manifests itself in the regime.

How Are Women Portrayed in LOAC?

LOAC and women

Theoretically, women benefit from all the provisions of LOAC. In common with the civilian population, they enjoy the rules of LOAC that provide protection against the effects of hostilities and during times of occupation (Kinsella 2005). As combatants they are covered to the same extent as men by the provisions relating to the legitimate means and methods of combat and those in favor of prisoners of war, the wounded, the sick, and the shipwrecked.

The four 1949 Conventions and their two Additional Protocols establish a system of equality in the sense that no adverse distinction can be drawn between individuals on the basis of, *inter alia*, sex. Differentiation on the basis of sex is thus permissible as long as its impact is favorable. This approach to equality permits the rules providing specific protections for women that are contained in all four 1949 Geneva Conventions and both their Additional Protocols. These provisions are all located in the Law of Geneva dealing with the victims of armed conflict, and none are found in the rules regulating the actual conduct of hostilities (ICRC 2016).

The system of special protection for women is founded in broad provisions that deal with the "regard" or "consideration due to women on account of their sex," and require that they be accorded special respect and protection (First Geneva Convention, art. 12(2); Second Geneva Convention, art. 2(2); Third Geneva Convention, art. 16; Fourth Geneva Convention, arts. 13, 27(3); Protocol I, arts. 9(1), 69(1), 70(1), 75(1); Protocol II, arts. 2(1), 4(1); Gardam 1993). Standing alone, the provisions in relation to "regard," "consideration," or "special respect" are statements of general principle and impose no concrete obligations. They are supplemented by more detailed rules. For example, women prisoners of war and internees are entitled, where feasible, to separate quarters and sanitary conveniences and to supervision by women. Other provisions are designed to directly protect women from sexual assault; and pregnant women and mothers of young children are the beneficiaries of a number of provisions dealing with such matters as early repatriation, priority in medical care, emergency relief, and the provision of food and medical supplies. Overall the rules are designed to either reduce the vulnerability of women to sexual violence, to directly prohibit certain types of sexual violence, or to protect them when pregnant or as mothers of young children.

Common Article 3 to the four 1949 Geneva Conventions and Additional Protocol II makes some provision for the treatment of women in non-international armed conflicts, but their focus is also on pregnant women and the vulnerability of women to sexual violence.

The influence of gender

Gender manifests itself in LOAC in a number of ways (Chinkin 2014). For a start, its operation can be seen in the arbitrary nature of its boundaries. LOAC predominantly operates only during periods of actual hostilities. Apart from the provisions of the 1949 Fourth Geneva Convention and those of Additional Protocol I that deal with the treatment of civilians in occupied territories, LOAC does not concern itself with the aftermath of conflict. The limitations arising from the boundaries of LOAC are shared by all victims of armed conflict. However, in common with those of international law generally, they have a differential impact on men and women (Gardam and Jarvis 2001). They have been drawn up to reflect the experience of combatants and male civilians. Traditionally, it is during hostilities, or when they are *hors de combat*, that combatants and male civilians are most seriously affected by armed conflict. They are most at risk of death, injury, torture, summary execution, and mistreatment generally during hostilities or when wounded, sick, or prisoners of war. LOAC provides detailed provisions dealing with all these situations. Although vulnerable during conflict, women have a distinctive (and in many ways harsher) post-conflict experience than that of men. Women, generally speaking, are more likely to initially survive the hostilities, only to then experience sexual violence, starvation, and other hardships after conflict. They are particularly vulnerable to the disintegration of societal structures that accompanies armed conflict due to the endemic discrimination they experience in virtually all societies, which renders them less able to cope with its challenges (Gardam 1997). Armed conflict exacerbates existing inequalities experienced globally by women and, moreover, may lead to new forms of discrimination against them, such as in the allocation of scarce emergency relief in conflict situations where women are frequently disadvantaged, either deliberately, or because their needs are not properly understood. There are few provisions of LOAC that reflect this overall experience of women in times of armed conflict (Gardam 1997).

The so-called special provisions for women in LOAC are a further example of how gender permeates LOAC. Over the years they have undoubtedly constituted a major obstacle to addressing the question of whether LOAC is in fact adequate to respond to the situation of women in times of armed conflict, as they appear to provide "favorable" treatment for women. Consequently, it remains the generally accepted view that LOAC is a satisfactory regime for women, as not only does the system require that its general rules be applied without discrimination, but there are additional "special provisions" of LOAC dealing with the particular needs of women.

What is overlooked in this assessment is gender (Sjoberg 2006). The so-called general provisions of LOAC in addressing humanitarian needs in armed conflict assume as their norm a certain male experience and a population in which there is no systemic gender inequality. As for the regime of special protection for women during armed conflict, it reveals a picture of women that is drawn exclusively on the basis of their perceived weakness, both physical and psychological, and their sexual and reproductive functions. This is the case whether we are dealing with women civilians or women combatants. Although some forty-two provisions of the four 1949 Geneva Conventions and their Additional Protocols specifically deal with women and the effects of armed conflict, nineteen concern women as "expectant mothers," "maternity cases," or "nursing mothers." The protection of the unborn child and small children is the rationale for many of these provisions. Women are included in their scope as they are integral to that protection.

The other major category of special rules relating to women deals with the prevention of sexual violence, and the protection of the chastity and modesty of women. Many of the provisions dealing with sexual violence are couched in terms of the honor of women (Lindsey 2001). For example, the Fourth Geneva Convention stipulates that women must be "especially protected against any attack of [sic] their honor, in particular against rape, enforced prostitution, or any form of indecent assault." The honor of both women and men is a pivotal concept in LOAC. The honor of women, as depicted in LOAC, is constituted solely on the basis of certain assumed sexual attributes, the characterizing features of which are chastity, modesty, and weakness. This interpretation of the meaning of honor in relation to women is confirmed in the original ICRC official Commentaries on the four 1949 Geneva Conventions and their Additional Protocols, which are regarded as an important source for interpreting these documents and as a useful aid in clarifying the intended scope and operation of their provisions. Such qualities are not based on any individualistic, autonomy-based concept belonging to the female person, but rather are a product of patriarchal honor belonging to the men to whom she is attached. In contrast, the honor of men in LOAC has many facets and encompasses both mind and bodily attributes, as illustrated by the prohibition on the parading of prisoners of war and their employment in work of a humiliating nature.

On its face, LOAC presents a picture of women that is distorted and far from the reality of their lives. It not only reinforces stereotypes of women but also fails to take into account in any way the underlying systemic discrimination that women experience in all societies (Gardam and Jarvis 2001). LOAC is predicated on the assumption that apart from their roles as mothers and in the context of sexual violence, women not only have the same experience of armed conflict as men, but also are able to avail themselves equally of the existing protections offered by LOAC. This is in fact not the case. The law regulating hostilities also assumes the homogeneity of the civilian population and that their experience of attacks, for example, has no gender dimensions (Sjoberg 2006). Once again, this assumption is not based on factual evidence of the actual experience of women during hostilities. For example, traditionally women are responsible for the care and protection of children and the extended family. Consequently, women tend to be less mobile than men and are often hampered in their efforts to flee from actual or impending armed attacks. The result is that women are more vulnerable in practice to direct harm from targeting than might be assumed, underscoring the value of a gendered assessment of LOAC and its relationship to the actual experiences of women during hostilities.

Having argued that LOAC takes no account of the endemic discrimination that women experience globally, there are some rare examples in the case of prisoners of war in which LOAC demands true equality of outcome and recognizes the potential for discrimination against women. One such case is Article 13 of the Third Geneva Convention, which requires that women prisoners of war be treated at least as well as men irrespective "of the practices of the detaining power."

In the next section I outline the issues that dominate the feminist agenda with respect to LOAC and explain what I regard as some of the obstacles to progress. My focus is the well-organized political campaign by a group of feminists to criminalize and prosecute sexual violence against women at the international level (Chinkin 2003). This may appear to be a somewhat narrow lens with which to view feminist encounters with LOAC, but it is the only area in which there has been concerted feminist engagement with the regime, and, moreover, remarkable changes have been achieved. Nevertheless, these achievements, although significant, have had some very negative consequences that I explore in the discussion that follows.

Feminist Encounters with LOAC

The highly effective feminist campaign to criminalize and punish sexual violence against women at the international level, which led to major developments in the interpretation of the existing provisions of LOAC by international criminal courts, represents a remarkable partnership between scholarship and advocacy (Copelon 1994). Its results can be seen as an unprecedented success story in which the traditional leading role of the ICRC in the development of LOAC was taken over by feminists and sympathetic states. This is not to suggest that the ICRC did not support these initiatives, but in this case it did not play a leading role.

But these achievements in the criminal punishment of sexual violence against women in ICL came at a price, including deep and sometimes bitter debates between feminists (see Nesiah, Chapter 22 in this volume). These differences are primarily attributable to fundamental theoretical disagreements as to how women should be portrayed (Engle 2008; Halley 2009). This is, of course, a familiar dilemma present in all feminist work. Having discarded one vision of woman as flawed, a prime item on the feminist agenda has always been how to clothe her replacement. The dilemma is stark in the case of international law that seeks a universal category of woman.

The campaign regarding sexual violence against women has brought these disagreements sharply into focus (Grahn-Farley 2010). There is the perception in some quarters that the process of achieving the developments in ICL has had significant negative consequences. In particular, not only has the fundamental challenge for feminist international lawyers of reconciling the complex intersections of race and gender been overshadowed, but also the vision of women as passive victims in need of protection has been reinforced (Engle 2005; Buss 2007).

Most would agree that lively debate is healthy and productive. Sometimes, however, deep divisions can play into the hands of those who oppose changes in the status quo. The internal disarray among feminists over the issue of sexual violence in armed conflict seems to have opened the door to suggestions that a great deal has been achieved for women, but that in the process the experience of men of armed conflict, in particular sexual violence against them, has been overlooked (Carpenter 2006). This sense of progress for women in terms of LOAC is misleading. There remains indifference in all quarters, including among feminists themselves, to the potential benefits that might ensue from developments in the law and its interpretation to take account of the overall different experience of women in armed conflict beyond sexual violence.

It is in this situation that the influence of the ICRC is important. The military has little motivation in improving the protection of women or indeed civilians in general from the impact of armed conflict. Its approach to LOAC is essentially pragmatic and its task is military victory (US Department of the Army 2007). Protecting civilians is seen as, if anything, hampering the achievement of this result, although, as I recount later, this is not always the case. It thus falls to the ICRC primarily to lead the way in relation to civilians. That organization, however, has always taken the view that the law in relation to women is adequate and what is needed is better implementation of its provisions. Moreover, a concept of equality that recognizes the insights that feminists have brought to this idea remains somewhat difficult for the ICRC to accommodate. The institution has come a long way in recent times and does accept the impact of gender and systemic discrimination on the way that women experience warfare (Lindsey 2001; ICRC 2016). However, the demands of its core principle of neutrality appear to prevent it from adopting an approach designed to recognize and take into account discrimination against women. This is particularly evident in the role of the ICRC in providing humanitarian assistance to women during times of armed conflict and its aftermath, but inevitably must flow through to its interpretation of the law and any suggestions for developments. As feminists have demonstrated, however, laws that were drawn up in an era that neither recognized this discrimination nor took account of it when the provisions were adopted do not qualify as neutral in their impact (Charlesworth 1999). For example, is it so unreasonable in this day and age to envisage a change in the law or in its interpretation to aspire to the equal participation of women in the decision-making as to the allocation and distribution of humanitarian aid during times of armed conflict? Accepting that there may be major obstacles in the implementation of such a strategy in many states, a provision of LOAC to that effect would at least provide a basis for such efforts.

It is also worth bearing in mind that much can be achieved through the reinterpretation of existing provisions of LOAC, rather than undertaking the hazardous path of persuading states to adopt new law (Gardam 2013). The developments in ICL on sexual violence against women are a testament to this process. A promising initiative in this context is the ICRC project that commenced in 2012 to revise the Commentaries on the four 1949 Geneva Conventions and their Additional Protocols (see ICRC 2016). It is to be expected that the changing attitudes over the past sixty years within the ICRC itself and among other international institutions to such ideas as the "modesty" and "honor" of women and other aspects of LOAC will be reflected in all the new documents.

In the case of LOAC, whatever strategy feminists adopt to achieve change and whatever the vision of women that emerges from these efforts, it would be wise not to underestimate the challenge that lies ahead and the impact of systemic power on efforts to achieve change. LOAC deals with the conduct of war, and women's voices are particularly muted in the intensely masculine environment that surrounds decision-making about such issues as national security and the resort to force. Women may have found a provisional place at the peace-building and post-conflict reconstruction table, but any meaningful participation in debates centering on the strategic and tactical issues of the conduct of hostilities continues to elude them.

New Challenges

The majority of the discussion so far has related to humanitarian law proper, that is, the protection of victims of armed conflict. That has without doubt been the major focus to date of feminist engagement with LOAC, and one gets the sense that those working in the area are more comfortable in that environment, and particularly so in the narrow area of sexual violence against women (MacKinnon 2006). This work should continue and hopefully with a broader focus on addressing the adequacy of LOAC to address the overall experiences of women in times of armed conflict. At the same time, however, feminists should turn their attention to that part of LOAC that has been almost completely neglected, namely the legal provisions that regulate the actual conduct of hostilities. This aspect of LOAC warrants a close study given the nature of the conflicts that occur in the world today, in which civilians and women in particular are so frequently at the frontline and are caught up directly in hostilities. It will not be an easy task. The actual means and methods of conflict are very much the domain of the military: feminism and that institution have never enjoyed an easy relationship. On the very few occasions that feminists have engaged with the law governing the conduct of hostilities, they have criticized the assumption by those applying the law that the protection of the civilian population is subsidiary to that of the combatant (Kinsella 2005). This approach is illustrated by the "zero casualties" policy adopted by NATO in the 1999 Kosovo conflict—"casualties" in that case being those of NATO combatants. Such an assumption has considerable influence on how the fundamental LOAC principle of proportionality is applied. Proportionality requires a balance to be struck between the anticipated military advantage of a particular attack and the likely number of incidental civilian casualties thereof. If the protection of combatants is a priority of those making the calculation, it will assume more significance in the assessment of the military advantage component of the equation and the consequent downplay of the risk of collateral (or civilian) casualties. Any realigning of this balance may serve to increase the protection of civilians during actual hostilities with a flow-on effect for women.

There is some evidence that in certain circumstances the military may be prepared to reconsider some aspects of force protection. For example, the approach to counterinsurgency warfare in the 2007 US Army/Marine Corps Counter Insurgency Field Manual (COIN) centers on minimizing civilian casualties rather than destroying the enemy, and it underpinned coalition efforts in both Iraq and Afghanistan (US Department of the Army 2007; Gardam and Stephens 2014). Such a strategy calls for including an increased assumption of risk by combatants, among other things, in the assessment of whether a particular attack satisfies the requirements of proportionality. According to the COIN Manual, its underlying premise is that the exposure of combatants to increased risk in the short term, although it may lead to more immediate military casualties, is more likely to result in winning the war. In the case of counterterrorism, military victory is measured less in terms of insurgent casualties than in a reduction of civilian casualties and a correlative investment in the legitimacy of the host government. It would be naive in the extreme, however, to see this as the start of a brave new world. The rationale of the COIN strategy is securing military victory in counter-insurgency situations, not the protection of the civilian population. So there just happened in this case to be a coalescence of interests that may never be repeated.

CONCLUSION

In conclusion, there are many aspects of LOAC that await concerted feminist action. The priority should be addressing the fundamental question as to whether the numerous provisions of LOAC not concerned with sexual violence are adequate to respond to the ways in which women experience armed conflict. There are pitfalls to avoid in such a project. In particular, denouncing the law as not reflecting the needs and aspirations of women and putting forward proposals for reform can all too readily be criticized as erasing differences between women by creating a feminist norm of the universal woman. This is, in fact, exactly what some feminists argue has occurred in the context of the developments in LOAC relating to the criminalization and punishment of sexual violence against women (Engle 2005).

Whatever the conclusion, however, major structural change in the regime will not be forthcoming. A more modest proposal would be to advocate an interpretation and application of the existing provisions that more accurately and effectively respond to the overall experience of women during times of armed conflict. A fundamental prerequisite to achieving this outcome is the recognition that what is required in such a process is more than working within the limits of formal equality as measured against a gendered male norm. Such an appreciation opens the way for progress toward a more gender-neutral regime. LOAC is a "protective" regime for all individuals, so it will always reflect its purpose and so it should. In their encounters with LOAC, however, feminists could articulate and encourage an approach to its provisions that reinforces a view of women not as passive, weak, and helpless victims, but rather as entitled to be regarded as equal participants with men in society.

REFERENCES

Buss, Doris. 2007. "The Curious Visibility of Wartime Rape: Gender and Ethnicity in International Criminal Law." *Windsor Yearbook of Access to Justice* 25, no. 1: 3–22.

Carpenter, R. Charli. 2006. *Innocent Women and Children: Gender Norms and the Protection of Civilians*. London: Ashgate.

Charlesworth, Hilary. 1999. "Feminist Methods in International Law." *American Journal of International Law* 93, no. 2: 379–394.

Chinkin, Christine. 2003. "Feminist Reflections on International Criminal Law." In *International Criminal Law and the Current Development of Public International Law*, edited by Andreas Zimmermann, 125–160. Berlin: Duncker and Humblot.

Chinkin, Christine. 2014. "Gender and Armed Conflict." In *The Oxford Handbook of International Armed Conflict*, edited by Andrew Clapham and Paola Gaeta, 675–699. Oxford: Oxford University Press.

Copelon, Rhonda. 1994. "Surfacing Gender: Re-Engraving Crimes against Women in Humanitarian Law." *Hastings Women's Law Journal* 5, no. 2: 243–266.

Engle, Karen. 2005. "Feminism and Its (Dis)contents: Criminalizing Wartime Rape in Bosnia and Herzegovina." *American Journal of International Law* 99, no. 4: 778–816.

Engle, Karen. 2008. "Judging Sex in War." *Michigan Law Review* 106, no. 6: 941–961.

Gardam, Judith. 1993. "The Law of Armed Conflict: A Gendered Regime?" In *Reconceiving Reality: Women and International Law*, edited by Dorinda G. Dallmeyer, 171–202. Washington, DC: The American Society of International Law.

Gardam, Judith. 1997. "Women and the Law of Armed Conflict: Why the Silence?" *International and Comparative Law Quarterly* 46, no. 1: 55–80.

Gardam, Judith. 2005. "The Neglected Aspect of Women and Armed Conflict: Progressive Development of the Law." *Netherlands International Law Review* 52, no. 2: 197–219.

Gardam, Judith. 2010. "War, Law, Terror, Nothing New for Women." *Australian Feminist Law Journal* 32, no. 1: 61–75.

Gardam, Judith. 2013. "A New Frontline for Feminism and International Humanitarian Law." In *The Ashgate Research Companion to Feminist Legal Theory*, edited by Margaret Davies and Vanessa Munro, 217–231. London: Ashgate.

Gardam, Judith, and Michelle Jarvis. 2001. *Women, Armed Conflict and International Law*. The Hague: Kluwer Law International.

Gardam, Judith, and Dale Stephens. 2014. "Concluding Remarks: Establishing Common Ground between Feminism and the Military." In *Rethinking Peacekeeping, Gender Equality, and Collective Security*, edited by Gina Heathcote and Dianne Otto, 265–279. London: Palgrave, Macmillan UK.

Geneva Convention for the Amelioration of the Condition of the Wounded and Sick in Armed Forces in the Field (First Geneva Convention). 1949. 6 U.S.T. 3114, 75 U.N.T.S. 31 (August 12).

Geneva Convention for the Amelioration of the Condition of Wounded, Sick and Shipwrecked Members of the Armed Forces at Sea (Second Geneva Convention). 1949. 6 U.S.T. 3217, 75 U.N.T.S. 85 (August 12).

Geneva Convention Relative to the Treatment of Prisoners of War (Third Geneva Convention). 1949. 6 U.S.T. 3316, 75 U.N.T.S. 135 (August 12).

Geneva Convention Relative to the Protection of Civilian Persons in Time of War (Fourth Geneva Convention). 1949. 6 U.S.T. 3516, 75 U.N.T.S. 287 (August 12).

Grahn-Farley, Maria. 2010. "The Politics of Inevitability: An Examination of Janet Halley's Critique of the Criminalisation of Rape as Torture." In *Feminist Perspectives on Contemporary International Law: Between Resistance and Compliance?*, edited by Sari Kouvo and Zoe Pearson, 109–132. Oxford: Hart.

Halley, Janet. 2009. "Rape at Rome: Feminist Interventions in the Criminalization of Sex-Related Violence in Positive International Criminal Law." *Michigan Journal of International Law* 30, no. 1: 1–123.

Hague Convention IV, Declaration I. 1899. Concerning the Prohibition, for a Term of Five Years, of the Launching of Projectiles and Explosives from Balloons or Other New Methods of a Similar Nature. 32 Stat. 1839 (July 29).

Hague Convention IV, Declaration II. 1899. Concerning the Prohibition of the Use of Projectiles Diffusing Asphyxiating Gases. 187 Consol. T.S. 453 (July 29).

Hague Convention IV, Declaration III. 1899. Concerning the Prohibition of the Use of Expanding Bullets. 187 Consol. T.S. 459 (July 29).

Hague Convention IV. 1907. Laws and Customs of War on Land. 36 Stat. 2277 (October 18).

Henckaerts, Jean-Marie, and Louise Doswald-Beck, eds. 2006. *Customary International Humanitarian Law*. Geneva: International Committee of the Red Cross.

International Committee of the Red Cross (ICRC). 2016. *Updated Commentary on the First Geneva Convention: Convention (I) for the Amelioration of the Condition of the Wounded and Sick in Armed Forces in the Field*. Accessed December 22, 2016. https://ihl-databases.icrc.org/ihl/full/GCI-commentary.

Kinsella, Helen. 2005. "Securing the Civilian: Sex and Gender in the Laws of War." In *Power in Global Governance*, edited by Michael Barnett and Raymond Duvall, 249–272. Cambridge: Cambridge University Press.

Lindsey, Charlotte. 2001. *Women Facing War*. Geneva: International Committee of the Red Cross.

MacKinnon, Catharine A. 2006. "Defining Rape Internationally: A Comment on *Akayesu*." *Columbia Journal of Transnational Law* 44, no. 3: 940–958.

Protocol Additional to the Geneva Conventions of 12 August 1949 and Relating to the Protection of Victims of International Armed Conflicts (Protocol I). 1977. 1125 U.N.T.S. 3 (June 8).

Protocol Additional to the Geneva Conventions of 12 August 1949 and Relating to the Protection of Victims of Non-International Armed Conflicts (Protocol II). 1977. 1125 U.N.T.S. 609 (June 8).

Sjoberg, Laura. 2006. "The Gender Realities of the Immunity Principle: Why Gender Analysis Needs Feminism." *International Studies Quarterly* 50, no. 4: 889–910.

UN Charter. 1945. 59 Stat. 1031, 1 U.N.T.S. XVI (October 24).

US Department of the Army. 2007. *The US Army/Marine Corps: Counterinsurgency Field Manual.* Chicago: University Chicago Press.

CHAPTER 4

....

HOW SHOULD WE EXPLAIN THE RECURRENCE OF VIOLENT CONFLICT, AND WHAT MIGHT GENDER HAVE TO DO WITH IT?

....

JUDY EL-BUSHRA

MOST conflicts in the world in this century have been civil wars taking place in poor and fragile states: in 2010 it was reported that every conflict started since 2003 had been a recurrence of a previous one (Walter 2010). With this realization in mind, the international community now devotes much attention to understanding how interventions in "post-conflict" settings might be designed more effectively to minimize relapse. However, given the persistence of war globally, it is pertinent to ask how much progress has been made.

The field of gender and conflict, no less than that of state fragility and conflict, similarly faces the challenge of reality-testing. As others detail in this *Handbook*, more than a decade and a half after the passing of UN Security Council resolution 1325 on women, peace, and security, little progress has been made in improving security for women in conflict-affected environments, or increasing their participation in peace negotiations (see, e.g., in this volume, Otto, Chapter 8; Goetz and Jenkins, Chapter 9; and Bell, Chapter 32).

To explore some of the factors that might contribute to our continued inability to prevent conflict and build peace, this chapter describes some of the ways in which the international community has sought to conceptualize persistent conflict, and asks whether incorporating a gender dimension into this analysis can enhance understanding and expand options for effective intervention. It argues that neither conflict analysis nor gender analysis are unproblematic categories; however, the potential for better understanding will not be realized as long as conflict analysis is dominated by the "liberal peace" model, and gender analysis means simply "add women and stir." For conflict analysis to comprehend the breadth and depth of social relations, and in the process to generate more tailored interventions that better comprehend realities, it must undergo a paradigm shift and reconceptualize conflict and peace as complex, iterative, multilayered, and dynamic processes, thereby opening up opportunities to be enriched by a nuanced understanding of gender relations.

The first section of the chapter reviews how cycles of conflict are described in orthodox conflict analysis, how gender has been situated within this, and the influence of this analytical framing on approaches to peace-building and state-building. The second section presents alternative approaches, and suggests that interpretations of conflict that stress the importance of social process and identity would have positive advantages, including more fruitful integration of gender analysis.

CYCLES OF CONFLICT: THE ORTHODOX VIEW

Mainstream understandings of violent conflict

To understand how the international community views recurring conflict, we must first examine its overall approach to conflict analysis. Mainstream approaches to understanding conflict, such as those evidenced in the work of the World Bank and the Stockholm International Peace Research Institute (SIPRI), focus on drawing conclusions based on rigorous quantitative evidence, and thus fall largely within an econometric perspective. For example, SIPRI defines "conflict" as an event leading to at least twenty-five battle-related deaths in one calendar year, as compared to "war," which requires at least 1,000 battle-related deaths in one calendar year. SIPRI's annual yearbook documents conflict trends and events, identifying the major timelines, players, and causal factors, and providing information on numbers of state-based (including inter-state, intra-state, and internationalized intra-state) conflicts, non-state conflicts, and "one-sided" conflicts, as well as the numbers of battle-related deaths in each conflict category (Themner and Wallensteen 2014).

Analysis of this type has typically been carried out at a national level. For example, conflict assessment guidelines developed by the UK government's Department for International Development (DFID) focus on "structures," "actors," and "dynamics" and on an assessment of the DFID's own and other international actors' interventions; no mention is made of either the global political dimensions of conflicts or how men and women at the community level contribute to, are violated by, and respond to the conflict (DFID 2002).

This "classical" approach assumes that conflict has a progressive trajectory, moving from latent to violent conflict and thence (under the benign influence of the international community) to peace negotiations, post-conflict transition, and eventually to permanent peace and stability. The distinction often made by the international community between ongoing conflict and post-conflict contexts is a key one: categorizing a particular conflict in these terms has implications for intervention and financing decisions. In ongoing conflicts, the aim is to support military containment, thereby helping to create conditions for a political solution.

In post-conflict situations (i.e., after the signing of a formal peace agreement and a suitable period of "transition"), the aim is to support the rebuilding of institutions in a way that minimizes the risk of a return to war. Much work on post-conflict reconstruction and development is based, implicitly or explicitly, on a desire to preempt a recurrence of conflict, thus addressing the issue of conflict cycles. However, in reality the international community may be equally influenced by pragmatic imperatives that limit sustainability of outcomes. For example, perhaps conscious of the high levels of financial investment expected of it, the international community is sometimes overly hasty in encouraging a transition from ongoing to post-conflict, before underlying conflict factors have been satisfactorily addressed. In this case it is likely that violence will continue to disrupt attempts at normalization. As a case in point, men and women in Eastern Democratic Republic of Congo (DRC) continued to experience their situation as "war" long after the government and the international community had categorized the country as "post-conflict" (Dolan 2010).

Peace-building and diplomacy can bring conflicts to an end in some circumstances, as it has in Northern Ireland, though even here grievances continue unresolved and break out in unrest from time to time. These exceptions notwithstanding, contrary examples abound: of conflicts that the international community has misinterpreted in various ways, largely as a result of allowing facts on the ground to be obscured in conflict analysis by wishful thinking on the part of donors, often with disastrous effect: DRC and Somalia are notable among these (Autesserre 2012; Harper 2012).

Conflict cycles and the "conflict trap"

Paul Collier, commenting from the perspective of a World Bank economist, sought to identify the circumstances under which some countries were perpetually unable, without major reform, to control the tendencies toward violent conflict. Collier asserted that countries with poor economic and governance indicators were those most likely to be caught in a "conflict trap" and to experience a recurrence of conflict, since conflict was the enemy of development, and vice versa (Collier et al. 2003). His analysis was highly influential for a number of years and was adopted by a number of UN and other international agencies; for example, it was cited as grounds for the establishment of the UN Peacebuilding Commission (Suhrke and Samset 2007).

Despite this, both Collier's methodology and conclusions have been repeatedly contested. Suhrke and Samset, using Collier's own figures, revised his conclusion from "half of conflicts recur within 5 years" to "a quarter of conflicts recur within 10 years," a shift which they pointed out might have significant policy implications. Further, they suggest that conclusions based on this statistical evidence are illusory to the extent that they "convey certainty and factual 'truth' even though this may be false security" (Suhrke and Samset 2007, 199). Critics of Collier also note that exclusionary politics are as important as economic factors, if not more so (Call 2010), as is attention to micro-level political relations (Kreutz 2012; Moe 2010). Barbara Walter concluded that political and economic unresponsiveness, not previous exposure to conflict, was the determining factor in war recurrence, a point of ambiguity in Collier's account (Walter 2010), and lack of political responsiveness was featured as the main explanation for cyclical conflict in the eventual definitive World Bank statement on conflict, the 2011 World Development Report (WDR) (World Bank 2011).

The 2011 WDR represents a small but observable shift in the international discourse around conflict, away from the rigidity of linear models and toward a stronger interest in addressing complexity, suggesting a view of conflict as an evolving and shifting process. It proposes that, globally, conflict may change its nature, and notes an increasing trend toward large-scale organized criminal violence as distinct from politically driven rebellion. It cautions that cause and effect can be difficult to tease out, and that the move away from fragility and violence to institutional resilience should be expected to take place in spiral fashion, rather than in a neat linear progression (World Bank 2011). However, the overall tenor of global discourse continues to be unidirectional, econometric, and macro-focused, and, as we see in the following, masculinized.

The orthodox view as policy frame

Orthodox thinking continues to drive international responses to specific conflict contexts. Collier's "conflict trap" feeds directly into the concept of the "liberal peace" (Suhrke and Samset 2007), a policy approach that provides justification for the international community to intervene (including militarily) in the affairs of countries whose governments it labels as morally or politically unacceptable. Spiral diagrams or not, the overall model in orthodox thinking continues to be one in which repeated cycles of conflict are the result of weak state institutions unable to replace the dynamics of war with dynamic state-citizen interaction. It still aspires toward a progressive pathway from pre-conflict, through active conflict, to post-conflict, and thence to social and economic reconstruction via "liberal peace" interventions from the international community, leading ultimately to the re-establishment of a permanently viable state. Reality, on the other hand, tends to be messier, driven by local dynamics rather than—and sometimes in direct conflict with—global policy imperatives (Campbell et al. 2011).

The orthodox conflict model finds further expression in the state-building approach currently favored under the New Deal for Fragile and Conflict Affected States (FCAS).[1] The concept of FCAS reflects the concern of major donors that their investments in post-conflict recovery have failed to lead countries emerging from civil war to the golden dawn predicted for them. State-building, with its five key goals (legitimate politics/political settlements, security, justice, economic foundations, and revenues and services), has emerged as a key policy response to the phenomenon of FCAS, promoting the reform of institutions and encouraging measures to improve state functionality and responsiveness, specifically in cases where persistent conflict threatens global security (OECD 2011).

"Add gender and stir?"

Does the concern with the metrics of conflict duration and recurrence share a common cause with the Women, Peace, and Security Agenda? Belatedly and occasionally, yes. Some examples merely provide further illustration of the incongruity of reducing complex debates to a percentage. Laurel Stone, for example, reviewing official records of peace negotiation processes, concludes that "encouraging [women's] participation increases the probability of violence ending within a year by 24 percent.... implementing gender quotas for national legislatures could increase the probability of violence ending within five years by 27 percent" (Stone 2014). Somewhat more substantially, Mary Caprioli has demonstrated statistical correlations between certain gender equality indicators and a country's propensity for peacefulness (Caprioli 2000, 2005). And although the World Bank's 2011 WDR is essentially a gender-free zone, subsequent research within the World Bank explored what gender-disaggregated evidence might add to the analysis of "conflict traps."

Resulting from this research, Myra Buvinic and colleagues (Buvinic et al. 2012) assert that gender difference adds an important dimension to conflict analysis and has implications for intervention design, especially since one of their findings is that the gendered impacts of conflict are not necessarily consistent across cases. Based on a review of quantitative evidence gathered from a wide range of conflict contexts, the authors frame their analysis around two levels of conflict impact, both of which have gendered implications. For them, first-round impacts differ between men and women and include (a) an increase in mortality and morbidity (mainly of young men and children) and widowhood (for women); (b) forced migration; (c) loss of assets and income; and (d) sexual and gender-based violence. Second-round impacts consist of household adaptations to the loss of male breadwinners and to the demographic imbalance that results; these include, in many cases, increased economic and political activity on the part of women (see Justino, Chapter 6 in this volume). These first- and second-round impacts themselves have further repercussions for the economic, political, and social fabric, and hence for recovery capacity. They should therefore be taken into account in the design of interventions, for example in projects addressing needs for education or financial or judicial services, if the international community is to make inroads into the "conflict trap." The review suggests that "gender inequalities shape and are shaped by the responses of households to violent conflict" (Buvinic et al. 2012, 131). It concludes that gender is an important variable; giving it sufficient attention would enhance the macropolicy community's efforts to understand the dynamics of conflict and to develop more effective means of supporting people affected by it.

Policy frames falling within the orthodox discourse, as well as associated practice, have also had trouble incorporating a gender dimension. Women's rights and well-being (and if gender is taken into account at all, it is generally in the form of "women's issues") frequently find themselves at the center of the potentially destructive convergence of two forces, local dynamics and global policy, with the managers of the liberal peace seemingly at a loss mediating the tension between them (Chaudhary et al. 2011). As far as the state-building discourse is concerned, this has been spectacularly ungendered, and the component processes of the state-building framework have largely excluded women (Castillejo 2011). This is in spite of the Organisation for Economic Co-operation and Development's own emphasis on the need for inclusivity and state-citizen dialogue at all stages of the process (OECD 2011). As with WDR 2011, gender has been added in at a late stage (OECD 2013); however, there has been little investment to date in researching the potential links between gender and state-building, and hence little hard evidence to support gender policy in state-building (Domingo et al. 2013)—or indeed to support state-building as a strategy for gender equality.

The exclusion of women (and other politically subaltern groups) as state-building participants has particularly grave outcomes when it occurs in the (typically early) phases of the state-building process, which are concerned with political settlements. Those engaged in peace negotiations and in the establishment of political settlements are generally under pressure to satisfy the demands of the previously warring parties, as a first and most urgent step in maintaining security, and to postpone the introduction of broader and more inclusive settlements until post-transition. Indeed, participants in peace negotiations have been known to exclude women explicitly, on the grounds that they did not form a defined party to the armed conflict (Itto 2006), thus ignoring both the fact of their active participation in armed groups and their legitimate interests in the terms of post-conflict settlements. As the OECD itself acknowledges, the time for broadening opportunities for participation is at the negotiation stage, before the shape and culture of newly-formed institutions becomes established. Once reconstruction begins, the practices and norms of the power-holders are likely to dominate the conduct of state–citizen relations (OECD 2013).

In summary, the way in which cyclical or recurrent conflict is described in the mainstream is shaped by an econometric approach, which seeks to measure the incidence of conflict, define its typologies, and assess the factors that contribute to it based on quantifiable data. Although conclusions based on statistical evidence may be useful as contributions to arguments around macro policy, they throw little light on the complexities of lived realities. Orthodox analysis, which forms the basis of resourcing and policy decisions governing international action on conflict, falls within, and supports, a "liberal peace" approach to international relations, ultimately seeking to identify the scope for "Western" responses to and intervention in conflict hotspots. Despite the "moral capital" that the liberal peace approach seeks to gain from the discourse around women's rights, mainstream conflict analysis retains a masculinized character. Where gender figures at all within this framework, it merely offers an additional—though valuable—layer of data disaggregation, constrained by its conceptual parameters in its ability to interpret and explain, as well as record, the data it uncovers. Little attempt has been made within this framework to draw on feminist or peace-building traditions (see Otto, Chapter 8 in this volume) that might assist with understanding the social processes that are involved in conflict and peace, rather than simply with their measurement.

A Broader Approach

Opening up the framework

The mainstream approach to conflict analysis tends to focus on situations of mass organized violence, specifically those that display features triggering identification by the international community as "conflict" or "post-conflict." Alternative approaches see "war" as one manifestation of conflict among many—one end, perhaps, of a continuum that also includes other forms of organized and unorganized violence, and which stretches to situations that are neither, but that have potential for violence if mismanaged. This broader framing permits "stabilizing points" (people or institutions who can provide stability when all around them is collapsing; Roche 1996) or "connectors and local capacities for peace" (Anderson 1999) to be acknowledged as key to conflict management and violence prevention.

The orthodox framework overlooks a broad spectrum of dimensions, including the social and psychosocial dimensions and related issues of cohesion, identity, and history. Violent conflict is more likely in contexts where integration between different forms of social capital is weak—social capital being composed of vertical linkages (between citizens and state) and horizontal linkages (membership of and networking across institutions such as the family or clan). Social cohesion is manifested in high levels of civic engagement and a well-functioning state, *both* being requirements for social and economic development and for effective conflict management (Colletta and Cullen 2000). Much ink has been spilled in contentions over the issue of ethnicity—or perhaps more accurately, the manipulation of ethnic identity and ethnic discourse—as a possible explanation for recurrent genocides, for example in Central Africa (Lemarchand 2009). History shows that underlying tensions and grievances often recur cyclically, possibly in different forms, over decades if not centuries; the knowledge of violence can be transferred from one generation to another, and informs not only the fact of war but also the intensity of the violence. For example, it has been suggested that some of the roots of the civil war in Liberia can be found in the experience of slavery undergone by American Liberians (Boas 1997), and that the cruelty inflicted by the Belgian colonial power in the Congo found later expression in present-day civil war behavior (Dummett 2004). The roots of recurring conflict, then, may be sought in the behavior of past generations as well as in current structures.

Infusing a gender analysis

In what way has gender informed less orthodox approaches to explaining conflict recurrence? To explore this further, we first need to examine differences in perspectives

within the "gender and peace-building" field between those who see the need to prioritize a women-centered approach and those who advocate a broader gender analytical
approach (O'Gorman 2014).

The former finds its main expression in the "women, peace, and security" (WPS) policy field (see, in this volume, Otto, Chapter 8; Goetz and Jenkins, Chapter 9). These resolutions have strengthened the international community's commitment to addressing
the needs of women and girls in war, and have legitimized women's voice and activism
in conflict and peace issues at the highest levels. However, large components of international discourse and practice have remained impervious to WPS, and it has not necessarily led to material changes for women on the ground (Anderlini 2010).

The broader approach, often termed "gender-relational," insists that gender analysis
needs to address relationships within the "whole society." Moving away from equat-
ing gender with women, it incorporates aspects of intersectionality theory (see, in this
volume, Žarkov, Chapter 2; and Rooney, Chapter 25) since it seeks to deepen analysis
by linking gender to other identity markers, such as age, social class, sexuality, disability, ethnic or religious background, marital status, or urban/rural setting (Cohn 2012;
Myrttinen et al. 2014).

The distinction between these two understandings is relevant to a consideration
of cyclical conflict. While the main emphasis of WPS is on identifying the impact
of war on women and on strengthening policy to ensure their protection and their
engagement in seeking remedies, the "gender-relational" perspective sets this goal
within a broader frame and hence encourages, among other things, an examination
of gender as a contributory factor in violent conflict. Gender may be seen as "causal
in militarization and war," with gender relations based on violent masculinities
"tend[ing] to feedback perennially into the spiraling continuum of armed conflict"
(Cockburn 2010, 152). Social processes that have accompanied civil wars have often
"reshaped a wide range of local social networks, destroying some, breaking others
into subnetworks, and creating new ones" (Wood 2008, 555), with impacts and further impacts sometimes being noted decades later. In all these processes, however,
no clear generalizations can be made about cause and effect, since the transformation of gender relations can go either forward or backward under different conditions (Wood 2008).

Similar themes can be seen in the outcome of research by the development agency
ACORD (Agency for Cooperation and Research in Development) addressing the connection between gender and conflict in specific communities in Sudan, Somalia, Mali,
Angola, and Uganda (El-Bushra 2003). First, the study found that the gender division of
labor generally changed as a direct result of violent conflict, often drastically, though not
necessarily permanently. In particular, men, having lost access to the resources (such as
land, labor, or commercial networks) on which their power was formerly based, found
great difficulty in adapting to changed economic circumstances, and fell into a state of
despondency. In contrast, women tended to rise to the occasion by exploiting whatever
economic niches could be found, and often took over practical responsibility for pro-
visioning and protecting their families, whether or not their menfolk were with them.

Other studies have reached similar conclusions (see Bennett et al. 1996 for a comprehensive study of conflicts in twenty different countries).

In assessing changes to gender relations, however, a distinction needs to be made between gender *roles*, which the ACORD study identified as being highly responsive to the demands of a changing environment, and gendered *institutions and ideologies*, which were more or less impervious to change. In particular, to the extent there was any change in women's standing within the household and community, it was only partial. The general impact of conflict on women was to widen their responsibilities and increase their workload (albeit in ways they often relished) while *not* providing them with decision-making remits concomitant with that increased responsibility. Whatever adaptations were necessary for practical reasons to the gender division of labor, these did not necessarily shake the ideological foundations of gender relations. The much-vaunted "window of opportunity" presented by the post-conflict moment was therefore shown to be illusory, as long as conscious efforts permanently to restructure social relations were not made.

The study also identified a range of other impacts, including increased reliance of households on petty commerce, changes to patterns of marriage and courtship, including the deployment of sexuality (for both men and women) as a means of achieving economic security, a reduction in the authority of older men, a breakdown in traditions of socialization of children within the household and increased intergenerational mistrust, and increased levels of domestic and sexual violence, especially where the availability of light weapons was accompanied by poor employment opportunities for young men. Many of these impacts have a demonstrable effect on the future coping capacities of societies emerging from violent conflict, generating the need for further adaptations and creating further stress in populations already coping with overwhelming disruption. These insights undermine the presumption of orthodox conflict analysis that conflict is to be measured in numbers of battle deaths and to be explained exclusively by the machinations of warlords and financiers, whose elimination will herald a sustainable peace.

A further finding was that although the differential impacts of conflict on men and women were significant, these went hand in hand with differential impacts on other categories—on different ethnic groups, on different economic classes, or on displaced as against settled population groups. In northern Mali, for example, armed conflict contributed to the detachment of ex-slaves from their erstwhile masters, thus reducing the workloads of ex-slave women while obliging noble women to take up economic roles within the household. Vulnerability is not confined to women, nor is it universal among women: war tends to bring particularly savage disadvantage to those who are already vulnerable, whether they are male or female. This conclusion lends relevance to an understanding of gender that incorporates intersectionality, and supports the call for a multidimensional and relational understanding of gender that is not exclusively focused on women.

In all five case study areas, patriarchal struggles for power and control of resources were implicated in war, both at the macro-political level and in terms of local and domestic violence. Much violence was driven by intolerance, greed, intransigence over religion, national-level struggles for armed supremacy, and aggressive forms of masculinity aiming to "restore the possibilities of ethnic and gender identity" (Bennett et al. 1996, 262). A key question, then, is how the emergence of this aggressive masculinity was enabled. At the individual level, it is not hard to trace the links between perturbations of masculine ideals on the one hand and violence on the other: indeed, a different ACORD study focusing on men in Uganda had identified "thwarted" gender identities as a key generator of domestic violence and self-harm by men: while male gender identities might not have changed radically, the possibilities of attaining masculine ideals had been severely curtailed (Dolan 2002). This insight suggests one way in which the examination of relational gender dynamics may prove fruitful in teasing out complex and cross-cutting interactions between conflict impacts.

In the panoply of consequences and further knock-on effects identified through these studies, gender and ethnic identities are either threatened or reinforced by conflict processes, with multiple possibilities for the further consequences of each. The violence of war typically leads to loss of life, loss of livelihood, poverty, humiliation and frustration, failures of governance, political manipulation, and a breakdown of inter-communal relations; in turn, these effects generate further manifestations of violence, including, for example, domestic and sexual abuse, alcoholism and drug abuse, depression, suicide, armed criminality, and adherence to militias. These in turn reinforce poverty and humiliation, further embedding conditions that perpetuate war, and leading to a general reduction in social cohesion and social capital, rendering the communities concerned vulnerable to continuing fragmentation. Gender identities are deeply implicated in this cycle, being key factors in people's perceptions of their social roles and positions. This suggests that they must be implicated equally in the processes whereby societies pull out of conflict cycles to build peace.

Gender and peace-building

Conflict analysis is a useful activity inasmuch as it forms a basis for identifying actions that contribute toward peace. Peace happens when "people are anticipating and managing conflicts without violence, and are engaging in inclusive social change processes that improve the quality of life" (International Alert 2010, 15), and peace-building is a "range of measures targeted to reduce the risk of lapsing or relapsing into conflict . . . to lay the foundations for sustainable peace and development" (UN PBSO 2010, 5).

If gender is implicated in ongoing cycles of violence, the test of this is to be seen in efforts to reduce violence by renegotiating gender relations. As mentioned earlier, statistical correlations have been identified that suggest that countries scoring highly on women's rights criteria may be relatively immune to either international or internal war (Caprioli 2000, 2005). There is also contextualized evidence that at the level of households and communities, dialogue processes that support a rethinking of gender identity can help bring an end to cycles of violence. In Namibia, the "bad behavior" of young men (and to a lesser extent, young women), which community members had identified as having reached crisis proportions, was seen to stem from the long history of apartheid in Namibia. Even in remote rural areas, apartheid had created extreme power inequalities between men and women, as well as between ethnicities. The communities then concluded that the focus should be on unraveling these historic power inequalities, rather than on blaming the young men concerned (Kandirikirira 2002); the results were so powerful that they eventually led to major changes in the Namibian education system. Second, an education project in Northern Uganda achieved significant reductions in domestic violence, as well as other positive impacts, through a year-long process of dialogue between young and old men and women, aimed at improving gender and intergenerational relations (Harris 2012). This demonstrates how vicious circles of conflict can be transformed into virtuous ones, since they contain stabilizing points as well as thresholds for new departures—points at which gender identities can, with sufficient will, be turned around to generate new and more constructive sets of relationships. They further suggest that the potential for gender analysis to contribute to peace is maximized when "gender' is understood not only as a campaign for women's rights (important though that may be), but rather as a framework for analyzing situations from the points of view of a wide range of actors, thereby opening up new possibilities for turning situations around (Myrttinen et al. 2014).

Conclusion: Thoughts about Gender and the Cyclical Nature of Conflict

Mainstream conflict analysis has tended to be positivist, reductionist, and masculinist, serving the interests of global power structures and the institutions that represent them, and failing to acknowledge the centrality of local actors or to recognize the complex, iterative, multilayered, and dynamic nature of the processes of conflict and peace. Belated attempts at engendering the mainstream approach have extended the paradigm to some extent and have opened up opportunities for women-supportive policy, but have been unable to escape from the narrow confines of the framework, thus limiting the envisioning of creative peace-building solutions.

Gender is deeply implicated not only in the immediate impacts of violent conflict, but also in the knock-on effects and beyond, including those that facilitate the perpetuation of violence for several generations into the future. Conceptualizing both conflict and gender in broad terms, recognizing their complexity and fluidity, does make a difference in terms of the richness and accuracy of the picture that analysis is able to paint. Applying a relational and intersectional understanding of gender to conflict analysis permits important insights into its social, psychosocial, and cultural, as well as political and economic, dimensions to be incorporated into peace-building strategies and practice.

NOTE

1. The New Deal for Engagement in Fragile States, agreed in Busan in November 2011, brought fragile states and donors together around five peace-building and state-building goals (PSGs) and set out agreed road maps for their implementation in specific countries. See "International Dialogue on Peacebuilding and State-building," accessed June 1, 2016, http://www.pbsbdialogue.org/.

REFERENCES

Anderlini, Sanam Naraghi. 2010. *What the Women Say: Participation and UNSCR 1325.* Washington, DC: International Civil Society Action Network and MIT Center for International Studies.

Anderson, Mary B. 1999. *Do No Harm: How Aid Can Support Peace—or War.* Boulder, CO: Lynne Reiner.

Autesserre, Séverine. 2012. "Dangerous Tales: Dominant Narratives on the Congo and Their Unintended Consequences." *African Affairs* 111, no. 443: 202–222.

Bennett, Olivia, Jo Bexley, and Kitty Warnock, eds. 1996. *Arms to Fight, Arms to Protect: Women Speak Out about Conflict.* London: Panos Institute.

Boas, Morten. 1997. "Liberia—the Hell-Bound Heart? Regime Breakdown and the Deconstruction of Society." *Alternatives* 22, no. 3: 353–379.

Buvinic, Mayra, Monica Das Gupta, Ursula Casabonne, and Philip Verwimp. 2012. "Violent Conflict and Gender Inequality: An Overview." *The World Bank Research Observer* 28, no. 1: 110–138.

Call, Charles. 2010. *Why Peace Fails: The Causes and Prevention of Civil War Recurrence.* Washington, DC: Georgetown University Press.

Campbell, Susanna, David Chandler, and Meera Sabaratnam, eds. 2011. *A Liberal Peace? The Problems and Practices of Peacebuilding.* London: Zed Books.

Caprioli, Mary. 2000. "Gendered Conflict." *Journal of Peace Research* 37, no. 1: 51–68.

Caprioli, Mary. 2005. "Primed for Violence: The Role of Gender Inequality in Predicting Internal Conflict." *International Studies Quarterly* 49: 161–178.

Castillejo, Clare. 2011. "Building a State That Works for Women: Integrating Gender into Post-Conflict State Building." FRIDE Working Paper 107, Fundación para las Relaciones Internacionales y el Diálogo Exterior, Madrid.

Chaudhary, Torunn Wimpelmann, Orzala Ashra Nemat, and Astri Suhrke. 2011. "Promoting Women's Rights in Afghanistan: The Ambiguous Footprint of the West." In *A Liberal Peace? The Problems and Practices of Peacebuilding*, edited by Suzanna Campbell, David Chandler, and Meera Sabaratnam, 106–120. London: Zed Books.

Cockburn, Cynthia. 2010. "Gender Relations as Causal in Militarization and War." *International Feminist Journal of Politics* 12, no. 2: 139–157.

Cohn, Carol, ed. 2012. *Women and Wars.* Cambridge: Polity Press.

Colletta, Nat, and Michelle Cullen. 2000. *Violent Conflict and the Transformation of Social Capital: Lessons from Cambodia, Rwanda, Guatemala and Somalia.* Washington, DC: The World Bank.

Collier, Paul, V. L. Elliott, Havard Hegre, Anke Hoeffler, Marta Reynal-Querol, and Nicholas Sambanis. 2003. *Breaking the Conflict Trap: Civil War and Development Policy.* Washington, DC: The World Bank.

Department for International Development (DFID). 2002. *Conducting Conflict Assessments: Guidance Notes*. London: DFID.

Dolan, Chris. 2002. "Collapsing Masculinities and Weak States: A Case Study of Northern Uganda." In *Masculinities Matter! Men, Gender and Development*, edited by F. Cleaver, 57–83. London: Zed Books.

Dolan, Chris. 2010. *"War Is Not Yet Over": Community Perceptions of Sexual Violence and Its Underpinnings in Eastern DRC*. London: International Alert.

Domingo, Pilar, Rebecca Holmes, Alina Rocha Menocal, Nicola Jones, and Jill Wood. 2013. *Assessment of the Evidence of Links between Gender Equality, Peacebuilding and State-building: Literature Review*. London: Overseas Development Institute.

Dummett, Mark. 2004. "King Leopold's Legacy of DR Congo Violence." *BBC*. February 24. http://news.bbc.co.uk/2/hi/africa/3516965.stm.

El-Bushra, Judy. 2003. "Fused in Combat: Gender Relations and Armed Conflict." *Development in Practice* 13, no. 2–3: 252–265.

Harper, Mary. 2012. *Getting Somalia Wrong? Faith and War in a Shattered State*. London: Zed Press.

Harris, Colette. 2012. "The Importance of Post-Conflict Socio-Cultural Community Education Programmes: A Case Study from Northern Uganda." MICROCON Research Working Paper 64.

International Alert. 2010. *Programming Framework for International Alert: Design, Monitoring and Evaluation*. London: London: International Alert.

Itto, Anne. 2006. "Guests at the Table? The Role of Women in Peace Processes." In *Peace by Piece: Addressing Sudan's Conflicts*, edited by Mark Simmons and Peter Dixon, 56–59. London: Conciliation Resources.

Kandirikirira, Nikki. 2002. "Deconstructing Domination: Gender Disempowerment and the Legacy of Colonialism and Apartheid in Omaheke, Namibia." In *Masculinities Matter: Men, Gender and Development*, edited by F. Cleaver, 112–137. London: Zed Books.

Kreutz, Joakim. 2012. "Dismantling the Conflict Trap: Essays on Civil War Resolution and Relapse." PhD diss., Uppsala University.

Lemarchand, Rene. 2009. *The Dynamics of Violence in Central Africa*. Philadelphia: University of Pennsylvania Press.

Moe, Louise Wiuff. 2010. *Addressing State Fragility in Africa*. Helsinki: Finnish Institute of International Affairs.

Myrttinen, Henri, Jana Naujoks, and Judy El-Bushra. 2014. *Rethinking Gender in Peacebuilding*. London: International Alert.

Organisation for Economic Co-operation and Development (OECD). 2011. *Supporting State-Building in Situations of Conflict and Fragility: Policy Guidance*. Paris: OECD.

Organisation for Economic Co-operation and Development (OECD). 2013. *Gender and State-Building in Fragile and Conflict-Affected States*. Paris: OECD.

O'Gorman, Eleanor. 2014. *Independent Thematic Review on Gender for the UN Peacebuilding Support Office (PBSO): Final Report*. New York: UN Peacebuilding Support Office.

Roche, Chris. 1996. "Operationality in Turbulence: The Need for Change." In *Development in States of War*, edited by Deborah Eade, 15–25. Oxford: Oxfam.

Stone, Lauren. 2014. "Can Women Make the World More Peaceful?" *The Guardian*. August 11. https://www.theguardian.com/global-development-professionals-network/2014/aug/11/women-conflict-peace-society.

Suhrke, Astri, and Ingrid Samset. 2007. "What's in a Figure? Estimating Recurrence of Civil War." *International Peacekeeping* 14, no. 2: 195–203.

Themner, Lotta, and Peter Wallensteen. 2014. "Patterns of Organised Violence 2001–2011." In *SIPRI Yearbook 2013*, 41–60. Stockholm: Stockholm International Peace Research Institute.

UN Peacebuilding Support Office (PBSO). 2010. *UN Peacebuilding: An Orientation.* New York: PBSO.

Walter, Barbara F. 2010. *Conflict Relapse and the Sustainability of Post-Conflict Peace.* Washington, DC: The World Bank.

Wood, Elisabeth Jean. 2008. "The Social Processes of Civil War: The Wartime Transformation of Social Networks." *Annual Review of Political Science* 11, no. 1: 539–561.

The World Bank. 2011. *Conflict, Security and Development.* Washington, DC: The World Bank.

CHAPTER 5

THE GENDERED NEXUS BETWEEN CONFLICT AND CITIZENSHIP IN HISTORICAL PERSPECTIVE

JO BUTTERFIELD AND ELIZABETH HEINEMAN

THE profoundly gendered nature of citizenship stems, in large part, from the historical rooting of citizenship in armed conflict. The modern practices of citizenship that came to dominate the West and strongly influence its former colonies emerged during two generations of transatlantic warfare between 1775 and 1830. During the "wars of liberation and revolution," revolutionaries in Europe and North and South America drew on both Enlightenment thought and the classical ideal of the citizen-soldier in staking claims for republican government. Republican revolutionaries contrasted the *subject*, who was literally subject to the authority of the ruling body (usually a monarch), with the *republican citizen*, who played a role in self-governance, for example by electing representatives to governing bodies. Revolutionaries were also committed to the ideals of *liberal citizenship*, most centrally the protection of individual rights from state intrusion. Citizenship also came to be understood as incorporating a sense of belonging, involving not only individual rights and the duties associated with governance, but also full participation in social, economic, and cultural life. With the formalization of the passport system over the course of the nineteenth and twentieth centuries, *national citizenship* or *nationality* came to refer to the state in which, at a minimum, an individual had the right to reside, regardless of the form of citizenship practiced within that state.

The variety of meanings of citizenship, their potential for overlap, and the high stakes of inclusion or exclusion mean that "citizenship" has, historically, been a very fluid term. During the wars of liberation and revolution, and in the centuries since, the meanings of republicanism, liberalism, and citizenship have been contested in forums ranging from courts of law to the battlefield. So has the question of who qualifies for what sort of citizenship. Initially, the paradigmatic citizen was a virtuous, propertied, white man whose means, abilities, and moral virtue justified the protection of his individual rights and enabled him to participate freely and responsibly in all spheres of life, including both governance and defense. Colonial subjects, women, (ex-)slaves, and the property-less were among those considered to lack the qualities of independence and reason necessary for the full exercise of citizenship.

The association of citizenship with warfare has been an opportunity as well as a hurdle for those excluded from full citizenship. Through the nineteenth and twentieth centuries, the property-less, (ex-)slaves, colonial subjects, and women made citizenship claims by pointing to their contributions to war. States, and later international bodies, recognized claims to the rights of citizenship on the basis of contributions to and sacrifices made on behalf of military efforts. Thus even the expansion of citizenship has frequently served to reinforce the linkage between citizenship and the highly gendered activity of war.

Although liberal citizenship initially referred to rights guaranteed by the (nation)-state, the gendered nexus between citizenship and conflict also shaped emerging international legal frameworks. Beginning in the nineteenth century, international humanitarian laws aimed to regulate the conduct of war and ameliorate its consequences, a process informed by ideas about masculine citizenship. Following World War II, the international community drafted human rights law as a means to promote peace and to guarantee rights outside the context of the nation-state. Citizenship status positioned individuals in relationship to expanding international bodies of law even as the creation of international forums enabled feminists to challenge the links binding conflict to citizenship at the national level.

This chapter begins with the wars of revolution and liberation of the late eighteenth and early nineteenth centuries. Race-based slavery, colonialism, and decolonization were defining factors in these wars, and so race and colonialism, like gender, were deeply embedded in emergent practices of liberal and republican citizenship as well as notions of national belonging. The chapter then examines the ways rival systems of government, such as conservatism, socialism, colonial rule, and fascism, further elaborated the gendered and militarized nexus of citizenship, even as they rejected liberal or republican models of citizenship. The second half of this chapter traces the extension of gendered citizenship to international humanitarian and human rights frameworks, as well as feminists' efforts to challenge the mutually constitutive nature of conflict and citizenship by positioning women as subjects—not objects—of international laws forged in the wake of conflict. Yet the persistence of the deeply embedded nexus between gender, conflict, and citizenship helps to explain the greater success of feminist claims regarding wartime violence against women over securing women's human rights outside the context of war.

Republican and Liberal Citizenship in the Nation-State

The years 1775 to 1830 saw nearly continuous warfare across the transatlantic world. The wars of revolution and liberation transformed European monarchies and American colonies into republics. Subjects became citizens. Both the scale of warfare and the widespread adoption of republican and liberal citizenship were novel, and so the two phenomena developed in tandem. Even as larger patterns emerged, the forms of citizenship varied according to local context.

In 1775 the first shots were fired in the American Revolutionary War. The French Revolution, which began in 1789, launched a generation of political experimentation and warfare across Europe. A 1791 slave revolt in the French colony of Saint-Domingue sparked twelve years of warfare, resulting in the new state of Haiti. A series of conflicts, mainly in the 1810s and 1820s, launched independent states in Central and South America. By 1830, the geopolitics of the Atlantic world had been transformed, tens of millions of people lived in newly founded republics, even empires and monarchies had to grapple with the language and claims of citizenship, and populations had endured up to a full generation of warfare.

The scale of mobilization, the nationalist and revolutionary aims of the wars, and the entanglement of political belonging with race helped to establish enduring gendered frameworks of citizenship (Hagemann 2010). Previously, fighting in Europe and its colonies had been the preserve of mercenary soldiers led by aristocratic officers bound to their monarch. Now fighting became the patriotic duty of all men, who were understood as bound to their nation. Where such men were newly constituted citizens, citizenship became inextricably tied to military availability. Where they continued to be constituted as subjects or as slaves, the promise of a future expansion of rights adhered to military service.

Nearly 40 percent of able-bodied men served in the American Continental Armies. France introduced mass conscription in the metropole; enemy regimes across Europe followed suit. Armies in the Spanish Americas and the Caribbean were likewise large and diverse, including both enslaved and free men of varying races and ethnicities. This level of mobilization could not be achieved by compulsion alone. Military reforms made service less onerous: the Prussian military banned corporal punishment, while Russia reduced conscripts' term of service from life to twenty-five years. The aristocratic officers' corps were opened to commoners. Constraints on enlisted men's right to marry were relaxed, fostering masculine ideals that combined military and familial roles. Thus, even anti-republican states recognized an exchange whereby men's military service warranted greater rights.

Patriotic propaganda bound masculinity to bearing arms and, for nationalist or revolutionary armies, demanding and accepting the responsibilities of citizenship. In France and the United States, this meant citizenship for white men; in much of the Caribbean and Latin America, the promise of masculine citizenship based on military service extended to free black men and newly freed male slaves. But after the wars, many states reneged on their promise of citizenship to slaves who had borne arms (Chambers 2000). The Prussian monarch revoked his promise of citizenship for *any* man, reinforcing men's status as subjects—yet military service remained the patriotic duty of all men. Military masculinity defined the patriotic subject *and* citizen, even as the ideal of the *citizen*-at-arms provided a powerful language for those whose struggle for national independence or republicanism continued.

The scale of the wars diminished the putative division between military and civilian realms. Furthermore, nationalist ideologies demanded that women not only contribute to the war effort, but also turn their reproductive labor to creating and sustaining the nations on whose behalf the wars were fought. Yet women were constituted as physically, morally, and spiritually inferior to men and thus incapable of bearing arms, participating in governance, or exercising full rights. Women's place in new citizenship frameworks thus emerged as a foundational problem of the modern era.

Authority over the domestic domain was intrinsic to republican manhood, an especially important development for emancipated men who as slaves had lacked the right to marry. Yet women's dependency also formed a basis for citizenship claims. Thus, in Saint Domingue, the wife of a citizen was a citizen; an enslaved woman was not (Colwill 2009). Widows across war-torn regions demanded state pensions on the grounds that they had sacrificed their husbands to the national cause. Underscoring their role in raising children in a republican spirit and in motivating men to fight, women articulated a feminine form of citizenship based on the public significance of their duties as wives and mothers (Kerber 1976).

With rare exceptions, proponents of a female form of citizenship assumed that women's citizenship could not be equivalent to men's, as it did not rest on bearing arms. Yet women of all political directions participated in national and revolutionary struggles. They wrote, read, and discussed political texts; they formed patriotic associations to organize boycotts, collect and disseminate funds, care for the wounded and refugees, and celebrate returning soldiers. And women went to war. Some bore arms under male disguise. Far more moved with armies in supportive capacities, continuing early modern patterns in which wives (often with children) followed their husbands to war and provided services such as laundering, cooking, dispensing drink, and bandaging wounds. Most of these so-called camp followers could not sustain their families in their husbands' absence; some were refugees (De Pauw 1998).

Military authorities distrusted camp followers, who carried on illegal activities like smuggling and were especially associated with illicit sex. They strained resources: like soldiers, camp followers had to be transported and fed. Yet the scale of warfare expanded more rapidly than the military's ability to modernize its support systems. As a result, authorities alternately defamed camp followers and strove to recruit, reward, and professionalize them (Cardoza 2010). Only with the development of railways in the late nineteenth century were European and North American armies able to dispense with women's logistical support; in later-industrializing regions, the shift was delayed.

Young republics worked to recover from war's upheaval and consolidate citizenship while maintaining military preparedness for new threats. For US slave-holding states, memories of Haiti aggravated fears of slave revolt. A notion of white male citizenship based on political participation and military readiness thus unified an ethnically and linguistically diverse white population. Across the Atlantic world, women remained disenfranchised, and their political organizations were disbanded. Newly independent states struggling to recover economically described not only military readiness but also labor as the citizen's duty. Much of this burden fell on women because of military casualties, yet bourgeois ideological frameworks established productive labor, like soldiering, as the duty of the male citizen.

ALTERNATIVE MODELS OF NATIONAL CITIZENSHIP

The model of the citizen-soldier proved adaptable to alternative systems of government, including conservatism (which in the nineteenth century meant a reactionary rejection of both liberalism and republicanism), colonial domination, socialism, and fascism. The model of the citizen-soldier also had salience in postcolonial states with varied forms of governance.

A rejection of republican structures of government and liberal rights frameworks characterized much of Latin America and Central and Eastern Europe in the decades following the wars. Economic and social reforms had not accompanied independence in much of Latin America, and landed elites engaged in internecine violence. National belonging was more meaningful than political structures of republicanism, but political agency continued to depend on the ability to bear arms. *Caudillos* (strongmen) emphasized military and patriarchal authority to legitimize violence against political enemies (Lynch 1992). In Central and Eastern Europe, some states slowly developed parliamentary structures whose powers were constrained by the monarch; in others, even this development waited until the twentieth century. A common feature, however, was the development of ethnically and linguistically based nationalism. Women's role in reproducing the nation increasingly involved not only the political socialization and cultural education of children, but also the transmission of a biological or metaphysical national essence. In the aftermath of World War I, fascist states likewise rejected both republican and liberal models of citizenship in favor of an exaltation of national belonging. Fascist states varied on the centrality of biological racism to nationhood, but they shared a highly militaristic ethos that elevated warrior masculinity while increasingly regimenting women's support roles.

Westerners' imaginative feminization of colonized men justified imperial rule in regions like South Asia that remained under European domination (Sinha 1995). New colonial conquests reinforced the link between inadequate military masculinity and subaltern status in colonizers' eyes. Within colonized populations, the political status that had once attended armed resistance to colonization shifted to those who collaborated with colonial authorities, sometimes by bearing arms to quell anti-colonial rebellions (Iliffe 2005; Moyd 2014). Confirming colonized men's patriarchal authority over colonized women (or granting such powers in new guises, for example by the imposition of Western-style family structures) helped to compensate colonized men for their loss of authority vis-à-vis the colonizer. Concubinage privileged some colonized women while degrading colonized men and created mestizo offspring whose citizenship status was subject to close scrutiny (Stoler 2002). In the metropole, European feminists cited their (non-military) contributions to imperialism to make claims to full citizen-ship (Burton 1994).

While the sentiment of national belonging helped to mobilize large armies in states ranging from republics to authoritarian empires in World War I, massive casualties and privations eventually prompted socialist revolution from Central Europe to Russia. The militant industrial worker of nineteenth-century Marxism thus became the radi-calized soldier, and revolutionaries established "Workers' and Soldiers' Councils" to found socialist states. Revolutionary socialism—like revolutionary republicanism over a century earlier—linked political belonging to the armed promulgation of revolution (Wood 1997).

Socialist programmatic statements had included women's suffrage since the late nine-teenth century; by the mid-twentieth century, socialist visions of women's belonging sometimes included military activity. In practice, arming women was a last resort, and military women faced harassment. Nevertheless, socialist states and movements cele-brated the armed woman as proof of women's emancipation under socialism, a promise that was meaningful to female recruits, whether in Soviet armies in World War II or in Marxist-Leninist liberation movements in sub-Saharan Africa and Latin America in the 1970s and 1980s (Krylova 2011; Lyons 2004).

By the era of decolonization, universal male and female suffrage had become an inter-national norm, a way for newly established states to demonstrate legitimacy, even as it also reflected many freedom fighters' commitment to political voice. But the gender-ing of postcolonial citizenship was also shaped by the wars that accompanied inde-pendence. Following the 1947 partition of the Indian subcontinent, for example, the Indian state's claim to be the rescuer of raped and abducted Hindu women established the state as patriarchal protector of its women—thus limiting their rights in a liberal framework—even as women gained the franchise (Das 1995). In settings where nation-alists interpreted women's emancipation as a colonial import, anti-colonial struggles often strengthened the hand of those who linked national identity to women's inferior status.

Even in republican settings, expansions of the franchise continued to be linked with conflict throughout late modernity. With industrialization and urbanization, reformers, including feminists, strove to better women's status by calling on the state to be a better patriarch, for example by protecting women and children from abusive labor conditions. By the end of the nineteenth century, however, many feminists demanded that women be not just objects of the law, but also political subjects. Yet across Europe and North America, only women's contributions to World War I finally convinced legislatures that had remained unmoved by decades of suffragist activity. Other examples of the linkage of armed conflict and the expansion of the franchise include the elimination of property restrictions for French men with the revolutions of 1848, suffrage for African American men following the American Civil War, universal suffrage for Mexican men following the Mexican Revolution, universal suffrage following wars of independence in Africa, and the lowering of voting age in the United States during the Vietnam War. Once gained legally, access to the vote was not always stable in practice: African-American men, for example, effectively lost the franchise during the era of Jim Crow. Yet the pattern remains: successful claims to national citizenship have been consistently tied to contribution to the militarized state.

CONFLICT, GENDERED CITIZENSHIP, AND INTERNATIONAL HUMANITARIAN LAW

At the 1815 Congress of Vienna following the Napoleonic Wars, European leaders sought to forge a balance of power to preserve peace, establishing the foundations of modern state-centered international cooperation. The Crimean War (1853–1856)—the first industrialized war—prompted an international movement that established the first humanitarian regulations intended to govern states' wartime behavior. Hoping to improve care for wounded citizen soldiers, Henri Dunant organized the International Committee of the Red Cross in 1863. By 1864, several European nations had signed the Geneva Convention for the Amelioration of the Condition of the Wounded in the Field, which entitled soldiers to care and protected the medical personnel treating them.

International jurists worked to strengthen wartime regulations as an expression of civilized masculine behavior. The first Hague Convention (1899, expanded 1907) incorporated the 1864 convention and articulated international rules of conduct for warfare. Civilized masculinity assumed rational, temperate men not inclined to uncontrolled aggression and emphasized the protection of women, societal order, progress, and economic engagement. European jurists contrasted ideas about civilized masculinity to racialized notions of the feminized colonial subject who failed to abide by Western ideas about state formation, property rights, or the gendered division of labor (Koskenniemi 2002). States' failure to extend international humanitarian laws to their colonial possessions distinguished colonizers from the colonized and rationalized violent subjugation.

The gendered nexus between conflict and citizenship meant that women entered the framework of international humanitarian law as objects of protection, not as subjects of the law. An important model for the 1899 Hague Convention was the 1864 Lieber Code, a compendium of humanitarian ideals adopted by the Union during the US Civil War. In articles repudiating the destruction of private property, the Lieber code prohibited "rape, wounding, maiming or killing inhabitants" of occupied territories. Likewise, the 1899 Hague Convention insisted that "[f]amily honors and rights, individual lives and private property . . . must be respected." The subject of the law was family honor, not a woman's right to bodily integrity. The inviolability of a woman's body was constitutive of the patriarch's family honor in a way that paralleled the inviolability of his private property.

With the creation of the League of Nations following World War I and the extension of suffrage to some Western women, white women from liberal/republican frameworks continued to dominate international feminist organizing. International feminists claimed expanded rights in the international sphere by pointing to gender-specific service and sacrifice in war and their potential role in maintaining peace. Female peace activists cited male leaders' failure to prevent war; feminists who had supported national war efforts highlighted their contributions. Both groups pointed to the loss of sons, husbands, and fathers (Harris 1993).

Feminists active in international forums did not focus on reforming humanitarian laws to ameliorate the conditions women confronted in war, but rather on preventing future wars; they held neither war nor its dire consequences as inevitable. Most pointedly, feminists insisted that securing peace demanded women's increased political participation (Rupp 1997). They also used international forums to challenge laws binding women's nationality to that of their husbands. In presuming that a woman's obedience to her husband could not coexist with loyalty to a different nation (a particular fear in the event of war), such laws codified the gender-citizenship-conflict nexus in a way that could cost women the citizenship of their birth—or even leave them stateless (DuBois 2010).

The expansion of humanitarian law—a process that excluded feminist voices—aimed to restrain, not eliminate war, and it reflected anxieties about wartime martial and domestic masculinity. Industrialized technologies, greatly expanded in World War I, required that visions of courageous battlefield acts performed against a worthy opponent adapt to the actualities of invisible enemies, poisonous gas, and trench warfare. Thus, the 1925 Geneva Protocol restricted the use of asphyxiating gases in war. The 1929 Geneva Convention might be seen in part as an effort to address anxieties about men's wartime inability to their fulfill patriarchal obligations by calling on states to provide women prisoners "all the considerations due to their sex."

Following World War II, the 1949 Geneva Conventions further elaborated humanitarian law. Still highlighting the state's role as a substitute patriarch, the Convention called on parties to protect expectant women and mothers with small children. Informed by evidence of sexual violence introduced at the Nuremberg and Tokyo Trials, the 1949 Conventions incorporated a prohibition of rape, enforced prostitution, and "indecent" assault, though none of these harms was considered a grave breach. Although more explicit than the 1929 Conventions, the 1949 Conventions nonetheless prioritized gender-based propriety by rebuking "outrages on personal dignity" and tying a woman's "honor" to her sexual inviolability.

By the 1970s, wars of decolonization and intra-state conflicts—often tied to colonial legacies—prompted an expansion of the Geneva Conventions. The 1977 Protocol (II) extended the Geneva Conventions beyond international conflict to include internal wars. The Protocols also incorporated the 1949 prohibition against enforced prostitution and indecent assault. Yet both Protocols persisted in conceptualizing women as objects in need of protection, not as subjects under the law of armed conflict. Despite expanded international feminist organizing in the 1960s and 1970s, women's voices remained largely marginalized from the elaboration of humanitarian laws.

HUMAN RIGHTS, PEACE, AND
THE GENDERED CITIZEN

After World War II, the language of human rights created a new opportunity to destabilize the gendered nexus between citizenship and conflict. Although doctrines of racial
superiority had long denied citizenship rights to the colonized, racial minorities, and
indigenous populations, Nazi Germany's race-based denial of rights to Europeans
finally put the connection between war and citizenship on the international agenda.
The 1945 United Nations Charter not only established the rights and responsibilities of
states, but also emphasized the rights of individuals by linking the promotion of human
rights to peace (Lauren 2011). The human rights project suggested rights based on membership in the human family, instead of rights tethered to national citizenship, which
were potentially destabilized by war and by rights-denying regimes.

Following World War II, feminists again emphasized war's cost and consequences
for women (Alonso 1993). Like their predecessors in the League of Nations, feminists
working in the early years of the United Nations prioritized creating peace through a
just postwar order over ameliorating wartime conditions. Women's full citizenship in
all spheres of life was essential to this peaceful world order. Activists insisted that UN
human rights doctrines, particularly the 1948 Universal Declaration of Human Rights
(UDHR), recognize that women's responsibilities as (potential) wives and mothers
necessitated rights—not protections. Most internationally minded feminists involved in
the drafting process did not conceptualize equal rights as meaning identical rights: contrary to later frameworks that distinguished sharply between "sameness" and "difference" feminism, early UN feminists did not consider "difference" and "sameness"
arguments to be contradictory. Women's and men's common humanity warranted identical political and civil rights, but women also required distinct rights (not protections)
to mitigate against the social and economic disadvantages that their childbearing and
rearing responsibilities engendered. Feminist delegates involved in the early UN human
rights project distinguished between protections, entitlements, and rights, arguing that
the entitlements and protections reinforced dependency and were all too often interpreted as "charity," instead of rights granted to self-determinate beings.

Yet encroaching Cold War politics intervened. At the United Nations, the US delegation promoted a liberal agenda focused on individual political and civil rights; the
Soviet Union's socialist platform highlighted state responsibility to secure economic
and social rights. Each state argued that women's citizenship was best secured under
its political and economic system. Women's rights thus became an object of Cold War
rivalry, undermining feminists' ability to situate women firmly as the subjects of international human rights law. Rather than employing the stronger language of rights, the
UDHR and the subsequent International Covenant on Economic, Social and Cultural
Rights (1966) entitled women to "special assistance" and "protections" as (potential)
mothers (Butterfield 2012).

The Cold War dimmed pacifists' hope for a peaceful postwar order built on inter-nationalism and human rights. Some had envisioned the United Nations as evolving into a world government where belligerent nationalism would be replaced by a global community of international citizens, thus eradicating war. Others anticipated the development of a robust organization capable of securing the rights of individuals as international citizens, alongside the framework of national state-based citizenship and rights. When the Cold War rivalry initially thwarted agreement on binding human rights conventions, feminists turned their attention to shoring up women's rights as national citizens via international standards in areas such as nationality, political rights, education, employment, and non-discrimination.

A CONTINUUM OF VIOLENCE: WOMEN AS SUBJECTS OF INTERNATIONAL LAW

With the collapse of the Cold War system between 1989 and 1991 and the eruption of regional and civil wars stoked by ethic nationalism, the United Nations renewed its commitment to human rights by convening the 1993 Second World Conference on Human Rights in Vienna. Feminists' work at Vienna shifted from preventing future wars to securing women's rights not only in times of peace, but also during war. Activists challenged androcentric interpretations of international human rights that had taken root during the Cold War and established an international humanitarian law framework that recognized violence against women as an assault on women's bodily integrity, not their (or their families') honor. Feminist activists and legal scholars demonstrated that violence against women defied the dichotomy between conflict and peace; for women, both were often marked by violence.

Feminist activism at Vienna built on the foundation laid by international organizing since the 1970s. Yet that organizing had exposed power differentials between Western-based feminists schooled in UN bureaucracy and activists from the global South, many of whom had engaged in national liberation struggles and who focused on development. At Vienna, however, activists from the North and South forged common ground through a shared commitment to ending violence against women by challenging long-standing distinctions between war and peace, humanitarian and human rights law, and the so-called public and private spheres (Reilly 2009). Abuser impunity and state failure to prevent violence exposed how the emphasis on public human rights violations obscured egregious violations against women in the so-called private spheres of the workplace and home. Furthermore, the international human rights regime's privileging of political and civil rights over economic and social rights bolstered social systems that devalued women's productive and reproductive labor, which placed them at greater risk for other, often sexualized, human rights violations. Vienna highlighted feminists' commitment to moving women's human rights from the "margins to the center" of the international human rights framework (Bunch and Fried 1996).

Vienna prompted expanded feminist activism in the realm of humanitarian laws regulating wartime behavior. In the context of reports of systematic rape in the former Yugoslavia and amidst new revelations about sexual slavery in East Asia during World War II, survivors joined with activists to demand international action against gender-based wartime violence. Thus, present crimes met past abuses at Vienna, creating a sense of urgency about the need to incorporate the rights of women into international humanitarian law (Copelon 2011). The Vienna Platform demanded an immediate halt to "systematic rape of women in war" and the punishment of perpetrators.

Unlike the more recent innovation of human rights law, humanitarian law had a tradition as a legitimate international subject dating back to the nineteenth century. But it was one in which women had historically entered as objects of protection, not legal subjects with affirmative rights. Humanitarian law offered feminist activists the opportunity to gain recognition for women as the subjects of laws prioritized by the international community. To this end, and in the wake of the rapes perpetrated during the Rwandan genocide, feminist legal scholars and activists collaborated to ensure that the 1998 Rome Statute (which created the International Criminal Court) and its attending Rules and Annexes incorporated explicit prohibitions against sexualized violence—as crimes against bodily integrity, not gendered propriety—into humanitarian law, including war crimes, crimes against humanity, and genocide. Thus, through laws that criminalized breaches in the sanctioned conduct of war, feminist activists gained recognition for women as subjects of international law, even as discursive practices reiterated the language of protecting women from violations.

The nexus of conflict, widespread violence against women in war *and* peace, and a renewed commitment to international human rights sparked a new era of UN feminist activism. Feminists' success in shaping humanitarian law, however, has come at a cost. Attention to wartime violence has created space to address sexualized violence against men and boys in conflict and to consider women's role as perpetrators. Yet feminists' traction in humanitarian law and the concomitant UN attention to gender-based issues in conflict and post-conflict settings, symbolized by Security Council resolution 1325, has drawn enforcement attention almost exclusively to the conflict end of the violence spectrum (see, e.g., Engle, Chapter 10 in this volume), and echoed a tacit hierarchy that privileges humanitarian over human rights law (see Patten, Chapter 13 in this volume). Although humanitarian law seeks to end impunity for gender-based crimes in conflict, earlier feminists' concentration on eradicating war and promoting human rights as a means to fostering a peaceful world order has gone from the center to the margins. For women, recognition as citizens with international rights continues to hinge on the nexus between gender and conflict, a mutually constitutive relationship forged during the revolutions and wars of national liberation of previous centuries.

REFERENCES

Alonso, Harriet. 1993. *Peace as a Women's Issue: A History of the U.S. Movement for World Peace and Women's Rights*. Syracuse, NY: Syracuse University Press.

Bunch, Charlotte, and Susana Fried. 1996. "Beijing '95: Moving Women's Human Rights from Margin to Center." *SIGNS: Journal of Women in Culture and Society* 22, no. 1: 200–204.

Burton, Antoinette. 1994. *Burdens of History: British Feminists, Indian Women, and Imperial Culture*. Chapel Hill: University of North Carolina Press.

Butterfield, Jo. 2012. "Gendering Universal Human Rights: International Women's Activism, Gender Politics, and the Early Cold War, 1928–1952." PhD diss., University of Iowa.

Cardoza, Thomas. 2010. *Intrepid Women: Cantinères and Vivandières of the French Army*. Bloomington: Indiana University Press.

Chambers, Sarah C. 2000. *From Subjects to Citizens: Honor, Gender, and Politics in Arequipa, Peru, 1780–1854*. State College: Penn State University Press.

Colwill, Elizabeth. 2009. "'Fêtes de l'hymen, fetes de la liberté': Marriage, Manhood, and Emancipation in Revolutionary Saint-Domingue." In *World of the Haitian Revolution*, edited by David Patrick Geggus Norman Fiering, 125–155. Bloomington: Indiana University Press.

Copelon, Rhonda. 2011. "Toward Accountability for Violence against Women in War." In *Sexual Violence in Conflict Zones: From the Ancient World to the Era of Human Rights*, edited by Elizabeth Heineman, 232–256. Philadelphia: University of Pennsylvania Press.

Das, Veena. 1995. "National Honour and Practical Kinship: Of Unwanted Women and Children." In *Critical Events: An Anthropological Perspective on Contemporary India*, edited by Veena Vas, 55–83. Delhi: Oxford University Press.

De Pauw, Linda Grant. 1998. *Battle Cries and Lullabies: Women in War from Prehistory to the Present*. Norman. University of Oklahoma Press.

Dubois, Ellen. 2010. "Internationalizing Married Women's Nationality: The Hague Campaign of 1930." In *Globalizing Feminisms, 1789–1945*, edited by Karen Offen, 204–216. London and New York: Routledge Press.

Hagemann, Karen. 2010. "Introduction." In *Gender, War and Politics: Transatlantic Perspectives 1775–1830*, edited by Karen Hagemann, Gisele Metelle, and Jane Rendall, 1–40. London: Palgrave Macmillan UK.

Harris, Ruth. 1993. "'The Child of the Barbarian': Rape, Race, and Nationalism in France during the First World War." *Past and Present* 141: 170–206.

Iliffe, John. 2005. *Honour in African History*. Cambridge: Cambridge University Press.

Kerber, Linda K. 1976. "The Republican Mother: Women and the Enlightenment—An American Perspective." *American Quarterly* 28, no. 2: 187–205.

Koskenniemi, Martti. 2002. *The Gentle Civilizer of Nations: The Rise and Fall of International Humanitarian Law 1870–1960*. Cambridge: Cambridge University Press.

Krylova, Anna. 2011. *Soviet Women in Combat: A History of Violence on the Eastern Front*. Cambridge: Cambridge University Press.

Lauren, Paul Gordon. 2011. *The Evolution of International Human Rights: Visions Seen*, 3rd ed. Philadelphia: University of Pennsylvania Press.

Lynch, John. 1992. *Caudillos in Spanish America, 1800–1850*. Gloucestershire, UK: Clarendon Press.

Lyons, Tanya. 2004. *Guns and Guerilla Girls: Women in the Zimbabwean National Liberation Struggle*. Trenton, NJ: Africa World Press.

Moyd, Michelle. 2014. *Violent Intermediaries: African Soldiers, Conquest, and Everyday Colonialism in German East Africa*. Columbus: Ohio State University Press.

Reilly, Niamh. 2009. *Women's Human Rights: Seeking Gender Justice in a Globalizing Age*. Malden, MA: Polity Press.

Rupp, Leila J. 1997. *Worlds of Women: The Making of an International Women's Movement*. Princeton, NJ: Princeton University Press.

Sinha, Mrinhalini. 1995. *Colonial Masculinity: The "Manly Englishman" and the "Effeminate Bengali" in the Late Nineteenth Century*. Manchester: Manchester University Press.

Stoler, Ann Laura. 2002. *Carnal Knowledge and Imperial Power: Race and the Intimate in Colonial Rule*. Berkeley: University of California Press.

Wood, Elizabeth. 1997. *The Baba and the Comrade: Gender and Politics in Revolutionary Russia*. Bloomington: Indiana University Press.

CHAPTER 6

....

VIOLENT CONFLICT AND CHANGES IN GENDER ECONOMIC ROLES

Implications for Post-Conflict Economic Recovery

....

PATRICIA JUSTINO

VIOLENT conflict affects the lives and livelihoods of hundreds of millions of people in the world, exacting substantial direct and indirect costs at the time of the conflict and for many years thereafter. Beyond the loss of life and injury to millions of people every year, wars and conflict destroy infrastructure, services, markets, assets, and livelihoods; displace populations; break families, communities, and overall social cohesion; and create fear and distrust. Each of these has economic implications. Economic reconstruction, like other post-conflict reconstruction undertakings, presents major challenges for development policy in post-conflict societies, and the extent to which women and men are differently affected and challenged by the economic consequences of collective violence is an important and under-explored matter.

People who live in areas affected by violent conflict display various degrees of resilience (Justino 2012a). Some will simply get by in a variety of ways, through their ability to navigate and negotiate the economic and political vacuum that often plagues this context (Vigh 2006). Others may actually do well in the war economies that emerge during armed conflict (Petesch, Chapter 26 in this volume). Levels of resilience depend on a series of factors both within and outside of the control of those affected by violence, shaped by the profound institutional changes that take place during armed conflict (Cramer 2006; Justino, Brück, and Verwimp 2013; Tilly 1990).

One of these potential forms of institutional change relates to gender roles and aspirations. The lives of women and men can adjust dramatically and in very different ways in response to changes in their households and their communities, as well as a direct response to fighting and violence. Women in particular may take up new economic and social roles, and provide essential economic and social support to the reconstruction of communities affected by violent conflict, in ways that would not have been possible before the conflict. One risk, however, is that after the war, social pressures and post-conflict processes limit the long-term ability of women to participate fully and take advantage of new opportunities (Justino et al. 2012). This may well be an important missed opportunity, but there is limited evidence on the impact of violent conflict on gender roles (but see Petesch, Chapter 26 in this volume).

This chapter assesses empirical evidence on the differential effects of violent conflict on the economic welfare and livelihoods of men and women, and the implications of these findings for development and economic recovery policies in the post-conflict period.[1] The analysis is based on quantitative research on the micro-level effects of violent conflict,[2] and focuses mostly on evidence from civil wars, largely because most empirical evidence to date has been generated from these contexts. The chapter is organized as follows: the first section reviews emerging evidence on the welfare impact of violent conflict across gender (boys and girls, women and men). The second section discusses how adaptation to the effects of violent conflict at the household level results in profound changes in gender roles within the family across time and throughout the conflict cycle. The section examines in particular the increase in female labor market participation observed in a large number of conflict-affected countries, the reversal of this effect in the post-conflict period, and the potential implications of these changes for the economic recovery of households and communities after the conflict. The third section concludes by discussing how economic recovery policies in post-conflict countries may benefit from further inclusion of stronger gender awareness in their objectives. In particular, this section argues that supporting new gender roles in the post-conflict period may not only be central to improving women's rights and aspirations, but also make economic sense in extremely fragile economies.

EMERGING EVIDENCE ON THE WELFARE IMPACT OF VIOLENT CONFLICT ACROSS GENDER

Empirical findings have highlighted the differentiated impact of violent conflict across gender, suggesting that men and women may participate in different ways in economic recovery and sustainable peace efforts (Buvinic et al. 2012; Justino et al. 2012). Despite important advances, there is still limited understanding about the ways in which interventions can strengthen the inclusion of women, alongside men, in economic recovery processes. This is due in part to a lack of systematic and rigorous evidence on the differential impact of violent conflict on gender roles (Justino et al. 2012).

Armed conflicts affect the lives and livelihoods of individuals and households through both direct and indirect channels. Direct channels include changes in household composition caused by deaths, injuries, and displacement; changes in household economic status, when economic opportunities are reduced (or improved in some cases); and social and economic changes caused by forced displacement and migration. Indirect channels refer to changes that take place at the local (community) level or at the national level, and can include changes in local markets, in social networks, and in local institutional structures, for instance, local political, social, and economic organizations, local forms of conflict resolution around property rights, and local social norms. In particular, armed violence is often associated with profound changes in how family members, neighbors, and friends interact, how communities relate internally and with other communities, the operation of local markets and civic and political organizations, and their relation with state-level institutions. National-level indirect channels consist of changes in economic growth and distribution that may impact on household welfare directly (through incomes and consumption opportunities) or through how local institutions operate. Notably, armed conflicts commonly have large adverse effects on economic growth and development due to the destruction of physical, human, social, and political capital, and the reduction in the capacity of states to provide key public goods and services, such as education, health care, and security (Blattman and Miguel 2010).

These various direct and indirect impacts of armed violence are closely associated with important changes in how households behave and are organized. Notably, injuries, deaths, and overall changes in household composition often force men and women to adopt new roles within the household, leading to profound social, cultural, and economic changes. One of the main changes is the substantial increase in female household heads in conflict-affected contexts, such as Nepal and Rwanda (Menon and Rodgers 2011; Schindler 2010). Women also tend to marry and have children at younger ages due to male shortages (Schindler 2010; Shemyakina 2009). As a result, violent conflict is often associated with increased household responsibilities for women and in changes with respect to the gender division of tasks and activities. These gendered changes have important implications for how individuals, households, and communities cope with and recover from violent conflict.

COPING STRATEGIES AND ECONOMIC RECOVERY: THE IMPORTANCE OF CHANGES IN GENDER ROLES DUE TO VIOLENT CONFLICT

The scale and duration of the welfare effects of violent conflict depend largely on how different people respond and adapt to the direct and indirect effects of violence outlined in the preceding section. The effectiveness of household coping and adaptation strategies is shaped in turn by initial household conditions (e.g., level of income, type of livelihoods, and social and human capital), the severity of exposure to violence, and the type of opportunities and alliances available to the household in the post-conflict period (Justino 2009).

Even though most common coping strategies are considerably restricted in contexts of conflict, people are often able to adopt a myriad of economic risk-management and risk-coping strategies amidst violence. These include the use of savings and the sale of assets (including land), resorting to subsistence agriculture, using or creating informal markets, reallocating labor within the household, and economic migration (Azam, Collier, and Cravinho 1994; Ibáñez and Moya 2006; Justino 2009, 2012a; Verpoorten 2009). Coping strategies during violent conflict may also include fighting, looting, support for armed groups, and participation in illegal activities (Justino 2009). Internal or cross-border migration may also result, creating its own set of challenges with large numbers of internally displaced persons or refugees. Across these scenarios, one of the most significant coping strategies adopted by households in conflict-affected countries is a change in traditional gender divisions of labor.

Most conflict-affected countries experience significant increases in female participation in labor markets (see reviews in Iyer and Santos 2012; Justino et al. 2012). This is a result of two factors. The first is the increase in the number of female-headed households due to the death or disappearance of male workers. The second is the fact that the income-generating opportunities men relied on before the conflict (such as land, animals, and other assets) may not be available, particularly when these assets are targeted by armed groups, or when people are forced into displacement and refugee camps. These effects have important implications for post-conflict economic recovery among affected populations, but are often either unacknowledged or explicitly reversed.

CHANGES IN GENDER ROLES DURING ARMED CONFLICT

The literature on the impact of violent conflict on female labor supply can be traced to the effects of World War II. Female labor force participation grew from 28 percent in 1940 to 34 percent in 1945 in the United States as a consequence of the military mobilization of males (Acemoglu, Autor, and Lyle 2004). Similar findings have been reported in most inter- and intra-state conflicts since the Cold War (see review in Justino et al. 2012). This finding has motivated large policy investments in female employment programs in conflict-affected countries (Justino et al. 2012). These interventions are based on the assumption that increases in the labor market participation of women will lead to increases in female empowerment within households and communities, and to subsequent welfare and social gains for women. This assumption is based on a body of evidence accumulated over the last several decades showing how changes in intra-household distributions of resources, assets, or power that favor women are often associated with positive household effects in terms of child survival rates (Thomas 1990) and spending on education and health (Duflo 2003; Qian 2008; Rangel 2006; Thomas 1997). One important mechanism leading to increases in female empowerment is the participation of women in the labor market and associated increases in earnings (Duflo 2012).

On the other hand, there is limited evidence that increases in female participation in the labor market *in areas affected by violent conflict* have been associated with long-term female empowerment. Women in Germany, for example, returned to their traditional roles once World War II was over (Akbulut-Yuksel 2009). In the United States, this appears less true—though subject to many fluctuations across the years—due to structural shifts in family and labor market structures that led to increased female labor market participation (Acemoglu, Autor, and Lyle 2004). During more recent civil wars, where increases in female labor market participation have been reported during conflict, women seem to be particularly active in low-skilled jobs and within the informal sector (Justino et al. 2012; Kumar 2000), and they tend to lose their jobs once the conflict is over, especially in the organized formal sector (Kumar 2000). Female- and widow-headed households living in many conflict-affected countries, such as Burundi, Rwanda, Mozambique, and Bosnia, also face significant social and economic constraints, such as the lack of property rights over the land that belonged to parents or dead husbands, and rules related to privatization (Greenberg and Zuckerman 2009; Kumar 2000; Schindler 2010). As a consequence, the increase in female labor market participation observed during conflict has not been necessarily accompanied by expected rises in female empowerment or improved levels of household economic security over time. In fact, female-headed households often report increased levels of vulnerability and poverty in the longer term (Ibáñez and Moya 2006; Justino and Verwimp 2013).

Gender Roles in the Post-Conflict Period and Implications for Economic Recovery

Moreover, because so many of the jobs available to women are in the informal sector, require very low skills, and pay badly, increases in female labor supply during conflict are rarely associated with rising female empowerment. Instead, rapid shifts in bargaining power within families that are driven by external violent shocks like conflict exposure and displacement have at times been associated with increases in domestic violence against women (Aizer 2010; Calderón, Gáfaro, and Ibáñez 2011).

In my empirical work on six countries (Bosnia and Herzegovina, Colombia, Kosovo, Nepal, Tajikistan, and Timor Leste), one of the only systematic studies available to date on the effect of changes in gender roles on women's empowerment and household economic recovery, evidence showed that although women participated more actively in labor markets during conflict, overall they also face strong restrictions in access to employment, particularly to jobs not deemed suitable for women. On average, women also tend to earn lower wages when employed in comparison to men employed in similar jobs, and they tend to lose their jobs once the conflict is over due to pressures to return to traditional roles. Economic vulnerability among women also tends to increase on average during armed conflict, particularly among female-headed households. This is due to an increase in dependency rates during the conflict (as a result of the increased number of orphans and injured and incapacitated household members), the rise in the labor market participation of women without any visible reduction in other household obligations, and the type of low-skilled, low-paid jobs available to women.

Despite these overall challenges, labor participation of women in conflict-affected areas is in some cases associated with increases in overall household and community welfare, when compared with households and communities in areas less affected by violence, and measured in terms of higher per capita consumption. For example, in Bosnia, Colombia, and Timor Leste, greater participation of women in labor markets during conflict seemed to be associated with overall positive household welfare effects. No association was found in Kosovo, Nepal, and Tajikistan. Greater participation of women in labor markets was found to be associated with positive community-level welfare outcomes in Bosnia and Colombia. These results are reported with some important caveats. First, the empirical analysis is noting association, not causation. Second, benefits are more significant when women are employed in better-paid jobs.[3] However, the results suggest that, under some circumstances, improvements in women's access to employment markets may facilitate the economic recovery of households and communities in the post-conflict period, particularly when employment is more stable, salaries are fair, and women remain in the labor market over time.

These findings are important because post-conflict economies face enormous recovery challenges in terms of rebuilding infrastructure, re-establishing the operation of exchange markets, supporting social reconciliation, promoting social cohesion, and establishing fully functioning political institutions. In addition, large groups of people face tremendous deprivation and multiple vulnerabilities following the end of violence. The physical and human destruction caused by violent conflicts is compounded by the return of large numbers of combatant, displaced, and refugee populations in the post-conflict period who need shelter, food, and employment (Justino 2012b). Supporting the small-scale economies generated by women during the war to sustain their households could potentially offer an entry point to the economic recovery of millions of families and communities affected by armed violence every year across the world. These issues are, however, not well understood in conflict-affected contexts, indicating an important area for future empirical research. It is also a critical policy matter, which is addressed in the next section.

POLICY IMPLICATIONS

The labor supply of women is an important economic coping strategy for households affected by the direct and indirect effects of violent conflict. Despite potential benefits for the economic recovery of households and communities in the post-conflict period, most evidence from conflict-affected countries suggests that in the post-conflict period, women tend to lose their jobs due to substantial societal and policy pressure to return to pre-conflict status quo, and the return of men to what often is a very competitive labor market due to violence-induced economic contraction. The social acceptance of women as income providers is often only temporary, due to war needs. Part of the solution to support the continuing employment of women and stronger empowerment effects requires changes in social attitudes, stronger investment by national and international development actors in creating laws to support equal opportunities in the labor market, as well as creating the opportunities themselves, and the assurance that men are not left out from formal employment.

Recent evidence in the context of India, though not explicitly dealing with conflict, has shown that when economic opportunities are made available locally, cultural norms around gender roles may change quite rapidly and women may join the labor market, may stay there, and may even be encouraged by their families to do so (Beaman et al. 2012; Jensen 2010). Even though we do not have any evidence to date of similar mechanisms operating in conflict-affected settings, this finding is important because it suggests that supporting new gender roles in the post-conflict period may lead to important economic gains in the context of vulnerable economies, in addition to improving women's rights and aspirations. Notably, increases in labor market participation among women in areas affected by conflict may spur local economic recovery in the post-conflict period by generating higher aggregate wealth, sustaining the functioning of markets, and increasing productivity in the use of resources.

These arguments are supported by a body of evidence that has highlighted the beneficial role of increased women's economic participation on aggregate growth and local development patterns (in peaceful settings). For example, agricultural outputs in developing countries could be increased by 2.5 to 4 percent by granting male and female farmers equal access to productive resources (FAO 2011). Gender inequality in education and employment in the Middle East and North Africa and in South Asia has negatively affected economic growth directly by lowering the average level of human capital (Klasen and Lamanna 2009). Education gender gaps may impede economic development and growth (Knowles, Lorgelly, and Owen 2002), and gender equality has been shown to be at the heart of long-run economic and demographic development in Europe (Lagerlöf 2003). In India, children in villages headed by female leaders have experienced higher immunization rates and improved school attendance rates (for girls) (Beaman et al. 2006), while increases in women's political representation have resulted in significant reductions in neonatal mortality because women politicians are more likely to build public health facilities, support antenatal care, provide conditions for safer deliveries, and encourage the immunization of children (Bhalotra and Clots-Figueras 2011). These findings suggest that the support for female labor market participation in the post-conflict period—beyond the immediate household needs generated during the conflict—may make economic sense and may facilitate the economic recovery of households affected by armed violence. Some new studies support this argument. For instance, recent research has shown that in conflict settings, once the violence has ended, the set of conflict-affected communities that experience the most rapid economic recovery and poverty reduction tend to be those that had more women reporting higher levels of empowerment (Petesch 2011, Chapter 26 in this volume). Gender equality has also been linked empirically to lower risks of inter-state conflicts (Caprioli 2003, 2005; Regan and Paskeviciute 2003), improved respect for human rights (Melander 2005), the promotion of democracy (Barro 1997), and lower corruption in society (Dollar, Fishman, and Gatti 2001; Swamy et al. 2001), factors that are arguably central to successful economic recovery and peace-building processes.

Evidence on the links between the small-scale economies generated by women during the conflict and the need to re-employ millions of men returning from wars is, however, too scarce. Limited, too, is evidence on whether the benefits of promoting gender equality will ever be observed in conflict-affected settings, where women may not be as actively involved in fighting as men (though in many cases they are), but may be responsible for how social norms around violence may be embedded within households and across generations (Moser and Clark 2001). We currently know too little about how to generate employment and rebuild markets in economies affected by widespread armed violence, how gender programming may work in those circumstances, and how conflicts may affect how norms and behavior are transmitted within households and across generations.

These gaps in knowledge mean that gender interventions in conflict-affected contexts are being designed on the basis of little hard evidence on fundamental processes linking armed conflict and the economic welfare and behavior of men and women affected by violent conflict. Yet, the identification of the mechanisms and determinants of the differentiated contribution of women and men to peace-building and economic recovery processes is a necessary step to improve the design and targeting of future interventions, in order to identify and mitigate costs and negative impacts of violence, as well as to better reap the benefits of positive changes in gender roles. As a starting point, policymakers spending their money on post-conflict recovery programs should invest first in gathering the data necessary to understand how their proposed programs will impact communities and women and men differently.

This is a challenging but not impossible task given the recent improvements in data availability and in analytical qualitative and quantitative methods to better understand different types and levels of armed conflict, and their consequences. There is, however, much to be done in terms of linking this new knowledge to long-term development processes and the design and implementation of effective recovery policies. Further improvements require considerable investment in appropriate methodological systems, as well as serious engagement between researchers, the international policy community, and local governments. Better knowledge will in turn result in better and more effective policy interventions to provide economic and physical security to the millions of women, men, and children who continue to live under violence and instability, even after conflicts have formally ended.

NOTES

1. While these may not answer macro questions about the functioning, rationale, and beneficiaries of the war economy, they offer significant insights and a way to address a wide variety of gender gaps in understanding.
2. See www.hicn.org and www.microconflict.eu.
3. However, positive household benefits were still observed in Bosnia, despite the low-status jobs performed by women affected by conflict, and the fact that women earn on average less than men (Justino et al. 2012).

REFERENCES

Acemoglu, Daron, David H. Autor, and David Lyle. 2004. "Women, War, and Wages: The Effect of Female Labor Supply on the Wage Structure at Midcentury." *Journal of Political Economy* 112, no. 3: 497–551.

Aizer, Anna. 2010. "The Gender Wage Gap and Domestic Violence." *American Economic Review* 100, no. 4: 1847–1859.

Akbulut-Yuksel, Mevlude. 2009. "Children of War: The Long-Run Effects of Large-Scale Physical Destruction and Warfare on Children." The Institute of Development Studies at the University of Sussex, Households in Conflict Network, HiCN Working Paper No. 62, Brighton, UK.

Azam, Jean-Paul, Paul Collier, and Andrea Cravinho. 1994. "Crop Sales, Shortages and Peasant Portfolio Behaviour: An Analysis of Angola." *Journal of Development Studies* 30, no. 2: 361–379.

Barro, Robert J. 1997. *Determinants of Economic Growth: A Cross-Country Empirical Study.* Cambridge, MA: MIT Press.

Beaman, Lori, Esther Duflo, Rohini Pande, and Petia Topalova. 2006. "Women Politicians, Gender Bias, and Policy-making in Rural India." Background Paper for UNICEF's The State of the World's Children Report 2007.

Beaman, Lori, Esther Duflo, Rohini Pande, and Petia Topalova. 2012. "Female Leadership Raises Aspirations and Educational Attainment for Girls: A Policy Experiment." *Science* 335: 582–586.

Bhalotra, Sonia, and Irma Clots-Figueras. 2011. "Health and the Political Agency of Women," Institute for the Study of Labor, IZA Discussion Papers 6216, Bonn, Germany.

Blattman, Christopher, and Edward Miguel. 2010. "Civil War." *Journal of Economic Literature* 48, no. 1: 3–57.

Buvinic, Mayra, Monica Das Gupta, Ursula Casabonne, and Philipa Verwimp. 2012. "Violent Conflict and Gender Inequality: An Overview." The Institute of Development Studies at the University of Sussex, Households in Conflict Network, HiCN Working Paper No. 129, Brighton, UK.

Calderón, Valentina, Margarita Gáfaro, and Ana María Ibáñez. 2011. "Forced Migration, Female Labour Force Participation, and Intra-Household Bargaining: Does Conflict Empower Women?" The Institute of Development Studies at the University of Sussex, MICROCON Research Working Paper No 56, Brighton, UK.

Caprioli, Mary. 2003. "Gender Equality and State Aggression: The Impact of Domestic Gender Equality on State First Use of Force." *International Interactions* 29, no. 3: 195–214.

Caprioli, Mary. 2005. "Primed for Violence: The Role of Gender Equality in Predicting Internal Conflict." *International Studies Quarterly* 49, no. 2: 161–178.

Cramer, Christopher. 2006. *Civil War Is Not a Stupid Thing: Accounting for Violence in Developing Countries.* London: Hurst.

Dollar, David, Raymond Fishman, and Roberta Gatti. 2001. "Are Women Really the 'Fairer' Sex? Corruption and Women in Government." *Journal of Economic Behavior & Organization* 46, no. 4: 423–429.

Duflo, Esther. 2003. "Grandmothers and Granddaughters: Old-Age Pensions and Intrahousehold Allocation in South Africa." *World Bank Economic Review* 17, no. 1: 1–25.

Duflo, Esther. 2012. "Women Empowerment and Economic Development." *Journal of Economic Literature* 50, no. 4: 1051–1079.

Food and Agriculture Organization of the United Nations (FAO). 2011. *The State of Food and Agriculture, 2010–2011: Women in Agriculture, Closing the Gender Gap for Development.* Rome: FAO.

Greenberg, Marcia E., and Elaine Zuckerman. 2009. "The Gender Dimensions of Post-Conflict Reconstruction: The Challenges in Development Aid." In *Making Peace Work: The Challenges of Social and Economic Reconstruction*, edited by Tony Addison and Tilman Brück, 101–135. Helsinki: Palgrave MacMillan and UNU-WIDER.

Ibáñez, Ana María, and Andrés Moya. 2006. "The Impact of Intra-State Conflict on Economic Welfare and Consumption Smoothing: Empirical Evidence for the Displaced Population in Colombia." The Institute of Development Studies at the University of Sussex, Households in Conflict Network, HiCN Working Paper No. 23, Brighton, UK.

Iyer, Lakshmi, and Indhira Santos. 2012. "Creating Jobs in South Asia's Conflict Zones." The World Bank Human Development Department, South Asia Region, Policy Research Working Paper No. 6104.

Jensen, Robert. 2010. "Economic Opportunity and Gender Differences in Human Capital: An Experimental Test for India." NBER Working Paper No. 16021, Cambridge, MA.

Justino, Patricia. 2009. "Poverty and Violent Conflict: A Micro-Level Perspective on the Causes and Duration of Warfare." *Journal of Peace Research* 46, no. 3: 315–333.

Justino, Patricia. 2012a. "War and Poverty." In *The Oxford Handbook of the Economics of Peace and Conflict*, edited by Michelle R. Garfinkel and Stergios Skaperdas, 676–705. Oxford: Oxford University Press.

Justino, Patricia. 2012b. "Nutrition, Governance and Violence: A Framework for the Analysis of Resilience and Vulnerability to Food Insecurity in Contexts of Violent Conflict." The Institute of Development Studies at the University of Sussex, Households in Conflict Network, HiCN Working Paper No. 132, Brighton, UK.

Justino, Patricia, Tilman Brück, and Philip Verwimp, eds. 2013. *A Micro-Level Perspective on the Dynamics of Conflict, Violence and Development.* Oxford: Oxford University Press.

Justino, Patricia, Ivan Cardona, Rebecca Mitchell, and Catherin Müller. 2012. *Women Working for Recovery: The Impact of Female Employment on Family and Community Welfare after Conflict.* New York: UN Women.

Justino, Patricia, and Philip Verwimp. 2013. "Poverty Dynamics, Violent Conflict, and Convergence in Rwanda." *Review of Income and Wealth* 59, no. 1: 66–90.

Klasen, Stephan, and Francesca Lamanna. 2009. "The Impact of Gender Inequality in Education and Employment on Economic Growth: New Evidence for a Panel of Countries." *Feminist Economics* 15, no. 3: 91–132.

Knowles, Stephen, Paula K. Lorgelly, and P. Dorian Owen. 2002. "Are Educational Gender Gaps a Brake on Economic Development? Some Cross-Country Empirical Evidence." *Oxford Economic Papers* 54, no. 1: 118–149.

Kumar, Krishna. 2000. *Women and Women's Organizations in Post-Conflict Societies: The Role of International Assistance*. Washington, DC: USAID.

Lagerlöf, Nils-Petter. 2003. "Gender Equality and Long-Run Growth." *Journal of Economic Growth* 8, no. 4: 403–426.

Melander, Erik. 2005. "Political Gender Equality and State Human Rights Abuse." *Journal of Peace Research* 42, no. 2: 149–166.

Menon, Nidhiya, and Yana van der Meulen Rodgers. 2011. "War and Women's Work: Evidence from Conflict in Nepal." The World Bank Policy Research Working Paper 5745, Washington, DC.

Moser, Caroline O. N., and Fiona C. Clark, eds. 2001. *Victims, Perpetrators or Actors? Gender, Armed Conflict and Political Violence*. London: Zed Books.

Petesch, Patti. 2011. *Women's Empowerment Arising from Violent Conflict and Recovery: Life Stories from Four Middle-Income Countries*. Washington, DC: USAID.

Qian, Nancy. 2008. "Missing Women and the Price of Tea in China: The Effect of Sex-Specific Earnings on Sex Imbalance." *Quarterly Journal of Economics* 123, no. 3: 1251–1285.

Rangel, Marcos A. 2006. "Alimony Rights and Intrahousehold Allocation of Resources: Evidence from Brazil." *The Economic Journal* 116, no. 513: 627–658.

Regan, Patrick M., and Aida Paskeviciute. 2003. "Women's Access to Politics and Peaceful States." *Journal of Peace Research* 40, no. 3: 287–302.

Schindler, Kati. 2010. "Who Does What in a Household after Genocide? Evidence from Rwanda" The Institute of Development Studies at the University of Sussex, Households in Conflict Network, HiCN Working Paper No. 90, Brighton, UK.

Shemyakina, Olga. 2009. "The Marriage Market and Tajik Armed Conflict." The Institute of Development Studies at the University of Sussex, Households in Conflict Network, HiCN Working Paper No. 66, Brighton, UK.

Swamy, Anand, Stephen Knack, Young Lee, and Omar Azfar. 2001. "Gender and Corruption." *Journal of Development Economics* 64, no. 1: 25–55.

Thomas, Duncan. 1990. "Intra-Household Resource Allocation: An Inferential Approach." *Journal of Human Resources* 25, no. 4: 635–664.

Thomas, Duncan. 1997. "Incomes, Expenditures and Health Outcomes: Evidence on Intrahousehold Allocation." In *Intrahousehold Resource Allocation in Developing Countries*, edited by Lawrence Haddad, John Hoddinott, and Harold Alderman, 142–164. Baltimore, MD: Johns Hopkins University Press.

Tilly, Charles. 1990. *Coercion, Capital, and European States, AD 990–1990*. Oxford: Blackwell.

Verpoorten, Marijke. 2009. "Household Coping in War- and Peacetime: Cattle Sales in Rwanda, 1991–2001." *Journal of Development Economics* 88, no. 1: 67–86.

Vigh, Henrik E. 2006. *Navigating Terrains of War: Youth and Soldiering in Guinea-Bissau*. Oxford: Berghahn Books.

CHAPTER 7

···

VICTIMS WHO ARE MEN

···

CHRIS DOLAN

IT remains difficult to give consideration to victims of conflict-related violence who are civilian men—and virtually impossible to see that militarized men can also be victims. Culture, laws, a conflagration of institutional and media interests, and the internalization of their related norms by survivors themselves, along with their spouses, children, and communities, militate against challenging this status quo. Service providers in conflict and post-conflict zones experience tension between a properly humanitarian, rights-based and victim-centered response to human need, and funding that prioritizes one gender and related stereotypes of vulnerability to the exclusion of others.

Some major developments, notably the United Nations Security Council resolution (UNSCR) 1325 (2000) and its successors, up to and including UNSCR 1960 (2010), have raised awareness of sexual violence against women and girls in conflict settings. At the same time, they have deepened the silence around sexual violence against men. The absence of any mention of men and boys prior to UNSCR 2106 (2013) underscored a gender-binary lens in which gender inequality and gender vulnerability were fundamentally conflated, and contextual specifics that deviated from this script were systematically silenced (Dolan 2014a). Caught between evidence-based approaches and normative beliefs about gender as well as gender equality, policymakers in the United Nations Security Council erred on the side of norms (Dolan 2014c).

By contrast, the Rome Statute of the International Criminal Court, emerging from the experience of ad hoc tribunals dealing directly with some of the most appalling conflicts of the 1990s, suggests that gender inequality and gender vulnerability are not automatically coterminous and that assumptions about who can or cannot be a victim must be suspended if justice is to be done on the basis of available evidence. From the 2007 judgment by the International Criminal Tribunal for the Former Yugoslavia (ICTY) in the case of Cesic,[1] through the International Criminal Court's development of a progressive policy on gender crimes in 2014 (ICC 2014), and up to the ICC judgment in the case of Jean Pierre Bemba in March 2016,[2] it is clear that victims of sexual violence who are men can now be recognized in international criminal law.[3]

Overall, while the position adopted in UNSCR 1325 has been rolled out and to a certain extent operationalized through, *inter alia*, the establishment of the Office of the Special Representative of the Secretary General on Sexual Violence in Conflict, as well as domesticated through National Action Plans on UNSCR 1325 (2000) (see Castillo Díaz and Cueva Beteta, Chapter 14 in this volume), the broader understanding of gender-based crimes as affecting men as well as women has yet to enter domestic legislation, where it matters. Specifically, if domestic penal codes were to adopt the Rome Statute's definition of rape and other forms of sexual violence, this would drive norm change (see Kapur, Chapter 17 in this volume). Breaking the silence on men's experiences of sexual violence in particular would also help open up discussion about men's experiences of gender and conflict more broadly.

This chapter begins by identifying some key points in gender and conflict debates to make the case that, despite repeated attempts to challenge the silencing of men's experiences, progress has been far from linear. It then brings additional critical elements to bear in a bid to open up new exit pathways from a seeming impasse and polarization between those who believe we should see victims first and their gender second (and therefore can acknowledge "victims who are men"), and those who question the very possibility of "men as victims."

The first of these elements is conflict-related sexual violence, a reality confronting men that has largely been excluded from the dominant discourse.[4] Within that reality, the fact that men can be victimized through being forced to "perpetrate" sexual acts against others is highlighted. Extrapolating from the evident harms that victims experience in doing harm to others, the chapter argues that it is not realistic to attribute "the harms of doing harm" in conflict settings to civilian victims only. Notwithstanding what gender norms, legal frameworks, and the Geneva Conventions would have us believe and allow us to see, military psychiatry indicates that it is an experience shared by militarized men also (see also Theidon, Chapter 11 in this volume). As such, it is argued, the tacit exclusion of men in general from the category of (civilian) victim, the delinking of militarized men specifically from the subcategory of victims who are men, and the manner in which this exclusion and delinking fuel cycles of violence and the continuum of conflict to post-conflict violence constitute major blind spots in debates about gender and conflict.

"FEMINISMS, GENDER, AND CONFLICT": A CONFLICTED RELATIONSHIP

The tensions arising from contemplating men as victims of gendered violence in conflict settings (rather than simply as the perpetrators of the same) are not new. Indeed, as will be shown, these tensions have been discussed within academia for decades. Whether or not the ontological, epistemological, and normative commitments of feminism are compatible with gender analysis is possibly the core question. In a provocative article published in 1996, Adam Jones argued that in practice they had proven incompatible. He called for feminist methodologies that would "isolate the gender variable but not leap so readily to the tacit equation of gender issues with women's issues." This would include exploring the gender dynamics behind variables in which men generally appear to fare worse than women. These range from peacetime suicide rates, life expectancy, and death by violence, to more directly conflict-related practices: "conscription; prisoners of war; under-age troops; 'civil defence patrols' in societies riven by civil war; mutiny and desertion; and post-battle trauma" (Jones 1996, 420–424).

In a critique of Jones's critique of feminist international relations (IR), Terrell Carver, Molly Cochran, and Judith Squires pointed to the diversity of feminist theorizing and the existence of "a very large and complex literature on men and masculinities." As well as effectively accusing Jones of constructing a straw woman, they also accused him of

> the fault that he claims to find in feminists, in that his "contribution" amounts merely *to stacking male bodies and male suffering up against female bodies and female suffering.* Indeed, there is an odious and otiose discourse of "fairness" operating in Jones's "Gender" article by which he seems to accuse feminists of "unfairness" in focusing on women-as-victims, whereas he apparently sees himself justly redressing their supposed sins of omission. For most of us, though, feminisms' predominant focus on women is hardly a surprise, and indeed it is self-consciously a response to the comparative (and still continuing) invisibility of women. (Carver, Cochran, and Squires 1998, 296; emphasis added)

While Carver et al.'s review remains helpful in highlighting the breadth and diversity of feminist theorizing within academia, it fails to address the vexing question of why what is received and perceived to be a "gender analysis" in policy and practice (notably in the area of so-called "gender mainstreaming") is generally about women, not about men. Their review did not explore the analytical and practical implications of focusing only on embodied women, privileging women's narratives, and exhibiting a normative commitment to addressing male–female gender inequalities writ large. In particular, they did not thoroughly explore the consequences of a pronounced reluctance to deal with those situations where the numbers do not "stack up" in line with a narrative of all-pervasive and unidirectional gender inequality and vulnerability. They may have been right to say that Jones's representation of the state of gender in IR was "unrepresentative of the totality of the field," but they missed the point. Bluntly put, the totality of the theoretical field is irrelevant to victims of gender violence; what matters to victims is that part of the field—or those specific "feminisms"—has succeeded in shaping dominant policy and practice to the benefit of particular gendered categories of victim and the detriment of others.

In a subsequent review of several substantive works on gender and conflict,[5] Carpenter argued that feminist IR is not only marginalized within mainstream IR theory but "also contributes to this marginalization by resisting the co-optation of gender as an explanatory framework separate from feminist normative commitments." She noted that "[w]omen's subordination and victimization is [*sic*] too often assumed by feminists rather than examined contextually." She highlighted the resultant risks to "nonfeminists" of integrating gender into their analysis and being given a "icy" reception of the kind experienced by Jones (Carpenter 2001, 156).

Carpenter also pursued her analysis further, by considering how gender beliefs that frame civilian protection advocacy interlock with underlying gender norms held by the belligerents themselves. Using the case of Srebrenica, in which nearly 8,000 men were massacred, she demonstrates how the use of "women and children" both as a proxy for civilians and as a synonym for vulnerability reduces the need for belligerents to distinguish male civilians from male combatants, and thus "encourages" them "to target and act contrary to the immunity norm itself" (Carpenter 2005). She went on to conclude that a shift by women's rights advocates toward an emphasis on women's social vulnerabilities arising from gendered inequality "has not tended to include an emphasis on the gender-based vulnerabilities that some males . . . also face due to social attitudes in times of war" (Carpenter 2005, 308). Paradoxically, therefore, "the strategic use of gender essentialisms as a persuasion tactic itself reproduces the set of ideas that make civilian males particularly vulnerable" (Carpenter 2005, 315). Zarkov's (2007) important work, *The Body of War*, particularly chapter eight on "The Body of the Other Man," in many respects details the interconnection and construction of gender and ethnic essentialisms by the media—and external interveners. Commenting on the United Nations Commission of Experts final report on Bosnia and Croatia, she observes that while it detailed many instances of sexual violence against men, it was received by "the public, already familiar with the large-scale sexual violence against women, as 'referring to women only'" (155).

Various research findings further demonstrate that, despite variations in the absolute difference between male and female figures, civilian men are, to borrow a phrase, "disproportionately affected" by premature deaths. One systematic attempt to establish gendered conflict-related civilian deaths found that, while comprehensive global data sets are simply not available, where data does exist, it indicates that "men are more likely to die during conflicts, whereas women die more often of indirect causes after the conflict is over" (Ormhaug, Hernes, and Meier 2009). More recently, an independent inquiry found that in Syria "males of fighting age have emerged as the main targets of violence," constituting 85.1 percent of recorded victims of the Syrian conflict between March 2011 and April 2014.[6] The report further noted that "men of fighting age are not granted any of the protections afforded to civilians by any of the parties" (IICISAR 2015, paras. 54, 58). These findings appear to corroborate Carpenter's statement that "of all war-affected noncombatants worldwide, those most at risk of summary execution are adult civilian males" (Carpenter 2003, 661). Turning to militarized men, one study of war and mortality in Kosovo found that men of military age (15–49) were "8.9 times more likely to die from war-related trauma than women," and appeared to add weight to this line of inquiry (Spiegel and Salama 2000).

Despite such male-to-female ratios of death by violence, the gendered nature of the underlying violence is not considered holistically. Instead, the added burdens accruing to women as a result of men's premature deaths are at times presented as important additional evidence of women's gendered disadvantage.[7] While this recognition of the gendered distribution of certain of the multiple impacts of violence is important, it is problematic insofar as the deaths themselves are not understood as also being gendered.

Where statistics do destabilize received narratives about unidirectional gender vulnerability related to conflict, there is a tendency to utilize language to deflect attention from this. In the case of unaccompanied minors coming to Europe in flight from conflict in the Middle East, for example, media headlines repeatedly refer to "children" rather than "boys," despite the fact that 90 percent of these minors are male, and the knowledge that sexual exploitation is undoubtedly a feature of their flight.[8] If the ratio were 90 percent girls to 10 percent boys, would the headline still talk of "children," or would it refer to "girls?"

The reasons that such findings are given little prominence in discussions of the gender-conflict nexus require further analysis that are beyond the scope of this chapter; suffice to say that the discussion about gender-based violence in conflict settings has largely been focused on conflict-related sexual violence in which the "disproportionate" victimization of women is often taken as a less controversial given (notwithstanding a number of feminist critiques of "the fixation on wartime rape" [Henry 2013] and "hyper-attention to sex" [Engle 2013]).

Many of the events before, during, and after the Global Summit on Ending Sexual Violence in Conflict held in London in 2014 reflected the dominant epistemological, ontological, and normative positions on conflict-related sexual violence described by Jones some twenty years earlier. An important departure from these was the G8 Declaration of April 11, 2013, that preceded the Summit. In this, "[m]inisters underlined the importance of responding to the needs of men and boys who are victims of sexual violence in armed conflict, as well as to the needs of those secondarily traumatized as forced witnesses of sexual violence against family members." They also "recognised that further action . . . is imperative to end sexual violence in armed conflict . . . to provide comprehensive support services to victims, be they women, girls, men or boys" (UK-FCO 2013).

The commitments made in the G8 statement were quickly diluted, though not lost entirely, by the more conservative UN Security Council in its new resolution 2106 (2013). This rehearsed the familiar trope that sexual violence in conflict and post-conflict "disproportionately affects women and girls, as well as groups that are particularly vulnerable or may be specifically targeted," but went on to state that this happens "while also affecting men and boys and those secondarily traumatized as forced witnesses of sexual violence against family members." While this phrasing implies that men and boys are less affected than women and girls (the very kind of "stacking-up" of numbers in an "otiose" manner that Carver accused Jones of back in 1996) and that they are not among particularly vulnerable or targeted groups when it comes to sexual violence, it was nonetheless progress toward recognizing that the category of victims can include men and boys.

During the summit itself, several plenary speakers drew on the language of the G8 declaration; William Hague, then British Foreign Secretary, admired the courage of "any survivor, woman, man, girl or boy, who can talk about their experiences of rape and turn suffering into strength and wisdom and compassion for others" while the US Secretary of State, John Kerry, argued that "[i]t is time for us . . . to write a new norm . . . . One that protects women, girls, men, boys, protects them from these unspeakable crimes." One of eight expert panels—chaired by the Special Representative of the Secretary-General on Sexual Violence in Conflict (SRSG-SVC) Zainab Bangura—occupied itself with the question of male victims of sexual violence, and only one of more than one hundred civil society organizations presenting in the fringe focused exclusively on presenting its work with male survivors.[9]

These rather limited instances of explicit focus on men and boys nonetheless prompted the former Chief, Peace and Security at UN Women, Anne-Marie Goetz, to write:

> The recent focus on male victims of domestic abuse and of war rape can have the unfortunate effect of further postponing the feminist social change project. The exposure of the ways in which men and boys also experience these types of violence (and we still do not know the full extent) has helped to attract new allies in the prevention effort . . . . *Wartime rape has been framed as an almost gender-neutral weapon of war. Taking the feminist social change project out of the definition of and the solutions to these problems makes response effort patronizing and in the end, ineffective.* (Goetz 2014b; emphasis added)

Goetz (2014a) positions herself explicitly as a "feminist policy activist." Her perspective on "the feminist social change project" (which nearly twenty years earlier Jones described simply as a "social project") exemplifies the normative dimensions of some feminisms and what Carpenter identifies as a "distortion" of gender as an analytical frame that also hollows out the very core of humanitarian and human rights frameworks and an understanding of victims *qua* victims.

LOCATING THE TENSIONS: NORMS OR EVIDENCE?

The preceding review highlights emblematic instances of a spectrum of positions on the possibility of men as victims in conflict, as well as key theoretical tensions. It suggests that while there are some moves toward a more comprehensive and inclusive understanding of gender and conflict, something of a theoretical-political-evidential impasse remains.

Notwithstanding Carver et al.'s dismissal of Jones's attempts at "stacking male bodies and male suffering up against female bodies and female suffering" as "odious," (296) the lack of systematic and cross-country statistics on victims who are men is undoubtedly a major factor in sustaining the evidential impasse. In the absence of well-researched and documented figures for the victimization of men, sweeping assertions about numbers will continue to nestle at the heart of claims to the victimhood of women as a category.

Nonetheless, such claims are used to bolster the case for particular types of intervention. Goetz (2014b), for example, argues that "an appropriate response [to sexual violence] involves a feminist project of emancipation," and that this is so because of "the basic fact that women are its principal victims." First, we do not know whether this "basic fact" is actually true (and in some contexts, such as the migrant male victims of sexual exploitation, it appears to be false). Second, whether men are or are not the principal victims, an appropriate response to sexual violence will *always* require a project of emancipation from the gender norms that made such violence so effective against all genders.

The prospects of filling the evidence gap are mixed. Key policy instruments such as the Inter-Agency Standing Committee's Guidelines on Gender-Based Violence (GBV) interventions, in a radical departure from otherwise widely held notions of evidence-based planning, argue that "[w]aiting for or seeking population-based data on the true magnitude of GBV should not be a priority in an emergency" (IASC 2015, 2). While at first sight this appears admirable, the problem lies in the Inter-Agency Standing Committee's guidance on who to consider at risk, in which women are heavily front-loaded. This is liable to divert attention away from male victims, who tend to be hidden anyway. On a more positive note, the revised edition of the International Protocol on the Documentation and Investigation of Sexual Violence in Conflict is set to include a specific chapter on men and boys.

The importance of critically interrogating the manner in which data is collected is evident in two recent reassessments of sexual violence statistics, both of which concluded that the women–men numbers gap for the situations examined is considerably narrower than previously thought. The first found that re-coding transcripts of testimonies in the Peruvian Commission for Truth and Reconciliation to include sexual humiliation, sexual mutilation, sexual torture, and rape raised the percentage of cases of sexual violence that included male victims from 2 percent to 29 percent and suggested that 22 percent of all male witnesses had experienced sexual violence. As the author noted, "the proportion of male to female victims can change according to how sexual violence is understood and recorded" (Leiby 2009, 82). The second, a review of five federal surveys conducted in peacetime in the United States by three distinct institutions, found "a high prevalence of sexual victimization among men—in many circumstances similar to the prevalence found among women" (Stemple and Meyer 2014, 1).

Primary data collected in conflict settings (see, for example, Johnson et al. 2008, 2010) supports the argument that women are more affected than men by sexual violence in conflict settings, but it also provides evidence that men are considerably more affected by sexual violence than is generally assumed and should therefore be correspondingly factored into GBV interventions.

Such studies are still rare. Clearly, "gender ideas" (Carpenter 2003, 663) rather than gender evidence continue to determine who is assumed to be vulnerable. Indeed, for some actors, sustaining an absence of numbers may be more strategically advantageous than promoting their presence.

Conflict-Related Sexual Violence against Men and the Harms of Doing Harm

Mindful that the political economy of the institutions that should be generating data on gendered patterns of victimization is such that they have little interest in doing so, and that the question of actual proportions of victims who are women, men (and others) in any given context is therefore unlikely to be "mainstreamed" for some time to come, it is necessary to consider alternative strategies for drawing attention to victims who are men (Dolan 2014b). In this the "gender-based violence of gender-based violences," namely conflict-related sexual violence, is a useful entry point.

As depicted in the aptly entitled film *Men Can Be Raped Too*, this form of violence exemplifies the disjuncture between widely held assumptions about male invulnerability and understandings of perpetratorship on the one hand, and men's lived experiences of vulnerability on the other (Refugee Law Project 2015). It is also an important example of a gender issue that is regularly silenced—or "disappeared" under the term "torture" (see Leiby 2009). The assumption that men are invulnerable to sexual violence and that women cannot be perpetrators is codified in many legal systems around the world that do not cater to male victims or female perpetrators (Sivakumaran 2007), and these assumptions are reflected in the training of both lawyers and medical personnel (Ongwech 2013).[10] These recent experiences suggest that Jones's (2000a) finding that only 3 percent of humanitarian agencies reported working with male victims of sexual violence, while yet to be updated, is unlikely to be very different today. The IASC's 2005 Guidelines for Gender-Based Violence Interventions in Humanitarian Settings, for example, were exclusively concerned about the safety of women and children (Dolan 2014c), and the 2015 revision, while acknowledging men and boys as possible victims, gave little concrete guidance on how to address their needs. Writing in 2010, Sivakumaran observed that sexual violence against men was "lost in translation" when it came to UN responses (Sivakumaran 2010). The manner in which the Extraordinary Chambers in the Cambodian Court (ECCC) is considering only those victims of forced marriage under the Khmer Rouge who were women offers another example (see Oosterveld, Chapter 18 in this volume). Notwithstanding this generally slow progress, the issues are gradually being discussed in policy spaces and documents.

There is also a slowly growing academic literature on conflict-related sexual violence against men. Solangon and Patel (2012) provide a useful overview. Legal dimensions are well addressed (Hennessey and Gerry 2012; Lewis 2009; Oosterhoff, Zwanikken, and Ketting 2004; Oosterveld 2013; Manivannan 2014; Sivakumaran 2007). Psychological issues for male survivors in general are raised by Walker, Archer, and Davies (2005). Psychosocial dimensions are addressed by Loncar and Bretic (1995), Loncar, Henigsberg, and Hrabac (2010), and Onyango and Hampanda (2011), with Johnson et al. (2008, 2010) making an important contribution regarding mental health. Zarkov's "The Body of the Other Man" considers both patterns of sexual violence against men and their (non-)portrayal in the media in the former Yugoslavia (Zarkov 2007).

The forms and locations that sexual victimization of men can take are extensive and have been listed elsewhere (Dolan 2014d). They include, but are not limited to, forced nudity, various forms of rape, genital mutilations, forced masturbation, and blunt trauma to the genitalia (Carlson 2006).[11] Within the multiple forms of sexual violence perpetrated against men, one of the most striking features of some men's experiences is the manner in which they are forced to "perpetrate" sexualized violence against others, including family members, friends, and fellow detainees. Generally, the scenarios shared by victims are of extreme coercion: "do it or be killed."

The following example is one of several collected by the author since 2013. The respondent described his experience as follows:

> In 2006 people from [a rebel group], soldiers, told us to help them carry food to the bush where they were fighting. By then I had a wife and children. Some of us helped them carry the guns to the bush. We were many people. Women carried food items. When we reached there they said "let the males come here." They told us, "you bend" (we were six men). Then they said "you remove your clothes." We thought they wanted to beat us. [But actually] they wanted to penetrate us from behind. They raped all of us. For me it was even more difficult, I was raped by two men. I felt a lot of pain in the abdomen. What pained me was that they said "don't think we are the only people to do that, you should also do that." They told us to rape others among ourselves.
>
> Q: Why do you say you are a woman?
> A: Firstly, I remember how I was sexually abused as a woman. Secondly, I cannot perform family sex life—my reproductive organs don't function normally. When I remember what I did I feel no longer a human being, it has never happened for a Burundian to do that.[12]

Detailed accounts such as this, over and above illustrating the obvious fact of men's victimization, also tell us about (1) targeting of heteronormative men: "By then I had a wife and children"; (2) deliberate steps taken by the perpetrators to compromise the victim's sense of self: "don't think we are the only people to do that, you should also do that"; (3) the manner in which the victim's vulnerability is exacerbated by internalized gender norms in which being penetrated equates with being feminized: "I was sexually abused as a woman"; (4) reproductive impact: "I cannot perform family sex life—my reproductive organs don't function normally";[13] (5) dehumanization of the victim through being made to "perpetrate": "When I remember what I did I feel no longer a human being"; and (6) the related attack on his sense of national identity: "it has never happened for a Burundian to do that."

Clearly, sexual violence in this shape tells us something about the rape of men as a weapon of war to which a nationality-ethnicity-sexuality nexus is central and in which the attack on the victim's sense of self and personhood is approached from each of these angles. For the victim, it can also be experienced as an attack on his moral identity, his sense of humanness. It is the fact of what he did, of being made to "perpetrate" with his own body, that makes him feel no longer a human being, even as what was done to him makes him feel no longer a man.[14]

In the ICTY case of *Prosecutor v. Ranko Cesic*, Cesic was convicted of rape as a crime against humanity and humiliating and degrading treatment as a war crime. The rape involved two Muslim brothers who were forced to perform fellatio on each other in front of others. The judgment also concluded that since the two victims were brothers and had been forced to do these acts in public, "the violation of the moral and physical integrity of the victims justified that the rape be considered particularly serious as well."[15] What one sees in these cases is that, just as women's bodies can be utilized by the perpetrators as a vehicle for "the enemy's child," so male victims' bodies can be turned against themselves by the perpetrators as the direct instrument of sexual violence and an extreme form of divide and rule. The Rome Statute recognizes that men in such scenarios can be victims if "[t]he perpetrator committed an act of a sexual nature against one or more persons or caused such person or persons to engage in an act of a sexual nature by force."[16] The implications of recognizing that the male body, in a state of apparent arousal, can in fact be an instrument of coerced self-harm are considerable, not only for male victims of sexual violence, but also for explaining the high levels of trauma seen among Vietnam "vets" and ex-combatants around the world.

THE HARM OF DOING HARM AND ITS MILITARIZED VICTIMS

This dynamic of victims being forced to perpetrate, and the evident harm that doing harm causes to them, should oblige us to raise the critical question of whether it is a dynamic restricted to civilians, or whether, in fact, it also bridges the divide between civilians and combatants as constructed, *inter alia*, by the Geneva Conventions of 1949.

The latter, even insofar as they cover "non-international armed conflict" are structured around a clear-cut civilian-military binary, and indeed, the laws of armed conflict are constructed around this binary. But how true is the binary? In many respects, it appears to ride roughshod over the realities of military groupings and structures. We know that many such groupings are built through abduction, forcible recruitment, or conscription involving degrees of coercion that nullify the likelihood of subsequent actions being attributed to free will. Even where people join of their own accord, induction can be brutal (see, for example, Belkin 2012). Second, there is an extensive literature on what one seminal work described as "killology" (Grossman 1995). This discusses men's reluctance to kill one another,[17] the difficulties faced by militaries in getting them to do so, the various strategies of desensitization (including the creation of "physical and psychological distance"), and the enduring post-conflict psychological and social costs both to the soldier-victim and to wider society.

When applied to armed groups such as the Lords' Resistance Army in Uganda, or the RPF (Rwandan Patriotic Front) in Sierra Leone, it is well established that new abductees are coerced into brutal acts of "hands-on" killing as part of an induction process. What is less reflected on is the extent to which these desensitization and brutalization processes are themselves forms of inhumane and degrading treatment. Equally, the degrading and humiliating nature of fear that soldiers are coerced to experience is given little attention as a form of gender-based violence.[18]

It is perhaps time that the growing literature on the hugely harmful impacts on militarized men of being coerced to harm others (Meagher 2014; Shephard 2003) be given a more central place in the analysis of gender and conflict. It was these impacts, as witnessed in thousands of veterans of the US army returning from Vietnam, that gave rise to the concept of post-traumatic stress disorder in the 1970s. One analyst argued that "for the combatants in every major war fought in this century, there has been a greater probability of becoming a psychiatric casualty than of being killed by enemy fire" (Gabriel 1987, quoted in Grossman 1995, 43). The dramatic impacts on the physiology of traumatized combatants can include "a recalibration of the brain's alarm system, an increase in stress hormone activity, and alterations in the system that filters relevant information from irrelevant" (Van der Kolk 2014).

Meagher (2014), looking into the "runaway suicide rates" among US soldiers returning from the Middle East (twenty-two per day in February 2013), found that "we are also especially good at killing our own, killing them 'from the inside out,' silently, invisibly." His far-reaching critique of just-war theory centers around "the violation, by oneself or another, of a personally embedded moral code or value resulting in deep injury to the psyche or soul" (Meagher 2014). He argues that "those who work with veterans to help heal their inner, invisible wounds know that the deepest and most intractable PTSD has its roots in what veterans perceive as the evil they have done and been part of" (Meagher 2014, 2). One is reminded here of the civilian man in Burundi whose victimization included being forced to rape other captives, and who stated, "When I remember what I did I feel no longer a human being."

DISCUSSION AND CONCLUSIONS

In the long-standing tug of war between gender norms that are multiply co-opted and numbers that do not always support a simple narrative of women's gender inequality and suffering in times of conflict (at least not in terms of premature deaths), norms currently hold the balance of power. Yet it is shifting, not least thanks to advances in ICL (International Criminal Law) jurisprudence that recognize victims of sexual violence who are men.

Within that lie the seeds of consideration not only of the role that gender norms and related ideas of masculinity and femininity play in men's sexual victimization, but also of the peculiarities of the men's embodied experience of sexual violence and how these are utilized and exploited by the perpetrators.

Some civilian men's experiences of sexual violence, notably being forced to "perpetrate" sexual acts under extreme duress, illustrate the complex ways in which gender, sex, and sexed bodies interact. They alert us to the paradox that men can be simultaneously victim and perpetrator, depending on the angle from which an act is perceived. The men in question, like women who conceive out of rape, are victims not only of those giving the commands, but of their own physiology.

Furthermore, though our starting point lies with civilian men's experiences, these insights can generate theoretical and empirical space for understanding men as victims of gender-based violence more broadly, for they open our eyes to a broader landscape (and related literature) of gendered coercion of men in conflict, particularly that experienced by militarized men. It is a landscape that obliges us to reappraise and destabilize not only an erroneously simplified male–female gender binary, but also the military–civilian and perpetrator–victim binaries with which the gender binary has been overlaid and made synonymous. For if civilian men can be made to rape in the absence of any wish whatsoever to do so, should we not also qualify our assumption that just because a man is in uniform and has committed a rape, he wished to do so—particularly given what we know about the work of coercion that goes into making people break their own moral norms and the psychological harms of doing harm that these "perpetrators" suffer? The debate thus has to come to grips with qualitative and quantitative evidence indicating that, to the extent that men being coerced to harm others is itself a gender-based form of violence, then it is one that disproportionately affects men.

International criminal law has been presented here as one of the discursive and policy spaces in which advances have been made in the direction of recognizing victims who are men. Despite its focus on individual responsibility, it does, through the concept of command responsibility, offer some limited avenues to shift emphasis from the intention of individual perpetrators and toward systemic culpability as operationalized by those in charge. It remains unable, however, to deal with the legions of men whose bodies have been commandeered for purposes of war and the inherently ambiguous nature of intent under situations of extreme duress and systemic coercion. Nor can it deal with the fact that—collectively, if not always individually—we remain unable or unwilling to surface the gender norms we have so successfully internalized. Indeed, by focusing on the individual "bad apples," it only helps to reinscribe the norms and absolve the systems.

If the low-ranking perpetrators of acts of violence are generally the victims of gender systems, then alternative models of doing justice will be required to deal with the groups, states, and institutions that perpetuate these systems. Recognizing victims who are men is a critical first step in constructing these alternatives.

Notes

1. *Prosecutor v. Ranko Cesic*, Case No. IT-95-10/1-S. 2007. Sentencing Judgment, paras. 13–14, 35, 107. March 11.
2. *Prosecutor v. Jean-Pierre Bemba Gombo*, Case No. ICC-01/05-01/08. 2016. Judgment Pursuant to Article 74 of the Statute. March 21.
3. This is notwithstanding the decision of the pre-trial judges in the Kenyatta case not to consider as sexual violence the castration and forcible circumcision occurring as part of the post-election violence in Kenya in 2008, a decision which suggests there is still a long way to go.
4. By dominant discourse, I refer simply to the discourse that is found in policy documents and reports, as well as those strands of academic theorizing that support them. Besides the UNSCRs discussed earlier, a prominent example of policy documents would be the IASC's 2005 and 2015 guidelines for humanitarians preventing and responding to GBV in emergency settings. UN Action's website (www.stoprapenow.org) also gives very little space to male experiences. In the testimonies section, only one out of twelve testimonies is male, and that is of a twelve-year-old boy. There is none by an adult male.
5. Goldstein (2001); Moser and Clark (2001); Tickner (2001).
6. The statistical analysis by Price, Gohdes, and Ball (2014) considered 191,369 documented killings (85.1 percent male, 9.3 percent female, 5.6 percent of records sex not indicated).
7. For example, the IASC Guidelines, while noting that "men and boys make up a larger number of those directly affected by landmines/ERW," go on to focus on the fact that "[e]ven if not directly injured, women, girls, and other at-risk groups may find themselves in a precarious economic situation if the primary breadwinner in the household is killed or injured by landmines/ERW" (IASC 2015, 187)
8. See, for example, Daniel Howden, July 14, 2016, "Refugees Caught Up in Child Prostitution in Athens," *News Deeply: Refugees Deeply*, https://www.newsdeeply.com/refugees/articles/2016/07/14/refugees-caught-up-in-child-prostitution-in-athens#.V4lIFLmHpHE. twitter; Jessica Steventon, August 26, 2016, " 'Less Than Human': Does Asylum System Harm Child Refugees' Mental Health?" *Open Democracy*, https://opendemocracy.net/child-refugee-mental-health-asylum-seeker-crisis.
9. Author's personal observations, both as one of the presenters for Refugee Law Project, and as one of the experts called to present on the "expert panel."
10. This is further reflected in the repeated failure of Refugee Law Project's attempts to identify a surgeon specialized in the needs of male survivors of conflict-related sexual violence.
11. Specific studies include Croatia and Bosnia (Loncar and Bretic 1995; Bassiouni and McCormick 1996); Sri Lanka (HRW 2013; Peel et al. 2000); DRC (Johnson et al. 2008); Liberia (Johnson et al. 2010); and Syria (IICISAR 2015).
12. Interview conducted by the author in Mbarara, September 2013.
13. It is important to note that the reproductive impacts may be intentional, raising questions about when such intent could be described as genocidal. In one case reported by the Commission of Inquiry into Syria, for example, the respondent described being told "we do this so you won't have children" as electric shocks were administered to his genitals (IICISAR 2015, annex IV, para. 11).

14. Other instances include a brother who was forced to have sex with his own sister, who subsequently gave birth to his child, and a young man who, as well as being raped anally himself, was forced to have sex with his aunt, who subsequently committed suicide rather than remain living in the same house (client interviews conducted by the author, Kampala, 2016).

15. *Prosecutor v. Ranko Cesic*, Case No. IT-95-10/1-S. 2007. Sentencing Judgment, paras. 13–14, 35, 107. March 11.

16. ICC Elements of Crimes, art. 7(1)(g)-6.

17. "Only 1 percent of U.S. fighter pilots accounted for nearly 40 percent of all enemy pilots shot down in World War II; the majority apparently did not shoot anyone down or even try to" (Grossman 1995, chap. 2).

18. Joanna Bourke's *Fear* provides many examples of the psychosomatic impacts of fear on soldiers, including incontinence, uncontrollable shaking, anorexia, etc. (Bourke 2005).

REFERENCES

Bassiouni, M. Cherif, and Marcia McCormick. 1996. *Sexual Violence: An Invisible Weapon of War in the Former Yugoslavia*. Chicago: International Human Rights Law Institute, DePaul University.

Belkin, Aaron. 2012. *Bring Me Men: Military Masculinity and the Benign Facade of American Empire, 1898–2001*. New York: Columbia University Press.

Bourke, Joanna. 2005. *Fear*. London: Virago.

Carlson, Eric Stener. 2006. "The Hidden Prevalence of Male Sexual Assault during War." *British Journal of Criminology* 46, no. 1: 16–25.

Carpenter, R. Charli. 2001. "Gender Theory in World Politics: Contributions of a Nonfeminist Standpoint?" *International Studies Review* 4, no. 3: 153–165.

Carpenter, R. Charli. 2003. "'Women and Children First': Gender, Norms, and Humanitarian Evacuation in the Balkans, 1995–95." *International Organization* 57, no. 4: 661–694.

Carpenter, R. Charli. 2005. "'Women, Children and Other Vulnerable Groups': Gender, Strategic Frames and the Protection of Civilians as a Transnational Issue." *International Studies Quarterly* 49, no. 2: 295–334.

Carver, Terrell, Molly Cochran, and Judith Squires. 1998. "Gendering Jones: Feminisms, IRs, Masculinities." *Review of International Studies* 24, no. 2: 283–297.

Dolan, Chris. 2014a. "Has Patriarchy Been Stealing the Feminists' Clothes? Conflict-Related Sexual Violence and UN Security Council Resolutions." *IDS Bulletin* 45, no. 1: 80–84.

Dolan, Chris. 2014b. "Into the Mainstream: Addressing Sexual Violence against Men and Boys in Conflict." *Overseas Development Institute* (May): 1–12.

Dolan, Chris. 2014c. "Letting Go of the Gender Binary: Charting New Pathways for Humanitarian Interventions on Gender-Based Violence." *International Review of the Red Cross* 96, no. 894: 485–501.

Dolan, Chris. 2014d. *Report of Workshop on Sexual Violence against Men*. New York: United Nations.

Engle, Karen. 2013. "The Grip of Sexual Violence: Reading United Nations Security Council Resolutions on Human Security." In *Rethinking Peacekeeping, Gender Equality and Collective Security*, edited by Gina Heathcote and Dianne Otto, 23–47. Basingstoke: Palgrave Macmillan UK.

Gabriel, R. A. 1987. *No More Heroes: Madness and Psychiatry in War*. New York: Hill and Wang.

Goetz, Ann Marie. 2014a. "Stopping Sexual Violence in Conflict Gender Politics in Foreign Policy." *Open Democracy*. www.opendemocracy.net/5050/anne-marie-goetz/stopping-sexual-violence-in-conflict-gender-politics-in-foreign-policy.

Goetz, Anne Marie. 2014b. "Preventing Violence against Women: A Sluggish Cascade?" *Open Democracy*. https://www.opendemocracy.net/5050/anne-marie-goetz/preventing-violence-against-women-sluggish-cascade.

Goldstein, Joshua. 2001. *War and Gender: How Gender Affects the War System and Vice-Versa*. Cambridge: Cambridge University Press.

Grossman, David A. 1995. *On Killing: The Psychological Cost of Learning to Kill in War and Society*. New York: Open Road Integrated Media.

Hennessey, Tom, and Felicity Gerry. 2012. *International Human Rights Law and Sexual Violence against Men in Conflict Zones*. London: Halsbury's Law Exchange.

Henry, Nicola. 2013. "The Fixation on Wartime Rape: Feminist Critique and International Criminal Law." *Social & Legal Studies* 1, no. 19: 93–111.

Howden, Daniel. 2016. "Refugees Caught Up in Child Prostitution in Athens." *News Deeply: Refugees Deeply*. https://www.newsdeeply.com/refugees/articles/2016/07/14/refugees-caught-up-in-child-prostitution-in-athens#.V4lIFLmHpHE.twitter.

Human Rights Watch (HRW). 2013. *"We Will Teach You a Lesson": Sexual Violence against Tamils by Sri Lankan Security Forces*. New York: Human Rights Watch.

Inter-Agency Standing Committee (IASC). 2015. *Guidelines for Integrating Gender-Based Violence Interventions in Humanitarian Action*. Geneva: IASC.

International Criminal Court (ICC). 2014. *Policy Paper on Sexual and Gender-Based Crimes*. The Hague: ICC Office of the Prosecutor.

Independent International Commission of Inquiry on the Syrian Arab Republic (IICISAR). 2015. *Ninth Report of the Independent International Commission of Inquiry on the Syrian Arab*. UN Doc A/HRC/28/69 (February 5).

Johnson, Kirsten, Jana Asher, Stephanie Rosborough, Amisha Raja, Rajesh Panjabi, Charles Beadling, and Lynn Lawry. 2008. "Association of Combatant Status and Sexual Violence with Health and Mental Health Outcomes in Postconflict Liberia." *JAMA: The Journal of the American Medical Association* 300, no. 6: 676–690.

Johnson, Kirsten, Jennifer Scott, Bigy Rughita, Michael Kisielewski, Jana Asher, Ricardo Ong, and Lynn Lawry. 2010. "Association of Sexual Violence and Human Rights Violations with Physical and Mental Health in Territories of the Eastern Democratic Republic of the Congo." *JAMA: The Journal of the American Medical Association* 304, no. 5: 553–562.

Jones, Adam. 1996. "Does 'Gender' Make the World Go Round? Feminist Critiques of International Relations." *Review of International Studies* 22, no. 4: 405–29.

Jones, Adam. 2000a. "Gendercide and Genocide." *Journal of Genocide Research* 2, no. 2: 185–211.

Leiby, Michele. "The Promise and Peril of Primary Documents: Documenting Wartime Sexual Violence in El Salvador and Peru." In *Understanding and Proving International Sex Crimes*, edited by Morten Bergsmo, Alf Butenschøn Skre, and Elisabeth J. Woods, 315–366. Berlin: Forum for International Criminal and Humanitarian Law.

Lewis, Dustin. 2009. "Unrecognized Victims: Sexual Violence against Men in Conflict Settings under International Law." *Wisconsin Journal of International Law* 27, no. 1: 1–49.

Loncar, Mladen, and Petra Bretic. 1995. *Characteristics of Sexual Abuse of Men during the War in the Republic of Croatia and Bosnia and Herzegovina*. Zagreb: Medical Centre for Human Rights.

Loncar, Mladen, Neven Henigsberg, and Pero Hrabac. 2010. "Mental Health Consequences in Men Exposed to Sexual Abuse during the War in Croatia and Bosnia." *Journal of Interpersonal Violence* 25, no. 2: 191–203.

Manivannan, Anjali. 2014. "Seeking Justice for Male Victims of Sexual Violence in Armed Conflict." *Journal of International Law and Politics* 46: 635–679.

Meagher, Robert Emmet. 2014. *Killing from the Inside Out: Moral Injury and Just War*. Eugene, OR: Cascade.

Moser, Caroline, and Fiona Clark, eds. 2001. *Victims, Perpetrators or Actors: Gender, Armed Conflict and Political Violence*. London: Zed Books.

Ongwech, Onen David. 2013. *Report on the 1st South-South Institute on Sexual Violence Against Men and Boys in Conflict and Displacement: Refugee Law Project*. Kampala: Refugee Law Project.

Onyango, Monica Adhiambo, and Karen Hampanda. 2011. "Social Constructions of Masculinity and Male Survivors of Wartime Sexual Violence: An Analytical Review." *International Journal of Sexual Health* 23, no. 4: 237–247.

Oosterhoff, Pauline, Prisca Zwanikken, and Evert Ketting. 2004. "Sexual Torture of Men in Croatia and Other Conflict Situations: An Open Secret." *Reproductive Health Matters* 12, no. 23: 68–77.

Oosterveld, Valerie. 2013. "Sexual Violence Directed against Men and Boys in Armed Conflict or Mass Atrocity: Adressing a Gendered Harm in International Criminal Tribunals." *Journal of International Law and International Relations* 10: 107–128.

Ormhaug, Christin, Helga Hernes, and Patrick Meier. 2009. *Armed Conflict Deaths Disaggregated by Gender*. Oslo: International Peace Research Institute.

Peel, Michael, Gill Hinshelwood, Duncan Forrest, and A. Mahtani. 2000. "The Sexual Abuse of Men in Detention in Sri Lanka." *Lancet* 355, no. 9220: 2069–2070.

Price, M., Gohdes, A., and Ball, P. 2014. *Updated Statistical Analysis of Documentation of Killings in the Syrian Arab Republic*. Los Angeles: Human Rights Data Analysis Group.

Refugee Law Project. 2015. "Men Can Be Raped Too." Refugee Law Project film. Posted November 16. http://refugeelawproject.org/component/allvideoshare/video/latest/men-can-be-raped-too.

Shephard, Ben H. 2003. *A War of Nerves: Soldiers and Psychiatrists in the Twentieth Century*. Cambridge, MA: Harvard University Press.

Sivakumaran, Sandesh. 2007. "Sexual Violence against Men in Armed Conflict." *The European Journal of International Law* 18, no. 2: 253–276.

Sivakumaran, Sandesh. 2010. "Lost in Translation: UN Responses to Sexual Violence against Men and Boys in Situations of Armed Conflict." *International Review of the Red Cross* 92, no. 877: 259–277.

Solangon, Sarah, and Preeti Patel. 2012. "Sexual Violence against Men in Countries Affected by Armed Conflict." *Conflict, Security & Development* 12, no. 4: 417–442.

Sooka, Yasmin. 2014. *An Unfinished War: Torture and Sexual Violence in Sri Lanka 2009–2014*. London: The Bar Human Rights Committee of England and Wales & The International Truth & Justice Project, Sri Lanka.

Spiegel, Paul, and Peter Salama. 2000. "War and Mortality in Kosovo 1998–99: An Epidemiological Testimony." *The Lancet* 355, no. 9222: 2204–2209.

Stemple, Lara, and Ilan H. Meyer. 2014. "The Sexual Victimization of Men in America: New Data Challenge Old Assumptions." *American Journal of Public Health* 104, no. 6: 1–8.

Steventon, Jessica. 2016. "'Less Than Human': Does Asylum System Harm Child Refugees' Mental Health?" *Open Democracy*. https://opendemocracy.net/child-refugee-mental-health-asylum-seeker-crisis.

Tickner, J. Ann. 2001. *Gendering World Politics: Issues and Approaches in a Post-Cold War Era*. New York: Columbia University Press.

United Kingdom Foreign and Commonwealth Office (UK-FCO). 2013. "Declaration on Preventing Sexual Violence in Conflict." UK Government. www.gov.uk/government/news/g8-declaration-on-preventing-sexual-violence-in-conflict.

Van der Kolk, Bessel. 2014. *The Body Keeps the Score: Mind, Brain and Body in the Transformation of Trauma*. New York: Penguin Books.

Walker, Jayne, John Archer, and Michelle Davies. 2005. "Effects of Male Rape on Psychological Functioning." *British Journal of Clinical Psychology* 44: 445–451.

Zarkov, Dubravka. 2007. *The Body of War: Media, Ethnicity, and Gender in the Break-up of Yugoslavia*. Durham, NC: Duke University Press.

PART II

THE SECURITY
COUNCIL'S
WPS AGENDA/
CONTEMPORARY
SURVEY

CHAPTER 8

....

WOMEN, PEACE, AND SECURITY

A Critical Analysis of the Security Council's Vision

....

DIANNE OTTO

THE Charter of the United Nations (UN Charter) makes forty-five references to the word "peace." In the vast majority of these references, peace is coupled with security—rather than with development or human rights—in the interdependent phrase "international peace and security." It is no surprise, then, that the Security Council continues this linkage in its Women, Peace, and Security (WPS) Agenda, which commenced in 2000 with the adoption of Security Council resolution 1325, the first of its thematic resolutions on WPS. In this critical analysis, I historicize the WPS Agenda and argue that long-standing feminist conceptions of positive peace—which at least some members of the coalition of nongovernmental organizations (NGOs) who lobbied the Security Council to adopt resolution 1325 had hoped to thereby promote—have become captive to the militarized security frame of the Council's operation.

The UN Charter includes a small number of other references to peace, which provide a starting point for reimagining peace outside the "frames of war" (Butler 2010) and creating the conditions of possibility for nonviolence rather than militarism, and an appreciation of the equal value of every life. In the preamble, the "peoples" of the United Nations commit to "liv[ing] together in peace with one another" (para. 2); among the listed purposes of the United Nations is the achievement of "universal peace" (art. 1(2)); UN membership is open to "peace-loving states" (art. 4(1)); and the "peaceful" or "pacific" settlement of disputes is prioritized (arts. 1(1), 2(3), 14, 33–38, 52(2), and 52(3)). These references accord with a feminist agenda for peace, the core components of which were identified a hundred years ago by the Hague Congress of Women (Hague Congress), held in 1915 during World War I, to develop strategies to bring the conflict to a speedy conclusion. The Congress participants outlined a wide-ranging vision of the measures they thought necessary to bring an end to "the madness and horror of war" and build a "permanent peace" (Costin 1982, 310; International

Congress of Women 1915). They established an International Committee of Women for Permanent Peace to pursue their goals, which was renamed the Women's International League for Peace and Freedom (WILPF) in 1919 (Rupp 1997). In 2000, WILPF played a leading role in persuading the Security Council to adopt resolution 1325, and the group remains actively involved in the NGO Working Group on Women, Peace and Security (NGO Working Group), which promotes the implementation of all the WPS resolutions.

While there is much to celebrate about the Security Council's WPS Agenda in terms of policy and institutional developments, admission into the inner sanctum of the Security Council's work has come at some cost to feminist goals (Otto 2010). One cost has been a softening of feminist opposition to war, evidenced by a shift in the focus of feminist peace advocates from strengthening the laws that make armed conflict illegal (*jus ad bellum*) to seeking to humanize the laws that govern the conduct of armed conflict (*jus in bello*); from aiming to end all wars to making wars safer for women. The idea that lawful justifications for the use of force might even be expanded to include protection of the rights of women has been endorsed and, while some of the long-term goals of feminist peace advocates appear to have been embraced, this engagement has proved to be largely "ritualistic," involving the formal acceptance of norms that are then undermined through inaction (Charlesworth and Larking 2015). Rather than brokering substantive change in the dominant ideas and practices of international peace and security that conceive of peace primarily in military terms, feminist arguments have been manipulated to support the expanding exercise of unaccountable power by the Security Council since the end of the Cold War and to legitimize its militaristic and carceral approach, in the name of protecting women, mostly from sexual violence, and promoting their rights. Far from reframing our obligations to each other in light of our shared (human) precariousness, as Judith Butler suggests (2010), the Security Council's approach to peace supports the continued expansion of the international market for arms, increased powers of state security institutions, and more coercive policing of expressions of sexuality and gender (Kapur 2013).

In order to critically examine the Security Council's vision of WPS and its impact on feminist aspirations for peace, I track the fortunes of three of the components of permanent peace identified a hundred years ago by the Hague Congress: calls for the equal participation of women and men in conflict-related decision-making; universal disarmament; and the adoption of measures to prevent the many adverse effects of war on women, especially sexual violence. In conclusion, I argue for rejecting conceptions of peace that are framed solely or largely in terms of militarized security and, instead, for reviving all of the elements of the permanent peace imagined by the Hague Congress in 1915, and building on their traces that can be found in the UN Charter. Feminist peace advocates need to rework these elements in light of present-day arrangements of power and contemporary feminist perspectives informed by queer, indigenous, and postcolonial politics, and think again about the wisdom of looking to the Security Council as a vehicle for promoting permanent peace.

TRACING THE AGENDA FOR PEACE
BROKERED BY THE HAGUE CONGRESS
OF WOMEN

Twenty interlinked resolutions adopted by the Hague Congress provide the backdrop for my critique of the Security Council's selective engagement with feminist ideas through its work on WPS. Although these resolutions bear many markings of their time, including maternalist assumptions about women's "natural" proclivity to peace, condescending references to colonized peoples (Rupp 1997, 75), and reliance on the system of "neutrality" that was then in place (Upcher 2014), they nonetheless outline some of the essential elements of an international system in which resort to arms becomes unthinkable. They propose that the right of conquest no longer be recognized, that international disputes be resolved by mediation or conciliation, that states assume obligations to exert social, economic, and moral pressure on any country that resorts to arms, that transfer of territory only occur with the consent of the men and women residing therein, that foreign policy be democratically determined through systems that ensure the equal representation of women and men, that children be educated in "ideals of constructive peace," and that a series of permanent international institutions be established in order to settle questions of law relating to war, to develop practical proposals for international cooperation among states, and to settle economic and commercial disputes (International Congress of Women 1915). The resolutions explicitly reject the approach of developing legal and customary conventions of law to "humanize" war (International Congress of Women 1915, resolution 2),[1] and focus squarely on transforming the laws of war so that the use of force can never be justified. The women who adopted them understood peace in the positive sense of creating global conditions in which all lives are valued and can be lived in dignity and equality, emphatically rejecting the idea that peace is merely the absence of war.

Eighty-five years later, still committed to the hope of a world without armed conflict, in which women enjoy equality with men, WILPF assembled a coalition of NGOs to persuade the Council to adopt a more feminist agenda, by individually lobbying its members and drafting an initial version of Security Council resolution 1325 (Gibbings 2004; Cohn, Kinsella, and Gibbings 2004). The resolution that was eventually adopted in October 2000 was widely welcomed by feminist scholars and activists, who described it as a "landmark resolution" representing a "new, daring, and ambitious strategy for anti-war feminists" (Cohn 2004, 3–4), a "watershed political framework" (Rehn and Sirleaf 2002, 3), and a "significant success story" for gender mainstreaming (True 2003, 373) (for discussion of all the WPS UNSCRs following on 1325, including their broad groupings under participation/empowerment and protection/sexual violence resolutions, see Goetz and Jenkins, Chapter 9, and Engle, Chapter 10, in this volume).

Among the Hague resolutions are three proposals that I will use to critically assess the Security Council's WPS Agenda. The first, evident in many of the 1915 resolutions and linked to the goals of the suffrage movement at the time, is the demand for the equal participation of women in conflict-related decision-making (International Congress of Women 1915, resolutions 3, 5, 8, 9, 14, 17, 18, and 19). The second proposal is the call for universal and complete disarmament and, as an initial step, nationalizing the arms industry in order to remove it from private ownership and profit-making (International Congress of Women 1915, resolution 12). The third is to halt the "odious wrongs" perpetrated against women during armed conflict, especially "the horrible violation of women that attends all war" (International Congress of Women 1915, resolution 2). These three concerns map onto the three core themes of the Security Council resolutions—participation, prevention, and protection—identified initially by WILPF (Cook 2009) and, since then, utilized by the Secretary-General to structure his annual reports on WPS (a fourth pillar—peace-building and recovery—is also reflected in Secretary-General's reports).

The Equal Participation
of Women and Men

From a historical perspective, it is clear that the Security Council's promotion of women's increased participation in conflict-related decision-making is far from novel. There are many earlier examples of international institutions formally endorsing this goal. They include the League of Nations in 1931 ("Spanish resolution," September 24, 1931), which called for increased cooperation with women's organizations in the "peace" work of the League, based on the assumption that this was an area for which women had a special affinity (Rupp 1997, 216–217). The disconnection between these repeated commitments and the continuing reality of women's exclusion from formal processes of international peace and security can aptly be described as a form of "ritualism," whereby states subscribe to institutionalized rituals that repeatedly affirm certain goals, despite having little or no commitment to their substantive realization—a term that has been used to describe UN human rights processes (Charlesworth and Larking 2015).

Yet despite the experience of ritualism, and the eventual realization that the achievement of voting rights for women in domestic politics was not going to make war an impossibility, feminist advocacy for peace has continued to call for the equal participation of women and men in decision-making associated with conflict resolution and peacemaking. Feminists have, however, disagreed about the justifications for this goal. Some argue for the importance of gender equality as a value in itself (Permanent Representative of Namibia to the UN 2000), while others, like the Hague Congress participants, take the view that women are "naturally" predisposed to peace and thus a stronger force (than men) for preventing war (di Leonardo 1985). Yet other feminists have sought to project a more social constructionist rationale for increasing women's participation—as bringing perspectives to bear on decision-making from outside the frame of military thinking because of their social experiences of inequality and disadvantage (Tickner 1992). However, even this approach does not entirely resolve the dilemma that has always haunted this aspect of the feminist agenda for peace: that mobilizing as women, to demand inclusion in peacemaking processes on the basis of women's present gendered experience, as mothers, as victims, and, more broadly, as marginalized from elite power structures, works against the feminist agenda for peace, which requires disrupting those same gender identities because they have served to legitimate militarism and women's inequality (Otto 2006).

Despite this conundrum, women's "increased" participation is promoted by all eight of the WPS resolutions, although the language of "equal" participation is undeniably patchy.[2] The hope of many feminists is that these references mark a break in the entrenched practice of "seeing" women in the context of armed conflict, if they appear at all, only as a vulnerable group needing, in particular, (military) protection from sexual violence.

In opening these opportunities for women's voices to be heard, and their agency as full participants in civil and political life to be recognized, it is important to examine exactly how, and for what purposes, the WPS resolutions anticipate that women's perspectives will be engaged. Will women's participation be limited to making "feminized" contributions, for example by assuming domesticating and pacifying roles in the immediate post-conflict period or contributing to the design of "civilized" rules and practices aimed at saving or protecting women in the Global South (Orford 2003)? Or will women be admitted as full and equal participants in conflict prevention and resolution, and in peace-building, able to question militarism and promote the positive peace envisaged by the women's peace movement? The rationale for women's participation offered in the sexual violence resolutions provides a salutary answer. For example, employing more women in peacekeeping military and police contingents is promoted instrumentally, as a way to provide better protection for local women and children against sexual violence (Security Council resolution 1820 [2008]) and to increase their willingness to report sexual violence (Security Council resolution 1960 [2010]), as if these are contributions that women are inherently predisposed to making (Simić 2014). Further, as Sheri Gibbings has found, even in their role as "peacemakers," women are severely constrained by the United Nations' discursive norms of speech and conduct, which make it impossible for critical, anti-imperial, and anti-militarist views to be "heard" within the terms of the Security Council's WPS Agenda (Gibbings 2011). This clearly makes it impossible for women's participation to make a difference to the Security Council's existing lexicon of peace.

Mimicking the earlier commitments to women's increased participation in promoting and securing international peace—whether in an empowered, protective, or instrumental sense—the Security Council's endorsement has so far proved ritualistic, with few tangible effects. Since the adoption of resolution 1325, the Security Council has repeatedly reiterated its frustration at the slow pace of change in this regard. Perhaps the problem lies in the top-down, imperial direction of promoting change through Security Council resolutions.

Moreover, the idea that the WPS resolutions provide new leverage for local women's peace and human rights organizations to insist on their inclusion in peace processes, and to craft their own peacemaking and peace-building projects, has also been questioned. There are certainly hopeful accounts of local activists managing to breathe life into the resolutions—to demand women's participation in peace negotiations (CARE International 2011), to ensure that women's rights are recognized in new constitutions (UN Secretary-General 2010), to promote the rights of widows (Owen 2011), to gain support for local women's projects (Bhagwan Rolls 2014), and to foster feminist reconceptualizations of security (McLeod 2011). Yet, on closer inspection, much of the activism by local women's organizations has involved raising awareness about the resolutions themselves, and lobbying governments and UN agencies to implement them, rather than using them as a means to support locally resonant community-controlled peace-building work outside the discursive limits of the resolutions (Farr 2011). A six-country field study, which sought women's views about the relevance and impact of resolution 1325, found that civil society organizations, despite security threats and few resources, "have been the engine behind the UNSCR 1325 movement," but noted "the pressure to adopt the women, peace and security agenda and be seen to be 'doing something,'" which has resulted in groups "basically repackaging existing programmes under the UNSCR 1325 umbrella . . . the substance [of which] is not necessarily well-adapted or tied to ongoing policy processes" (Anderlini 2010, 42–43). The pressure to deliver a "result" that is recognizable as such by the Security Council threatens to disempower women's grassroots movements for peace—the very subjects of feminism's transformative hope.

UNIVERSAL DISARMAMENT (PREVENTION)

In contrast to the ritualistic engagement of the Security Council with women's participation, the WPS resolutions are completely silent about the long-standing feminist goal of general disarmament. This silence is even more glaring when the numerous formal commitments to disarmament during the Cold War are recalled (see, e.g., UN General Assembly 1946). References to feminist support for disarmament have been made in many multilateral statements, including at the 1985 Nairobi World Conference on Women, where states called for women to actively support "the halting of the arms race, followed by arms reduction and the attainment of a general and complete disarmament" (World Conference 1985, para. 250) and, as recently as 1995, at the follow-up conference in Beijing, where states undertook to "work actively towards general and complete disarmament under strict and effective international control" and to foster a "culture of peace" (World Conference 1995, paras. 143(f)(i) and 146).

Yet by 2000, general disarmament did not even rate a mention in resolution 1325 or subsequent WPS resolutions. Even the Security Council's own responsibilities under the UN Charter, to establish systems to regulate weapons in order to ensure "the least diversion for armaments of the world's human and economic resources" (art. 26), are not referred to. The only references to disarmament in the WPS resolutions are in the context of disarmament, demobilization, and reintegration (DDR) of former combatants, which, while important, is disarmament on a very small scale. Three of the empowerment resolutions are concerned that women and girls who have been combatants, or otherwise directly associated with supporting armed forces and groups, have access to DDR programs, and that their "different needs" are addressed (e.g., Security Council resolution 1325 (2000), para. 13). Also, three of the sexual violence resolutions highlight the need for mechanisms that provide protection for women from violence in DDR processes, particularly sexual violence (e.g., Security Council resolution 1820 [2008], para. 10). One positive consequence of these provisions is that the large numbers of women and girls involved directly in providing services, supporting, and fighting alongside men and boys on the front lines has become increasingly apparent, which also serves to counter the stereotype that women do not participate actively in armed conflict. While it is important to ensure that women are included in DDR processes, the focus is on disarming individuals in the post-conflict environment, rather than preventing the use of arms in the first place and dismantling the burgeoning arms industry.

Even worse, instead of limiting the justifications for the use of arms, several of the WPS resolutions suggest that systematic violations of women's rights could provide a new trigger for the collective use of force, particularly where sexual violence is used as a "tactic of war." In three of the sexual violence resolutions, the Security Council expresses its "readiness," "where necessary," to take steps to address widespread or systematic sexual violence in situations on its agenda (resolutions 1820 [2008], 1888 [2009], and 1960 [2010]). Violations of women's rights have also been proffered as a new justification for military occupation.[3] As Gina Heathcote has argued, feminist ideas are being used by the Security Council to expand the legal justifications for the use of force (*jus ad bellum*) (Heathcote 2011)—a profoundly anti-feminist project. While it could be argued that, in this move, women's lives are more highly valued than previously—that their lives have come to matter and are thus "grievable" (Butler 2010)—the *quid pro quo* is that women are again conceived in protective terms and are "valued" for their chastity and honor, rather than for their humanity. Further, I am not convinced that finding new pretexts for justifying the use of force can ever be defended as valuing human life more fully.

Closely related to disarmament, in the sense of avoiding the use of force, is the goal of conflict prevention. However, prevention is given little attention in the WPS resolutions. While there are a number of references to the "important" and "vital" role of women in conflict prevention, they show all the signs of ritualism, appearing mostly in preambular paragraphs and lacking any substantive content. The few operative paragraphs that do refer to conflict prevention do not go beyond reiterating the need to invite women to participate in related discussions. All the other references to "prevention" are about the need for measures to prevent sexual violence—and most of these, by contrast, appear in operative paragraphs that give them substance, such as calling for the establishment of monitoring and reporting mechanisms (Security Council resolution 1888, para. 11;

resolution 2106, para. 6; resolution 2242, para. 10) and better prevention training for peacekeepers (resolution 2106, para. 14; resolution 2242, para. 9). This provides a dramatic illustration of the way that the WPS Agenda has served to refocus feminist attention from *jus ad bellum*, as a means of making armed conflict impossible, to making armed conflict safer for women (*jus in bello*)—as an end in itself.

Today, the amassing of nuclear and conventional weapons is the preferred means of establishing international peace and security. The adoption of the Arms Trade Treaty in 2013 concedes as much, setting out to eradicate only the "illicit" trade in arms in an effort to keep weapons out of the hands of "untrustworthy" actors who intend to use them for illegal purposes (UN General Assembly 2012). Clearly, it is necessary to reaffirm the earlier connection between disarmament and peace. Yet the Security Council is the least likely of all international institutions to revive this connection, given that its five permanent members are host to the world's largest arms producers. Other institutional locations must be found, or created, where thinking outside the frames of war is not only possible, but also can be actively fostered, and where transformative anti-militarist and anti-imperial cultures and practices of peace can be nurtured. The current work of the Human Rights Council toward drafting a Declaration on the Right to Peace (UN Human Rights Council 2013), which includes promotion of general disarmament (Bailliet and Larsen 2013), perhaps points to a better location, although member states are politically divided about the wisdom of this development (UN Watch 2014).

Measures to Prevent the Adverse Effects of War on Women (Protection)

Although the Hague Congress of Women rejected the idea that it was possible to humanize war through the development of *jus in bello*, and thereby protect women from harm, they nevertheless protested the adverse effects of armed conflict on women (International Congress of Women, resolution 2). These concerns, especially about sexual violence, were for many decades dismissed as unavoidable collateral damage and/or as the inevitable result of "boys being boys," enjoying the spoils of war, despite its ubiquity (Heineman 2011). The condemnation of sexual violence, both during armed conflict and in its aftermath, in all of the WPS resolutions presents a striking contrast. Further, that four of the resolutions are entirely devoted to addressing the problem attests to the inordinate focus—I would suggest panic (Otto 2007)—which sexual violence in armed conflict attracts today (see Engle, Chapter 10 in this volume). Even the empowerment resolutions employ their strongest language when it comes to condemning sexual violence, insisting that criminal justice must be applied and impunity must not be tolerated, shadowing successful feminist campaigns in international criminal law (Halley 2008). For example, resolution 1325 urges parties to armed conflict to take "special measures" to protect women and girls from gender-based violence (para.

10), and to end the impunity that attaches to perpetrators of war crimes, genocide, and crimes against humanity involving violence against women and girls (para. 11). Clearly, the Security Council is more at ease with casting women in a protective frame than with treating them as equal participants in peacemaking and peace-building. This protectionism serves to reinforce a general sense of the Security Council's (masculine) fortitude and dependability and provides reassurance about its commitment to protecting those vulnerable (feminized) civilians who need it, despite many indications to the contrary (Otto 2010).

While Security Council resolution 1325 urges the importance of addressing the broad band of "gender-based violence," all of the following resolutions concern themselves with the narrower category of "sexual violence." As Karen Engle has argued, this identifies sexual violence as the quintessential harm of war and deepens the sense of sexual panic (Engle 2014; Engle, Chapter 10 in this volume). The four resolutions that are concerned exclusively with sexual violence clearly support the view that the harm suffered is of the worst kind. They condemn the use of sexual violence not only as a "tactic of war," but also as an impediment to the restoration of international peace and security. According to Security Council resolution 1820 (2008), the horror of sexual harm even warrants "evacuation of women and children under imminent threat of sexual violence" (para. 3), which grants sexual violence victims a new position of privilege in communities affected by armed conflict. Their lives appear to have become lives that matter. But what purposes are being served by this heightened concern for some people's safety? What about the women facing imminent death from a non-sexual armed attack, or the men who are at imminent risk of sexual violence, or the children who need emergency medical treatment? Prioritizing the rescue of women and children who are at risk of sexual violence does a lot of symbolic work for the Security Council, providing further reassurance about its determination to protect women and children, despite its "masculinized" military methods of securing and maintaining peace. The panic about sexual violence also serves the larger interests of the Security Council's permanent members by diverting attention from the failure to attend to the underlying structural causes of armed conflict, in particular the inequitable distribution of global power and wealth, which continues to be reflected in poverty-stricken peacekeeping economies and the imposition of punishing free market economic systems by international economic institutions.

While many feminists applauded the Security Council's newfound concern with addressing sexual violence as a "historic achievement" (Human Rights Watch 2008) and a long overdue admission that sexual violence during armed conflict is a matter that falls within its purview (PeaceWomen 2008), others worry that the fixation on sexual violence has distilled the multiplicitous issues associated with women's experiences of armed conflict to the single issue of their sexual vulnerability (Heathcote 2011), reducing the broad agenda of Security Council resolution 1325 to the goal of making war safer for women, as if this were possible. Thus, engagement with the Security Council has shifted feminist attention from preventing war to attempting to ameliorate its adverse impacts on women. This development reflects a wider shift in anti-war activism, from concern with aggression to concern with "atrocity" (Moyn 2016). While the more recent empowerment resolutions work hard to make up some of the lost ground, demanding attention to improving women's socioeconomic conditions through, *inter alia*, access to education, justice, and basic health services (Security Council resolution 1889 [2009]), and affirming that "sustainable peace" requires a holistic approach that integrates political, security, development, human rights, the rule of law, and justice activities (Security Council resolution 2122 [2013]), the larger goal of making resort to armed force impossible has been lost in the panic about sexual violence and the focus on *jus in bello*.

CONCLUSION

In many respects, the Security Council's WPS Agenda has cemented the idea that securing international peace relies on military strength and securitized states. Feminist aspirations for permanent peace have been reduced to seeking women's participation in the decision-making structures of the existing frames of war, supporting disarmament only at the local level in post-conflict communities, and urging legal and practical reforms aimed at making armed conflict safer for women. This is not to deny the value of many of the hard-won achievements that have been made possible despite, more than because of, the Security Council's vision. Among these achievements I would include the new openings for women's participation, increased pressure to reduce conflict-related sexual violence, and long-overdue recognition of the importance of local women's projects aimed at peacemaking and peace-building. However, my argument is that, ultimately, these achievements are not enough—that the *quid pro quo* of the sacrifice of many components of the permanent peace that were identified by the Hague Congress in 1915 weighs heavily against feminist change. The result has been a weakening of feminist opposition to war, the solidification of protective stereotypes of women that lend support to military ways of thinking, and the loss of the hope for a world in which its "peoples" commit to "liv[ing] together in peace with one another" (UN Charter, preamble para. 2).

So, I return to the dilemma of gender that has always haunted feminist strategies for peace, and the importance of critically examining how gender is being engaged and what it is that women's increased participation in conflict and post-conflict decision-making is expected to achieve. I have argued elsewhere that the Security Council hopes thereby to improve its "gender legitimacy" and shore up support for its exercise of unaccountable power (Otto 2010). Building its social capital in this way relies heavily on the gendered paradigm that men fight wars in order to protect women (and children), and that women are naturally predisposed to peace. The sexual violence resolutions clearly reinforce these ideas, while the women's empowerment resolutions all slide into protectiveness as well (Otto 2009). Instead of promoting increased women's participation in the existing framework, feminist peace advocates need to expose the role that gendered ways of thinking play in framing armed conflict as inevitable, and to develop strategies that contest and disrupt such certainties. This means fully embracing gender as a social category and engaging men and other genders, as well as women, in the project of peace. Dichotomous conceptions of gender need to be jettisoned if security institutions are ever to demilitarize, and only then will it be possible for people of all gender identities to enjoy equal political participation in all of its senses. In the context of the WPS Agenda, men too must be engaged as peacemakers and recognized as potential victims of sexual violence, and peace must be conceived as a multi-gendered project, if the conservative moorings of biological determinism, which support the gendered grammars of war and peace, strength, and vulnerability, are ever to be dislodged.

In order to extricate the idea of peace from the frames of war, we need to disrupt the relentless certainties of militarized security and gender dichotomy that have stifled change and kept us locked in the perpetual violence of "dirty peace," justifying the production of ever more deadly weapons. We need to understand how to work against feminist ideas becoming bound up in global relations of inequitable power. We need to reframe peace as the creation of conditions that would make the response of violence unintelligible and nonsensical, drawing on all the resources at our disposal, including the rich history of feminist imaginaries of permanent peace, Third World visions of friendly relations, indigenous relations of harmony between people and land, and queer dreams of gender and sexual multiplicities. Engaging with the Security Council's work on WPS reminds us of the urgency of the task of creating conditions conducive to positive peace, as well as its complexity, even as this experience suggests that we think again about the wisdom of looking to the Security Council as a vehicle for promoting permanent peace.

NOTES

1. "This International Congress of Women opposes the assumption that women can be protected under conditions of modern warfare" (International Congress of Women 1915, resolution 2).
2. Apart from preambular references to women's equal participation in most of the WPS resolutions, only three resolutions make reference to equal participation in operative paragraphs: see S.C. Res. 1820, para. 12 (peace and security decision-making); S.C. Res. 1889, para. 19(c) (peace-building processes); S.C. Res. 2122, para. 7(c) (peace talks) and para. 8 (electoral processes).
3. See, for example, the reference to resolution 1325 in Security Council resolution 1483, the resolution adopted by the Security Council that provided belated endorsement to the invasion and occupation of Iraq by the United States and its allies in 2003.

REFERENCES

Anderlini, Sanam N. 2010. *What the Women Say: Participation and UNSCR 1325–A Case Study Assessment*. Washington, DC: International Civil Society Action Network and the MIT Center for International Legal Studies.

Bailliet, Cecilia M., and Kjetil Mujezinović Larsen. 2013. "Nordic Expert Consultation on the Right to Peace: Summary and Recommendations." *Nordic Journal of Human Rights* 31, no. 2: 262–278.

Bhagwan Rolls, Sharon. 2014. "Thinking Globally and Acting Locally: Linking Women, Peace and Security in the Pacific." In *Rethinking Peacekeeping, Gender Equality and Collective Security*, edited by Gina Heathcote and Dianne Otto, 118–130. London: Palgrave-Macmillan.

Butler, Judith. 2010. *Frames of War: When Is Life Grievable?*, 2nd ed. London: Verso.

CARE International. 2011. *From Resolution to Reality: Lessons Learned from Afghanistan, Nepal and Uganda on Women's Participation in Peacebuilding and Post-Conflict Governance*. London: CARE International.

Cohn, Carol. 2004. "Mainstreaming Gender in UN Security Policy: A Path to Political Transformation?" Boston Consortium on Gender, Security and Human Rights Working Paper No. 204, University of Massachusetts, Boston, MA.

Cohn, Carol, Helen Kinsella, and Sheri Gibbings. 2004. "Women, Peace and Security: Resolution 1325." *International Feminist Journal of Politics* 6, no. 1: 130–140.

Charlesworth, Hilary, and Emma Larking, eds. 2015. *Human Rights and the Universal Periodic Review: Rituals and Ritualism*. Cambridge: Cambridge University Press.

Cook, Sam. 2009. "Editorial." In *WILPF 1325 PeaceWomen E-News* 111. http://www.peace-women.org/assets/file/ENews/enews_issue111.pdf.

Costin, Lela B. 1982. "Feminism, Pacificism, Internationalism and the 1915 International Congress of Women." *Women's Studies International Forum* 5, no. 3: 301–315.

di Leonardo, Micaela. 1985. "Morals, Mothers and Militarism: Antimilitarism and Feminist Theory." Review of *Over Our Dead Bodies: Women against the Bomb*, edited by Dorothy Thompson; *Reweaving the Web of Life: Feminism and Nonviolence*, edited by Pam McAllister; and *Does Khaki Become You? The Militarisation of Women's Lives*, by Cynthia Enloe. *Feminist Studies* 11, no. 3: 599–617.

Engle, Karen. 2014. "The Grip of Sexual Violence: Reading UN Security Council Resolutions on Human Security." In *Rethinking Peacekeeping, Gender Equality and Collective Security*, edited by Gina Heathcote and Dianne Otto, 23–47. London: Palgrave-Macmillan.

Farr, Vanessa. 2011. "UNSCR 1325 and Women's Peace Activism in the Occupied Palestinian Territory." *International Feminist Journal of Politics* 13, no. 4: 539–556.

Gibbings, Sheri Lynn. 2004. "Governing Women, Governing Security: Governmentality, Gender-Mainstreaming and Women's Activism at the UN." Master's thesis, York University.

Gibbings, Sheri Lynn. 2011. "No Angry Women at the United Nations: Political Dreams and the Cultural Politics of United Nations Security Council Resolution 1325." *International Feminist Journal of Politics* 13, no. 4: 522–538.

Halley, Janet. 2008. "Rape at Rome: Feminist Interventions in the Criminalization of Sex-Related Violence in Positive International Criminal Law." *Michigan Journal of International Law* 30, no. 1: 1–123.

Heathcote, Gina. 2011. "Feminist Politics and the Use of Force: Theorising Feminist Action and Security Council Resolution 1325." *Socio-Legal Review* 7: 23–43.

Heineman, Elizabeth D., ed. 2011. *Sexual Violence in Conflict Zones from the Ancient World to the Era of Human Rights*. Philadelphia: University of Pennsylvania Press.

Kapur, Ratna. 2013. "Gender, Sovereignty and the Rise of a Sexual Security Regime in International Law and Postcolonial India." *Melbourne Journal of International Law* 14, no. 2: 317–345.

McLeod, Laura. 2011. "Configurations of Post-Conflict: Impacts of Representations of Conflict and Post-Conflict upon the (Political) Translations of Gender Security within UNSCR 1325." *International Feminist Journal of Politics* 13, no. 4: 594–611.

Moyn, Samuel. 2016. "What Are the Political Aims of Anti-Impunity?" In *Anti-Impunity and the Human Rights Agenda*, edited by Karen Engle, Zinaida Miller, and Dennis Davis, 68–94. Cambridge: Cambridge University Press.

Orford, Anne. 2003. *Reading Humanitarian Intervention: Human Rights and the Use of Force in International Law*. Cambridge: Cambridge University Press.

Otto, Dianne. 2006. "A Sign of 'Weakness'? Disrupting Gender Certainties in the Implementation of Security Council Resolution 1325." *Michigan Journal of Gender & Law* 13, no. 1: 113–175.

Otto, Dianne. 2007. "Making Sense of Zero Tolerance Policies in Peacekeeping Sexual Economies." In *Sexuality and the Law: Feminist Engagements*, edited by Vanessa Munro and Carl F. Stychin, 259–282. New York: Routledge-Cavendish.

Otto, Dianne. 2009. "The Exile of Inclusion: Reflections on Gender Issues in International Law over the Last Decade." *Melbourne Journal of International Law* 10, no. 1: 11–26.

Otto, Dianne. 2010. "The Security Council's Alliance of Gender Legitimacy: The Symbolic Capital of Resolution 1325" In *Fault Lines of International Legitimacy*, edited by Hilary Charlesworth and Jean-Marc Coicaud, 239–276. New York: Cambridge University Press.

Owen, Margaret. 2011. "Widowhood Issues in the Context of United Nations Security Council Resolution 1325." *International Feminist Journal of Politics* 13, no. 4: 616–622.

PeaceWomen. 2008. "Security Council Resolution 1820: A Move to End Sexual Violence in Conflict." In *1325 PeaceWomen E-Newsletter* 102: 4–7.

Permanent Representative of Namibia to the UN. 2000. Letter dated July 12, 2000, from the Permanent Representative of Namibia to the United Nations, Addressed to the Secretary-General. UN Doc. A/55/138–S/2000/693 (May 31).

Rehn, Elizabeth, and Ellen Johnson Sirleaf. 2002. *Women, War and Peace: The Independent Experts' Assessment on the Impact of Armed Conflict on Women and Women's Role in Peace-Building*. New York: UNIFEM.

International Congress of Women. 1915. "Resolutions Adopted by the International Congress of Women at The Hague, 1 May, 1915." In *Women at the Hague: The International Congress of Women and Its Results*, edited by Jane Addams, Emily G. Balch, and Alice Hamilton, 123–130. New York: Macmillan.

Rupp, Leila J. 1997. *Worlds of Women: The Making of an International Women's Movement*. Princeton, NJ: Princeton University Press.

Simić, Olivera. 2014. "Increasing Women's Presence in Peacekeeping Operations: The Rationales and Realities of 'Gender Balance.'" In *Rethinking Peacekeeping, Gender Equality and Collective Security*, edited by Gina Heathcote and Dianne Otto, 185–199. London: Palgrave-Macmillan.

Tickner, J. Ann. 1992. *Gender in International Relations: Feminist Perspectives on Achieving Global Security*. New York: Columbia University Press.

True, Jacqui. 2003. "Mainstreaming Gender in Global Public Policy." *International Feminist Journal of Politics* 5, no. 3: 368–396.

Human Rights Watch. 2008. "UN: Finally, a Step Toward Confronting Rape in War." June 18. https://www.hrw.org/news/2008/06/18/un-finally-step-toward-confronting-rape-war.

UN General Assembly. 1946. G.A. Res. 41 (I). Principles Governing the General Regulation and Reduction of Armaments (December 14).

UN General Assembly. 2012. G.A. Res. 67/234. The Arms Trade Treaty (December 24).

UN Human Rights Council. 2013. Res. 23/16. UN Doc. A/HRC/RES/23/16 (June 24).

UN Secretary-General. 2010. *Women's Participation in Peacebuilding*. UN Doc. A/65/354–S/2010/446 (September 7).

UN Watch. 2014. "The Proliferation of 'Human Rights': A Dictator's Best Friend." *UN Watch*. July 4. http://blog.unwatch.org/index.php/category/right-to-peace/.

Upcher, James. 2014. "Collective Security and Sovereign Equality: The Debates over the Discriminating Concept of War and the Limits of Non-Participation." Paper presented at the 22nd annual ANZSIL Conference, Canberra, Australian Capital Territory (July 3–5).

World Conference on Women. 1995. *Report of the Fourth World Conference on Women*, UN Doc. A/CONF.177/20 (October 17).

World Conference to Review and Appraise the Achievements of the United Nations Decade for Women: Equality, Development and Peace (World Conference). 1985. *Nairobi Forward-Looking Strategies for the Advancement of Women*. UN Doc. A/CONF.116/28/Rev. (July 26).

CHAPTER 9

....

PARTICIPATION
AND PROTECTION

*Security Council Dynamics, Bureaucratic
Politics, and the Evolution of the Women,
Peace, and Security Agenda*

....

ANNE MARIE GOETZ AND ROB JENKINS

THIS chapter analyzes the political and institutional factors that have shaped the implementation of UN Security Council resolution (UNSCR) 1325, on Women, Peace, and Security (WPS), since its passage in October 2000. The focus is on differing levels of political emphasis and financial resources assigned to two different elements of the WPS Agenda—participation and protection—as it has evolved since then.

UNSCR 1325 articulated two fundamental principles: (1) that gender inequality (in social, economic, and political power) is linked to insecurity; and (2) that successfully preventing, resolving, and rebuilding after conflict requires both women's participation and the incorporation of gender-equality concerns, in local, national, and international processes. Practice has rarely conformed to either principle. First, women remain seriously underrepresented in peace negotiations and post-conflict political settlements, and there are few opportunities for women's organizations and gender experts to influence mediation processes or post-conflict planning bodies. International efforts at state-(re)building rarely strike at the legal and institutional foundations of gender inequality. This is evident in chronic underfunding for public action to increase women's economic security, whether through stand-alone programs or gender-aware administrative provisions. Service-delivery priorities and modalities rarely address women's post-conflict needs, and there is insufficient attention to gender-specific crimes or the gendered impacts of crimes in the mandates, staffing, and operational practices of transitional justice institutions.

A second component of the WPS Agenda, less tied to the imperative of women's *participation*, concerns women's *protection* in fragile, conflict, and post-conflict situations.

The focus here has been war's consequences for women's insecurity, not how manifestations of gender inequality themselves may contribute to conflict propensity. The energy of donor governments and UN entities engaged in peace and security work has been targeted at reducing the rate at which women are subjected to violations of physical integrity as defined under international humanitarian and human rights law.

In contrast to the Security Council's halting progress in ensuring that women's organizations and gender experts are regularly consulted in UN-mediated peace processes, the Council has in recent years responded robustly to the imperative of protecting women from conflict-related sexual violence (CRSV) and responding to its aftermath. The Council's country-specific instructions to UN missions are more specific on CRSV than on participation (UN Women 2015, chap. 11). Monitoring and accountability systems ensure that alleged perpetrators of CRSV are named and sanctioned, and a system champion, the Special Representative of the Secretary-General on Sexual Violence in Conflict (SRSG-SVC), has been endowed with staff and resources to keep the issue on the radar of international bodies (operational and intergovernmental) within and beyond the United Nations. UN peacekeepers receive training in the prevention of sexual violence, and UN mediators are encouraged to ensure that it is addressed in various types of peace agreements (Jenkins and Goetz 2010).

A combination of political and institutional factors helps to explain differences in implementation between these "participation" and "protection" elements of the WPS Agenda. At the political level, the opposition to the participation agenda is part of a backlash from mainly developing country member-states against using donor-funded post-conflict state-building to advance what they consider Western agendas of social transformation. At the bureaucratic level, issues of women's participation in peacebuilding have lacked a powerful champion within the UN system, as well as functional accountability systems to ensure that entities charged with advancing women's participation have sufficient incentive to fulfill their responsibilities. In this chapter we review the divergence between participation and protection in the WPS resolutions, show how this reflects political differences between Security Council members, and how the divergence is being institutionalized within the UN bureaucracy.

PARTICIPATION AND PROTECTION

UNSCR 1325 does not specify what the proportion of women among peace and security decision-makers should be, or how to achieve that goal. Nor does it say what a "gender perspective" entails. UNSCR 1325 was in part driven by gender essentialism, in which women are conceived of as inherently peaceful (Otto 2006). Essentialist arguments were subsequently backed with evidence to support the suggestion that women make a positive difference to the project of peace-building. For instance, quantitative studies have found that peace processes involving civil society last longer than closed, exclusive processes (Nilsson 2012). Peace processes that involve women, and agreements that include provisions for women's post-conflict political participation, last even longer (O'Reilly, Sullebhain, and Paffenholz 2015; Stone 2014). However, the precise direction and dynamics of causality between women's participation, gender equality, and peace remain unclear. In general, it appears that basic security, the rule of law, and functioning governance institutions are prerequisites for building gender equality, not the other way around.

By 2005, it was apparent that neither the Council nor the United Nations' lead peace and security departments were taking UNSCR 1325 seriously. Although on other thematic issues on the Council's regular agenda—refugees, protecting civilians, and Children and Armed Conflict (CAAC)—the initial, broadly defined "breakthrough" resolutions were swiftly followed by additional resolutions establishing institutional mechanisms for implementation and accountability, this was not true for 1325. Indeed, in 2005, less than a third of relevant Security Council resolutions that year (on country situations, sanctions regimes, etc.) even mentioned 1325, let alone included implementation instructions (Butler, Mader, and Kean 2010). While the Department of Peacekeeping Operations (DPKO) had deployed senior gender advisors to some UN missions, it still lacked standardized training for peacekeepers, or guidance on how to improve the security environment for women in conflict situations. The Department of Political Affairs (DPA), which supports conflict resolution and post-conflict elections, relied primarily on a loose network of "gender focal points," whose responsibilities for women's participation was an add-on to their regular jobs.

The deficit of accountability mechanisms linked to the WPS Agenda was thrown into sharp relief when evidence of the lack of international response to the exceptionally high levels of sexual violence in conflicts in the Democratic Republic of Congo (DRC) and Darfur triggered condemnation from observers (Lewis 2007). Lacking a core institution with the mandate or operational capacity to address this issue, the UN treated CRSV as a humanitarian problem, addressed only after attacks had taken place, not as a feature of fighting, meriting a tactical response. In 2007 a group of mid-level bureaucrats from several UN agencies formed a coalition (eventually including twelve UN entities) called UN Action Against Sexual Violence in Conflict. Among other things, it encouraged DPKO to charge peacekeepers with preventing sexual violence. It also pressed DPA to encourage greater attention to CRSV in internationally mediated peace processes (UNIFEM et al. 2009).

UN Action sought to reframe CRSV as a tactic of warfare, not an unfortunate but inevitable byproduct of war. When viewed as a tactic, CRSV could be met with preventive deployments and other strategies; command responsibility could be invoked in seeking prosecutions; CRSV could be identified as a prohibited act in ceasefire agreements; and measures could be taken to address its long-term consequences. In early 2008, it suddenly seemed possible to promote a new Security Council resolution built around this understanding of CRSV. The initial draft came from the UK and US missions, with support from within the United Nations and from prominent civil society networks. UNSCR 1820, passed in April 2008, enumerated Council, UN, and member-state responsibilities for preventing and responding to "widespread or systematic sexual violence in conflict."

After UNSCR 1820 was passed, further resolutions on CRSV came relatively quickly, creating the kinds of implementation and accountability mechanisms that were still lacking with respect to the women's-participation/gender-perspective commitments specified in UNSCR 1325. UNSCR 1888 (2009) created the office of the SRSG-SVC. UNSCR 1960 (2010) empowered the SRSG to monitor conflicts worldwide and maintain an annually updated list of warring parties credibly suspected of engaging in CRSV to be presented to the Security Council. After the United Kingdom's Foreign Secretary made CRSV a personal priority in 2012, UNSCR 2106 (2013) was passed, addressing impunity and other concerns. Since then, CRSV has been the main focus of Council instructions to peacekeeping missions, crowding out other issues faced by conflict-affected women. Statements by Council members in WPS debates increasingly focused on CRSV (e.g., Gasana 2013).

The participation agenda had not entirely disappeared, and indeed a reaction against the over-focus on sexual violence had been developing momentum. UNSCR 1889 (2009) presented by Vietnam called for improved responses to women's needs for basic public services, economic security, and access to decision-making. UNSCR 2122 (2013) urged improved reporting from UN field missions on women's participation in elections and greater member-state support to women's organizations in conflict situations. Other proposals—a requirement that newly deployed UN envoys establish consultations with women's organizations within thirty days, or that gender quotas in post-conflict elections be regularly advocated—were dropped during the 2122 negotiations because of a view, shared by some member states and DPA, that the idiosyncrasies of conflict situations militate against imposing formal participation requirements on mediators or governments. Another "participation" resolution, 2242, which passed on October 13, 2015, while falling short of establishing mandatory procedures to ensure women's participation in peace or recovery processes, laid the ground for an oversight mechanism to track the Council's performance in this area, an informal working group on WPS, which could not only ensure consistent Council responses to abuses of women's rights, but also spur it to promote women's engagement in conflict resolution and recovery.

COUNCIL DYNAMICS AND THE WOMEN, PEACE, AND SECURITY AGENDA

The implementation of the "participation" component of the WPS resolutions is extremely sensitive to existing divisions in the Council between members that favor a broader "human security" approach to peacebuilding, and those seeking to minimize the scope of external influence on the choices facing post-conflict authorities. By contrast, the "protection" component is widely regarded as more firmly within the Council's mandate. By linking peacebuilding with the long-term project of gender equality, UNSCR 1325 could be understood to implicate the Council in a major project of social change. As a result, some Council members have criticized what they regard as Council "mission creep" into "developmental" (and even cultural) matters. During the annual Open Debate on UNSCR 1325, Russia and China have regularly reminded the Council that the Commission on the Status of Women, the Economic and Social Council, and other bodies are more appropriate forums for discussing women's rights and empowerment. They are joined periodically by non-permanent Council members, including many non-aligned states and the G77, who consider women's empowerment a development or human rights issue, not a matter of international peace and security. This group includes the most vocal advocates of Security Council reform—notably India, Brazil, and South Africa—all of which seek permanent membership.

This concern is linked to the broader worry that the Security Council will use new human rights–related doctrines to expand its mandate and, potentially, justify military intervention. The Council's 2011 authorization of air strikes in Libya was a major influence on this thinking. This intervention invoked the international community's "responsibility to protect" and was subsequently seen by Council members such as India as having transformed into a mission to effect "regime change"—that is, to overthrow Libyan leader Muammar Gaddafi. India and other countries expressed outrage at this turn of events. This sense of betrayal spilled over into debates over matters such as the Council's approach to the WPS Agenda.

Russia, China, and other Council members from the G77 have long resisted creating anything that might resemble an accountability mechanism for ensuring compliance with UNSCR 1325. However, UNSCR 1889 (2009), perhaps because it was sponsored by Vietnam, a country with impeccable anti-imperialist credentials, did call for the UN system to develop a set of statistical indicators to track the implementation of WPS commitments (see Castillo Díaz and Cueva Beteta, Chapter 14 in this volume). As a result, since 2010, the Secretary-General's annual 1325 report to the Council has included data that highlights trends in, for instance, the number of women in peace processes, the extent to which peacekeeping operations adopt measures to improve the security environment for women, and the degree to which national human rights bodies address conflict-related crimes against women. Each step on the gradual path toward institutionalizing this feature of the annual report has been fiercely resisted by G77 states. For instance, during 2012, when India and Pakistan both served on the Council, the two countries displayed unusual diplomatic unity in opposing (unsuccessfully) the further development of these indicators.

An important source of information regarding the Council's commitment to the protection and participation aspects of WPS is the instructions or "mandates" it issues to UN missions. Mandated actions for UN missions determine staffing and funding decisions and affect the balance between protection and participation on the ground. In principle, the content of these mission-specific resolutions are informed primarily by the regular reports to the Council from UN missions that contain recommendations for UN actions. One analysis of the mission reports to the Council found that less than 18 percent of those issued between 2000 and 2003 made multiple references to gender issues, and when they did, women were rarely mentioned as "potential dynamic actors," as opposed to victims of violence (OSAGI 2003). By 2013, according to "Security Council Report" (SCR), an NGO that analyzes the Security Council, references to gender issues were found in most reports to the Council, though nearly 40 percent of these were non-substantive mentions of "women and girls" (SCR 2014). Only one-third of UN field mission reports to the Council in 2013 contained a specific dedicated section on gender issues. Since the passage of the first resolution on sexual violence in 2008, however, these reports contain far more detail on sexual violence than on women's political participation and engagement in post-conflict priority-setting (SCR 2014).

Most country-specific resolutions passed by the Security Council—of which there were thirty in 2013—mention at least one WPS resolution in their preambular paragraphs. What matters, however, are the operational paragraphs (OPs). These contain specific instructions that trigger staff-appointment and funding-allocation mechanisms. Three patterns marked the Council's 2013 resolutions (SCR 2014). First, operational instructions relating to gender issues increasingly, often exclusively, address sexual violence. Second, when resolutions do mention women's participation as a mission responsibility, concrete instructions are noticeably absent. Third, instructions on gender issues are sometimes missing completely or are included inconsistently. The 2013 mission mandate renewals for Abyei (Sudan and South Sudan) and Iraq made no mention of women's participation in their operational paragraphs (SCR 2014).

Even when mandates on women's participation are substantive and specific, the Security Council rarely follows up with close scrutiny of the mission's performance to determine whether these instructions were carried out. For instance, the April 2013 resolution 2100 for Mali instructs the UN mission (MINUSMA) to work with the Malian government to ensure women's meaningful participation in the upcoming national political dialogue and elections. Despite MINUSMA's many implementation shortcomings on WPS issues, Security Council members failed to question UN officials about them in Council meetings.[1] This failure to monitor the implementation of mandated actions in this specific area sends a signal that UN missions can safely ignore this issue because a lack of action will be neither noted nor condemned.

The 2014–2015 period saw a shift at least at the rhetorical level in the attention the Council devoted to the issue of women's participation. In part, this came from the focus on issues of participation highlighted in negotiations over resolutions 2122 (2013) and 2242 (2015). In part, it was a response to international debates on women's participation by women's groups to mark the fifteenth anniversary of the passage of resolution 1325 in October 2015. While a detailed analysis of this heightened attention to participation on recent Council actions has not yet been conducted, we would predict an improvement in the number and quality of instructions regarding women's participation in elections and in governance reform processes in mission contexts since the end of 2013. This is particularly likely as the composition of the Council in 2014 and 2015 included countries that made a point of insisting on attention to women's rights—countries like Australia, Chile, Argentina, South Korea, and Spain. Unfortunately, the incoming non-permanent members in 2016 included fewer gender-equality champions and some that have aligned themselves to conservative negotiating blocs at the United Nations, such as Egypt and Malaysia.[2]

If women's participation is not to be held hostage to the random chance of a favorable alignment of gender-equality champions on the Council, it is critical that within the UN system itself there is clear support for the women's participation agenda and consistent supply of relevant information on which the Council can base its instructions to missions. However, the flow of data and analysis to the Council on the full range of issues relevant to implementing the WPS resolutions is remarkably uneven. This reflects considerable variation in institutional investment in WPS capacities at UN headquarters, where the leading peace and security institutions—notably DPA and DPKO—have few incentives to prioritize gender issues, and in the field, where the positioning and professional background of gender advisors in UN missions, whatever form their deployment takes, are often inadequate to ensure the collection of necessary data, the production of high-quality gender and conflict analyses, or the delivery of critical information to the Council.

BUREAUCRATIC POLITICS AND THE UN SYSTEM

The analytical and operational capacity of UN bodies with a mandate to promote women's empowerment is of central importance to the implementation prospects of Security Council WPS resolutions, and helps explain the tension between their protection and participation elements. UN system entities have a strong interest in providing data, analysis, and recommendations for actions to Security Council members. Doing so can help to sustain international attention to the group, process, or issue in question (e.g., refugees, children, mediation, the environment), and can validate the work of the entity in question, thus ensuring donor support and inclusion in key policymaking forums.

However, providing these inputs is a challenge for some UN entities, particularly agencies, funds, and programs that operate outside the UN secretariat. DPKO and DPA are the key Secretariat entities on peace and security: DPKO coordinates and manages UN peacekeeping missions and delivers assessments from these missions to the Council of threats of conflict escalation or prospects for resolution and mission drawdown; DPA conducts analytical work on country situations (including technical assessment missions to support post-conflict elections) and provides experts—including mediators—to support conflict-resolution efforts. Most UN agencies, by contrast, are not nearly as well structured to support the Security Council's normative and operational work, focusing instead on country-level programming. One constraint on their capacity to provide objective information to the Council is that they are governed by executive boards composed of UN member states that prefer not to see information about their country's performance aired in intergovernmental forums.

This perverse institutional incentive led the Security Council to create specialized reporting positions (SRSGs) on specific abuses, including on Children and Armed

Conflict in 1999, and a decade later, on Sexual Violence in Conflict (SVC). Offices for these SRSGs monitor and report on abuses and brief the Council periodically. A lesser-known function is to support the inclusion of mandate language in country resolutions so that UN missions have instructions to take action to prevent atrocities. There is no UN entity providing the same "service" to the Council on issues of women's participation and empowerment, whether in terms of simply providing text, or providing valuable political analysis, data, and arguments to support the case for women's inclusion. Up to 2010 there was no agency dedicated to advancing the rights of women equipped with the same resources, or mandate to provide services ranging from advocacy to humanitarian relief to long-term development assistance, as for instance UNICEF has enjoyed in its work on behalf of children. This was precisely the rationale for the creation of the UN Entity for Gender Equality and Women's Empowerment (UN Women) in mid-2010. UN Women has the same status as other major UN agencies—its chief executive is an Under Secretary-General who participates in all of the UN's top decision-making forums. But UN Women lacks adequate funding—falling far short of the estimated minimum half billion dollars needed to meet its mandate—and the kind of field presence that can make a difference on the ground (Bunting 2011).

UN Women's founding mandate provides for the organization to inherit the mandates of its precursor entities, but these were relatively weak on peace and security—1325, for instance, and UN Women's relationship to the Security Council are not mentioned in its founding General Assembly resolution (United Nations 2010). UN Women set out to concretize its mandate on WPS via country-level programming to support women's peace organizations and to ensure that gender issues were addressed in transitional justice, security sector reform, and post-conflict electoral processes. It also worked with OHCHR to add WPS to the CEDAW framework, supporting the consultations and production of draft text for General Recommendation 30 (2013) on "Women in Conflict Prevention, Conflict and Post-Conflict Situations" (CEDAW 2013; Swaine and O'Rourke 2015).

Most striking was an increasingly ambitious engagement with the Security Council itself, via UN Women's annual responsibility to draft the Secretary-General's report to the Council on women and peace and security. This was used strategically to recommend priority actions to advance women's participation (many of which are included in resolutions 2122 and 2242) and to intensify the Council's focus on women's voice in conflict resolution, for instance through securing invitations by the Council for briefings from the UN Women executive director. Staff of UN Women's small "Peace and Security" section also functioned as the Secretariat for the production of the 2015 Global Study on the implementation of 1325 (which was called for in resolution 2122). And these same individuals identified the political opening provided by the fifteenth anniversary of resolution 1325 to insert a Council working group on WPS in the draft of resolution 2242. This is an institutional innovation, with the potential to balance the protection and participation elements of the WPS Agenda. The working group will be "informal," which means it will have much more flexibility than the Council's formal working groups on sanctions against regimes or on thematic issues such as Children and Armed Conflict or Conflict Prevention in Africa. While it will lack authority to *require* (as opposed to *recommend*) Council actions, it will be free to bring a wide range of information on WPS to the Council's attention, information not subject to the legal evidentiary requirements that circumscribe the knowledge base and actions open to other working groups.

UN Women's limited funding and thin field presence means that it has not been able to systematically to engage with the Security Council to the extent needed to ensure consistency or timeliness in the information base on which country-specific Council recommendations are made. UN Women also still lacks the ability to provide the direct service to Security Council members offered by the Office of the SRSG on SVC—that is, to offer on a routine basis precise, carefully formulated language (and justifications) for instructions to be contained within Council mission mandate renewals.

While UN Women is an obvious actor to offer gender-relevant political analysis to the Council, it lacks the field presence to provide the gender advisors in peacekeeping and political missions with useful intelligence to feed into regular reporting to the Council. The Department of Political Affairs (DPA), by contrast, is much better positioned to generate data on women's engagement in conflict resolution and recovery. DPA's country desk officers conduct analyses of "fragile" situations; its officials and special envoys convene national dialogue and peace processes; and its Electoral Assistance Division (EAD) draws on the considerable expertise of its regional missions and (where present) country-level political missions to assist post-conflict countries in organizing elections. Despite this wide-ranging remit, DPA has never provided the Security Council with a dedicated briefing on women's role in preventing, resolving, and recovering from conflict, not even in the now defunct periodic "horizon-scanning" briefings (introduced in 2011), in which the Under Secretary-General for Political Affairs provided the Council with conflict trend analysis on topics such as elections in Africa, concerns with instability, or power-sharing mechanisms.

Yet, DPA has power within the system to avoid taking action on agenda items that it deems of lesser priority, and it has clearly signaled that this is the case with regard to gender. Beyond a lack of leadership commitment, institutional design and culture explain why gender issues have received such low prioritization within DPA. DPA's gender unit is not located in the core areas of country-specific political analysis (the country desks under the regional divisions), but in its peripheral Mediation Support Unit, and is not funded by its core budget. Its gender policy formulation relies, to an unusually large extent, on inputs from external consultants on non-permanent contracts, most of whom face few incentives for engaging in the difficult task of pressing upper management for a more robust approach.

While we have focused here on the deficit in gender and conflict analysis to broaden Council attention beyond issues such as sexual violence, it is nested within a broader crisis in the quality of political analysis of conflict situations within the United Nations. This issue rose to international concern in 2015, where the low capacity of the UN to identify both spoilers and social forces supportive of peace-building in UN mission contexts was identified in two massive investigations as a major reason for the high failure rate of peace-building efforts. In *Uniting Our Strengths for Peace,* the much-anticipated report of the High-Level Independent Panel on United Nations Peace Operations (2015b), a key recommendation is to strengthen the United Nations' conflict and political analysis capacity. Astonishingly, this report's political analysis section does not address the need to incorporate an analytical capability on gender issues in conflict contexts (Goetz and Jenkins 2015). A second major assessment, the 2015 Peacebuilding Architecture Review, similarly neglects this issue (Goetz and Jenkins 2015; UN Advisory Group 2015a).

Both reports do, however, mention the need to improve the performance of gender advisors in field missions, who are frequently marginalized from mission decision-making. However, while these two reports mention UN Women's potential role in building field-mission capacity in this area, they remain vague about how UN Women, puny in resources and institutional clout in relation to DPA and DPKO, might achieve this. During inter-agency consultations to input to the peace operations review in early 2015, UN Women suggested that this could be accomplished by adopting a similar model used by the Office of the High Commissioner for Human Rights (OHCHR), but adapted so that UN Women would support the recruitment of gender expertise in the missions, and provide technical support to the experts as needed in the areas of strategic assessment, planning, design, benchmark creation, deployment, implementation, and evaluation, but with a single line of accountability to the head of mission and no budgetary implications (UN Women 2015). However, the suggestion was met with considerable resistance, leaving UN Women, the main interested party, on its own to handle this difficult negotiation for improved collaboration with DPA and DPKO.

Conclusion

The differing levels of enthusiasm with which two aspects of the WPS Agenda (women's protection and participation) have been implemented reflect trends in the domains of both bureaucratic and intergovernmental politics. In terms of bureaucratic politics—within and across international organizations—a key factor that helps to explain the relative weakness of efforts to institutionalize the participation agenda is the performance of DPA, the UN lead on mediation and post-conflict elections, two critical elements of the participation agenda. DPA's institutional commitment to women's participation in peace processes or post-conflict elections is uneven, judging from outcomes, but is hard to assess, because the secretive nature of mediated peace talks, or of discussions with governments about the design of their electoral systems, makes it difficult to monitor DPA's actions. A lack of institutional transparency, along with resistance to UN Women's efforts to improve coherence and coordination on these matters within the UN, continues to have an adverse effect on the prospects for accountability among the actors responsible for delivering on the promise of UNSCR 1325 (Goetz and Jenkins 2016).

At the intergovernmental level, Security Council composition determines whether it invests as much in women's participation as in protection. Even when Council composition includes gender-equality champions, it is limited in the extent to which it can craft detailed instructions on women's participation in elections, or in transitional justice measures, or in security sector reform, because of the uneven quality and quantity of useful information on gender and conflict dynamics locally. More broadly, a narrow focus on violence against women and on protection fits more readily into widely shared assumptions about gender and conflict than does an emphasis on women's political empowerment. Some Council members not only cannot accept gender equality—even in the context of post-conflict states—as essential to international peace and security; they regard efforts to empower women as potentially triggering (or exacerbating) conflict. Afghanistan, where girls' education is viewed as inciting Taliban militancy, is a primary example. Russia, China, and several non-permanent Security Council members (e.g., India, Pakistan, and Azerbaijan in the 2012–2013 period) see the Council's embrace of women's empowerment as moving the Council far outside its remit. Russia has consistently argued that the Security Council should not get involved in issues of political participation, traditionally the prerogative of sovereign states. Such matters, they claim, should be referred to the UN Human Rights Council or humanitarian agencies (e.g., Karev 2013).

It is no surprise that protecting women from danger is a bigger winner politically than investing in their political access and capacities. It is not easy to engage in sustained coalition-building with women's organizations, or to encourage post-conflict countries to consider the benefits of adopting a nationally appropriate quota system to fast-track women into elected office. The idea of protection, on the other hand, situates women as sexually injured subjects, not agents demanding institutional changes to enhance their political participation (see Engle, Chapter 10 in this volume). Unlike victims, women leaders do not fit predefined gender-role categories. Protecting women from CRSV is not incompatible with conservative views on women's roles and rights prevailing in many countries. Unfortunately, UNSCR 1325's emphasis on empowering women to engage substantively—including as leaders—in all aspects of peace and security work is often regarded as revealing the Council's Western bias.

While there is no avoiding the political tensions on women's rights in the Council, the informal working group on WPS to which the Security Council has now committed under resolution 2242 will perhaps force an overdue convergence of the protection and participation concerns. To be effective, the working group will need access to up-to-date analyses of gender issues and women's political engagement in situations on the Council's agenda and beyond. It will also need to monitor Council actions and request explanations for failures to advance women's participation. To combat the inevitably powerful tug of attention to sexual violence in conflict, and to balance the strong presence and capacity of the OSRSG (Office of the Special Representative of the Secretary-General on Sexual Violence in Conflict), UN Women, which functions as the Secretariat for this new group, will have to make a capacity leap in analytical and coordination capabilities. At a minimum, it will have to assemble information from across the United Nations on a wider range of protection issues than sexual violence, such as the gender-differential impact of depriving populations of food, shelter, health care, and education, and the deliberate targeting of hospitals and schools. It will need to generate gender-disaggregated data on forced disappearances, forced displacement, arbitrary arrest and detention, torture, restrictions on dress and freedom of movement, forced marriage, and the targeting and punishment of women because of their own activism or activism by male relatives.

Beyond this, it will need a close working relationship on the ground with the DPKO/DPA gender advisors to support women's civil society organizations and to enable women's participation in peace and security processes, including through the engagement of women and gender experts in planning peace talks, donor conferences, constitutional reform, and the like. At this time of writing, eight out of the United Nations' nine integrated multidimensional peacekeeping missions lacked a senior gender advisor, indicating a crisis in the gender architecture in conflict countries. Ultimately, institutionalizing sustained attention to gender equality issues in ways that keep women's agency and empowerment at the forefront of interventions requires that the two UN entities with field leadership in conflict contexts accept UN Women's coordinating and analytical role.

NOTES

1. Information learned during private communications with staff in missions of members serving on the Council.
2. The "Group of the Friends of the Family" is a growing collection of countries (initially eleven) that declared its intention in early 2015 to bargain as a group to defend an undefined, but implicitly conservative, version of "the family" in international negotiations, for instance at the Commission on Population and Development. See Friends of the Family, "Statement of the Group of Friends of the Family" (New York). https://sustainabledevelopment.un.org/content/documents/12348Joint%20statement-friends%20of%20the%20family.pdf.

REFERENCES

Butler, Maria, Kristina Mader, and Rachel Kean. 2010. *Women, Peace, and Security Handbook: Compilation and Analysis of United Nations Security Council Resolution Language, 2000–2010*. New York: PeaceWomen Project, International League for Peace and Freedom.

Bunting, Madeline. 2011. "Women's Rights Are in Danger of Becoming a Wordfest." *Poverty Matters* (blog), *The Guardian*. January 27, 2011. http://www.theguardian.com/global-development/poverty-matters/2011/jan/27/un-women-funding-commitment.

Committee on the Elimination of Discrimination Against Women (CEDAW). 2013. *General Recommendation No. 30 on Women in Conflict Prevention, Conflict, and Post-Conflict Situations*. UN Doc. CEDAW/C/GC/30 (October 18).

Gasana, Eugène-Richard. 2013. "Statement of Government of Rwanda." Statement given during Security Council Open Debate on Women, Rule of Law, and Transitional Justice in Conflict-Affected Situations, New York (October 18).

Goetz, Anne Marie, and Rob Jenkins. 2015. "Missed Opportunities: Gender and the UN's Peacebuilding and Peace Operations Reports." *Global Peace Operations Review.* July 30. http://peaceoperationsreview.org/thematic-essays/missed-opportunities-gender-and-the-uns-peacebuilding-and-peace-operations-reports/.

Goetz, Anne Marie, and Rob Jenkins. 2016. "Agency and Accountability." *Feminist Economics* 1, no. 22: 211–236.

Jenkins, Rob, and Anne Marie Goetz. 2010. "Addressing Sexual Violence in Internationally Mediated Negotiations." *International Peacekeeping* 17, no. 2: 261–277.

Karev, Sergei. 2013. "Statement of Government of Russia." Statement given during Security Council Open Debate on Women, Peace and Security, New York, November 30, 2012.

Lewis, Stephen. 2007. "Congo-Kinshasa: End Sexual Violence in Eastern Region." *AllAfrica.* September 13. http://allafrica.com/stories/200709130788.html.

Nilsson, Desirée. 2012. "Anchoring the Peace: Civil Society Actors in Peace Accords and Durable Peace." *International Interactions* 38: 243–266.

O'Reilly, Marie, Andrea Ó Súilleabháin, and Thania Paffenholz. 2015. *Reimagining Peacemaking: Women's Roles in Peace Processes.* New York: International Peace Institute.

Office of the Special Advisor on Gender Issues and the Advancement of Women (OSAGI). 2003. *An Analysis of the Gender Content of Secretary-General's Reports to the Security Council: January 2000–September 2003.* New York: OSAGI.

Otto, Diane. 2006. "A Sign of 'Weakness?' Disrupting Gender Uncertainties in the Implementation of Security Council Resolution 1325." *Michigan Journal of International Law* 13: 113–175.

Security Council Report (SCR). 2014. *Cross-Cutting Report: Women, Peace and Security.* 2014. New York: Security Council Report.

Stone, Laurel. 2014. "Women Transforming Conflict: A Quantitative Analysis of Female Peacemaking." Master's thesis, Seton Hall University, New Jersey.

Swaine, Aisling, and Catherine O'Rourke. 2015. *Guidebook on CEDAW General Recommendation No. 30 and the UN Security Council Resolutions on Women, Peace and Security.* New York: UN Women.

United Nations. 2010. G.A. Res. 64/289 (July 2).

UN Advisory Group of Experts on the 2015 Review of the UN Peacebuilding Architecture. 2015a. *The Challenge of Sustaining Peace.* New York: United Nations.

UN Development Fund for Women (UNIFEM), UN Department of Political Affairs, UN Department of Peacekeeping Operations, UN Development Programme, and Centre for Humanitarian Dialogue. 2009. *Conflict Related Sexual Violence and Peace Negotiations: Implementing Security Council Resolution 1820: Report on the High-Level Colloquium.* New York: UNIFEM.

UN High-Level Independent Panel on Peace Operations. 2015b. *Report on Uniting Our Strengths for Peace: Politics, Partnership and People.* UN Doc. A/70/95-S/2015/466 (June 1).

UN Women. 2015. "Gender Architecture in Peace Operations and Integration with the UN Country Team." Submission to the High-Level Independent Panel on Peace Operation. New York: UN Women.

CHAPTER 10

A GENEALOGY OF THE CENTRALITY OF SEXUAL VIOLENCE TO GENDER AND CONFLICT

KAREN ENGLE

OVER the past two decades, discussion of gender and conflict has increasingly focused on sexual violence, primarily against women. Indeed, the following two statements can be seen as representative of the dominant legal, political, and even popular understandings of the relationship between gender and conflict today: (1) sexual violence is the predominant, if not paradigmatic, concern regarding gender and conflict, and—at times—conflict in general; and (2) sexual violence is a tactic of war that both accompanies and is fueled by a culture of impunity, and should be primarily responded to with criminal sanctions.

This chapter demonstrates and contests the power of these assumptions, or what I have elsewhere called the "grip" of sexual violence, on gender and conflict discourse (Engle 2014). It does so by first considering a series of representative events on sexual violence in conflict—at the G8, the UN Security Council and General Assembly, and a special UK-hosted international summit—that reflect the mainstreamed perspectives on the centrality of sexual violence to conflict, and the need for and effectiveness of carceral responses to it. Next the chapter traces these views to a number of international legal and political changes beginning in the late 1980s. In particular, consideration is given to the centrality of sexual violence to the early women's human rights movement and of criminalization to post–Cold War law reform. Finally, it concludes with some critiques of these portrayals.

DOMINANT UNDERSTANDINGS OF GENDER, CONFLICT, AND SEXUAL VIOLENCE

On April 11, 2013, then-UK Foreign Secretary William Hague shared the stage in London with Zainab Bangura, who was the UN Secretary-General's Special Representative on Sexual Violence in Conflict, and well-known movie star Angelina Jolie, who serves as Special Envoy of the United Nations High Commission on Refugees. Although the G8 summit that had just concluded had failed to reach agreement on some of the issues at the top of its agenda, including Syria and North Korea, the three appeared together to launch an initiative that all eight states had agreed upon—the G8 Declaration on Preventing Sexual Violence. This press conference came nearly one year after Hague and Jolie announced their Preventing Sexual Violence Initiative (PSVI). In the ensuing few months, Jolie, Hague, and Bangura successfully advocated for a new UN Security Council resolution on sexual violence in conflict, resolution 2106, which recognized the G8 declaration. Hague and Bangura also promoted a UN General Assembly Declaration of Commitment to End Sexual Violence in Conflict ("Declaration of Commitment") that was eventually signed by 155 UN member states. And in June 2014, Hague and Jolie co-hosted in London the Global Summit to End Sexual Violence in Conflict. These events and some of the documents produced from them are used here to demonstrate the dominant understandings about gender and conflict with which this chapter began.

CENTRALITY OF SEXUAL VIOLENCE TO ARMED CONFLICT

In their statements at the G8 press conference, Hague and Bangura respectively stated that sexual violence in conflict "is one of the greatest and most persistent injustices in the world" and "is a fundamental threat to international peace and security, and as such requires an operational and strategic security and justice response" (Foreign & Commonwealth Office 2013). Later documents reiterate that sexual violence is not only the greatest issue concerning gender and conflict, but conflict more generally. Security Council resolution (SCR) 2106, for example, repeating similar language in earlier resolutions on the same issue, states that sexual violence "can significantly exacerbate and prolong situations of armed conflict and may impede the restoration of international peace and security" (para. 1). The UN Declaration of Commitment also notes that "[p]reventing and responding to sexual violence is vital to resolving conflicts, enabling development and building sustainable peace" (U.N. General Assembly 2013). The chair's summary of the June 2014 London summit, elaborates: "Sexual violence in conflict poses a grave threat to international peace and security. It exacerbates tension and violence and undermines stability" (Foreign & Commonwealth Office 2014a).

An animated video released by the UK Foreign and Commonwealth Office prior to the London summit further suggests the centrality of sexual violence to conflict. The roughly one-minute video depicts a rape occurring during armed conflict in an unidentified place (Foreign & Commonwealth Office 2014b). The two-dimensional animation begins with an apparent nuclear family—man, woman, boy, and girl—in front of a house surrounded by green trees and blooming flowers. The father is barbecuing on one side of the screen, while the rest of the family is playing on the other. Birds are chirping and the family's dog is making playful noises. By the third second of the video, the scene begins to change dramatically. Black clouds move in, with military helicopters following. The family members run inside the house as ground military vehicles arrive. Soldiers shoot the dog and enter the house firing their weapons into the air. They rape the woman.

As I discuss further in the following, the video promotes a carceral response to rape in conflict, indicating that the way to end sexual violence in conflict is simply to jail the perpetrators. And with no sexual violence, the animation further suggests, armed conflict will not otherwise threaten the ability of civilians to live their lives freely and peacefully.

RESPONSE OF CRIMINALIZATION

The dominant strategic response to sexual violence in conflict is increasingly penal in nature, often with an unspoken (and always unproved) assumption that deterrence will result from bringing the perpetrators to justice. We see the emphasis on criminalization in the G8 declaration and press conference, as well as in SCR 2106 and the animated video promoting the Summit.

Criminalization is the thrust of much of the G8 declaration. Indeed, Hague claimed that the G8 "made a historic declaration that rape and serious sexual violence in conflict are grave breaches of the Geneva Convention, as well as war crimes," giving countries "the responsibility [to] actively to search for, prosecute or hand over for trial anyone accused of these crimes" (Foreign & Commonwealth Office 2013). And, so that the gains in international criminal law could make their way into local enforcement of international humanitarian law, the G8 "declared [its] support for the deployment of international experts to help build up the judicial, investigative and legal capacity of other countries in this area" (G8 2013, para. 23).

The focus on the importance of criminalization appears throughout the declaration (G8 2013, paras. 2, 4, 5, 6, 7, 10). It also marked all the speeches announcing it. Hague noted, for example, that, despite the severity of sexual violence, "the overwhelming majority of survivors never see any justice for what they have endured." By "justice," he clearly meant criminal penalties. Special Representative Bangura commented that "even as we concentrate on our obligations to the survivors of sexual violence . . . we now also throw a more concerted spotlight on the perpetrators. All those who commit, or command, or condone sexual violence in conflict." Jolie also praised the criminal response, expressing encouragement at the possible "start of a new global alliance against warzone rape and sexual violence; and finally an end to impunity" (Foreign & Commonwealth Office 2013).

One of the provisions of the G8 declaration "stress[es] the need to exclude crimes of sexual violence in armed conflict from amnesty provisions" (G8 2013, para.10). Similar language later made its way into the UN Declaration of Commitment and SCR 2106, and in fact had been in prior UN Security Council resolutions as well. Although some might contend that the prohibition on amnesty could hamper peace negotiations, Jolie denied it, contending that "[t]here is no choice between peace and justice: peace requires justice" (Foreign & Commonwealth Office 2013).

Anti-impunity discourse drove much of the advocacy of SCR 2106 by Jolie, Hague, and Bangura. In urging the Security Council to adopt and implement the resolution, for example, Jolie chided the world for not yet having "take[n] up war-zone rape as a serious priority" despite "hundreds of thousands—if not millions—of victims." After noting the dearth of prosecutions for sexual violence, Jolie continued: survivors "suffer most at the hands of their rapists, but they are also victims of a culture of impunity." Only when "perpetrators are finally held to account" will they "at last feel that they are on safer ground" (UN Security Council 2013, 6).

As with the G8 declaration, much of SCR 2106 focuses on criminalization. Although previous resolutions had called for individual accountability for crimes of sexual violence and even had created mechanisms by which to facilitate it,[1] SCR 2106 expresses concern with "the slow implementation" of resolution 1960, an earlier such resolution, and offers greater operational detail toward that end. Indeed, the United Kingdom titled the Security Council debate that preceded the passage of SCR 2106 "Addressing Impunity: Effective Justice for Crimes of Sexual Violence in Conflict." Beyond rejecting amnesty provisions, the resolution reminds states of their obligations to "fight impunity by investigating and prosecuting" those responsible for sexual violence, which can constitute war crimes, crimes against humanity, and acts of genocide. Through the resolution, the Security Council also recommits itself "to continue forcefully to fight impunity and uphold accountability with appropriate means" through international criminal institutions (para. 2, 3). Thus, the Security Council promotes the use of both domestic and international criminal law to prosecute and punish violations of international humanitarian, human rights, and criminal law. A later resolution, SCR 2242 (2015), though focused primarily on women as peacekeepers, continues to promote criminalization at both of these levels.

In fairness, these documents do not focus only on criminal justice mechanisms for addressing sexual violence in conflict. Other provisions, for example, call for social services and reparations for victims. The animated video to advertise the London summit, however, only offers incarceration as a response to sexual violence in conflict. And, as already suggested, it sees it as a wholly effective response, not only to sexual violence but to conflict in general.

During the rape scene in the video, the face of one of the perpetrators mutates into that of a monster. He bares his teeth and growls at the viewers, while a scream and wailing is heard in the background. The narrator of the video specifically refers to "monsters" who commit rapes and "are allowed to get away with it, even live near their victims." After the perpetrators have left the house, the girl in the family is shown looking out the window where a male figure can be seen. As the narrator says "even live near their victims," the male figure turns his head and moves toward the window. He transforms into a monster, baring his teeth and growling at the window. The young girl recoils and pulls down a yellow window shade.

Black scribbles then begin to be drawn over the shade and eventually take over the screen, as the narrator states: "But it doesn't have to be this way." Suddenly the black becomes the robe of a judge (of uncertain gender) in a courtroom. The judge is gesticulating toward the defendant, who is one of the monsters we have seen, now wearing his human face. The narrator states, "Rape and sexual violence are the worst crimes you can imagine. But they are not an inevitable part of war." The screen then zooms in on the perpetrator. "It's time to end sexual violence in conflict." Prison bars drop in front of him. The screen pans out, and is filled with repeating identical images of him behind bars. The narration continues: "Time to bring those responsible to justice."

The video ends by returning to the original idealized image of the house. The man and woman stand happily at the door together, while the children and dog once again play in the front yard. The family is depicted as feeling safe, notwithstanding the war that we can only assume continues to rage.

Despite the fanfare around the events and pronouncements I have described, the recognition of the illegality of sexual violence was not as path-breaking as the speakers, especially those at the G8 Summit, suggested. International criminal law has long prohibited rape as a war crime, which the G8 declaration itself acknowledges. What seems new here is the sense that impunity is the greatest threat to ending sexual violence in conflict and that ensuring that perpetrators are imprisoned will resolve not only sexual violence in conflict but perhaps conflict more generally. Recall that the G8 was able to achieve consensus on sexual violence but not on North Korea or Syria. If agreement around the former could somehow help resolve the latter, it would of course be a victory.

What might also seem new is a serious commitment to enforcing the criminal laws against sexual violence in conflict. Yet increased discourse about criminalization has not necessarily resulted in increased prosecutorial endeavors. Indeed, in June 2015, the *Observer* reported that the UK Foreign Ministry spent five times more money on the London Summit than it had on efforts to end sexual violence in conflict. The story suggested that the PSVI of the United Kingdom "has had negligible impact and that British funding has been withdrawn from vital projects" (Townsend 2015). The story led to the establishment of a House of Lords Select Committee on Sexual Violence in Conflict, which issued its report in April 2016. The report notes that the PSVI's "great emphasis on ending impunity for sexual violence in conflict and holding the perpetrators accountable" are "important objectives," but it also pays significant attention to other types of programs it believes should be "undertaken alongside" such efforts (Select Committee on Sexual Violence in Conflict 2016, para. 21).

The Committee's attention to non-criminal responses to sexual violence, even if they are meant to work in tandem with criminal ones, is welcome. Yet, many critics of the PSVI and similar efforts focus on the lack of follow-through in terms of criminal enforcement. This chapter suggests, in contrast, that the emphasis on criminalization is itself part of the problem.

ROOTS OF THE DOMINANT UNDERSTANDINGS

This section traces the roots of the problematic perceptions that sexual violence is the quintessential harm of war and that criminalization should be the primary response to it. It attributes these notions to a convergence of events and ideas in the early years following the Cold War. At that time, the slogan "women's rights as human rights" began to gain traction and to achieve mainstream recognition, and the establishment of criminal law institutions became a post–Cold War action on which members of the UN Security Council could agree. Both women's human rights and international criminalization discourses were soon gripped by sexual violence in conflict.

Women's rights as human rights

Since the mid-1980s, when feminists began to theorize women's human rights, violence against women (VAW) was central to their cause. They also began to achieve some international institutional support for their efforts. When, in 1993, they came to Vienna for the second World Conference on Human Rights with the slogan "women's rights are human rights," VAW was at the top of their agenda. Women's human rights advocates were mostly radical feminists who were eager to break down the public/private distinction they saw in human rights. They hoped to hold states accountable for the myriad ways in which women suffered in the so-called private sphere (see, for example, Bunch 1990).

Women's rights were not explicitly mentioned in the initial organizing documents for the conference. Charlotte Bunch, one of the main advocates for reconceiving human rights to include the private sphere, spearheaded the Global Campaign for Women's Human Rights, which helped initiate a petition "calling on the 1993 Conference to comprehensively address women's human rights at every level of the proceedings and demanding that gender violence be recognized as a violation of human rights requiring immediate action." The petition garnered over 300,000 signatures from over 120 countries (Keck and Sikkink 1998, 186). By the time it was presented on the floor of the conference, according to Bunch, half a million people had signed it (Bunch 2012, 30).

By most accounts, advocates were successful in their efforts at achieving recognition of women's human rights at Vienna. According to Bunch and collaborator Niamh Reilly (1994, 2), by the time the conference concluded, "gender-based violence and women's human rights emerged as one of the most talked-about subjects, and women were recognized as a well-organized human rights constituency." They point, in particular, to the number of pages of the Vienna Declaration and Programme of Action devoted to the equal status of women and to its call for the elimination of violence against women in both public and private (Bunch and Reilly, 104–106).

The 1993 conference took place in the shadow of revelations about rapes taking place during armed conflict in the former Yugoslavia. Although rape had been only one type of violence that those working on VAW had originally considered, rape in armed conflict became an integral part of women's human rights advocacy as feminists at the conference presented it as symptomatic of the violence against women that they urged human rights NGOs and governments to address. The issue soon dominated. A 1998 UN report on sexual violence and armed conflict would later describe Vienna as a "watershed for women's human rights," explaining that "[a]t that time, reports of sexual violence committed against women in the former Yugoslavia had flooded the media. The accompanying worldwide outrage provided powerful support for NGO arguments that violence against women is a fundamental human rights violation, of concern to the international community at large" (UN Division for the Advancement of Women 1998).

Feminist attention to sexual violence in conflict at Vienna served several functions, two of which are explored further here. First, it appeared to mediate a number of debates among feminists, particularly between those in the Global South and the Global North. Before and after Vienna, many feminists in the Global South complained that feminists in the Global North downplayed the extent and nature of women's rights violations in the North, failed to consider the role of Northern countries in Southern dispossession, and misunderstood "culture" as they inappropriately blamed it for the bulk of women's rights violations (Engle 2005b). For some feminists, the VAW focus was meant to avoid some of the North–South debates. As Bunch put it in an interview in 1997, "[i]f you look at economic issues, women have problems everywhere but the forms it takes are very different. However, it was very easy for women across different cultures to talk about their experiences of rape, their experiences of battering and their experiences of fear in the streets" (Bunch and Douglas 1997, 10). Because no one—feminist or otherwise—could claim that rape in war was culturally defensible, those debates did not resurface in the context of the treatment of rape in conflict. Moreover, the fact that the rapes were taking place in Europe meant that Northern feminists could attest that they were attending to issues "at home."[2]

Second, the focus on rape in armed conflict both tapped into and gave feminists power in the simultaneous development of international criminal law and institutions. Even though feminists inside and outside the former Yugoslavia were deeply divided over how to name and understand rapes that had taken place there and over whether military intervention was called for in terms of a response (Engle 2005a, 2007), they agreed that the acts were criminal and that perpetrators should be held accountable. That position was largely accepted by the mainstream, and was bolstered by the establishment of the

International Criminal Tribunal for the Former Yugoslavia (ICTY) one month before the conference (see Sellers, Chapter 16 in this volume).

The Vienna Declaration and Programme of Action reflects not only the extent to which VAW and women's human rights were recognized, but also how rape and other forms of what we now call sexual violence in conflict were explicitly condemned. The document states, for example, that "[v]iolations of the human rights of women in situations of armed conflict are violations of the fundamental principles of international human rights and humanitarian law. All violations of this kind, including in particular murder, systematic rape, sexual slavery, and forced pregnancy, require a particularly effective response" (UN OHCHR 1993, para. 38). Note that, with the exception of murder, the condemned violence in conflict is sexual in nature.

The ICTY would seem to be one possibility for "a particularly effective response." The importance of the ICTY was made explicit in a "Special Declaration on Bosnia and Herzegovina" included in the Conference report, which noted that "[o]ver 40,000 Bosnian women have been subjected to the gruesome crime of rape" (UN Secretary-General 1993). It called for UN Security Council intervention in the former Yugoslavia; among the mechanisms for such intervention was the ICTY.

Women's human rights and international criminal law

The previous section showed why and how sexual violence in conflict became central to women's human rights advocacy in the early 1990s. Although the conflict in the former Yugoslavia could have brought attention to a myriad of gender and conflict issues, the attention to rapes in the region, along with the VAW focus that feminists brought to Vienna, led to the centrality of sexual violence. Moreover, many of the women's human rights advocates came to the meeting with an emphasis on women's bodies as the primary locus of male domination and female subordination. The narrowing of VAW to sexual violence fit well with that focus.

But what about the criminal punishment response? Even with sexual violence emerging as the primary issue regarding gender and conflict, why would criminal law be the principal way to address it? Again, the ICTY is central to the story. When the UN Security Council unanimously voted in May 1993 to establish the ICTY to prosecute serious violations of international humanitarian law, it justified its creation in part on reports of "systematic detention and rape of women" (UN Security Council 1993, preamb. para. 3, para. 2). In doing so, it set the stage for a broader reliance on criminalization that has dominated responses to rape and sexual violence in conflict. It also strengthened emerging trends in that direction.

Rape in the former Yugoslavia received significant reporting and attention at an important historical moment. With the end of the Cold War, the UN Security Council was newly poised to use its Chapter VII intervention powers under the UN Charter after decades of stalemate wrought by the use or threatened use of the veto power held by the five permanent members of the Council. Some feminists and non-feminists alike called for military intervention in the former Yugoslavia, but—unable to agree on such intervention—Security Council member states reached a novel compromise to establish an international criminal tribunal.

Though novel, the result was not surprising, given a more general international governance trend toward the expansion of criminal legal institutions at both the international and domestic levels. Indeed, support for an international criminal court had been on the rise since 1989. And international human rights advocates increasingly expressed concerns about "the culture of impunity," a term rarely used before 1991 (Engle 2015, 1074–1079). Those advocates began to argue, with some success, that states had an international legal obligation to defy that culture by investigating, prosecuting, and punishing non-state actors for violations of human rights.[3] Many feminists lauded this move, seeing it as offering a way to hold states accountable for what had previously been considered private harms (Byrnes 1992, 229; Etienne 1995, 157; Spahn 1995, 1064).

The penal approach of women's human rights advocates also built upon feminist domestic strategies that were increasingly turning to the punitive state to protect women's rights, particularly those rights regarding bodily and sexual integrity. As Aya Gruber (2007) has documented in the context of domestic violence, feminists in the United States in the 1980s and 1990s began to turn away from social services and progressive grassroots resistance and toward the use and promotion of criminal prosecutions (749–751). Although the Violence Against Women Act in 1994 was a visible representation of that turn (Bernstein 2012, 239), Gruber notes that feminists were in fact aligning themselves with an approach toward domestic violence that had been pushed at least since 1984 by the Reagan administration, consistent with its broader war on crime and in the name of "family values" (Gruber 2007, 794–796). This approach was not unique to the United States. As Dianne Martin noted in 1998, "[f]eminists around the world identified and addressed the failures of the justice system in regard to wife abuse in remarkably consistent ways" so that "an almost irresistible pressure drove the movement toward criminal justice reform and solutions, and to make use of 'law and order' arguments to ensure that criminal justice actors will become involved" (168).

Meanwhile, feminist critiques of the treatment of rape victims often led to procedural reforms that made convictions more likely and to harsher penalties for perpetrators, at least for those accused of "stranger" rape (Martin 1998, 6). The internationalization of these responses was aided by the United States' increased exportation of its own criminal justice model throughout the 1990s to combat transnational crime (McLeod 2010).

SOME CRITIQUES OF THE DOMINANT UNDERSTANDING

The preceding analysis suggests a number of concerns about the portrayals of sexual violence as central to conflict and about the turn to criminal law as the primary, if not the only, means to address sexual violence in conflict. I consider some of these more explicitly here.

With regard to the centrality of sexual violence, a key question is what gets missed in this framing in terms of both conflict and gender. When we assume (whether consciously, as in the video, or unconsciously) that, in the absence of sexual violence, there will be peace, or at least law-abiding armed entities, we elide—as Maria Eriksson Baaz and Maria Stern (2013) have demonstrated in the context of the Democratic Republic of the Congo—many other important aspects of conflict, including its causes and possible remedies (also Eriksson Baaz and Stern, Chapter 41 in this volume). Some, but not all, of the causes might be gendered in important ways.

One of the greatest challenges to the focus on sexual violence within the gender and conflict realm has come from women's peace movement advocates who have spent a significant amount of time and energy encouraging greater female participation in peace processes. The women's peace movement has its own important genealogy, dating back at least to the inter-war period (Alonso 1993; Amos and Parmar 2005; Otto 2003; Rupp 1997; Wiltsher 1985). As recently as the 1970s, peace was central to the international women's movement, and was one of the three themes of the UN Decade on Women and subsequent conferences (the other two being equality and development). Yet, the women's peace and women's human rights movements have had remarkably little overlap or intersection. In fact, attention to women's peace has arguably declined as women's human rights have ascended (see Figure 10.1).

This inverse relationship was not inevitable. Indeed, one could easily have imagined that the conflict in the former Yugoslavia might have galvanized women's peace activists at Vienna and might even have led to a different understanding of human rights. But the fact that the issue was seized upon by those who had focused on VAW, with a particular interest in sexual violence, has continued to affect the strategies by which women's peace advocates have addressed women's participation in peace processes.

Many peace advocates, for example, have pursued these aims through the UN Security Council and other international bodies, in part with the explicit aim of contesting the emphasis on sexual violence. Nevertheless, even though they have achieved some success in calling attention to the need for greater women's participation, they have conceded much of the terrain by seeing sexual violence as an obstacle to that participation (Engle 2014). As a result, women's peace advocates have narrowed both their perception of the relationship between gender and conflict and their scope for imagining possibilities for peace—with or without greater female participation.

The carceral turn by women's human rights advocates is also problematic in that it has allied feminists with the police and with penal systems at the international and domestic levels. Criminalization is often done in a way that demonizes individual perpetrators (as in the video), has little justification beyond retribution, and makes little sense even to the victims (though it is generally done in their names). Moreover, to the extent that the war on crime, domestically and internationally, has been central to neoliberalism, feminists have often participated in neoliberal restructuring and the multiple harms that occur from it.

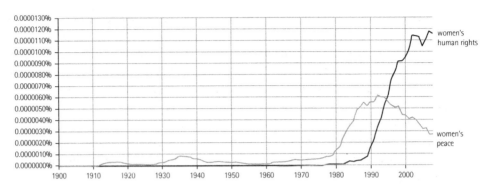

FIGURE 10.1. N-gram: References to "women's human rights" and "women's peace" (1900–2008).[*]

[*] An N-gram based on eight million of the titles digitized in Google Books demonstrates a sharp and steady increase in references to "women's human rights" and decline of "women's peace" during the mid-1990s.

Source: Michel et al. (2011).

The aim of this chapter is not so much to persuade readers of the critiques, but rather to call attention to the dominance of the mainstreamed understandings and to recognize that many of them reflect particular strategies devised by women's human rights advocates themselves. In many ways, they reflect the victory of particular feminist positions (perhaps surprisingly, radical feminist positions) that managed to have mainstream traction in ways that other positions did not. The task ahead is to recognize the limitations of the strategies we have come to rely upon, and perhaps even to reinvigorate some of the earlier positions that did not succeed. In short, we need to devise sharper tools for understanding and attending to both gender and conflict.

Notes

1. The first resolution specifically calling for a criminal justice response to sexual violence is SCR 1325 (2000), which is also the first resolution on women and security. It "[e]mphasizes the responsibility of all States to put an end to impunity and to prosecute those responsible for genocide, crimes against humanity, and war crimes including those relating to sexual and other violence against women and girls, and in this regard stresses the need to exclude these crimes, where feasible from amnesty provisions" (para. 11). SCR 1960 (2010), however, provides the first detailed attempt to hold individuals accused of sexual violence accountable through a Security Council "naming and shaming" mechanism (para. 3; see Heathcote 2012; see also Goetz and Jenkins, Chapter 9 in this volume).

2. Indeed, some argued that the rapes only received serious attention "because the Western world identified with the victims they were hearing about. It was not possible to dismiss the stories as concerned with distant cultural traditions or genders unfamiliar to the Western world" (Skjelsbaek 2011, 69). Regardless of the motive for attention, I would argue that Bosnia and Herzegovina was in fact often treated as a site of the Global South (on which Western feminists had long been focused).

3. A path-breaking case in this regard was *Velásquez Rodríguez v. Honduras*, Inter-Am. Ct. H.R. (Ser. C) No. 4 (July 29, 1988).

References

Alonso, Harriet Hyman. 1993. *Peace as a Women's Issue: A History of the U.S. Movement for World Peace and Women's Rights*. Syracuse, NY: Syracuse University Press.

Amos, Valerie, and Pratibha Parmar. 2005. "Challenging Imperial Feminism." *Feminist Review* 17: 3–19.

Bernstein, Elizabeth. 2012. "Carceral Politics as Gender Justice? The 'Traffic in Women' and Neoliberal Circuits of Crime, Sex, and Rights." *Theory and Society* 41, no. 3: 233–259.

Bunch, Charlotte. 1990. "Women's Rights as Human Rights: Toward a Re-Vision of Human Rights." *Human Rights Quarterly* 12, no. 4: 486–498.

Bunch, Charlotte, and Niamh Reilly. 1994. *Demanding Accountability: The Global Campaign and Vienna Tribunal for Women's Human Rights*. New Brunswick, NJ, and New York: Center for Women's Global Leadership and UNIFEM.

Bunch, Charlotte, and Carol Anne Douglas. 1997. "Interview: Charlotte Bunch on Global Feminism." *Off Our Backs* 17, no. 9: 10–12.

Bunch, Charlotte. 2012. "How Women's Rights Became Recognized as Human Rights." In *The Unfinished Revolution: Voices from the Global Fight for Women's Rights*, edited by Minky Worden, 29–39. Bristol, UK: The Policy Press.

Byrnes, Andrew. 1992. "Women, Feminism, and International Human Rights Law: Methodological Myopia, Fundamental Flaws or Meaningful Marginalisation?" *Australian Yearbook of International Law* 12: 205–240.

Engle, Karen. 2005a. "Feminism and Its (Dis)contents: Criminalizing Wartime Rape in Bosnia and Herzegovina." *American Journal of International Law* 99, no. 4: 778–816.

Engle, Karen. 2005b. "International Human Rights and Feminisms: When Discourses Keep Meeting." In *International Law: Modern Feminist Approaches*, edited by Doris Buss and Ambreena Manji, 47–66. Oxford: Hart.

Engle, Karen. 2007. "'Calling in the Troops:' The Uneasy Relationship among Women's Rights, Human Rights, and Humanitarian Intervention." *Harvard Human Rights Journal* 20: 189–226.

Engle, Karen. 2014. "The Grip of Sexual Violence: Reading UN Security Council Resolutions on Human Security." In *Rethinking Peacekeeping, Gender Equality and Collective Security*, edited by Gina Heathcote and Dianne Otto, 23–47. London: Palgrave-Macmillan.

Engle, Karen. 2015. "Anti-Impunity and the Turn to Criminal Law in Human Rights." *Cornell Law Review* 100: 1069–1127.

Etienne, Margareth. 1995. "Addressing Gender-Based Violence in an International Context." *Harvard Women's Law Journal* 18: 139–170.

Eriksson Baaz, Maria, and Maria Stern. 2013. *Sexual Violence as a Weapon of War?: Perceptions, Prescriptions, Problems in the Congo and Beyond*. London: Zed Books.

Foreign & Commonwealth Office. 2013. "G8 Declaration on Preventing Sexual Violence in Conflict." *Gov.uk*. April 11. https://www.gov.uk/government/news/g8-declaration-on-preventing-sexual-violence-in-conflict.

Foreign & Commonwealth Office. 2014a. *Chair's Summary—Global Summit to End Sexual Violence in Conflict*. London: Foreign & Commonwealth Office.

Foreign & Commonwealth Office. 2014b. "Animation Launched for Summit to End Sexual Violence in Conflict." *Gov.uk*. June 4. https://www.gov.uk/government/news/animation-launched-for-summit-to-end-sexual-violence-in-conflict.

G8. 2013. *Declaration on Preventing Sexual Violence in Conflict*. London: G8 UK.

Gruber, Aya. 2007. "The Feminist War on Crime." *Iowa Law Review* 92: 741–833.

Heathcote, Gina. 2012. "Naming and Shaming: Human Rights Accountability in Security Council Resolution 1960 (2010) on Women, Peace and Security." *Journal of Human Rights Practice* 4, no. 1: 82–105.

Keck, Margaret E., and Kathryn Sikkink. 1998. *Activists beyond Borders: Advocacy Networks in International Politics*. Ithaca, NY: Cornell University Press.

Martin, Dianne L. 1998. "Retribution Revisited: A Reconsideration of Feminist Criminal Law Reform Strategies." *Osgoode Hall Law Journal* 36, no. 1: 151–188.

McLeod, Allegra M. 2010. "Exporting U.S. Criminal Justice." *Yale Law and Policy Review* 29: 83–164.

Michel, Jean-Baptiste, Yuan Kui Shen, Aviva P. Aiden, Adrian Veres, Matthew K. Gray, the Google Books Team, Joseph P. Pickett, et al. 2011. "Quantitative Analysis of Culture Using Millions of Digitized Books." *Science* 331: 176–182.

Otto, Dianne. 2003. "International Peace Activism: The Contributions Made by Women." *Reform* 82: 30–36.

Rupp, Leila J. 1997. *Worlds of Women: The Making of an International Women's Movement*. Princeton, NJ: Princeton University Press.

Select Committee on Sexual Violence in Conflict. 2016. *Sexual Violence in Conflict: A War Crime Report*. London: House of Lords.

Skjelsbaek, Inger. 2011. "Sexual Violence in the Post-Yugoslav Wars." In *Women and War: Power and Protection in the 21St Century*, edited by Kathleen Kuehnast, Chantal de Jonge Oudraat, and Helga Hernes, 65–85. Washington, DC: US Institute of Peace Press.

Spahn, Elizabeth K. 1995. "Waiting for Credentials: Feminist Theories of Enforcement of International Human Rights." *American University Law Review* 44, no. 4: 1053–1083.

Townsend, Mark. 2015. "William Hague's Summit against Warzone Rape Seen as 'Costly Failure.'" *The Observer*. June 13. http://www.theguardian.com/global-development/2015/jun/13/warzone-rape-congo-questions-uk-campaign.

UN Division for the Advancement of Women. 1998. "Sexual Violence and Armed Conflict: United Nations Response." *Women2000*. http://www.un.org/womenwatch/daw/public/cover.htm.

UN General Assembly. 2013. *Declaration of Commitment to End Sexual Violence in Conflict*. UN Doc. A/68/633 Annex (December 3).

UN Office of the High Commissioner for Human Rights (OHCHR). 1993. *Vienna Declaration and Programme of Action*. Vienna: OHCHR.

UN Secretary-General. 1993. *Rep. to the World Conference on Human Rights*. UN Doc. A/CONF.157/24 (Part I) (October 13).

UN Security Council. 1993. S.C. Res. 827 (May 27).

UN Security Council. 2013. 68th Sess., 6984th mtg. UN Doc. S/PV.6984 (June 24).

Wiltsher, Anne. 1985. *Most Dangerous Women: Feminist Peace Campaigners of the Great War*. London: Pandora Press.

CHAPTER 11

1325 + 17 = ?

Filling in the Blanks of the Women, Peace, and Security Agenda

KIMBERLY THEIDON

IN 2015 the United Nations published the results of its *Global Study on the Implementation of UNSCR 1325*. Weighing in at 418 pages, the *Global Study* offers an assessment of where the Women, Peace, and Security (WPS) Agenda stood on the fifteenth anniversary of the passage of UN Security Council resolution 1325, which serves as the foundation for the United Nations' attempt to ensure the full involvement of women in all efforts for maintaining and promoting peace and security.

As noted elsewhere, the Security Council resolutions have overwhelmingly focused on women and girls as victims of sexual violence during armed conflict (see Theidon 2012, 2015, 2016; see also Engle, Chapter 10 in this volume). Strikingly absent in the agenda are men and boys as *victims* of sexual violence, and *children* born as a result of wartime rape and sexual exploitation. This chapter draws upon research that I have conducted in Peru and Colombia, the Final Report of the Peruvian Truth and Reconciliation Commission (PTRC), and relevant comparative research and literature to explore these two groups, which have scarcely figured in the WPS Agenda to date.

Men and boys appear as perpetrators hovering in the margins of the resolutions or, at best, as "those secondarily traumatized as forced witnesses of sexual violence against family members"[1] but rarely as victims of these same violations. I begin by discussing how rape between men has been used as a form of establishing relations of power and domination at the nexus of gender, ethnicity, and social class. The literature on male-dominant environments, such as armed groups, indicates that these groups utilize elaborate socialization mechanisms that are especially relevant to understanding the roles some men assume during conflict (e.g., Sanday 1990, discussing male fraternities; Goldstein 2001; Grossman 1996; and Holmes 1989, discussing military socialization; Peteet 1994, discussing torture and male authority). From illegal armed groups to state-sponsored militaries, induction into male-dominant groups frequently involves brutal or demeaning rites of passage, which in turn establish hierarchical relationships among the men. Exploring these internal dynamics forces us to reconsider "militarized masculinity" as a uniformly shared identity, and to question its explanatory or predictive value with regard to the use of sexual violence against civilians. This section concludes by illustrating how men are both perpetrators *and* victims of sexual violence, and what the erasure of the latter means in terms of gender-based violence, essentialisms, and the politics of victimhood.

The chapter then turns to children born of wartime rape and sexual exploitation, the second group largely missing from the WPS Agenda. During the last decade alone, it is estimated that tens of thousands of children have been born worldwide as a result of mass rape campaigns or wartime sexual exploitation (Carpenter 2007). What do we know about these children? While Security Council resolution 2122, one of the eight resolutions that form the WPS Agenda, specifically notes "the need for access to the full range of sexual and reproductive health services, including regarding pregnancies resulting from rape, without discrimination," there is nothing said about the outcome of those pregnancies, nor about their meaning for the mothers and their children. What about these living legacies of sexual violence? Although children born of wartime rape have remained largely invisible on the international agenda, empirical data indicates that they are not so invisible in the families and communities in which they live. At the local level, these children are frequently hidden in plain sight (Theidon 2015). Taken together, it is my hope that these reflections contribute to research and analysis on gender, violence, and justice in the years ahead.

ADD MEN AND STIR?

> Some of the recruits were really young. They were just adolescents. They didn't want to participate [in the rapes]. If someone refused, the rest of the men would take him aside and rape him. All of them would rape him, with the poor guy screaming. They said they were "changing his voice"—with so much screaming, his voice would lower and he wouldn't be a woman anymore. (Former member of the Peruvian Navy, cited in Theidon 2012)

There is a certain irony in the UN Security Council resolutions under consideration here. In much of the policy literature—including UN and World Bank documents— "gender" is frequently a code word for "women," leaving men as the unquestioned, unmarked category. When we turn to sexual violence, however, the logic of the default is reversed. As Stemple (2009) has noted in her analysis of Security Council resolution 1325, the foundational resolution of the WPS Agenda, "in the perambulatory language, boys are included through the use of the term 'women and children.' But as soon as sexual violence is addressed specifically, the instrument excludes them, switching to the term 'women and girls' " (622). Men and boys as victims of gender-based and sexual violence are all but erased.

A cursory reading of reports on sexual violence leads to a similar conclusion. There is generally the toss-away line or footnote acknowledging that, of course, men and boys may also be victims of sexual violence—and then the report returns to its main story-line, which one can gloss as "womenandgirls." One is reminded of the outmoded and critiqued Women in Development (WID) approach that was introduced in the 1970s, and which reached its apex during the UN Decade for Women. Later referred to face-tiously as "add women and stir," WID was criticized for its emphasis on women, rather than on gender relations, and for failing to address systemic gender inequality. As critics argued, WID did not "consider the underlying and often discriminatory gender struc-tures upon which these very projects are often built" (Chant and Gutman 2000, 6). In the new focus on women and girls and conflict-related sexual violence, men and boys figure as potentially violent actors or, as noted, "secondary victims" traumatized by wit-nessing the abuse of family members. This framework fails to grasp men as vulnera-ble to sexual violence, and raises older concerns about female honor and male offense creeping back into the conversation. But it is not enough to "add men and stir" to the hyper-focus on conflict-related sexual violence that has characterized the WPS Agenda thus far. That is one corrective and a necessary one; we need, however, to apply the pro-ductive insights of intersectionality to our exploration of men and masculinities, a proj-ect that extends beyond investigating sexualized forms of violence (see Crenshaw 1989).

Clearly, gender-sensitive research should include studying the masculinities forged both during armed conflict and as one component in reconstructing individual identities and col-lective existence in the aftermath of war (Hamber 2015; Theidon 2009). This means incor-porating a nuanced gender analysis into our research design and recommendations, and contemplating how our methods and questions would change if we included men and boys as both perpetrators *and* victim-survivors of gender-based and sexual violence. Additionally, given that women survivors of sexual violence are unjustly made to bear the narrative bur-den for these crimes, involving men in our research on sexual violence is crucial.

There is not just one explanation or motivation for sexual violence during armed con-flict. As with any sort of human action, the specificities matter. Indeed, the specificities are key to moving beyond the "boys will be boys" shrug of inevitability to understanding when and where sexual violence occurs; which individuals or groups are targeted and why; who the perpetrators are; and the types of sexual violence practiced, and how these may vary across time, space, and armed groups.

In her comparative research, Elisabeth Wood has employed the concept of a "rep-ertoire of violence" to refer to the range of violent acts that an armed group deploys. She then examines whether or not sexual violence figures in that broader repertoire. Wood has found that different forms of violence do not co-vary; in other words, even in highly violent conflicts, the use of sexual violence may be either very low or virtually nonexistent. This has led her to state that rape is not inevitable in war, a conclusion that should lead to a series of important consequences (Wood 2006). Investigating this var-iation moves beyond essentializing arguments about men, guns, and testosterone and allows us to identify those factors that encourage—or may serve to limit—the deploy-ment of sexual violence. It becomes easier to hold perpetrators accountable if we can demonstrate that rape and other forms of sexual violence are not "an unfortunate but inevitable by-product of the necessary game called war" (Brownmiller 1975).

My research and the Peruvian TRC's final report reveal that patterns of sexual violence varied across armed parties to the conflict. Shining Path guerrillas were more inclined toward sexual slavery and mutilation, forced nudity, and coerced abortions; the Peruvian armed forces were more likely to engage in sexual torture and gang rape. Indeed, as my research showed, when women described their experiences of rape, it was never one soldier, but rather several. "They raped the women until they could not stand up." The soldiers were mutilating women with their penises, and the women were bloodied. These were blood rituals (see Theidon 2012).

When analyzing gang rape, we should think about why the men raped this way. An instrumentalist explanation would indicate that the soldiers raped in groups in order to overpower a woman, or so that one soldier could serve watch while the others raped. However, it would be a limited reading to attribute this practice to the necessity for pure force or standing watch. When a soldier pressed his machine gun into a woman's chest, he did not need more force. When the soldiers came down from the bases at night to rape, "privacy" was not their primary concern. They operated with impunity.

Clearly there is a ritualistic aspect to gang rape (Enloe 1988; see also Gaca, Chapter 23 in this volume). Many people related that after killing someone, the soldiers drank the blood of their victim, or bathed their faces and chests with the blood. Blood ties were established between soldiers, and bloodied wombs birthed a lethal fraternity. These blood ties united the soldiers, and the bodies of the raped women served as the medium for forging those ties.

Gang rape not only breaks the moral codes that generally order social life: the practice also serves to eradicate shame. Committing morally abhorrent acts in front of others not only forges bonds between the perpetrators but also forges *sinvergüenzas*—shameless people—capable of tremendous brutality. To lose the sense of shame—a regulatory emotion because shame implies an "Other" in front of whom one feels ashamed—creates men with a recalibrated capacity for atrocity. Acts that obliterate shame also obliterate a sense of self, contributing to processes aimed at subsuming individuality to create group cohesion and "selflessness" in the service of a collective. Additionally, there is a temporal aspect to understanding these acts and the men who engage in them—and to understanding why the solidarity of guilt may give way to a deep sense of shame over time. In my research, I have been struck by the fact that "men don't talk," at least not in the first person, about their participation in rape.

But they certainly do talk during the act itself. Women (and men) emphasize what the soldiers said while raping them: *Terruca de mierda* (shitty terrorist), *ahora aguanta India* (now take it, Indian), *carajo, terruca de mierda* (damn it, terrorist of shit), and *India de mierda* (shitty Indian). The soldiers were marking their victims with physical and verbal assaults. Importantly, in my conversations as well as in the testimonies provided to the PTRC, acts of sexual violence were almost always accompanied by ethnic and racial insults, prompting me to consider the ways in which gender, racial, and military hierarchies converged during the internal armed conflict.

Where did the soldiers learn this behavior, and acquire such virulent disdain for people ethnically similar to themselves? I suggest we look to the barracks. Drawing upon her research in Guatemala, Diane Nelson has written that "reports of brutal barracks training suggest that internalized racism is a tool used to break the boys down so they may be remade as soldiers, in part by promising them marks of ladino identity (modern bourgeois practices like wearing shoes and eating meat) and of masculinity. Mayan men are often feminized in relation to traditional practices and in their limited power vis-à-vis the ladino" (Nelson 1999, 91).[2] Military service, for all of its abuses, is thus a way to become "less Indian" in a context in which "the Indian is often coded as female" (Nelson 1999, 182).

This holds true in Peru as well, where young rural men swelled the lowest ranks of the army, and were subject to brutal military socialization. *Los antiguos* (senior officers and more seasoned soldiers) referred to these young men as *los perros* (the dogs); the former soldiers we interviewed summed up their basic training as *la perrada*—a dog's life. They recount being forced to lick the floors of filthy latrines, to sleep with dirty flea-infested blankets, to kill dogs, and subsequently drink their blood and eat their raw flesh. These men also described severe beatings and lacerating verbal harassment as punishments for even minor infractions.

Included in the verbal harassment were ethnic insults. The recruits were darker-skinned men from the sierra, serving under lighter-skinned officers from the coast. Class standing and military rank magnified ethnic difference, which was further enforced by the use of sexual violence, especially rape. In our interviews, former soldiers assured us that "sex was 80 percent of the conversations we had every day." Who could *tirar* (rape) another was a determining factor in deciding who was the *más macho*, and the first one to anally rape another man came out, literally, on top. Just as rank determined who would go first when raping civilians, that same hierarchy was repeated within the barracks. The gang rapes began with the highest-ranking officer and ended with the lowliest recruit. Rape was a means of establishing hierarchies, between armed groups and the population, and within the armed forces themselves. Several former soldiers described the use of sodomy on young recruits who were reluctant to demonstrate the "appropriate" level of aggression vis-à-vis the civilian population. In other instances, we were told that if a recruit refused to participate in the raping, he would be shot and his family told that he died in combat. Thus, I stress again the importance of understanding men as both victims and victimizers during times of conflict, a recognition that need not devolve into a lack of accountability or endless moral elasticity.

Holding people accountable means having a clear understanding of the forms of violence practiced and suffered, by whom, and in what context. This may involve listening differently to male victim-survivors, which could change what we think we know about sexual violence. For example, political scientist Michelle Leiby (2009) reviewed a sample of 2,500 testimonies given to the Peruvian TRC, examining what people had said and how the acts they described were coded into the database. When she analyzed the original testimonies (and worked with native Quechua speakers to capture the nuances of language), Leiby found that 22 percent of the victims of sexual violence were men, strikingly at odds with the eleven male rape victims included in the PTRC's Final Report

(82). In the TRC's coding "the rape of men is treated inconsistently—coded as either sexual violence or torture, and sometimes not recorded at all"[3] (Leiby 2009, 82). Evidently, what determined whether a particular act was coded as sexual violence versus torture often depended not on the act itself, but on the gender of the body upon which the act was performed. The erasure of sexualized violence against men yields stereotypical victim-perpetrator binaries, and reinforces the image of women as persons to whom sexual crimes essentially occur. Women get raped; men, apparently, do not.[4]

For certain testimony takers and database designers in Peru, the idea of men as victims of sexual violence was "unthinkable," and the stories men told about being raped, sexually tortured, mutilated, or humiliated were largely erased. Thus, an important silence entered into and molded the archive. Statistics have powerful knowledge effects, and archives are more than a mere collection of documents that define a culture at a particular moment. As Foucault (1982) argued, archives are more than institutions neutrally established to preserve texts. Rather, the archive is "the law of what can be said," and the law of how what is said is transformed, used, and preserved (127). In this instance, the archive leaves us with essentialized notions of victims and perpetrators, categories too frequently assumed to map seamlessly onto gendered dichotomies as well. Gender is reduced to women; gender-based violence is reduced to rape; and the more complicated stories people tell about war are at risk of becoming unthinkable and, therefore, erased.

HIDDEN IN PLAIN SIGHT: CHILDREN BORN OF WARTIME SEXUAL VIOLENCE

When I began to work on the topic of children born of wartime rape, I returned to volume six of the Peruvian TRC's Final Report and to the chapter entitled "Sexual Violence against Women." In that chapter alone were thirty-seven references to girls and women impregnated as a result of wartime rape or exploitative sexual relationships. Mostly these are third-party reports, and the women speaking refer to the phenomenon of unwanted pregnancies in the plural. "They ended up pregnant," "they came out pregnant"—the army, the police, and guerrillas of the Shining Path and the Tupac Amaru Revolutionary Movement are all named in the women's testimonies about rape-related pregnancies. The TRC acknowledges that these children may suffer as a result:

> There are numerous cases of women who, being pregnant, were subjected to sexual violence and saw their pregnancies interrupted as a result of that violence. On the other hand, there are abundant cases of women who became pregnant as a result of the sexual violence they suffered at the hands of agents of the conflict; they found themselves obligated to assume a forced pregnancy and their children still continue to suffer the consequences of the violence. (PTRC 2003, vol. 6, 372; my translation)

The reader is left with no further information about those consequences. The women indicate that the guerrillas frequently forced the girls and women to have abortions, and when pregnancies were somehow carried to term, the babies were "forcefully taken away" (PTRC 2003, vol. 6, 310). There are fleeting references to babies who died shortly after birth. The Commission's singular focus on compiling first-person accounts of rape and sexual violence in order to "break the silence" about these crimes somehow reduced children to a mere coda. What happened to all of those babies? Who else was talking about them?

Abortions and infanticide are phenomena widely reported in post-conflict settings in which the use of rape was widespread. In Peru, some women tried to abort with herbs, attempting to rid their bodies of fetuses they could not bear. Others sought out *curanderos* (healers) who used various abortifacients to perform *limpiezas* (cleansings). In this instance, the word *limpieza* is a form of veiled speech that allowed women to maintain a useful ambiguity. *Limpiezas* of various sorts are common for a range of illnesses; it was only with time that my colleagues and I realized the women had visited *curanderos* to cleanse themselves literally—they complained of feeling "filthy" as a result of being raped—as well as to cleanse their uteri of unwanted pregnancies. Across a variety of post-conflict settings, the recurrent theme of children born with disabilities is striking. For example, Carpenter (2010) noted a number of children born to rape survivors in Bosnia who were disabled (24). I believe some of these disabilities may have been due to botched abortion attempts. The lack of safe, accessible, and affordable abortions does a grave disservice to these women, their fetuses, and babies.

Still other Peruvian women resorted to infanticide. There is a long-standing practice of "letting die" those babies who are unwanted, perhaps because they are born with congenital defects or are the product of rape. The idea is that *criaturas* (little babies) do not suffer when they die; one can leave them sleeping "mouth down," gently drifting off to death. Additionally, given women's concerns about the transmission of *llakis* (toxic memories) and *susto* (soul loss due to fright) from mother to baby, either in utero or via their mother's "milk of pain and sorrow," concerns about damage to their infants were omnipresent. How could a baby born of such suffering and fear be normal? Many women were certain they could not. Letting these babies die reflected a desire to spare them the violence of memory—and to spare their mothers these memories of violence.

In addition to women's testimonies about rape-related pregnancies, audible speech acts of another sort were playing out all around those of us working in the highlands. I am referring to the names given to children born of conflict-related sexual violence. In any community—this is in no way limited to Peru—there is the audible impact of names given to these children, both individual and collective, that are frequently of an injurious nature. Some examples of these are the following:

RWANDA: collectively labeled "unwanted children," "children of bad memories," "children of hate," "genocidal children"; the individual names include "little killer," "child of hate," "I'm at a loss," and "the intruder"
KOSOVO: "children of shame"

EAST TIMOR: "children of the enemy"
VIET NAM: "dust of life" and "American infected babies"
NICARAGUA: "monster babies"
GUATEMALA: "soldadito" (little soldier)
UGANDA: "Only God knows why this happened to me," "I am unfortunate," "Things have gone bad"
COLOMBIA: "paraquitos" (little paramilitaries).

In Peru, among other names, children are referred to as *los regalos de los soldados*, (the soldier's gifts), *hijo de nadie* (nobody's child), *fulano* (what's his name), and *chatarra* (stray cat). Time and again, across regions, names reveal the conjuncture of painful kinship and "poisonous knowledge" (Das 2000). These naming practices seem strikingly at odds with the secrecy and silence assumed to surround rape and other forms of sexual violence. Concealment is a leitmotif in the literature, and is generally understood as a way to avoid stigma for both the mother and her child.

And yet, names mark certain children and reveal their violent origins. Naming is verbal, audible, and interpersonal; naming practices are one way of expressing, perhaps projecting, the private into public space and laying claims upon others. These "entanglements" are worth contemplating. Every woman who spoke with me or with my research assistants about rape insisted, "I've never told anyone before." However, those of us who work amidst secrets and silences know that "I never told anyone" is not synonymous with "nobody knows." But for the moment, let us assume that some women did successfully conceal their pregnancies—did conceal this violence and its legacies. Even so, at some point, women give birth to the secret. In that process of emergence, who and what is being made public? Who and what is being named?

Over the years, I have known several children who were the result of rape. Here I mention one boy whose mother had been passed around by the soldiers in the base that had overlooked their community for almost fifteen years. I first noticed him because he was standoffish, never joining the growing group of children who made my room a lively place. I tried to speak with him a few times, but he had no interest in conversation. After months of living in the community, I finally asked someone about him. It was late afternoon and I saw him heading down the steep hill toward home, his three goats and one llama kept together with an occasional slap of a slender stick. The woman sitting at my side knew him by name: Chiki. My face must have expressed my surprise because she whispered that his mother was "one of those women."

Chiki is a painful name for a young boy, who in turn was a painful child for his mother. *Chiki* means "danger" in Quechua, and in daily usage refers to a warning that something bad is about to happen and should be averted. People recall the ways they learned to look for a sign that the enemy might attack. One such *chiki* was a strong wind that blew through the village, rattling the roofs and letting people know something evil was about to occur. This boy could not be a warning; it was too late to avert this particular danger. Rather, he was the product of an evil event his mother had been unable to escape. His mere being extends his mother's memory both to the past and into the future. Her son is a living memory of the danger she survived, and a reminder that nothing good could possibly come from this Chiki she had failed to avoid.

In a fascinating piece on children born to young women who had been abducted and made "wives" by the Lord's Resistance Army in Uganda, Apio (2007) briefly discusses naming practices. In a sample of sixty-nine children, she found that forty-nine of them had injurious names. These forty-nine children were all named by their mothers, while the other twenty had been named either by the father, or by medical staff who delivered the babies following their mother's reintegration. "These names compile all the bad experiences of a mother into a name and give it a life in the nature of her baby," Apio wrote. "In this way the baby is turned into a living reminder of her suffering" (101). Social workers made efforts to give these children new names such as "I am fortunate" or "things have turned good," but as Apio found in her interviews with World Vision staff, the women were reluctant: "*They prefer the old names*" (2007, 101; emphasis added). We are not told why. This example, however, is at odds with the idea that women inevitably seek to conceal the violent conception of these children. When it is the mother who does the naming, and in doing so names the violence she survived, poisonous knowledge is moved outward into the public domain. This appears to be less about shame than it is about pressing some sort of claim upon others—from poisonous knowledge to a demand for acknowledgment? Why are the mothers breaking this particular silence?

The concept of stigma is frequently applied to these children, yet is that really all we can say about these names? Stigma seems a thin explanation for a thick phenomenon, and forecloses a broader repertoire of potential meanings and motivations. While the evidence does not allow one to make totalizing claims, these names surely have something to do with memory and memorialization, and with theories regarding what is passed from parent to child—hence my insistence on who and what is being named and made public, and why.

In the literature on rape, women frequently appear as metonyms for the nation, the community—for some collective that is allegedly attacked via the rape of its female members. The "rape as a weapon of war" approach turns on this idea, and on the deployment of rape as a strategic means of achieving an end (Eriksson Baaz and Stern 2013). Eriksson Baaz and Stern rightly challenge this framework, noting that the uses and meanings of rape are far more variable than the "weapon of war" approach allows. If rape is, however, at times used to undermine the morale of the enemy and to destroy communities, then marking these children may be a way of bearing witness to the harm done to the collective. Naming is both a "saying" and a "doing," and speaking these names implicates others in an act of memorialization. Might this be, at times, a woman's refusal to accept shame and stigma, albeit at a cost to the well-being of her child? In my research, I found that women were frequently disruptive of communal histories that had been elaborated by community leaders, virtually all men (Theidon 2012). Women were "counter-memory specialists" whose versions of events often diverged from the seamless accounts of the war offered up to those who came around asking about the past. These children's names can be a form of narrating the past, of attesting to the legacies of violence in the present, and of denouncing the harm done, for which no redress has yet been found.

Ní Aoláin has noted that many acts of sexual violence during war are not private acts: "Unlike the experience of gendered violence during peacetime, which is predominantly located in the domain of the private, the home, sexual violence during war is strikingly public" (2000, 78). In Peru, women were raped in front of their families and communities; at times they were hauled off to nearby military bases and returned with their hair shorn as a mark of the gang rapes that they had endured. These violations frequently occurred with the complicity of local authorities—all male—and the neighbors who turned a deaf ear to the screaming next door. I have found that officials in the military bases demanded a "communal counterpart" in exchange for the "security" they provided to rural communities during the internal armed conflict. That counterpart consisted of food, wood, and *warmis* (women). At times this demand was veiled by the term *aynicha*, a diminutive of *ayni*. *Ayni* refers to reciprocal labor exchanges by which people work on one another's agricultural plots. It implies reciprocity, but with an element of hierarchy and obligation. Communal authorities would indicate to the military officials which houses were occupied by single mothers and widows; these homes would be the first targeted when the soldiers descended from the bases at night for *la carnada*—literally "bait," but in this context it refers to gorging on meat (*carne*), that is, the women they would rape. Again, who and what is being named and made public?

If names can implicate others in acts of memorialization, they may also implicate others in acts of betrayal and treachery. Communal contracts involved sexual contracts, and the burden of providing the communal counterpart fell heavily upon certain women and girls who were obliged to "service" the troops. These names disrupt the rules of the game—in this instance, that of knowing what not to know and what not to say. Rather than the "labor of the negative" that is vital to public secrets, with their reproductive labor women gave birth to, and insisted upon naming, a body of evidence. Taussig has argued that "truth is not a matter of exposure which destroys the secret, but a revelation that does justice to it" (1999, 2). The names—this revelation—may not do justice, but rather constitute a demand for it. Exploring the ways in which children born of wartime sexual violence are named, represented, marked, and, perhaps, loved could generate new insights into the intersection of gender, ethnicity, sexuality, violence, and identity. Combined with the previous discussion of men and boys as victims of sexual violence, evidence-based research on these issues could help fill in the certain blanks in the WPS Agenda as it currently stands, contributing to a greater measure of justice in the years ahead.

Notes

1. S.C. Res. 2106 (June 24, 2013).
2. The ladino population in Guatemala has been characterized as a group that expresses itself in the Spanish language as a maternal language, and that possesses specific cultural traits of Hispanic origin mixed with indigenous cultural elements, and dresses in a style commonly considered "Western."

3. The most frequent forms of sexual abuse suffered by men was sexual humiliation (46 percent), followed by sexual mutilation (20 percent), then sexual torture (15 percent) and rape (15 percent) (Leiby 2009).
4. Space limitations do not allow me to adequately address certain domestic legal systems and the gendered pronouns used in the rape laws. In some countries, men cannot "legally" be raped because the law only recognized female victims. In other cases, "sodomy" may be illegal, and thus a man who comes forward to denounce having been raped is a criminal, not a victim.

REFERENCES

Apio, Eunice. 2007. "Uganda's Forgotten Children of War." In *Born of War: Protecting Children of Sexual Violence Survivors in Conflict Zones*, edited by Carli Carpenter, 94–109. Bloomfield, CT: Kumarian Press.

Brownmiller, Susan. 1975. *Against Our Will: Men, Women, and Rape*. New York: Simon & Schuster.

Carpenter, R. Charli. 2007. *Born of War: Protecting Children of Sexual Violence Survivors in Conflict Zones*. Bloomfield, CT: Kumarian Press.

Carpenter, R. Charli. 2010. *Forgetting Children Born of War: Setting the Human Rights Agenda in Bosnia and Beyond*. New York: Columbia University Press.

Chant, Sylvia, and Matthew C. Gutman. 2000. *Mainstreaming Men into Gender and Development: Debates, Reflections and Experiences*. London: Oxfam.

Crenshaw, Kimberlé. 1989. "Mapping the Margins: Intersectionality, Identity Politics, and Violence against Women of Color." *Stanford Law Review* 43: 1240–1299.

Das, Veena. 2000. "The Act of Witnessing: Violence, Poisonous Knowledge and Subjectivity." In *Violence in Subjectivity*, edited by Veena Das, Arthur Kleinman, Mamphela Ramphele, and Pamela Reynolds, 205–225. Berkeley: University of California Press.

Enloe, Cynthia. 1988. *Does Khaki Become You? The Militarisation of Women's Lives*. London: Pandora Press.

Eriksson Baaz, Maria, and Maria Stern. 2013. *Sexual Violence as a Weapon of War? Perceptions, Prescriptions, Problems in the Congo and Beyond*. London: Zed Books.

Foucault, Michel. 1982. *The Archaeology of Knowledge*. New York: Vintage Books.

Goldstein, Joshua S. 2001. *War and Gender: How Gender Shapes the War System and Vice Versa*. New York: Cambridge University Press.

Grossman, David. 1996. *On Killing: The Psychological Costs of Learning to Kill in War and Society*. New York: Back Bay Books/Little Brown.

Hamber, Brandon. 2015. "There Is a Crack in Everything: Problematising Masculinities, Peacebuilding and Transitional Justice." *Human Rights Review*, 17, no. 1: 9–34.

Holmes, Richard. 1989. *Acts of War: Behavior of Men in Battle*. New York: Free Press.

Leiby, Michelle. 2009. "Digging in the Archives: The Promise and Perils of Primary Documents." *Politics and Society* 37: 75–99.

Nelson, Diane. 1999. *Finger in the Wound: Body Politics in Quincentennial Guatemala*. Berkeley: University of California Press.

Ní Aoláin, Fionnuala. 2000. "Sex-Based Violence and the Holocaust: A Reevaluation of Harms and Rights in International Law." *Yale Journal of Law and Feminism* 12, no. 43: 43–84.

Peruvian Truth and Reconciliation Commission (PTRC). 2003. *Informe Final de la Comisión de Verdad y Reconciliación*. Lima: Peruvian Truth and Reconciliation Commission.

Peteet, Julie. 1994. "Male Gender and Rituals of Resistance in the Palestinian 'Intifada': A Cultural Politics of Violence." *American Ethnologist* 21: 31–49.

Sanday, Peggy. 1990. *Fraternity Gang Rape: Sex, Brotherhood, and Privilege on the College Campus*. New York: New York University Press.

Stemple, Lara. 2009. "Male Rape and Human Rights." *Hastings Law Journal* 60: 605–645.

Taussig, Michael. 1999. *Defacement: Public Secrecy and the Labor of the Negative*. Stanford, CA: Stanford University Press.

Theidon, Kimberly. 2009. "Reconstructing Masculinities: The Disarmament, Demobilization, and Reintegration of Former Combatants in Colombia." *Human Rights Quarterly* 31, no. 1: 1–34.

Theidon, Kimberly. 2012. *Intimate Enemies: Violence and Reconciliation in Peru*. Philadelphia: University of Pennsylvania Press.

Theidon, Kimberly. 2015. "Hidden in Plain Sight: Children Born of Wartime Sexual Violence." *Current Anthropology* 56, no. 12: 191–200.

Theidon, Kimberly. 2016. "A Greater Measure of Justice: Gender, Violence and Reparations." In *Mapping Feminist Anthropology in the Twenty-First Century*, edited by Leni Silverstein and Ellen Lewin. New Brunswick, NJ: Rutgers University Press.

Wood, Elisabeth Jean. 2006. "Variation in Sexual Violence during War." *Politics and Society* 34, no. 3: 307–342.

CHAPTER 12

COMPLEMENTARITY AND CONVERGENCE?

Women, Peace and Security and Counterterrorism

NAUREEN CHOWDHURY FINK
AND ALISON DAVIDIAN

THE imperative for governments to prevent unpredictable civilian atrocities with the potential for mass-casualty attacks and diminish the appeal and recruiting potential of terrorist groups has generated greater attention by international counterterrorism (CT) actors to the roles of women in addressing terrorism and violent extremism.[1] The roles of women as prominent facilitators and recruiters, even perpetrators, has prompted an increasing focus on the grievances, recruitment techniques, and intervention points for prevention that underpin their actions. At the same time, women are also playing active roles in the prevention of, and response to, terrorism, from supporting early warning efforts as well as challenging extremist narratives. Yet, the discourse remains characterized by gender stereotypes that impede a more nuanced assessment of the roles of women and constrain the scope of policy responses. While the evolution of the international CT toolkit to include efforts to prevent and counter violent extremism (CVE) has created more opportunity to address these issues, critics argue that the Women, Peace, and Security (WPS) Agenda is at risk of marginalization, instrumentalization, and securitization. Without fully integrating a gender perspective into CT and CVE efforts, across the analysis, implementation, and evaluation phases, this risk will prove difficult to mitigate.

This chapter explores the gendered dimension of today's terrorism threat and the gendered dynamics of the violent extremist ideologies that underpin it. It analyzes the WPS Agenda in relation to terrorism and counterterrorism, as well as the emerging focus on CVE, looking in particular at integration efforts as called for in Security Council resolution 2242 (2015). While noting the risks and criticisms associated with an integrated approach, the chapter concludes that the WPS and CVE agendas are characterized more by complementarity and convergence than dissonance, where efforts to reduce the impact of terrorism and violent extremism can reinforce efforts to support women's empowerment, and where women's meaningful inclusion and participation can inform more contextually relevant and sustainable responses. Indeed, terrorism and violent extremism is part of the current peace and security environment affecting women and women's rights. As a growing body of evidence highlights, women's leadership and participation increase operational effectiveness in all areas of peace and security and humanitarian engagement, including in preventing and countering terrorism and violent extremism (UN Women 2015), making it a critical component of our efforts in this regard.

GENDERED NARRATIVES, GENDERED IMPACT

Groups like Al-Qaeda and the so-called Islamic State (ISIS, which includes references to ISIL, IS, Daesh and other associated translations) have used a highly gendered narrative to bolster their appeal—not only to women, but also to men. In 2005, the leader of Al-Qaeda in Iraq, Abu Musab Al-Zarqawi, called for Sunni supporters, asking, "Where is your sense of honor, your zeal, and your manliness?" (Al-Zarqawi 2005). Similarly ISIS's recruitment narrative employs hyper-militarized, hyper-masculinized, and particularly violent motifs to portray its fighters as the epitome of "real men." This image draws on gendered expectations of the male as head of the household and, by extension, the community, empowered to protect women from the brutalities of outsiders (Van Leuven, Dallin, Mazurana and Gordon 2016, 117–118). The promises of a wife, home, and monthly allowance also appear to be motivating factors. Such prospects can be particularly appealing to young men who feel marginalized or cut off from traditional rites of passage into adulthood, such as securing a job and starting a family. In Mali, terrorist and violent extremist groups are reportedly utilizing highly gendered (and repressive) narratives to appeal to supporters, urging them to join in the restoration of women to their (traditional) roles.[2]

The Internet and social media platforms, including messaging apps and private chat forums, have created spaces in which women who may otherwise be cautious about public interaction can become active virtual participants. Through Twitter, for example, accounts reportedly belonging to women living in ISIS-controlled territory extol the virtues of sisterhood, freedom to live under their interpretation of Sharia, and the pleasure derived from supporting jihad. The objective of an Islamic Utopia, a state that answers the calling of the *ummah* (community), has led ISIS to diverge from Al-Qaeda's previous practice and actively pursue female recruits. They are critical incentives—wives, sexual slaves, ideological partners—for the young men they hope to attract, but also play an important role in securing the loyalty of fighters. By marrying the women off, ISIS keeps the men and makes it less likely that they will go back to their home countries (Van Leuven, Dallin, Mazurana and Gordon 2016, 107). Moreover, female recruits also play a key role in ISIS's state-building enterprise, which has a critical need for women as mothers, wives, teachers, and nurses. The manifesto on the role of women in ISIS, developed by the Al-Khansaa Brigade, the all-female wing of ISIS, reaffirms notions of traditional male and female roles and positions them as an objective lost to modern Western societies; this has been often reaffirmed, including, for example, in long articles produced for *Dabiq*, ISIS's English-language glossy magazine clearly developed for Western recruits (Winter 2015). The core ideas in these have been reflected throughout a range of social media messages posted in support of joining ISIS.

Terrorists targeting women

Despite the glorification of female roles in their narratives, control over women, their lives, and their bodies lies at the heart of the agenda of many violent extremist and terrorist groups. In addition to physical attacks and the use of sexual violence as a tactic of terror, epitomized most starkly in the sexual slavery of Yazidi women and girls, groups like ISIS, Boko Haram, and the Taliban also use violence to curtail women's rights and prospects for development, attacking the core principles of the women's movement and its hard-won gains. By targeting schools, cutting off access to health care, social services, and employment, and imposing harsh codes of conduct on dress, movement, and expression, such violent extremist groups deny women access to the rights and freedoms encapsulated in the UN Charter, as well as international humanitarian and human rights law. This is not confined to transnational groups. In Bangladesh, for example, initiatives to empower women and promote their rights and education have been attacked by violent extremist groups; in 2013, Hefazat-e-Islam's demand that men and women not mix in public was greeted with alarm bells in a country where women are active in public life and commerce (Burke and Hammadi 2013). While violence against women by conflict actors and their utilization of a gendered narrative is not new, the institutionalization of sexual slavery and the use of young children for sex, and the routinization of kidnappings for ransom, violent executions, and graphic punishments, mark a significant development in the modus operandi of terrorist groups like ISIS and Boko Haram. These dynamics highlight that violence against women can be an important "warning sign" for terrorism because "groups that engage in these sorts of attacks on civilians as a whole often pursue misogynist agendas and carry out, or advocate, severe forms of violence against women" (Bennoune 2008). In 2012 in Mali, for example, groups including Ansar Dine, the Movement for Unity and Jihad in West Africa, and Al-Qaeda in the Islamic Maghreb (AQIM) seized control of the north and immediately curtailed women's rights to employment, education, and access to basic social services (Human Rights Watch 2012; Nossiter 2012). Similar restrictions have also been reported by women and girls living under Al Shabaab in Somalia (Albin-Lackey and Tayler 2010). The imposition by ISIS of a strict interpretation of Sharia law on all aspects of life, from dress to movement, employment, and religion, has particularly impacted women (UN Human Rights Council 2015, para. 161). The restrictions are especially pronounced as the conflict in Syria continues and the numbers of Syrian men killed and disappeared increases, leading directly to a rise in female-headed households in the midst of a systemic oppression on women's rights. This renders these households more vulnerable to abuse and violence, as well as poverty from lack of access to means of economic survival and public life.

Women as preventers

Women are often on the frontlines of violence and terrorism, forced to navigate complex relationships and circumstances to meet the expectations that they will hold families and communities together in the face of conflict. Their roles are multifaceted and range from female imams to community mobilizers and educators to women police officers. In places like Kenya, Nigeria, Pakistan, and Indonesia, for example, women's civil society organizations are working to promote women's rights, and support gender mainstreaming and inclusion in efforts to prevent and respond to terrorism and violent extremism.

As mothers, they are often uniquely positioned in homes and communities to identify changes in the household and the behaviors of children, and to provide powerful countervailing incentives (Schlaffer and Kropiunigg 2016). However, in many instances, mothers may not be culturally empowered to take on such a role, and it is important to balance support for mothers with efforts to promote women's meaningful participation in a range of capacities (Oudraat 2016). Where there is deep mistrust of the police or state security agencies, women may also be unwilling to bring attention to potential signs of radicalization among family members for fear of the consequences, particularly where early warning mechanisms are linked not to assistance, but to criminal justice responses. It is critical that these risks are taken into account when designing and implementing programs.

Women as supporters, perpetrators

Despite the threat posed by groups like ISIS to women and their rights, women have also emerged as supporters and perpetrators, as evidenced by the number of foreign female recruits. One estimate suggests that up to 15–20 percent of foreigners joining ISIS are women (USAID 2015). In the United States, for example, there has been a discernible rise in the numbers of women openly supporting terrorist groups (Alexander 2016). There are numerous accounts of women shaming friends and family into supporting or joining the jihad, and extolling the virtues of a caliphate where they are free to practice their interpretation of their religion unmolested. Although to date their roles have been within gendered parameters and limited to the private, domestic sphere, there are hints that this may not always be the case, with some expressing desires to perpetrate attacks and participate in brutally violent actions. However, to date, ISIS has been clear regarding their expectations of women's behavior, devoting several columns in *Dabiq* magazine to detailing the prescribed protocols (Dabiq 2016). While in certain circumstances they are permitted to engage in jihad (i.e., "if the enemy is attacking her country and the men are not enough to protect it and the imams give a fatwa for it"), the primary role of women living in ISIS-controlled territory is to be wives and mothers until such time as the jihad is deemed *fard'ayn*, or the duty of every Muslim (Winter 2015).

While the participation of women in terrorism is by no means a novelty, their very public roles as recruiters, enablers, and even perpetrators in the cause of violent extremist groups, particularly via social media platforms, appears in contrast with the worldview articulated by ISIS. Little research is available about the direct impact of their voices on patterns of recruitment and participation, particularly regarding the flow of foreign fighters and migrants to ISIS-controlled territory, but if their public Twitter feeds are to be believed, there is a keen sense of agency and empowerment that accompanies their decisions to travel (Saltman and Smith 2015). This would align with the motivations of many women to join other armed groups such as the Liberation Tigers of Tamil Eelam (LTTE) in Sri Lanka, the Maoists in Nepal, and the Red Brigades in Italy, for example, in the past. In other cases, coercion, manipulation, and abuse may inform women's decisions to knowingly or unknowingly perpetrate attacks—in Nigeria, for example, where the motivations of young female suicide bombers remains unclear (Searcey 2016). Stories of women whose only path to social salvation was through violence, believed to cleanse both individuals and families of shame, also highlight the complex dynamics that underpin women's roles as perpetrators (Bloom 2011).

Applying the "Women, Peace, and Security" Lens to Counterterrorism

The international community has been quick to respond to the rise of terrorist/violent extremist groups with military power. These tools alone, however, cannot address the drivers of extremist violence and the spread of radical ideologies that are conducive to terrorism. Nor can they build conflict-resilient communities. Instead, they can perpetuate structural inequalities that disadvantage women and girls and create an insecure environment that can be exploited by terrorist groups.

Since the adoption of resolution 1325, many stakeholders have tended to prioritize the inclusion of women and their concerns into existing militarized systems for maintaining peace and security, while deprioritizing efforts to challenge the very nature of those systems (Wright 2015). In consultations for the Global Study on the implementation of resolution 1325, women explicitly stated that the only way to truly make the world safe for all is to bring about an end to conflict and focus more on prevention. This aligns with the WPS Agenda, and its assertion that sustainable peace will only be possible when stakeholders focus on addressing the root causes of conflict and violence, as well as demilitarization and disarmament.

The reviews of the United Nations on peace operations and peace-building made similar findings. The High-Level Independent Panel on UN Peace Operations (2015) stated, "the prevention of armed conflict is perhaps the greatest responsibility of the international community and yet it has not been sufficiently invested in" (ix); and the report of the advisory group of experts on the UN peace-building architecture underscored that while militarized responses to conflict "can prove effective in the immediate context of violence, they tend to address symptoms rather than root causes" (Advisory Group of Experts 2015).

The core of the WPS Agenda is about protecting and promoting women's rights in conflict and post-conflict situations, including the right to equal and meaningful participation. Indeed, the central finding of the Global Study is that women's leadership and participation increase our operational effectiveness in all areas of peace and security and humanitarian engagement, including in preventing and countering terrorism and violent extremism. Goal 16 of the new 2030 Agenda for Sustainable Development makes it clear that the global community cannot build peace on the basis of exclusion, inequality, or marginalization. Consequently, women's participation in all efforts to prevent and resolve conflict, including CT, is not an option. Rather, it is a prerequisite for sustainable and effective responses.

While the institutional architecture of the United Nations on CT was created almost in parallel to the WPS Agenda, with key resolutions passed only a year after resolution 1325 and in the wake of September 11, 2001, the two agendas have largely developed with little interaction. In recent years, however, gender advocates have increasingly grown aware of the impact of both terrorism and counterterrorism on women's rights, and the WPS Agenda itself is beginning to grapple increasingly with these issues. Security Council resolution 2122 explicitly mentions terrorism as one of the thematic areas where the Council intends to increase its attention to women, peace, and security issues. A Presidential Statement issued during the 2014 Open Debate reiterated the role of women's participation and empowerment to prevent the spread of violent extremism, while noting its consequences on the rights of women and girls (UN Security Council 2014).

Most significantly, Security Council resolution 2242 (2015) provides one of the most important pronouncements of this body to date on the issue of countering terrorism and violent extremism, and the linkages to women, peace, and security. The resolution specifically calls for greater integration by member states and the United Nations of their agendas on women, peace, and security, counterterrorism, and countering violent extremism that can be conducive to terrorism. By doing so, it commits the Security Council and key actors to integrating a gender perspective. It is also an opening—if the tools of the WPS Agenda are applied, this increasing convergence could be an avenue to ensure a focus on prevention, demilitarization, and human rights.

Key elements of the resolution include requesting CT bodies to integrate gender as a cross-cutting issue throughout their respective mandates, and urging member states and relevant UN entities, in collaboration with UN Women, to conduct gender-sensitive research and data collection on the drivers of radicalization for women and the impact of CT strategies on women's human rights and women's organizations. Member states and the UN system are urged to ensure the participation and leadership of women and women's organizations in developing strategies to counteract terrorism and violent extremism and in building their capacity to do so effectively. The resolution also calls for adequate financing and for committing an increased amount, within UN funding for countering terrorism and violent extremism, to projects that address gender dimensions, including women's empowerment. The 2015 Secretary-General's report on Women, Peace and Security recommends that a minimum of 15 percent of all funds dedicated to countering violent extremism are committed to projects that address women's needs, or that empower women.

The roles of women have increasingly garnered the attention of CT and CVE practitioners, who have emphasized the importance of integrating a gender dimension in policies and programs. For example, in March 2016, Ambassador Mara Marinaki, EEAS Principal Advisor on Gender and on UNSCR 1325/WPS, co-hosted an event on Gender and CVE with the Organization of the Islamic Conference (OIC). There she asserted that women are important actors in Preventing/Countering Violent Extremism (P/CVE) efforts and, reflecting a core value of UNSCR 1325, called for greater understanding of how to advance more inclusive policy development and programming. Echoing those sentiments, US Under-Secretary of State Sarah Sewall affirmed that ". . . empowered women provide powerful antidotes to violent extremism. They are able to refute extremist narratives and nihilistic visions with independence and authenticity. Societies that respect the rights of all and fully engage the participation of all have no room for violent extremism. So women's empowerment is not only essential for defeating violent extremism; defeating violent extremism is essential for women's empowerment. The two go hand-in-hand" (Sewall 2016, n.p.). Civil society experts have also echoed these views, with Sureya Roble, working on prevention efforts in Kenya, underscoring that

> [t]he mis-conception that women are not involved in extremism or terrorist radicalization has often shaped counter terrorism strategies, excluding women from decision making process and their significant under representation among law enforcement officers and security meetings. Intelligence operations on getting information should be enhanced to include women. Gender equality and women empowerment should not be valued only to the extent that it helps national security. Gender equality should be promoted in its own right and women should be empowered to participate fully in society. This is because women have been frequently victims of both terrorist attacks and counter terrorism measures. (Roble 2016)

These views were also reinforced by women working on efforts to promote resolutions 1325 and 2242 in contexts where terrorism and violent extremism were posing an increasing threat, for example, in Indonesia, Nigeria, and Bosnia-Herzegovina (Global Center on Cooperative Security 2016).

The changing normative landscape of counterterrorism

The international CT frameworks established by UNSCR 1373 (2001) and the UN Global Counterterrorism Strategy (2006) were gender-blind. There was no discussion about gender in terms of implementation, nor was there outreach to women's groups and relevant entities within the multilateral system on reflecting their expertise and experiences in developing or assessing responsive strategies. Security Council resolution 2178, adopted with over a hundred co-sponsors and notable for the first mention of CVE in a Chapter VII resolution, recognized for the first time the need to empower women as a mitigating factor to the spread of violent extremism and radicalization in the context of addressing foreign terrorist fighters. Reviews of the Global Counterterrorism Strategy, particularly in 2014, and revisions of mandates for entities such as Counter Terrorism Executive Directorate (CTED)[3] have also provided opportunities for integrating a gender dimension into UN CT frameworks. However, the increased focus by many governments on expanding the CT toolkit to encompass preventive approaches, reflective of Pillars 1 and 4 of the Global Strategy and the emergent area of practice known as "countering violent extremism" (CVE) have prompted engagement with a broader range of stakeholders than were associated with traditional law-enforcement-centric CT. This includes, for example, focusing on development, governance, human rights, education, psychology, and media. While the impact of CVE on CT policies and practices remains to be seen, a proliferation of initial efforts, including the establishment of a CVE Working Group within the Global Counterterrorism Forum (GCTF), institutions such as *Hedayah* and the Global Community Engagement and Resilience Fund (GCERF), and networks such as RESOLVE and YouthCAN are indicative of growing interest in this approach, as was the development of the UN Secretary-General's *Plan of Action to Prevent Violent Extremism*, which was presented to the General Assembly in January 2016. The recognition of sexual violence as a tactic of terrorism and a "threat to international peace and security" has further heightened consideration of women in the CT discourse.

The path from UNSCR 2122 to 2242 is also reflective of the increased focus on the intersection between WPS and CT/CVE. This has been in part because of the *deliberate* targeting of terrorist and violent extremist groups of women and women's rights, as described earlier. Global and national efforts to promote education, reduce the age of child marriage, and promote resilient and inclusive communities, exemplified in the adoption of the Sustainable Development Goals, cannot flourish where such violence occurs. Governments are also desperate to better understand the dynamics of radicalization, recruitment, and rehabilitation in relation to their own security concerns, and this is reflected in calls for enhancing research and engagement outlined in resolution 2242. For example, it appears that while some motivations may be similar for males and females, economic motivators appear to be less common among women (USAID 2015). Understanding and verifying such differences are critical in developing effective government responses and rehabilitation efforts.

The evolution of CVE has created openings for greater consideration of women's roles in relation to terrorism. For example, the adoption of a GCTF good practices memorandum on "Women and Countering Violent Extremism," developed with the Organization for Security and Cooperation in Europe (OSCE), reflects the concern that applying a label of "CT" or "CVE" to their work in the field will jeopardize the integrity of the program of work or the partners they engage with, and may compromise their security by fueling a perception that civil society groups, and women's groups, are the long arm of law-enforcement actors, national or foreign. We have heard differing views from a range of contexts. Where conflict is raging and where communities are daily confronting the ill effects of increased violent extremism or terrorism, women are already engaged in efforts to secure rights, services, and pathways to political partic- ipation (Chowdhury Fink and Barakat 2013). The increased focus on the intersection of the WPS and CT/CVE agendas came about in part through efforts on the ground to ensure the inclusion of women at all levels of CVE policy and programmatic responses, and to consider the impact of these initiatives on women (see, e.g., Peters 2015). These need not be labeled "CVE," but many objectives are aligned with the objective of pre- venting and countering violent extremism, and a number of these programs pre-date the emergence of CVE and continue under their original rubric, with their possible relevance to CVE being noted by policymakers and practitioners. While some have preferred not to work in the CVE space, other civil society actors have underscored that not engaging offers them no protection in their environments, and that they see potential benefit in drawing on the resources and political attention given to CVE, if it supports them in achieving their core objectives (Global Center on Cooperative Security 2016).

Without local and grassroots insights and expertise integrated into the development of CT and CVE efforts, the risks are likely to increase. Experts have already highlighted the negative impact of anti-terrorism legislation and financial controls on women's groups, and the chilling effects of civil society writ large of many government efforts to quell dissent in the name of countering terrorism (Huckerby and Fakih 2011). Stringent domestic and international regulations to combat the financing of terrorism have cur- tailed the ability of many diaspora communities to send remittances home. Commercial banks, for example, have responded to the increased regulations by refusing to do busi- ness with Somali money transfer operators altogether, because they are considered too high risk. This has specific gendered impacts. Remittances from the Somali diaspora, estimated at USD 1.2 billion a year, are an essential lifeline for populations in Somalia and are used to cover basic expenses including food, clothing, education, and health care. Somali women depend more on remittances than men: remittances account for 64 percent of their income, compared with 59 percent for men. Remittances are often the only funds that female caregivers are able to access and control, making them a vital tool for women's economic empowerment (Kidder, Bright, and Green 2014). For these harmful impacts to be minimized or eliminated, greater understanding is critical about the consequences of CT and CVE interventions, and how these may be undertaken to do no harm in the process.

Instrumentalization, securitization and negative backlash are crucially important risks to consider, and CT and CVE efforts must be developed in a way to best mitigate them. At the same time, without women's participation and a closer understanding of gender dynamics in peace and conflict, we know that any resolution reached will be nei- ther effective nor sustainable.

INTEGRATING A GENDER DIMENSION
INTO CT AND CVE EFFORTS

As a practical matter, what does it mean to integrate gender into CT and CVE? Adopting a gender-sensitive approach to this issue requires analyzing the impact on women's rights of both terrorism and counterterrorism. It reveals where the promotion of women's rights has been tied to national security goals in ways that undermine gender equality (Satterthwaite and Huckerby 2013). Furthermore, a gender-sensitive approach helps to understand. Ideally, it would mean understanding where the inclusion of women in prevention and response strategies will be too unsafe, unprincipled, or counterproductive. It also involves considering how labeling activities as "counterterrorism" may create an unsafe and overly securitized space for women (see Shalhoub-Kevorkian, Chapter 43 in this volume). At the same time, integrating a gender dimension into CT/CVE efforts means ensuring women's participation and leadership in decision-making processes at all levels. Women and women's organizations are already engaged in preventing violent extremism and mitigating its impact in many locales. Excluding women from the processes where relevant policies are discussed and developed leads to gaps on how they affect their rights.

Counterterrorism measures have had gendered collateral effects that are often neither acknowledged nor compensated. Enforced disappearances of male detainees in the name of countering terrorism negatively impact female family members, who bear the burden of harassment, social exclusion, and economic hardship caused by the loss of the breadwinner. Similar effects ensue from the prolonged detention without trial and forced deportation of male family members, and the practice of extraordinary rendition. Women and children are also unlawfully detained and ill treated to either gain information about male family members or to compel male terrorism suspects to provide information or confessions (Scheinin 2009). Militarized responses to terrorism are often marked by violations of international law, including gross violations of human rights, with specific negative impacts on women's human rights, thus enhancing the vulnerability of women and girls to crimes committed by both state and non-state actors. For example, attacks by security forces against Boko Haram have resulted in civilian casualties, extrajudicial and summary executions, torture, arbitrary detention, enforced disappearance, and rape (UNHCHR 2015, para. 56). In addition, women and girls in captivity who had been forced to marry Boko Haram fighters were killed when the group was forced to retreat by the African Union joint forces, reportedly so that they would not marry "infidels" or provide information to regional forces (UNHCHR 2015, para. 27).

Although the increased integration of the WPS and CVE agendas has been welcomed by many, there is concern that in bodies like the Security Council, for example, the dominance of the security objective might ensure that only those parts of the

WPS Agenda that are deemed necessary for CT/CVE will be adopted (Ní Aoláin 2015). Moreover, gender stereotypes prevail in CT efforts, with female radicalization often reduced to the idea of a seduction, coercion, or an irrational response to personal circumstances, stripped of political agency. While states in the Council appear more at ease with acknowledging the role of mothers, the issues of human rights, gender mainstreaming, and women's mobilization remain uncomfortable topics and therefore are sidelined in discussions on women and CVE. Explicit references to women's roles and gender in the context of negotiations reviewing the Global Strategy over the past years have been contentious and resulted in no mentions of the issue in the resultant resolution in 2014.

CONCLUSION

Given the impact of violent extremism and terrorism on women, as well as the critical roles women can play in prevention or perpetration, we do not see the WPS and CT/CVE agendas as mutually exclusive; nor do we believe that they are necessarily overlapping in their entirety. We see instead several points of convergence and complementarity, where efforts to reduce the burden and impact of terrorism and violent extremism can reinforce efforts to support women's empowerment. In the current threat landscape, it is likely the attention to terrorism and violent extremism will not abate. It is therefore critical that responses are undertaken in such a way that they apply the principles of the WPS Agenda, in order to not only continue efforts to empower women, but also ensure an inclusive and sustainable peace.

Better research is critically important on the impacts of interrogating female family members left behind as a result of the detention of male suspects (Kassem 2013), as well as the treatment of women terrorist suspects in custody (Ní Aoláin 2013). However, we also believe that there are important lessons learned from fifteen years of WPS work and in the area of human rights that can and must inform policy and programming. While CVE may be an emerging field, there are already experts in the WPS space whose expertise and insights can inform interventions.

Resolutions and policies will, however, only be as good as the political will and commitments that underpin them. It is crucial that all the work done to bring a gender perspective into CVE actually shape CT efforts, and that governments do not insulate gender-related discussions from broader decisions on security interventions, thus ensuring that conflict analyses and risk assessments, implementation plans and evaluations are based on a deeper understanding of the context and dynamics, including gender perspectives. Just as resolution 1325 made the powerful argument for consulting with women and ensuring them a place at the table, these are universal principles that apply to all peace and security threats and contexts, and are critical for current-day CT and CVE efforts.

Notes

1. The views in this chapter represent those of the authors and not the institutional positions of the Global Center on Cooperative Security or UN Women, respectively. The authors would like to thank Franziska Praxl for her support and inputs into this chapter.
2. Authors' discussion with senior UN official, New York, 2016.
3. The Counter-Terrorism Committee, comprising all fifteen Security Council members, is tasked with monitoring the implementation of resolutions 1373 (2001) and 1624 (2005). These resolutions obligate countries to implement a number of measures intended to enhance their legal and institutional ability to counter terrorist activities, and prohibit incitement to commit acts of terrorism. The Counter-Terrorism Committee Executive Directorate (CTED) provides the Committee with expert advice on all areas covered by resolution 1373, and technical assistance to countries, as well as promoting closer cooperation and coordination, both within the UN system of organizations and among regional and intergovernmental bodies.

References

Advisory Group of Experts. 2015. *The Challenge of Sustaining Peace: 2015 Review of the United Nations Peacebuilding Architecture.* Geneva: United Nations.

Albin-Lackey, Chris, and Letta Tayler. 2010. *Harsh War, Harsh Peace: Abuses by Al-Shabaab, the Transitional Federal Government, and AMISOM in Somalia.* New York: Human Rights Watch.

Alexander, Audrey. 2016. *Cruel Intentions: Female Jihadists in America.* Washington, DC: The Program on Extremism, George Washington University.

Al-Zarqawi, Abu Mus'ab. 2005. "Declaration of Total War on Shi'ites." *Jihad Media Battalion.* September 14. http://thesis.haverford.edu/dspace/bitstream/handle/10066/4810/ZAR20050914P.pdf.

Bennoune, Karima. 2008. "Terror/Torture." *Berkeley Journal of International Law* 26, no. 1: 1–61.

Bloom, Mia. 2011. *Bombshell: Women and Terrorism.* Philadelphia: University of Pennsylvania Press.

Burke, Jason, and Saad Hammadi. 2013. "Bangladesh Simmers as Islamic Conservatives and Progressives Clash." *The Guardian.* April 16. https://www.theguardian.com/world/2013/apr/16/bangladesh-hefazat-e-islam-women.

Chowdhury Fink, Naureen, and Rafia Barakat. 2013. *Strengthening Community Resilience against Violence and Extremism: The Roles of Women in South Asia.* Goshen, IN: Center on Global Counterterrorism Cooperation.

Dabiq. 2016. "The Fitrah of Mankind and the Near-Extinction of Women." July 31. http://clarionproject.org/factsheets-files/islamic-state-magazine-dabiq-fifteen-breaking-the-cross.pdf.

Global Center on Cooperative Security. 2016. "Advancing Integrated Approaches to Women and Countering Violent Extremism." April 28. http://www.globalcenter.org/events/advancing-integrated-approaches-to-women-and-countering-violent-extremism/.

High-Level Independent Panel on United Nations Peace Operations. 2015. *Uniting Our Strengths for Peace: Politics, Partnership and People.* Geneva: United Nations.

Huckerby, Jayne C., and Lama Fakih. 2011. *A Decade Lost: Locating Gender in US Counter-Terrorism.* New York: New York University School of Law, Center for Human Rights and Global Justice.

Human Rights Watch. 2012. "Mali: War Crimes by Northern Rebels." *Human Rights Watch.* April 30. https://www.hrw.org/news/2012/04/30/mali-war-crimes-northern-rebels.

Kassem, Ramzi. 2013. "Gendered Erasure in the Global 'War on Terror': An Unmasked Interrogation." In *Gender, National Security and Counter-Terrorism,* edited by Margaret Satterthwaite and Jayne Huckerby, 15–35. New York: Routledge.

Kidder, Thalia, David Bright, and Caroline Green. 2014. *Meaningful Action: Effective Approaches to Women's Economic Empowerment in Agriculture.* London: Oxfam.

Ní Aoláin, Fionnuala. 2013. "Situating Women in Counterterrorism Discourses: Undulating Masculinities and Luminal Femininities." *Boston University Law Review* 93: 1085–1112.

Ní Aoláin, Fionnuala. 2015. "Counter-Terrorism Committee: Addressing the Role of Women in Countering Terrorism and Violent Extremism." *Just Security.* September 17. https://www.justsecurity.org/25983/counter-terrorism-committee-addressing-role-women-countering-terrorism-violent-extremism/.

Nossiter, Adam. 2012. "In Timbuktu, Harsh Change under Islamists." *New York Times.* June 2. http://www.nytimes.com/2012/06/03/world/africa/in-timbuktu-mali-rebels-and-islamists-impose-harsh-rule.html.

Oudraat, Chantal de Jonge. 2016. "Preventing and Countering Violent Extremism (CVE): The Role of Women and Women's Organization." In *A Man's World? Exploring the Roles of Women in Countering Terrorism and Violent Extremism,* edited by Naureen Chowdhury Fink, Sara Zeiger, and Rafia Bhulai, 18–35. Abu Dhabi and Washington, DC: Hedayah and the Global Center on Cooperative Security.

Peters, Allison. 2015. *Creating Inclusive National Strategies to Counter Violent Extremism.* Washington, DC: Inclusive Security.

Saltman, Erin Marie, and Melanie Smith. 2015. *"Till Martyrdom Do Us Part": Gender and the ISIS Phenomenon.* London: Institute for Strategic Dialogue.

Satterthwaite, Margaret L., and Jayne Huckerby. 2013. *Gender, National Security, and Counter-Terrorism: Human Rights Perspectives.* New York: Routledge.

Scheinin, Martin. 2009. *Report of the Special Rapporteur on the Promotion and Protection of Human Rights and Fundamental Freedoms While Countering Terrorism.* UN Doc. A/HRC/13/37 (December 28).

Schlaffer, Edit, and Ulrich Kropiunigg. 2016. "A New Security Architecture: Mothers Included." In *A Man's World? Exploring the Roles of Women in Countering Terrorism and Violent Extremism,* edited by Naureen Chowdhury Fink, Sara Zeiger, and Rafia Bhulai, 54–75. Abu Dhabi and Washington, DC: Hedayah and the Global Center on Cooperative Security.

Roble, Sureya. 2016. "Women against Violent Extremism." Remarks at the Gender and Countering Violent Extremism Conference, New York, March 17.

Searcey, Dionne. 2016. "Boko Haram Turns Female Captives Into Terrorists." *New York Times.* April 8. http://www.nytimes.com/2016/04/08/world/africa/boko-haram-suicide-bombers.htnll?_r=0.

Sewall, Sarah. 2016. "Women and Countering Violent Extremism." Remarks at the Gender and Countering Violent Extremism Conference, New York, March 17. https://2009-2017.state.gov/j/remarks/254868.htm3.

UN High Commissioner for Human Rights (UNHCHR). 2015. *Report of the UN High Commissioner for Human Rights on Violations and Abuses Committed by Boko Haram and the Impact on Human Rights in the Affected Countries.* UN Doc. A/HRC/30/67.

UN Human Rights Council. 2015. *Ninth Report of the Independent International Commission of Inquiry on the Syrian Arab Republic.* UN Doc. A/HRC/28/69 (February 5).

UN Security Council. 2014. *Statement by the President of the Security Council.* UN Doc S/PRST/2014/21 (October 28).

UN Women. 2015. *Preventing Conflict, Transforming Justice, Securing Peace: A Global Study on the Implementation of United Nations Security Council Resolution 1325.* New York: UN Women.

US Agency for International Development (USAID). 2015. *People Not Pawns: Women's Participation in Violent Extremism across MENA.* Washington, DC: USAID.

Van Leuven, Dallin, Dyan Mazurana, and Rachel Gordon. 2016. "Analysing the Recruitment and Use of Foreign Men and Women in ISIL through a Gender Perspective." In *Foreign Fighters under International Law and Beyond,* edited by Andrea de Guttry, Francesca Capone, and Christophe Paulussen, 97–120. The Hague, The Netherlands: ASSER.

Winter, Charlie, trans. 2015. *Women of the Islamic State: A Manifesto on Women by the Al-Khanssaa Brigade.* London: Quillam Foundation.

Wright, Hannah. 2015. "The High-Level Review of Women, Peace, and Security: A Tale of Two Viewpoints." *Women for Women International.* October 21. http://www.womenforwomen.org/node/737.

CHAPTER 13

UNLOCKING THE POTENTIAL OF CEDAW AS AN IMPORTANT ACCOUNTABILITY TOOL FOR THE WOMEN, PEACE AND SECURITY AGENDA

PRAMILA PATTEN

ON October 18, 2013, the Security Council met for its annual open debate on Women, Peace, and Security (WPS). It unanimously adopted resolution 2122, which puts in place a road map for a more systematic approach to the implementation of its WPS commitments. This seventh WPS resolution acknowledges that women will remain underrepresented in conflict prevention and resolution, protection, and peace-building for the foreseeable future without a "significant" implementation shift.

On that same day, the Committee on the Elimination of All Forms of Discrimination Against Women (the Committee) adopted the landmark *General Recommendation No. 30 on Women in Conflict Prevention, Conflict, and Post-Conflict Situations* (CEDAW 2013). *General Recommendation 30* (GR 30) asserts that protecting women's rights at all times and advancing substantive gender equality before, during, and after conflict, including through full participation in all peace-building, peacemaking, and reconstruction processes are important objectives of the Convention on the Elimination of All Forms of Discrimination Against Women (CEDAW).

Based on these two important mechanisms for furthering women's rights—the (now) eight Security Council resolutions on WPS and CEDAW itself—GR 30 advocates for improved use of both sets of standards as a substantive framework to ensure that gender equality is integral to conflict prevention, peace-building, and post-conflict reconstruction and accountability. This chapter explores the relevance and application of CEDAW to situations of conflict and post-conflict as detailed in GR 30, and describes how CEDAW's reporting procedure serve as a critical accountability tool to improve the implementation of the WPS Agenda.

APPLICATION OF CEDAW TO CONFLICT-
RELATED SITUATIONS

CEDAW is the authoritative legal instrument on women's human rights and a binding source of international law for its current 189 states parties. The Convention imposes obligations on states parties to condemn discrimination against women in all its forms and to take all appropriate measures to ensure the full exercise and enjoyment of all human rights and fundamental freedoms. It recognizes that discrimination can occur through the failure of states to take necessary legislative measures to ensure the full real-ization of women's rights, the failure to adopt national policies aimed at achieving equal-ity between women and men, and the failure to enforce relevant laws. Under Article 2, states parties are obliged to react actively against discrimination against women, regard-less of whether such acts or omissions are perpetrated by the state or by private actors.

CEDAW contains a reporting procedure whereby states parties must submit reports every four years, and the Committee on the Elimination of All Forms of Discrimination Against Women, a body composed of twenty-three experts, monitors progress on implementation. Since its early sessions, in its concluding observations to states parties following the examination of reports, the Committee has expressed concern about the gendered impacts of conflict and women's exclusion from peace- and security-related processes.

It was because of the failure of many states parties to understand the relevance and application of CEDAW to situations of conflict and post-conflict that the Committee adopted GR 30. The recommendation's primary aim is to highlight the gendered impacts of conflict and to provide authoritative guidance to states parties on legislative, policy, and other measures to ensure full compliance with their obligations under CEDAW during conflict and post-conflict situations.

GR 30 stresses that the implementation of CEDAW as a whole is critical for protect-ing women, ending impunity, providing redress for rights violations in the transitional period, and advancing women's rights in all spheres in the post-conflict context. It high-lights the broad application of the Convention, which goes beyond international and non-international armed conflicts to include situations of foreign or other forms of occupation and other situations of concern, such as internal disturbances, protracted and low-intensity civil strife, political strife, ethnic and communal violence, states of emergency and suppression of mass uprisings, war against terrorism, and organ-ized crime. Some unique features of the recommendation include its clarification of CEDAW's scope of application, its extraterritorial application, and its emphasis on the accountability of states parties for non-state actors.

GR 30 also addresses the interplay between international humanitarian law (IHL) and human rights law and endorses the principle of complementarity, namely that the two legal regimes are mutually reinforcing and that states parties must respect all their obligations under CEDAW to the extent that these obligations do not conflict with their obligations under IHL. This complementary model can ensure significant protection to women by holding perpetrators accountable and delivering justice and reparations to survivors of conflict-related violations, particularly in the absence of protracted or traditional modes of conflict and where the application of IHL is contested.

CEDAW AND CONFLICT PREVENTION

With new sources of instability, including rising violent extremism, the need to reduce suffering, prevent violent conflict, and identify nonviolent means of resolving tensions has become one of today's most pressing issues. CEDAW'S preamble affirms that conflict prevention lies at the core of strengthening international peace and that this goal requires the maximum participation of women on equal terms with men "in all fields." Research indicates that the security of women is one of the most reliable indicators of the peacefulness of a state (Hudson 2015). Yet women's participation in conflict prevention remains persistently low, and women's experiences, or indeed a gendered lens on conflict, are dismissed as not having predictive relevance.

Recognizing the limited role of women in conflict prevention, GR 30 addresses states parties' obligations under CEDAW relating directly to women's rights to representation and participation in the public and political life of the country. Article 1 of CEDAW, which defines discrimination against women as meaning any distinction, exclusion, or restriction made on the basis of sex, recognizes that women suffer both direct and indirect discrimination simply because they are women. This principle is directly applicable to the consistent calls for the inclusion of a gender perspective in all processes related to conflict prevention. It requires that prevention policies be non-discriminatory, and that efforts to prevent or mitigate conflict neither voluntarily nor inadvertently harm women nor create nor reinforce gender inequality. Similarly, Article 7, which deals with participation of women in the political and public life of the country on equal terms with men, is critical for advancing women's equal and meaningful participation in conflict prevention. GR 30 recommends that states parties reinforce and support women's formal and informal conflict-prevention efforts and ensure their equal participation in national, regional, and international organizations, as well as in informal, local, or community-based processes charged with preventive diplomacy.

APPLICATION OF CEDAW TO CONFLICT AND POST-CONFLICT SITUATIONS

GR 30 reaffirms that the obligations of states parties do not cease in periods of armed conflict or in states of emergency due to political events; that such situations have a deep impact on the equal enjoyment and exercise by women of their fundamental rights; and that states parties should adopt strategies that address the particular needs of women, including those outlined in the following.

Sexual and gender-based violence

Conflicts exacerbate existing gender inequalities, placing women at a heightened risk of various forms of sexual and gender-based violence by both state and non-state actors (Theidon, Chapter 11 in this volume). In post-conflict environments, the violence does not stop with the official ceasefire or the signing of the peace agreement, and widespread sexual violence can often continue or even increase as a consequence of insecurity and impunity, as well as the absence of effective institutions to protect citizens and bring perpetrators to justice.

Gender-based violence is discrimination within the meaning of Article 1 of CEDAW, and states parties are obligated to take appropriate and effective measures to overcome these violations, whether by public or private act. The threat posed by non-state actors, such as armed groups, warlords, insurgents, paramilitaries, corporations, private military contractors, organized criminal groups, and vigilantes, is of increasing concern. Article 2(e) mandates states parties to take all appropriate measures to eliminate discrimination against women perpetrated not only by state agents but also by non-state actors, including private individuals, organizations, and enterprises. It requires states parties to regulate non-state actors under the duty to protect, such that states must exercise due diligence to prevent, investigate, punish, and ensure redress for the acts of private individuals or entities that impair the rights enshrined in CEDAW. The exercise of due diligence under Article 2(e) requires that national systems effectively respond to women's experiences of sexual violence, which involves the institutionalization of independent courts, protective laws, policies, and penal provisions for rape and sexual violence, a functional security sector, and health care services.

GR 30 recommends that states parties engage with non-state actors to prevent human rights abuses, in particular sexual and gender-based violence, and to establish effective accountability mechanisms. It also reaffirms the extraterritorial application of CEDAW requiring states parties to regulate the activities of domestic non-state actors who operate extraterritorially.

Some states parties are weakened in their ability to respond to the rise of targeted violence and human rights violations linked to terrorism and violent extremism, such as the scale and brutal methods used by some armed groups such as the Islamic State (ISIS). Even for fragile, failed, or collapsed states, the Committee takes the position that although implementation of CEDAW can be seriously challenged, state obligations continue. For example, with regard to the systematic violations of human rights in the Central African Republic by various armed groups and the "quasi-collapse" of the state, the Committee stressed that the implementation of CEDAW is the most effective safeguard to ensure full respect for and enjoyment of women's rights at all times. It reminded the state party that its obligations under CEDAW are non-derogable and continue during conflict situations, and it recommended a drastic increase in support from the international community to enable the government to rebuild state institutions, including the national security forces and the judiciary (CEDAW 2014c).

Trafficking in women

Both conflict and post-conflict situations develop particular war-related demand structures for women's sexual, economic, and military exploitation (see Vandenberg, Chapter 31 in this volume). Indeed, trafficking in women is exacerbated during and after conflict due to the breakdown of political, economic, and social structures and increased militarism. The lack of livelihood opportunities, economic disparity, and the weakened rule of law in many post-conflict environments make women and girls particularly vulnerable to trafficking and sexual exploitation. Article 6, which obligates state parties to take all appropriate measures, including legislation, to suppress traffic in women, in conjunction with Article 2(e), provides the framework for designing and implementing specific measures to combat trafficking in women in conflict and post-conflict situations, including peacekeeping operations. GR 30 recommends measures for the prevention, prosecution, and punishment of trafficking and related human rights violations, whether perpetrated by public authorities or private actors.

Internally displaced persons and refugees

Contemporary, brutal, prolonged, and disorderly conflicts afflict many civilians, entailing a huge rise in the number of refugees and internally displaced persons (IDPs), the majority of whom are women and children (Hovil, Chapter 21 in this volume). These populations are regularly denied access to health care, education, and economic opportunities and suffer human rights abuses throughout their displacement. Discrimination against women in the distribution of food, the lack of recognition of their particular needs, attacks, and acts of violence or extortion in the camps perpetuate this insecurity.

   In addition to the Convention and Protocol Relating to the Status of Refugees, the provisions of CEDAW offer a broad range of protections to both internally displaced and refugee women. GR 30 spells out that the obligations of states parties under CEDAW apply without discrimination to refugees within their territory or effective control, as well as to IDPs at every stage of the displacement cycle. It recommends measures to ensure the following: protection against forced displacement; the protection of human rights; the prevention of gender-based violence; and adoptions of mechanisms for accountability (CEDAW, arts. 1, 2, 5); meaningful inclusion and participation in all

decision-making processes, including in all aspects related to the planning and implementation of assistance programs and camp management (arts. 4(1), 7, 8); and equal
access to health-care services, education, and economic opportunities (arts. 10, 11, 12).
States must also address the specific risks and particular needs of different groups of
refugees and displaced women, including women subjected to multiple and intersecting forms of discrimination, such as rural women, elderly women, widows, and women
with disabilities (arts. 2, 14).

Participation

Central to the advancement and protection of women's human rights in the immediate aftermath of conflict and in the long-term post-conflict setting is their ability
to effectively participate in the public life of their country. Barriers to this participation persist, however, and women continue to be excluded or marginalized in peace
and security decision-making, as confirmed by a growing body of research reflected
in the Global Study on the implementation of Security Council resolution (SCR)
1325 (see, in this volume, Bell, Chapter 32; McWilliams and Kilmurray, Chapter 42;
Coomaraswamy 2015). Articles 7 and 8 provide the normative framework for
advancing women's equal and meaningful participation in all processes related to
conflict prevention, resolution, and the maintenance and promotion of peace. GR 30
spells out that the fulfillment of states parties' obligations to ensure women's equal
representation in political and public life (art. 7) and at the international level (art.
8) requires measures, including temporary special measures under Article 4(1) in the
form of quotas, to address the full participation and involvement of women in formal peace processes. The implementation of these obligations also applies to other
states parties involved in peacemaking processes, including in a supporting role. In
its examination of reports, the Committee expressed serious concerns at the marginalization of Syrian women from participating in peace negotiation efforts, such as the
Geneva peace talks, and recommended their meaningful and inclusive participation
at all stages of the peace process, including through the use of quotas. Similarly, it
recommended better representation of Afghan women in the High Peace Council, as
well as their full and effective involvement at all stages of the peace and reconciliation
process.

Access to education, health, and employment

Armed conflicts have a devastating impact on economic life, destroying infrastructure,
markets, and livelihoods (see Ng and Betancourt, chap. 27, this volume). At the cessation
of hostilities, women tend to be the most neglected in formal economic reconstruction
activities, suffering gross violations of their socio-economic rights aggravated by discriminatory attitudes and practices.

Girls' access to education has been the target of different forms of discrimination, including sexual violence, abduction, intimidation, and harassment. Targeted attacks and threats against girls and their teachers, occupation of schools by state and non-state actors, or closures owing to insecurity, seriously impede girls' access to school. There are harrowing reports of poisoning and acid attacks against schoolgirls in Afghanistan, abduction of girls from their schools in northern Nigeria by Boko Haram, as well as the forced removal of girls from schools in Somalia to become wives of Al-Shabaab fighters (GCPEA 2014; Human Rights Watch 2012).

Similarly, inadequate infrastructure and lack of professional medical care workers and basic medicines and health-care supplies in conflict-affected areas are compounded by the deliberate targeting of health-care systems. According to the International Committee of the Red Cross (ICRC), within three years, 2,400 attacks against patients, health personnel, facilities, and transports occurred in eleven conflict-affected countries (Maurer 2016). The disruption of health care, including reproductive health services, place women and girls at a greater risk of unplanned pregnancy, severe sexual and reproductive injuries, and sexually transmitted infections, including HIV and AIDS, as a result of conflict-related sexual violence.

At the cessation of hostilities, in spite of their active role in war, women are often neglected in formal economic reconstruction activities and experience problems in both the formal and informal sector as men return for previous jobs, and pre-conflict gender attitudes and patterns of discrimination resume.

CEDAW provides the relevant framework to address these violations with its substantive provisions dealing with education (art. 10), employment opportunities (art. 11), and access to health care and services (art. 12). Article 10 obliges states parties to eliminate discrimination against women in order to ensure equal rights with men in the field of education. In contextualizing this to conflict settings, GR 30 recommends: programs for conflict-affected girls who leave school prematurely; prompt repair and reconstruction of school infrastructure; and measures to prevent the occurrence of attacks and threats against girls and their teachers and to ensure that perpetrators of such acts are promptly investigated, prosecuted, and punished. Under Article 11, state parties must ensure an enabling environment comprising appropriate laws, regulations, and institutions that promote gender equality in formal and informal employment with gender-sensitive employment-creation, income-generation, and reintegration programs set up through the post-conflict needs assessment analysis and integrated into national development strategies.

Access to health care, including reproductive health, is a basic right under Article 12 of CEDAW, and states parties must ensure that adequate protection and health-care services are provided for women in especially difficult circumstances, such as those trapped in situations of armed conflict. Sexual and reproductive health care must include access to psychosocial support; family planning services, including emergency contraception; safe abortion services; post-abortion care; prevention and treatment of HIV and other sexually transmitted infections; as well as care to treat injuries such as fistula arising from sexual violence.

ACCESS TO JUSTICE

In the aftermath of conflict, securing justice and accountability for gender-based crimes committed during conflict and strengthening domestic justice systems remains a challenge. The most egregious violations that occur during armed conflict often remain unpunished and ultimately are normalized in the post-conflict environment. Challenges faced by women prior to conflict in accessing justice, including legal, procedural, institutional, social, and practical barriers, ingrained gender discrimination, and impunity for perpetrators, are exacerbated during conflict, persist during the post-conflict period, and operate along with the breakdown of the police and judicial structures to deny or hinder women's access to justice. Transitional justice mechanisms fail women by (1) not delivering justice or reparations for harms suffered; and (2) inadequately involving women in the design, implementation, and monitoring of mechanisms that could otherwise have potentially transformative impacts.

Article 2 provides an important framework for delivering justice to victims and survivors of the conflict. Articles 2(c) and (d) mandate states parties to establish legal protection of the rights of women on an equal basis with men and to ensure through competent national tribunals and any other public institutions the effective protection of women against discrimination. Justice systems must monitor the enforcement of appropriate, effective, and timely remedies. Article 2(b) obliges states parties to provide reparation to women whose rights have been violated. Forms of justice should provide individual redress and should include different forms of reparation, such as recognition of the truth; monetary and non-monetary compensation; restitution, rehabilitation, and reinstatement; measures of satisfaction, such as public apologies, public memorials, and guarantees of non-repetition; medical and psychological care and other social services. GR 30 recommends a comprehensive gender-sensitive transitional justice process that incorporates both judicial and non-judicial measures and guarantee women's access to justice by mandating bodies to address all gender-based violations and by rejecting amnesties for gender-based violations.

CEDAW's Reporting Procedure

Article 18 obliges states parties to submit to the Committee a report on the legislative, judicial, administrative, or other measures that they have adopted to give effect to the provisions of CEDAW. These reports are due within a year of ratification and thereafter every four years. Although the Committee cannot sanction states who fail to report, the reporting requirement remains an important accountability mechanism. Due to the Committee's compliance procedures, which include the use of reminders and examination in the absence of a report as a measure of last resort, states tend to honor their reporting obligations. The "exceptional report" procedure under Article 18(1)(b), which allows for requests for a report outside the reporting cycle, is an important tool that the Committee could use to address the situation of women in conflict and post-conflict situations. It is unfortunate that this procedure remains under-utilized and has been resorted to in only a few instances, namely in the Federal Republic of Yugoslavia (Serbia and Montenegro); Bosnia and Herzegovina; Croatia; Rwanda; and the Democratic Republic of Congo (formerly Zaire) (CEDAW 1994a, 1994b, 1995, 2004, annex VI). It was used in 2010 to address the communal violence in Gujarat, India (CEDAW 2007).

Because the reporting procedure remains the primary mechanism for monitoring the implementation of CEDAW, an effective follow-up procedure is critical. In 2008, the Committee adopted its follow-up procedure, which entails the selection of two priority recommendations for implementation within a year or two. This procedure is increasingly used to address the situation of women in conflict or post-conflict situations (CEDAW 2011, paras. 40–41; 2014a, 2014b, 2014c). In connection with both regular and follow-up reports, the Committee receives information from several sources, including NGOs, UN specialized agencies, and national human rights institutions.

The Committee has been quite innovative in bringing urgent issues to the attention of states parties through the use of statements. In 2010, in a Statement to the Afghan Government, it expressed deep concern about the exclusion of women from the International Conference on Afghanistan in London in 2010 and urged the government and its international allies to ensure that women are included in the peace talks with the Taliban and that any agreement reached include a clear commitment for the respect and protection of women's human rights (CEDAW 2010). The Committee has adopted statements on the situation of women in conflict-affected settings such as Iraq, Palestine, Northern Mali, and Syria.

OPTIONAL PROTOCOL TO CEDAW

The Optional Protocol to CEDAW, adopted by the General Assembly in 1999 and ratified by 107 states parties, has great potential as an additional accountability tool, especially in post-conflict settings. It contains two procedures: (1) a communications procedure, which allows individual women or groups of women to submit claims of violations of rights protected under CEDAW; and (2) an inquiry procedure, whereby the Committee can initiate an inquiry upon receipt of reliable information indicating grave or systematic violations of any of the rights set out in CEDAW. Whereas for the first procedure the Committee can only act upon receipt of a communication, it can initiate the second procedure on its own. Although the Committee has not received any individual complaint, nor has it initiated any inquiry in the context of a conflict or post-conflict setting, the Optional Protocol remains an important tool in the toolkit.

SYNERGY BETWEEN CEDAW AND SECURITY COUNCIL RESOLUTIONS ON WOMEN, PEACE, AND SECURITY

The Security Council's WPS Agenda is an important framework to promote and strengthen women's participation, protection, and rights in conflict prevention through post-conflict reconstruction contexts. All the areas of concern addressed in those resolutions find expression in the substantive provisions of the Convention. Since the adoption of SCR 1325 and the evolution of the WPS Agenda, heavily premised on CEDAW, a substantive synergy has emerged between the two normative frameworks. They share a common agenda that recognizes women's human rights and gender equality as central to the maintenance of international peace and security. They also demand women's full participation in decision-making at national, regional, and international levels as a critical component in the achievement of gender equality and repudiate the pervasive nature of violence against women, which impedes their advancement and maintains their subordinate status.

In spite of wide acknowledgment of their respective particularities, both sets of standards have been hailed as important in their own right, complementary in many instances, and with great potential to reinforce each other (UNIFEM 2006). The WPS Agenda undeniably expands the reach of CEDAW and broadens its application to states that either have not ratified CEDAW, such as conflict-affected states like Sudan and Somalia, or have ratified CEDAW with reservations. In addition, states are increasingly operationalizing the WPS resolutions through the adoption of national action plans, as well as regional action plans on women, peace, and security, and by so doing, enhancing the visibility of national efforts to implement WPS policies. However, CEDAW remains the treaty body with the highest number of reservations and declarations, some of which affect core provisions central to its purpose, affecting the state accountability for the rights enshrined here.

The proliferation of non-state armed groups in conflicts raises serious issues of accountability and impunity. Although under Article 2(e), states parties are obligated to regulate non-state actors under the duty to protect, CEDAW does not bind non-state actors. On the other hand, SCR 1325 demands that all actors engaged in every stage of conflict, peace negotiations, and post-conflict reconstruction protect and respect women's human rights, and be held accountable. The impact of the Committee's calls to non-state actors, such as the one to non-state armed groups in Syria, to abide by the declaration of Commitment in compliance with International Humanitarian Law and the Facilitation of Humanitarian Assistance (which they signed), remains to be seen (CEDAW 2014b).

Similarly, the WPS Agenda can be enhanced through an integrated approach, especially given the lack of a monitoring and accountability framework to assess its implementation enforceability. The strategic framework developed in 2010 establishing indicators to track progress still fails to hold any specific entity responsible for achieving outcomes (see Castillo Díaz and Cueva Beteta, Chapter 14 in this volume).

Although the adoption of SCR 1820, which recognized sexual violence as a tactic of war and a threat to international peace and security, was celebrated as a major achievement of feminist advocacy, the Security Council is criticized for its uneven focus on sexual violence at the expense of promoting women's participation, as per the original intention of SCR 1325. In addition, most of the sexual violence perpetrated during times of conflict does not fit the narrow criterion of "conflict-related sexual violence." CEDAW, which addresses all forms of sexual and gender-based violence, provides an important complement to the resolutions' narrow focus.

Enhancing the Convergence between CEDAW and the WPS Agenda

The call of GR 30 is fundamentally for a concerted and integrated approach. It recommends that the implementation of Security Council commitments reflect a model of substantive equality, take into account the impact of conflict and post-conflict contexts on all rights enshrined in CEDAW, and enact the WPS Agenda through national action plans and strategies complying with the Convention. This is based on its own consistent integration of the WPS Agenda in the work of the Committee.

Nonetheless, CEDAW is not necessarily central to deliberations behind the closed doors of the Security Council. Although the bold language of SCR 2122 reaffirms the Council's commitment to the continuing and full implementation of the WPS Agenda in a "mutually reinforcing manner," SCR 2106 (2013), which affirms the centrality of gender equality, made no reference to CEDAW and its Optional Protocol. Subsequent resolutions did not, however, repeat this omission. SCR 2242 (2015) not only reaffirmed the obligations of states parties to CEDAW and its Optional Protocol, but made explicit reference to GR 30 and highlighted the "important complementary role of United Nations entities and regional organizations." The impact of the operationalization of both SCR 2122 and 2242 remains to be seen.

It is now appreciated that the WPS Agenda is not only relevant for the Security Council. There is also a need for greater convergence between the CEDAW and the range of human rights mechanisms; the WPS Agenda was highlighted in the Global Study on the implementation of Security Council resolution 1325, which stressed that as long as the WPS Agenda operates in isolation and in a fragmented fashion, it will not succeed in translating its rhetoric into reality (Coomaraswamy 2015, 328, 350). In that respect, SCR 2122 (2013) is significant for its recognition of implementation deficits, its elements of concern about the Council's working methods, and in setting out the Council's own commitments to implementation and action. While the resolution does stand out with its identification of ways to consolidate its working methods and in requesting the consolidation of some of its practices, it did not go far enough in addressing all the challenges to a more concrete and consistent implementation of the WPS Agenda.

More than ever, it is incumbent on the Committee to maintain the momentum of both GR 30 and the Global Study in affirming that the WPS Agenda is relevant beyond the Security Council and in stressing the importance of all intergovernmental bodies and human rights mechanisms, including treaty bodies such as CEDAW, to act in synergy. After all, GR 30 ambitiously aims to strengthen both the application of CEDAW to conflict-affected contexts, as well as the accountability of states on the implementation of the WPS resolutions. In positioning itself as a key actor in the "implementation shift" called for by SCR 2122, the Committee must consistently engage with states parties on the implementation of their WPS commitments, for example by including pertinent questions in its List of Issues and Questions to them, and making concrete recommendations in its concluding observations. Such actions would strengthen both frameworks.

Given that the Security Council is the master of its own procedure and determines its own practices,[1] the Committee will gain in exploring other paths, such as participating in Arria-formula meetings, which are informal, confidential gatherings that enable Security Council members to engage in a dialogue on matters with which they are concerned. The aim of such meetings, which may include other relevant treaty bodies and special mandate holders, might be to provide a gender analysis of the situation of women in conflict and post-conflict situations based on examination of states parties' reports, country missions, commissions of inquiry, and fact-finding missions. The Task Force on GR 30 could initiate requests for such meetings and could further establish some formal links with both the WPS section of UN Women and the Office of the Special Representative of the Secretary-General on Sexual Violence in Conflict (SRSG-SVC) for better information sharing. Acting fully within its mandate, more importantly, as recommended in the Global Study, the Committee should consider a better use of its exceptional reporting procedure and hold special sessions to examine the situation of women in conflict-affected settings.

Both SCR 2122 and GR 30 pave the way toward holding states parties accountable on their approach to women's rights in situations of conflict and post-conflict; GR 30 potentially enables substantive equality provisions of the WPS Agenda to be taken forward, while SCR 2122 strengthens enforcement of the equality and non-discrimination norms of CEDAW in conflict and post-conflict contexts. On the other hand, the willingness of states parties to implement GR 30, as well as the extent of openness of the Security Council, remains to be seen, even though the recommendations of the Global Study create an enabling environment for a more integrated use of both frameworks. More interestingly, the complementarity of the two agendas shows how the WPS Agenda can be coordinated with a rights-based approach and can be understood and articulated from a human rights perspective.

NOTE

1. Article 30, Charter of the United Nations.

REFERENCES

Committee on the Elimination of Discrimination Against Women (CEDAW). 1994a. *Summary Record of the First Part (Public) of the 253rd Meeting: Special Report of Bosnia and Herzegovina.* UN Doc. CEDAW/C/SR.253 (March 18).

Committee on the Elimination of Discrimination Against Women (CEDAW). 1994b. *Consideration of Reports Submitted by States Parties under Article 18 of the Convention: Federal Republic of Yugoslavia (Serbia and Montenegro).* UN Doc. CEDAW/C/YUG/SP.1 (December 10).

Committee on the Elimination of Discrimination Against Women (CEDAW). 1995. *Summary Record of the 279th Meeting: Special Report of Croatia.* UN Doc. CEDAW/C/SR.279 (January 31).

Committee on the Elimination of Discrimination Against Women (CEDAW). 2004. *Report of the Committee on the Elimination of Discrimination Against Women: Thirtieth Session and Thirty-First Session.* UN Doc. A/59/38, supplement no. 38.

Committee on the Elimination of Discrimination Against Women (CEDAW). 2007. *Concluding Comments of the Committee on the Elimination of Discrimination Against Women: India.* UN Doc. CEDAW/C/IND/CO/3 (February 2).

Committee on the Elimination of Discrimination Against Women (CEDAW). 2010. "Inclusion of the Afghan Women in the Process of Peace Building, Security and Reconstruction in Afghanistan." Statement given at the CEDAW Committee 45th Session, Geneva, Switzerland (January).

Committee on the Elimination of Discrimination Against Women (CEDAW). 2011. *Concluding Observations of the Committee on the Elimination of Discrimination Against Women: Sri Lanka.* UN Doc. CEDAW/C/LKA/CO/7 (April 8).

Committee on the Elimination of Discrimination Against Women (CEDAW). 2013. *General Recommendation No. 30 on Women in Conflict Prevention, Conflict, and Post-Conflict Situations.* UN Doc. CEDAW/C/GC/30 (October 18).

Committee on the Elimination of Discrimination Against Women (CEDAW). 2014a. *Concluding Observations on the Combined Fourth to Sixth Periodic Reports of Iraq.* UN Doc. CEDAW/C/IRQ/CO/4-6 (March 10).

Committee on the Elimination of Discrimination Against Women (CEDAW). 2014b. *Concluding Observations on the Second Periodic Report of Syria.* UN Doc. CEDAW/C/SYR/CO/2 (July 18).

Committee on the Elimination of Discrimination Against Women (CEDAW). 2014c. *Concluding Observations on the Combined Initial and Second to Fifth Periodic Reports of the Central African Republic.* UN Doc. CEDAW/C/CAF/CO/1-5 (July 24).

Coomaraswamy, Radhika. 2015. *Preventing Conflict, Transforming Justice, Securing Peace: A Global Study on the Implementation of United Nations Security Council Resolution 1325.* New York: UN Women.

Global Coalition to Protect Education from Attack (GCPEA). 2014. *Education under Attack.* New York: GCPEA.

Hudson, Valerie. 2015. "Summary of Research Findings: Establishing the Relationship Between Women's Insecurity and State Insecurity." Speech given at panel on Gender Equality and Peaceful Societies: From Evidence to Action, New York (March).

Human Rights Watch. 2012. *No Place for Children: Child Recruitment, Forced Marriage, and Attacks on Schools in Somalia*. New York: Human Rights Watch.

Maurer, Peter. 2016. "Even Wars Have Limits: Health-Care Workers and Facilities Must Be Protected." Speech given at the UN Security Council Briefing, New York (May).

UN Development Fund for Women (UNIFEM). 2006. *CEDAW and Security Council Resolution 1325: A Quick Guide*. New York: UN Women.

CHAPTER 14

....

THE PROMISE AND LIMITS
OF INDICATORS ON WOMEN,
PEACE AND SECURITY

....

PABLO CASTILLO DÍAZ AND HANNY
CUEVA BETETA

IN 2009, nine years after the adoption of Security Council resolution 1325, the Council adopted two resolutions on consecutive days calling for the development of indicators and better data on women, peace, and security, including indicators to track the implementation of resolution 1325 and a system to monitor trends and patterns of sexual violence.[1] Days later, during a hearing at the Canadian Senate, Anne Marie Goetz (see Goetz and Jenkins, Chapter 9 in this volume) ended her presentation with a similar call for numbers:

> It is a truism among monitoring and evaluation specialists that what doesn't get counted, doesn't count. It is time for us all to count the numbers of women at the peace table, the numbers of women raped in war, the numbers of internally displaced women who never recover their property, the numbers of perpetrators of sexual violence who are never removed from armies and police, the numbers of women human rights defenders killed for their efforts to stand up and be counted. (Goetz 2009)

It became one of the most repeated quotes of the following twelve months. The slogan used by the United Nations Development Fund for Women (UNIFEM) was "Women Count for Peace," a wordplay on women being perennially pushed aside and counted out during and after armed conflict, on the one hand, and the belief that stronger data on women, peace, and security issues would help change this reality, on the other.

In this context, and for the first time, the United Nations produced a list of indicators meant to measure implementation of its commitments on women, peace, and security to be presented every year to the Security Council. Several regional organizations followed suit with their own lists of indicators and monitoring frameworks. At the national

---

Box 14.1 What Are Benchmarks and Indicators?

In broad terms, benchmarks and indicators are colloquially and in the context of the United Nations used interchangeably, even though they are not strictly synonymous. Benchmarks are agreed points of reference in the form of a value, a state, or a characteristic (e.g., two dollars a day to define the poverty line in global development), and indicators are measurement units that can be used to collect relevant and specific data and determine the extent of change in that benchmark. Indicators typically measure something in absolute terms, whereas benchmarks are normative standards or criteria that provide a meaningful point of comparison, and that are often formulated as targets. For example, decisions about a peacekeeping mission's eventual drawdown and withdrawal are sometimes informed by benchmarks agreed on by the Security Council and that mission's host government, and these benchmarks are often expressed in broad terms (e.g., "national security forces operate lawfully and legitimately and are capable of ensuring a safe and secure environment for all citizens"), which require collecting specific data through multiple indicators (e.g., "number and frequency of attacks against security forces" and "share of population feeling insecurity at market places").

---

level, countries rushed to adopt action plans on women, peace, and security, many of them replete with indicators, benchmarks, and targets (see Box 14.1).

As in other policy areas that have been taken over by a focus on quantification and measurements in recent decades, the rapid proliferation of these indicators has led to important debates about their limitations, risks, and potential benefits (see, e.g., Hoover Green, Chapter 24 in this volume). For some, these indicators can never capture the richness and complexities of the phenomena they are meant to measure, and are vulnerable to co-optation and political manipulation. For others, the emergence of these monitoring tools is a breakthrough, the first step toward meaningful accountability that could turn the words of resolution 1325 into actions, after a decade of little progress. This chapter summarizes this debate and its implications for the Women, Peace, and Security (WPS) Agenda, gives an overview of the existing data gaps in the field of gender and conflict and the challenges in addressing these gaps, and puts into perspective the importance and benefits of these indicators, both globally in the Security Council and in national action plans, to move the WPS Agenda forward.

WHERE IS THE DATA?

In the first decade after its adoption, resolution 1325 revealed an alarming divide between policy and practice. Policymakers paid lip service to this agenda, and plans and policies proliferated, but this had little impact on the lives of women and girls. While it was a known fact that women's participation in peace processes, security institutions, or post-conflict recovery remained unacceptably low, concrete evidence that could be used to inform policymaking and hold anyone accountable was negligible. Unlike the Convention for the Elimination of All Forms of Discrimination Against Women (CEDAW) (see Patten, Chapter 13 in this volume), which established elaborate systems to monitor implementation and for public accountability, the resolutions on women, peace, and security did not have such a system. To turn resolution 1325 into a reality, many actors in the international community lobbied for and supported the adoption of national action plans, but many of those plans included few means of monitoring. By the end of 2009, only six national action plans had indicators and other ways of evaluating whether the plan was being implemented, and the plans lacked an effective connection to national policies on security, justice reform, or poverty reduction (UN Women 2015a, 248).[2]

By then, the accounting culture that had emerged from management methods in the private and nonprofit sectors had moved to the human rights and development fields. Since the 1990s, results-based management had become the gold standard in the international community for designing, monitoring, and evaluating projects, and this system had been progressively embraced by broader frameworks, such as the Millennium Development Goals and its quantitative targets, or the new UN peace-building architecture, with its stated need for objective criteria or benchmarks to transition from peacekeeping missions to peace-building support to normalization, and even by human rights frameworks (Merry 2016, 35–41).

The impetus behind the turn-of-century call for indicators on women, peace, and security came from the realization that there were no baselines, no systems to track implementation, and no numbers to provide a frame of reference for the issues that were at the center of resolution 1325. No one kept track of the numbers of women in peace talks, the numbers and type of gender-related provisions in peace agreements, and the percentage of resources and estimated budget allocations devoted to women's empowerment or gender equality in post-conflict planning and financing instruments.

Conversely, when indicators and benchmarks were being added to monitoring frameworks on other issues, they frequently ignored gender issues or gender equality. For example, by the end of 2014, out of a total of thirty-three benchmarks adopted in previous years by five of the largest peacekeeping missions, none referred to gender-specific issues. These benchmarks alluded to a broad range of issues, from security and stabilization to national reconciliation, free and fair elections, an independent and credible judiciary, effective disarmament and dismantling of militias, and even more technical matters such as border management, but the sole oblique reference to gender equality could be found in the benchmarks for the United Nations-African Union mission in Darfur, which speaks of an "inclusive peace process" and defines it as an "internal dialogue and consultations that seek to reflect the views of the civilian population, including women" (UN Secretary-General 2014). Furthermore, of the 105 indicators used to measure these benchmarks, only five referred to gender issues, and most of these related to sexual violence, such as "relevant parties support monitoring and reporting mechanisms on cases of sexual violence in conflict and such conflict-related cases are reduced"

(UN Secretary-General 2012, 25) or "reduction in human rights violations, including incidents of sexual and gender-based violence" (UN Secretary-General 2014, 18).

Although all kinds of social and economic indicators had emerged in previous decades, and an interest in gender-related statistics had grown considerably in the 1980s and 1990s, women's role on matters of war and peace was relatively less prominent in global policy before the adoption of resolution 1325 in 2000. Although advocates could cite a great deal of data on women's education and literacy, domestic violence, maternal mortality, and HIV prevalence (despite the complications and imperfections of these measurements), few numbers on women, peace, and security were available, other than highly disputed victimization statistics related to indirect conflict deaths, displacement, and sexual violence.

By definition, women, peace, and security issues deal with conflict-affected settings that lack reliable statistics as well as systems to collect them periodically, or even the safety and necessary infrastructure to conduct one-time data collection exercises. This challenge is common to all measurements in conflict or post-conflict settings, as record-keeping is interrupted and resources are diverted away from data collection and statistics. But it is especially difficult to measure decision-making power and substantive equality and violations of women's rights, particularly given the unreliability of gender-based violence data in countries with non-functioning states, police, or health care. For example, access by women and girls to services, from shelters and transitional housing to paralegals and courts, can be verified if those service providers undertake reliable book-keeping, but these services are often so limited, and the mobility of women in the area so restricted, that their records cannot possibly say anything meaningful about the effectiveness of these services or women's ability to use them. Very few security institutions in conflict-affected settings, typically undergoing massive reform processes, have up-to-date sex-disaggregated data on women's presence in the military or the police. Even women's participation in peace processes is difficult to count. The composition of negotiating teams is usually fluid. Records are typically not kept. If no one thought of counting the women in the room, chances are this data point was lost forever, with the exception of the many times in which there are no women at all (Duerto Valero 2014).

Assessments of women's interests and needs in conflict and post-conflict environments are rare. For example, out of a list of 145 assessments on Iraq's humanitarian situation compiled at the end of 2015, only four focused explicitly on gender-related issues. In more general assessments, a lack of gender analysis and sex-disaggregated data continues to obscure the differential impact of conflict or humanitarian disasters on women and girls, as well as their specific priorities and concerns. Furthermore, these assessments typically show only a snapshot in time, whereas women's daily needs, priorities, and preferences about security, justice, reconciliation, or accountability vary over time. Stronger understanding and a better programmatic response are only possible through quality data, which can only be produced through periodic and comparable assessments.

However, compared to 2000, when resolution 1325 was adopted, we now have better and more widely available data on gender equality and women's rights, and this positive trend is likely to continue. In 2013, the UN Statistical Commission adopted fifty-two standard indicators for measuring gender equality and, for the first time, nine standard indicators for measuring violence against women. The monitoring framework for the new sustainable development goals, adopted in 2015, have gender-focused targets and indicators in eleven of seventeen goals (Buvinic, Furst-Nichols, and Koolwal 2014; Data2X and Open Data Watch 2016; UN Women 2015b). In 2016, unprecedented financial investments on closing the gender data gap promised to bring a wealth of new statistics on women and girls.[3]

To help implement the WPS Agenda, in 2010 the United Nations compiled up to 2,500 indicators, ultimately whittled down to a list of twenty-six, which are now used to collect data that is presented annually to the Security Council. These indicators (listed in Box 14.2) try to measure, *inter alia*, sexual violence, perceptions of women's safety, sexual exploitation and abuse by peacekeepers and humanitarians, maternal mortality, girls' school enrollment, women's participation in a range of public sector roles, and percentage of benefits for women from various post-conflict programs. But some of them track process-related issues, and act as less meaningful markers of bureaucratic compliance with requirements, which has been one of the main sources of criticisms that have been levied against the recent focus on indicators.

Objecting to "the Tyranny of Indicators"

The emphasis on data and indicators has not been without its critics. As expected, some countries have objected to the scrutiny that they bring, and particular indicators have been the subject of political contestation or have been blocked altogether. But the value and adequacy of these indicators have also been questioned by gender advocates and practitioners (Chowdhury 2010; Merry 2006; Scully 2014).

As soon as the first generation of national action plans started adding indicators, it was evident that these were often measuring *process* rather than results, or completion of specific activities. In spite of guidance to the contrary, this pattern has continued, and more than 80 percent of indicators in national action plans, on average, are about process rather than impact. A focus on process fails to get to the heart of gender issues. For example, simply counting the number of new regulations or legal provisions says little about their content or whether they are enforced. Counting the number of women trained on specific issues, or participating in political and military structures, is more an indication of formal equality rather than substantive equality, and says nothing about the quality of such participation and its effects on women and girls in general. This problem affects even more broadly used indicators, such as school enrollment: school enrollment figures say nothing about actual attendance, sex segregation, the curriculum, or any of the multiple context-specific factors that determine the quality of education and its effect on girls and the wider society (Rosga and Satterthwaie 2009).

Box 14.2 UN Indicators on Resolution 1325

Number	Indicator
1a	Prevalence of sexual violence
1b	Patterns of sexual violence in conflict and post-conflict situations
2	Extent to which United Nations Peacekeeping and Special Political Missions include information on violations of women and girls' human rights in their periodic reporting to the Security Council
3a	Extent to which violations of women's and girls' human rights are reported, referred, and investigated by human rights bodies
3b	Number and percentage share of women in governance bodies of National Human Right Bodies (NHRB)
4	Percentage of reported cases of sexual exploitation and abuse allegedly perpetrated by uniformed, civilian peacekeepers and/or humanitarian workers that are acted upon out of the total number of referred cases
5a	Extent to which measures to protect women's and girls' human rights are included in Peacekeeper Heads of Military Components and Heads of Police Components Directives
5b	Extent to which measures to protect women's and girls' human rights are included in national security policy frameworks
6	Number and type of actions taken by the Security Council related to resolution 1325 (2000)
7	Number and percentage share of women in the executive leadership of relevant regional and subregional organizations involved in preventing conflict
8	Percentage of peace agreements with specific provisions to improve the security and status of women and girls
9	Women's share of senior UN positions in field missions
10	Percentage of field missions with senior-level gender experts
11a	Representation of women among mediators, negotiators, and technical experts in formal peace negotiations
11b	Women's participation in an official observer status at the beginning and the end of formal peace negotiations
12a	Women's political participation in parliaments and ministerial positions
12b	Women's political participation as voters and candidates
13	Extent to which Security Council missions address specific issues affecting women and girls in the Terms of Reference and Mission Reports
14	Index of women's and girls' physical security. Survey-based indicator to measure three dimensions: • Perceptions of physical security of women and girls (by location, time of day) • Proxy variables measuring how women's and girls' ability to participate in public life has been affected • Proxy variables measuring how women's and girls' regular activities have been affected
15	Extent to which national laws to protect women's and girls' human rights are in line with international standards
16	Level of women's participation in the justice and security sector

17	Existence of national mechanisms for control of illicit small arms and light weapons (SA/LW)
18	Percentage of (monetary equivalent, estimate) benefits from temporary employment in the context of early economic recovery programs received by women and girls
19	Percentage of referred cases of sexual and gender-based violence against women and girls that are reported, investigated, and sentenced
20	Hours of training per capita of decision-making personnel in security and justice sector institutions to address SGBV cases
21a	Maternal mortality ratio
21b	Net primary and secondary education enrollment ratios, by sex
22a	Proportion of budget related to indicators that address gender equality issues in strategic planning frameworks
22b	Proportion of budget related to targets that address gender equality issues in strategic planning framework
23a*	Proportion of total disbursed funding to civil society organizations that is allocated to address gender-equality issues
23b*	Proportion of total disbursed funding to support gender-equality issues that is allocated to civil society organizations
24a	Proportion of disbursed multi-donor trust funds (MDTFs) used to address gender equality issues
24b	Proportion of total spending of UN system used to support gender-equality issues
25	Extent to which Truth and Reconciliation Commissions include provisions to address the rights and participation of women and girls
26a	Percentage of (monetary equivalent, estimate) benefits from reparation programs received by women and girls
26b	Percentage of (monetary equivalent, estimate) benefits from DDR programs received by women and girls

* For exact formulation, see http://www.un.org/en/ga/search/view_doc.asp?symbol=S/2010/173 (pp. 15–24).

Source: UN Indicator chart from Duerto Valero (2014).

Moreover, the choice of indicators by policymakers explicitly defines—and potentially delimits—the WPS Agenda. In the case of the indicators on resolution 1325, women's protection and empowerment in conflict are narrowed down to the specific issues being counted and reported on. For example, an overemphasis on police reports and convictions in courts to measure progress on addressing violence against women in national action plans, or on increasing the percentage of women in the armed forces, may not correspond with the priorities of women's civil society organizations and feminist activists, or the gender equality priorities of ordinary women and girls.

Many of the indicators can be deliberately chosen by governments to feign compliance. For example, the adoption of a national action plan has often been interpreted by many to be an indicator of progress in itself, regardless of whether the plan was implemented, had an adequate (or any) budget allocation, and reflected the priorities of women and girls in that country. Other indicators are simply chosen because they reflect existing limits to data collection, and they are the only things that are measurable. To date, most of the indicators that are being reported to the Security Council concern the efforts carried out by UN entities and other international actors, rather than data for the numerous indicators that measure actual outcomes for women and girls at the country level (UN Women 2015a, chap. 10). Both approaches risk perpetuating the status quo, rather than bringing about radical reform and transformative change. Forward-looking goals like gender equality are not easily translated into narrow, time-bound planning tools that often reflect the limitations of transient government bureaucracies.

The Promise of Numbers on Women, Peace, and Security

These objections are important, but they do not negate the value of these indicators. Indicators on women, peace, and security allow advocates to use the language of science and objectivity as a powerful tool to lobby governments, expose their shortcomings, and hold them accountable. It is more difficult to dismiss the allegations of civil society, for example, when they are simply pointing to governments' failures to live up to their own signed commitments and plans. Monitoring frameworks, indicators, and statistics open up the possibility of weaving gender equality issues into the very fabric of development, humanitarian, and peace and security practice. And the fact that these are directly reported to parliaments or even presidents, as in the case of some national action plans, or, most significantly, to the Security Council, as in the case of the global indicators adopted by the United Nations, represents one of the most significant steps forward for implementation of this agenda.

Recent decades have witnessed an emphasis on evidence-based policymaking and quantification in all fields. The political and cultural force of numbers is powerful. Numbers move policy development and fundraising. While attention-grabbing statistics are still the subject of much contestation on technical and political grounds by interest groups and other experts, they are helpful advocacy tools with both the general public and policymakers. Students all over the world can recite numbers about women's illiteracy, maternal mortality, HIV/AIDS, and lack of access to land titles or education, to illustrate the gross injustice behind gender inequality. For example, the fact that women invest 90 percent of their income on their family's health, education, and nutrition needs—whereas men invest only 30 to 40 percent of their income on these needs—is a convenient starting place to advocate for women-led economic recovery (World Bank 2001).

Since the resolution 1325 indicators have been in place, implementation of women, peace, and security commitments has improved. The United Nations now fields investigations on international crimes with the presence of one or multiple gender experts, resulting in a proliferation of gender justice milestones in national and international tribunals. Evidence of stagnation in women's representation in UN field missions has led to reviews of recruitment procedures and the launch of special initiatives targeting women. The language of peace agreements and mission mandates now reflects gender-equality issues more comprehensively and specifically, and women's meaningful and significant participation in peace talks, national dialogues, and other peace and security processes has improved. The international community is now reaching hundreds of thousands of survivors of gender-based violence in conflict-affected settings with assistance programs that did not exist two decades ago. The publication and dissemination of data on women, peace, and security and the increasing use of gender markers has improved funding allocations (Duerto Valero 2014), and this translates into more attention focused on women receiving reparations, or benefiting from temporary employment and economic recovery programs. The Secretary-General's action plan on gender-responsive peace-building stood out precisely because it contained concrete negotiated targets, such as the commitment to allocate a minimum of 15 percent of all peace-building funding to women's empowerment.

And in spite of the prevalent criticism about national action plans, suggesting that they are not much more than pieces of paper, they have become better at building in accountability tools. Currently, many of them report annually or biannually to the head of the government or the parliament. Often, this data is made public. And it is precisely the need to publicly and periodically account for implementation of these resolutions that makes it impossible for this issue to be pushed off the table. States will not want to reproduce data that is unreliable and inaccurate, and producing good data requires significant investments on their part that should have knock-on effects further along. The act of having ministries report to parliament, for example, or having countries report to the Security Council, is not meaningless, even if these commitments cannot be directly enforced. Comparability with other states adds pressure to show compliance, and all the information that is recorded can be used by the public. Further, in several countries, civil society organizations produce shadow reports or are invited to comment on annual implementation reports and participate in national monitoring mechanisms.

There is great value in the systematic collection of information on these indicators. It is true that the number and percentage of women in governance bodies of national human rights institutions, in truth and reconciliation commissions, at the peace table, in parliaments, as gender advisors and in senior leadership positions in peacekeeping and special political missions, in regional organizations working on conflict prevention, and in security and justice institutions does not tell us whether any of them are furthering gender justice. But women's participation in these forums is a central goal of resolution 1325, and one that is independent of outcomes from such participation.

It is equally true that scoring projects to know how many have indicated that gender equality is a significant objective says nothing about how that project is then implemented. But such scoring slowly drives up funding allocations and provides information on gaps in specific sectors. For example, a study of six post-conflict countries showed that the United Nations was targeting women in their support for elections, but not in their support for security sector reform, information that can be subsequently used by advocates to push for greater attention and resources in this area (Kundu 2013).

Perhaps most important, the very act of systematically tracking these indicators, imperfect as they are, can lead to more interesting findings and lines of inquiry and even better policy. For example, the indicator on women's political participation in parliaments and ministerial positions can help advocates of special measures for women's political participation. In 2011, post-conflict countries that had elections and do not have an electoral gender quota averaged only 7 percent of women in parliament (such as DRC, Cote d'Ivoire, Haiti, Liberia, Central African Republic). Countries with a quota undergoing elections that same year (for example, Rwanda, South Sudan, East Timor) returned an average of 30 percent of women in parliament. An analysis of elections in twenty-six post-conflict countries between 1991 and 2011 indicates that women's political representation leaps upward once gender quotas are used. This is as expected. But here's the powerful finding: in countries with quotas, women tend to build on their electoral successes over time, gradually achieving, then exceeding, quota levels in successive elections, while in post-conflict countries without quotas, women's participation tends not to increase over time (Lukatela 2012).

Similarly, counting the number of women in peace negotiations does not tell you how those women fared at the peace table, or whether their views were represented—just as the indicator on gender provisions of peace agreements does not tell you whether these came about as a result of women's participation. But the consistent finding that women's percentage of peace negotiators remains in the single digits does send a compelling message about how conflict resolution is practiced. And that sparks interesting, qualitative studies on the different modalities of women's participation and their impact, or about the language of gender-responsive provisions and their usefulness in the implementation of peace agreements. These studies build a powerful and empirical case for the positive influence of women's participation in the success and durability of peace talks (UN Women 2015a, chap. 3).

A UN Women study in 2012 revealing that the percentage of budget allocations in a sample of post-conflict needs assessments, poverty-reduction strategies, and multi-donor trust funds devoted specifically to women's needs and gender equality was under 5 percent helped build the case for the Secretary-General's call to earmark 15 percent of all UN funds related to peace-building for these matters (Kuonqui and Cueva Beteta 2012). Case studies on women's economic vulnerability, the rate of female-headed households after conflict, and the relatively greater impact that women's rather than men's participation in the labor force has on household and community welfare have provided the evidence base to support what would otherwise have been a hard-fought policy target across the United Nations of ensuring that at least 40 percent of beneficiaries from post-conflict employment programs are women (Justino 2012). A positive correlation between the presence of women police and the reporting of sexual assault provides an incentive for greater efforts to have a more inclusive security sector. And in all cases, they have led to significant policy results: UN entities reaching the previously mentioned 15 percent target for the first time, an increase in the percentage of women as beneficiaries from temporary employment programs, and a proliferation of initiatives to recruit women to the security sector or establish special units and protocols to address gender-based violence.

Data showing that the inclusion of women in water and infrastructure committees can make women and girls more than 40 percent less likely to have to walk for an hour or longer to fetch water can drastically change the attitude that more traditional humanitarians may have about the importance of gender equality and women's leadership in the effectiveness of humanitarian relief programs (Humanitarian Unit, UN Women 2015). New data on election-related violence against women, which was rarely assessed in the past, has led to a proliferation of specific initiatives and programs targeting this issue.

Conclusion

For a political struggle like gender equality, in a male-dominated sector like peace and security that actively resists it, evidence is key. Even if the indicators that populate these monitoring frameworks are sometimes objectionable or improvable, their mere existence makes it possible to review them and replace them with better ones.

This is particularly true of women, peace, and security and the inclusion of relevant indicators in the reports to the Security Council. In a crowded policy arena, where different issues compete for time, attention, and funding, the indicators ensure that resolution 1325 has a prominent place on the agenda by virtue of establishing a regular reporting system, populating these reports with actual information that is available to the public, policymakers, and gender advocates, and, perhaps most significant, presenting them to the Security Council every year, a feature that is unique to the WPS Agenda. The full impact of such a remarkable development lies ahead.

Notes

1. Security Council resolution 1888 "requests that the Secretary-General ensure more systematic reporting on incidents of trends, emerging patterns of attack, and early warning indicators of the use of sexual violence in armed conflict in all relevant reports to the Council." resolution 1889 "requests the Secretary-General to submit to the Security Council within 6 months, for consideration, a set of indicators for use at the global level to track implementation of its resolution 1325 (2000), which could serve as a common basis for reporting by relevant United Nations entities, other international and regional organizations, and Member States."
2. This number soared to thirty out of forty-seven NAPs reviewed in 2014 (UN Women 2015a).
3. For example, see the following gender data initiatives: WomanStats (http://www.womanstats.org/); Data2X (http://data2x.org/); the World Bank's Women, Business, and Law Project (http://wbl.worldbank.org/); UN Women and UN Statistics Divison's EDGE Project

(http://unstats.un.org/unsd/gender/EDGE/about.html); PRIO Centre on Gender, Peace, and Security (https://www.prio.org/Projects/Project/?x=1681); and the OECD Gender Data Initiatives (http://www.oecd.org/gender/).

References

Buvinic, Mayra, Rebecca Furst-Nichols, and Gayatri Koolwal. 2014. *Mapping Gender Data Gaps.* Washington, DC: Data2X.

Chowdhury, Anwarul K. 2010. "Doable Fast-Track Indicators for Turning the 1325 Promise into Reality." *PeaceWomen.* August 26. http://www.peacewomen.org/content/international-doable-fast-track-indicators-turning-1325-promise-reality.

Data2X and Open Data Watch. 2016. *Ready to Measure: Sixteen Indicators for Monitoring SDG Gender Targets.* Washington, DC: Data2X.

Duerto Valero, Sara. 2014. *Women Peace and Security Statistics: Where We Stand and How to Move Forward.* New York: UN Women.

Goetz, Anne Marie. 2009. "Statement to the Canadian Senate's Standing Committee on Human Rights." Statement presented on October 19, 2009, Ottawa (on file with author).

Humanitarian Unit, UN Women. 2015. *The Effect of Gender Equality Programming on Humanitarian Outcomes.* New York: Institute of Development Studies and UN Women.

Justino, Patricia. 2012. *Women Working for Recovery: The Impact of Female Empowerment on Family and Community Welfare after Conflict.* New York: UN Women.

Kundu, Sudarsana. 2013. "Budgetary Baselines and Methodology Development for the Strategic Results Framework and the Seven-Point Action Plan." Report commissioned by UN Women and the UN Development Programme.

Kuonqui, Christopher, and Hanny Cueva Beteta. 2012. *Tracking Implementation of Security Council Resolution 1325 (2000).* New York: UN Women.

Lukatela, Ana. 2012. *Gender and Post-Conflict Governance: Understanding the Challenges.* New York: UN Women.

Merry, Sally Engle. 2016. *The Seductions of Quantification: Measuring Human Rights, Gender Violence, and Sex Trafficking.* Chicago: University of Chicago Press.

Rosga, AnnJanette, and Margaret L. Satterthwaie. 2009. "The Trust in Indicators: Measuring Human Rights." *Berkeley Journal of International Law* 27, no. 2: 253–315.

Scully, Pamela. 2014. "Measuring the Unmeasurable or the Tyranny of Indicators: A Case Study of Liberia's National Action Plan to Address Gender-Based Violence." Paper presented at the IPSA Conference, Montreal (July).

UN Secretary-General. 2012. *Report of the Secretary-General on South Sudan.* UN Doc. S/2012/486 (June 26).

UN Secretary-General. 2014. *Report of the Secretary-General on the African Union-United Nations Hybrid Operation in Darfur.* UN Doc. S/2014/279 (April 15).

UN Women. 2015a. *Preventing Conflict, Transforming Justice, Securing the Peace: A Global Study on the Implementation of United Nations Security Council Resolution 1325.* New York: UN Women.

UN Women. 2015b. *Monitoring Gender Equality and the Empowerment of Women and Girls in the 2030 Agenda for Sustainable Development: Opportunities and Challenges.* New York: UN Women.

World Bank. 2001. *Engendering Development: Through Gender Equality in Rights, Resources, and Voice.* Washington, DC, and New York: The World Bank and Oxford University Press.

PART III

LEGAL AND
POLITICAL
ELEMENTS

CHAPTER 15

HUMANITARIAN INTERVENTION AND GENDER DYNAMICS

GINA HEATHCOTE

THE intervention of military force to resolve a humanitarian crisis, such as the intervention in Libya authorized by the UN Security Council in 2011, raises a host of questions regarding the usefulness of military force to secure humanitarian goals. Within the discipline of international law, however, debates have centered on the legality of interventions as a response to humanitarian crises. Considerably less attention has been given to the usefulness of a military intervention in resolving complex emergency situations, the gendered consequences of interventions, or the gendered model that humanitarian interventions deploy (see Heathcote 2012). In this chapter, I analyze the nexus between the gendered effects and gendered practice of humanitarian intervention, identifying a need for collective security strategies that attend to the politics of "the everyday" and the necessity of working in concert to disrupt these gendered dynamics.

In focusing on humanitarian interventions, I narrow the attention of the chapter to a very specific range of conflicts. Although all conflicts have humanitarian dimensions and consequences, humanitarian intervention refers to the use of military force to halt either state-led violence against its citizens or a significant group of citizens within the state, or the use of force to intervene when a state is unwilling or unable to respond to the widespread violence of non-state actors or a non-human-made disaster. Within international law, the use of military force is only legal as a response to humanitarian crises if it has been authorized by the Security Council under Chapter VII of the United Nations Charter (see Abass 2001).[1] While in the 1990s Security Council authorizations of humanitarian force were considered exceptional and unique, by 2011—when the Security Council authorized the deployment of military force to Libya—the authorization of humanitarian force was broadly accepted as within Security Council powers. Over this same period, international legal debate centered on whether states might unilaterally exercise a right to humanitarian intervention, without Security Council authorization. Rather than enter debates on whether states should act outside of the Security Council when a humanitarian emergency exists, this chapter considers the gendered dynamics of authorized interventions present in decision-making structures of the Security Council, as well as the narratives that the Council produces.

In advocating strategies for working in concert, I highlight the need for attention to power dynamics, including and beyond gender, within international structures to develop mechanisms to respond to the needs of all members of a community. Contemporary debates on humanitarian intervention focus on the legal rights and responsibilities of intervening states and generally neglect the diverse understanding of humanitarian crises held by those living within the crisis. This approach is inspired by Article 2(3) of the UN Charter, which directs states to "settle their international disputes by peaceful means in such a manner that international peace and security, and justice, are not endangered." A primary focus on Article 2(3), rather than the potential authorization of force under Article 42 of the UN Charter, requires states to consider the immediate and long-term consequences of the deployment of military force.

By contrast, the politics of "the everyday" requires responses to the continuum of violence, from the intimate to the international, from public to private spaces, that ultimately, as Charlesworth writes, requires "a methodology to consider the perspectives of non-elite groups" (Charlesworth 2002, 370, 399). In thinking through such a strategy, I contextualize interventions in terms of the gendered consequences, acknowledging sexual exploitation and abuse, sexual violence and trafficking post-intervention, as well those demonstrated via the "web of harms" model (a multilayered notion of gendered harm) advocated by O'Rourke (2013) that alerts us to the gendered consequences of periods of military activity. This gender-based contextualization of humanitarian interventions leads toward reimagining how decisions to authorize interventions are made. The need for such a transformation of the collective security architecture is particularly acute in the context of humanitarian crises, where poverty, human rights abuses, environmental degradation, the flow of refugees, and tolerance of gender-based violence create an unlikely space for military solutions. Both strategies, working in concert and through the lens of a politics of "the everyday," invite reflection on the nexus between feminist messages and feminist methods (Charlesworth 2011; also see Elias and Roberts 2016). The analysis in this chapter demonstrates how the take-up of feminist messages on women's insecurity in humanitarian crises has reinforced, rather than transformed, gendered laws due to insufficient incorporation of feminist methods within the Security Council.

Justifying Interventions

The Security Council has, since the 1990s, while demonstrating its readiness to intervene in humanitarian crises, increasingly justified these interventions via articulation of a need to protect vulnerable groups. The attention to vulnerable groups is visible in the Security Council's Women, Peace, and Security (WPS) Agenda and resolutions, the resolutions on children and armed conflict, and the resolutions on the protection of civilians. Security Council resolutions that authorize the use of military force now include substantial references to the protection of civilians, the protection of women from conflict-related sexual violence, and the protection of children in armed conflict. These components substantiate the credibility of the Security Council, yet do not facilitate the participation or perspectives of these groups to inform the decision to intervene with military force. As such, these provisions contribute to the production of a gendered narrative in which a feminized population (composed of civilians, women, and children) requires rescue and/or protection through the deployment of masculine violence, via military interventions. This structural gendering of humanitarian interventions both propels international law toward the resolution of crisis through force, rather than pacific methods, and reinstates gender binaries that ultimately negate women's full participation in local, national, and international decision-making structures.

In addition, despite the development of the WPS framework within the Security Council's work, decisions to authorize the use of force have not been subject to gender analysis by the Council. A gender analysis might involve consulting local women with respect to the potential consequences of any intervention, understanding that it is unlikely that "local women" speak with a unified voice *qua* woman, while also attending to the further intersection of gender with other power dynamics in discussions. Yet the participation of women is not valued as important when "hard" security choices are on the table, and the notion that a gender analysis might be vital when decisions to deploy force are made has not been acknowledged by the Security Council. The consequence is that women are cast as the silent victims of humanitarian crises, rather than decision-makers, reinscribing the gendered decision-making structures of the collective security system. When the gendered architecture is highlighted, the international narratives on humanitarian intervention are understood as depending on the unspoken construction of feminine vulnerability and a narrative of masculine rescue. As such, the continued perception of women in need of saving during periods of unrest connects to traditional masculine understandings of the relationship between law and violence. These gendered power relations are further perpetuated within new institutional forms, such as the responsibility to protect, leading to a preservation of gendered understandings of law that I address in this chapter. The following section examines the impact that the WPS resolutions have had on decisions to authorize military force as a response to humanitarian crisis. This is followed by a discussion of the gendered understanding of violence embedded in humanitarian intervention authorizations.

THE GENDERED CONTOURS OF SECURITY COUNCIL DECISION-MAKING

The transformative potential of the WPS framework has been well documented, and I do not wish to diminish or dismiss the living qualities of the eight resolutions on women, peace, and security as feminist tools and as mechanisms for challenging the thinking of mainstream international institutions and actors. At the same time, feminist reform strategies are caught in a paradox: the Security Council's women, peace, and security Agenda has contributed to very specific understandings of women's need for protection during crisis that might constitute a reason for authorizing force (as sexual violence victims or as civilians) despite the history of feminist anti-militarism from which the WPS Agenda derives (see Otto, Chapter 8 in this volume). The constructed, and real, vulnerability of women during humanitarian crises is reinforced by the further distinction in the resolutions between women who require saving or protection and those who are to be given access to decision-making forums.

In the following section I focus on the sequence of resolutions authorizing the use of military force in Libya in 2011 to demonstrate the construction of the feminized Libyan population and the failure of the Security Council to consult women or gender experts regarding the decision to authorize force on humanitarian grounds. I then examine how the participation requirements of the WPS resolutions reinforce a formal equality model that gives access to decision-making for a very small group of women, potentially undermining feminist politics. This gendered model functions in nexus with the additional gendered narrative produced through arguments for humanitarian interventions. As such, this sequence of Security Council resolutions demonstrates the perpetuation of a gendered status quo, rather than a genuine transformation within collective security in the period after the establishment of the WPS framework. The Security Council's actions on Libya can also be explained by the narrow range of women's groups and individual women that have access to the Security Council when consultations occur, some of whom have been willing to align their projects with that of the Security Council, perhaps due to their own status as elite actors within states.

Libya

At the commencement of 2011, the Security Council made the decision to take action under Chapter VII of the Charter, authorizing a no-fly zone (Security Council resolution 1970 [2011]), followed by the use of military force in Libya (resolution 1973 (2011). The use of force in Libya consolidated the role of the Security Council in responding to humanitarian crises, as well as the crystallization of the responsibility to protect as an accepted component of the international legal landscape. As is discussed throughout this *Handbook*, it is clear that by the year 2011, the Council had established a normative framework on women, peace, and security through resolutions 1325, 1820, 1888, 1890, and 1960. Despite the existence of the WPS framework, the Council made no reference to it in the resolution authorizing force in February 2011, although the intervention was articulated as necessary to protect civilians in Libya from the violence of the Gaddafi regime.

The failure of the Security Council to address women's experiences of the Libyan crisis in this initial authorization of force demonstrates the Council's approach to women in humanitarian emergencies. It perceives women as within the category of civilians in need of protection and in need of being saved, not as part of the decision-making structures either within local communities or within international forums.

It was not until resolution 2040 was adopted, one year later, that the influence of the WPS framework was visible in the Libya resolutions. In resolution 2040 (2012), the Council condemns sexual violence (against men, women, and children) in the preamble, addresses issues of protection from and accountability for acts of sexual violence in paragraph 3, and encourages the United Nations Support Mission in Libya (UNSMIL) to promote "the empowerment and the political participation of women," as well as identifying the need for protection of women and children's human rights. This sequence of resolutions in response to the humanitarian crisis in Libya demonstrates how the references to women function as a subset of rule of law concerns for the Libyan state in transition, rather than a security issue per se (Security Council resolution 2095 [2013]). Instead of integrating gender perspectives across the responses to the Libyan violence, the WPS framework is used as a forward-looking requirement for the future of Libya, after the military intervention, and as a response to crimes of sexual violence previously committed, but not until after the military intervention has concluded. By 2016, the situation had reverted back to one where WPS was not deemed relevant to the security situation in Libya, with a sequence of four resolutions in the first six months failing to mention the gender dimensions of the measures implemented. The first resolution, 2273 (2016), extending UNSMIL's mandate for a further six months, is silent on WPS, as is resolution 2278 (2016) on the arms embargo, the oil industry, and the appointment of a panel of experts. The following two resolutions, 2291 (2016), which further extends UNSMIL's mandate for six months, and 2292, which authorizes all member states to inspect sea vessels off the Libyan coast, are also silent with respect to WPS. The Security Council had issued, by this stage, its strongest WPS resolution yet, in resolution 2242 (2015), with paragraph 5(b) asserting the need "to integrate women, peace and security concerns across *all country specific situations* on the Security Council's agenda, taking into account the specific context of each country" (emphasis added). The dissonance between the Council's approach under WPS and country-specific situations is stark here, not least given the reassertion of the humanitarian dimensions of the 2016 security threats in Libya.

Furthermore, the collective security focus on protection narratives, in terms of protecting states subject to humanitarian crises and the emergent protection of civilians' agenda, displaces the diversity of women's lives during humanitarian situations. The tendency to produce gendered tropes of women as victims and women as vulnerable, primarily to sexual crimes (Otto 2006), is compounded by further strategies of including women as civilians (Heathcote 2012) and women as peacemakers (Charlesworth 2008, 347). This displaces women from spaces that could recognize women's continued political agency and fails to address the capacity of women to support (and to further) unjust causes, as well as the multitude of roles women have in transforming their communities from within.

The Security Council's recognition of the need for participation by a range of representatives, including women, in the pursuit of a peaceful settlement of the humanitarian crisis in Syria is not matched by an examination of the Security Council's internal decision-making structures. The Council maintains limited opportunities for women to participate: either creating special "women's" meetings, such as was conducted with respect to Syria in January 2014, segregating women's concerns from broader security issues in the process, or facilitating access for a small group of elite female actors. The Libyan resolutions discussed earlier show how the call in resolutions 2122 (2013) and 2242 (2015) for consultations with civil society actors and for the Council's own decision-making structures to be subject to WPS strategies often simply do not translate into situation-specific strategies that include WPS consultations.

While the Security Council has not always acknowledged the need for participation requirements to be applied to its own structures, this does not mean that women have not and do not participate in Council decision-making. For example, at the time of the decision to authorize force in Libya, the United States was represented in the Council by then Secretary of State Hillary Clinton. Yet this can hardly be what is required under the Council's WPS framework: elite women from powerful states given access to represent their own state's (not women's) interests in the Council and other key decision-making forums (compare Heilbrunn 2011 and Krikorian 2011). Other actors that were given audience in Council during the decision to use force in Libya included the Arab League, the African Union, and the Organization of the Islamic Conference. The perspectives of women's groups working in Libya, of women from Libya or women from the Middle East and North Africa (MENA) region, were not specifically addressed and consequently the specific, yet varied, needs and expectations of local women were not concretely considered in terms of how the crisis was to be resolved. Furthermore, across the series of meetings with respect to Syrian women's security, only one focused on women's participation rather than vulnerability, and when the Council authorized the use of force in Syria (in regions under the control of Da'esh or the Islamic State group) in resolution 2249 (2015), no reference to any aspect of the WPS Agenda was made, including the need for the Council's decision-making structures to be sensitive to the need for gender participation, as stipulated in resolution 2122 (2015), or the need for consultation with local civil society groups and women's NGOs, as stipulated in resolution 2242 (2016).

An alternative, integrated understanding of gender within Security Council dynamics themselves would require attention not only to the additional privileges of women who have access to decision-making bodies, but also a concerted strategy to appreciate the very different and complex needs of women local to a community. (When acknowledging difference, I am referring to cross-cultural differences and women's diversity within a specific state.) The consequence for decision-making processes in relation to the use of force would potentially be a new tier of consultations that work from the premise that women's diversity within and across communities is intimately integrated into additional power relations. Failure to attend to women's diversity and a failure to take the time to listen to the perspective of those to be "protected" risks the perpetuation of the perception that military force can be used to save at-risk populations.

GENDERED DYNAMICS AND NARRATIVES ON HUMANITARIAN INTERVENTIONS

Alongside the gendered contours of Security Council practice, the spectrum of women's experience before and during a humanitarian intervention is not adequately attended to in the current collective security process. For example, when the Council does address women's participation and specific gendered violence (primarily the risk of sexual violence) in the Libyan post-intervention resolutions, there is a diminishing rather than expansive understanding of the types of roles women take up during armed conflict, as the Libyan resolutions center primarily on conflict-related sexual violence, with only brief references to women's participation (and, of course, once security risks re-emerge, these references disappear altogether).

Warring factions and combatant groups are often given priority places in consultative processes, even though past practice indicates the important role of women in attaining local peace and security. The collective security regime does not see women as leaders, women as perpetrators, women as strategic partners, women as survivors, women as active community shapers. Yet we know from experience—from Liberia to Bougainville, from Cambodia to Haiti, from Libya to Timor Leste—that women take up roles during and after conflict that include, but are not limited to, leading their communities (Sirleaf 2009), as military actors (McDougall 2013), as landowners (Heathcote 2014), as perpetrators (Brown 2013), as survivors, as peaceworkers (Gbowee 2011), as key actors, and as agitators for change (Cristalis 2002), throughout, during and after conflict and crisis. These are not one-off, isolated stories from specific conflicts, although they are often presented as such. Stories of women's roles during conflict are as diverse, as complex, and as facilitative as those of men. The key difference between the roles of men and women, however, is the limited institutional recognition of women's contributions and the relegation of women's actions to informal structures rather than formal decision-making bodies. Recognition of the diversity of women's experiences, however, is an inadequate strategy if the gendered dynamics they occur within are not also recognized and reimagined.

Consequently, contemporary debates on the responsibility to protect and humanitarian intervention appear to create the means to circumvent the excesses of state violence. But they do not: the masculine binaries that international law has threaded into its structures and histories, as well as additional privileges associated with assumptions regarding class, race, heterosexuality, religion, and ability are reasserted, rather than diminished, when linked with military force (Otomo 2011). Authorized humanitarian interventions function through acceptance of law as a model premised on the ideal masculine subject that preserves coercive force as a last resort in times of crisis. To build an alternative approach that is attentive to feminist method, in addition to feminist messages about the discrimination and harm that women experience globally, facilitates understanding of the flawed persistence of humanitarian intervention in our global imaginings and the need to concretely challenge force as a means to save women, civilians, or "other" communities. To fully interrogate the gender dynamics of humanitarian interventions, women's experiences of armed conflict (Charlesworth 2010) require attention. However, this risks a reassertion of gendered law if the gendered structures that inform international law are not interrogated at the same time. The latter project goes to the center of debates on when violence should be tolerated, regulated, prohibited, or authorized.

To this end, Charlesworth draws a distinction between feminist method and feminist messages, as well as the need for a politics of "the everyday" (Charlesworth 2011), all of which seem to have a role in forward-looking strategies for disrupting the gendered male model of law that prioritizes violence as the ultimate enforcement capability. Contemporary approaches to women, peace, and security within the Security Council are then seen as indicators of how feminist messages about specific harms women experience, particularly sexual violence, have been picked up and mobilized within the international legal system. The emergence of authorized humanitarian interventions within the international systems require a feminist method that springboards beyond attention to the harm and discrimination women experience to interrogate the gendered dynamics that couple law with coercion and law with violence. Humanitarian intervention can then be understood as a gendered tool that relies upon the invocation of a series of feminized victims, depleted of agency, to permit the violence of powerful states to "save" civilians, including women, at risk of sexual violence. This model preserves, within international law, the notion of white knights (Orford 2003) and Western warriors (Buchanan and Johnson 2005), who retain force as the ultimate enforcement model.

To take seriously the gendered violence through which law acts, we need to move to strategies for change, rather than description of known reality; that is, there is a need to think through how to respond to humanitarian crises and to question how decisions to authorize force are made, rather than focus solely on women's experiences of armed conflict as the only site where gendered dynamics are to be apprehended. Adding women, as international stateswomen and as voices on the ground, respecting the disagreements between women, and acknowledging that women must be equal participants in peace negotiations are partial steps in a politics of working in concert. To move also toward a politics of "the everyday" means to take seriously the link between private, domestic, and daily violence that women encounter as gendered violence and international attempts to use violence to solve crisis. The links between violence against women, as a gendered structure connected to power relations, and limited methods of dispute resolution, must be connected to the use of military violence to solve complex humanitarian crises.

To challenge the status quo, feminist engagements with humanitarian intervention narratives need to return to law's foundational structures to interrogate the gendered forms that populate our assumed means of legal thinking, in particular the assumption that force sits at the apex of legal regulation.

The creation of the WPS framework within the work of the Security Council demonstrates precisely the type of risk that feminist attention to "woman" and "women" as political subject entails; that is, this captures the message but not the methods of feminist thinking and activism. The category of women is over-inclusive so that actors with additional privileges, for example, high-level US officials who are female and have access to the Council, may be included as examples of the access women have to decision-making structures, creating a perpetuation rather than dismantling of global privilege. Yet the focus on women can be under-inclusive because it assumes a heterosexual ordering, with subjects knowingly identified as male or female, in order for the WPS framework to function. A gender approach would be more interested in the dismantling of heterosexual or cis-privilege to understand the persistent discrimination and harm associated with gender binaries. In addition, the focus on the female subject is insufficiently attentive to feminist method (Charlesworth 2011), which enlarges on women's diversity, critical engagement with structures and institutions, deconstruction of liberal political frameworks, and the links between colonial histories and contemporary international legal interventionist projects.

CONCLUSION

Numerous issues are raised by the manner in which the Security Council has approached humanitarian interventions, not in terms of legality, but rather in terms of how this intertwines with the WPS Agenda.

The first issue is centered on where the WPS framework "fits" with regard to decisions to authorize force on humanitarian grounds. The Libya resolutions demonstrate the space between the authorization of force and the focus on women's security. During the Libyan intervention, the WPS Agenda was designated a space after the military intervention concludes and the post-conflict rebuilding commences under the auspices of UNSMIL. At least two sites of feminist engagement seem urgent as a result. First, the network of women, women's groups, and peace advocates linked to Security Council resolution 1325 must commence discussions on the costs, consequences, and benefits of military interventions for women. Consultation with women, and men, in communities where interventions have occurred in the past would be an important mechanism for appreciating the diverse gender effects of interventions. Second, the potential of Security Council resolution 2122 as a renewed space for women's agency and consultation within the Security Council itself might be mobilized to develop procedural mechanisms that attach to Security Council decision-making processes before force is authorized.

The second issue revolves around who participates as decision-makers when the use of force is to be authorized, including on humanitarian grounds; this interlocks with additional privileges that determine who has access to the Council and its decision-making structures. The absence of local and regional women and women's organizations from the Security Council decision-making process needs to be juxtaposed with the privileged women who do have access to the Council. The formal equality gestures of liberal states thus reify privilege, rather than dismantling it, while perpetuating global divisions between women in the Global North and South, economically privileged actors, and the legacies of colonial power. Consequently, non-Western women remain voiceless, without sufficient agency to participate in "hard" security decisions, and are represented as primarily in need of protection (from the men in their own communities), rather than as significant and important potential contributors to decisions to authorize military force. Later Security Council resolutions on women, peace, and security acknowledge the need to consult women's leaders (resolution 2122 [2013] in particular) and to make efforts to further consult women's leaders representing socially and economically excluded groups of women. Yet these resolutions are addressed to the work of the Secretary-General and the Special Representatives of that office, not to the Security Council itself.

Moreover, the decision to use force does not look at the substantial consequence of military force on women within a community. While humanitarian interventions are premised on a need to intervene on behalf of those who are no longer protected sufficiently by the state, it is not clear that the arrival of foreign militaries produces a safer outcome for women (Al-Ali and Pratt 2009). The gendered consequences of interventions include a "web of harms" that require attention to how existing gendered harms are often invisible during periods of military violence, yet interlock with public violence to maintain and produce insecurity for women (O'Rourke 2013). These harms may occur in the private sphere, such as reproductive health, intimate partner violence, or access to justice for gender-based violence, yet they exist in a peculiar relationship to public violence, and in times of humanitarian crises are often simultaneously neglected and prevalent. At the same time, increased public harms for women also emerge during and after military interventions, regardless of their humanitarian credentials. Risks have been documented to include the emergence of transnational trafficking industries and the increased sexual exploitation and abuse of women, including from intervening militaries (see Vandenberg, Chapter 31 in this volume). The use of military violence abroad also brings additional gendered consequences to states that contribute troops, where long-term mental health issues among veterans often impact on families in gendered ways. Yet, collective security interventions have, as yet, paid no attention to these aspects of women's security and the everyday, intimate nature of the harms women face, alongside public violence.

Finally, analysis of humanitarian intervention narratives and the preservation of the masculine model of law that military interventions retain within international law are feminist projects that demand a broader engagement with the structures and foundations of international law. This is by no means a simple task; this is a politics of "the everyday" that relies on a politics of seeing, hearing, listening, and asking women and peripheral subjects to be full participants in our reimaginings of global relationships, actions, and institutions. At the core of challenging the gendered dynamics of humanitarian intervention, and by extension the foundational structures of international law, is a commitment to the difficulties of acting in concert to challenge violence as enforcement or as law.

As a strategy for engaging and disrupting gendered dynamics in conflict situations and humanitarian crises, this would require slow, concerted conversations regarding the relationship between force and feminist politics. This is the politics of acting in concert, rather than acting through coercion, humanitarian or otherwise.

NOTE

1. There may also be a role for regional organizations to play.

REFERENCES

Abass, Ademola. 2001. *Regional Organisations and the Development of Collective Security: Beyond Chapter VIII of the UN Charter*. Oxford: Hart.

Al-Ali, Nadje, and Nicola Pratt. 2009. *What Kind of Liberation? Women and the Occupation of Iraq*. Berkeley: University of California Press.

Brown, Sara E. 2013. "Female Perpetrators of the Rwandan Genocide." *International Feminist Journal of Politics* 16, no. 3: 448–469.

Buchanan, Ruth, and Rebecca Johnson. 2005. "The 'Unforgiven' Sources of International Law: Nation-Building, Violence and Gender in the West(ern)." In *International Law: Modern Feminist Approaches*, edited by Doris Buss and Ambreena Manji, 239–283. Oregon: Hart.

Charlesworth, Hilary. 2002. "International Law: A Discipline of Crisis." *Modern Law Review* 65, no 30: 377–390.

Charlesworth, Hilary. 2008. "Are Women Peaceful? Reflections on the Role of Women in Peacebuilding." *Feminist Legal Studies* 16, no. 3: 347–361.

Charlesworth, Hilary. 2010. "Feminist Reflections on the Responsibility to Protect." *Global Responsibility to Protect* 2, no. 3: 232–249.

Charlesworth, Hilary. 2011. "Talking to Ourselves? Feminist Scholarship in International Law." In *Feminist Perspectives on Contemporary International Law: Between Resistance and Compliance?* edited by Sari Kouvo and Zoe Pearson, 17–32. Oxford: Hart.

Cristalis, Irena. 2002. *Bitter Dawn: East Timor A People's Story*. London: Zed Books.

Gbowee, Leymah. 2011. *Mighty Be Our Powers: How Sisterhood, Prayer, and Sex Changed a Nation at War*. Philadelphia: Beast Books.

Elias, Juanita, and Adrienne Roberts. 2016. "Feminist Global Political Economies of the Everyday: From Bananas to Bingo." *Globalizations*: 787–800.

Heathcote, Gina. 2012. *The Law on the Use of Force: A Feminist Analysis*. New York: Routledge.

Heathcote, Gina. 2014. "Participation, Gender, and Security." In *Rethinking Peacekeeping, Gender Equality and Collective Security*, edited by Gina Heathcote and Dianne Otto, 48–69. London: Palgrave Macmillian.

Heilbrunn, Jacob. 2011. "America's Foreign Policy Valkyries: Hillary Clinton, Samantha Power, and Susan Rice." *National Interest*. March 21. http://nationalinterest.org/blog/jacob-heilbrunn/americas-foreign-policy-valkyries-hillary-clinton-samantha-p-5047.

Krikorian, Mark. 2011. "They Know Who Wears the Pants in This Country." *National Review Online*. March 31. http://www.nationalreview.com/corner/262607/they-know-who-wears-pants-country-mark-krikorian.

McDougall, Clair. 2013. "When Liberian Child Soldiers Grow Up." *Newsweek*. July 31. http://www.newsweek.com/2013/07/31/when-liberian-child-soldiers-grow-237780.html.

Orford, Anne. 2003. *Reading Humanitarian Intervention: Human Rights and the Use of Force in International Law*. Cambridge: Cambridge University Press.

O'Rourke, Catherine. 2013. *Gender Politics in Transitional Justice*. Abingdon, Oxon: Routledge.

Otomo, Yoriko. 2011. "Searching for Virtue in International Law." In *Feminist Perspectives on Contemporary International Law: Between Resistance and Compliance?*, edited by Sari Kouvo and Zoe Pearson, 33–45. Oxford: Hart.

Otto, Dianne. 2006. "A Sign of 'Weakness'? Disrupting Gender Certainties in the Implementation of Security Council Resolution 1325." *Michigan Journal of Gender and Law*, 13 no.1: 113–175.

Sirleaf, Ellen Johnson. 2009. *The Child Will Be Great: Memoir of a Remarkable Life by Africa's First Woman President*. New York: HarperCollins.

CHAPTER 16

....

(RE)CONSIDERING GENDER JURISPRUDENCE

....

PATRICIA VISEUR SELLERS

THE modern era of international criminal law is in full throttle, spurred by the judicial decisions of the International Criminal Tribunal for the Former Yugoslavia (ICTY) and the International Criminal Tribunal for Rwandan (ICTR) and the Sierra Leone Special Court (SCSL), and furthered by litigation at the Extraordinary Criminal Chambers of Cambodia (ECCC) and the International Criminal Court (ICC). Even though gender-centric considerations inform the adjudication of genocide, crimes against humanity, and war crimes, identifying a so-called gender jurisprudence is an elusive endeavor. Should gender jurisprudence be narrowly understood and focused on judgments relating to wartime rapes or sexual violence? Or is gender jurisprudence more panoramic, inclusive of virtually all international criminal judgments that pronounce on crimes committed against men and women protected under international humanitarian law and international criminal law (IHL and ICL)? In essence, the panoramic view would acknowledge an inherent gendered dimension in all international crimes.

That armed conflicts, or periods of genocide, operate in a gendered manner is not a startling revelation. Societies enmeshed in such atrocities are often imbued with gendered norms in their pre-atrocity existence, and war and genocide spur distinct gendered conduct. However, the correlation of pre-atrocity gendered patterns with gendered conduct that occurs during atrocity periods, while useful, cannot fully account for the gendered nature of atrocities. International criminal law judgments are replete with details that implicate gender. The Nuremberg Judgment, often assailed for its woeful lack of explicit passages regarding sexual violence, nevertheless recounted gendered facts. In reference to Nazi defendant Bormann's participation in the Nazi slave labor, it held that

> Bormann was prominent in the slave labor program .... A report of 4 September
> 1942 relating to the transfer of 500,000 female domestic workers from the East to

Germany showed that control was to be exercised by Saukel, Himmler and Bormann. (Bormann 1946)

Decisions generated by the Yugoslav and Rwandan Tribunals elicited similar gendered descriptions of illicit harms. In the ICTR case of *Kayishima*, the trial chamber observed:

> Not only were Tutsis killed in tremendous numbers, but they were also killed regardless of gender or age. Men and women, young and old were killed without mercy. Children were massacred before their parents' eyes, women raped in front of their families. No Tutsi was spared, neither the weak nor the pregnant. (Kayishema 1999, para. 532)

These factual, gender-detailed judicial pronouncements or holdings provide more than visual power. They demonstrate, first, that vicious crimes were perpetrated against both males and females. In Rwanda, all Tutsis, irrespective of age, or gender-specific conditions such as pregnancy, were killed. Second, the descriptions validate that, at times, gender determined who would be victimized. Frequently, certain crimes produced distinct gendered patterns of victims, such as imprisonment, killings, shelling of civilians, deportation, or enslavement. Under the Nazi slave labor policy, females were deported as household workers. In Rwanda, females were raped. Third, the gender descriptions of crimes include non-sexually violent gender-based acts, such as killing, as well as gender-based acts of sexual violence such as rapes. Moreover, such gender-descriptive factual holdings had legal significance. They were tendered into evidence and invariably met the admissibility standard of relevance, probative value, and reliability. The gendered descriptions recited in judgments often attest to their value as material evidence going to the proof of war crimes, crimes against humanity, or genocide.

What I reference as the narrow view of gender jurisprudence consists of international criminal law decisions about sexual violence. During the past twenty years, the narrow view of gender jurisprudence has set legal precedents and has garnered much scholarly attention. It commenced with the *Tadić* case's pronouncement about the sexual mutilation of a male detainee committed under force by two fellow male prisoners. That strand of cases, exemplified by the SCSL's convictions for conjugal slavery in *Taylor* (Taylor 2012, paras. 427–428; see Oosterveld, Chapter 18 in this volume) continues through to the ICC case of *Bemba* (2016) and the ICTY judgment in *Karadžić* (2016).

Albeit more identifiable and accompanied by reasoned legal observations about sexual violence, the narrow strand of gender jurisprudence can myopically be seen as a case-by-case endeavor to primarily redress rapes. This narrow focus often misreads the breadth of victims harmed and of acts of sexual violence. It is all too commonly assumed that overwhelmingly females are the targets of sexual violence, even though gender jurisprudence started with acts of sexual violence inflicted upon males (in *Tadić*) (Sellers and Nwoye 2018). This perspective conflates gender and female and inconsistently acknowledges that males, children, groups of detainees, or entire communities are subjected to distinct forms of sexual violence, such as terrorization by sexual violence.

To date, the narrow view of gender jurisprudence does not contain sexual violence cases that understand gender in a non-binary manner (namely, in terms of gender identity or expression or sexual orientation as related to sexual violence). Also, while cases in the narrow strand highlight the redress of sexual violence, critical analysis of other gendered facets of a decision, such as the gendered composition of the detainee population, tend to be overlooked. Thus, focus on the narrow strand's sexual violence pronouncements can obscure the examination of the full range of gender considerations within a judgment.

The panoramic view highlights factual holdings in judgments that illustrate the intertwined fate of men and women. Most relevant facts in international criminal law adjudication are distorted when devoid of expressions of gender of the victim population or the perpetrators. For example, separation of the sexes, a gendered factual observation, frequently happens within the context of detention, forced transfers, or deportation, and comprises a material fact. Nonetheless, the panoramic view, while admittedly replete with descriptions of gendered scenarios, is often remiss of any reasoned legal conclusions about such gender configurations. Also, cases from the panoramic view can obscure the sexual violence or reproductive implications of international crimes that on their face appear to be non-sexual. Routinely, the gender impact wrought by illegal military operations, such as the targeting of cultural, religious, educational, or scientific objects, tends to be minimally analyzed or critiqued.[1] A panoramic view of gender jurisprudence should necessitate more than a compilation of gender-descriptive pronouncements about atrocities.

Neither the panoramic nor the narrow view of gender jurisprudence is theoretically a consummate means to understand it. Ultimately, the dichotomy between the narrow and the panoramic strand is false.

As the third decade of modern international criminal law takes form, its gender jurisprudence bears reconsideration. How many cases or series of cases evade critical gender critique or commentary? Is this an oversight, or an inability to grasp what gender jurisprudence entails? Perhaps, identification of gender jurisprudence can progress beyond the facile counting of sexual assault charges included in an indictment, or singling out a judgment's descriptive passages about atrocities inflicted upon males or females. At a minimum, it must be affirmed that gender holdings in judgments serve to support the ultimate verdicts of guilt or innocence of an accused. Should not gender jurisprudence, again, at a minimum indicate the extent to which international criminal law is gender competent—meaning whether it diligently is accountable when addressing crimes committed against females as well as males? However, is it facetious or a foregone prerequisite to inquire whether gender jurisprudence plays a role beyond the individual case-related adjudicative function? Ultimately, does a holistic and integrated gender jurisprudence not merit a further elaboration of its significance?

This chapter envisages a *de nova* approach to gender jurisprudence. It posits that gender holdings are per se instructive of certain tenets of the IHL and ICL legal regimes. Accordingly, gender jurisprudence provides a means to simultaneously gauge the adherence to, interpretation of, and evolution of war crimes, crimes against humanity, and genocide—a utilitarian function.

To illustrate, the next two sections will examine aspects of the crime of genocide. The ICTR cases, such as *Akayesu* and *Nahimana*, embody the narrow strand and are noted for jurisprudence on sexual assault acts committed during the Rwandan genocide. The ICTY's Srebrenica cases concern the massacre of more than seven thousand males and are representative of the panoramic strand of gender jurisprudence. When examined holistically, these cases have affirmed and, yet, seemingly have redeployed the doctrinal bases of genocide law.

A third section consolidates this utilitarian approach. It advances that gender jurisprudence acts as a measurement of genocide, war crimes, and crimes against humanity and extends our appreciation of its legal safeguards. In so doing, the comprehensive reading of gender jurisprudence provides a fresh, analytical tool for practitioners and scholars alike to further conceptualize redress under international criminal law.

GENOCIDE: THE NARROW VIEW OF GENDER JURISPRUDENCE

The narrow jurisprudence approach challenges redress of sexual assault under ICL and IHL. It was the perceptible forerunner to the proposed approach. The narrow view of gender jurisprudence attests to the proscription of sexual violence as genocide (Muhimana 2005), and direct and public incitement to commit genocide (Media Case 2003), torture (Delalić 1998; Kvocka 2001), persecution (Media Case 2003), enslavement, other inhumane acts (AFRC Case 2008), sexual slavery as a crime against humanity (RUF Case 2009), as well as cruel treatment (Tadić 1997), inhumane treatment (Tadić 1997), outrages upon personal dignity (AFRC Case 2007, paras. 1068, 1188; Furundzija 1998), and slavery (Kunarac 2001) as war crimes. *Akayesu, Furundzija*, and *Kunarac*, the iconic triumvirate, represent gender jurisprudence that produced such *de novo* rulings.

The first ICTR case concerned the criminal conduct of a local, rural, politician, Jean-Paul Akayesu, who presided over the Taba commune (Akayesu 1998). The killings in Rwanda were inflicted upon males and females of all ages and even fetuses. However, depending on the local context, the sequence of killings might be determined by gender. In the Taba commune, intellectuals, male or female, such as schoolteachers, were killed first, followed by the remaining Tutsi men and boys. Tutsi females were the last to die. Pregnant women, even Hutus who carried babies fathered by Tutsi men, were forced to abort and often, like Tutsi females, were killed. Along with massive killings, Akayesu was indicted for the rampant rapes and sexual mutilation committed against Tutsi females. Tutsi women and girls endured multiple rapes by multiple perpetrators throughout the duration of the genocide. The rapes occurred even if the victims were visibly pregnant. Often, the sexual violence was inflicted immediately before they were killed.

Although Mr. Akayesu was not a physical perpetrator, it was alleged that he encouraged and instigated the rapes and and knew they were committed on the compound in front of his office. He was charged for the rapes under the genocide provision of "causing serious bodily or mental harm to members of the group." The *Akayesu* judgment, indeed, held that the rapes and mutilations *did* satisfy each alternative prong of the provision, causing both serious bodily or mental harm to Tutsi women and girls. The chamber interpreted that provision to be inclusive of, but not limited to, acts of torture, be they bodily or mental, or acts of inhumane or degrading treatment, or acts of persecution. Equally importantly, the chamber did not require that the harm be permanent and irremediable. As such, the *Akayesu* judiciary found that the infliction of rapes and sexual violence caused both serious bodily harm and mental harm to Tutsi females.[2] The destructive psychological effects of crimes of sexual violence were thus granted the same importance as the physical consequences of the acts. Lauded as an exception and legal departure—that rapes were condemnable as acts of genocide—the *Akayesu* judiciary delivered their decision assured of its sound legal bearings. Harms such as the rapes and sexual mutilation, according to their interpretation of genocide safeguards, conformed squarely to the conduct that the drafters intended to reach when penning this provision.

The origins of causing serious bodily or mental harm arose from the biological experiments conducted by the Nazi regime on concentration camp inmates. Experiments entailed devising insemination techniques, sterilization procedures, and, of course, the genetic trials conducted on twins. These sexualized and reproductive experiments, based on the Nazi eugenics policies and undertaken to cause group annihilation, were purposely condemned under genocide law. Article 1 (II)(1)(c) of the initial draft of the Genocide Convention sanctioned "mutilations and biological experiments imposed for other than curative purposes." What was encapsulated in Article 2(b) of the Genocide Convention covered biological experiments that attacked the sexual integrity of members of the group. Thirty years prior to the *Akayesu* case, Israeli judges had ruled in the *Eichmann* case that the provision "causing serious bodily or mental harm" captured a plethora of vile conduct, such as inhumane treatment and torture.[3] The drafters of the Genocide Convention consciously enumerated non-killing provisions as equivalent means to destroy a group. Causing serious bodily or mental harm joins other non-killing acts, such as those that forbid measures to impede birth or the transfers of children to other groups that would result in the eradication of the targeted group. The *Akayesu* trial chambers opined that the rapes and sexual violence comprised, and were consistent, with other acts of genocide committed against the Tutsi population.

Akayesu cannot be surmised as recognizing what has been termed genocidal rape. The holding was actually more poignant and profound. The gendered sexual violence is recognized as an act of serious bodily or mental harm to members of the group and acknowledged as a manner to destroy a group that is contemplated by genocide law. Stated otherwise, the very gendered sexual violence is integral as a means employed to effectuate the genocide. Years into the ICTR's existence, these aggregate holdings on rapes and sexual mutilation shaped the judiciary's understanding of the Rwandan genocide. Accordingly, repeated ICTR litigation such as *Muhimana* (2005), *Gacumbitsi*

(2004), and *Karemera* and *Ngirumpaste* (2012) led the chambers to conclude that rapes and killings constituted the two integral, and almost numerically equivalent, components of the Rwandan genocide. *Kayishema*, an ICTR case that did not charge sexual violence as genocide, nevertheless held rapes to be evidence of the intent to destroy a people in whole or part. As such, sexual violence can constitute both an underlying act of genocide, as well as part of the specific intent to commit genocide.

The ICTR cases that observed the gendered nature of mutilating and killing pregnant females and that interpreted the rapes as acts of causing serious bodily or mental harm reinvigorated important principles of the Genocide Convention. The rapes and sexual violence cohered with genocide tenets aimed at penalizing biological and reproductive tortures. *Akayesu* presented a doctrinal circling back, if you will, to reaffirm genocide's fundamental grounding in prohibition of sexualized degradation and assaults of the targeted group, both in forming the genocidal intent and committing the underlying acts.

Another ICTR case of *Nahimana*, commonly called the Media Case (2005), also exemplifies the narrow strand of gender jurisprudence. The Media Case addressed allegations of direct and public incitement to commit genocide, an untested provision of the Genocide Convention. Direct and public incitement to commit genocide is not dependent upon a genocide having happened. Its purpose is to prevent genocides by condemning their public incitement, even if, thankfully, genocide does not materialize.

Defendant Nahimana chaired the board of the radio station Mille Collines, while Barayagwiza chaired the legal committee. Radio Mille Collines broadcast sexually denigrating propaganda programs. Ngeze founded *Karunga*, a newspaper with articles that aimed to incite rapes and other sexual assaults against Tutsi females. Such sexually violent acts later occurred during the Rwandan genocide. Each defendant was convicted of direct and public incitement to commit genocide.

The Media Case substantiates two core aspects of genocide law. First, it illustrates that constant calls for sexual violence and sexual degradation of a targeted group when coupled with specific intent to commit genocide satsify the elements of the crime. Prior to the Media Case, whether sexual violence propaganda could be considered a form of genocidal incitement was never raised in the genocide commentaries, nor addressed, even by *obiter dicta*, in the case law.

Second, direct and public incitement to commit genocide aims to *prevent* genocides. Prevention is a driving objective of the Genocide Convention, proclaimed in the convention's title: The Convention on the Prevention and Punishment of the Crime of Genocide. Incendiary verbal sexual attacks, as used in the Rwandan scenario, were precursors to or early warning signs of genocide. The Media Case, accordingly, illustrates how condemnation of sexual propaganda is integral to the prevention of genocide. Such condemnation would function similarly to the condemnation of calls to kill off a group, prevent its future births, or transfer its children to another group. Fueling sexual violence *is* incitement to commit genocide, and condemnation of such incitement *is* a means to prevent genocide. The Media Case forces a legal "double take," as it fully bores into the core of the law's aim to avert genocides.

The narrow strand of gender jurisprudence's focus on sexual violence surfaces key aspects of genocide's legal foundation. While highlighting the rapes, the *Akayesu* and other ICTR chambers also noted that the killings aimed to eradicate the replenishing of the Tutsi population. This was especially apparent in the killing of pregnant females and children. Sexualized violence and the sexualized targeting of the Tutsi population was core to distinct components of the genocide. Sexual violence honed the intent to commit genocide and manifested in killings, in the act of causing serious or bodily harm to members of the group, as well as in the objective to publicly incite genocide. Beyond counting the incidences of rape, these gender holdings serve to measure the adherence to and development of the doctrinal bases of genocide—a notable contribution. The panoramic view exhibits a similar legal propensity.

GENOCIDE: THE PANORAMIC VIEW
OF GENDER JURISPRUDENCE

At a more overarching and analytical level, the panoramic view of gender jurisprudence surfaces international criminal law's fundamental doctrinal components, as shown by the ICTY's Srebrenica jurisprudence (see Erdemović 1998; Krstić 2001; Obrenović 2003; Blagojević 2005; Nikolić 2006; Popović 2010; Tolimir 2012; Karadžić 2016). Its gender-centered analysis of the acts committed against males and females, separately and collectively, unveils the doctrinal essence of genocide. It recounts the execution of nearly eight thousand Bosnian Muslim military-aged males in eastern Bosnia in 1995 and the forced transfer of women, children, and elderly men out of the Srebrenica safe area. *Krstić*, an early Srebrenica case, held that the killings of the military-aged males constituted genocide, and that the shooting of males who nonetheless miraculously survived constituted another act of genocide, namely, causing serious mental or bodily harm to members of the group. It further ruled that the forcible transfer of the overwhelmingly female population of refugees was not an act of genocide, but amounted to evidence of the perpetrators' intent to commit genocide against the males. In essence, *Krstić* held that the Srebrenica genocide had been committed only against the Bosnian Muslim males.

On appeal, *Krstić* upheld the two acts of genocide and, moreover, confirmed the trial chamber's considered observation of the gendered impact of the killings. The appeals chamber opined that

> [i]n examining these consequences, the Trial Chamber properly focused on the likelihood of the community's physical survival. As the Trial Chamber found that the massacred men amounted to about one-fifth of the overall community. The Trial Chamber found that given the patriarchal character of the Bosnian Muslim society in Srebrenica, the destruction of such a sizable number of men would "inevitably result in the physical disappearance of the Bosnian Muslim population in Srebrenica." Evidence introduced at trial supported this finding, by showing that

with the majority of the men killed officially listed as missing, their spouses are unable to remarry and consequently to have children. The physical destruction of the men therefore had severe procreative implications for the Srebrenica community, potentially consigning the community to extinction. (Krstić 2004, para. 28)

The *Krstić* trial and appeals chambers, in distinguishing the gender-differentiated treatment of the males and females, conceded that the diminished reproductive capacity of the Srebrenica Muslim community was integral to their contemplation of the Srebrenica genocide. The appeals chamber affirmed that the trial chamber had correctly ruled upon the elements of genocide, inclusive of the specific intent. The appeals chamber was satisfied that the requisite intent was based, *inter alia,* upon the reproductive impact caused by killing the males. It stated that

> some members of the VRS Main Staff devised the killing of the male prisoners with full knowledge of the detrimental consequences it would have for the physical survival of the Bosnian Muslim community in Srebrenica further supports the Trial Chamber's conclusion that the instigators of that operation had the requisite genocidal intent. (Krstić 2004, para. 29)

To correctly discern the breadth of the gendered nature of the Srebrenica genocide, *Krstić*'s holdings must be situated among the other Srebrenica cases.

In *Blagojević* (2005), a subsequent Srebrenica case, the commander of the Brautinac brigade was convicted for aiding and abetting in the crime of complicity in genocide. In addition to the killings, *Blagojević* held that (1) the separation of males from their families, with the realization that they would be executed, (2) the wounding and mental anguish of the male survivors of the executions, and (3) the forcible transfer of the females, children, and elderly constituted separate acts of genocide, under the provision of causing serious bodily or mental harm to members of the group. Moreover, the *Blagojević* trial chamber found that the dire reproductive consequences faced by the surviving community members also comprised part of their mental suffering. On appeal, while the conviction was reversed, the exceedingly gendered analysis of the acts that comprised the genocide were not challenged.

In *Popović*, another Srebrenica case, the prosecution charged acts of genocide similar to those found in *Krstić*. In addition, the prosecutor formally submitted that the forcible transfer of the women, children, and elderly contributed to the failure of the remaining population to live and reproduce normally (Popović 2010, para. 850). Accordingly, it alleged two other acts of genocide, namely "deliberately inflicting conditions calculated to bring about physical destruction of the group in whole or part;" and "imposing methods to prevents births within the group." (Popović 2010, para. 851–853). The *Popović* trial chamber entered convictions for acts of genocide similar to those condemned in *Krstić*; however, it did not enter convictions on the newly framed counts. The chamber considered that forced transfer of the mainly female population without alleging, under the same count, the killing of the men, did not represent "conditions" as intended under that provision. Likewise, it held that, objectively, forced transfers were not, strictly speaking, a "measure" that was intended to prevent births. Nonetheless, the *Popović* chamber acknowledged that the killing of the men broached issues of biological group survival. Overall, *Popović* reaffirmed Srebrenica's gendered jurisprudence regarding killings and the different acts of serious bodily or mental harm. It demonstrated the unsuccessful pleading of two heretofore untested provisions of genocide to redress continuing reproductive harms.

In *Tolimir*, a subsequent Srebrenica case, the prosecution revised the pleading. It argued that the forced displacement in *combination* with killing of males amounted to the act of genocide of inflicting conditions of life calculated to bring about the group's destruction. The *Tolimir* trial chamber entered a conviction for the count holding that

> [t]he Majority finds that the combined effect of these operations had a devastating effect on the physical survival of the Bosnian Muslim population of Eastern BiH, . . . and is satisfied that the goal of . . . these operations were aimed at destroying this Bosnian Muslim community and preventing reconstitution of the group in this area. (Tolimir 2012, para. 766)

Tolimir examined the genocide, based upon the long-term reproductive implications of the combined acts endured by male and female members of the Srebrenica Muslim community. Nevertheless, and similar to *Popović*, the *Tolimir* trial chamber did not qualify the forcible transfer as a measure to prevent births within the group. The *Tolimir* appeals chamber overturned the conviction based on inflicting a condition calculated to bring about physical destruction. Moreover, it ruled that the forcible transfer alone did not amount to a condition calculated to bring about physical destruction.

Karadžić is the latest Srebrenica judgment. There, the trial chamber pronounced Radovan Karadžić guilty of genocide for the killing of the males and the causing of serious mental and bodily harm to these individuals, who suffered in the final days and hours of their lives, knowing death was imminent. The trial chamber also found that for the males who did not succumb to their wounds, their shooting likewise comprised acts of genocide. Furthermore, it found that the pervasive anguish caused to the females, boys, and elderly men by their forcible removal and the killing of their male family members had long-lasting impacts that impaired their abilities to envision the future and "to live normal and constructive lives," amounting to acts of genocide of causing serious bodily or mental harm (Karadžić 2016, para. 5664).

In specific regard to the reproductive consequences of the Srebrenica genocide, *Karadžić* opined, that

> viewing the evidence in its totality, the Chamber considers that the Bosnian Serb Forces must have been aware of the detrimental impact that the eradication of multiple generations of men would have on the Bosnian Muslims in Srebrenica in that the killing of all able-bodied males while forcibly removing the remainder of the population would have severe procreative implications for the Bosnian Muslims in

Srebrenica and thus result in their physical extinction. The Chamber therefore finds beyond reasonable doubt that these acts were carried out with the intent to destroy the Bosnian Muslims in Srebrenica as such. (Karadžić 2016, para. 5671).

Karadžić characterizes the reproductive consequences as evincing the specific intent that undergirds the entire genocidal destruction of the targeted group. The killings embody the intent to affect the reproductive capacity of the Bosnian Muslims in the immediate and long term. To that extent, it could be posited that the Srebrenica genocide was not a punctual event, but one that continues to be perpetrated.

Hence, contemplated holistically, the gendered journey extends from *Krstić*'s initial observation of the reproductive consequences as evidence of intent to commit genocide, through *Blagojević, Popović,* and *Tolimir*'s interpretation of several distinct genocide provisions, to *Karadžić*'s reassertion of the diminished reproductive capacity of the group as evidence of specific intent of genocide. A meticulously gendered examination of the mental and physical acts, inflicted individually and collectively on the group, shaped the chambers' varying interpretation of the genocide. The analysis undermines the simplification of the Srebrenica genocide as an event confined to unpardonably egregious massacres.

Utilitarian Tool: Reconsideration of Gender Jurisprudence

The moment to reconsider the body of what is considered gender jurisprudence is upon us. After two-plus decades of litigation at the ad hoc Tribunals and internationalized courts, and while still on the cusp of a maturing ICC, the very concept and role of gender jurisprudence begs reconsideration. The analysis in the previous sections broached a reassessment and offered two primary observations. First, instead of examining individual judgments, whether in the narrow or panoramic strands of gender jurisprudence, case observations should be aggregated and their holdings probed jointly and comparatively. Second, rather than being studied only for their immediate judicial pronouncements, gender holdings should be viewed through the doctrinal prism of specific international crimes.

Furthermore, aggregating the narrow and panoramic strands of gender jurisprudence permits a more acute analysis of international criminal law. A brief revisit of the ICTY and ICTR cases is insightful. *Akayesu* resuscitated the genocide provision of "causing serious bodily and mental harm to members of the group" when ruling that mental and physical harm was innate to the rapes of Tutsi females. The provision, originally pegged to Nazi-conducted reproductive experiments and other forms of torture, allowed wide berth for similar harms. *Akayesu* and subsequent ICTR cases, by logical extension, ruled that the identical provision of the ICTR statute encompassed sexual violence. The Srebrenica cases eventually ruled that the act indeed enveloped the psychological harm that precedes impending executions, or that inures to survivors of such executions, or that inflicted upon the deported members of the group who have a diminished reproductive capacity. The *Krstić* trial chamber and subsequent Srebrenica cases and the *Akayesu* interpretation of these gender-centric psychological harms speak to the breadth of gender analysis in deciphering the respective genocides. The eventual reckoning with the mental harm of the Srebrenica deported population offers congruent aspects of mental anguish and suffering, similar to those endured as a result of biological or genetic experiments geared toward stifling reproduction within a group. Hence, read in the aggregate, *Akayesu* and the Srebrenica cases lucidly signal the breadth of the provision of causing serious bodily or mental harm to members of the group. Jointly, they fortify legal aperture consistent with genocide law and securely tether genocide law to its doctrinal objectives—the prevention and suppression of genocide.

From this vantage point, gender jurisprudence performs a critical utilitarian function to enlighten our knowledge of the boundaries of genocide. The conscientious gendered appraisal of the Rwanda and Srebrenica genocides defy the simplistic narrative that they were rooted solely in killings. Dissecting the gender-inflicted harms, such as rapes, and reconfiguring the killings as gendered harms, whether committed against the Srebrenica males or Rwandan pregnant women, led to the chambers' fuller comprehension of the acts of genocide and the manifestation of its specific intent. Invoking gender jurisprudence as a tool to delineate doctrine readily applies to other crimes under IHL and ICL.

Kunarac (2001), an ICTY case squarely situated within the narrow strand of gender jurisprudence, when aggregated with *Krnojelac* (2002), an infrequently examined ICTY case in the panoramic strand, illuminates the utilitarian approach. Read in tandem, the decisions expose the gendered patterns of the military occupation that were emblematic of the armed conflict in the former Yugoslavia. Males and females endured detention under the control of Bosnian Serb forces, albeit in different locations, and each population was forcibly transferred separately. The common charges of enslavement as a crime against humanity seemingly are justified given the simultaneous operations to detain persons. However, the underlying patterns of detention diverge according to gender. The key doctrinal element of enslavement is a determination of whether the perpetrator exercised "any or all the powers of ownership over a person." *Kunarac* asserted that legal basis of enslavement comprised the perpetrators exercising, *inter alia*, sexual ownership over certain females. Two accused in *Kunarac* were convicted of enslavement as a crime against humanity after the chamber determined that they indeed exercised the powers attaching to ownership over detained females. *Krnojelac* asserted exercise of ownership over the manual (non-sexual) labor of male prisoners. The trial chamber acquitted *Krnojelac* of enslavement, noting that the forced labor inflicted upon the men, while a discriminatory act, was not reliant upon exercising powers of ownership over the males.

Kunarac and *Krnojelac* confirm the utility of an aggregate appraisal of gendered holdings, especially when filtered through the doctrinal prism of enslavement's requirement of exercising powers attached to ownership. Jointly, they offer a critical assessment of international criminal law. Such use of gender jurisprudence as a normative analytical tool upholds and strengthens the guarantees and identifies the limits of international criminal law's protection. The doctrinal foundations of genocide, enslavement, torture, terrorizing the civilian population, or persecution remain to be more acutely distilled by gender jurisprudence. Modes of liability, such as superior responsibility, also await the assessment of their gendered effectiveness.

CONCLUSION

When envisioned as a vibrant analytical tool, gender jurisprudence of conflict moves beyond a recitation of sexual assault holdings or gendered descriptions of atrocities. Reconceptualized, it can function as a deft measurement of the current state of international criminal law. Nonetheless, gender jurisprudence itself must rectify its elusive, ill-defined status. The plausibility of a utilitarian approach is weakened when gender jurisprudence woefully conflates women and gender, or restricts gender to a binary approach, or diminishes the scope and frequency of male-directed sexual violence, or ignores sexual orientation. Each oversight, in turn, insufficiently examines the true scope of the available doctrinal protections. Gender descriptions that omit the breadth of gender identity and sexual orientation actually reinforce and perpetuate the lack of redress under international criminal law. Gender jurisprudence, in order to be a viable and valuable analytical tool for practitioners and scholars, must acknowledge its fragility and inabilities, and then seek to further hone its analytical tools.

NOTES

1. Security Council resolution 2122 (2013) makes an effort to address this, in recognizing the need for justice to address the differentiated impacts of violations on women and girls, including forced displacement, enforced disappearances, and destruction of civilian infrastructure.
2. The chamber held that
   [n]umerous Tutsi women were forced to endure acts of sexual violence, mutilations and rape, often repeatedly, often publicly and often by more than one assailant. Tutsi women were systematically raped, as one female victim testified to by saying that "each time that you met assailants, they raped you." Numerous incidents of such rape and sexual violence against Tutsi women occurred inside or near the Bureau communal. It has been proven that some communal policemen armed with guns and the accused himself were present while some of these rapes and sexual violence were being committed. Furthermore, it is proven that on several occasions, by his presence, his attitude and his utterances, Akayesu encouraged such acts, one particular witness testifying that Akayesu, addressed the Interahamwe who were committing the rapes and said that "never ask me again what a Tutsi woman tastes like."
   In the opinion of the Chamber, this constitutes tacit encouragement to the rapes that were being committed. In the opinion of the Chamber, the above-mentioned acts with

which Akayesu is charged indeed render him individually criminally responsible for having abetted in the preparation or execution of the killings of members of the Tutsi group
and the infliction of serious bodily and mental harm on members of said group. (Akayesu
1998, paras. 707–708)

3. *Akayesu* directly referred to the Eichmann case's holding that a plethora of conduct
to establish "causing serious bodily or mental harm to members of the group" could be
established

by the enslavement, starvation, deportation and persecution [. . .] and by their detention
in ghettos, transit camps and concentration camps in conditions which were designed to
cause their degradation, deprivation of their rights as human beings, and to suppress them
and cause them inhumane suffering and torture. (Akayesu 1998, para. 503)

REFERENCES

Prosecutor v. Akayesu, Case No. ICTR-96-4 (Akayesu). 1998. Judgment. September 2.
Prosecutor v. Bemba Gombo, Case No. ICC-01/05-01/08-3343 (Bemba). 2016. Judgment.
    March 21.
Prosecutor v. Blagojević et al., Case No. IT-02-60-T (Blagojević). 2005. Judgment. January 17.
Prosecutor v. Brima et al., Case No. SCSL-04-16-T (AFRC Case). 2007. Trial Chamber
    Judgment. June 20.
Prosecutor v. Brima et al., Case No. SCSL-04-16-A (AFRC Case). 2008. Appeals Judgment.
    February 22.
Prosecutor v. Delalić et al., Case No. IT-96-21-T (Delalić). 1998 Judgment. November 16.
Prosecutor v. Erdemović, Case No. IT-96-22 (Erdemović). 1998. Judgment. March 5.
Prosecutor v. Furundzija, Case No. IT-95-17/1-T (Furundzija). 1998. Judgment. December 10.
Prosecutor v. Gacumbitsi, Case No. ICTR-2001-64-T (Gacumbitsi). 2004. Judgment. June 17.
Prosecutor v. Karadžić, Case No. IT-95-5/18-T (Karadzic). 2016. Judgment. March 24.
Prosecutor v. Karemera et al., Case No. ICTR-98-44-T (Karemera). 2012. Trial Judgment.
    February 2.
Prosecutor v. Kayishema et al., Case No. ICTR-95-1-T (Kayishema). 1999. Sentence. May 21.
Prosecutor v. Krnojelac, Case No. IT-97-25-T (Krnojelac). 2002. Judgment. March 15.
Prosecutor v. Krstić, Case No. 98-33-T (Krstić). 2001. Trial Chamber Judgment. August 2.
Prosecutor v. Krstić, Case No. 98-33-A (Krstić). 2004. Appeals Judgment. April 19.
Prosecutor v. Kunarac et al., Case No. IT-96-23-T and IT-96-23/1-T (Kunarac). 2001. Judgment.
    February 22.
Prosecutor v. Kvočka et al., Case No. IT-98-30/1 (Kvocka). 2001. Judgment. November 2.
Prosecution v. Muhimana, Case No. ICTR-95-1B-T (Muhimana). 2005. Judgment. April 28.
Prosecutor v. Nahimana et al., Case No. ICTR-99-52-T (Media Case). 2003. Judgment.
    December 3.
Prosecutor v. Nikolić, Case No. IT-02-60/1 (Nikolić). 2006. Judgment on Sentencing Appeal.
    March 8.
Prosecutor v. Obrenović, Case No. IT-02-60/2-S (Obrenović). 2003. Sentencing Judgment.
    December 10.
Prosecutor v. Popović et al., Case No. IT- 05-88-T (Popović). 2010. Judgment. June 10.
Prosecutor v. Sesay et al., Case No. SCSL-04-15-T (RUF Case). 2009. Trial Chamber Judgment.
    March 2.

Prosecutor v. Tadić, Case No. IT-94-1-T (Tadić). 1997. Judgment. July 14.

Prosecutor v. Taylor, Case No. SCSL-03-01-T (Taylor). 2012. Trial Chamber Judgment. April 26.

Prosecutor v. Tolimir, Case No. IT-05-88/2-T (Tolimir). 2012. Judgment, December 12.

Sellers, Patricia Viseur, and Leo C. Nwoye. 2018. "Conflict-Related Male Sexual Violence and the International Criminal Jurisprudence." In *Sexual Violence Against Men and Boys in Global Politics*, edited by Marysia Zalewski, Paula Drumond, Elisabeth Prügl, and Maria Stern. London: Routledge.

The Trial of Martin Bormann (Bormann). 1946. Judgment (International Military Tribunal at Nuremberg). October 1.

CHAPTER 17

COMPLEMENTARITY AS
A CATALYST FOR GENDER
JUSTICE IN NATIONAL
PROSECUTIONS

AMRITA KAPUR

THE Rome Statute established the International Criminal Court (ICC) with an ambitious objective: to end impunity for international crimes and deter future perpetrators from committing them. As the first permanent international court with jurisdiction over genocide, crimes against humanity, war crimes and aggression, the ICC is a landmark in the continuing evolution of international criminal justice. Relevant to this *Handbook*, the ICC has two institutional features that offer as yet unexplored potential to account for international crimes of sexual and gender-based violence (SGBV) committed in conflict. First, the Rome Statute establishes a new standard of gender justice in international law, evidenced by its inclusion of a broad range of gender-based crimes, gender-sensitive procedural rules, and institutional pursuit of gender parity. Second, while the Rome Statute includes elements from statutes of other tribunals for international crimes, like those created to prosecute crimes committed in the Rwandan and Yugoslav conflicts, it clearly establishes the ICC as a mechanism to complement, rather than override, the primary responsibility of states to prosecute international crimes.

This chapter considers the opportunities presented by the complementarity regime contained in the Rome Statute to promote justice for victims of SGBV crimes and gender justice more generally. First, the concept and contours of complementarity are explored to identify where the ICC's greatest potential for catalyzing prosecutions of international crimes lies. Second, the chapter describes the ICC's approach to sexual violence and gender, including its developing jurisprudence and its impact on national treatment of sexual violence crimes. Third, the chapter discusses how to maximize complementarity's catalytic impact on national prosecutions of sexual violence, given the legislative, procedural, and sentencing shortcomings of local criminal justice systems; recent shifts in national prosecutions within Colombia and Guinea reveal some cause for cautious optimism. Finally, contemplating the broader gender potential of the complementarity regime, this chapter suggests that there may be benefits for women and victims of SGBV beyond the prosecution and punishment of post-conflict criminal perpetrators.

It is important to acknowledge at the outset that ensuring criminal accountability for international crimes is a crucial but limited aspect of resolving conflict and preventing its recurrence. Other mechanisms to establish the truth and acknowledge responsibility for individual criminal acts are equally essential to promote reconciliation, and they may offer more effective redress for victims of gender-based harms. The ICC (and indeed prosecutions generally) as a transitional justice tool has only ever represented one aspect of a multifaceted approach encompassing diverse judicial and non-judicial accountability mechanisms such as truth-seeking and reconciliation projects, symbolic and material victim reparations, and institutional rebuilding (see Bueno-Hansen, Chapter 35 in this volume). As an international prosecutorial mechanism, the ICC was always intended to address only the most exceptional criminal cases and further the aim of building domestic justice capacities. More specifically, as a criminal instrument, the Rome Statute defines and applies to crimes of sexual violence, rather than gender-based violence more broadly, such that its *direct* effects on national criminal justice systems discussed here are similarly limited. This traditional framing reduces women's experiences of harm to the narrow prism of sexual violence without acknowledging broader gender-based harms committed within armed conflict, and in so doing exposes the inadequacy of criminal responses to redress them (Ní Aoláin, Haynes, and Cahn 2011a). While some of the discussed considerations can apply and are applied equally to sexual violence and gender-based violence, this chapter also identifies how the ICC's complementarity regime could *indirectly* encourage improved modes of redressing gender-based harms beyond the scope of the sexual violence crimes included in the Rome Statute. While recognizing the need for greater attention to sexual violence experienced by men and boys in conflict, the discussion here focuses on women, who comprise the majority of victims of sexual violence in conflict and whose access to justice is impacted by broader gender inequalities.

Notwithstanding the inherent limitations of a criminal justice response to gender-based harms, there are unexplored opportunities for the ICC to facilitate improved responses through developing a gender-sensitive approach to complementarity.

DIFFERENT FACETS OF COMPLEMENTARITY

The term "complementarity" explicitly defines the relationship between the ICC and its states parties, confirming the primacy of state jurisdiction and limiting admissibility of cases before the ICC. Article 17 of the Rome Statute identifies three circumstances in which a case is admissible before the ICC: when it is not being investigated or prosecuted nationally, or when the state is unwilling, or unable genuinely to carry out the investigation and prosecution of the case. The case must also be of sufficient gravity to justify investigation and prosecution by the ICC. Complementarity reinforces "the duty of every State to exercise its criminal jurisdiction over those responsible for international crimes" (Rome Statute, preamble), which is integral to the Rome Statute system's long-term efficacy. Indeed, from the outset, the ICC's first prosecutor linked the success of the ICC to the number of international prosecutions avoided through the increased effectiveness of national prosecutions for international crimes, which the ICC is expected to catalyze.

A decade of operation, resulting in only twenty-three cases, three convictions, and one acquittal, has proven beyond doubt that the ICC's institutional capacity will be limited to a few exemplary trials. This necessarily means that its actions are intended to be part symbolic, but also catalytic (ICC ASP 2012). Together with the principle of complementarity, ICC trials are expected to motivate genuine national prosecutions; the extent to which the ICC has achieved this is still contested.[1]

To achieve this goal, the ICC Office of the Prosecutor (OTP) adopted a policy of "positive complementarity," "encouraging genuine national proceedings where possible, relying on national and international networks, and participating in a system of international cooperation" (ICC Office of the Prosecutor 2006, 5). One aspect of the OTP's implementation of complementarity is the use of preliminary examinations pursuant to Article 15 to ascertain if there is a reasonable basis to proceed with an investigation on the basis of the inactivity, inability, or unwillingness of national authorities. This is also the OTP's first opportunity to catalyze national proceedings through its positive complementarity approach, by monitoring situations, sending missions, requesting information, and assisting stakeholders to better identify the steps required to meet national obligations under the Statute.

The first, narrow construction of complementarity involves a three-stage case-specific assessment as to whether genuine investigations and prosecutions have been or are being conducted with respect to cases identified by the OTP that would likely arise from an investigation into the situation. According to the OTP's 2013 *Report on Preliminary Examination Activities*, the first stage comprises an empirical assessment as to whether there are or have been any relevant national investigations or prosecutions (cases): the absence of national proceedings is sufficient to make the case admissible, and there is no need to consider inability or unwillingness (ICC Office of the Prosecutor 2013, 12).

The ICC has defined "case" as proceedings against the same person of interest to the ICC Prosecutor, for the same conduct the ICC Prosecutor seeks to prosecute.[2] Importantly, this means it is sufficient for a state to prosecute the subject's conduct as a domestic crime rather than as an international crime, as long as it is the same conduct at issue. The implications of this definition for sexual violence crimes would be that rape, even where undertaken as part of a systematic or widespread attack or with genocidal intent, could be prosecuted as a domestic offense, not as a crime against humanity, rendering the case inadmissible before the ICC. The comparative ease of prosecuting domestic crimes compared to international crimes incentivizes national prosecutors to forgo identifying crimes in their broader societal context in favor of increasing prospects of convictions.

If there are national proceedings, then the OTP will consider unwillingness or inability to investigate or prosecute a case. Unwillingness is evidenced by an unjustified delay in proceedings; lack of impartiality or independence; or proceedings undertaken to shield the person concerned from criminal responsibility. Factors showing "unwillingness" include, but are not limited to: ignoring evidence or giving it insufficient weight; intimidation of victims, witnesses, or judicial personnel; manifest inadequacies in charging; flawed forensic examination; and lack of resources allocated to proceedings compared to overall capacities (ICC Office of the Prosecutor 2013, 13).

State inability to investigate or prosecute a case is assessed with respect to factors including the absence of secure conditions for witnesses, investigators, prosecutors, and judges; the absence of the required legislative framework; and the lack of adequate resources for effective investigations and prosecutions (ICC Office of the Prosecutor 2013, 14). Interestingly, a failure to implement the Rome Statute crimes into local law does not itself amount to inability,[3] presumably because prosecuting conduct as a domestic crime rather than an international crime satisfies the ICC's requirement for genuine justice.

The broader effects of complementarity are closely tethered to and dependent on ICC articulations of the terms contained in Article 17. This is where the real potential lies for the ICC to promote genuine justice at the national level, including for SGBV crimes.

GENDER AT THE INTERNATIONAL CRIMINAL COURT

Laws and practice in the courtroom

The ICC has a solid foundation from which to promote accountability for sexual violence crimes, due to gender-progressive substantive and procedural provisions in its constituent instruments. The Rome Statute consolidates previous international legal developments in its recognition of rape, sexual slavery, enforced prostitution, enforced sterilization, and other forms of sexual violence as war crimes and crimes against humanity; and rape and sexual violence as acts of genocide. It also extends international criminal law through its inclusion of forced pregnancy as a new act constituting a war crime.

Procedurally, both the Statute and the ICC's Rules of Procedure and Evidence include provisions to protect witnesses and victims and to reduce the impact of participation on their physical and mental well-being (Rome Statute, art. 68(2), (3); ICC Assemb. of States Parties 2002, rules 70, 71, 89–93). The OTP has specific obligations under the Rome Statute to apply and interpret the law in a manner consistent with international human rights, to investigate crimes of sexual and gender violence, and to appoint specialist advisers on sexual and gender violence. The Statute's significant and more con-troversial innovations were the introduction of victim participation in court proceed-ings, accompanied by the power to award reparations to victims, including through the establishment of a Trust Fund (see Kalla, Chapter 19, this volume).[4] Other provisions require staff in the Victims and Witnesses Unit in the Registry, responsible for witness protection and well-being, to have expertise in sexual violence–related trauma, as well as protection measures during proceedings.

Institutionally, the ICC pursues gender parity in its staffing, including providing for a fair representation of female and male judges, OTP, and registry staff, and recognizing the need to include judges with legal expertise on violence against women and children. The ICC's current composition reflects these aspirations: women currently hold 47 per-cent of all staff positions, including the senior position of prosecutor, and women com-prise ten of the eighteen judges.

The track record of ICC indictments and successful prosecutions for sexual violence crimes is more mixed. By 2012, only 50 percent of SGBV charges had been confirmed by the pre-trial chamber; and across nine cases, while only seven of 204 requested charges did not include arrest warrants or summonses to appear, five of these seven charges related to sexual or gender-based violence (Women's Initiative for Gender Justice 2012). As a litmus test, the OTP initially failed to charge SGBV crimes in its first case against Lubanga,[5] despite available evidence confirming their occurrence and supporting their characterization as international crimes. Despite referencing evidence of sexual vio-lence in its *Lubanga* judgment, the trial chamber made no findings of fact because there were no allegations of sexual violence in the indictment.

The trial chamber's acquittal of all sexual violence charges against Katanga[6] com-pounds this disappointing conviction track record. Even though the trial chamber found the relevant witnesses credible and believed that sexual violence crimes had been committed, it did not find that these formed part of the common purpose of the attack compared to murder, attacking a civilian population, destruction of property, and pil-laging. Beyond immediate concerns of inconsistent expectations of standards of proof between sexual violence and other crimes, is the longer-term potential to entrench impunity for sexual violence crimes at both the international and domestic levels, as well as the damage to the ICC's (and particularly the judiciary's) credibility with victims of sexual violence in conflict zones.

The effects of this jurisprudence will not only be felt by victims of future proceed-ings, but also those facing similar changes in national jurisdictions. The OTP and all three ICC chambers need to adopt broad, rather than narrow, interpretations of sexual violence offenses, to consider new categories of crimes in a more progressive manner, and to be conscious of latent discrepancies in evidentiary requirements across different categories of crimes. Otherwise, complementarity's success will be limited not only by national inability or unwillingness, but also by inadequate international standards that make it easier to justify the continued disparity in impunity for sexual violence com-pared to other international criminal conduct.

Legal effect beyond the courtroom

Improving the ICC's courtroom achievements is important directly and symbolically, but does not on its own guarantee parallel improvements in national jurisdictions, which continue to retain primary jurisdiction over sexual violence crimes.
There is evidence of legislative reform to include a broader range of sexual violence
crimes recognized under international law. A survey of states parties to the Rome
Statute evidences a modest positive correlation between state ratification and subsequent modification and augmentation of domestic laws regarding sex-based harms
against women (Ní Aoláin 2014, 627–628). Acknowledging the many other potential
causal factors and a time lag in ratification across some states, the coincidence rates
nevertheless suggest that ratification creates an opportunity to remedy contradictory domestic laws and expands the political space to take advantage of such legislative progress. One example is Kenya's enactment of the Sexual Offences Act in 2006,
following its ratification of the Rome Statute in March 2005. The new law redefined
rape to include both males and females as possible victims and perpetrators, and it
included new offenses such as gang rape, sodomy, trafficking for sexual exploitation, and pornography.[7] Two years later, Kenya enacted the International Crimes
Act as part of its Rome Statute obligations, which conferred jurisdiction for genocide, war crimes, and crimes against humanity on domestic courts, but referred to
the Rome Statute for definitions of these crimes.[8] Consequently, all the sexual violence crimes contained in the Rome Statute may now be prosecuted before Kenyan
courts.

Practice beyond the courtroom

More important and more challenging than legislative reform is meaningful improvement in enforcement of the law, including punishing sexual violence crimes and
providing adequate protection for its victims. For example, while the Democratic
Republic of Congo (DRC) amended its domestic law to incorporate definitions of
international crimes according to international law, subsequent continuing large-
scale attacks involving sexual violence committed with impunity belie any international legal influence on DRC armed actors. In other situations under ICC
investigation, notwithstanding more limited definitions of sexual violence, the same
danger exists. Sexual violence continues to be blatantly and consistently used to perpetrate genocide, war crimes, and crimes against humanity, despite the specter of an
ICC investigation. In fact, there are ongoing ICC investigations in six of the worst ten
countries in the 2013 Sexual Violence in Conflict Index (measuring the risk of sexual violence),[9] highlighting the continuing disparity between the ICC's legal influence
and its practical effects.

Maximizing Complementarity's Effect on Criminal Justice Responses to Sexual Violence

Positive complementarity, through engagement with national authorities and preliminary examinations, provides a mechanism that the ICC can and should strategically use to compel reluctant states to pursue an acceptable measure of accountability for key categories of crimes, including sexual violence. Through its scrutiny of criminal legislation, procedures, and outcomes as discussed in the following, the OTP can prompt domestic regimes to prioritize prosecution of these crimes. The mandate for this specific consideration comes from the OTP's public commitment to "pay particular attention to methods of investigations of crimes committed against children, and sexual and gender-based crimes" (ICC Office of the Prosecutor 2006, 7).

The OTP's public commitment is undoubtedly motivated in part by the fact that worldwide, national jurisdictions continue to struggle to sensitively and effectively codify, prosecute, convict, and punish SGBV crimes: challenging structural gender inequality, discrimination, and the consequent systemic violence against women has been even less effective. It is generally understood that SGBV crimes are underreported, often inadequately investigated, less likely to reach court, and result in disproportionately high numbers of acquittals. These challenges are reflected within international criminal law, which draws upon domestic legislation, jurisprudence, and practices. They are compounded in post-conflict contexts by extremely scarce financial, human, and technical resources, collapsed or dysfunctional institutions, and an overwhelming number of criminal cases within the justice system.

Legislative limitations

In terms of legislation, a UN Women report observes: "While almost all countries criminalize rape, penal codes often define sexual violence very narrowly, with many still framing the problem in terms of indecency or immorality, or as a crime against the family or society, rather than a violation of an individual's bodily integrity" (UN Women 2011, 33). To take an example from a country in which the ICC is investigating and prosecuting individuals, rape in the Ugandan Penal Code is located in the chapter entitled "Offences Against Morality," and is defined as "unlawful carnal knowledge of a woman or girl."[10] The definition is limited to penetration of the penis into the vagina of a woman or girl and excludes forced oral sex, rape with an object, anal rape, and other common forms of sexual violence, which are characterized merely as indecent assault. Narrow domestic legislative provisions may in turn create both evidentiary and due process challenges at the point of prosecution.

The Penal Code in Guinea (a country under preliminary examination by the ICC) does not recognize any forms of sexual violence beyond rape. Under such domestic laws, a range of sexual violence crimes, including sexual slavery and sexual mutilation, are either unable to be prosecuted, or must be prosecuted as less serious crimes. Moreover, the characterization of such offences as contrary to morality or dignity fundamentally misconceives them as a violation of male status (Ní Aoláin 2014).

Beyond the characterization of physical acts, the legal concept of consent and the effect of surrounding circumstances are particularly important in prosecuting crimes of sexual violence. Conceptions of non-consent for sexual offenses have evolved to varying degrees and in different directions across national jurisdictions. The requirement of resistance to prove non-consent; the admissibility of previous sexual behavior; the existence of marital rape as a crime; the sufficiency of recklessness to prove the requisite *mens rea*; and the relevance of any delay in complaint are treated diversely and remain controversial in many national jurisdictions (Klein 2008).

Procedural limitations and problematic outcomes

Procedural limitations to effectively prosecuting sexual violence are less visible, but also contribute to low rates of prosecution and conviction. For example, in the absence of witness protection programs, sexual violence complainant witnesses are at particular risk of intimidation and are likely to refuse to testify at trial. Without police and prosecutorial procedures to guarantee that trained women officers conduct witness interviews in these cases, continuity in case management, psychosocial support, ensuring that the complainant does not encounter the defendant at court, and ensuring that she is not questioned on matters irrelevant to proving the crime (such as her sexual history and failure to physically resist), the risk of re-traumatization is high and the likelihood of conviction low (Kelly, Lovett, and Regan 2005). Re-traumatization reduces the chance that women will in fact testify in trial, and in the event that they do, it reduces their confidence, the believability of their testimony, and consequently the likelihood of a conviction.[11]

Even limited improvements, such as changing testimony locations, providing private hearings, and judicial guidance through explicit minimum sentences and sentencing guidelines, can improve imperfect criminal justice systems enough to encourage women to testify and increase the chances of convictions and appropriate sentences.

Maximizing complementarity's effect

The predominant suggestion to augment the ICC's impact is through a gender-sensitive interpretation of the terms "unwillingness" and "inability" contained in Article 17 that addresses the inadequacies of the criminal justice system mentioned earlier. Unwillingness could be interpreted to encompass rules that discriminate against victims of sexual violence, such as valuing a woman's testimony less than a man's, or lacking procedures to protect rape victims from re-traumatization (Chappell, Grey, and Waller 2013). Inability could be understood in terms of gender incompetency, including systemic elements such as laws, procedures, and policies governing the investigation and prosecution of sexual violence crimes (SáCouto and Cleary 2009) and the failure to provide gender-sensitive witness protection (Chappell, Grey, and Waller 2013).

As a cautionary note, these suggestions are in tension with the OTP policy, based on ICC jurisprudence, to assess the outcomes for cases against particular individuals, rather than systematic aspects of domestic legal systems as a court of judicial review might. In some cases, impunity enjoyed by individuals may be a result of systemic legislative or procedural loopholes with respect to SGBV, which make it difficult to conclude inability or unwillingness without assessing the background causes. Nevertheless, an interrogation about the legal architecture is a substantial extension of the OTP's scrutiny to date, and there is some conceptual overlap in the suggested aspects capable of constituting both inability and unwillingness—namely, legal rules and procedures.

To harmonize these distinct interpretations, a more nuanced approach would continue to interpret "unwillingness" with respect to specific individuals, but would incorporate systemic elements into the concept of inability, such as legal definitions, discriminatory legal rules or procedures that make it difficult, if not impossible, to prosecute and punish sexual violence crimes. Such an interpretation is more consistent with the text of Article 17, where unwillingness relates to bringing an individual to justice, and inability relates to the obstruction of obtaining evidence and testimony or court proceedings due to the unavailability of the justice system. Indeed, if an individual is prosecuted and punished for a range of crimes but not for sexual violence, it may be difficult to prove an unwillingness to bring her or him to justice per se; it would be necessary to imply a requirement for justice for the entire range of crimes for which she or he is responsible in Article 17.

For example, inability to collect the necessary evidence and testimony to prosecute sexual and gender-based crimes could be shown by the absence of procedural regulations requiring interviews with women victims of sexual violence to be conducted in secure and confidential settings. A failure to allocate resources to gender sensitization training of interviewers of women victims of sexual violence or recruitment of female law enforcement officers may amount to the constructive unavailability of the judicial system with respect to these crimes, resulting in an inability to prosecute them. Further, since victims of sexual violence are more likely to face discrimination, social stigma, exclusion from their community, or physical harm, protection systems that may be adequate for victims who do not face these additional risks may be inadequate to protect victims of sexual violence, either because the risk of harm is realized or because witnesses refuse to testify. The likely national resource constraints compounding these risks highlight the importance of capacity-building support offered by other states or institutional donors as part of a broader project to enhance complementarity's impact.

Unwillingness to prosecute sexual violence crimes could include the failure to use other available evidence in the absence of DNA forensic evidence, or giving insufficient weight to the victim witness's testimony and requiring corroborative evidence. Charging sexual violence acts as less serious crimes, such as an indecent assault or an act of indecency, may be an example of inadequate charging in relation to the gravity of the alleged conduct. Further, if sexual violence crimes in a situation under preliminary examination are well documented and evidenced as systemic and/or widespread, and yet there are no national prosecutions for these crimes despite ongoing proceedings for other international crimes, this would suggest unwillingness based on the selective allocation of resources.

Regardless of the method, an explicitly gender-sensitive OTP policy can "broadcast" minimum standards beyond the states with which it engages directly, prompting broader improved domestic post-conflict responses to sexual violence. Just as the crimes, definitions, procedures, and conceptions of liability within the Rome Statute have prompted state parties to be on notice of the types of crimes requiring prosecution and punishment, a gender-sensitive OTP approach to unwillingness and inability sets clear expectations that neglecting sexual violence crimes is unacceptable and has consequences. The general trend for states to improve domestic laws related to sexual-violence harms in response to an articulated international standard as embodied by the Rome Statute could well be replicated in post-conflict country responses to an OTP policy that similarly identifies sexual violence crimes as an essential aspect of its assessment.

CAUSES FOR CAUTIOUS OPTIMISM

Upon her appointment as the second ICC Prosecutor in June 2012, Fatou Bensouda publicly declared that SGBV crimes would be a priority focus for the OTP; this is now reflected in a formal policy for sexual and gender-based crimes, which defines these key terms and identifies what may constitute inability or unwillingness with respect to them (ICC Office of the Prosecutor 2014). Consistent with the approach considered earlier, such factors include discriminatory attitudes and gender stereotypes in substantive law and/or procedural rules that limit access to justice for victims of such crimes, such as inadequate domestic law criminalizing conduct proscribed under the Statute; the existence of amnesties or immunity laws and statutes of limitation; the absence of protective measures for victims of sexual violence; official attitudes of trivialization and minimization or denial of these crimes; manifestly insufficient steps in the investigation and prosecution of sexual and gender-based crimes, and the deliberate focus of proceedings on low-level perpetrators, despite evidence against those who may bear greater responsibility.

The 2012 OTP interim report on Colombia reflects this shift in emphasis by explicitly noting the limited number of national proceedings concerning rape and sexual violence despite the scale of their commission, and specifically recommending that the Colombian authorities prioritize the investigation and prosecution of these crimes (ICC Office of the Prosecutor 2012b). The OTP December 2012 report on preliminary examinations reinforced this message by listing rape and sexual violence as one of five focus issues in Colombia (2012a).

Subsequent to two 2013 ICC missions regarding these focus issues, Colombian authorities broadened their investigations to include sexual violence crimes (ICC Office of the Prosecutor 2013). Clearly, enhanced scrutiny is capable of promoting prioritization of sexual violence prosecutions, accompanied by greater transparency and accountability regarding their progress and a state desire to prove such progress to the international community. Maintaining this scrutiny may ensure that superficial commitments gradually evolve into more substantial and enduring systemic improvements of national criminal justice systems.

In Guinea, ICC scrutiny has coincided with more general progress to prosecute the most senior perpetrators of international crimes. After opening a preliminary examination into the 2009 Conakry stadium massacre on February 8, 2010, the ICC has made eight visits to assess investigative and prosecutorial progress made by authorities, including two visits in 2013. While it is possible the fourteen indictments and 400 victim hearings (including 50 victims of sexual violence) may have occurred regardless of ICC engagement, Guinean human rights lawyers note that charges are laid around ICC visits, that security for judges increases when ICC staff are in Guinea, and that the continuing liberty enjoyed by some of the defendants indicates the government's underlying reluctance to pursue genuine justice.[12] Sexual violence was a prominent type of crime committed in the 2009 massacre, but it is difficult to conclude that this category has been neglected when cases are proceeding so slowly. Nevertheless, ICC visits and engagement have empowered civil society to mobilize more effectively and to articulate their concerns at national and international levels.[13]

Both the Colombian and Guinean examples suggest that the OTP's approach to complementarity can have broader, and subtler, implications for women's access to justice, if strategically cultivated. This approach of overtly increasing the visibility of and prioritizing SGBV crimes is justified in any dialogue the OTP has with states in which SGBV has been committed as international crimes. If we accept that SGBV crimes frequently occupy an integral position in the strategy of potential ICC suspects, then it follows that the OTP's criteria or conceptual framework for evaluating what constitutes sufficient justice must explicitly include and prioritize the domestic prosecution and conviction of international SGBV crimes.

The requirement to be willing and able to prosecute international crimes generally has led states to either incorporate the Rome Statute in its entirety into domestic law, or to select sections, or merely to adopt its terms for the purposes of prosecuting international crimes. This can create a two-tiered justice system, where certain crimes can be prosecuted if they constitute a war crime, crime against humanity, or genocide, but not if they are charged as domestic crimes. However, such a discrepancy can also provide an opportunity and foundation for women's advocates to lobby for domestic law reform to reflect ICC standards.

For example, in both Colombia and Uganda, national actors (members of the legislature and women's organizations) have used Rome Statute standards to argue for law reform. In Uganda the sections of the 1951 Penal Code Act relating to sexual acts are being reviewed for consistency with the 2010 ICC Act; and in Colombia, the parliament passed a bill proposed by two representatives to promote access to justice for victims of sexual violence on the basis of international criminal law definitions.

EXTENDING COMPLEMENTARITY'S EFFECTS

Beyond the more obvious discussion around complementarity and sexual violence, the broader gender dimension of the ICC's impact on national legal systems and prosecutions is also complex and largely unexplored (Chappell, Grey, and Waller 2013). A more active OTP approach to the broader aspect of complementarity has potential for improved catalyzing effects, including on restorative justice initiatives, as supported by the Assembly of States Parties and the community of post-conflict donors and stakeholders.

While the ICC's reparations are linked to convictions within its courtroom, the trial chamber has adopted a broad and gender-inclusive approach to their distribution, including both collective and individual reparations for direct and indirect victims. As such, ICC reparations may help address some of the underlying inequalities and could contribute (see Kalla, Chapter 19 in this volume), albeit in a limited way, to transforming gender relations within local communities. As a subtle extension of complementarity, this approach could influence how reparations are perceived and designed at the national level: reparations that further entrench gender inequality are harder to justify when international experience demonstrates their proven capacity to successfully empower women. Reparations have already been used to challenge systemic gender inequality in certain contexts, including women's access to land in Morocco; the ICC principles on reparations provide additional material to advocate for this approach more universally.

Finally, incorporation of Rome Statute criminal law standards also provides leverage to advocate for more general gender equality within legal systems. For example, procedures guaranteeing that women's testimony is treated equivalent to men's in criminal cases could prompt matching civil law reform to ensure consistency across other areas of the law typically discriminatory against women, including marriage, land, and inheritance. The need for gender expertise to prosecute SGBV crimes as recognized at the international level could support similar arguments nationally for a fair representation of women and men judges and lawyers, and for their training on gender-related legal issues.

CONCLUSION

To achieve effective individual criminal responsibility for SGBV crimes committed in conflict, domestic criminal justice inadequacies must be identified and remedied. The complementarity mechanism of the ICC provides the OTP with both the scope and leverage to encourage reforms to achieve this, and may promote gender justice beyond the criminal accountability. For example, by explicitly prioritizing rape and sexual violence in its scrutiny of the Colombian situation, the OTP created an unprecedented dynamic, requiring prosecution of these crimes to meet OTP standards of willingness. Notwithstanding the complex legal, political, and social pressures that undoubtedly contribute to national criminal justice reform, significant progress occurring now or in the immediate future in Colombia will be too closely linked to greater OTP scrutiny on sexual violence to deny the influence of the ICC. The Colombian precedent may well prove a valuable tool to promote criminal accountability in other post-conflict jurisdictions that encompasses, rather than excludes, SGBV.

The ICC is only one external actor: a standard-setting institution promoting particular outcomes within a complex post-conflict domestic political and legal context. As such, the OTP's engagement with and support of civil society to promote justice for victims of SGBV can provide powerful leverage for reform of legislation and prosecutorial practices. Introducing Rome Statute standards into national law and prosecutorial practices for international crimes in turn creates reform opportunities for prosecuting domestic SGBV crimes, and pressure for governments to ensure consistency across different bodies of law.

The continued failure to prosecute international crimes necessarily becomes more obvious under long-term international scrutiny. The expanding membership of the Rome Statute treaty regime increases its normative force, adding weight to such scrutiny and institutional evaluations of states' commitments to genuine justice for international crimes. Both through direct engagement and its representation of international normative standards, the ICC, and especially the OTP, can continue to improve its catalytic potential on national prosecution of SGBV crimes committed during conflict.

This has important implications for domestic efforts to promote gender justice more broadly. From requiring sexual violence expertise in victim and witness support units to reparations that challenge structural gender inequalities, to gender-sensitive legislation for land rights and other civil law areas, the standards and principles embedded in the Rome Statute are capable of creating ripple effects. The political space created by ICC scrutiny and the increased relevance of its instruments provides civil society with useful benchmarks beyond criminal justice and the capacity to amplify these ripple effects. Understanding the mutually reinforcing relationship between and impact of the ICC, other international actors, and local actors is critical to maximizing the potential of the complementarity regime, not only to improve criminal justice outcomes for victims of SGBV, but also to facilitate more meaningful improvements in their daily lives.

NOTES

1. For an overview of the complementarity framework and its implementation, see Stahn and El Zeidy (2011).

2. *Situation in the Democratic Republic of Congo*, Case No. ICC-01/04-520-Anx2, Decision on the Prosecutor's Application for Warrants of Arrest, Article 58, ¶ 31 (February 10, 2006).

3. *Prosecutor v. Gaddafi*, Case No. ICC-01/11-01/11-344-Red, Decision on the Admissibility of the Case Against Saif Al-Islam Gaddafi, ¶¶ 85–88 (May 31, 2013).

4. Rome Statute Article 68(3) permits the views and concerns of the victims to be presented and considered in court proceedings, and Article 75 permits reparations to be awarded to victims, including through the ICC Trust Fund, established by Article 79.

5. *Prosecutor v. Lubanga*, Case No. ICC-01/04-01/06-2842, Judgment Pursuant to Article 74 of the Statute (March 14, 2012).

6. *Prosecutor v. Katanga*, Case No. ICC-01/04-01/07-3436-tENG, Judgment Pursuant to Article 74 of the Statute (March 7, 2014).

7. Sexual Offences Act (Ken), §10, §5(1), §18, and §16, respectively.

8. International Crimes Act 2008 (Ken), §6.

9. This index is created by Verisk Maplecroft, and a more recent index is not publicly accessible.

10. Penal Code Act (Ug), Art. 123.

11. The impact of witness confidence on believability is well documented; for a foundational explanation, see Fox and Walters (1986).

12. Interviews with human rights lawyers, Conakry, Guinea, May 2013, on file with author.

13. Interviews with representatives of victims' associations, May 2013, on file with author.

References

Chappell, Louise, Rosemary Grey, and Emily Waller. 2013. "The Gender Justice Shadow of Complementarity: Lessons from the International Criminal Court's Preliminary Examinations in Guinea and Colombia." *International Journal for Transitional Justice* 7, no. 3: 455–475.

Fox, Steven G., and H. A. Walters. 1986. "The Impact of General versus Specific Expert Testimony and Eyewitness Confidence upon Mock Juror Judgment." *Law and Human Behavior* 10, no. 3: 215–228.

ICC Assembly of States Parties (ASP). 2002. *Rules of Procedure and Evidence*. ICC-ASP/1/3/Part.II-A (September 3–10).

ICC Assembly of States Parties (ASP). 2012. *Report of the Bureau on Complementarity*. ICC-ASP/11/24 (November 7).

ICC Office of the Prosecutor. 2006. *Report on Prosecutorial Strategy*. September 14. The Hague: International Criminal Court.

ICC Office of the Prosecutor. 2012a. *Report on Preliminary Examination Activities*. The Hague: International Criminal Court.

ICC Office of the Prosecutor. 2012b. *Situation in Colombia: Interim Report*. The Hague: International Criminal Court.

ICC Office of the Prosecutor. 2013. *Report on Preliminary Examination Activities*. The Hague: International Criminal

ICC Office of the Prosecutor. 2014. *Policy Paper on Sexual and Gender-Based Crimes*. The Hague: International Criminal Court.

Kelly, Liz, Jo Lovett, and Linda Regan. 2005. "A Gap or a Chasm? Attrition in Reported Rape Cases." Home Office Research, Development and Statistics Directorate, Home Office Research Study 293, London.

Klein, Richard. 2008. "An Analysis of Thirty-Five Years of Rape Reform: A Frustrating Search for Fundamental Fairness." *Akron Law Review* 41, no. 4: 981–1057.

Ní Aoláin, Fionnuala. 2014. "Gendered Harms and Their Interface with International Criminal Law: Norms, Challenges and Domestication." *International Feminist Journal of Politics* 16, no. 4: 622–646.

Ní Aoláin, Fionnuala, Dina Francesca Haynes, and Naomi Cahn. 2011a. "Gender and the Forms and Experiences of Conflict." In *On the Frontlines: Gender, War, and the Post-Conflict Process*, edited by Fionnuala Ní Aoláin, Dina Francesca Haynes, and Naomi Cahn, 40–56. Oxford: Oxford University Press.

SáCouto, Susana, and Katherine Cleary. 2009. "The Importance of Effective Investigation of Sexual Violence and Gender-Based Crimes at the International Criminal Court." *American University Journal of Gender, Social Policy & The Law* 17, no. 2: 337–359.

Stahn, Carsten, and Mohamed M. El Zeidy, eds. 2011. *The International Criminal Court and Complementarity: From Theory to Practice*. Cambridge: Cambridge University Press.

UN Women. 2011. *2011–2012 Progress of the World's Women: In Pursuit of Justice*. New York: UN Women.

Women's Initiative for Gender Justice. 2012. *Gender 2012 Report Card on the International Criminal Court*. The Hague: Women's Initiatives for Gender Justice.

CHAPTER 18

....

FORCED MARRIAGE DURING CONFLICT AND MASS ATROCITY

....

VALERIE OOSTERVELD

FORCED marriage has occurred, and continues to occur, in conflicts around the world, such as in the Democratic Republic of the Congo, Iraq, Mali, Myanmar, Somalia, South Sudan, Sudan, Syria, and Yemen (UN Secretary-General 2015). Despite its prevalence, it has only been prosecuted as a criminal offense within two international criminal tribunals: the Special Court for Sierra Leone and the Extraordinary Chambers in the Courts of Cambodia. The armed conflict in Sierra Leone of the 1990s saw widespread use of women and girls forced to serve as so-called 'bush wives' to fighting forces (Coulter 2009; Human Rights Watch 2003; McKay and Mazurana 2004). During the 1975–1979 reign of the Khmer Rouge, group weddings between men and women who did not know each other took place throughout Cambodia as part of the ruling party's attempts to regulate marriage and procreation (Case 002 Closing Order 2010). While the circumstances in Sierra Leone and Cambodia were different, similar charges were brought by the prosecution in both situations, accusing senior leaders of the crime against humanity of "other inhumane acts" for allowing or encouraging subordinates to force women and girls into non-consensual relationships deemed to be marriage or akin to marriage, resulting in forced labor and rape.

This chapter begins with an examination of how forced marriage has been defined under international human rights law, and yet largely overlooked in refugee law, even when evaluating claims by those fleeing conflict. The chapter then turns to an analysis of how forced marriage has been delineated in international criminal law by the Special Court for Sierra Leone and the Extraordinary Chambers in the Courts of Cambodia. The Special Court has produced divergent jurisprudence, while the Extraordinary Chambers have not yet definitively interpreted that jurisprudence. The result is some conceptual confusion on how to define and charge forced marriage, leading to differing views on the gendered harms it causes and a debate on whether the terminology is even useful in the context of conflict and mass atrocity.

Definitions of Forced Marriage in International Human Rights and Refugee Law

International human rights law defines forced marriage as marriage occurring without the consent of one or both of the parties to the marriage. This section explores how international human rights treaties approach the requirement of consent in marriage, then considers the challenges inherent in applying the consent requirement. Finally, I turn to a consideration of how international refugee law interprets the consent requirement when considering whether an individual's situation qualifies as persecution.

International human rights law adopts a relatively uniform approach to consent in marriage. For example, the International Covenant on Civil and Political Rights states at Article 23(3): "No marriage shall be entered into without the free and full consent of the intending spouses." This approach is replicated, sometimes also with the right to free choice of spouse (with certain limits on age and consanguinity), in other treaties and international law documents, such as the Universal Declaration of Human Rights, the International Covenant on Economic, Social and Cultural Rights, the Convention on Consent to Marriage, and the Convention on the Elimination of All Forms of Discrimination Against Women. International human rights law's focus on freely given spousal consent and selection appears to be straightforward, but in reality operates in complex contexts (Freeman 2012). These contexts include "cultural expectations of marriage based on class, ethnic, religious and other identity factors," including the involvement of the family in spousal choice, and economic transactions (such as dowry) (Freeman 2012, 423). Thus, the actual application of the rights to free and full consent and free choice of spouse are affected by gendered role expectations, creating pressure on women to marry and become mothers, and by gendered power relations, resulting in greater familial (frequently fathers') assertion of control over young women's choice of spouse (Freeman 2012). These pressures and control occur along a continuum and sometimes rise to the level of forced marriage. Forced marriage occurs when "parents or other individuals in a position of control determine when and whom a woman [or, frequently, a girl] will marry without consulting her in any way," and has been condemned by the Committee on the Elimination of Discrimination Against Women (Freeman 2012, 424 and n74). The Committee has noted situations in which women or girls have been threatened with, or subjected to, force, exile from the family, or death for refusing (Freeman 2012). The Committee has recognized the occurrence of forced marriage in conflict and post-conflict situations (CEDAW 2013; see Patten, Chapter 13 in this volume).

Like international human rights law, international refugee law considers the role of non-consensual marriage through a determination of whether a particular individual, "owing to a well-founded fear of being persecuted for reasons of race, religion, nationality, membership of a particular social group or political opinion" has left his or her country of nationality and is unable or unwilling to return (1951 Refugee Convention, art. 1A(2)). In the case of forced marriage, the central question is whether non-consensual marriage rises to the level of persecution for the purposes of refugee law. In this manner, the international human rights law definition of forced marriage informs the refugee law analysis. Forced marriage has been recognized as a gender-related form of persecution by the United Nations High Commissioner for Refugees and by some refugee-receiving countries (Dauvergne and Millbank 2010; UNHCR 2002, 2012).

Unfortunately, that recognition at the level of policy has not necessarily translated into widespread recognition in practice of forced marriage as a valid ground on which to claim refugee status. In a leading study on the topic, Dauvergne and Millbank (2010) researched cases involving actual and threatened forced marriage and found that "the harm feared was often construed [by refugee adjudicators] as social, familial and privately motivated when family members were the agents of persecution, with little or no consideration of the willingness or ability of the state to protect applicants from such harm" (69, 76). As well, refugee decision-makers often did not consider the persecutory consequences of the imposed marriage itself (Dauvergne and Millbank 2010). In other words, refugee adjudicators did not adequately concentrate on the issue of consent or non-consent, as one would expect given the definition of forced marriage in international human rights law (Dauvergne and Millbank 2010). The result was an extremely low rate of recognition that forced marriage in and of itself is a form of persecution (4 of 120 cases) (Dauvergne and Millbank 2010). These trends, combined with the fact that some refugee decision-makers also classify conflict-related rape as privately motivated or a common crime, and tend not to focus on the impact of conflict on the gender-based claims, appear to disadvantage refugees fleeing forced marriage in situations of conflict or mass atrocity (Oosterveld 2012).

Clearly, the pivotal focus on non-consent in international human rights law is not being adequately considered at the level of practice in refugee case determination. In contrast, the approach of international criminal law to forced marriage takes the non-consent requirement seriously, even as it becomes confused in its application of the term "marriage" and its linkage of non-consent to a criminal label.

FORCED MARRIAGE IN CONFLICT AND MASS ATROCITY IN INTERNATIONAL CRIMINAL LAW

The term "forced marriage" has a recent, but complex, history within international criminal law. The term first came into widespread use within the Special Court for

Sierra Leone, when the prosecutor charged six individuals from two different rebel groups with forced marriage (AFRC Indictment 2005; RUF Indictment 2006). The term "forced marriage" was not listed within the Special Court's Statute, so the charge was incorporated through the count referring to the crime against humanity of "other inhuman acts."[1]

Forced marriage jurisprudence of the Special Court for Sierra Leone

Since the term "forced marriage" was new to the Special Court and had not been litigated at any prior international criminal tribunal, the Special Court's judges needed to define the term before pronouncing on the guilt or innocence of the accused in this respect. It did so in its first case, involving three accused who were affiliated with the Armed Forces Revolutionary Council. In that case, the prosecutor advanced this definition of forced marriage: "words or other conduct intended to confer a status of marriage by force or threat of force or coercion, such as that caused by fear of violence, duress, detention, psychological oppression or abuse of power against the victim, or by taking advantage of a coercive environment, with the intention of conferring the status of marriage" (AFRC Trial Judgment 2007, para. 701). In explaining this definition, the prosecutor identified two types of harm suffered by victims of forced marriage: first, the non-consensual conferral of the status of marriage and the resulting long-lasting physical, psychological, and cultural damage; and second, the harms stemming from the consequent forced duties associated with being a "wife" (Oosterveld 2011). This explanation of dual harms was rejected by a majority of the judges in the 2007 trial chamber judgment. While neither side was explicit, this rejection seems to stem from differences in the manner in which the prosecutor and the majority judges used the term "marriage." The prosecutor seemed to use the term not in its strict legal sense as defined in international human rights law, but as a proxy for a perverted version of pre-war peacetime marriages in Sierra Leone, in which women and girls were largely treated as subordinate to men (Oosterveld 2011). For this reason, one of the accused argued that forced marriages were more akin to "cultural understandings of implicit conjugal contracts" than to a crime against humanity (Kanu Defence Brief 2006, para. 60; Kelsall 2009, 246–255). The trial chamber judges, however, defined marriage as "establishing mutual obligations inherent in a husband[-]wife relationship," which seems to imply either consent by, or equality between, spouses. This approach led the majority judges to conclude that witnesses gave evidence that they had been "taken as wives," but not that they considered themselves to be married. As a result, the majority judges concluded that the acts instead amounted to sexual slavery (AFRC Trial Judgment 2007, paras. 711–713).

The conclusion by a majority of the trial chamber judges that the evidence amounted to sexual slavery was controversial. On the one hand, the "wives" were indeed sexually enslaved, as they were subjected to rape on demand by their "husbands." This fulfilled the definition of sexual slavery: a state in which "[t]he perpetrator exercised any or all of the powers attaching to the right of ownership over one or more persons" and caused the victim "to engage in one or more acts of a sexual nature" (AFRC Trial Judgment 2007, para. 708). On the other hand, it did not describe the totality of the experience of the "wives," who were often captured or abducted and were forced to provide labor in the form of cooking, cleaning, portering, child-bearing, child-rearing, and protection of her "husband's" possessions. Many were physically and psychologically assaulted, infected with sexually transmitted diseases, and subsequently stigmatized (AFRC Trial Judgment 2007, Sebutinde J. and Doherty J. judgments).

Forced marriage has many facets, or effects, outside of those captured by the definition of sexual slavery. It is for this reason that the appeals chamber rejected the collapse of the analysis of forced marriage into sexual slavery. The appeals chamber identified two types of harms stemming from forced marriage: first, violations related to having the label "wife" imposed upon the victims, including social stigmatization; and, second, injuries resulting from being raped, forced into domestic labor, and forced to bear and rear children (Oosterveld 2011). It adopted a new definition of forced marriage: "a situation in which the perpetrator through his words or conduct, or those of someone for whose actions he is responsible, compels a person by force, threat of force, or coercion to serve as a conjugal partner resulting in severe suffering, or physical, mental or psychological injury to the victim" (AFRC Appeals Judgment 2008, para. 196). While the appeals chamber moved away from a definition reliant on the term "marriage" by using "conjugal partner," the term "conjugal" is defined in the *Oxford English Dictionary* as "relating to marriage or the relationship between a married couple." Thus, a focus on conjugality does not resolve the question of what "marriage" means in the term "forced marriage," nor does it resolve variances in social and cultural understandings of marriage.

The second Special Court case in which forced marriage was considered involved three accused from the Revolutionary United Front who were ultimately convicted in 2009 of responsibility for forced marriages. That case avoided the issue of the meaning of "marriage" entirely by focusing on whether the acts described by the witnesses satisfied the relevant elements of crime for the category "other inhumane acts" within crimes against humanity, under which the forced marriage charges were laid. It found a "pattern of conduct" by the Revolutionary United Front in which women and girls were captured or abducted, assigned to specific commanders or soldiers, and, in fear of violent retribution, forced to submit to sex on demand and maintain an exclusive relationship, expected to carry out domestic duties and housework for the "husband," carry the "husband's" possessions and supplies as the rebels moved around, and bear and raise any children of the relationship. The Trial Chamber also found that the Revolutionary United Front used the term "wife" deliberately and strategically, "with the aim of enslaving and psychologically manipulating the women and with the purpose of treating them like possessions" (RUF Trial Judgment 2009, para. 1466). This was done not only to ensure that rebels had domestic and sexual slaves (see Coulter 2009; discussing the need for women's labor for, among other needs, food production during the war), but also to disempower the civilian population, instill fear in entire communities, and break down all preexisting social bonds. The terminological focus of the trial chamber in this case was on "wife," and not on "marriage."

The issue of terminology came to the fore in the Special Court's 2012 trial judgment in the *Charles Taylor* case. Charles Taylor was charged with responsibility for sexual slavery and other forms of enslavement, and it was in this context that evidence of forced marriage was considered. The trial chamber took the opportunity to express its views again on forced marriage, reconsidering its position somewhat since the Armed Forces Revolutionary Council trial judgment. In particular, it focused on the issue that had been left unclear or avoided in the earlier judgments: Why describe the situation as forced *marriage* when no marriage under domestic law actually occurred? The Trial Chamber deemed the use of the term "marriage" as inaccurate. It then redefined the harms suffered by the victims as sexual slavery plus enslavement through forced labor. It proposed the term "conjugal slavery" to jointly capture these two forms of slavery (Taylor Trial Judgment 2012, para. 428). In this manner, the *Taylor* trial judgment seemed to clarify the definition of what had previously been referred to as forced marriage, but did not, in fact, do so, given that the term "conjugal" is usually defined in relation to marriage.

In sum, the Special Court for Sierra Leone's jurisprudence has resulted in two different definitions: sexual slavery + forced labor = conjugal slavery from the *Taylor* trial judgment, and the appeals chamber's "situation in which the perpetrator . . . compels a person . . . to serve as a conjugal partner" (AFRC Appeals Judgment 2008, para. 196). As well, the Special Court's trial chambers have taken three different analytical approaches, with the Armed Forces Revolutionary Council judgment's focus on whether acts of forced marriage amount to a separate legal violation, the Revolutionary United Front judgment's method of evaluating the results of forced marriage as amounting to inhumane acts, and the *Taylor* judgment's tactic of classifying all aspects of forced marriage as falling within different forms of enslavement. The Special Court has created legal uncertainty as to which, if any, definition and analytical approach should be applied in other circumstances also referred to as forced marriage.

Forced marriage jurisprudence of the Extraordinary Chambers in the Courts of Cambodia

Forced marriage has also been considered by the Extraordinary Chambers in the Courts of Cambodia, set up to prosecute genocide, crimes against humanity, war crimes, and certain other violations committed during the 1975–1979 Khmer Rouge regime in Cambodia. Forced marriage was not initially investigated by the Extraordinary Chambers due to incorrect assumptions that sexual violence was not condoned by the Khmer Rouge (Studzinsky 2013), but the court was prompted into consideration of this type of violation by the filing of a request by the civil parties and their legal representatives and subsequent orders (Case 002 Forced Marriage Order 2009; Case 002 Supplementary Submission 2009). As a result, the practice was considered by the co-investigating judges in the Closing Order for Case 002.

The Closing Order described the ways in which the Khmer Rouge regulated marriage by whatever means necessary to advance the cause of the revolution by increasing population growth and by building up a society matching the Khmer Rouge ideals. Individuals were only permitted to marry and have sexual relations as approved or ordered by the Khmer Rouge, and most of these marriages were involuntary. The practice was to assign men and women with similar political status to each other, or to assign women to marry Khmer Rouge soldiers. Wedding ceremonies involving anywhere from two couples to over 100 couples took place in official buildings or public places. The forcibly married individuals were expected to have sex with each other in order to promote procreation, and sometimes Khmer Rouge representatives would spy on the couple to ensure that this happened (Case 002 Closing Order 2010).

Forced marriage in the Cambodian situation bears some factual similarities to, and differences from, forced marriage during Sierra Leone's civil war. In both contexts, the joining of one person to another took place without traditional rituals or the customary presence of the bride and groom's parents or relatives. The forced marriages often occurred in groups among individuals who did not know each other and who had no choice of partner (Jain 2008, 1013). Refusal to be forcibly married was punished by violence or death. Forced marriage was institutionalized in both settings. In Sierra Leone and Cambodia, young people were the target victims of forced marriage. There were also factual differences. In Sierra Leone, the Special Court only recognized girls and women as victims of forced marriage. The legal discussion did not focus on whether boy soldiers assigned "bush wives" without their consent and under group coercion might also be victims (Bunting 2012). In Cambodia, the individuals married without their consent were both male and female, and the victims were identified as such. Second, there were marriage ceremonies in the Cambodia situation and not in Sierra Leone.

The Extraordinary Chambers' consideration of the legal elements of forced marriage acts was influenced by the Special Court. As in the Special Court, forced marriage was seen by the Extraordinary Chambers as part of a larger goal: in this case, regulation of marriage by the Khmer Rouge. As was done in the Special Court, the Extraordinary Chambers analyzed forced marriage through the crime against humanity of "other inhumane acts." The Extraordinary Chambers found that forced marriage did indeed amount to an inhumane act, as "victims endured serious physical or mental suffering" and "were forced to enter into conjugal relationships in coercive circumstances" (Case 002 Closing Order 2010, para. 1443). There was also a significant focus on the sexual aspects of forced marriage, with the Extraordinary Chambers focusing on the crime against humanity of rape and its definition (sexual slavery was not included in its Statute).

Given the overlapping approaches between the Special Court and the Extraordinary Chambers to forced marriage, the approach in Cambodia might be viewed as helping to resolve the internal incoherence of the Special Court on the definition of, and legal approach to, forced marriage. The Chambers might be seen as taking the position that forced marriage can be viewed as a combination of the crime against humanity of "other inhumane acts" and rape (or sexual slavery). However, the Extraordinary Chambers' Closing Order, in which forced marriage is discussed at length, was issued in 2010. This was prior to the Special Court's 2012 trial judgment in *Taylor*, in which the Trial Chamber expressed the view that forced marriage was actually conjugal slavery consisting of forced labor plus sexual slavery. It is unclear whether the *Taylor* approach will influence the Extraordinary Chambers' ongoing cases,[2] or whether the Extraordinary Chambers will determine that the Khmer Rouge violations differ in substance from those in Sierra Leone.[3] The outcome will either entrench or resolve a key question: What criminal acts are covered by the terminology of "forced marriage?" If the Extraordinary Chambers create a clear differentiation between the Sierra Leonean and Cambodian contexts—for example, based on the fact that marriage ceremonies took place in Cambodia—then this will call into question the characterization of the Sierra Leonean situation, and all other similar situations, as forced marriage.

Issues arising from the analysis of forced marriage by the Special Court and Extraordinary Chambers

The dissonant analyses of forced marriage within the Special Court for Sierra Leone and the differing Sierra Leonean and Cambodian scenarios have led commentators to grapple with the meaning of the term "forced marriage" under international criminal law. They have raised three main questions: First, is marriage the central focus of the crime? Second, where does forced marriage fit within already existing international criminal legal categories? And third, is there any legal benefit to labeling an act (or group of acts) as forced marriage?

The first question is a fundamental one: Is marriage the central focus of the crime? In turn, this raises the question: What is marriage? Toy-Cronin (2010) has argued that forced marriage should be understood as the forced conferral of the status of marriage, and the attendant consequences of that marriage status. Under this approach, other prohibited acts that occur following this marriage, such as rape, should always be considered as separate offenses (Toy-Cronin 2010). The benefit of this approach is that it brings specificity to the label of forced marriage because the category does not overlap with other prohibited acts, such as rape, sexual slavery, and forced labor (Toy-Cronin 2010). The drawback of this approach is that, in the view of some, it is too narrow: the expressive benefit of the term "forced marriage" is that it captures a constellation of harms that cumulatively equal more than the sum of the parts (Oosterveld 2011). These commentators argue that the harm in forced marriage is not simply the conferral of the status of spouse plus the resulting effects (such as social stigmatization); it is the conferral of that status *plus* all of the violations that follow (such as rape, forced domestic labor, cruel treatment, forced pregnancy, etc.) (Frulli 2008; Jain 2008; Scharf 2014). Others take the more limited view that it is the forced conferral of the status of marriage, with the consequence of certain exclusive obligations or rights (including sexual exclusivity) between the spouses that do not exist between those not forcibly married (Haenen 2014). In the latter vein, Carlson and Mazurana (2009) feel that "the lived experiences and longer-term consequences of forced marriage demand different justice responses" than for those who suffered rape but not forced marriage (15).

Regardless of which approach is taken, there is the related question of what is meant by the term "marriage" in "forced marriage": Is a marriage recognized by domestic law required, or are "marriage-like" scenarios also included? If the answer is that only marriage as recognized under domestic law is captured, then the mass wedding ceremonies referred to in the Cambodian situation would qualify as forced marriage, but not the "bush wife" phenomenon in Sierra Leone. This was the view of the majority trial chamber judges in the Special Court's Armed Forces Revolutionary Council case. If, however, something other than marriage under domestic law is included (such as the owner-slave relationship or a relationship qualified as "marriage" by the perpetrator, the victim, the subculture of war, and/or by society at large), then the Sierra Leone experience would likely qualify (Haenen 2014; Toy-Cronin 2010). The Special Court's appeals chamber and commentators such as Belair (2006) take this view:

> Why was the concept of "marriage" used to refer to the type of union that prevailed between rebels and their captives during the conflict in Sierra Leone? . . . [Because] "bush wives". . . were required to perform the same functions as wives under customary law: to carry out all of the domestic tasks and be sexually submissive. Thus, "bush wives" played the traditional role of wives to the combatants, but under extreme circumstances. (573, 575, 576)

On the other hand, others have argued that the "bush wives" situation did not resemble any form of marriage in any meaningful way (Gong-Gershowitz 2009). Rather, it was a perversion of the concept of marriage, and there was no continuum from peacetime marriage (Mibenge 2013; Scharf 2014). The challenge for international criminal law of accepting "marriage-like," or perversion of "marriage-like," scenarios as amounting to forced marriage is that it may inadvertently reinforce patriarchal views of peacetime marriage (Toy-Cronin 2010; Oosterveld 2011) and may consequently inadvertently undermine the international human rights law definition of marriage.

The debate over terminology has also raised the question of where forced marriage fits within already existing international criminal legal categories. A number of critics have argued that the term "forced marriage" as a legal term is misleading and unhelpful (e.g., Bunting 2012; Park 2006), and that the acts would be better described as enslavement (Sellers 2011). In Sellers's view, this categorization is more likely to better capture the multifaceted harms faced by the victims and to lead to adequate judicial redress (Sellers 2011). Bunting similarly argues that enslavement better captures the institutionalized process of forced marriage during conflict and refocuses the judges on the manner in which the victims' various forms of labor (and not only sexual labor) were used as a tactic of war or control (Bunting 2012).

On the other hand, Scharf (2014) posits that the use of the category "enslavement" obscures the sexual violence inherent in the crime. Related to this is the risk that, given that enslavement potentially captures a host of different sexual and non-sexual acts, judges may lose sight of the distinct effects of certain of the acts when evaluating the whole (Toy-Cronin 2010; Oosterveld 2011). Scharf (2014) also argues that the definition of enslavement requires the exercise by the perpetrator of the right of owner-ship, whereas forced marriage requires the exercise by the perpetrator of a "perversion of the protected institution of marriage" (212). Haenen (2014) similarly maintains that enslavement does not capture the act of forcing someone to enter into a conjugal associ-ation. In response to these concerns, some raise the possibility that gender-based perse-cution may be a helpful category (Oosterveld 2011; Haenen 2014).

The final question asked by commentators on the subject of forced marriage within international criminal law is whether there is any legal benefit to labeling an act (or group of acts) as forced marriage. The OTP of the International Criminal Court has taken two different approaches. Under one approach, violations are not charged as "forced marriage"; rather, they are disaggregated into sexual slavery and enslavement.[4] This also implicitly appears to be the approach in the OTP's groundbreaking 2014 Policy Paper on Sexual and Gender-Based Crimes due to the absence of discussion of forced marriage (e.g., para. 34). While understandable—such an approach avoids critiques of mislabeling of crimes—this decision also has possible side effects. One of the per-ceived benefits of the "forced marriage" (or "conjugal slavery") category is that it brings together a number of prohibited acts under a "meta-label" and demonstrates how this confluence results in greater harm to victims and communities (Oosterveld 2011). Such overarching labels can help to express the breadth and depth of harm done to victims by particular combinations of prohibited acts, potentially resulting in higher sentences and increasing understanding and awareness of the violations within and outside of the courtroom (Oosterveld 2011). In addition, a "meta-label" can also assist in identifying broader patterns of violation in armed conflict and could potentially lead to change in the enforcement of gendered forms of harm within international law. On the other hand, these outcomes could be undercut by the ambiguous nature of the term. Perhaps recognizing these benefits and drawbacks, the OTP subsequently charged an accused in *Prosecutor v. Ongwen* with forced marriage under the crime against humanity of "other inhumane acts." The pre-trial chamber accepted this classification, finding that the central element of forced marriage is "the imposition, regardless of the will of the victim, of duties that are associated with marriage" as well as the social stigma associated with being the perpetrator's "wife," regardless of whether the marriage was illegal under domestic law (Ongwen Confirmation of Charges 2016, para. 93).

CONCLUSION

International human rights law, international refugee law, and international criminal law both converge and diverge on the topic of forced marriage. On the one hand, all three fields agree that marriage without consent of one or both spouses is a violation of international law (even though this is not applied consistently in refugee law). On the other hand, international criminal law has introduced uncertainty into the content and definition of the term. This demonstrates that international criminal law has not yet developed an underlying theory, or a coherent practical analysis, of whether, how, and when individuals should be charged with forced marriage occurring in conflict. In a wider sense, the questioning is reflective of the need for more consideration within international law of whether and how human rights, refugee, and criminal conceptions of non-consensual marriage fit together. At the moment, the criminal approach, as an attempt to capture compounded harms not even necessarily linked to the performance of legal marriage, is very different from the peacetime human rights approach, yet potentially similar to the refugee approach to persecution. Additionally, significantly more thought should be given by scholars and legal practitioners to the links between forced marriage in different conflicts and situations of mass atrocity: the commonality appears to be the use of humans for production and/or reproduction deemed necessary during times of upheaval, often implemented through violence, including sexual violence (e.g., Coulter 2009). This attribute invites further contemplation of the role that preexisting gender and other forms of discrimination play in consensual marriage, and how these are replicated or distorted in conflict-related forced marriage. The "surfacing" of forced marriage represents progression in international law (Copelon 1994), but the remaining questions indicate that the law in this area has not yet matured.

Notes

1. This category was chosen because of its "catch-all" nature and the perceived differences with the other enumerated crimes against humanity (Scharf 2014, 204–211).
2. Forced marriage is alleged in Cases 002/02, 003, and 004, which are ongoing at the time of writing.
3. If the *Taylor* approach is considered by the Extraordinary Chambers, the Chambers will need to identify the enslaver(s): if both of those forcibly married are considered to be victims, then the enslavers would be Khmer Rouge officials external to the marriage.
4. E.g., forced marriage was characterized as sexual slavery in *Prosecutor v. Katanga*, Case No. ICC-01/04-01/07, Decision on the Confirmation of Charges, para. 431, September 30, 2008.

References

Belair, Karine. 2006. "Unearthing the Customary Law Foundations of 'Forced Marriages' during Sierra Leone's Civil War: The Possible Impact of International Criminal Law on Customary Marriage and Women's Rights in Post-Conflict Sierra Leone." *Columbia Journal of Gender and Law* 15, no. 3: 551–607.

Bunting, Annie. 2012. "'Forced Marriage' in Conflict Situations: Researching and Prosecuting Old Harms and New Crimes." *Canadian Journal of Human Rights* 1, no. 1: 165–185.

Carlson, Khristopher, and Dyan Mazurana. 2009. *Forced Marriage within the Lord's Resistance Army, Uganda.* Somerville, MA: Feinstein International Center, Tufts University.

Committee on the Elimination of Discrimination Against Women (CEDAW). 2013. *CEDAW General Recommendation No. 30: Women in Conflict Prevention, Conflict and Post-Conflict Situations.* UN Doc. CEDAW/C/GC/30 (October 18).

Copelon, Rhonda. 1994. "Surfacing Gender: Re-Engraving Crimes against Women in Humanitarian Law." *Hasting's Women's Law Journal* 5: 243–265.

Coulter, Chris. 2009. *Bush Wives and Girl Soldiers: Women's Lives through War and Peace in Sierra Leone*. Ithaca, NY: Cornell University Press.

Dauvergne, Catherine, and Jenni Millbank. 2010. "Forced Marriage as a Harm in Domestic and International Law." *The Modern Law Review* 73, no. 1: 57–88.

Frulli, Micaela. 2008. "Advancing International Criminal Law: The Special Court for Sierra Leone Recognizes Forced Marriage as a 'New' Crime against Humanity." *Journal of International Criminal Justice* 6: 1033–1042.

Freeman, Marsha A. 2012. "Article 16." In *The UN Convention on the Elimination of All Forms of Discrimination against Women: A Commentary*, edited by Marsha A. Freeman, Christine Chinkin, and Beate Rudolf, 409–442. New York: Oxford University Press.

Gong-Gershowitz, Jennifer. 2009. "Forced Marriage: A 'New' Crime against Humanity?" *Northwestern Journal of International Human Rights* 8, no. 1: 53–76.

Haenen, Iris. 2014. *Force and Marriage: The Criminalisation of Forced Marriage in Dutch, English and International Criminal Law*. Antwerp: Intersentia.

Human Rights Watch. 2003. *"We'll Kill You if You Cry": Sexual Violence in the Sierra Leone Conflict*. New York: Human Rights Watch.

Jain, Neha. 2008. "Forced Marriage as a Crime Against Humanity: Problems of Definition and Prosecution." *Journal of International Criminal Justice* 6: 1013–1032.

Kelsall, Tim. 2009. *Culture under Cross Examination: International Criminal Justice and the Special Court for Sierra Leone*. Cambridge: Cambridge University Press.

McKay, Susan, and Dyan Mazurana. 2004. *Where Are the Girls? Girls in Fighting Forces in Northern Uganda, Sierra Leone and Mozambique: Their Lives during and after War*. Montreal: International Centre for Human Rights and Democratic Development.

Mibenge, Chiseche Salome. 2013. *Sex and International Tribunals: The Erasure of Gender from the War Narrative*. Philadelphia: University of Pennsylvania Press.

Oosterveld, Valerie. 2011. "Forced Marriage and the Special Court for Sierra Leone: Legal Advances and Conceptual Difficulties." *Journal of International Humanitarian Legal Studies* 2: 127–158.

Oosterveld, Valerie. 2012. *Women and Girls Fleeing Conflict: Gender and the Interpretation and Application of the 1951 Refugee Convention*. Geneva: UN High Commissioner for Refugees.

Park, Augustine S. J. 2006. "'Other Inhumane Acts': Forced Marriage, Girls Soldiers and the Special Court for Sierra Leone." *Social & Legal Studies* 15, no. 3: 315–337.

Prosecutor v. Brima, Kamara and Kanu, Case No. SCSL-04-16-PT (AFRC Indictment). 2005. Further Amended Consolidated Indictment, para. 57 (February 18).

Prosecutor v. Brima, Kamara and Kanu, Case No. SCSL-04-16-T (AFRC Trial Judgment). 2007. Judgment (June 20).

Prosecutor v. Brima, Kamara and Kanu, Case No. SCSL-04-16-A (AFRC Appeals Judgment). 2008. Judgment, para. 196 (February 22).

Prosecutor v. Brima, Kamara and Kanu, Case No. SCSL-04-16-T (Kanu Defence Brief). 2006. Public Version: Kanu–Defence Trial Brief (December 8).

Prosecutor v. Nuon, Ieng, Khieu and Ieng, Case No. 002/19-09-2007-ECCC-OCIJ (Case 002 Closing Order). 2010. Closing Order (September 15).

Prosecutor v. Nuon, Ieng, Khieu and Ieng, Case No. 002/19-09-2007-ECCC-OCIJ (Case 002 Forced Marriage Order). 2009. Order on Request for Investigative Action Concerning Forced Marriages and Forced Sexual Relations (December 18).

Prosecutor v. Nuon, Ieng, Khieu and Ieng, Case No. 002/19-09-2007-ECCC-OCIJ (Case 002 Supplementary Submission). 2009. Supplementary Submission, Office of the Co-Prosecutors (April 30).

Prosecutor v. Ongwen, Case No. ICC-02/04-01/15 (Ongwen Confirmation of Charges). 2016. Decision on the Confirmation of Charges against Dominic Ongwen (March 23).

Prosecutor v. Sesay, Kallon and Gbao, Case No. SCSL-04-15-PT (RUF Indictment). 2006. Corrected Amended Consolidated Indictment, para. 60 (August 2).

Prosecutor v. Sesay, Kallon and Gbao, Case No. SCSL-04-15-T (RUF Trial Judgment). 2009. Judgment, paras. 164–172, 682–687, 1466–1472 (March 2).

Prosecutor v. Taylor, Case No. SCSL-03-01-T (Taylor Trial Judgment). 2012. Judgment, paras. 422–430 (May 18).

Scharf, Michael. 2014. "Forced Marriage as a Separate Crime against Humanity." In *The Sierra Leone Special Court and Its Legacy: The Impact for Africa and International Criminal Law*, edited by Charles Chernor Jalloh, 193–214. New York: Cambridge University Press.

Sellers, Patricia Viseur. 2011. "Wartime Female Slavery: Enslavement?" *Cornell International Law Journal* 44, no. 1: 115–143.

Studzinsky, Silke. 2013. "Victims of Sexual and Gender-Based Crimes before the Extraordinary Chambers in the Courts of Cambodia: Challenges of Rights to Participation and Protection." In *Sexual Violence as an International Crime: Interdisciplinary Approaches*, edited by Anne-Marie de Brouwer, Charlotte Ku, Renée Römkens, and Larissa can den Herik, 173–186. Antwerp: Intersentia.

Toy-Cronin, Bridgette A. 2010. "What Is Forced Marriage? Towards a Definition of Forced Marriage as a Crime against Humanity." *Columbia Journal of Gender and Law* 19, no. 2: 539–590.

United Nations High Commissioner for Refugees (UNHCR). 2002. *Guidelines on International Protection: Gender-Related Persecution within the Context of Article 1A(2) of the 1951 Convention and/or Its 1967 Protocol Relating to the Status of Refugees*. UN Doc. HCR/GIP/02/01 (May 7).

United Nations High Commissioner for Refugees (UNHCR). 2012. *Guidelines on International Protection: Claims to Refugee Status Based on Sexual Orientation and/or Gender Identity within the Context of Article 1A(2) of the 1951 Convention and/or Its 1967 Protocol Relating to the Status of Refugees*. UN Doc. HCR/GIP/12/09 (October 23).

United Nations Secretary-General. 2015. *Conflict-Related Sexual Violence*. UN Doc. S/2015/203 (March 23).

CHAPTER 19

....

ADVANCING JUSTICE AND MAKING AMENDS THROUGH REPARATIONS

Legal and Operational Considerations

....

KRISTIN KALLA

SOCIETIES undertake a range of responses to deal with the legacies of widespread or systematic human rights violations as they move from violent conflict toward peace: reconstruction, reconciliation, rule of law, and respect for individual and collective rights. In the realm of justice, reparations are unique, as they directly address the situation of the victims themselves and are essential in the delivery of justice and redress for harm caused by gross human rights crimes (see, e.g., Hadzimesic, Chapter 39 in this volume). These programs serve a variety of important functions and can help victims to manage the material aspect of their loss, repair individual psychosocial and physical injuries, and restore social and political institutions. They can also serve to publicly acknowledge wrongdoing, restore victims' dignity, raise public awareness about the impact of the violence on victims and their communities, and, when appropriate, assist with enabling positive social transformation. For this reason, reparations for victims and communities are often a psychologically necessary component of the healing and reconciliation process.

Reparations may be conceptualized as monetary compensation, memorials, or material, medical, psychological, and social welfare support, and can range from specialized health services and education programs to land restitution, formal apologies, and victim commemoration days (OHCHR 2008). Their design and delivery must be formulated in human rights–based approaches, meaning they should be equitable and universal in application, and just, if they are to make a meaningful contribution to reconciliation in post-conflict societies. Grievances that are not addressed fairly, or are attended to inappropriately, are likely to result in additional harm and possibly fuel renewed cycles of violence. Reparations not only provide benefits to victims, but also can ensure accountability and recognition that injustices have occurred, which are essential steps toward making amends, healing, and reconciliation. Therefore, from the perspective of the victims and affected communities, reparations have significance in any transition where mass atrocities and other human rights violations have occurred.

This is especially true for vulnerable victims with special needs, including, *inter alia*, certain groups of women and girls, rural and slum inhabitants, victims of sexual and gender-based crimes, disabled, mutilated persons, orphans and other vulnerable children, elderly, and the illiterate, who will often face challenges in accessing reparations. Reparations programs need to pay special attention to facilitating effective access to the reparations regime for these groups, as well as adequate consideration of their needs in designing both the process and the substance of reparations and in avoiding stigmatization and discrimination. Accordingly, reparation principles may include affirmative measures to redress any inequalities affecting vulnerable victims.

Because of the nature of their experience, and their social and cultural surroundings, female victims may need distinct mechanisms that facilitate their recovery, reintegration, and redress in a different way than their male peers. The specific trauma related to sexual and gender-based violence, and the subsequent social alienation that follows, may affect the possibility of these victims to fully participate in and benefit from reparation.

This chapter provides an overview of the legal and operational considerations for reparations, while highlighting programmatic details for special categories of victims, such as women and victims of sexual and gender-based violence.

REPARATIONS IN INTERNATIONAL HUMANITARIAN LAW AND CRIMINAL LAW

The right to reparation was originally a right of states; however, this has evolved into a right of individuals. Under international law, gross violations of human rights and serious violations of international humanitarian law give rise to a right to reparation for victims (OHCHR 2008). In 2005, the United Nations General Assembly adopted resolution 60/147, *Basic Principles and Guidelines on the Right to a Remedy and Reparation for Victims of Gross Violations of International Human Rights Law and Serious Violations of International Humanitarian Law*, which provided a significant contribution to a normative framework on the obligation to provide reparations by recognizing reparations as a right and describing several forms of redress. This framework described five categories of reparation: *restitution, compensation, rehabilitation, satisfaction*, and *guarantees of non-repetition* (UN General Assembly 2005).

Most of these legal instruments, however, are silent on how they should be interpreted for vulnerable categories of victims such as survivors of sexual and gender-based violence and others, as previously described. Some guidance is available in relevant jurisprudence of human rights courts, and in particular, the Inter-American Court of Human Rights (IACtHR).

Judicial reparations in the context of mass human rights violations are becoming a reality. These forms of reparations are linked to individual criminal accountability of alleged perpetrators, which may be included as part of a transitional justice processes. The design and implementation of judicial reparations in these cases belong to the discretion of a court, and not the state.

The increase in judicial reparations for mass human rights crimes is due in no small part to the creation and work of the International Criminal Court (ICC). The recognition of the plight of victims of the most serious crimes is a cornerstone of the Rome Statute, which created the ICC. The rights of victims to participate in proceedings and benefit from Court-ordered reparations are without international precedent. The establishment of a Trust Fund for Victims, linked to the Court, with mandates to redress harm to victims of crimes within the jurisdiction of the Court, is generally accepted to be an important innovation of international criminal law.

The reparation regime described in Article 75 of the Rome Statute is based on individual criminal responsibility, and in accordance with Article 75(2) presupposes a conviction. In other words, before embarking on a reparations process, the ICC must establish the culpability of the convicted person for specific crimes, thus linking him or her to the harm suffered by the victims.

While the centrality of reparations in the work of the ICC is one of the most laudable advances in international criminal law, it has not been without criticism—much of it stemming from tensions between the expectations of victims and the reality of the appropriateness of reparations ordered by a court in any particular case. This is due to an inherent tension between the limitations of judicial reparations as a right under criminal court proceedings and the kinds of harm and the large number of victims usually associated with international gross human rights violations. Judicial reparations for gross human rights violations are limited to individual criminal responsibility for specific charges, as a result of a prosecutorial strategy, which may not necessarily be geared toward addressing this tension adequately. Also, a judicial approach does not necessarily support forms of reparations that have the potential to challenge preexisting gender hierarchies, including those that result in women holding less property than men, and women having fewer educational opportunities and, hence, less income-generating potential (Manjoo 2010).

Regardless of the reparations mechanism, designing multifaceted reparations programs maximizes impact, resources, and victim satisfaction. Programs that combine a variety of benefits, ranging from rehabilitative to material to symbolic, and that are delivered both individually and collectively, may cover a larger universe of victims as compared to programs that distribute only monetary compensation (OHCHR 2008). Since victims of different categories of violations may not receive exactly the same kinds of benefits, having a broader variety of reparations means reaching more victims and ensuring that multiple types of harm are redressed.

Ultimately, reparations should redress past harm and not create any further harm. In particular, they should not result in fueling further tension and conflict in communities. If reparations are administered without regard to local contexts, victims may be harmed again by stigmatizing them or putting them in danger with their families and communities.

GENDER-SENSITIVE PROGRAMMING

Many reparations programs have been criticized for ignoring the needs of women, and there are few examples where programs have defined and operationalized gender-sensitive responses. Discrimination against women, based on gender stereotypes, stigma, harmful and patriarchal cultural norms, and gender-based violence, has an adverse impact on the ability of women to gain access to justice on an equal basis with men. Most women have derived their compensation as heirs and dependents through reparations provided to men, and not as victims in their own right (Rubio-Marin 2009).

Gender analyses of the effects of serious human rights violations are necessary to understand how conflict-related violence impacts men, women, boys, and girls differently; and this information should inform both development and reparations programs that target those most affected by serious human rights violations. Reparations programs can ensure gender-sensitive approaches and even recognize and challenge gender inequalities in the way they design benefits for victims. There must be provisions in any reparations program to ensure attention to concepts of gender, gender equality and non-discrimination on a normative, procedural, and substantive basis. Empirical and normative standards attest to the need for reparation provisions to be delivered in ways that address the conditions of discrimination experienced by women and girls prior to and relative to when the events occurred, as they were occurring, and in the current context of reparations delivery. Lack of attention to these dynamics may prevent the full repair and rights fulfilment of female victims.[1]

There are examples of gender-sensitive forms of redress in Columbia, Guatemala, Morocco, Peru, Rwanda, Sierra Leone, South Africa, and Timor-Leste. For example, Colombia developed policies guiding how gender issues are to be incorporated throughout the reparations process and how sexual and gender-based violence is to be addressed. Recent developments have challenged the taboos of publicly acknowledging sexual violence, paving the way to addressing the impact of the conflict on women and girls. A broader discussion on gender-sensitive approaches to truth and accountability, as well as on promoting women's active participation in decision-making processes to redress victims of human rights violations, is growing in Colombia. In Timor-Leste, the truth commission recognized that women whose husbands had died during the occupation and conflict were particularly vulnerable because they had limited access to jobs, and prioritized widows as direct recipients of reparations benefits.

In 2007, women's groups mobilized to examine how reparations policies could be more responsive to women, girls, and victims of sexual and gender-based violence. Their efforts led to the Nairobi Declaration on Women's and Girls' Right to a Remedy and Reparation, which states that "reparations must go above and beyond the immediate reasons and consequences of the crimes and violations; they must aim to address the political and structural inequalities that negatively shape women's and girls' lives" (Nairobi Declaration 2007). In addition, the first thematic report submitted to the Human Rights Council by the Special Rapporteur on Violence Against Women focused on the topic of reparations to women who have been subjected to violence in contexts of both peace and post-conflict (Manjoo 2010).

Neither of the foregoing is formally binding (as soft law), merely aspirational; however, gender considerations for reparations were further articulated in the legal filing in the case of the *Prosecutor v Thomas Lubanga Dyilo* submitted by the Women's Initiatives for Gender Justice, the only civil society organization to substantively address gender issues in relation to reparations before the ICC.[2] They argued in the context of the closing arguments that "[d]espite the many challenges in this case, . . . [a] decision which recognizes the gender dimensions of enlistment, conscription and the forced participation of children in hostilities, could transform the legal definition of child soldiers and pave the way for similar prosecutions" (Inder 2011).

The *United Nations Guidance Note of the Secretary-General on Reparations for Conflict-Related Sexual Violence* also reaffirms these issues and emphasizes the need to invest in gender equality as a foundation of reparations programs in order to address inequality that renders women vulnerable to conflict-related violence and to the consequences of its aftermath (United Nations 2014).

When designing reparations programs, it is important to consider the individual and collective consequences of violence associated with gross and systematic human rights violations because these can translate into different attitudes toward concepts of healing, justice, reconciliation, and accountability. Women's experiences of conflict and transition often differ from those of men; yet for many reasons, several of which are discussed in this *Handbook*, women's experiences of violence and needs for justice have until recent times largely been ignored.

Gender-sensitive approaches to programming reparations imply consciously creating an environment that reflects an understanding of the realities of the lives of women and men within their social setting. Furthermore, gender sensitivity includes attempts to adequately respond to women's and men's strengths and challenges while they seek justice.

Reparations programs have great potential for empowering women in general by addressing social and economic inequality linked to gender and contributing to a broad social justice agenda (Valji 2009). For example, key priorities for post-conflict reconstruction and peace-building include establishing political governance, security, justice and the rule of law, and the administrative institutions of the state. Early state reconstruction should integrate gender-equality measures and ensure women's participation in political, social, and economic development processes. These efforts can provide opportunities to shape new social, economic, and political dynamics that can break existing gender norms and stereotypes. Not focusing on gender early on in reconstruction and transitional justice initiatives can entrench systems that discriminate against women, which are much harder to challenge later.

Lack of access to justice, scarcity of participation in peace-building, and economic inequity and inequality are some of the key challenges faced by women in conflict and post-conflict situations. Unfortunately, gender discrimination is deeply rooted in most social and cultural contexts, including those giving rise to reparations proceedings. Reparations programs should take into account the manner in which women's marginalized status negatively affects their ability to access justice within their own local settings. For example, women are often widowed or left to care for children and other family members during and following conflict, and tracing the fate of missing family members and finding out where their remains were buried is considered a form of reparation. This can also be a basis for other restorative measures, such as the issuing of a death certificate, which may enable women and the family to then draw a state pension.

TAILORING ACCESS FOR VICTIMS OF SEXUAL AND GENDER-BASED CRIMES

The general breakdown in law and order that occurs during conflict and displacement leads to an increase in all forms of violence. The underlying acceptance of violence against women that exists within many societies becomes more outwardly acceptable in conflict situations. Sexual violence in armed conflict settings, predominantly committed against women and girls, is the most common form of gender-based violence and one of the most widespread forms of criminality experienced in armed conflicts. However, the devastating physical and psychological impact of sexual violence, compounded by the stigma attached to it, often prevents victims from participating in transitional and criminal justice efforts or from seeking or obtaining reparations (United Nations 2014).

The inclusion of sexual violence in many reparations programs is a victory against a tradition that minimizes its importance as collateral, private, or non-political damage (Manjoo 2010). However, the specific trauma related to sexual and gender-based violence, and the subsequent social alienation, may affect the ability of these victims to fully participate in and benefit from reparations proceedings. Therefore, reparations programs should acknowledge this challenge and ensure that the reparations process, procedures, and awards are sensitive to the special needs and circumstances of both female and male victims of sexual and gender-based violence (and in the case of female victims, their children). Reparations processes should enable children born of rape and their siblings to be considered for the purposes of reparations, but this must be handled with sensitivity and within a child-centered approach, with complete confidence that neither the victim of sexual violence nor the child's identity will be disclosed (but see contra, Theidon, Chapter 11 in this volume).

Meaningful consultation with victims of sexual and gender-based crimes requires designing tailored reparations processes and systems to ensure safe environments and confidentiality measures. Equally important are transport provisions and child-care facilities so women can register as beneficiaries (United Nations 2014). For example, reparations programs must account for

> women's greater difficulties in complying with formal requirements for obtaining reparations (such as identification, certificates, official documents, etc.); their greater difficulty in accessing information (linguistic barriers, illiteracy, etc.); or having a bank account; their degree of involvement in civil society organizations that function as intermediaries in either the identification and registry of victims or the delivery of services; and their geographical distance from the agencies that decide on reparations or deliver services. (Rubio-Marin 2009, 2010)

Importantly, requiring victims of sexual violence to apply for reparations under the label of "victim of sexual violence" may deter many and may cause additional harm given the shame, stigma, and discrimination associated with this crime in their communities. It may be preferable to identify victims of sexual violence under the umbrella of other forms of injury or violence.

Reparations Aimed at Transformation

Past reparations programs have tended to emphasize restoring victims to the position they were in before the conflict began, usually through the award of restitution, compensation, or rehabilitation measures. Yet for many women and girls, this focus fails to acknowledge the structural and economic inequality experienced before the conflict and the contribution of such inequality to sexual violence before, during, and after conflict. Combining reparations with a structural transformative approach will be of particular importance to victims who have suffered irreparable harm and who are marginalized in their communities.

One goal of reparations for sexual violence is to address the conditions that existed prior to the conflict that may have contributed to these crimes and that may prevent the full rehabilitation and restoration of the rights of victims. Collective reparations can address existing gender inequalities within societies, advancing gender equality through the types of programs funded and the type of support provided to affected communities (but see, Hadzimesic, Chapter 39 in this volume).[3] Ordering reparations in the *Cotton Field* case, the IACtHR stated that, bearing in mind the context of structural discrimination in which women had been sexually abused and murdered, "re-establishment of the same structural context of violence and discrimination is not acceptable."[4]

If appropriately designed and delivered, and with the aim of addressing underlying gender inequalities, reparations can play a significant role in bringing about this societal transformation. For example, educating communities so women are better able to participate in reparations programs can enable social transformation. Raising awareness is often the cornerstone of women's empowerment because it can transform the way that communities think about women's roles, rights, and responsibilities. Community outreach as part of a reparations process must provide women and girls with the knowledge and skills they need to participate, and must create an enabling environment for them to actually do so.

Frequently community structures—including local government, law enforcement, justice, and health-care institutions—are unresponsive to women's rights and needs, and thus perpetuate inequality. When this happens, reparations programs could support these structures by mainstreaming gender considerations in order to transform the necessary systems and empower women.

Reparations that support women's economic empowerment can also contribute to transformative justice by placing women in a better position to break with historic patterns of subordination and social exclusion, with a view to eliminating the preexisting structural inequalities that have led to or encouraged violence (UN Women 2011). Economic independence is often cited as key to empowering women. Women's economic participation and empowerment are fundamental to strengthening women's rights and enabling women to have control over their lives and exert influence in society. Promoting business-enabling environments, village savings and loan schemes as part of reparations programs can transform women's economic empowerment in ways that traditional vocational training simply cannot (see Justino, Chapter 6, and Petesch, Chapter 26, in this volume).

But women's economic empowerment cannot be examined in a vacuum. Widespread cultural and economic practices work to prevent empowerment, and women experience specific social and economic obstacles in many societies, such as limited access to land, property, formal banking, inheritance, and marriage rights. To fully assess the opportunities and obstacles that exist, the intersection of political, sociocultural, and environmental conditions must be analyzed alongside traditional economic indicators if this type of response is to be included in reparations programs.

If possible, reparations should also be linked to anti-corruption measures, in fulfillment of the obligation to provide guarantees of non-repetition as a central component of redress measures and to ensure that reparations are transformative in nature. This is important given the disproportionate effect of corruption on women in many societies.

If reparations are associated with anti-corruption and gender-sensitive governance efforts, then this may help lead to improved service delivery, increased access to justice, and decreasing levels of corruption, conflict, and poverty. International practice on transitional justice is moving toward an approach that includes economic and social rights abuses. Tunisia's new structure for inter-ministerial collaboration on anti-corruption and transitional justice has demonstrated clear and deliberate formulation and coordination of inter-ministerial efforts; a committee to build off of and implement the work of the Joint Consultative Committee which drafted Tunisia's Action Plan; the elaboration of a strategy which takes into account financial resources required and evaluates progress; the engagement of governorates and municipalities through consultations and evaluative measures; and two-way communication to promote trust in government and enable citizens and civil society to come up with and propose solutions. (OECD 2016)

These efforts offer opportunities to integrate gender-sensitive approaches and support joint efforts for greater impact.

THE RELATIONSHIP BETWEEN REPARATIONS, GENDER, AND DEVELOPMENT

For most victims from resource-poor settings, the demands for both reparations and development assistance often arise concurrently, but they are generally conceptualized, resourced, and operationalized independently. In these circumstances, the issue of social and economic exclusion is central to both development and reparations programming.

The intersection of development, gender, and reparations programming within post-conflict and reconstruction settings should ensure integrated efforts and include analyses on how conflict has affected gender relations in affected communities (de Greiff 2013; UN Women and UNDP 2012). Issues of compensation and rehabilitation of victims could be incorporated into plans for post-conflict reconstruction and economic revitalization. Integrating transitional justice initiatives not only addresses the culture of violence and impunity, but also begins a healing process within the community through rehabilitation, truth and reconciliation, accountability, and reparations (Samuels 2006).

Reparations programs should be designed to be closely linked with other transitional justice initiatives—for example, criminal justice, truth-telling, and reconciliation processes. While development assistance allows for far-reaching responses to victimized communities, it does so in the absence of accountability and the associated satisfaction for victims. Reparations can provide that accountability.

The highest rates of victim satisfaction in reparations programs are achieved when victims take an active role in the process, and where offenders are encouraged to take responsibility for their actions (Sherman and Strang 2007). Therefore, if reparations are integrated as part of development and humanitarian efforts in the absence of state or offender accountability, then it is difficult to guarantee victim satisfaction.

RECOMMENDATIONS AND CONCLUSIONS

Unlike other transitional justice measures, reparations programs are designed to do something not just against perpetrators, but also on behalf of victims directly. Reparations, if well-designed, acknowledge victims' suffering, and offer measures of redress and some form of compensation for crimes and human rights violations. Reparations not only provide material benefit to victims, but also recognition that the injustices have occurred, which is an important step toward making amends, healing, and reconciliation.

Redressing harm requires multidimensional and multidisciplinary responses, involving medical, psychological, social, and legal measures that are gender sensitive. The challenge for any transitional justice initiative is in integrating women and other marginalized communities into the structure of justice. For reparations to be successful and effective, they need to address the needs of female victims in their complexity with respect to both victimhood and agency.

Adopting a gender perspective does not mean only prioritizing sexual crimes committed again female victims and thus ignoring other types of victimization to which women are exposed. This approach also underestimates the possibility that men and boys can be the victims of sexual crimes. Moreover, reparations programs should give due consideration to ensuring that indirect victims may benefit, such as the children of child mothers and former child soldiers, or those who suffered harm because they tried to protect direct victims from suffering crimes. Reparations should further underline that family members may be eligible for receiving redress where the direct victims were killed or have disappeared, with a view to ensuring that women and girls receive their rightful benefits without being subjected to discriminatory laws or customs.

Community mobilization and outreach for raising awareness are also essential as part of reparations programs, and these efforts must make victims aware of their rights in a language they understand. Reparations ought to be closely linked with other transitional justice initiatives for both pragmatic and conceptual reasons. Such connections provide an incentive for victims to interpret reparations benefits in terms of justice, rather than as an exchange of money and services for appeasement or acquiescence (OHCHR 2008).

Justice also demands that the concerns of victims take center stage in any reparations program. If structural injustices that triggered or worsened armed conflict are left unaddressed in reparations programs, then gender-based violence and other atrocities could be repeated, undermining the goal of reparations to support lasting peace and security.

NOTES

1. *Prosecutor v. Lubanga*, ICC-01/04-01/06-3177-Red, Trust Fund for Victims Redaction of Filing on Reparations and Draft Implementation Plan (November 3, 2015).

2. *Prosecutor v. Lubanga*, ICC-01/04-01/06-2876, Observations of the Women's Initiatives for Gender Justice on Reparations (May 10, 2012).

3. *Prosecutor v. Lubanga*, ICC-01/04-01/06-2876, Observations of the Women's Initiatives for Gender Justice on Reparations (May 10, 2012).

4. In the case *Cotton Field v. Mexico*, the IACtHR held that that "the concept of 'integral reparation' (*restitutio in integrum*) entails the re-establishment of the previous situation and the elimination of the effects produced by the violation, as well as the payment of compensation for the damage caused. However, bearing in mind the context of structural discrimination in which the facts of this case occurred, which was acknowledged by the State [. . .], the reparations must be designed to change this situation, so that their effect is not only of restitution, but also of rectification. In this regard, re-establishment of the same structural context of violence and discrimination is not acceptable" *Gonzales ("Cotton Field") v. Mexico*, Admissibility, Merits and Reparations, Inter-Am. Ct. H.R. (ser. C) No. 205, 450 (November 16, 2009).

REFERENCES

de Greiff, Pablo. 2013. *Rep. of the Special Rapporteur on the Promotion of Truth, Justice, Reparation and Guarantees of Non-Recurrence.* UN Doc. A/68/345 (August 23).

Inder, Brigid. 2011. *Reflection: Gender Issues and Child Soldiers: The Case of* Prosecutor v. Thomas Lubanga Dyilo. The Hague: Women's Initiatives for Gender Justice.

Manjoo, Rashida. 2010. *Rep. of the Special Rapporteur on Violence against Women, Its Causes and Consequences.* UN Doc. A/HRC/14/22 (April 19).

"Nairobi Declaration on Women's and Girls' Right to a Remedy and Reparation." 2007. International Meeting on Women's and Girls' Right to a Remedy and Reparation, Nairobi, Kenya.

Organisation for Economic Co-operation and Development (OECD). 2016. *Open Government Review of Tunisia* (February 8). Paris: OECD.

Office of the UN High Commissioner for Human Rights (OHCHR). 2008. *Rule of Law Tools for Post-Conflict States: Reparations Programmes.* New York and Geneva: United Nations.

Rubio-Marín, Ruth, ed. 2009. *The Gender of Reparations Unsettling Sexual Hierarchies While Redressing Human Rights Violations.* Cambridge: Cambridge University Press.

Rubio-Marín, Ruth. 2010. "Gender and Reparations: Challenges and Opportunities." Paper presented at Open Society Institute Roundtable on Gender and Transitional Justice, February 7, New York.

Samuels, Kirsti. 2006. "Rule of Law Reform in Post-Conflict Countries: Operational Initiatives and Lessons Learnt." World Bank, Social Development Papers, Conflict Prevention & Reconstruction, Paper No. 37, Washington, DC.

Sherman, Lawrence W., and Heather Strang. 2007. *Restorative Justice: The Evidence.* London: The Smith Institute.

United Nations. 2014. *Guidance Note of the UN Secretary-General: Reparations for Conflict-Related Sexual Violence.* New York: United Nations.

UN General Assembly. 2005. *Basic Principles and Guidelines on the Right to a Remedy and Reparation for Victims of Gross Violations of International Human Rights Law and Serious Violations of International Humanitarian Law.* UN Doc. A/RES/60/147 (December 16).

UN Women. 2011. *2011–2012 Progress of the World's Women: In Pursuit of Justice.* New York: UN Women.

UN Women and UNDP. 2012. *Reparation, Development and Gender*. Kampala, Uganda: UN Women and UNDP.

Valji, Nahla. 2009. "Gender Justice and Reconciliation." In *Building a Future on Peace and Justice: Studies on Transitional Justice, Peace and Development: The Nuremberg Declaration on Peace and Justice*, edited by Kai Ambos, Judith Large, and Marieke Wierda, 217–236. Berlin: Springer.

CHAPTER 20

COLONIALISM

AMINA MAMA

THIS chapter sets out to demystify the prevalence of violence against women in postcolonial conflicts by excavating the intertwined histories of militarization and women's subordination in postcolonial African states. Militarism and gender oppression emerge as mutually reinforcing features of the nineteenth- to twentieth-century European states that drove the expansion of capitalism, together with its associated sociocultural regimes.

The particular sex and gender regimes that accompanied nineteenth-century European imperialism were deeply contradictory sex-negative cultures that construed sexuality as a threat to social order, and therefore a matter for regulation through disciplinary, sometimes punitive, social practices. Existing analyses suggest that social policies of the day were motivated by ruling-class fears of contagion and degeneracy, both of which were blamed on the poorer classes, and in some cases—the most obvious being sexually transmitted diseases—often blamed specifically on the "corrupting" bodies of poor women (Stedman Jones 2013). However, the most influential histories of sexuality do not address the concurrence of nineteenth- to twentieth-century European sexual politics with imperialism, or the normative proclivity for racialized sexual abuse and gender-based violence in Western patriarchal states (Foucault 1978). They therefore fail to attend to the extension of such violence by the colonial regimes established by European empires.

Gender studies of colonialism have, to an extent, addressed the inculcation of Western bourgeois culture through ideologies of domesticity and the importation and naturalization of capitalist gender divisions of labor (Hansen 1992). The colonizing effects of the introduction of political institutions premised on an inequitable social contract that relied on a gendered separation of the private from public spheres are yet to be assessed. This gender division, referred to as the "sexual contract" by Pateman (1989), lies at the heart of women's marginalization in modern political, legal, and economic systems, such that the expansion of these systems ensured male domination in colonial and postcolonial states (Bond 2007). A focus on the appalling record of violence perpetrated against colonized women illuminates the centrality of sex and gender coercion, the use of force being central to the entire process. As a profoundly gendered and gendering phenomenon, militarism cultivates aggressive and violent expressions of masculinity for the purposes of war.

This chapter explores the manner in which imperialism—conceptualized as a militarized expansion of capitalism—worked to insinuate a patriarchal gender regime at the heart of the modern state in Africa. The consequences of this have been profound, but my focus here is on the manner in which the history of imperialism has bequeathed a systemic vulnerability to militarism, and to repeating cycles of conflict, characterized by sexual and gender-based violence (SGBV). This anti-imperialist perspective frames the US-led "Global War on Terror" as the global expansion of the genocidal US doctrine of "Manifest Destiny." In African contexts, militarism has many manifestations: coups d'état, military rule, civil war, and other forms of conflict and insecurity. The normalization of violence has particularly negative consequences for sex and gender relations, and targets women in particular ways.

IMPERIAL ANTECEDENTS

Prior to colonization, the transatlantic slave trade instigated and fueled numerous conflicts within and between existing political entities and economic systems, depopulating entire regions of the continent, and trafficking an estimated 12–15 million African women, men, and children across the Atlantic. Conservative estimates based on available records suggest that over 12 percent (1.5 million or more) met their deaths in transit.

Class formation was thus an intrinsic feature of European capitalist industrialization, reliant on the exploitation of labor drawn from the men, women, and children who constituted the poorer classes in Europe. The class- and gender-based exploitation of labor reached new extremes through transatlantic slavery and the various systems of indentured and forced labor in the African colonies. Imperialism also offered an outlet for the discontents that may otherwise have given rise to unrest, as Cecil Rhodes explicitly recognized when he remarked,

> I was in the East End of London yesterday and attended a meeting of the unemployed. I listened to the wild speeches, which were just a cry for "bread," "bread!" . . . in order to save the 40,000,000 inhabitants of the United Kingdom from a bloody civil war, we colonial statesmen must acquire new lands to settle the surplus population, to provide new markets for the goods produced in the factories and mines . . . . If you want to avoid civil war, you must become imperialists. (Cecil Rhodes, 1895, cited in Young 2001, 22)

Clearly the establishment of overseas colonies provided a safety valve, facilitated by a supremacist, patriarchal ideology that undermined any possibility of class solidarity by grandly positioning even the poorest white men as "heads of households." White men were therefore complicit, being personally invested in a patriarchal-racist system that appeared to afford them command over their own households, and the world (McClintock 1995, 42–51).

The early twentieth-century world was dominated by the interests of an emerging capitalist class that can be credited as much for their technological inventiveness as for the industrialization of violence and warfare, through increasingly deadly arsenals. Overall, the century saw wars claim over 231 million lives (Leitenberg 2003). Nordstrom (2004) further notes that 50–100 million indigenous people were killed in the *undeclared* wars of the twentieth century. Imperialism and colonialism thus violently restructured the world, giving rise to a deeply competitive, male-dominated capitalist world order in which war preparedness and war making were to remain integral to modern statecraft (Giddens 1987).

COLONIAL PACIFICATION

The African continent offers a particularly powerful vantage point from which to analyze colonial legacies. The region was colonized relatively late, rather incompletely, and for the most part for relatively short periods of time that formally ended just fifty or so years ago. By the mid-1970s—just a decade after the various declarations of flag independence that took place between the 1950s and 1960s—more than half of Africa's new nations were under military rule, and coups d'état had become a regular impediment to political development.[1] The rise of military rulers was not so much a new development as a relapse, because colonial rule was itself a militarist and authoritarian mode of governance that structurally prepared and predisposed the new nations to military rule. At the same time, this entirely masculine mode of governance systematically excluded and marginalized women in accord with ideologies of domesticity that were gender-divisive and elitist, part and parcel of colonial state-formation processes. Colonial policies therefore excluded girls from education and employment in state institutions, while health and welfare policies pathologized African women (Vaughan 1991).

It is a general fact of African experience that the revolutionary optimism that informed earlier visions of freedom and independence has remained largely unrealized. Instead, military interventions have repeatedly stalled democratic political development, while armed conflicts of various kinds have cost the continent billions of dollars and millions of lives (Hutchful and Bathily 1998). No amount of national security spending appears to change the fact that the majority of Africa's people lead precarious lives, or that African military expenditure grows in inverse proportion to investment in social, educational, welfare, and health services (SIPRI 2013). Because they rely on public services to alleviate the burden of care work and for employment, women bear the heaviest costs.

Walter Rodney (1972) makes the compelling argument that Africa's underdevelopment and Europe's development emerge as the conjoined consequences of an unequal colonial relationship that drained African human and material resources to the advantage of Europe. However, the role of gender and race or ethnicity in the colonizing processes that institutionalized these global dynamics of development and underdevelopment can be further elaborated through a gender analysis. Colonial armies paved the way for the administrative and social regulatory policies.

Colonial armies

Initially all-male institutions, colonial armies were established to patrol borders and protect the economic interests of rivaling Europeans against perpetual threats of insurrection and dissent. While there were some initial concerns over arming the natives, many of the territories claimed as colonies were simply too vast for European armies to control. For instance, the area that was amalgamated to form modern Nigeria was eight times the size of Britain and included large areas in the northern region that remained "no-go" zones. The West African Frontier Force (WAFF) was established in 1897 by amalgamating the various Chartered Company constabularies from Nigeria and Gambia, the Gold Coast Regiment, and the Sierra Leone Battalion. Their first mission was to arrest the French influence, at that time extending from the French Sudan down the River Niger. In 1914 the WAFF was dispatched to invade the German Cameroons in the first of a series of World War I punitive expeditions. WAFF men were later to fight in Ethiopia and Burma during World War II, and to return as men accustomed to the hyper-masculine chain-of-command culture of the barracks (Gutteridge 1975).

In another telling example, La Force Publique was established in King Leopold's Congo, an area eight times the size of Belgium itself. Hochschild (1998) details the tactics that this notorious militia used to terrorize local men into forced labor. The extraction of ivory, rubber, and other lucrative resources was carried out using summary executions, floggings, incarceration in prison camps, the amputation of limbs, and a specific strategy of gendered terror. To force men to work, La Force Publique raided villages to abduct women and confine them in prison camps until their male relatives delivered the specified quantities of latex to secure their release (Hochschild 1998). Parts of today's Democratic Republic of Congo (DRC) still suffer exceptionally high levels of rape and brutality to women, perpetrated by men fighting to vanquish other men.

Military history suggests that the imperialists established colonial armies with the additional goal of winning support for imperial rule through a masculine pact. Colonial powers grafted the structures of an all-male modern army onto local warrior practices, such as praise singing and the use of protective talismans. Women warrior traditions— such as the elite all-women guard responsible for protecting the king of Dahomey— did not survive colonialism (Alpern 1998). Social historical studies suggest a gender dynamic that went deeper than the men-only conscription and recruitment practices, to inform the emergence of modern masculinities more broadly. For example, Miescher (2005) details how individual men sought careers in colonial security forces to escape economic hardships inflicted by empire, noting that colonial service offered a route to more mobile, urbane, and authoritative masculinities.

Colonial military service separated men from their communities, their relationships, and their responsibilities to women and children, schooling them in unquestioning obedience to the military chain of command and colonial values. This disrupted indigenous gender relations and introduced economic changes, too; for example, because no catering facilities were provided for soldiers, they relied on purchasing food, laundry, and sexual services from women. Women also left their homes either to follow menfolk who had been recruited or conscripted, or to find new livelihoods for themselves, away from the physical drudgery of rural life. Women who entered informal relationships with recruits were thus tacitly tolerated among the ranks in peacetime, where they supported and serviced the soldiers, through various monetary transactions.

By the 1930s, soldiers were allowed to marry, once they had completed their training, albeit subject to approval by their commanding officers, partly because marriage was considered conducive to stability in the troops. In KAR (Kings African Rifles) and WAFF (West African Frontier Force), officially recognized wives were placed under the authority of a "head woman"—*maguja* in Hausa. *Maguja* was usually the wife of the most senior African soldier, appointed and recognized by the commanding officer, and afforded the right to mete out corporal punishments—usually flogging— to her subordinates, just as her husband was mandated with regard to his junior ranks. In West Africa, child marriage and polygamy were tolerated and regulated within the military—privates could have one wife and non-commissioned officers (NCOs) could have two, while senior NCOs could have three.

Extramarital liaisons that would have been anathema to most Africans were encouraged to minimize the service costs of maintaining colonial troops:

> If a young askari was not sufficiently wealthy to afford a wife . . . the Africa CSM saw that he took a concubine unto himself—the policy being that for disciplinary reasons all askaris in the lines should have a wife—the concubine also cooked for him. (Clayton 1999, 242)

The women in such informal relationships were often handed over from draft to draft as the battalions were moved from one location to another. Some regiments went further, to maintain brothels for the use of soldiers, as was the case for the 4/6th KAR in Somaliland, the 5th battalion in Ethiopia, and the pre-Burma training camp in Sri Lanka. However, where such provisions attracted official scrutiny, the women were dispersed, to be re-enrolled as "laundresses" or "millet-shakers."

In sum, the African colonial armies performed their service well. They maintained order, suppressed rebellions, carried out punitive expeditions, and ensured the collection of taxes for empire. The preceding evidence points to a highly patriarchal order that was institutionalized within the barracks by colonial officers intent on "making men" of the natives, with far-reaching consequences for gender relations across the society.

Administrative pacification: Confinement, taxation, and social regulation

> The administrator who ruled by reports and decrees in more hostile secrecy than any oriental despot grew out of a tradition of military discipline in the midst of ruthless and lawless men: for a long time he had lived by the boyhood ideals of a modern knight in shining armour sent to protect the helpless and primitive people.
>
> (Arendt 1976, 186)

Apart from military subjugation, various other institutions carried out mass detention and confinement, forced labor, and torture, with and without the backing of European and international laws. The German genocide of the Herero peoples between 1904 and 1907 exemplified extreme cruelty, and cost somewhere between 24,000 and 100,000 lives—about three-quarters of the total population. The military strategy saw men slaughtered outright, women and children raped, and survivors driven out into the Namib Desert to die of thirst, in an effort to exterminate them entirely (Olusoga and Erichsen 2010). The administrative strategy saw survivors confined to concentration camps and other forms of internment, to be used as slave labor. Thousands died from malnourishment, disease, and physical abuses such as flogging. The legalities of genocide, not to mention the first concentration camps, were not addressed until the same technologies of coercion and control were turned on Europeans during World War II.

This was not just a German administrative practice. Elkins (2005) reports that the British confined over a million forcibly displaced Gikuyu people to detention camps that were little different from concentration camps, in order to acquire their lands and eliminate competition from highly successful indigenous farming. The conditions of the camps left inmates to eke out livelihoods on land so arid and poor that severe malnourishment became the norm, and life expectancies among the Gikuyu were significantly lowered.

In other parts of the continent, existing social and economic systems were attacked in similar ways. Numerous corrupt deals and unfavorable treaties and settlements exploited local rivalries in order to ensure imperialist economic domination. When these did not prove adequate to the task, punitive expeditions were carried out by the military on the slightest pretext, leaving little room for doubts about who was in charge.

Once they had established military supremacy, the colonial states introduced new capitalist labor and taxation regimes to pursue their economic interests. Modeled on the idea of industrial man—a hard-working, disciplined servant of industry—male labor and remuneration were premised and dependent on the idea of a stay-at-home wife. Housewifery was not only a completely alien idea in regions where women had been responsible for many kinds of production and trade, but it was also a luxury that few Africans would ever be able to afford. This did not prevent the ideology of female domesticity from having material consequences. Women were not admitted into the colonial economy to any significant degree. To date, women across Africa remain underrepresented in the formal sector, left to eke out marginal livelihoods in an unregulated and exploitative informal sector, valorized under the spurious guise of "entrepreneurialism."

Colonial administration relied on the collection of taxes to force local peoples into the wage economy through debt, obliging them to contribute products and labor to empire. Administrative pacification added a layer of governance to military regimes. Initially only men were taxed, in keeping with European gender ideology. However, once the extent of women's productive labor was realized, census-taking and taxation were extended to colonized women. The carrying out of censuses and plans to extend taxation to married women (seen as double taxation) often provoked resistance. Both were factors in the Igbo Women's War during the 1920s, which saw the colonial troops kill fifty-three women (Mba 1982).

During the World War years, colonial administrations imposed heavier taxes, and at times resorted to forcibly seizing goods to support the war effort. Byfield (2003) reports on the Great Upheaval (1947–1948), during which Egba women held several months of organized protests against hardships suffered as a result of the heavy taxes imposed on women traders during Europe's Great Depression and World War II. These conditions explain why census-taking and excessive taxation became the focus of women's anti-colonial activism.

The development of colonial civil services presented new opportunities and mobility for a male elite, but they systematically discriminated against women, institutionalizing gender inequalities in the colonial bureaucracies. Historical research shows that local women were initially completely excluded from colonial service, only to be later admitted on unfavorable terms. So, for example, in the West African British colonies of the 1930s only European women would be employed in secretarial-type positions. When more women were admitted into the service, they were only allowed menial positions, from which they were required to resign upon marriage (Denzer 1989).

By the early twentieth century, European women's involvement in colonial rule had increased. Most of the European women who came to West Africa did so through their status as the lady-wives of British colonial administrators, whereas in the settler colonies of East and Southern Africa colonial wives were drawn from a wider class spectrum, to adapt to the rigors of settler life as well as its many privileges. The growing literature on gender and empire reveals the manner in which European women were brought in variously to curb the perceived excesses of European men, and to assist in the instruction of an emerging elite of African women schooled in European domesticity, to provide suitable wives for male African clerks and administrators (Hansen 1992). It was hoped that European women would contribute a "soft touch" to the broader domestication of native populations that were proving slow to adopt Western culture and ways of life. In colonial Tanganyika, for example, British wives established the Tanganyikan Women's Union, partly because they feared that Kenyan women joining and supporting the nationalist movement across the border would influence local women (Geiger 1997). In French Algeria, this strategy went further during the bloody national liberation war, with the deployment of ordinary working-class French women to offer soap and hygiene classes to rural Algerians, in an effort to subvert the resistance. Before the French lost the war to the Algerian nationalists, the accoutrements of modern femininity on offer included "freedom from the veil," as demonstrated in the French tactic of staging public unveiling ceremonies in city centers (Lazreg 2007).

As a supplement to colonial armies, colonial bureaucracies were administered according to imperial interests. Although these came to include colonial organizations for women, the European colonial administrators who "ruled by reports and decrees" left Africa with authoritarian bureaucratic structures that were modeled on military hierarchy.

Men's service to empire and nation

During World War I and II, hundreds of thousands of African men were recruited to fight on the side of their respective colonial masters. The French led the way, conscripting over 200,000 able-bodied men from a population of 11 million in French Sudan to fight in the trenches of World War I, while the British mustered 30,000 men (Echenberg 1991). By the end of World War II, Britain had enlisted over 400,000 men, of whom as many as 166,000 were dispatched overseas to fight in Burma, Abyssinia, and Italian Somalia (Killingray and Rathbone 1986). Echenberg records that 30,000 French West African soldiers died in the trenches of World War I. He estimates that as many as 20,000 participated in the Allied landing of 1944 alone. However, at the end of the war, President De Gaulle ordered the *enblanchissment* of the Free French, 50 percent of whom were Africans. To ensure that African soldiers did not appear in the Victory Day Marches, they were detained before being shipped back to the colonies. In Senegal the failure of the French to pay the meager sums of money due to returned soldiers at Camp Thiaroye led them to protest. The French response is recorded as a massacre, which left thirty-five veterans shot dead (Echenberg 1991).

In her appraisal of the role played by returning World War II veterans in the Guinean nationalist movement, Schmidt (2005) notes that most of the men recruited had been drawn from the underprivileged and uneducated classes, who joined up in the hope of attaining dignity and upward mobility—interests that were not met when they found themselves returned to colonial racism. Mann (2003) notes that instead of returning as the "special men" that they might have aspired to become, veterans returned home to find themselves in complicated and often subservient relationships with the men emerging as new political, religious, and economic elite. This became a source of dissatisfaction that threatened civilian governments.

The removal of large numbers of able-bodied men must have had dramatic effects on the gendered social, economic, and cultural fabric of the lands from which they were drawn, burdening and changing the lives of women in many ways that have remained undocumented. The nation-states that were established—whether they aspired to ideals of women's emancipation or not—were thus imbued with a militarist gender order that relegated women to the margins and reinscribed male dominance within all of its institutions.

To summarize, while nineteenth- and early twentieth-century theaters of war were largely located within Europe, African men were mustered into the service of their respective European masters.

Colonial militarism therefore escalated dramatically during the World Wars, indoctrinating Africans into male-dominant institutions that were to persist after independence. African men embraced nationalism as an assertion of masculine prowess, such that even today, post-independence politicians invoke colonial customary laws—such as the right to beat wives—in the name of masculine renditions of "African culture."

CONCLUSION

Colonial legacies of militarized governance are implicated in the speed with which flag independence gave way to military rule across the region. Because colonial regimes were all-male systems that governed despotically on behalf of distant powers, they did not include institutions conducive to democracy, nor did they allow women's participation in political or economic life. With the all-male army as the strongest state institution, and administrative structures that did little for the people in general, the social contract necessary for democratic governance remained underdeveloped. It further created and then constrained hyper-masculine, militarized political cultures that marginalized women from government and neglected their social and economic contributions. This analysis of colonial rule gives new salience to its militaristic nature, and therefore offers new insight into the rapidity with which a number of African nations descended into military rule and civil war following flag independence. I have argued that this was a relapse, not an African improvisation. Indeed, the institutional dominance of all-male colonial security systems, more accustomed to detaining political actors than being accountable to them, suggests a degree of inevitability. African men who had fought and killed Europeans returned home disconnected from diverse indigenous gender cultures, and the statuses some of these afforded to women. Indoctrinated into despotic militarist notions of authority, Africa's not-so-new military men disrespected democratic governance, civilian leaders, and women.

Beyond the armies, colonial legal and policy regimes regulated and informed the gender distortions that have continued post-independence. Continuing injustices have provoked women to mobilize into numerous movements dedicated to challenging gender discrimination and all forms of violence, and advocating powerfully for more peaceful, just, and democratic modes of governance, with some important successes.

NOTE

1. The apartheid regimes in the Southern subregion represent a particularly unpleasant militaristic legacy affecting neighboring countries as well as the inhabitants of Rhodesia and South Africa, one that was to persist until the formal end of apartheid in 1994.

REFERENCES

Alpern, Stanley B. 1998. *Amazons of Black Sparta: The Women Warriors of Dahomey.* New York: New York University Press.

Arendt, Hannah. 1976. *The Origins of Totalitarianism.* London: Harcourt.

Bond, Johanna E. 2007. "Constitutional Exclusion and Gender in Commonwealth Africa." *Fordham International Law Journal* 31, no. 2: 289–342.

Byfield, Judith A. 2003. "Taxation, Women, and the Colonial State: Egba Women's Tax Revolt." *Meridians* 3, no. 2: 250–277.

Clayton, Anthony. 1999. *Frontiersmen: Warfare in Africa since 1950.* London: University College London Press.

Denzer, LaRay. 1989. "Women in Government Service in Colonial Nigeria, 1862–1945." African Studies Centre Working Paper No. 136, Boston University, Boston, MA.

Echenberg, Myron. 1991. *Colonial Conscripts: The Tirailleurs Sénégalais in French West Africa, 1857–1960.* Portsmouth, NH: Heinemann.

Elkins, Caroline. 2005. *Imperial Reckoning: The Untold Story of Britain's Gulag in Kenya.* New York: Henry Holt.

Foucault, Michel. 1978. *History of Sexuality*, Vol. 1: *An Introduction.* Translated by Robert Hurley. London: Allen Lane.

Geiger, Susan. 1997. *TANU Women: Gender and Culture in the Making of Tanganyikan Nationalism, 1955–1965.* Portsmouth, NH: Heinemann.

Giddens, Anthony. 1987. *The Nation-State and Violence: Volume Two of a Contemporary Critique of Historical Materialism.* Berkeley: University of California Press.

Gutteridge, William F. 1975. *Military Regimes in Africa.* London: Methuen.

Hansen, Karen Tranberg, ed. 1992. *African Encounters with Domesticity.* New Brunswick, NJ: Rutgers University Press.

Hochschild, Adam. 1998. *King Leopold's Ghost: A Story of Greed, Terror, and Heroism in Colonial Africa.* Boston: Houghton Mifflin.

Hutchful, Eboe, and Abdoulaye Bathily, eds. 1998. *The Military and Militarism in Africa.* Dakar: CODESRIA.

Killingray, David, and Richard Rathbone, eds. 1986. *Africa and the Second World War.* New York: St. Martin's Press.

Lazreg, Marnia. 2007. *Torture and the Twilight of Empire: From Algiers to Baghdad.* Princeton, NJ: Princeton University Press.

Leitenberg, Milton. 2003. "Deaths in Wars and Conflicts in the 20th Century." Center for Peace Studies Occasional Paper 29, Cornell University, Ithaca, NY.

Mann, Gregory. 2003. "Old Soldiers, Young Men: Masculinity, Islam, and Military Veterans in Late 1950's Soudan Francais (Mali)." In *Men and Masculinities in Modern Africa*, edited by Lisa A. Lindsay and Stephan Miescher, 69–86. Portsmouth, NH: Heinemann.

Mba, Nina E. 1982. *Nigerian Women Mobilized: Women's Political Activity in Southern Nigeria, 1900–1965.* Berkeley: University of California Press.

McClintock, Anne. 1995. *Imperial Leather: Race, Gender and Sexuality in the Colonial Conquest.* New York: Routledge.

Miescher, Stephan F. 2005. *Making Men in Ghana.* Bloomington: Indiana University Press.

Nordstrom, Carolyn. 2004. *Shadows of War: Violence, Power, and International Profiteering in the Twenty-First Century.* Berkeley: University of California.

Olusoga, David, and Casper W. Erichsen. 2010. *The Kaiser's Holocaust: Germany's Forgotten Genocide and the Colonial Roots of Nazism*. London: Faber and Faber.

Pateman, Carole. 1989. *The Sexual Contract*. Cambridge: Polity Press.

Rodney, Walter. 1972. *How Europe Underdeveloped Africa*. London: Bogle-L'Ouverture.

Schmidt, Elizabeth. 2005. *Mobilizing the Masses: Gender, Ethnicity, and Class in the Nationalist Movement in Guinea, 1939–1958*. Portsmouth, NH: Heinemann.

Stockholm International Peace Research Institute (SIPRI). 2013. *SIPRI Year Book*. Oxford: Oxford University Press.

Stedman Jones, Gareth. 2013. *Outcast London: A Study in the Relationship between Classes in Victorian Society*. London: Verso.

Vaughan, Megan. 1991. *Curing Their Ills: Colonial Power and African Illness*. Palo Alto, CA: Stanford University Press.

Young, Robert J. C. 2001. *Postcolonialism: An Historical Introduction*. Oxford: Blackwell.

CHAPTER 21

··

CONFLICT, DISPLACEMENT, AND REFUGEES

··

LUCY HOVIL

DISPLACEMENT is one of the most tangible indicators of conflict. It represents a visible human cost as individuals and families are physically uprooted from their homes and are forced to seek safety either over an international border as refugees, or within their country as internally displaced persons (IDPs). The nature of a conflict and the trajectory it follows have an impact on all stages of displacement: the root causes of conflict have a direct bearing on whether or not populations are likely to be displaced; the consequences of the conflict follow refugees and IDPs into exile when they fail to find safety; and the resolution of the conflict (or its failure) is intricately connected to discussions around the resolution of displacement.

Refugee policy is relatively well established and provides a clear theoretical framework for responding to the plight of exile. It is governed by the 1951 Refugee Convention and the 1967 Protocol, and falls under the mandate of the United Nations High Commissioner for Refugees (UNHCR). IDP policy is more recent and less formally established—though it is widely endorsed by governments and international actors and is gaining increasing traction. In practice, however, the legal and policy frameworks for both refugees and IDPs alike fail to deliver on that mandate to protect those who are displaced. On the ground, forced displacement, whether it results in cross-border movement or remains internal, is a highly complex and variable process, and policy often remains poorly implemented and discordant with lived realities.

All displaced persons face the prospect of similar rights violations. However, these violations are experienced in different ways: just as conflict can impact men and women, and girls and boys, differently, the same can be said of displacement. Therefore, while it is important not to create hierarchies of suffering, key to any effective response is an understanding of the specific contextual dynamics that are present given the various intersectionalities differently impacting those displaced. Within this context, viewing displacement through a gender lens provides one framework for creating a more nuanced and contextually relevant understanding. A gender perspective can highlight specific issues that are present in any situation of displacement, including those that were exported into exile with displaced populations, as well as new power dynamics that are created as a consequence of exile. Thus, while displacement is a phenomenon that has a strongly negative impact on *all* those who are displaced regardless of gender, age, ethnicity, or any other categorization, a gender lens provides a contextually relevant understanding of specific experiences of displacement.

It is important to point out that the notion of gender here refers broadly to injustices that can be suffered by men, women, boys, and girls. A gender lens helps us to understand patterns of violations and responses that are not necessarily limited to women and girls and reflects an increasing recognition of the need for a more nuanced understanding of masculinities and their relationship to issues of forced displacement.

In reality, however, as this chapter shows, the opportunity to use gender as one means of providing improved understanding and responses to displaced persons, although internationally recognized as relevant and important, has been poorly realized at both a theoretical and practical level. The chapter begins by examining how gender is relevant within a forced migration context and critiques the extent to which the international community, responding to the plight of refugees and IDPs, has failed to adequately address entrenched gender-related problems. Next, it considers the extent to which the gender response in refugee policy has been understood and implemented principally through a humanitarian paradigm that has focused primarily on gender mainstreaming, and has therefore been ineffective in addressing the structural issues that cause gendered harm throughout the displacement trajectory. The chapter then considers specific gender-based harms throughout the trajectory of displacement, including statelessness. It concludes by asserting that as long as refugees and IDPs remain caught within a humanitarian paradigm that leaves little room for engagement with some of the deeper, political dynamics associated with exile, the protection of those who are displaced will continue to be compromised. At the same time, it also asserts that a gender-sensitive approach points to the possibilities of a paradigm shift in refugee protection more generally. In this respect, a gender lens has the potential to precipitate a genuinely transformational response to the broader debate on conflict and displacement.

THE EVOLUTION OF GENDERED HUMANITARIAN RESPONSE AND ITS IMPACT ON REFUGEES AND INTERNALLY DISPLACED PERSONS

Engagement with gender issues within the field of forced displacement has generally been both selective and superficial. From as early as the 1970s, UNHCR and other humanitarian organizations made intermittent attempts to recognize the specific needs of refugee women. However, these attempts were initially concerned only with protection due to insecurity in refugee settlements or camps, and the focus of UNHCR's gendered protection was primarily on combating the sexual and gender-based violence (SGBV) against women and girls common in refugee settings (Grabska 2011).

Even with an exclusive focus on SGBV, there was a dearth in understanding of not only its root causes, but also the many other gender issues confronting refugees. Indeed, until the mid-1980s, there was little research or analysis of forced displacement trends that focused on gender issues in any way. Not surprisingly, this lack of attention to and consideration of gender was reflected in a number of detrimental policies and programs in operation. For instance, an admirable commitment to respecting "culture" did not come to terms with the fact that some cultural practices perpetuated gender inequality and discrimination in the name of "tradition"; other approaches were simply "gender blind" (Hyndman 1998). Thus, until the mid- to late 1990s, instead of recognizing displacement contexts as opportunities for supporting the development of transforming gender roles in order to better address the vulnerabilities faced by women and girls in situations of conflict and displacement, UNHCR tended to rely on traditional gender hierarchy structures that already existed within the refugee communities to disseminate aid and resources in refugee camps, or to make decisions around camp management and design.

At least in theory, this gender-blind or gender-absent approach to humanitarian programing began to change in the early 1990s, reflecting global changes in international law and policy and the ascendency of the human rights movement, the women's rights movement, and the feminist movements (see Žarkov, Chapter 2 in this volume). But gender goals alone, of course, yield few results without consistent implementation.

The advent of the *Gender Guidelines*

In the early 1990s, UNHCR issued a policy on refugee women, the *Guidelines on the Protection of Refugee Women*, representing an important breakthrough (UNHCR 1991). The *Guidelines* demonstrated a stronger awareness of the need to promote the protection of individual rights of women despite cultural or traditional practices that might undermine the realization of these rights. As it acknowledged, moving slightly beyond the prior exclusive focus on SGBV, "[i]n addition to these basic needs shared with all refugees, refugee women and girls have special protection needs that reflect their gender: they need, for example, protection against manipulation, sexual and physical abuse and exploitation, and protection against sexual discrimination in the delivery of goods and services" (UNHCR 1991, para. 3).

As a result of the increased awareness resulting from the *Guidelines*, there has been greater commitment to the need to explicitly include women in decision-making and food distribution, as well as greater awareness of other gender-specific humanitarian needs over the past two decades. For instance, the *Guidelines* state that women should take a lead role in local decision-making committees on food aid management, as well as the management of assets created through food-for-work programs (UNHCR 1991, para. 86). The World Food Programme (WFP) policies now state that women should control the family food aid entitlement in 80 percent of WFP food distributions. Yet such tokenism, while arguably an improvement inasmuch as it shows a degree of gender awareness, nonetheless essentializes women and assumes that they are "more responsible."

This increased gender awareness has impacted not only humanitarian programing for those in exile, but is also in evidence in a growing understanding of the extent to which gender dynamics are often interlinked with *causes* of flight. Gender is not included as one of the five grounds upon which someone can be considered a refugee, which require demonstrating "a well-founded fear of being persecuted for reasons of race, religion, nationality, membership in a particular social group, or political opinion" (1951 Refugee Convention, art. 1(A)(2)). But, in 2002, UNHCR issued *Gender Guidelines* for state parties and those conducting refugee status determinations, specifying the need for gender-sensitive assessment of cases (UNHCR 2002). This approach is crucial both in sensitizing adjudicators with regard to their interaction with refugee and asylum applicants, and in encouraging them to think more broadly about gender in their application of the law. In the context of conflict, the 2002 *Gender Guidelines* have been particularly helpful where, for instance, women have been specific targets of military attacks or where they have been put in danger as a result of the political activities of male relatives. Furthermore, the *Gender Guidelines* note that although gender is not specifically referenced in the refugee definition, "it is widely accepted that it can influence, or dictate, the type of persecution or harm suffered and the reasons for this treatment. The refugee definition, properly interpreted, therefore covers gender-related claims. As such, there is no need to add an additional ground to the 1951 Convention definition" (UNHCR 2002, para. 6). Though soft law, this statement effectively circumvented the need for adding a sixth gender ground, which would have been highly unlikely to receive enough support from member states. Since the issuance of the *Gender Guidelines*, many countries have begun to consider gender asylum claims under the "social group" category of the refugee definition contained within the Convention.

Limitations of the *Gender Guidelines*

As revolutionary as they were in some respects, both sets of *Guidelines* fall short of explaining for adjudicators the complex gender-related issues that can precipitate displacement. For instance, in cases where perpetrators were non-state actors, which is often the case with gender-based claims, asylum cases are still often seen as lacking legitimacy. Thus, despite the growing awareness of the need to be responsive to gender dynamics among displaced populations, legal interpretation, policy, and implementation have in many respects all remained fundamentally flawed. While some of the ideas and policies behind gender mainstreaming have the potential to generate positive change, in practice there has been low compliance with UNHCR guidelines on the ground and an inadequate understanding of the nuanced gendered realities of displacement that could have, in turn, been translated into effective policies.

The Impact of a Narrow Interpretation of Gender on Refugee Women and Men

One of the cross-cutting issues that has stunted progress in addressing gender discrimination has been a limited interpretation of gender by those working in the area of forced displacement. Gender has often been exclusively equated with women, resulting in inadequate recognition of the fact that gender is also about men and boys. This unequal emphasis has had a negative impact on both men and women: in the case of the latter, women are viewed as being more "true" refugees, stereotyped as the victims of war rather than the perpetrators (Malkki 1995). This limited understanding and recognition have often created gender discrimination, rather than removed it, by exiling women into the "vulnerable group" category favored by humanitarian actors wherein women can be robbed of their agency.

At the same time, all too frequently male refugees and IDPs are left to cope alone, not only with the violations that led to their displacement, but also with the layers of injustice that are added by their experience of exile. Men also have to make adjustments in exile, particularly with regard to their economic and domestic roles. Traditional male roles are often effectively taken over by agencies such as UNHCR and the WFP, which provide families with tents to sleep in and food to eat, to such an extent that women have observed that they find UNHCR to be a "better husband" (Turner 2000). Sometimes refugee men are expected to take on tasks traditionally assigned to women. Although this can be interpreted as positive inasmuch as it challenges gender power dynamics, the context in which this takes place—and the fact that it is driven by circumstances, rather than an expressed desire to transform unequal gender power dynamics—often exacerbates rather than alleviates gender discrepancies.

Furthermore, where there is a narrow interpretation of gender, everyone loses out. Research conducted in northern Uganda's IDP camps, for instance, showed that both women and men blamed high levels of domestic violence within the camps on the fact that men felt emasculated and disempowered by displacement (Okello and Hovil 2007). This fact obviously does not justify domestic violence, but needs to be acknowledged—and should be taken into account in any response. The extent to which displacement disempowers men, therefore, has received inadequate attention and has been poorly understood.

Gender-Based Harms: The Trajectory of Displacement for Refugees and Internally Displaced Persons

Gender-specific issues can be both the *cause* of displacement and part of the broader *context* in which it takes place. This section explores the causes of displacement;

gender-based harms in exile; and some of the specific gender-related issues at the point of ending displacement. It also looks briefly at the response, or lack of response, to these problems.

Gender harms as a cause of displacement and during flight

Conflict at varying levels generally lies at the heart of causes of displacement. But gender discrimination and power dynamics are inevitably part of the context in which people flee. In addition, specific gender harms—particularly sexual violence—can also be the direct *cause* of flight. SGBV as a cause of displacement—as both a real harm and as a threat—has gained increasing prominence within discourses on forced displacement. While the majority of conflicts today take a heavy toll on the civilian population in general, displacement can have a strongly gendered dimension, with sexual violence perhaps the most tangible example. Notoriously high levels of sexual violence in the eastern Democratic Republic of Congo, for example, have become the focus of international academic and media attention, where vast numbers of people have been displaced as a result. While sexual violence is often non-discriminatory in its reach, it is likely that certain groups will be at particular risk. For instance, Mayan women were specifically targeted in Guatemala, their minority status and their gender both factors in their vulnerability and consequently their displacement (Rosser 2007). It is important to note that the *threat* or fear of rape can be as real a driver to flight as actual rape.

The process and duration of flight and transit are also a time of extreme vulnerability in an already volatile context, but having a gendered understanding of some of these dynamics can be crucial. Families are often separated, either in the chaos of conflict-induced flight, or as a deliberate decision on the part of families to flee separately for strategic reasons. In these circumstances, women and girls who are on their own can be particularly vulnerable, not only with regard to access to assistance, but also with regard to sexual violence by those they meet along the way—whether they be pirates, border guards, army or rebel combatants, male refugees, or others with whom they come in contact.

GENDER HARMS IN EXILE

Once in exile, the risk of gender harms often continues, despite the fact that those who flee conflict do so in order to find safety—indeed, the very notion of the status of "refugee" (and, more recently, the recognition of IDPs as a specific category of concern) is constructed around the notion of protection. However, and as outlined earlier, empirical research in camps suggests that responses are still hugely inadequate as specific gender needs continue to be responded to in token ways by UNHCR and its implementing partners.

Indeed, much of what has passed for gender mainstreaming remains relatively palliative for refugees and IDPs. While "fixing" the provision of assistance can deal with some gender issues and economic disparities impacting those in exile, the ideological underpinnings that feed gender discrimination are far harder to address (El-Bushra 2000). For instance, too often humanitarian actors believe that they have ticked the gender-sensitive "protection" box by locating a borehole for a well or a toilet in an accessible location. This important but nevertheless superficial adherence to gender-specific concerns does little to address the deep-rooted systemic injustice that lies behind gender divisions, and thus fails to assist displaced women (Hovil 2012). Some note that the humanitarian paradigm is not well-suited to supporting gender equality, as humanitarian contexts are inherently hierarchical—with all refugees, regardless of gender, dependent on international institutions and actors for their livelihoods (Grabska 2011). By contrast, recent research by the Institute of Development Studies found that placing gender equality at the center of humanitarian assistance planning makes assistance more effective for all (IDS 2015).

The inertia in implementing real gender responses in part reflects a broader problem in which refugee protection has evolved from its more political roots into an overtly humanitarian enterprise. As a result, humanitarian responses have often treated gendered issues as "symptoms" of conflict and/or displacement: deep-rooted gendered power dynamics have remained ignored, and gender issues get placed again at the bottom of the priority list. Gender-mainstreaming, when seen as a solution to all gender-related issues, fails to acknowledge that many gender issues are the result of deeply entrenched and pervasive gender inequalities that require more than symptomatic responses. While it goes beyond the mandate of UNHCR to address root issues per se, at the very least it is clear that there is a need for greater awareness of the broader gender context in this regard.

In addition to these deeper, structural issues that drive gender harms and to some extent flight, many of the gender harms in exile are specific to the circumstances in which people find themselves living. Refugee camps and settlements often put demands on survival that force women and girls to take considerable risks to their own safety. The well-documented risks taken by those who go to the outskirts of the camp to collect ever diminishing supplies of firewood is one example. Where settlements and camps are located in remote areas, women are vulnerable to sexual violence from armed elements (both government and rebel groups) when leaving the center of the camp. Even within the "safety" of the camp, girls and women are often in danger of being forcibly abducted into rebel groups to be used as soldiers, porters, and/or sex slaves (Okello and Hovil 2007, documenting abduction from camps in northern Uganda).

People uprooted from their homes are extremely vulnerable as a result of the problems that led to the displacement, but especially due to their dependency on outsiders for provisions and assistance. The internally displaced are further at risk because "the abuses they seek to escape are often being committed by the very government that should afford them protection" (Nowrojee 2008, 125). In addition, inadequate services and lack of access to humanitarian assistance can lead women and girls into prostitution.

A word of caution needs to be sounded here, however. It is possible for gender concerns and stereotyping to be attached to specific conflicts as a means to access funding from an international donor community that sees a concern for women as currently fashionable. Indeed, the international community has read its gender obligations as necessitating that it target funds for assistance that has a gender-based dimension. In this environment it is crucial that international actors use reliable data and not allow sensationalism on the part of the media to create truisms about specific conflict situations or to drive funding and program creation.

Furthermore, women and girls are not the only targets of sexual violence in exile. Indeed, the stereotype that sexual violence can only be inflicted on women has had a strong impact on humanitarian workers who fail to see and acknowledge the realities of sexual violence against men and boys. Although there is a slow but growing realization of the realities of sexual violence suffered by boys and men, there has yet to be a significant paradigm shift in the way in which this reality is dealt with on the ground. Instead, male victims remain unsupported, and their suffering remains largely hidden.

These different vulnerabilities can too often be exploited in the context of camp settings, in which access to justice is generally poor. It means that those suffering from gender harms have few, if any, places to turn. In particular, the stigma of rape within a settlement environment—where privacy is often compromised—is an ongoing concern. UNHCR reports situations in which refugee families have begged them to relocate their daughters to another camp after rape because of the stigma on the family—as much out of concern for their own honor as for the well-being of their female relative (Nowrojee 2008). Lack of access to justice within camps is compounded by the fact that refugee or IDP camps and settlements are often perceived and run as if they were isolated islands outside national jurisdiction, particularly in cases where UNHCR or other international actors effectively run the camps in a context of limited national host country capacity (Verdirame and Harrell-Bond 2005). Linked to this is the notion that what takes place inside the camp is irrelevant to wider national processes unless it has a direct bearing on the "outside." As a result, the response to gender-related injustices is often both inadequate and inappropriate.

URBAN-BASED DISPLACEMENT: SPECIFIC CHALLENGES

As stated earlier, refugees and IDPs are seen primarily as a humanitarian problem that demands a humanitarian response. Keeping those who are displaced in camps is a logical development within this paradigm. Yet refugees and IDPs have continually subverted this approach and have voted with their feet for alternative responses. In reality, an estimated 50 percent of all refugees live in urban settings (Thomas et al. 2011), not in camps. In some settings, that percentage is higher.

Despite the launch of UNHCR's urban refugee policy in 2009, the needs of urban-based refugees and IDPs continue to be poorly understood and badly responded to. Of particular relevance to this chapter, while the challenges of being displaced in an urban setting are considerable for everyone, there are a number of gender-specific dynamics that need to be taken into account in urban settings. While many of these gender-specific challenges are similar to those outlined earlier in relation to settlement environments, an urban setting—in which refugees and IDPs often receive no assistance—can be particularly challenging, and gender inequalities that were confronted prior to exile can be exacerbated. Women heads of household are particularly vulnerable to exploitation and victimization in unfamiliar labor markets; they might not have relatives or friends to assist them with child care; and many do not have the skills or language relevant in a new environment.

In the urban setting, displaced men and boys also face problems on the basis of their gender. Beyond being forced to make many of the same adjustments as women, they are more vulnerable to arbitrary arrest and can be targeted by government agents (both host government and those from their country of origin) as a result of the negative associations of men with armed conflict. Burundian refugees in Tanzania were harassed by the host country's authorities, who associated them with rebel groups (IRRI and CSFM 2008). Likewise, Rwandan men living in Uganda who were considered old enough to have participated in the Rwandan genocide in 1994 were allegedly targeted by Rwandan government operatives: the assumption was that, because they have not returned to Rwanda, they must be *génocidaires* (IRRI and RLP 2010). The same feelings of provider inadequacy felt by refugee men in settlements can occur in an urban environment where men are unable to provide for their families.

A better understanding of these gender-specific dynamics within an urban context is important as a means not only to generate a gender-appropriate response to urban-based refugees and IDPs, but also to lead to a more appropriate response to displacement generally. It points to some of the nuances within a context of local integration and strengthens the discussion on local integration as an alternative approach to the settlement structure—one in which empowerment and agency, rather than dependence and lack of opportunity, are the norm.

STATELESSNESS: A PARTICULAR CONCERN

Statelessness, as a subcategory of displacement, is one specific area in which gender can play a role. Many African states, for instance, inherited citizenship laws from European colonizers that discriminated on the basis of gender. Female citizens were not able to pass on their citizenship to their children if the father was not also a citizen and were unable to pass their citizenship to their spouse (Manby 2009). Although considerable progress has been made since the 1960s to amend many of these laws with regard to the inheritance of citizenship, the right of women to pass citizenship to their husbands has proved more elusive. In situations of displacement, where a refugee man marries a woman from the host community, considerable problems can arise, at times leading to the breakup of families (Hovil and Kweka 2008, describing families split when only some were offered Tanzanian citizenship). Positively, significant attention has been brought to this issue through UNHCR's Global Campaign to end Statelessness, launched in 2014, which emphasizes the fact that equitable nationality laws are key to ending statelessness.

The Implications of Gender Harms at the Point of Return

At the point of repatriation, problems relating to gender harms often arise. The point of return can be a moment of extreme economic vulnerability: lack of infrastructure, a wrecked economy, the presence of land mines, and numerous other infrastructural hazards all make the return process fraught. And specific groups face particular challenges. For instance, recovering property lost through displacement can be highly problematic for women heads of household, particularly with regard to land reclamation, which is often dependent on proof of ownership that was held by a now missing male. In patriarchal societies, women are often excluded from owning land, leaving them landless and without livelihoods.

Equally, for those who have suffered sexual violence, returning to an area in which perpetrators are still living is likely to be both painful and dangerous. In many contexts, perpetrators are unlikely to be physically removed, either as a result of (1) amnesties and ex-combatant reintegration programs, or (2) from a broader deficit of justice that has created a culture of impunity and a lack of attention to gendered harms. Impunity can generate enormous fear, as the silence that surrounds unacknowledged crimes can be utterly devastating for returnees. The point of return, without more thoughtful provision of gendered assistance, can thus underscore the marginalization that victims of violence suffer, making them increasingly vulnerable as a result.

Conclusion

This chapter has given an overview and broad critique of some of the key ways in which gender has been understood and misunderstood in situations of displacement. It has explored the generally well-intentioned but often badly misplaced understanding of, and response to, gender dynamics in relation to displacement. It has specifically pointed to the way in which refugees and IDPs have remained caught within a humanitarian paradigm that leaves little room for engagement with some of the deeper political, cultural, and social dynamics associated with exile.

In response to this somewhat stunted understanding of gender, this chapter has also explored ways in which a gendered understanding of displacement in situations of local integration might provide for a better response to gender challenges faced by refugees and IDPs specifically, and may also point to broader possibilities that go beyond the narrow understanding of refugees and IDPs within a humanitarian context. In other words, a gender-sensitive approach to these issues might not only present the opportunity to allow for responses to displacement that are more gender-appropriate, but also point to the possibilities of a paradigm shift in more general responses. In this respect, a gender lens has the potential to precipitate a genuinely transformational response to the broader debate on conflict and displacement.

References

El-Bushra, Judy. 2000. "Gender and Forced Migration: Editorial." *Forced Migration Review* 9: 4–8.

Grabska, Katarzyna. 2011. "Constructing 'Modern Gendered Civilised' Women and Men: Gender-Mainstreaming in Refugee Camps." *Gender and Development* 19, no. 1: 81–93.

Hovil, Lucy. 2012. "The Nexus between Displacement and Transitional Justice: A Gender-Justice Dimension." In *Transitional Justice and Displacement*, edited by Roger Duthie, 329–359. New York: Social Sciences Research Council.

Hovil, Lucy, and Opportuna Kweka. 2008. "Going Home or Staying Home? Ending Displacement for Burundian Refugees in Tanzania." Working Paper, Series on Citizenship and Forced Migration in the Great Lakes Region, International Refugee Rights Initiative and Social Science Research Council, New York.

Hyndman, Jennifer. 1998. "Managing Difference: Gender and Culture in Humanitarian Emergencies." *Gender, Place and Culture* 5, no. 3: 241–260.

Institute of Development Studies (IDS) and UN Women. 2015. *The Effect of Gender Equality Programming on Humanitarian Outcomes*. New York: UN Women.

International Refugee Rights Initiative (IRRI) and the Centre for the Study of Forced Migration (CSFM). 2008. *Going Home or Staying Home? Ending Displacement for Burundian Refugees in Tanzania*. Dar es Salaam and New York: IRRI and CSFM.

International Refugee Rights Initiative and Refugee Law Project. 2010. *A Dangerous Impasse: Rwandan Refugees in Uganda*. New York and Kampala: IRRI and RLP.

Malkki, Liisa. 1995. *Purity and Exile: Violence, Memory, and National Cosmology among Hutu Refugees in Tanzania*. Chicago: University of Chicago Press.

Manby, Bronwen. 2009. *Struggles for Citizenship in Africa*. London: Zed Books.

Nowrojee, Binaifer. 2008. "Sexual Violence, Gender Roles, and Displacement." In *Refugee Rights: Ethics, Advocacy, and Africa*, edited by David Hollenbach, 125–136. Washington, DC: Georgetown University Press.

Okello, Moses Chrispus, and Lucy Hovil. 2007. "Confronting the Reality of Gender-Based Violence in Northern Uganda." *International Journal of Transitional Justice* 1, no. 3: 433–443.

Rosser, Emily. 2007. "Depoliticised Speech and Sexed Visibility: Women, Gender and Sexual Violence in the 1999 Guatemalan Comisión para el Esclarecimiento Histórico Report." *International Journal of Transitional Justice* 1, no. 3: 391–410.

Thomas, Fiona C., Bayard Roberts, Nagendra P. Luitel, Nawaraj Upadhaya, and Wietse A. Tol. 2011. "Resilience of Refugees Displaced in the Developing World: A Qualitative Analysis of Strengths and Struggles of Urban Refugees in Nepal." *Conflict and Health* 5: 20–31.

Turner, Simon. 2000. "Vindicating Masculinity: The Fate of Promoting Gender Equality." *Forced Migration Review* 9: 8–10.

United Nations High Commissioner for Refugees (UNHCR). 1991. *Guidelines on the Protection of Refugee Women.* Geneva: UNHCR.

United Nations High Commissioner for Refugees (UNHCR). 2002. *Guidelines on International Protection: Gender-Related Persecution within the Context of Article 1A(2) of the 1951 Convention and/or Its 1967 Protocol Relating to the Status of Refugees.* UN Doc. HCR/GIP/ 02/01 (May 7).

Verdirame, Guglielmo, and Barbara Harrell-Bond. 2005. *Rights in Exile: Janus-Faced Humanitarianism.* New York: Berghahn Books.

CHAPTER 22

GENDER AND FORMS
OF CONFLICT

The Moral Hazards of Dating the Security Council

VASUKI NESIAH

IN May 1993, the Security Council passed resolution 827, creating the International Criminal Tribunal for the Former Yugoslavia (ICTY).[1] The resolution identified three crimes as catalyst for the establishment of the court: mass killings, ethnic cleansing, and the "massive, organized and systematic detention and rape of women." Rape emerged as a prominent dimension of battlefield atrocities in the former Yugoslavia (see Gaca, Chapter 23 in this volume). Sexual violence in the context of armed conflict was not new; what was new was the attention it garnered from influential Western feminists and human rights advocates, and the impact that feminism and criminal tribunals subsequently had on the accepted application of international humanitarian law (IHL) (Copelon 1995a). Hitching feminism to Security Council agendas brought about a transformation in the place of contemporary feminism in the discourse of global governance, but it also heightened the tensions and contradictions internal to this effort.

This chapter reviews the far-reaching legal and policy stakes inherent in alternative mappings of gender and forms of conflict. It argues that too often International Conflict Feminism (ICF) defines, advocates for, and represents the notion of conflict victims and the landscape of "women, peace, and security" (WPS) in ways that empower globally hegemonic structures and ideas. ICF is used as a shorthand reference to feminist initiatives aimed at strengthening the international law and policy arena's response to women's experience of war through measures that expand recognition and redress for harms suffered, and increased inclusion of women in justice and peace measures addressing contexts of conflict (Nesiah 2012b). The first part of this chapter describes the challenges that ICF launched against the classical IHL regime for not adequately addressing women's experience of conflict and for rendering invisible the gendered experience of conflict. The second part turns the gaze back to interrogate the "conflict maps" of ICF. It describes the achievements of ICF in highlighting sexual violence in conflict, and mapping those dynamics in ways that augment our accounting of the resultant injury. This section also addresses how this focus has made other kinds of gendered conflict dynamics less visible, while "overinvesting" in the victimhood narrative. Further, ICF's focus on contexts of extraordinary forms of conflict has empowered particular institutions (such as the Security Council) and responses (such as humanitarian intervention). From IHL to ICF, the aim of the chapter is to identify and analyze what is privileged and what is marginalized in different taxonomies of conflict, and the implications of a political, constructivist understanding of conflict mapping.

Mapping Forms of Conflict: From International Humanitarian Law to International Conflict Feminism

The international system has generated taxonomies of conflict through international law, the institutional arrangements that structure the global economy, and the dominant political imaginaries of bodies such as the UN Department of Peacekeeping Operations or NGOs focused on human rights, humanitarianism, and peace-building. Approaches to gender become fused into these efforts at categorization with complex and significant impacts (Mackinnon 2006a).[2] I use the metaphor of "mapping" to convey that the process of categorization can be foundational in defining the legal and policy landscape. The international community's engagement on gender and, particularly, the engagements of ICF inhabit this landscape; it is shaped by, and in turn impacts, the boundaries, routes, and topology through which conflict is imagined and categorized, and different legal and policy interventions are triggered. Conflict mapping is a contested, political process with significant stakes for feminism and its engagement with the dominant world order.

International humanitarian law

International humanitarian law is the regulatory regime that defines the rules applicable to different forms of conflict. Framed through a mid-twentieth-century sovereignty lens, the Geneva Conventions are focused primarily on international armed conflict. This preoccupation and, concomitantly, the relative neglect of internal armed conflict have resulted in the IHL framework investing in the international/non-international distinction as a central legal and political anchor for defining forms of conflict. The international/non-international distinction has been challenged from many quarters, including by those interested in integrating the human rights and humanitarian law regimes (Lubell 2007), by those focused on the changing nature of contemporary conflict (Beerli 2015), by those interested in advancing or challenging "counterterrorism" policies (Becker 2006), and by those highlighting the gendered nature of conflict from an ICF perspective (MacKinnon 2006b). The war in the former Yugoslavia catalyzed challenges to the received IHL regime; the wars in Iraq and Afghanistan also have been occasions for revisiting critical IHL precepts.

Within the IHL regime, demarcation of a conflict as being on one or the other side of the international/non-international line has implications for the rights and responsibilities of belligerents and the protections afforded to civilians in the conflict zones (Gardam, Chapter 3 in this volume). IHL also defines roles for the International Committee of the Red Cross (ICRC), neutral states, and other actors. Common Article 2 of the Geneva Conventions defines the scope of international conflict, and Common Article 3 speaks to conflicts that are "not of an international character." The Geneva Conventions define the form of conflict and the relevant rules on the basis of factors that include the actors involved and the duration and intensity of conflict. Not only is the international/non-international distinction a matter of interpretation, the attendant implications are a matter of context. In some cases, civilians or other actors would gain more protection if the distinction was interpreted to enable additional engagement by the international community; yet in other cases, civilians may be better off if the matter were deemed internal, and sovereignty issues were raised to deter international intervention. For instance, the politically charged classification by the Security Council of Iraq and Afghanistan as non-international conflicts (in the case of Iraq, a shift from classification as "international armed conflict" to the post "mission accomplished" moment when the Security Council recognized the new Iraqi government) rendered the status of different IHL rules regarding the treatment of detainees ambiguous. In addition to other consequences, this has left civilians in those countries exposed to legal black holes (Modirzadeh 2010).

The IHL regime for the classification of forms of conflict had different consequences in the context of the war in the former Yugoslavia. The ICTY treated what were (still contested) "embryonic states" as "states" in classifying that conflict as one where the laws of international conflict were applicable. This treatment of a conflict as one that is international rather than internal can itself be a significant step to constituting it as such. Thus the role of international humanitarian law is not merely one of "discovering" the form of conflict, but one of producing particular forms through the reach of its regulatory apparatus.

The Geneva Conventions have laid out rules of war that outline important provisions for the protection of civilians in all forms of conflict, often specifically identifying women and children, and further specifying the prohibition of sexual violence (pertaining to men and women) as a key element of those protections (Sellers 2008). The protection framework highlights women primarily in their role as civilians, in their roles within the family unit, and in their vulnerability to sexual violence (Fourth Geneva Convention, art. 14). Moreover, the Geneva Conventions declare a clear prohibition of rape, but do not describe it as a grave breach. Thus the first three Geneva Conventions urge that "(w)omen shall be treated with all consideration due to their sex" and the Fourth Geneva Convention declares that "women shall be protected from any attack against their honor, in particular against rape, enforced prostitution or any form of indecent assault"; grave breaches are enumerated without reference to rape in the list of these most serious crimes such as "willful killing, torture or inhuman treatment, including biological experiments, willfully causing great suffering or serious injury to body or health, unlawful deportation . . . ," etc. (Fourth Geneva Convention, arts. 27, 147). In provisions detailing humane conditions during incarceration, there was attention to women not only as civilians, but also as combatants, particularly when incarcerated as prisoners of war.

Feminist engagements with IHL have highlighted language regarding violations of honor and approaches to sex that are evocative of, if not embedded in, patriarchal notions of family and nation—Patricia Sellers describes it as "Victorian code language" (Sellers 2008). From the early 1990s on, there has been an effort to "de-Victorianize" IHL, including a reinterpretation of the grave breach "willfully causing great suffering or serious injury to body or health" to include rape. ICF has been pivotal to this effort.

International Conflict Feminism

International Conflict Feminism developed and was consolidated through efforts to bring attention to sexual violence in the wars in the former Yugoslavia and the genocide in Rwanda. ICF pushes for an international law and policy scaffolding for sexual violence that would trigger the highest scrutiny, strongest legal sanction, and most forceful international response, irrespective of the form of conflict that was the context for sexual violence. To this end, ICF highlights and frames sexual violence violations in ways that give it legal weight and recognition across lines of sovereignty and the international/non-international distinction. ICF has included two distinct strategies: (1) a focus on patterns of sexual violence against women as a challenge to both the IHL and international human rights (IHR) frameworks, and (2) a focus on women's human rights (with particular focus on sexual violence) as a legal and policy framework that challenges and complements the IHL framework. Both these approaches to ICF are motivated by overlapping claims about the limitations of IHL; however, they are shaped by different analyses of the gender politics of international law.

In advancing the first strategy, Catherine MacKinnon, Diana Russell (2012), and others use terms such as "femicide" and "genocide" to convey that women are under attack on all fronts, from the bedroom to the battlefield, requiring urgent and concerted attention. MacKinnon argues that the Bosnian rapes should be situated not only in relation to "this particular ethnic war of aggression" but also as continuous "with the gendered war of aggression of everyday life . . . . These rapes are to everyday rapes what the Holocaust was to anti-Semitism. Without everyday anti-Semitism a holocaust is impossible but anyone who has lived through both knows the difference" (MacKinnon 2006a, 183). This is an argument that patterns of gendered violence (not just sovereignty) constitute a (if not *the*) critically relevant context in determining the form of conflict and appropriate response. MacKinnon argues that the field of human rights is premised on treating the male experience of being human as the "universal" ground of the human experience;

thus, for MacKinnon, the received human rights framework is an inadequate entry into understanding gendered patterns of violence.

In contrast, those advancing the second approach are more hopeful about the human rights framework and highlight human rights as the relevant normative and legal context for understanding different forms of violence. To this end, they participate in a broader challenge to IHL that has emerged from the human rights community, which argues for approaching all rights through a notion of universality and core entitlements irrespective of sociopolitical context and individual circumstances. Moreover, while sexual violence emerges as their primary preoccupation, advocates of the second approach are also invested in a broader accounting of human rights violations in conflict contexts and the potential of the human rights framework as the entry point into such contexts. For instance, Sellers (Chapter 16 in this volume) highlights the universalist form of human rights norms as enabling a unified approach with a core set of rules that apply in different contexts of conflict. This approach pushes toward the convergence of international human rights law, international humanitarian law, and international criminal law by focusing on the yield that convergence offers for plugging the holes in the gender justice landscape of IHL (Sellers 2008)—holes that resulted at least partly from how the IHL framework attached different rights and remedies to different forms of conflict, including its investment in the line between internal and international conflicts.

Whether the starting point was the preeminence of gendered patterns of sexual violence, or whether the starting point was the universalist promise of the human rights framework, all strands of ICF's mapping of conflict seek to dissolve the differences between multiple regimes of laws and norms that pertain to different forms of conflict. Thus, while these two approaches are distinct, they yielded mutually reinforcing insights and interventions that broke new and complementary ground for how we map gender and conflict.

International Conflict Feminism's challenge to international humanitarian law

The most significant challenge that ICF brought to IHL's mapping of forms of conflict focused on the two-tiered treatment of sexual violence entailed by IHL's bifurcation of conflict into international and non-international. A victim of a rape that occurred in what was deemed an international conflict was eligible for a different degree of protection than someone suffering the same crime in a conflict classified as non-international. Rape was prohibited under both regimes, but the dual-regime approach continued to be accompanied by divergent state recognition of the customary law applicable for each form of conflict (Sellers 2008).

ICF criticized the IHL conflict maps for ignoring context where it mattered (i.e., the gendered experience of war), while formulaically deferring to context when it didn't matter (i.e., the international/non-international dimension of conflict). On the one hand, ICF insisted that the gendered context of conflict mattered, because "women experienced conflict differently than men; indeed, that conflict exacerbates gendered inequalities and oppressions in ways that brought human rights into abeyance and rendered women 'major victims in these situations'" (Gardam 1998). On the other hand, there was an insistence that particular acts transcended the *form* of conflict; and indeed, that the IHL international/non-international classification led to an underappreciation of the gendered dimension of conflict (of all forms) and the continuities between background structures and ideologies of gendered power relations.

The challenge to bifurcation was also a challenge to the role and relevance of sovereignty in engaging with rape in conflict. In the course of engaging with the ICTY, ICF challenged (with considerable success) IHL's understanding of gender in conflict as involving a sovereignty fetishism that minimized the import of gendered patterns of sexual conflict, or framed them in ways that remained mired in patriarchal constructions of honor and familial roles. From the perspective of ICF, the pre-ICTY IHL maps were part of the problem, not the solution, and the Geneva Conventions offered few resources to challenge the normalization of sexual violence in war. For instance, in an early article on the potential of the ICTY, Rhonda Copelon (1995b) noted that just as rape was rendered invisible within the nation because it was seen as a private matter, it was rendered invisible on the international stage because it was seen as a domestic crime, but not the most serious of war crimes. If the family unit screened rape from visibility in one context, sovereignty offered a parallel screen in the other. In taking sovereignty as the most important determinant of rights and responsibilities, classical IHL also was seen to contribute to a background perception that wartime sexual violence was inevitable, even if it was to be condemned and prohibited.

The developments in the 1990s, from the battlefield of the former Yugoslavia to the courtrooms of The Hague, changed all this. There was a marked trend toward erosion of the international/non-international distinction and what the International Law Association refers to as "growing convergence" in the rules that obtain in both forms of conflict (ILA 2010, 8). The move toward convergence was complemented also by ICF analysis bringing sexual violence into sharper focus by connecting the dots between gendered structural conditions, and the enabling dynamics of sexual violence across these distinctions. ICF maps sought to investigate how conditions of extraordinary violence were facilitated by conditions of ordinary violence and, equally, the long-term consequences that the former will hold for the latter. Relatedly, ICF maps of forms of conflict were sometimes productive in generating an intersectional analysis of those dynamics, and the way gender interacted with ethnicity, race, religion, and other fault lines. Thus ICF facilitated legal and policy responses that went further than IHL in responding to sexual violence, heightening its visibility and pushing for concerted action. Months after the war broke out in the former Yugoslavia, the ICRC's 1992 *Aide-memoire* proposed that the grave breaches provisions of Article 147 of the Fourth Geneva Conventions should be interpreted to include rape (Sellers 2008). With the ICTY established in 1993, feminist groups prodded the court to incorporate the ICF challenge to the received legal architecture of conflict. Thus, in 1998, the ICTY *Celebici* ruling interpreted the language of grave breaches to include rape even if there is no express inclusion of the crime in the grave breaches listed in the Conventions (Delalić 1998). Moreover, with the Rome Statute drafting process taking place, ICF pushed for the ICC to go beyond Article 27 of the Fourth Geneva Convention in its treatment of rape. Finally, ICF also achieved traction in the halls of the United Nations; thus the Security Council WPS resolutions from resolution 1325 (2000) onward were hugely significant in reorienting conflict maps (see Otto, Chapter 8, and Goetz and Jenkins, Chapter 9, in this volume).

REPRESENTATIONS AND CONSEQUENCES: INTERROGATION OF INTERNATIONAL CONFLICT FEMINISM MAPS

The preceding sections highlighted how ICF challenges to IHL conflict mapping catalyzed more robust responses to sexual violence. However, ICF maps are not without costs, and this concluding section will examine these, including the representation of gender and human rights.

Representation of gender in the context of conflict in ICF maps

ICF enters the conversation by shining a light on sexual violence, and highlighting the invisibility of gender in IHL conflict maps. This has had numerous implications and consequences. First, it neglected non-sexual gendered injuries that accompany conflict, such as displacement, loss of livelihood, and the deprivation of political rights. ICF did not attend adequately to the multiple dimensions of gender in conflict contexts and the historically specific analysis that would require consideration of sociopolitical conditions, cultural dynamics, and political economy. Ironically, in focusing on sexual violence to the neglect of other gendered injustices, ICF appears to reflect the very priorities of Victorian morality that feminists had condemned as a feature of the IHL discourse on honor. This preoccupation is shared across ICF, but the dominance of the first strand, described earlier (identified by MacKinnon), has accentuated this focus.

Second, and relatedly, within ICF a focus on gender has been conflated with a focus on women as victims. However, women are not the only victims, and victimhood is not the most applicable register of gendered analysis. Yet, in the international community's engagement with conflict and conflict zones, the category of victim often emerges as one that is *a priori* feminized. The embrace of victimhood as the dominant entry point to gendered analysis has gained sympathy and attention for an ICF agenda on a humanitarian register. Significantly, however, this has taken ICF on a trajectory in tension with feminist challenges to the politics of victimhood as denying agency, and invested in a politics of *ressentiment* that cramps feminisms' political futures (Brown 1993).

The simplification of the categories of victim and perpetrator into binary oppositions and the gendering of that opposition has functioned in ways that have neglected sexual violence against men (see Dolan, Chapter 7, and Theidon, Chapter 11, in this volume). Moreover, there has been inadequate analysis within ICF of the role of masculinity and the impact of gendered dynamics on men. Many of these problems in ICF maps of forms of conflict suggest that ICF, in effect, has translated gender into a species of women's interest group politics, with women's interests translated even more narrowly into a focus on sexual violence.

Third, it has privileged criminalization, with prosecutions serving as the indicator that "gender" (aka sexual violence against women) is taken seriously and is getting the attention it warrants. While criminal justice is one arena for justice struggles, overinvestment in prosecutions and harsh sanctions may prove a poor response to the complex dynamics of conflict, including questions of accountability. In addition to prosecutions, in some cases ICF has turned to other transitional justice responses, including truth commissions and reparations; however, over the last decade, these have also incorporated key elements of the criminal justice field—individualized, legalized, and focused overwhelmingly on justiciable injuries (see Engle, Chapter 10 in this volume).

Fourth, ICF conflict mapping has often approached gender as the organizing cartographic principle that travels across diverse conflict contexts with a discrete set of analytical preoccupations, policy prescriptions, and legal strategies. In effect, mapping conflict on the basis of gender as an independent and overdetermining fault line has neglected the multifaceted nature of conflict, as well as impacts that are not captured by the focus on gender. It has often meant divorcing gender analysis from the analysis of specific historical contexts and relevant structural conditions. This often treats women transnationally as having a shared gender-defined agenda, even when the causes and consequences of particular conflicts may have been better served with attention to issues such as the international political economy of resource wars, and an intersectional focus on gender's intertwining with other fault lines such as class, ethnicity, empire, or other factors.

The assumption of a gender-defined global agenda risks authorizing interventions to "save brown women from brown men," to invoke Gayatri Spivak's memorable phrase for imperial feminism (Spivak 1988, 297). In this context, gendered mappings of forms of conflict can collude with the military, political, and economic landscape of North–South dynamics. The US administration's formulation of a National Action Plan (NAP) on WPS illustrates these concerns. Some could argue that it potentially weaponizes gender and renders it a foreign policy tool for the biggest military power in the world. At the very least, it renders ICF and US foreign policy symbiotic in ways that are at odds with more dissident and anti-imperial traditions of feminism. On December 19, 2011, President Barack Obama signed an Executive Order making the NAP official US policy, requiring that government agencies undertake "a gender responsive approach to its diplomatic, development, and defense-related work in conflict-affected environments"

(Executive Order 13595, 2011). The NAP provides a window into the reach of ICF in shaping the linkages between the policy apparatus of the most powerful countries of the world to the battlegrounds of some the most vulnerable places in the world. The foundation of NAP's sweeping approach was laid by ICF advocacy of Security Council resolution 1820 (2008). While the scope of resolution 1820 is narrower than the US NAP, it points in the same direction in formulating a legal and policy framework for Security Council members to respond to sexual violence; and it identifies rape in the context of conflict as a threat to international peace and security and therefore (in conjunction with other factors) as a potential trigger for Security Council engagement in the countries under its purview.

Finally, to the extent that there has been a focus on gender outside of sexual violence, it has been a stress on the inclusion of women in peace and justice processes. Beyond broad policy statements advocating such inclusion, there has been little attention to the context-specific institutional arrangements that would enable more opportunities for women's political participation. There has been attention to women's participation in international justice processes; however, with a few notable exceptions (Coomaraswamy 2015), the focus has been on numerical equity and neglect of the more substantively significant dimensions of participation, and the ways that may complicate and pluralize our understanding of women's agendas (however, see Bell, Chapter 32 in this volume, who presents a different view). While ICF has done much to reveal the entrenched biases of IHL maps and classical taxonomies of forms of conflict, it has not examined its own biases and will to power with equal rigor.

Representation of human rights in the context of humanitarian crisis in International Conflict Feminism maps

The challenge to received IHL maps through the increased convergence of human rights and humanitarian law was a notable dimension of the post–Cold War international law landscape. In the preceding decades, when human rights discourse experienced a resurgence through its affiliation with Eastern European dissidence (Moyn 2010), it focused primarily on human rights in the everyday, such as civil liberties critical to democratic vitality in the course of ordinary circumstances. However, with the war in the former Yugoslavia and the genocide in Rwanda driving the development of international law in the early 1990s, it was the stage of extraordinary circumstances, of "human rights in the context of humanitarian crises," that dominated the human rights field. ICF has been a co-traveler in this shift in emphasis on human rights in the context of extraordinary violence rather than ordinary violence, and this has had several adverse consequences.

First, it (unintentionally) shifted the preoccupations and priorities of feminist engagements in international law and policy from human rights to the peace and security agenda. In 1979, a decade before the end of the Cold War, the General Assembly adopted the Convention on the Elimination of All Forms of Discrimination Against Women (CEDAW). The central thrust of CEDAW was the establishment of a legal and policy framework for women's rights in the everyday. A decade after the end of the Cold War, in 2000, the Security Council adopted resolution 1325 (2000) on WPS. resolution 1325 aimed at both victimhood and agency, namely, the protection of women in contexts of conflict and their participation in peace processes. The discourse of victimhood gained traction in the WPS resolutions of the early 2000s—perhaps most prominently embodied in resolution 1820 (see Goetz and Jenkins, Chapter 9, and Engle, Chapter 10, in this volume). This moment signals a marked change in emphasis from agency to victimhood, from CEDAW's more multifaceted engagement with women's rights to a predominant focus on women's vulnerability to sexual violence in war.[3] More generally, this shift from a "women's rights" framework to the "peace and security" framework is paradigmatic of the extent to which humanitarian crises emerged as the dominant context for human rights in this period. Today, even CEDAW mechanisms are increasingly focusing on peace and security issues and crisis contexts (see Patten, Chapter 13 in this volume). With the continued privileging of violent conflict, nonviolent social justice struggles do not receive the support and solidarity that other women's rights causes have attracted.

Second, while ICF maps valuably highlighted gaps in IHL maps, they may have disempowered valuable elements of the IHL framework in ways that inadvertently contributed to dynamics that heightened the vulnerability of geopolitically weaker communities. For instance, in the *Dark Side of Convergence*, Naz Modirzadeh (2010) notes that in a context where political authority is unstable and shifting (with no "clear duty bearer who is capable of responding to the rights claims"), a civilian is rendered even more vulnerable if we focus on her as a rights holder and distract from the IHL notion that parties to a conflict have clear obligations to that civilian—particularly when such parties are powerful countries that invoke IHR to evade responsibility. Thus in situations such as Basra, Iraq, post–US intervention we found ourselves more likely to trip over the legal black hole that accompanied the new ambiguity in the convergence landscape. While ICF looked to IHR to fill in the gaps in the IHL regime's treatment of gender, the lack of a clear duty bearer rendered the promise of human rights illusory, while inadvertently handicapping critical focus on IHL protections. Human rights, premised as they were on universal applicability, offered ICF an avenue to overcome the dichotomies and distinctions of international/non-international. However, in underscoring the universality of the response, this ICF approach treated all conflicts as essentially similar, while powerful states who were protagonists to a conflict could foreground IHR discourse to duck IHL obligations. While earlier in the twentieth century it may have seemed that it was non-international conflicts that had weaker protections, today, with increased use of IHR as a shield against accountability, it may well be that civilians are equally—and, in some cases, more—vulnerable in international conflicts.

This problem is rendered even more acute when we consider initiatives such as the US government's NAP described earlier, where IHR is used not only as a shield, but also as a weapon of intervention. NAP encourages deeper, multipronged intervention to protect women's rights in ways that may exacerbate a humanitarian crisis, without enabling accountability for IHL violations by parties to that conflict. For instance, while ICF challenged the deployment of sovereignty to entrench impunity, it also (and here not always inadvertently) legitimated powerful nations' infringements on the sovereignty of weaker nations. Thus it was not that it corroded sovereignty so much as the fact that it had distributive impacts that empowered some sovereigns (such as members of the Security Council) and disempowered others (such as countries deemed to be "in conflict"). This dynamic is not only a product of, but also engenders an alliance between powerful states and the nongovernmental ICF community. For instance, while resolution 1820 may have emerged from the nongovernmental ICF community, it also had strong US support, and the United States is the "penholder" on sexual violence in conflict in the Security Council. Arguably, the US approach marries US foreign policy to a narrow version of IHL while minimizing international human rights; ICF proves remarkably adaptable to this agenda. In 2015 the Security Council passed resolution 2242 and brought these dynamics full circle by focusing on the role of women in counterterrorism efforts as a part of its work implementing the WPS Agenda (see Chowdhury Fink and Davidian, Chapter 12 in this volume).

Finally, and relatedly, a significant feature of humanitarian crisis–focused approaches to human rights is attention to violence—of "putting cruelty first," as Ignatieff (following Judith Shklar) famously described it (Brown 2004). This emphasis on the most brutal violence reflected a narrowing of the human rights gaze to focus on "bare life" (Agamben 1998). This was the universalizable normative rationale for intervention that rendered it attractive to ICF. As Modirzadeh (2010) notes, resolution 1820 has to be read alongside resolution 1373, passed in 2001, which created binding obligations on all states to adopt all international conventions on terrorism and take on a range of counterterrorism measures. As illustrated by resolution 2242, the dynamic that may turn out to be most relevant in the conflict maps that ICF advances is the ways in which these maps converge with those generated by counterterrorism efforts (Satterthwaite and Huckerby 2012). In this same period, the Security Council became especially significant in countries that were labeled "failed" states, or conflicts that were deemed threats to peace and security and therefore warranting Security Council engagement. Sovereignty continues to have weight in ICF maps, but it has a double life—countries deemed to be in conflict, be it internal or international, are treated as if they have abdicated sovereignty, and countries that are part of the Security Council are authorized by ICF to exercise imperial sovereignty—or what Ignatieff describes as a "humanitarian empire." Significantly, from Iraq to Chechnya to Afghanistan, this twinned thrust, abdicated sovereignty and imperial sovereignty, has shielded Security Council member countries from sustained ICF challenge and critique. Thus the ICF map of forms of conflict may further entrench the misdistribution of sovereign powers by empowering members of the Security Council, even as it disempowers sovereignty in "conflict zones."

ICF and its co-travelers empower advocates of the rights of women in conflict. As rights and responsibilities converge, as IHL and IHR converge, "the rights of victims, the rights of those who were unable to enact any rights or even any claim in their name" become a new right to "humanitarian interference" in the name of responsibilities (Rancière 2004, 298). This suggests, then, that even the sovereignty rights of some can be wielded by others in their name. While Rancière may have Kosovo or Iraq in mind when he speaks of invasion, there is value in also highlighting non-military intervention through specific institutional engagements, such as the priority given to the prosecution of sexual violence, or the more multipronged diffusion of WPS-related laws and norms that travel through human rights discourse in manifesting the hegemonic reach of what some commentators have described as "governance feminism" (Halley et al. 2006).

CONCLUSION

The two different dimensions of ICF maps that I have highlighted here—gender and "human rights in humanitarian crisis"—have mutually reinforcing dynamics. The focus on violence has narrowed international feminist work and has neglected dynamics not captured by sexual victimization; similarly, it has reinforced a two-tier approach to human rights that distinguishes between injuries classified as "gross violations" and all other rights. In both areas, there is a trend toward universalist framings of gender dynamics in conflict, a deeper embedding of ICF in the political economy of transnational aid, and, concomitantly, greater centrifugal pressure for local organizations to formulate issues in ways that correspond to international agenda setting.

From IHL to ICF, the dominant approach to mapping forms of conflict has aimed at developing taxonomies that represent conflict and then assessing whether the operative laws and norms reflect the realities of the form of conflict—that is, researching a conflict situation to determine what is going on, and then, depending on how it gets classified, triggering the appropriate legal and policy responses. In contrast, this chapter has examined how different mappings of forms of conflict generate alternative approaches to gender issues. Thus we have described those maps as having a performative or constitutive role that shapes the very conflicts they claim to describe—laying out the boundaries, routes, and topology through which conflict is imagined and acted on.

Many have celebrated ICF efforts as a corrective to patriarchal mappings of the international legal and policy landscape, including the conflict maps of IHL. In contrast, my analysis of the conflict maps of ICF acknowledges the contributions of ICF, but also cautions against that celebration. While launching a compelling challenge of IHL's international/non-international distinction, ICF maps slip into the distinction between ordinary and extraordinary conflict, and empower a distinction between the sovereignty of powerful countries and weaker countries. Without attending adequately to questions of global power, to political complexity and historical specificity, too often ICF has framed the stakes of engagement in contexts of conflict in terms of clear ethical choices of right and wrong, good and evil, innocent victims and vile perpetrators. This illusory clarity emerges from problematically rendering contexts of conflict as political *terra nulles* where ICF can find common cause with institutions such as the Security Council and the agendas of powerful states. I suggest that it was not that sovereignty's significance dissolved when the international/non-international distinctions were challenged, but rather that some sovereigns were rendered more significant than others.

Notes

1. I borrow from the title of Katherine Franke's brilliant article, *Dating the State: The Moral Hazards of Winning Gay Rights.* This chapter benefited enormously from the input of Naz Modirzadeh, my guru in all things IHL related.
2. Consider the significance of categorizing a conflict as "war" versus "genocide" for how we understand sexual violence. Catharine MacKinnon argued for the distinction: "In war, the destructive effects of rape are largely beside the point. In genocide, the destruction is the point" (MacKinnon 2006a). MacKinnon won $745 million dollars in compensatory and punitive damages for a group of Bosnian and Bosnian Croat women and their children by arguing that rape resulting in forced impregnation was an actionable act of genocide, independent of rape as a war crime (Vullo 2001). In contrast, Rhonda Copelon famously expressed concern that this approach did not pay due attention to the gendered dimensions of rape and the ethnic dimensions of genocide (Copelon 1995a). This debate speaks to the stakes (even within ICF) of framing the context of sexual violence in accounting for the injury suffered.
3. Nahla Valji argues that this tilt gets partially corrected with the focus on participation in SCR 2122.

References

Agamben, Giorgio. 1998. *Homo Sacer: Sovereign Power and Bare Life.* Translated by Daniel Heller-Roazen. Stanford, CA: Stanford University Press.

Becker, Tal. 2006. *Terrorism and the State: Rethinking the Rules of State Responsibility.* Oxford: Hart.

Beerli, Christine. 2015. "The Distinction between International and Non-International Armed Conflict: Challenges for IHL?" Keynote address presented at the XXXVIII Round Table on Current Issues of International Humanitarian Law, International Institute for Humanitarian Law, Sanremo, Italy.

Brown, Wendy. 1993. "Wounded Attachments." *Political Theory* 21, no. 3: 390–410.

Brown, Wendy. 2004. "'The Most We Can Hope For . . .': Human Rights and the Politics of Fatalism." *South Atlantic Quarterly* 103, no. 2–3: 451–463.

Coomaraswamy, Radhika. 2015. *Preventing Conflict, Transforming Justice, Securing the Peace: A Global Study on the Implementation of United Nations Security Council Resolution 1325.* New York: UN Women.

Copelon, Rhonda. 1995a. "Gendered War Crimes: Reconceptualizing Rape in Time of War." In *Women's Rights, Human Rights: International Feminist Perspectives,* edited by Julie Peters and Andrea Wolper, 197–214. New York: Routledge.

Copelon, Rhonda. 1995b. "Women and War Crimes." *St. Johns Law Review* 65, no. 1: 61–68.

Executive Order No. 13,595. 2011. 76 Federal Register 80, 205 (December 19).

Gardam, Judith. 1998. "Women, Human Rights and International Humanitarian Law." *International Review of the Red Cross* 324.

Halley, Janet, Prabha Kotiswaran, Hila Shamir, and Chantal Thomas. 2006. "From the International to the Local in Feminist Legal Responses to Rape, Prostitution/Sex Work and Sex Trafficking: Four Studies in Contemporary Governance Feminism." *Harvard Journal of Law and Gender* 29: 335–423.

International Law Association (ILA). 2010. *The Hague Conference: Final Report on the Meaning of Armed Conflict in International Law.* London: ILA.

Lubell, Noam. 2007. "Parallel Application of International Humanitarian Law and International Human Rights Law: An Examination of the Debate." *Israeli Law Review* 40, no. 2: 648–660.

MacKinnon, Catharine A. 2006a. *Are Women Human? And Other International Dialogues.* Cambridge, MA: Harvard University Press.

MacKinnon, Catharine A. 2006b. "Women's September 11th: Rethinking the International Law of Conflict." *Harvard International Law Journal* 47, no. 1: 1–32.

Modirzadeh, Naz K. 2010. "The Dark Sides of Convergence: A Pro-Civilian Critique of the Extraterritorial Application of Human Rights Law in Armed Conflict." *International Law Studies* 86: 349–410.

Moyn, Samuel. 2010. *The Last Utopia: Human Rights in History.* Cambridge, MA: Harvard University Press.

Nesiah, Vasuki. 2009. "The Specter of Violence That Haunts The UDHR: The Turn to Ethics and Expertise." *Maryland Journal Of International Law* 24, no. 1: 135–154.

Nesiah, Vasuki. 2012a. "Uncomfortable Alliances: Women, Peace and Security." In *South Asian Feminisms,* edited by Ania Loomba and Ritty Lukose, 139–161. Durham, NC: Duke University Press.

Nesiah, Vasuki. 2012b. "Feminism as Counter-terrorism: The Seduction of Power." In *Gender, National Security and Counter-Terrorism: Human Rights Perspectives*, edited by Margaret Satterthwaite and Jayne Huckerby, 127–151. New York: Routledge.

Prosecutor   v.   Delalić et al., Case No. IT-96-21-T (Delalić). 1998. Judgment (November 16).

Rancière, Jacques. 2004. "Who Is the Subject of the Rights of Man?" *South Atlantic Quarterly* 103, no. 2–3: 297–310.

Russell, Diana. 2012. "Femicide Is a Lethal Hate Crime against Women." *50 Million Missing.* http://genderbytes.wordpress.com/2012/06/03/diana-russell-femicide-is-a-lethal-hate-crime-against-women/.

Satterthwaite, Margaret, and Jayne Huckerby, eds. 2012. *Gender, National Security and Counter-Terrorism: Human Rights Perspectives.* New York: Routledge.

Sellers, Patricia. 2008. *The Prosecution of Sexual Violence in Conflict: The Importance of Human Rights as Means of Interpretation.* Geneva: OHCHR.

Spivak, Gayatri. 1988. "Can the Subaltern Speak?" In *Marxism and the Interpretation of Culture*, edited by Cary Nelson and Lawrence Grossberg, 271–316. Urbana: University of Illinois Press.

Vullo, Maria T. 2001. "Prosecuting Genocide." *Chicago Journal of International Law* 2, no. 2: 495–501.

PART IV

··

CONFLICT AND POST-CONFLICT SPACE

··

CHAPTER 23

THE MARTIAL RAPE OF GIRLS AND WOMEN IN ANTIQUITY AND MODERNITY

KATHY L. GACA

How does the martial rape of women and girls in warfare fit into a historical under-standing of warfare in and since the societies of the ancient Mediterranean and nearby regions? In ancient warfare known as "ravaging a targeted populace" (Gaca 2015), rape and the coercive power relations pervading this aggression are best understood as mar-tial, to name these war customs now in retrospect for the war god Mars. Along with other diverse gods presented as approving, supporting, and giving the orders to carry out ravaging warfare in this region, Mars and his Greek counterpart Ares were believed to promote and authorize ravaging warfare, including "rapes and other uses of penetra-tive force" and "the corrupting and killing of women."[1] Ravaging forces and mobs are referred to in the following as ethno-religious groups, for historically their sense of eth-nic identity is shaped by being devoted to one or more such gods.

By my argument, martial or ravaging rape, a heterosexual kind of penetrative sexual assault,[2] is fundamental to the ravaging warfare that has afflicted the region of diverse Mediterranean cultures since antiquity. Further, martial rape later spread more globally through ravaging expeditions and colonizing occupations, such as the one that went eastward to what is now Afghanistan and India under Alexander the Great in the turn toward the Hellenistic period (Burstein 2012), and the later one that went westward across the Atlantic starting under Columbus in 1492. While I sketch trans-Atlantic rav-aging, my focus here is on the Mediterranean, in order to present continuities between ravaging warfare and martial rape from antiquity to the end of the Byzantine Empire to the modern Balkans and Darfur.

As explained in the following sections, first, specific patterns of sex and age inform the methods or approaches of ravaging warfare since antiquity. These patterns show that the practice was organized purposeful violence, and this is key to disclosing the cen-trality of martial rape therein. Second, ravaging warfare and its martial ethos should be distinguished from other kinds of warfare that arose in antiquity, largely in a struggle against war ravaging. Third, although warfare has been theorized since Clausewitz as an exercise in lethal force (Gaca 2011a), this provides only a partial story of ravaging warfare. War ravaging, though often described simply as massacre, also has violently coercive living functions and motives, such as when martial rape is an exercise to enslave captive girls and young women en masse and induce them to undergo forced impregnation and compulsory procreation. One of the main goals in forcibly impregnating rape is to augment the martial ethno-religious identity, numbers, and strength of the ravaging aggressors at the expense of the social identities and communities to which the ravaged girls and women used to belong. As argued in this chapter, this reproductive agenda of martial rape is traceable as a persistent and important continuity in ravaging warfare from ancient and Byzantine Greece to the Bosnian conflict in the early 1990s.

Ravaging Warfare since Antiquity and Its Organized Violence

Despite ancient poetic imagery that likens ravaging warfare to indiscriminate storms, ravaging is highly discriminate in who is killed or injured alive. In a martial tradition since antiquity, ravaging is an organized and purposeful aggression that culminates in the martial rape and enslavement of young female war-captives.

In ancient Mediterranean accounts, ravaging is explained in detail mainly in terms of the two approaches to killing the males of the targeted people. One approach is to kill the fighting-age males, that is, the males old enough to have pubic hair, conventionally fourteen years old, up to sixty years of age (Livy 26.25.11), described as killing males "from adolescence onward" (*hêbêdon*). This is the characteristic treatment of males in ravaging, named in ancient Greek primarily for the "andrapodizing" or "manhandling" of the slain men's women and children (Gaca 2011b). For example, when Athenian forces ravaged Melos in 415 BCE, during the Peloponnesian War, "they killed the men old enough to have pubic hair (*hêbôntas*) that they caught and they subjected the women and children to manhandling enslavement" (Thucyd. 5.116.4; Gaca 2010).

The other approach to killing males in war ravaging is known as "killing all the males," and it is geared toward terminating an entire male lineage from infancy (Gaca 2015, 281–283). For instance, when a ravaging Celtic contingent attacked the Callian Greeks of Aetolia in 279 BCE, "[t]hey cut down the entire male lineage (*genos pan to arsen*); both old men and little ones nursing at their mothers' breasts alike were slaughtered." The Celtic forces then gang raped and killed, or raped and enslaved, the women and girls among the Callians (Pausanias 10.22.3–4). Similarly, the Germanic Vindelici in their ravaging in northern Italy "did not kill only men in adolescence and older." Rather, "they went as far as killing male infants" (Strabo 4.6.8).

Testimonials from early twenty-first-century Darfur verify the persistence of ravaging with the aim of killing the entire male lineage. In Darfur, Arab Muslim militiamen known as the *janjaweed* were assigned to kill all the males among non-Muslim Nuba Africans, especially male infants. As stated by a Nuba man in his mid-thirties, who had eluded capture while trying to keep his extended family safe in hiding, "[t]he *janjaweed* would halt women with babies and force the women to show whether their children were boys or girls. And when the enemy caught a man, the man was killed. And if they caught a woman and she had a child, if the baby was a boy, they would kill him . . . . If the baby was a girl, they would leave them. The same for little girls" (Totten and Bartrop 2009, 219). War ravaging therefore is lethal force against the males of targeted people, whether the killing is directed at the entire male lineage or its fighting-age members.

Though often given scant notice, the corresponding female-targeting dimension of rape in ravaging warfare is of critical import, both historically and for making the aims of such warfare intelligible. Like war ravaging as a whole, martial rape is a directed aggression in compliance with top-down orders from superiors and with peer-pressure agreements in the ranks.[3] This rape is geared toward being lethal or enslaving. There is a notable emphasis on lethal rape and other ways of killing the mothers and maternal figures when the male killing is directed at the entire targeted male lineage, as in the Celtic ravaging of the Callian Greeks (cf. Midian and Jabesh-gilead, Num 31:1–54, Judg 21:6–12). To subject mothers and their young daughters to enslaving rather than lethal rape is more the norm in ravaging directed at killing fighting-age males and subjecting the women and children to manhandling enslavement, such as at Melos (cf. Abydos, Polyb. 16.32.6). Readers in antiquity readily understood, without needing to be told, that ravaging women and girls involved raping them, for this was implied by either approach to systematic male killing. As stated by the Greek historian Diodorus about an incident of fighting-age male massacre, "aggressors with the audacity by day to slaughter law-abiding men on the roads and in the marketplace do not need someone who will point out what they did by night privately in the men's houses." Ancient readers knew "how the men conducted themselves toward the virgin-aged girls deprived of their fathers and toward women bereft of those who could rescue them, now that the girls and women had fallen under the autocratic power of their bitter enemies" (Diod. *Sic.* 19.8.4–5). The Greek military historian Polybius further supports this observation (9.39.2, 16.32.4).

Often enough, ancient sources from the *Iliad* onward are explicit about martial rape, so modern readers need not guess about its customs. Since antiquity, martial rape has meant aggravated and penetrative sexual assault against war-captive women and girls who are held under death threats and can be killed with impunity if they resist or for other reasons are judged not deserving to live (Gaca 2016). For an explicit account, when the Greek city Pellene was taken by force and ravaged in around 600 BCE, "the women and daughters" were sexually assaulted en masse "as spear-taken war captives" by Greek forces. The mass rape of the girls and women of Pellene is described as subjecting them to "the total whore treatment" (Gaca 2012, 95–96). In modern Darfur, similarly, the Arab Muslim militiamen left baby girls and little girls with their mothers, but, the Nuba man later adds, "if the girls were thirteen, fourteen, fifteen or older, they often took them away" and serially raped and injured the girls before their mothers were able to rescue them. Regarding these girls, "some never came back and we still don't know what happened to them" (Totten and Bartrop 2009, 221).

Martial rape is integral to ravaging, done in compliance with top-down orders and peer-pressure agreements, with serious retaliation for soldiers who disobey. In the *Iliad*, Nestor threatens the Greek forces with death if they try to go home before conquering Troy and raping Trojan women (*Il.* 2.354–359). Similarly, in the ravaging 1913 Balkan War, a Greek soldier was almost killed by his comrades when he protested against six of them serially raping a young Bulgarian girl. His sergeant ordered him to stop interfering and moved him to another assignment (Carnegie 1993, 306). Consequently, martial rape since antiquity has not been random, anarchic, or opportunistic. It is built into, and central to, the organized violence of war ravaging.

Populace-ravaging warfare is a two-stage aggression: first, the "big slaughter," and then the pivotal but hitherto low-profile "big captivity" (Gaca 2014, 327; e.g., Theoph., *Chron.* 257), in which the girls and women who are not killed are enslaved.[4] To grasp the magnitude of ravaging captivity and enslavement, fighting-age males in antiquity numbered about 25 percent of a people. The rest were the women, children, and elders in the "non-fighting multitude" (*imbellis multitudo*, Livy 7.27.8, 9.15.5).[5] To follow military history research conventions and identify ancient warfare with its adult-male battles and massacres ignores what happens to the other 75 percent (e.g., Campbell and Trifle 2013; Carlton 1994; Sabin et al. 2007). By paying attention to the ravaging rape of the girls and women, we start correcting this imbalance toward better understanding the gendered aims and persistence of ravaging warfare in our social history.

Martial rape warfare is of two kinds. The first is unrestricted lethal gang rape, or other sadistic and severely injurious rape. This has been the historical norm against women of the targeted people not wanted alive or actively wanted dead, mainly the grown, mature, and resistant ones. Lethal rape functions in part as interrogative torture, such as Greek forces in the 1913 Balkan War coercing locals to inform them which Bulgarian households had girls and young women, and then gang raping the girls' mothers in an effort to force them to disclose where they had hidden their daughters. Similarly, in the Bulgarian village of Radovitch, female and male elders did their best to make "a vigorous intervention" to have "the young women and girls to run away and hide in the forest" to stop the ravaging forces from commandeering their female children. Knowing the likely tortures in store for themselves, the elders called out to the girls, "If the Serbians spare us, we will let you know, but . . . save yourselves and let God's will be done to us." Lethal gang rape is not the only way to torment and kill women in war ravaging, but it is a signature way to do so.[6]

The second kind is the more survivable single-assailant or limited serial rape. This has been the historical norm against girls and young women wanted alive, such as the ones fleeing Radovitch. Young female captives "make men rich" (App. *Hann.* 244) among the forces, and among additional recipients on the forces' side, through the compulsory procreation of exploitable offspring and the coerced performance of other non-sexual and sexual labors, including prostitution (Gaca 2014, 306–307; 2015, 281–291). This second kind of rape is life threatening, too. It includes beatings, death threats, and bludgeoning with weapons to induce and reinforce submission, a hazing known in the *Iliad* as "taking the day of freedom from women" (Hom., *Il.*

20.191–194; Gaca 2008, 159; 2014, 304). In antiquity, once girls and women were turned into enslaved martial drudges, their talents and capabilities to be empowered mothers and constructive social agents were revoked, along with their civil status and freedom. A lurid domination focused strictly on pleasing and pleasuring the men informs enslaving rape and contributes to the development of forced prostitution in antiquity.[7] These forms of aggravated and enslaving or lethal sexual assault against the girls and women constitute martial rape and are the second fundamental component of ravaging warfare.

RAVAGING AND ITS HISTORICAL PLACE IN WARFARE

Ravaging is historically one form of warfare, albeit prevalent in and since the ancient Mediterranean. Not all armies practiced ravaging warfare or committed martial rape when they took up arms, just as today not all armies practice such warfare. In antiquity, many soldiers fought to defend their peoples and neighboring allies from being ravaged. As ancient defense policy, children and mothers were the ones "for whom wars are customarily taken up" to protect them from martial aggressors (Justin 26.2.3; Synes. *Calv. encomium.* 21.9–11). Defenders prided themselves on being modest but effective and smart (Aesch., *Sept.* 447–452, 473–480). By contrast, martial aggressors were braggart soldiers, crowing about being killers of great renown and becoming rich and powerful in enslaved female war captives (*PMG* 26; Alciphron, *Epist.* 2.34.1–3).

Although much of ravaging in the ancient Mediterranean was an interchange of wars among peoples already caught up in martial power and its ravaging customs, this aggression and its power relations were transferable to new frontiers in martial colonizing, notably across the Atlantic starting under Columbus. Against the Arawak Taino on Hispaniola, "[t]wo principal customs have been employed by the Spaniards in extirpating the peoples. After having slain all the native-born lords and adult males, it is the Spaniards' custom in their wars to allow only young boys and females to live, and they oppress them with bondage" (de las Casas 2006, 12). This is ravaging as a conquistador export, the direct transfer of ravaging in the andrapodizing manner from the Mediterranean to the New World. This is the same aggression as that used by Roman forces under Licinius Lucullus when they ravaged a Celtiberian people of Spain known as the Caucaei in 151 BCE, slaying about 20,000 fighting-age males to oppress the more numerous women and children with enslavement (App., *Hisp.* 217–221). The transfer of ravaging colonization to the New World and one of its known ancient antecedents in Spain must suffice here to indicate that martial rape derives from ancient Mediterranean ravaging warfare; its modern global reach is well elucidated by de Brouwer (2005).

COMPULSORY PROCREATION FOR MARTIAL ETHNO-RELIGIOUS DOMINANCE

Ravaging historically functions to co-opt and redirect the targeted people's reproductive capacity and childrearing customs to serve the peoples exerting martial ethno-religious hegemony over them. Further, the regular forces and irregular mobs trained to conduct war ravaging since antiquity might seem like no-name rabble now, but they did not see themselves that way. These men likewise had strong martial ethno-religious identities, such as the Ionian Greeks in the early Iron Age and the Gallic Aegosagae in the Hellenistic period (Polyb. 5.78.1–4). Among these groups, to ravage targeted peoples on their superiors' command and to rape and impregnate their enslaved girls and young women functioned as collective one-upmanship to augment their ethno-religious identity and strength in population at the expense of their adversaries and their social identities.

For example, armed forces of Athenian men, an ethno-religious branch of the Ionian Greeks, carried out precisely this scoring against enemies when they ravaged the Carian city of Miletus in the early Iron Age. They killed the boys and men of all ages and colonized the city, which then became very prominent as Ionian Greek Miletus. In addition to killing all the Carian males they captured, the Athenian forces killed both parents, mothers and fathers, of the unmarried young Carian girls they seized for spear-conquest enslavement. The Athenian forces then used the girls as vessels for their Ionian Greek brand of ethno-religious reproduction (Hdt. 1.146.2–3). In so doing, the Athenians forcibly converted Miletus from the Carian city it used to be (Hom., *Il.* 2.867–875) to the Greek city they literally raped it into becoming, for the Athenian men brought no women with them on this colonizing expedition. Every first-generation Ionian Greek girl and boy born in Miletus came from raping Carian girls, whose families and people used to consider the city their homeland.

Several centuries later, the Persian king Darius ravaged his subject city of Greek Miletus in 494 BCE as punishment for instigating the Ionian Greek rebellion against him. The ravaging method he used was andrapodizing. His forces killed the fighting-age Milesian Greek males and enslaved the women and children, the women and girls partly as coerced procreative dispensers to strengthen the progeny of the Athenians' Persian enemies. The Athenians were grief-stricken and outraged (Hdt. 6.21.2), as though Miletus were their peaceably settled Ionian Greek daughter city.

The Greek tragedian Euripides understood this martial ethno-religious agenda of enslaving martial rape for the compulsory procreation of triumphal enemy groups. In 415 BCE, he presented onstage the classical Athenian view that just as in Miletus, the same sort of forced Hellenizing aim was at work when Greek forces ravaged Troy. The Greek forces wanted to seize the young women of Troy as their crown of victory and prosperity (*neanidôn stephanos*, Eur., *Troj. Wom.* 564–567). Their aim was to force them to bear and rear offspring to strengthen the Greeks and bring grief to remnant Trojans, that is, to subject the female captives to Hellenizing rape and deplete the girls' capacity to regenerate a Trojan populace and identity.

Since antiquity, ravaging martial projects of targeted male massacre, enslaving martial rape, and forced impregnation of the girls and young women have persisted with striking overtones of ethno-religious rivalry, as disclosed in late twentieth-century Bosnia. The andrapodizing approach characterized much of the martial Serbian or "Chetnik" ravaging under way by 1992 against the Bosnian Muslim peoples. As described by Emina, a young Bosnian Muslim woman, "Chetniks entered our village with their tanks and armored cars . . . . They killed men between the ages of fourteen and sixty right off"[8] (Stiglmayer 1994, 97; cf. Commission of Experts 1994, para. 230(i)). The killing of the entire male lineage was on display, however, during the massacre at Srebrenica in July 1995, a killing of men and boys alike. "Executed systematically, . . . three generations of Bosniak [i.e., Bosnian Muslim] men and boys disappeared within a matter of a week" (Subasic 2011, 134). From the martial Serbian viewpoint, the Bosnian Muslims were a still lingering and unwanted Turkish Muslim occupation—the men, women, and children alike—not fellow neighbors and citizens in a diverse civil society.

The Serbian martial forces sought to bring "death to all Turkish sperm" in what the ancients would call a "big slaughter" of the Bosnian Muslim males (Stiglmayer 1994, 109; Commission of Experts 1994, paras. 195–209, 230(i)). Once that semen was killed off along with the men, then it was time for the ravaging rapes of the girls and young women seized in the big captivity. Serbian forces saw it as their required mandate to sow "the seeds of Serbs in Bosnia," as one fighter declared to UN investigators in the town of Zvornik (Commission of Experts 1994, para. 261, cf. n625). Enslaving martial rapes were the seed-sowing kind to inflict forced impregnation on Bosnian Muslim female captives to gain boys and girls for the greater development of martial Serbia. The Bosnian Muslim girls and women subjected to enslaving rape for these ends were mainly child-bearing age, between twelve and thirty-five years old, generally closer to twelve, but also younger still (Commission of Experts 1994, paras. 150, 113, 115, 221).

The Serbian or Chetnik forces carried out their reproductive program in braggart soldier fashion, with declarations of purposeful ethno-religious domination over many formerly Bosnian Muslim towns and counties. Bosnian Muslim women and girls who were attacked and raped are the sources of the following testimonies. In Doboj, numerous martial rapes conducted by Serb forces were "to make Chetnik babies" (Commission of Experts 1994, para. 94, cf. nn175–176). In Foca and Kalinovik counties, twelve women abducted and raped were told, "Now you are going to have our children. You are going to have our little Chetniks" (paras. 110, 123). In Tesanj, twenty-five women were serially raped in a nearby forest. A Serbian guard told one of the women, "Now you will have Serbian babies for the rest of your life" (para. 223). Likewise, in Teslic, captive young women "were raped in front of each other and were told that they would bear Serbian children" (para. 226). These plans were reinforced by incarcerating the women and girls. In Grbavica, a fifteen-year-old girl and twenty other girls were kept by Serb forces in a small room and were raped until they were impregnated (para. 208). So too in Sokolac, local Serbs kept thirteen young women locked up and raped them, most of them eighteen years old or younger, but one of them only six, "saying they intended to have Muslim women give birth to Chetniks" (para. 221, cf. n526). In Kotor Varos, a number of the women were "impregnated and detained until it was not possible to obtain abortions" (para. 149). As a related ritual in this ethno-religious takeover and compulsory procreation of Chetniks or Serbs, a number of the girls and women were forced to renounce Islam and adopt Serbian Orthodox Christianity. As in antiquity, aggravated battery was standard practice in these rape ordeals. To have barracks for this compulsory procreation en masse, Serbian forces turned civil buildings, such as schools and hotels, into rape-camp detention sites.[9] These repurposed buildings echoed the debasing of the women and girls as agents of Bosnian civil society, such as having been teachers and students at the schools before their martial shutdown.

In addition, numerous Bosnian Muslim girls and young women were subjected to forced prostitution, and one was presented naked and called a "Chetnik whore" (Commission of Experts 1994, para. 164, cf. n334). This practice, soon after the killings, was not yet a mercantile sex trade, but still was focused on reproducing Chetniks. In the Vilina Vlas Hotel of Visegrad, known for its forced prostitution, "[t]he Chetniks were there with the girls. There was nothing they didn't do with them, you only had to stop and look. In every room there were women, men, screams, noise, songs, everything. They said they were bringing the women there to bear Chetnik kids . . . 'girls and women who'll carry our babies, babies for the Chetniks,'" as stated by the young woman Hasiba, who was incarcerated and repeatedly raped there (Stiglmayer 1994, 130). Just as Athenian forces in antiquity killed the males of all ages in Carian Miletus to rape a martial Greek Miletus into colonized existence, so too, in living memory, Serbian martial forces massacred fighting-age Bosnian Muslim males, and males of all ages in Srebrenica, to rape and reproduce a greater martial Serbia. The Athenian colonizers raped and used Carian girls as their enslaved vehicles for their martial procreative purposes. The martial Serbian forces raped and used Bosnian Muslim girls and young women for their like-minded reproductive agenda.

Conclusion

Martial rape in war ravaging shows persistent continuities from the ancient Mediterranean to the modern day. The ancient evidence about ravaging warfare makes the recent and modern testimonials about male massacre and martial rape clearer and more meaningful by situating them in their historical tradition. Conversely, the modern testimonials make massacre, martial rape, and the experience of female enslavement much better known from the perspective of girls, women, and male relatives who have lived to tell about being ravaged. Taken together, these accounts bear out that the enslaving martial rape of war-captive girls and young women has been a foundational purpose of ravaging warfare in conflicts to assert martial ethno-religious hegemony over an extensive time period—a time long antedating the early medieval rise of Islam and its martial ravaging expressions. As in the former Yugoslavia, the commandeering of girls and young women of targeted ethno-religious groups is at the epicenter of such warfare, for ravaging is focused on gaining them from conquered peoples and forcibly insemi-nating them as culturally effaced fertile bodies to build up their own martially run social groups and ethno-religious profiles. Through this aggression, society is reprocessed into bunkered and hostile groups of bellicose, martially observant, adult males with disem-powered ancillary groups of women and children.

By 1453 CE, the end of the Byzantine Roman Empire, the early Iron Age practice of ravaging targeted peoples to use their girls and young women as spear-taken slave con-cubines or wives had become an established custom in martial Muslim society (Chalc. 64d). This is the practice ISIS has recently reinstated by andrapodizing the Yazidi peo-ple of Iraq as syncretistic rebels. In 2014, news headlines read that ISIS "executed Yazidi men and kept the dead men's wives for unmarried jihadi fighters."[10] The next year, UN investigators found this practice systematic. However, just as in Miletus and Bosnia, the acquisitive preference of ISIS is not for the grown wives but for the young unmar-ried daughters of the Yazidi, girls as young as eleven. ISIS operatives openly call them "slaves" (*sabaya*). As acts of martial religious devotion, these agents of martial Islam have commandeered Yazidi girls and young women for systematic rape, procreation, and other exploitation. These enslaved girls are modern counterparts to the countless young women and girls ravaged by martial ethno-religious bands and armies since antiquity. The aggressors keep some of their female captives to forcibly produce their ethno-religious numbers and to serve the men with prestige in their hierarchies, and they trade the rest on a slave market developed and supplied by war ravaging (Gaca 2011b, 2015).

The prevalent idea that warfare, properly speaking, is an exercise of lethal force, what-ever its ulterior motives (e.g., Walzer 2006; Ferguson in de Souza 2008, 15), is too narrow to account for ravaging warfare. It focuses mainly on the male killing and defines that as warfare, leaving out the ravaging of girls and women. In addition to lethal rape, ravaging rape continues as an enslaving force against the girls and young women wanted alive to exert martial ethno-religious supremacy over them and their wombs in the destruction of their ravaged peoples and cultural heritage. This makes ravaging warfare as ruthless a compulsory vital force as it is a lethal force.

In studies on martial rape in modernity, the present consensus is that rape is an elec-tive instrumental weapon in wartime, utilized in some but not all modern wars, such as sexual terrorism to drive out a targeted people, or ruthless recreation for soldiers through forced prostitution (Branche and Virgili 2012). Yet martial rape is far more than simply a weapon or combat stress release. As shown by its forced reproductive agendas, martial rape is central to ravaging warfare and shapes the gendered ineq-uities of power and violence in martially run ethno-religious culture and society, as first developed in the ancient Mediterranean and spreading out in colonizing vectors from there.

Notes

1. Vett. Val., *Anthology* 3. Greek and Roman works are cited by the abbreviation list in the *Oxford Classical Dictionary*, 4th edition (2012).
2. As distinct from enslaving aggression against ravaged boys when kept alive, see Gaca (2015), 283.
3. Hom., *Il.* 2.354–359, 3.297–301, 6.55–60; cf. Gaca (2015), 306; Gaca (2008), 149; Deut 20:10–15; Paus. 10.22.2–4; App., *Pun.* 244.
4. Procop., *Goth.* 6.21.38–40; Gaca (2014), 309; Gaca (2012), 93–106; Gaca (2008), 149, 158, 167.
5. The percentages are from the Helvetii and allied census tablets in 58 BCE and the estimates of Persians and Armenians ravaged by Roman forces near Amida in 504 CE (Caesar *BG* 1.29.1–3; Joshua Stylites, *Chronicle* 75).
6. Hdt. 8.33, 4.202.1; Isocr., *epist. Archid.* 9.10; Diod. *Sic.* 33.14.1–5; Paus. 10.22.2–4; Tac., *Hist.* 3.33; Stiglmayer (1994), 141.
7. Dio Chrys. 7.132–36; ps.-Dem. 59.18–19; Sen., *Controv.* 1.2.3; Gaca (2014), 326; Gaca (2015), 280, 290–291.
8. So too, ISIS executing Yazidi males over fourteen years old (Nick Cumming-Bruce, "United Nations Investigators Accuse ISIS of Genocide over Attacks on Yazidis," *New York Times*, March 19, 2015). As with Emina, the names of most of the Bosnian Muslim witnesses are witness-protecting pseudonyms—a moral necessity, though not the preferred standard for historical research, and problematic for legal discovery (see Wing 1994; Kent 1997, 1107–1108, on Stiglmayer 1994 as a reliable source for Bosnian Muslim testimonials).
9. On renouncing Islam, see Stiglmayer (1994), 118, 128. On battery, see Gaca (2008), 158n35; Gaca (2012), 101–103. On compulsory procreation barracks, see Commission of Experts (1994), paras. 92, 114–15, 123, 164, 245; Searles and Berger (1995), 174–175.
10. See Tim Arango, "Jihadists Rout Kurds in North and Seize Iraqi Dam," *New York Times*, August 8, 2014, A1; Nick Cumming-Bruce, "United Nations Investigators Accuse ISIS of Genocide over Attacks on Yazidis," *New York Times*, March 20, 2015, A7; Rukmini Callimachi, "ISIS Enshrines a Theology of Rape, *New York Times*, August 14, 2015, A12.

References

Branche, Raphäelle, and Fabrice Virgili, eds. 2012. *Rape in Wartime*. New York: Palgrave Macmillan.

Burstein, Stanley M. 2012. "Whence the Women? The Origin of the Bactrian Greeks." *Ancient West and East* 11: 97–104.

Campbell, Brian, and Lawrence A. Tritle, eds. 2013. *The Oxford Handbook of Warfare in the Classical World*. New York: Oxford University Press.

Carlton, Eric. 1994. *Massacres: An Historical Perspective*. Brookfield, VT: Ashgate.

Carnegie Endowment for International Peace. 1993. *The Other Balkan Wars: A 1913 Carnegie Endowment Inquiry in Retrospect*. Washington, DC: Carnegie Endowment for International Peace.

Commission of Experts Established Pursuant to Security Council Resolution 780. 1994. *Final Report: Annex IX—Rape and Sexual Assault*. UN Doc. S/1994/674/Annex IX, Add.2 (Vol. V) (December 28).

de Brouwer, Anne-Marie L. M. 2005. *Supranational Criminal Prosecution of Sexual Violence: The ICC and the Practice of the ICTY and the ICTR.* Antwerp: Intersentia.

de las Casas, Bartolomé. 2006. *Brevísima relación de la destrucción de las Indias.* Edited by Jean-Paul Duviols. Buenos Aires: Stockcero.

de Souza, Philip, ed. 2008. *The Ancient World at War: A Global History.* London: Thames and Hudson.

Gaca, Kathy L. 2008. "Reinterpreting the Homeric Simile of *Iliad* 16.7–11: The Girl and Her Mother in Ancient Greek Warfare." *American Journal of Philology* 129, no 2: 145–171.

Gaca, Kathy L. 2010. "The Andrapodizing of War Captives in Greek Historical Memory." *Transactions of the American Philological Association* 140, no. 1: 117–161.

Gaca, Kathy L. 2011a. "Girls, Women, and the Significance of Sexual Violence in Ancient Warfare." In *Sexual Violence in Conflict Zones*, edited by Elizabeth D. Heineman, 73–88. Philadelphia: University of Pennsylvania Press.

Gaca, Kathy L. 2011b. "Manhandled and 'Kicked Around': Reinterpreting the Etymology and Symbolism of *andrapoda*." *Indogermanische Forschungen* 116: 110–146.

Gaca, Kathy L. 2012. "Telling the Girls from the Boys and Children: Interpreting *paides* in the Sexual Violence of Populace-Ravaging Ancient Warfare." *Illinois Classical Studies* 35–36: 85–109.

Gaca, Kathy L. 2014. "Martial Rape, Pulsating Fear, and the Sexual Maltreatment of Girls (*paides*), Virgins (*parthenoi*), and Women (*gunaikes*) in Antiquity." *American Journal of Philology* 135: 303–357.

Gaca, Kathy L. 2015. "Ancient Warfare and the Ravaging Martial Rape of Girls and Women: Evidence from Homeric Epic and Greek Drama." In *Sex in Antiquity: Exploring Gender and Sexuality in the Ancient World,* edited by Mark Masterson, Nancy Sorkin Rabinowitz, and James Robson, 278–297. New York: Routledge.

Gaca, Kathy L. 2016 "Rape and Tyranny in Martial Societies." In *Women in Antiquity: Real Women across the Ancient World*, edited by Stephanie Budin and Jean Macintosh Turfa, 1041–1056. New York: Routledge.

Kent, Sarah A. 1997. "Writing the Yugoslav Wars: English-Language Books on Bosnia (1992–1996) and the Challenges of Analyzing Contemporary History." *The American Historical Review* 102, no. 4: 1085–1114.

Sabin, Philip, Hans van Wees, and Michael Whitby, eds. 2007. *The Cambridge History of Greek and Roman Warfare.* Cambridge: Cambridge University Press.

Searles, Patricia, and Ronald J. Berger. 1995. *Rape and Society: Readings on the Problem of Sexual Assault.* Boulder, Colorado: Westview Press.

Stiglmayer, Alexandra. 1994. *Mass Rape: The War against Women in Bosnia-Herzegovina*, trans. Marion Faber. Lincoln: University of Nebraska Press.

Subasic, Munira. 2011. "Turning Darkness into Light: The Quest for Justice by Srebrenica's Mothers." In *Assessing the Legacy of the ICTY*, edited by Richard H. Steinberg, 133–138. Boston: Brill | Nijhoff.

Totten, Samuel, and Paul R. Bartrop, eds. 2009. *The Genocide Studies Reader.* New York: Routledge.

Walzer, Michael. 2006. *Just and Unjust Wars: A Moral Argument with Historical Illustrations*, 4th ed. New York: Basic Books.

Wing, Adrien Katherine. 1994. Review of *Mass Rape: The War against Women in Bosnia-Herzegovina*, by Alexandra Stiglmayer. *The American Journal of International Law* 88, no. 4: 849–851.

CHAPTER 24

···

"MIND THE GAP"

Measuring and Understanding Gendered Conflict Experiences

···

AMELIA HOOVER GREEN

As many of the authors in this volume persuasively argue, gender is—or should be—a key analytical category for researchers of armed conflict. Gender affects individual experiences of war and violence, and thus should also inform research and policy. This chapter considers how measurement practices shape our understandings of the relationships between gender and conflict experiences. While both academic and policy literatures frequently highlight substantive "knowledge gaps," this chapter focuses instead on two *methodological* gaps: (1) gaps between the parts of reality that have been observed (i.e., data) and the (frequently unobservable) underlying reality itself, and (2) gaps between isolated measurements of specific experiences and broader assessments of conflict and gender.

The overarching message of the chapter is as follows: if conflict researchers intend to use data to draw accurate conclusions about population-level patterns, then nuanced information about the construction of these data is absolutely vital. Moreover, even when nuanced information is available, the ability to draw inferences about population-level patterns of gendered conflict experiences is limited. Avoiding errors in both research and policy requires that we "mind the gap" between data gatherers, data analysts, and data users, as well as the gap between data and reality—a process that requires careful, multidisciplinary analysis.

By way of illustration, the chapter frequently considers a particular type of gendered conflict harm: conflict-related sexual violence (CRSV). As a topic of investigation, CRSV exemplifies both of the methodological gaps discussed in the preceding. Measured patterns of CRSV often provide incomplete and misleading information about the true underlying patterns of CRSV. In many cases, this is due to a related "gap" between those who produce data and those who employ it. Perhaps more important, it now appears clear that considering CRSV in isolation—without measuring other gendered harms and without considering potential gendered *benefits* of war—can produce both misleading analysis and mistaken policy.[1]

Moreover, it is difficult to evaluate data. Consider a hypothetical collection of data about CRSV, drawn from testimonies collected at a refugee camp. These testimonies (the data) can be analyzed to produce descriptive statistics, for example "10 percent of respondents reported experiencing sexual violence." However, if the reporting rate is poor—if, for example, the underlying reality is that 20 percent of testimony-givers experienced sexual violence, but only half of victims reported their experiences—then descriptive inferences about the *overall level* of sexual violence based on the "10 per-cent" statistic will be biased. If the reporting rate varies between victim groups (e.g., between younger and older victims or between males and females), then the data are unrepresentative, and consequently descriptive inferences about *patterns* of sexual vio-lence will be biased. If, on the other hand, we have reason to believe that the report-ing rate is high *and* the testimonies are representative of the broader camp population, then the descriptive statistics can be used to produce valid descriptive inferences about the level and patterns of sexual violence in the broader group. More generally, though, neither raw data nor descriptive inferences about patterns of CRSV can provide useful information about other gendered harms, about gendered wartime opportunities, or about gendered differences in felt need (e.g., for food, shelter, medical care, or psycho-social services).

GAP 1: DATA TO INFERENCE

While researchers across several disciplines have made important strides in understand-ing how to use data and in understanding when employing data is useful, and when it might instead be harmful (see, e.g., Cohen, Hoover Green, and Wood 2013, reviewing CRSV findings), a number of basic substantive questions about gendered violence dur-ing conflict remain unanswered. These include the following: How many incidents have occurred? What is the demographic profile of victims and perpetrators? What types of violence are most common, and how are they related to one another culturally, politi-cally, geographically, demographically, or temporally? Perhaps most important, how do those who have experienced such harms view their own experiences and needs? Data can serve as a starting point for researchers looking to answer these types of questions. However, the researchers and practitioners who interpret data may not fully under-stand the goals or methods of data collectors. Likewise, they may not fully appreciate the extent to which data collection methods may misrepresent underlying realities. This section considers some potential analytical pitfalls associated with common sources of conflict data.

Survey data

If the researcher's goal is to draw accurate (unbiased) descriptive inferences about population-level patterns from a given data source, then nuanced information about the source and construction of the data is perhaps her most important resource. This is particularly true for stigmatized or elusive phenomena. In particular, the researcher should ask whether the data were collected as part of a systematic, population-based sample (usually a survey). Roth, Guberek, and Hoover Green (2011) describe three key requirements for accurate, representative survey investigations: "(1) the sample population . . . is representative of the general population of interest . . . (2) responses to the survey are truthful and complete; and (3) each individual in the reference population has a known probability of selection into the sample . . . . [R]esearchers must know how large the target population is, how large relevant sub-populations are, and how to elicit a full and correct answer" (32).

These are stringent requirements. Many types of wartime violence are elusive phenomena: they are relatively rare with respect to the general population, and/or are clustered in certain subpopulations. Consequently, standard survey methods may produce underestimates (Watters and Biernacki 1989). Moreover, mass population movements and high mortality frequently mean that researchers cannot accurately estimate the likelihood that certain (types of) individuals will fall into the sample. Indeed, to assume representativeness, researchers must assume that there was no relationship between patterns of displacement and patterns of violence, that is, that a person who suffered violence was no more likely to flee than a person who did not suffer violence.

Even where a survey sample is carefully stratified and populations are relatively stable, accurately estimating the prevalence of violence, particularly its relative prevalence across different subpopulations, is far from guaranteed. Accurate inferences from surveys require that survey questions elicit complete and correct answers—but sharing "complete and correct" information about stigmatized experiences may create significant risks to respondents—risks that are often highly gendered. For example, even anonymous, confidential surveys generally undercount the true number of survivors of sexual violence, often because victims fear social ostracism or physical reprisal. This may be particularly true for male victims. Where reporting violence is risky—socially, physically, or otherwise—respondents are more likely to report violence that occurred in public (i.e., violence already known to others in the community) than violence that occurred in private.

In addition, whereas some conflict-related harms are easily identified by victims, others are not. For example, many victims of sexual violence do not identify their experiences as such, and/or identify their experiences as sexual violence only when cued in specific ways. Studies examining US women's responses to survey questions about sexual violence have shown that question wording, question order, interviewer sex, manner of interview (face-to-face versus phone, versus computerized), and a host of other factors can dramatically alter the estimated prevalence of sexual violence among American women (e.g., Fisher 2009). However, it is unclear whether these conclusions also apply to conflict settings, or to other forms of violence. For example, US researchers find that anatomically specific questions increase response rates, but it is unclear whether this tactic would have the same effect elsewhere. To date, no survey experiments have investigated the determinants of reporting in conflict or post-conflict settings.

More generally, surveys may or may not be crafted with an eye to advocacy efforts, causal inference, or policy effectiveness. This can limit the utility of surveys outside the academic disciplines or government offices for which they are (frequently) designed. While scholars or inter-governmental organizations may conduct surveys "in partnership" with human rights advocates, both design and implementation are often driven by funders' priorities. Thus, while surveys may produce very detailed data, they may not provide the *type* of detail that consumers of these data need. For example, many surveys ask respondents if they experienced sexual violence during a specific reference period, but do not ask for details about the date, location, or perpetrator of the incident—key information for researchers attempting to understand the causes as well as the prevalence of conflict-related violence. In addition to inferential difficulties, survey researchers face a host of ethical issues. Swiss and Jennings (2006) have questioned whether the benefits of precise estimates outweigh the potential costs to people who disclose sexually violent experiences but lack support services such as medical services, financial assistance, or mental health interventions.

Systematic survey data provide the only rigorous means of drawing population-level inferences about the incidence and patterns of sexual violence. However, researchers also frequently draw on several other types of data. These are "convenience samples," a general term for any data *not* gathered according to the requirements for systematic, population-based sampling. Convenience data can never be rigorously extrapolated to wider populations.

Media data

Collating and quantifying media reports is a common method of convenience sampling. Indeed, a number of data sources on CRSV are tied to media data. Yet media reports typically are not intended as "data"; indeed, media data have been shown to overrepresent large events, dramatic or unexpected events, events that occur in urban and otherwise accessible areas, and events whose victims are well-known (Davenport and Ball 2002). Media sources also may be prevented from reporting on some classes of events by social conventions, political pressure, or outright repression.

A number of data sources on CRSV are tied to media data. For example, while media-based research on sexual violence during the Syrian civil war (e.g., Wolfe 2013), has raised awareness of CRSV in Syria, these data may or may not accurately represent sexual violence in Syria.[2] Media data on sexual violence focus on particularly taboo or inescapably public events, such as sexual violence against small children, sexual mutilation, or public gang rapes, rather than on less salacious or more private events. Yet analyses based on media data may have significant effects on aid, intervention, or other policy choices. These effects are also observed for other types of violence. For example, media reports appear to overestimate the prevalence of crimes such as forced cannibalism, reinforcing stereotypes about civil wars in general and African civil wars in particular (Cohen and Hoover Green 2012).

Health sector data

In a number of conflicts, data drawn from hospitals, clinics, or government health ministries have provided important evidence about the physical and emotional consequences of CRSV (e.g., Bartels et al. 2013; Mukwege and Nangini 2009). However, clinical data describe just a small subset of the victim population: those whose injuries necessitate hospital treatment but who are not immediately killed, and who have the physical ability and means to travel, and who perceive that the benefits of seeking treatment outweigh the risks (e.g., travel in a conflict zone, abandonment, ostracism, destruction of marriage prospects, isolation, physical injury, or retaliation by one's abuser). In addition, hospital staff must identify and record the victim's injuries as related to CRSV.

Roth, Guberek, and Hoover Green (2011) considered health and medical data from Colombia, a conflicted country that nevertheless maintains a relatively strong health system, including multiple mandatory reporting systems and fairly clear communication between health-related governmental and NGOs. Colombian medical professionals are mandatory reporters of sexual violence; in addition, data are collected from forms designed to summarize every provider visit, and weekly reports from every hospital. In other conflict settings, such as the Democratic Republic of Congo (DRC), no effective reporting mandate exists, but clinics that treat sexual violence victims may gather their own data (e.g., Mukwege and Nangini 2009).

In Colombia, a number of human rights organizations indicated that reporting capacity was worst in areas of intense conflict (Roth, Guberek, and Hoover Green 2011). If this is so, then these data are particularly ill-suited for tracking sexual violence (whether conflict-related or not) over space and time. Moreover, victims seen in clinical settings may not identify themselves as sexual violence survivors, or may appear for seemingly unrelated reasons (Paras et al. 2009). Further, because public health data are primarily concerned with traditional public health indicators, rather than with the gendered harms of conflict, even effective mandatory reporting structures will not capture significant contextual details, such as the organizational affiliation of the perpetrator. More broadly, overreliance on clinical data produces a view of conflict violence that is skewed toward the most severely physically injured victims, toward those who risk little in seeking medical treatment, and/or toward those attacked nearer to clinics. Both injuries and the risks associated with reporting vary with the type of violence and, importantly, with the gender of the victim.

Data from legal mechanisms

In many conflicted countries, data collected from police or court reporting are absent or laughably incomplete. Nevertheless, law-enforcement data frequently play a major role in human rights monitoring, particularly where state presence in conflicted zones remains strong. However, much like medical data, all law-enforcement and court data rely on victim self-reports, and changes over time in factors such as urbanization, funding, and accessibility can lead to startling changes in reporting, which likely do not reflect changes in the underlying reality of conflict and conflict-related violence.

Recent research has starkly illustrated the extent of underreporting in official sources. Relying on Demographic and Health Survey (DHS) data from twenty-four countries, Palermo, Bleck, and Peterman (2014) find that, even among women who are willing to report experiences of sexual violence to a survey enumerator, very few have reported their experiences to any official source (see Figure 24.1). In addition, reporting rates varied dramatically from country to country. Among women who reported an experience of rape to the DHS, rates of reporting to any official source (police, medical, or social services) varied from about 1 percent (in India) to about 26 percent (in Colombia, an outlier). Rates of police reporting were still lower, varying from 0.1 percent (Mali) to about 17 percent (Colombia). Only three of twenty-four countries showed rates of police reporting over 10 percent. While it is possible that less-stigmatized forms of violence might be reported to police and other official sources more frequently, there is little evidence that police or legal data are representative of either true underlying patterns of violence or true underlying victim populations.

Beyond simple issues of trust or reporting capacity, a number of groups have reported that government data sources, in some countries particularly including the police, may actively obfuscate reports of sexual violence. Law enforcement agencies may be affiliated with groups responsible for committing large amounts of sexual violence, may themselves be perpetrators, or may have political or financial incentives to downplay reports of violence. While both courts and law-enforcement sources may benefit from creating and maintaining data sources, it is unclear whether researchers or advocates can derive useful, generalizable information from these sources.

In addition to traditional legal data sources such as police or courts, some transitional justice mechanisms have amassed considerable data collections. Testimonies to the Truth and Reconciliation Commission for Liberia, for example, were coded for dozens of types of violence (Cibelli, Krüger, and Hoover 2009) to create a data set with over 160,000 observed episodes of violence. Coding directly from testimonies represents an advance, in that coding procedures allow researchers to place episodes of particular types of violence in a broader context; in addition, transitional justice data may include causally relevant details about the perpetrators, timing, or location of the violence. However, while these data may be biased *differently* than, for example, police records, they are not *ex ante* more likely to accurately represent patterns of violence across a population.

Data from NGO case files

Organizations outside the government, particularly advocacy and civil society groups, are among the most important sources of information on conflict-related violence—often because official sources, such as law enforcement or medical facilities, lack the will or capacity to systematically document violence. Human rights organizations play

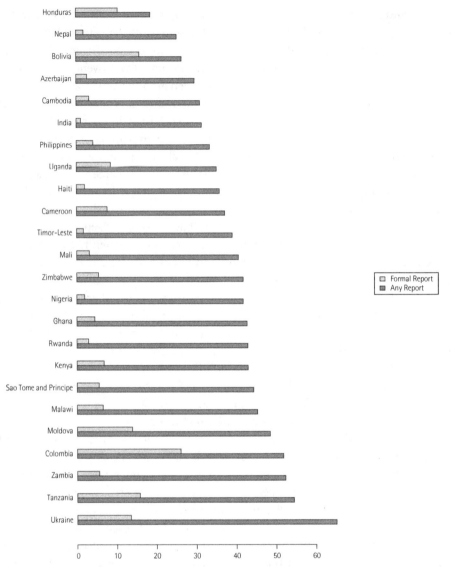

FIGURE 24.1. Estimated rate of rape reporting to formal and informal sources by country, female victims only, 2004–2011.

Data taken from Palermo, Bleck, and Peterman (2014), table 1.

an especially important role in contexts that pit government forces against a domestic opposition; here, violence by government forces or forces supporting the government may be elided almost completely in official records. More generally, political affiliation plays an important role in the social production of violence data: data from organizations that are politically opposed (or simply attach to different social networks within a conflicted area) may show radically different patterns of violence.

However, it should not be assumed that *any* of these opposing "statistical narratives" is correct; the magnitude of missing data (violence not reported to any source) frequently dwarfs variation between existing data sources. Nor does pooling several data sources help. This practice may mitigate some inaccuracies (for example, by pooling records from politically opposed organizations), but it amplifies others (for example, by pooling several sources that have similar geographic access issues).

Like media, health, and law enforcement data, NGO data represent an incomplete and biased set of reports. However, unlike health or law enforcement data, NGO files are often specifically geared to documenting the context, causes, and perpetrators of violence. This type of information is invaluable to researchers whose concern is causal inference; whereas police data may not distinguish between conflict-related and non-conflict-related sexual violence, and almost certainly will not record specific details of each episode of sexual violence, data collected by advocacy organizations may perform either or both of these functions. In some instances, however, NGOs' limited access to conflicted regions may virtually eliminate data from highly violent, inaccessible, or politically hostile areas, creating biases that may not be immediately evident. In many cases, NGOs' focus on political violence, combined with limited staff and resources, means that the total number of cases documented is quite low. For example, in the Colombian case, government data sources showed many more cases of sexual violence than did NGO data (Roth, Guberek, and Hoover Green 2011, 53). Yet NGOs, unlike government sources, included information about perpetrators and specifically focused on perpetrators' institutional affiliations—information that is invaluable to advocates, jurists, and academic researchers alike. Indeed, in a number of cases, NGO data have provided an important basis for later truth commission data collections.

GAP 2: ISOLATED MEASUREMENTS TO BROADER UNDERSTANDINGS

The gap between underlying truth and data production (and, thus, between description and inference) is considerable. Yet understandings of conflict experiences may be incomplete and misleading even when specific types of violence are measured with precision. This section addresses three issues arising from the gap between isolated measurements of specific types of violence and broader understandings of conflict: gendered misunderstandings of the repertoires of violence deployed against women and men during conflict, incorrectly inferring subjective experiences of violence from objective data about violence, and inability to identify potential gendered benefits of conflict.

Consider CRSV, one of the most extensively studied gendered conflict harms (e.g., Cohen 2013; Peterman, Palermo, and Bredenkamp 2011). While undoubtedly important in its own right, intense attention to CRSV as an isolated phenomenon can produce distortions in both academic understandings and policy responses. During the Liberian

civil war, CRSV against women was perhaps the most highly publicized form of gendered harm. Yet broader data suggest that sexual violence was not the most common
form of violence, and certainly not the most common conflict-related harm, suffered by
women in Liberia (Cohen and Hoover Green 2012). Both women and men were more
likely to report forced displacement, for example, than sexual violence, even where
definitions of sexual violence were quite broad. Thus, to the extent that CRSV against
women is measured in isolation, neither academic researchers nor practitioners are able
to identify the full extent and effects of wartime violence. This can lead to significant
policy distortions: Utas (2005) documents Sierra Leonean women's intense awareness of
the "best" types of violence to report to humanitarian organizations.

Moreover, measures of the incidence or prevalence of violence may not accurately
reflect survivors' or communities' felt needs. Qualitative research in several settings
suggests—*contra* most media narratives—that survivors of CRSV may not view this
experience as their most harmful or traumatic wartime violation. Theidon (2007;
Chapter 11 in this volume), for example, finds that Peruvian women who suffered
CRSV during civil war frequently identified other gendered harms (inability to feed
their children, threats to spouses, or the destruction of homes and property) as more
damaging than CRSV. Indeed, some viewed suffering sexual violence as the "best of
bad options" that might produce leverage with fighters or secure the release of family
breadwinners.

Similarly, Annan et al. (2011, examining the case of Uganda) show that violence is
far from the only determinant of postwar outcomes for ex-combatants. Exposures to
violence affect social and psychological outcomes, particularly for female former combatants. However, in terms of postwar well-being, these effects may be outweighed by
human capital effects. Moreover, these human capital effects are highly gendered. In
particular, Annan et al. find that female combatants had "less to lose," economically
speaking, and therefore that negative economic effects of ex-combatant status (lack of
formal education, joblessness, and so on) fall more heavily on males.

Theidon's and Annan et al.'s analyses also emphasize a third pitfall of focusing measurement efforts on a single form of violence: doing so ignores the potential for gendered
benefits, as well as gendered harms, during armed conflict (Fuest 2008). Scholars have
documented extensive changes in social structures during conflict (see Wood 2008).
In many settings, war shifts the balance of gender power as women join fighting forces,
head households in migration, or enter the workforce.

CONCLUSION

All data are socially produced. In addition to forms of bias to which *particular* data
sources are prone, several issues shape *all* data collections: social and political networks, cultural norms, individual incentives, community decision-making, and practical issues of access to people and places. Without stronger infrastructure for gathering

and analyzing data on conflict experiences and gender, it is difficult to assess or repair gaps between data and reality, or gaps between research on specific gendered harms and research that views gendered wartime experiences more broadly.

The gaps documented in this chapter clarify the need for several methodological improvements. First, both academic and policy researchers must acknowledge the likelihood that any conflict data source is incomplete and biased; in academic literature, this means engaging much more seriously with questions of data incompleteness, and insisting upon stronger evidence about data quality (for example, by conducting rigorous sensitivity testing). For many conflicts, while data are plentiful and have been gathered carefully, we lack systematic data on the data-gathering process itself. Different conflict data collections seldom converge on the same statistical narrative; when they do, it is impossible to know whether the convergence represents reality, or just a similar set of reporting errors.

To ameliorate these issues somewhat, Roth, Guberek, and Hoover Green (2011) advocate asking, effectively, "whose story is missing here?" In practical terms, this means considering whether some conflict-affected people are more likely to keep their experience private than others; whether some are more likely to have access to an organization that could report their stories; and whether changes in reported patterns reflect changes in actual patterns of experience—or simply changes in reporting (e.g., changes in season, access to urban areas, resources, staffing, political affiliation, social networks, military control, and so on). Unraveling these complexities is arduous, but it is a useful buffer against the false precision that often attends large-scale data-gathering projects (particularly quantitative projects). In this vein, it is also vital that funding bodies avoid incentivizing falsely precise claims by, for example, demanding certain types of data and measurement.

Of course, carefully considering gaps in individual data sources is not a prescription for improving data overall. It is, rather, a stopgap that may mitigate some inferential errors. The difficulties associated with assessing data accuracy, as well as the importance of contexts broader than single forms of violence, lead to a second implication: interdisciplinary engagement must become the rule, rather than the exception, in studies of conflict-affected populations. Gaps between researchers from different disciplines may be best solved in the context of in-depth, local investigations; here, experts across disciplines can reflect upon the potential biases in their data collections, multiple data sources may speak to one another directly, and researchers may arrive at some (albeit rather limited) conclusions about population-level patterns (Roth, Guberek, and Hoover Green 2011). In addition to local, multidisciplinary investigations, more comprehensive research into reporting patterns is necessary. For example, while survey experiments have illuminated important reporting issues in the context of US sexual violence (e.g., Fisher 2009), no such experiments have been carried out in conflict-affected settings. These methodological innovations—together with a disciplined awareness of the breadth and variety of gendered conflict experiences—may produce a view of gender and conflict that accurately represents specific patterns of harm *and* responds successfully to a broader set of experiences.

NOTES

1. Where possible, this chapter avoids specialized terminology. However, a few definitions are necessary to speak precisely about gaps between data and reality. "Description" (or "descriptive statistics") refers to information about data, not information about underlying reality. However, in some cases it is possible to use descriptions of data to arrive at conclusions about reality. The systematic process of reasoning from description to conclusions about the underlying reality is "descriptive inference" (although "inference" may refer to the conclusions themselves). Descriptive inference may fail for a number of reasons. One of the most common is uneven reporting rates across subpopulations. "Reporting rate" refers to the proportion of total incidents that are reported in a given data source; the reporting rate varies across victim populations, countries, and data sources. "Bias" refers to any non-random error in description; biases, unless understood and accounted for, can lead to extremely inaccurate descriptive inferences. "Causal inference," which relies fundamentally on accurate descriptive inference, is the systematic process of reasoning from conclusions about the state of the world (i.e., descriptive inferences) to conclusions about the causes of phenomena in the world.
2. Note that, while some data included in the Women Under Siege documentation project (Wolfe 2013) are "crowd-sourced," in the sense that individuals report them independently of media sources, the majority are coded from media reports. Consequently, I discuss this data collection under the heading "media data."

REFERENCES

Annan, Jeannie, Christopher Blattman, Dyan Mazurana, and Khristopher Carlson. 2011. "Civil War, Reintegration, and Gender in Northern Uganda." *Journal of Conflict Resolution* 55, no. 6: 877–908.

Bartels, Susan, Jennifer Scott, Jennifer Leaning, Denis Mukwege, Robert Lipton, and Michael VanRooyen. 2013. "Surviving Sexual Violence in Eastern Democratic Republic of Congo." *Journal of International Women's Studies* 11, no. 4: 37–49.

Cibelli, Kristen, Jule Krüger, and Amelia Hoover. 2009. *Descriptive Statistics from Statements to the Liberian Truth and Reconciliation Commission*. Palo Alto, CA: Benetech Human Rights Data Analysis Group.

Cohen, Dara Kay. 2013. "Explaining Rape during Civil War: Cross-National Evidence (1980–2009)." *American Political Science Review* 107, no 3: 461–477.

Cohen, Dara Kay, and Amelia Hoover Green. 2012. "Dueling Incentives: Sexual Violence in Liberia and the Politics of Human Rights Advocacy." *Journal of Peace Research* 49, no. 3: 445–458.

Cohen, Dara Kay, Amelia Hoover Green, and Elisabeth Jean Wood. 2013. *Wartime Sexual Violence: Misconceptions, Implications, and Ways Forward*. Washington, DC: US Institute of Peace.

Davenport, Christian, and Patrick Ball. 2002. "Views to a Kill: Exploring the Implications of Source Selection in the Case of Guatemalan State Terror, 1977–1995." *Journal of Conflict Resolution* 46, no. 3: 427–450.

Fisher, Bonnie S. 2009. "The Effects of Survey Question Wording on Rape Estimates Evidence from a Quasi-Experimental Design." *Violence Against Women* 15, no. 2: 133–147.

Fuest, Veronika. 2008. "'This Is the Time to Get in Front': Changing Roles and Opportunities for Women in Liberia." *African Affairs* 107, no. 427: 201–224.

Mukwege, Denis, and Cathy Nangini. 2009. "Rape with Extreme Violence: The New Pathology in South Kivu, Democratic Republic of Congo." *PLoS Medicine* 6, no. 12: e1000204.

Palermo, Tia, Jennifer Bleck, and Amber Peterman. 2014. "Tip of the Iceberg: Reporting and Gender-Based Violence in Developing Countries." *American Journal of Epidemiology* 179, no. 5: 602–612.

Paras, Molly L., Mohammad Hassan Murad, Laura P. Chen, Erin N. Goranson, Amelia L. Sattler, Kristina M. Colbenson, Mohamed B. Elamin, Richard J. Seime, Larry J. Prokop, and Ali Zirakzadeh. 2009. "Sexual Abuse and Lifetime Diagnosis of Somatic Disorders: A Systematic Review and Meta-analysis." *Journal of the American Medical Association* 302, no. 5: 550–561.

Peterman, Amber, Tia Palermo, and Caryn Bredenkamp. 2011. "Estimates and Determinants of Sexual Violence against Women in the Democratic Republic of Congo." *American Journal of Public Health* 101, no. 6: 1060–1067.

Roth, Francoise, Tamy Guberek, and Amelia Hoover Green. 2011. *Using Quantitative Data to Assess Conflict-Related Sexual Violence in Colombia: Challenges and Opportunities.* Bogotá: Corporación Punto de Vista and Human Rights Data Analysis Group.

Swiss, Shana, and Peggy J. Jennings. 2006. *Documenting the Impact of Conflict on Women Living in Internally Displaced Persons Camps in Sri Lanka: Some Ethical Considerations.* Albuquerque, NM: Women's Rights International.

Theidon, Kimberly. 2007. "Gender in Transition: Common Sense, Women, and War." *Journal of Human Rights* 6, no. 4: 453–478.

Utas, Mats. 2005. "Victimcy, Girlfriending, Soldiering: Tactic Agency in a Young Woman's Social Navigation of the Liberian War Zone." *Anthropological Quarterly* 78, no. 2: 403–430.

Watters, John K, and Patrick Biernacki. 1989. "Targeted Sampling: Options for the Study of Hidden Populations." *Social Problems* 36, no. 4: 416–430.

Wolfe, Lauren. 2013. "Syria Has a Massive Rape Crisis." *The Atlantic.* April 3, 2013. http://www.theatlantic.com/international/archive/2013/04/syria-has-a-massive-rape-crisis/274583/.

Wood, Elisabeth Jean. 2008. "The Social Processes of Civil War: The Wartime Transformation of Social Networks." *Annual Review of Political Science* 11, no. 1: 539–561.

CHAPTER 25

....

INTERSECTIONALITY

Working in Conflict

....

EILISH ROONEY

INTERSECTIONALITY has an extraordinary standing in contemporary feminist theorizing and activism within critical race studies, European equality discourse, international law, and reflections on uprisings in the Middle East (Crenshaw 2004; Möschel 2014; Phoenix and Pattynama 2006; Salem 2013).[1] This remarkable dispersal across disciplines and continents supports the view of it as a kind of fast-traveling theory (Knapp 2005; Said 1983). When taken up in conflict studies, intersectionality retains a characteristic feature of its US origins as a politically engaged form of feminist theorizing. As such, in conflict studies it is concerned with deep underlying structural inequalities and the social divisions and violence they give rise to (Möshel 2014; Yuval-Davis 2006).

Originally developed within critical race studies in the United States, the gender/ race/class framework was at that time used to reveal Black and ethnic minority women's concrete experience of race-based inequalities (Crenshaw 1991, 2004; Hill-Collins 2004; Žarkov, Chapter 2 in this volume). When used to study conflict, the framework enables the investigation of women's identity-based inequalities. In addition, it calls for a decisively deconstructive approach to the totalizing and repressive impulses of what is often referred to as identity politics (Knapp 2005).

This chapter builds upon a series of prior contributions to intersectional studies in conflict and transition (Rooney 2006, 2014). The chief goal of these studies has been to reveal and tackle women's inequalities in conflict and post-conflict sites (Ní Aoláin and Rooney 2007). A broader theoretical aim is to explain the gendered nature of armed conflict and its impacts in marginalized lives in deeply divided societies, particularly where a conflict is described as sectarian (Rooney 2013). Such conflicts commonly involve long-standing disputes over governance and the power to control resources. Structural inequality in these circumstances is a fundamental gender justice issue affecting everyday life. Globally, it is the most pressing issue of the twenty-first century (Hill-Collins and Bilge 2016); yet its investigation is often overlooked or avoided in transitional circumstances as being divisive. Intersectionality provides a framework for engaging in these challenging conversations (Rooney and Swaine 2012).

In intersectional analysis, conflict-related identities are treated as socially produced critical sites of power and oppression that govern women's access to resources and their visibility in conflict discourse. This enables us to deconstruct the apparent fixity of identity labels, to investigate their dynamics in everyday life, and to counter silence and avoidance as an inadequate response (Butler 2002). Identity categories that appear to be static are the unsettled product of unique circumstances (Hall 1993). They are neither permanent nor fixed, although they may seem to be so, especially within the context of conflict. This is the case for identities such as Catholic and Protestant in Northern Ireland, race and ethnicity in South Africa, and Sunni and Shia in the Middle East and North Africa (MENA) and elsewhere. Intersectionality helps to explain the everyday impacts and policy implications of deep-rooted intersectional inequalities. This approach affirms a view of feminist theory as an activity "whose strength is tested not by claims to internal coherence but by an ability to deliver" (Bottomley and Conaghan 1993; O'Rourke 2015). It is theory as critical engagement.

The theory-to-practice argument of this chapter is that gender is an intersectional concept that fundamentally structures the framework of understanding conflict (Rooney 2008). This chapter reviews the situation in Northern Ireland to provide data points for discussion on each of the following, and to apply that experience to other conflicts. The first section briefly explains how intersectional theory and method are useful for surfacing women's positioning within conflicts, including the role of the concept of masculinity in identity discourses. The following section illustrates intersectionality in practice as a method that is attentive to how gender, race, and class are understood within particular settings, using the site of Germany's post-1989 transition (Knapp 2004). The third section revisits Crenshaw's observations on institutional silence as an unacceptable response to women's domestic violence experience in the community of color. It stresses the significance of social institutions in shaping and tackling deep underlying structural inequalities that give rise to group grievance. The last section opens with some comments on intersectionality as a forceful tool of legal doctrine. It examines an intersectional study of a policing strategy for the protection of Muslim women in Canada and a preliminary study of conflict-related female fatalities in Northern Ireland. The latter affirms the centrality of gender, sect, and class to understanding the gender dimensions of conflict-related deaths and the wider social experience of conflict for women.

PRACTICAL THEORY

It is in Martha Fineman and Roxanne Mykitiuk's (1994) groundbreaking text on domestic violence in the United States that Kimberlé Crenshaw used intersectional analysis to test contemporary theory and practice in the field. She identified gender and race as the primary sites for the distribution of social resources such as housing, education, and jobs. The outcome amounts to race-based class differences that fundamentally "structure the experiences of battered women of color in particular ways [that require feminist] intervention . . . to be responsive to these systems" (Crenshaw 1994). The study revealed that the police and a then high-profile feminist strategy failed to acknowledge the experience of these women. Crenshaw's challenge is considerable. As Susan F. Hirsch notes in the Introduction, questioning the "fundamental assumptions of a theory or practice is an awesome undertaking" (Hirsch 1994, 4). It involves taking the risk of exposing a deficiency that may undermine fragile success (Hirsch 1994). Feminist success, in any field, is hard won, often fragile, and justifiably stoutly defended. The benefit of intersectional method, however, is critical for identifying conceptual gaps that have practical implications for theory and action. In this case, Crenshaw demonstrated that a conceptualization of gender harm that neglects the experience of the most marginalized women has limited validity, as well as serious legal consequences for battered women themselves.

When taken up in conflict studies, the concept of intersectionality augments a long-standing feminist practice of recognizing women as simultaneously positioned, for instance, as political actors, refugees, colonial subjects, combatants, and victims of gender violence in various contexts (Moyo 2012; Ní Aoláin 2016; Phoenix and Pattynama 2006). Intersectionality adds to this recognition an exacting combination of empirical method with concept analysis. It enables investigation of the concrete impacts of social division in marginalized lives. It calls for examining objective data relating to sectarian inequalities, for instance, in housing, education, or jobs. Such inequalities perpetuate underlying structural inequalities and the social divisions and civil unrest they give rise to. These structural conditions are allied to identity discourses and help to explain their class-based makeup. They do not fully explain the totalizing and patriarchal tendencies of identity discourse in conflicts. The analytical aim is to understand these repressive impulses as a function of the instability of social categories under pressure (Butler 2002; Knapp 2005). An allied aim is to examine the masculinity of social identities in conflict, recognizing the role of gender as an organizing principle of their articulation and practice. The repressive consequences in women's lives are often overwhelming and hidden. Intersectional analysis enables us to detail the corrosive effects in everyday life (Crenshaw 1991; MacKinnon 2013). It enables us to understand the importance of a social policy that aims to tackle social need and reduce sectarian differentials. Such policy helps to undermine the material basis of identity grievance and is intersectional in practice.

The theory-to-practice argument of the chapter—that gender is an intersectional concept that structures the framework of understanding conflict—incorporates the concept of masculinity as central to that understanding (Hutchings 2008). The concept of masculinity within this framework is deeply problematic. It functions to legitimize war as a normative male-only activity (Hutchings 2008). Furthermore, sectarian and other conflict-related identities are used in conflict discourse as essentially masculine categories. Accordingly, a persistent focus on male violence affirms the patriarchal norm that renders the significance of women's lives in conflict as immaterial. The concept of female gender is also problematic for different reasons. Female gender functions as a category of blamelessness. This is because the exceptional presence of femaleness in a conflict discourse commonly represents innocence and peacemaking as morally desirable and essentially female characteristics. This categorical blamelessness, allied to masculine *blamefulness*, sustains a fiction that social identities are gender free and combat is a male-only activity. Women are positioned as a homogenous category completely uninvolved in allied structural inequalities and without interest or agency in social divisions or violent conflict (Davis 2015). This also infers that men are essentially uninterested in nonviolent agency (Sharoni 1995). This helps to explain why the figure of "woman fighter," for instance, is such a powerful trope of gender displacement (Alison 2003; Hassim 1993). Women's active role in combat is consistently underplayed or invisible in mainstream discourse, despite documented and recent reports of recruitment of women by ISIS/ISIL (Ní Aoláin 2015). Narratives of female agency and innocence in conflict discourses carry significant rhetorical weight. They are employed by armed forces, and by women themselves, often to strong effect (Cockburn 2012; Hasso 1998; McEvoy 2009). The current binary framework of understanding gender in conflict tends to foreclose the possibility of making political settlements gender inclusive. The integration of women's agency and allied identity-based, socioeconomic circumstances into an analysis radically alters the framework of understanding armed conflict and women's absence from negotiations to end them (Bell, Chapter 32 in this volume).

CONCEPTS IN CONFLICT

Knapp's exploration of intersectionality, in the context of German reunification, may seem an unlikely place for exploring the practical usefulness of intersectionality for gender conflict studies. However, her homegrown analysis is valuable for advocating researcher reflexivity as a critical competence that is particularly important for feminist engagement in conflict settings where nuances of language may be unfamiliar. She explains, for instance, that when gender/race/class travels from its New World origins in the United States, to be taken up in feminist discourse in the Old World of European states, the concepts undergo a significant shift in meaning. In order to grasp the scale of the alteration, she cites Germany's World War II history of state division. In contemporary West German social science, class and gender have long been viewed as "zombie" categories—effectively dead and awaiting burial (Knapp 2004, 14). So, a West German feminist who undertakes gender research risks being viewed within the academy as engaged in a passé rhetoric long ago overtaken by the playful postmodern. For feminists from East Germany, on the other hand, the concept of class is unusable given its function in the Cold War narrative as a product of Western capitalism. As for the category of race, this poses another set of historically situated, deep-rooted problems within the German academy. The concept of racial categories is so negative a contemporary construct that it too is effectively unusable for feminists East or West. The process of employing intersectional concepts in the German context usefully exposes critical concept tensions and silences.

These "local" European apprehensions have wider ramifications for gender conflict studies. Intersectional analysis works as a reflexive reminder that within highly developed democratic states, human rights and universal equality *coexist* with discourses that normalize oppressive gender-, identity-, and class-based discrimination. The argument is more nuanced than this analysis allows. However, the point is that intersectionality helps to pinpoint conceptual silences that have practical repercussions for feminist engagement in situations of armed conflict. It helps to explain why feminists, speaking of the MENA region, see intersectionality as offering a framework for inclusive conversation (Salem 2013). At heart, this conversation is about how gender is understood, regulated, and *lived* in any deeply divided context and, moreover, whether or not and how it is investigated within the local and international academy.

Like other academic scholarship, whatever its provenance, feminist theory aims to provide explanatory tools that have practical and general application. The cautionary implications of adapting social theories from "elsewhere" for understanding the domestic is well developed within feminist subaltern and postcolonial studies (Cleary 2003; Moyo 2012). From this work we learn that "the local" is categorically neither central to nor the source of social theory. In a way that is reminiscent of feminist intervention in the academic mainstream, Joe Cleary's (2003) observation from Irish postcolonial theory is relevant: "dependent cultures are always interpreting their own realities with intellectual methods created somewhere else and whose basis lies in other social processes" (24). Many, if not most, conflict jurisdictions could be characterized as in some ways "dependent cultures." This is so in relation to the remit of the geopolitical interest or disinterest of powerful states and of international organizations commissioning research and intervention. The explanatory power of intersectionality in the local place is critical for comprehending the domestic dilemmas of women's empowerment that may otherwise be overlooked.

The practicalities of intersectional reflexivity in Germany have application for women's empowerment elsewhere. This is pointedly the case when we apply core feminist concepts or legal norms to lives in conflicted jurisdictions that are "other" to our own and that are dependent on international agencies. An international intervention may have unintended consequences and may be misunderstood or unwelcome (Otto 2009). In a reflection on the negative experience of Western feminist engagement in the Middle East, Sara Salem (2013) makes a case for intersectional theory to underpin future engagement. She contends that intersectionality "can be a powerful tool [for] women in the Middle East [to] reclaim a feminist project that has often excluded and objectified them" (para. 7). She suggests that the reflexivity of intersectional research also aids internal grassroots feminist advocacy. From this perspective, intersectionality travels to and from the Middle East as an adaptable framework for empowering domestic activism and international conversation.

Intersectional understandings of gender and the importance of including social and economic rights within peace agreements are also necessary (Chinkin 2003). If women's lives are to be improved, however, the enforcement of rights is required (Ní Aoláin and Rooney 2007). The Irish context adds an important tactical addendum. In Northern Ireland, local academic and feminist networks, along with women's groups from nationalist and unionist working-class districts, have developed activism around UN Security Council resolution (SCR) 1325 to mobilize women in a united front. This involves a strategic deployment of the sovereignty issue of partition as an effective entry point to elected assemblies in the North and South of Ireland. The women involved are both "representative" of opposed political positions and speak tactically for all women as a group that would benefit from the implementation of SCR 1325. The alliance calls on the UK government to engage SCR 1325 in the Northern Ireland context (Hannah's House 2012; Hoewer 2013; McMinn and O'Rourke 2012). This intersectional alliance affirms critical engagement as a smart tactic to advance unrealized commitments to women's equality made in the 1998 Agreement (Rooney and Swaine 2012).

An absence of women from negotiations and the masculinity of conflict discourses obscure the reality that many men and women have shared views about women's political participation. Their common interests in the outcome of negotiations generally reflect their socioeconomic and political positions (Rooney 2007). Men and women share an array of gender-differentiated experiences of discrimination, invasion, occupation, and violence. They also have significant stakes in the cessation of violence and the resolution of conflict. That women qua women may benefit less directly from a negotiated "deal" or may gain very little in practice does not lessen their stake in the outcome. Indeed, a lesser scale of benefit for those most marginalized in a conflict-affected community arguably intensifies the value and contentiousness of any redistributive gain involved, be it material, cultural, or symbolic (Crilly, Gordon, and Rooney 2002). This is a further reason to investigate structural inequality as a gender justice issue that plays a critical role in conflicts. On this matter, however, conflict discourses are generally silent.

SILENCE

Crenshaw's observation on silence as an unacceptable response to the domestic violence experience of marginalized women in the community of color is instructive. The Los Angeles Police Department refused to release community data because to do so, they claimed, would promote prejudice and would enable the crime to be dismissed as a "minority problem" (Crenshaw 2004, 409). Local community representatives agreed. They opposed the release of data because drawing attention to violent male abuse, they believed, would serve to reinforce Black male stereotypes. The scale of battering experienced by women of color was thereby hidden and suffered in a collective silence sanctioned by community leaders and institutionalized within the body responsible for law enforcement.

Germinal research into domestic violence during the Northern Ireland conflict similarly reported a police and community silence about the experience of nationalist (mainly Catholic) women living in disadvantaged districts (McWilliams and McKiernan 1993). The nature of the silences uncovered in these studies reflects the power dynamics at stake in differently divided societies. In Northern Ireland, sect and gender, as primary sites for the distribution of resources, structured the experience of battered women in particular ways during the conflict. Nationalist women did not report their abuse to the Royal Ulster Constabulary (unionist and chiefly Protestant) because of communal distrust. A woman's request for policing intervention, even in the case of her battering, could incur censure. Accordingly, the scale and impact of domestic violence during the conflict remain unknown.

The reformed Police Service of Northern Ireland (PSNI) is now largely accepted in nationalist areas. In this post-conflict period there has been a marked increase of violence in the Black, minority, and ethnic (BME) community. When McWilliams and Yarnell (2013) studied the community's experience of domestic violence, the Public Prosecution Service of Northern Ireland (PPS) could not provide data because of sectarian sensitivities. An official explained that reporting identity related data in Northern Ireland could lead to the PPS being questioned as to "whether more Catholics than Protestants were prosecuted" (McWilliams and Yarnell 2013, 18). The scale of battering experienced by BME and marginalized Catholic and Protestant women remains unknown. The PPS gave assurances that it would in future record BME data, but gave no such assurance on the experience of women from Catholic and Protestant backgrounds. Yet, as Crenshaw and others have argued, over many years, intervention needs to be based on empirical evidence. Institutional silence about the role of racism and sectarianism is unacceptable. It is not that race and sect are interchangeable categories. They are categories, however, that are readily associated with disdained masculinities. Intersectional method questions this ready association and its related silences about women's experiences of abuse.

The silence about domestic violence and women's intersectional identities in Northern Ireland is worrying, but it is neither unique nor recent (CAJ 2006). Social policy silence on sectarian inequalities is a long-standing form of "institutional denial of sectarianism" (Williamson and Darby 1978). Women themselves openly engage with the sectarian dynamics of their conflict experience when the opportunity arises (Rooney 2014). Social policy silence on the gendered impacts of sectarian inequality, however, looks set to continue (Fitzgerald 2004; Hinds 2011; Osborne and Shuttleworth 2004).

Violence against Women/Gender Harm

In the arena of international law, intersectionality is an effective method of surfacing the specific conflict harms experienced by women (Davis 2015; MacKinnon, 2013). This carries significant benefits for the women themselves and for legal doctrine in international and domestic contexts. In international human rights law, for instance, it aids the identification of human rights violations against women members of recognized minorities, be they racial, ethnic, national, or religious. This is significant for marginalized women, whose circumstances would not otherwise be explicitly recognized within remedy arrangements (Davis 2015; Hill-Collins and Bilge 2016). Intersectionality is also observable in the theory underpinning the recognition of genocidal rape as a crime against humanity (MacKinnon 2013). The identity of Bosnian Muslim women, per se, is not the issue. The critical issue for these women is "the consequences of how they are socially identified and hence treated" (MacKinnon 2013, 1027). The theory argument made by Davis, and MacKinnon's theory-to-practice contribution, underscore the adaptability of intersectional method for revealing conflict harm experienced by marginalized women.

The thorny question of conflict-related identity being viewed as an *outcome* of the dynamics that create the identity supports an important post–9/11 intersectional study of identity dynamics for Muslim women in Canada. Sherene H. Razack (2004) explains that a progressive women's equality discourse was deployed in a policing strategy to protect Muslim women from forced marriage. In practice, the strategy became a high-profile policing surveillance tool that focused on Muslim male violence. This made it impossible for Muslim women to "name and confront the violence that Muslim women (like all groups of women) experience at the hands of their men and families" (130). The focus on Muslim male violence was counterproductive for these women, but effective for further energizing the "War on Terror" rhetoric (Razack (2004). The deployment of aggression for the purpose of protecting vulnerable women from patriarchal threat has a long history in the promotion of war (see Kouvo and Levine in relation to Afghanistan, Chapter 37 in this volume). Razack adds a contemporary insight to how this discourse works on the home front for Muslim women in Canada. Intersectional research deepens our understanding of the everyday domestic and international dynamics of sectarian politics. Researchers seeking to illumine these dynamics, however, face complex challenges.

Women's conflict experience is an outcome of how they are socially identified and treated as members of social groups (Enloe 1998; MacKinnon 2013). In other words, this experience is constituted by systems of gender, sect, and class in a given time and place. This recognition broadens the prominent conceptualization of gender harm in conflict as a reference to sexualized violation (Ní Aoláin, O'Rourke, and Swaine 2015). The theory-to-practice implications are evident within Northern Ireland. Here, for instance, a study of gender harm as sexual violation during conflict would examine nationalist women's experience of public humiliation by "tarring and feathering" as punishment for alleged "fraternizing" with British Security Forces in working-class districts of Derry and Belfast in the 1970s (Harkin and Kilmurry 1985). Throughout the conflict, women were punished because they partnered or married a member of the "other community." In several instances this led to the woman's death. Women and men have documented their strip-searching prison experience as a political regime of sexualized humiliation (Aretxaga 1997; Moore and Scraton 2010).[2] The impact of sexualized violence and humiliation, as an extreme form of state and communal control, is largely unexamined in mainstream studies.[3] Moreover, in Northern Ireland the dominant cultural influence and repressive power of religious institutions on women's reproductive and sexuality rights throughout the conflict are arguably a form of sexualized control and gender harm that remains unexamined.

A focus on sexualized violation in conflict is vital for those who are violated and are entitled to legal redress (MacKinnon 2013). Hard-won legal advances that capture national and international attention, however, may also fail to encompass critical dimensions of marginalized experience. Intersectional analysis foregrounds the specific ways in which women's lives are bounded by gendered inequality, sexist oppression, and silence within conflicts regarded as sectarian.

A focus on female death as a category of gender harm works to disrupt the framework of understanding conflict as basically a matter of armed misogyny or ancient enmity. This is illustrated in the preliminary study of conflict-related female death in Northern Ireland that follows. In this situation, the concept of gender, far from being the "zombie" category of Knapp's Germany, is commonly a reference to women and innocence as overlapping categories. The already noted categorization of innocence as essentially female enters war discourse as an exploitable rhetoric of vulnerability requiring masculine protection.[4] This is explicit in war reports that dissolve femaleness to an infantilizing category of "women and children" (Enloe 1989). The discursive power of female gender, however, is in inverse proportion to women's actual presence or agency in conflict decision-making.

This discursive power extends to conflict-related female death in complicated ways. Reports of female deaths in conflict underscore the barbarity of conflict violence in ways that male deaths do not. A male death, however appalling, is viewed as normal or legitimate and to be expected in war, a deeply gendered paradigm in its own right. This is an additional reason for an individual woman's death to more readily become a high point of public interest. The narrative power of gender innocence and frailty is difficult to overestimate. Class is also a significant category, although the significance of social marginalization is largely overlooked and taken for granted. For instance, the death of a lawyer in circumstances of state collusion in his killing augments public concern in a way that the comparable death of a working-class man may not.[5] Similarly, and to powerful effect, the exceptional death of a middle-class woman can fortify the framework of understanding conflict as a competition between deviant working-class masculinities, precisely because the death of a woman with the tropes of presumed vulnerability and innocence captures attention in ways not opened up by "unremarkable" male death.[6]

These uncomfortable observations go some way to explain the powerful legitimizing and delegitimizing force of intersections of gender and class in conflict discourses. Additionally, the death of a woman may be used as evidence of enemy viciousness. On the other hand, the death of a woman "killed in action" is a negation of gender innocence that may be deployed to "unsex" her gender identity and delegitimize her purpose (Rolston 1989). A woman's death as a result of political activism may be utilized by armed forces as a powerful claim to political legitimacy. The analogous death of a man is generally without the equivalent discursive gender power. This also extends to the deaths of men and women in peacekeeping missions (Goetz and Anderson 2008). Intersections of gender, sect, and class do indeed shape the framework of understanding war to powerful effect. This strongly influences how women's gendered experience of harm is conceptualized and acted upon. Women's presence in conflict discourse can lend powerful moral authority and justification to war rhetoric, military action, and legal doctrine.

The following outline study of female fatalities in the Northern Ireland conflict unsettles the relationship between gender, harm, and sexual violation. In line with intersectionality theory, it introduces social disadvantage into the frame. Over 80 percent of violent trauma occurred in the most disadvantaged urban areas of Belfast and Derry. In other words, Catholic and Protestant people living in those areas with the highest levels of deprivation and poverty, which saw the outbreak of civil disturbance in the 1960s, experienced the worst impacts of the conflict. This supports a view of war as a gendered practice with the severest outcomes for the most marginalized people with the fewest resources.

The first casualty of the Northern Ireland conflict was that of Matilda Gould in June 1966 (McKitterick et al. 1999). Her death was acknowledged by the paramilitary actors to be a mistake. Some of its characteristics form the pattern of conflict-related deaths that followed.[7] She was a seventy-seven-year-old Protestant widow and mother who lived in a working-class, mainly Protestant, area. Her house adjoined a Catholic-owned bar that was the Ulster Volunteer Force (UVF) target. Her death sparked concerns of an emerging divide between a liberalizing middle-class unionist leadership and the mobilization of working-class unionist militancy in the UVF.

A calculation of the conflict data reveals approximately 340 female deaths (McKitterick et al. 1999). Of these, around 55 percent (185) are recorded as Catholic, 35 percent (119) as Protestant; 10 percent (36) from outside the jurisdiction are without a designation. Almost all conflict-related female deaths are identified as either Catholic or Protestant. One death is recorded as that of a Jewish woman. Almost all domestic female deaths are of working-class women. A pattern of conflict modality is also evident in these women's deaths. All "outsider" deaths, specifically deaths of women from outside the jurisdiction, like the majority of conflict-related domestic deaths, were caused by bomb and gun attacks on civilians in public places such as pubs, hotels, and shopping areas. Public bars frequented by women and men from a working-class community were recurrent targets. An armed organization carrying out violent attacks on a public place knew that females and often children would be present and might be killed or injured as a result. The discursive power of innocence and vulnerability was disregarded to compelling effect. Such violent action conveyed a powerful message of military strategy and political intent. Some women were the targets of planned attacks, though these were infrequent.[8] Also infrequent are the deaths of women members of the Irish Republican Army (IRA) who were transporting explosives that detonated prematurely. Republican women later explained how they moved armaments without raising the suspicion of nearby British soldiers (Aretxaga 1997). Here again, we see that assumed gender innocence is a material resource in the modalities of war.

An intersectional pattern of fatalities by gender, sect, and class in Northern Ireland is conspicuous. The data reveals a continuum between social class disadvantage, violent female deaths, and women's combat status (McKitterick et al. 1999). This begs obvious questions about how gender organizes social thought such that female experience is out of the frame and, for the most part, of no consequence. Social class, though sometimes noted, also makes little difference to analysis. Yet, it is a stark factor in the data. Using intersectionality in conflict studies is a pragmatic way of detecting silences about the realities of women's lives, and the injustice of ignoring their deaths.

Conclusion

Intersectionality is a fairly recent term for a feminist approach with a long history. It originates within critical race studies, but names a deep concern with social oppression shared by feminist movements across the world. It offers a reflexive methodology for feminist engagement and a framework for explaining relations between structural inequalities and identity dynamics within conflicts. Intersectionality fixes none of this, but it brings the realities of women's lives into sharp focus. The gender dimensions of deep-rooted social divisions associated with deprivation are evident in highly developed economies, as well as impoverished regions and oil-rich states. Intersectionality is a useful tool of empirical inquiry in each context. As a politically engaged form of feminist theorizing, it inspires activists and academics alike—not because it suggests simple answers or a one-size-fits-all approach to these problems, but precisely because it offers a way to understand and theorize complexity.

Notes

1. My thanks go to Séan Rooney, who developed the simplified data from *Lost Lives*, and to Hilary Bell, Michelle Clarke, Maureen Fitzgerald, and Dr. Erik Cownie for helpful reading of an earlier draft and providing useful references.
2. See "Female Prisoners in Northern Ireland/ Strip Searching," *Women and Global Human Rights*, accessed May 26, 2016, http://www2.webster.edu/~woolflm/ireland.html. The Northern Ireland Human Rights Commission explains that body searches may amount to "inhuman and degrading treatment" and contravene the European Convention on Human Rights (NIHRC 2012).
3. Though the campaign against the practice of strip-searching is primarily associated with the republican movement, noted female loyalist Hester Dunn also spoke out against the practice (Felo 2013). My thanks to Dr. Erik Cownie for this reference.
4. The Bush administration claimed that the protection of women's human rights and dignity in Afghanistan was a key reason for the invasion. High-profile backing by First Lady Laura Bush and Hillary Clinton was critical (Rawi 2004). Feminist opposition to the invasion subsequently collapsed into disarray (Butler 2002).
5. Prominent Northern Ireland lawyer Pat Finucane's professional role as a human rights lawyer is a significant factor in a long-term high-profile campaign for a judicial inquiry into his death, which involved the complicity and collusion of the state; compared with regular

civilian Gerard Slane's circumstances. "Slane Inquest Delays 'Unacceptable,'" *The Belfast Telegraph*, March 12, 2014.

6. The Ann Travers case and legislation on special advisors in the NI Assembly is an example.

7. Matilda Gould's advanced age make her death atypical in the data (Smyth 1998, chap. 3).

8. Those individually targeted for assassination include leading political and human rights activists, among them: Máire Drumm, vice president of Sinn Féin (d. 1976); Miriam Daly, an academic and leader of the Irish Republican Socialist Party (d. 1980); Bernadette Devlin-McAliskey, prominent republican activist (1981, survived); Sheena Campbell, Sinn Féin member and law student (d. 1992); Rosemary Nelson, human rights lawyer (d. 1999).

References

Alison, Miranda H. 2003. "'We Are Fighting for the Women's Liberation Also': A Comparative Study of Female Combatants in the Nationalist Conflicts in Sri Lanka and Northern Ireland." PhD diss., Queen's University Belfast.

Aretxaga, Begoña. 1997. *Shattering Silence: Women, Nationalism, and Political Subjectivity in Northern Ireland.* Princeton, NJ: Princeton University Press.

Bottomley, Anne, and Joanne Conaghan. 1993. "Feminist Theory and Legal Strategy." *Journal of Law and Society* 20, no. 1: 1–5.

Butler, Judith. 2002. "Explanation and Exoneration, or What We Can Hear." *Social Text* 20, no. 3: 177–188.

Committee for the Administration of Justice (CAJ). 2006. *Equality in Northern Ireland: The Rhetoric and the Reality.* Belfast: Shanways.

Chinkin, Christine. 2003. *Women, Nationality and Citizenship: Women2000 and Beyond.* New York: UN Division for the Advancement of Women.

Cleary, Joe. 2003. "Misplaced Ideas? Colonialism, Location, and Dislocation in Irish Studies." In *Ireland and Postcolonial Theory*, edited by Clare Carroll and Patricia King, 16–45. Cork: Cork University Press.

Cockburn, Cynthia. 2012. *Antimilitarism: Political and Gender Dynamics of Peace Movements.* London: Palgrave Macmillan.

Crenshaw, Kimberlé W. 1991. "Mapping the Margins: Intersectionality, Identity Politics, and Violence against Women of Color." *Stanford Law Review* 43, no. 6: 1241–1299.

Crenshaw, Kimberlé. 1994. "Mapping the Margins: Intersectionality, Identity Politics, and Violence against Women of Color." In *The Public Nature of Private Violence*, edited by Martha Albertson Fineman and Rixanne Mykitiuk, 93–118. New York: Routledge.

Crenshaw, Kimberlé. 2004. "Mapping the Margins: Intersectionality, Identity Politics, and Violence against Women of Color." In *Feminist Frontiers*, 6th ed., edited by Laurel Richardson, Verta Taylor, and Nancy Whittier, 405–412. Boston: McGraw-Hill.

Crilly, Anne, Hazel Gordon, and Eilish Rooney. 2002. "Women in the North of Ireland: 1969–2000." In *The Field Day Anthology of Irish Writing*, Volume V: *Irish Women's Writing and Traditions*, edited by Angela Bourke, Siobhán Kilfeather, Maria Luddy, Margaret MacCurtain, Gerardine Meaney, Máirín Ní Dhonnchadha, Mary O'Dowd, and Clair Wills, 1476–1545. Cork: Cork University Press.

Davis, Aisha N. 2015. "Intersectionality and International Law: Recognizing Complex Identities on the Global Stage." *Harvard Human Rights Journal.* 28: 205–242.

Enloe, Cynthia. 1989. *Bananas, Beaches, and Bases: Making Feminist Sense of International Politics*. London: Pandora Press.

Enloe, Cynthia. 1998. "All the Men Are in the Militias, All the Women Are Victims: The Politics of Masculinity and Femininity in Nationalist Wars." In *The Women and War Reader*, edited by Lois A. Lorentzen and Jennifer Turpin, 50–61. New York: New York University Press.

Felo, Joanna. 2013. "Everyone Can Help: Social Service Provision by the Ulster Defence Association, 1971–1988." PhD diss., Queen's University Belfast.

Fineman, Martha Albertson, and Roxanne Mykitiuk, eds. 1994. *The Public Nature of Private Violence*. New York: Routledge.

Fitzgerald, Garrett. 2004. "Foreword." In *Fair Employment in Northern Ireland: A Generation On*, edited by Ian Shuttleworth and R. D. Osborne, vii–xi. Belfast: The Blackstaff Press.

Goetz, Anne-Marie, and Letitia Anderson. 2008. *Report on Wilton Park Conference: Women Targeted or Affected by Armed Conflict: What Role for Military Peacekeepers?* New York: UN Fund for the Development of Women.

Hall, Stuart. 1993. "Cultural Identity and Diaspora." In *Colonial Discourse and Postcolonial Theory: A Reader*, edited by Patrick Williams and Laura Chrisman, 392–401. London: Harvester Wheatsheaf.

Hannah's House. 2012. *Feminist Visions of Peace, Justice and Transformation*. Belfast: Women's Research and Development Agency.

Harkin, Cathy, and Avila Kilmurry. 1985. "Working with Women in Derry." In *Women in Community Work in Northern Ireland*, edited by Marie Abbott and Hugh Frazer, 38–45. Belfast: Farset Press.

Hassim, Shireen. 1993. "Family, Motherhood and Zulu Nationalism: The Politics of the Inkatha Women's Brigade." *Feminist Review* 43: 1–25.

Hasso, Frances S. 1998. "The 'Women's Front': Nationalism, Feminism, and Modernity in Palestine." *Gender & Society* 12, no. 4: 441–465.

Hill-Collins, Patricia. 2004. "Some Group Matters: Intersectionality, Situated Standpoints, and Black Feminist Thought." In *Feminist Frontiers*, 6th ed., edited by Laurel Richardson, Verta Taylor, and Nancy Whittier, 66–84. Boston: McGraw-Hill

Hill-Collins, Patricia, and Sirma Bilge. 2016. *Intersectionality*. Cambridge: Polity Press.

Hinds, Bronagh. 2011. *The Northern Ireland Economy: Women on the Edge*. Belfast: Women's Research and Development Agency.

Hirsch, Susan F. 1994. "Introduction." In *The Public Nature of Private Violence*, edited by Martha Albertson Fineman and Roxanne Mykitiuk, 3–10. New York: Routledge.

Hoewer, Melanie. 2013. "UN Resolution 1325 in Ireland: Its Implication for Women's Rights." *Irish Political Studies*, 28, no. 3: 450–468.

Hutchings, Kimberly. 2008. "Making Sense of Masculinity and War." *Men and Masculinities* 10, no. 4: 389–404.

Knapp, Gudrun-Axeli. 2004. "Race, Class, Gender: Reclaiming Baggage in Fast Travelling Theories." Lecture presented at fifth conference in the series European Intertexts: A Study of Women's Writing as Part of a European Fabric, Szeged, Hungary (copy on file with author).

Knapp, Gudrun-Axeli. 2005. "Race, Class, Gender: Reclaiming Baggage in Fast Travelling Theories." *European Journal of Women's Studies* 12, no. 3: 249–266.

MacKinnon, Catherine A. 2013. "Intersectionality as Method: A Note." *Signs* 38, no. 4: 1019–1030.

McEvoy, Sandra. 2009. "Loyalist Women Paramilitaries in Northern Ireland: Beginning a Feminist Conversation about Conflict Resolution." *Security Studies* 18, no. 2: 262–286.

McKitterick, David, Seamus Kelters, Brian Feeney, Chris Thornton, and David McVea. 1999. *Lost Lives: The Stories of the Men, Women and Children Who Died as a Result of the Northern Ireland Troubles*. Edinburgh: Mainstream Publishing.

McMinn, Karen, and Catherine O'Rourke. 2012. "Baseline Study on UNSCR 1325: Women and Peacebuilding Toolkit: Sharing the Learning." Research Paper No. 14-02, Transitional Justice Institute, Belfast.

McWilliams, Monica, and Joan McKiernan. 1993. *Bringing It Out in the Open: Domestic Violence in Northern Ireland*. Belfast: H.M. Stationary Office.

McWilliams, Monica, and Priyamvada Yarnell. 2013. *The Protection and Rights of Black and Minority Ethnic Women Experiencing Domestic Violence in Northern Ireland*. Belfast: Northern Ireland Council for Ethnic Minorities.

Moore, Linda, and Phil Scraton. 2010. "From Conflict to Peace: The Rights Abuses of Women and Girls in Prison in Northern Ireland." *Current Issues in Criminal Justice* 22, no. 2: 269–286.

Möschel, Mathias. 2014. *Law, Lawyers and Race: Critical Race Theory from the United States to Europe*. Oxon: Routledge.

Moyo, Khanyisela. 2012. "Feminism, Postcolonial Legal Theory and Transitional Justice: A Critique of Current Trends." *International Human Rights Law Review* 1, no. 2: 237–275.

Ní Aoláin, Fionnuala. 2015. "On the Front Lines: Women and the Military." *Just Security* (blog). August 24. https://www.justsecurity.org/25527/front-lines-women-military/.

Ní Aoláin, Fionnuala. 2016. "The Gender Politics of Fact-Finding in the Context of the Women, Peace and Security Agenda." In *The Transformation of Human Rights Fact-Finding*, edited by Philip Alston and Sarah Knuckey. Oxford: Oxford University Press. August 7, 2017, https://www.justsecurity.org/25527/front-lines-women-military/.

Ní Aoláin, Fionnuala, Catherine O'Rourke, and Aisling Swaine. 2015. "Transforming Reparations for Conflict-Related Sexual Violence: Principles and Practice." *Harvard Human Rights Journal* 28: 97–146.

Ní Aoláin, Fionnuala, and Eilish Rooney. 2007. "Underenforcement and Intersectionality: Gendered Aspects of Transition for Women." *International Journal of Transitional Justice* 1, no. 3: 338–354.

Northern Ireland Human Rights Commission (NIHRC). 2012. *The 2012 Annual Statement: Human Rights in Northern Ireland*. Belfast: NIHRC.

O'Rourke, Catherine. 2015. "Feminist Scholarship in Transitional Justice: A De-Politicising Impulse?" *Women's Studies International Forum* 51: 118–127.

Osborne, Bob, and Shuttleworth, Ian, eds. 2004. *Fair Employment in Northern Ireland: A Generation On*. Belfast: Blackstaff Press.

Otto, Diane. 2009. "The Exile of Inclusion: Reflections on Gender Issues in International Law over the Last Decade." *The Melbourne Journal of International Law* 10, no. 1: 11–26.

Phoenix, Ann, and Pamela Pattynama. 2006. "Intersectionality." *European Journal of Women's Studies* 13: 187–192.

Rawi, Mariam. 2004. "Rule of the Rapists." *The Guardian*. February 12, 2004. https://www.theguardian.com/world/2004/feb/12/afghanistan.gender.

Razack, Sherene H. 2004. "Imperilled Muslim Women, Dangerous Muslim Men and Civilised Europeans: Legal and Social Responses to Forced Marriages." *Feminist Legal Studies* 12, no. 2: 129–174.

Rolston, Bill. 1989. "Mothers, Whores and Villains: Images of Women in Novels of the Northern Ireland Conflict." *Race and Class* 31: 51–57.

Rooney, Eilish. 2006. "Women's Equality in Northern Ireland's Transition: Intersectionality in Theory and Place." *Feminist Legal Studies* 14, no. 3: 353–375.

Rooney, Eilish. 2007. "Engendering Transitional Justice: Questions of Absence and Silence." *International Journal of Law in Context* 3, no. 2: 173–187.

Rooney, Eilish. 2008. "Critical Reflections: 'Documenting Gender and Memory.'" *Women's Studies International Forum* 31, no. 6: 457–463.

Rooney, Eilish. 2013. "Intersectionality: A Feminist Theory for Transitional Justice." In *Feminist Perspectives on Transitional Justice*, edited by Martha Albertson Fineman and Estelle Zinsstag, 89–114. Cambridge: Intersentia.

Rooney, Eilish. 2014. *Transitional Justice Grassroots Toolkit: User's Guide*. Belfast: Bridge of Hope.

Rooney, Eilish, and Aisling Swaine. 2012. "The 'Long Grass' of Agreements: Promise, Theory and Practice." *International Criminal Law Review: Special Issue: Transitional Justice and Restorative Justice* 12: 519–548.

Said, Edward W. 1983. *The World, the Text, and the Critic*. Cambridge, MA: Harvard University Press.

Salem, Sara. 2013. "Feminist Critique and Islamic Feminism: The Question of Intersectionality." *Academic Journal* 1, no. 1. August 7, 2017, http://postcolonialist.com/civil-discourse/feminist-critique-and-islamic-feminism-the-question-of-intersectionality/#.

Sharoni, Simona. 1995. *Gender and the Israeli-Palestinian Conflict: The Politics of Women's Resistance*. Syracuse, NY: Laurence Hill Books.

Smyth, Marie. 1998. *Half the Battle: Understanding the Impact of the Troubles on Children and Young People in Northern Ireland*. Londonderry: INCORE.

Williamson, Arthur, and John Darby. 1978. *Violence and the Social Services in Northern Ireland*. London: Heinemann Educational.

Yuval-Davis, Nira. 2006. "Intersectionality and Feminist Politics." *European Journal of Women's Studies* 13: 193–209.

CHAPTER 26

··

AGENCY AND GENDER NORMS
IN WAR ECONOMIES

··

PATTI PETESCH

PERIODS of violent political conflict and their aftermath disrupt local opportunity structures, including the normative environment for women's and men's roles and conducts. Yet, as this chapter brings to light, traditional gender norms remain present and powerful, resulting in strikingly divergent responses.

One might imagine conflict periods to be utterly debilitating times for gaining more freedom in one's life. But this study and the wider gender and conflict literature point to phases during and after horrific political violence as windows of opportunity when gender norms sometimes relax in ways that give women more control and authority in their lives (e.g., Bouta, Frerks, and Bannon 2005). Drawn from a large qualitative data set collected in twenty-four communities of Afghanistan, Liberia, Palestine, and Sudan, the evidence presented in this chapter reveals a large majority of women reporting a strong sense of empowerment from gaining more say in their households and greater economic independence as they strive to pull their families through the conflict.[1]

Yet, in these same localities where so many women speak of greater agency, men largely indicate feeling disempowered. Conflict shatters their gender-ascribed roles of leaders, protectors, and providers for their families and communities (Bannon and Correia 2006). Much less examined has been civilian men's struggles to cope with conflict, and this oversight has likely limited our understanding of why we do not see more lasting normative change resulting from women's new roles.

To address this gap in the literature, the chapter presents evidence of and then assesses more carefully how and why conflict has such strongly diverging effects on women's and men's agency and the implications for gender norms across varied contexts. An understanding of agency, defined here as an "ability to define one's goals and act upon them" (Kabeer 1999, 438), is necessary because women's wartime experiences require them to actively press against or resist gender norms, at the same time as these very processes often compel men to enforce norm compliance for women's roles—even as, or perhaps especially because, men are deeply insecure about their own roles. Shedding more light on how conflict fuels these competing agency processes and how gender norms strongly color individual agency lies at the heart of the following analysis.

The chapter opens with a review of the study approach, and sets forth the polarized findings on men's and women's perceptions of empowerment. The main narrative of the chapter is then framed by two case studies, each set in border towns. The first border town, in Palestine, highlights the polarized empowerment and limited gender norm change that is typical in this data set. The second case, from Liberia, an outlier, tells a hopeful story of the dual increase in both men's and women's agency and the more sweeping normative shifts and favorable development outcomes associated with this rarer change phenomenon. It notes that the ability of both genders to find pathways for participating in and benefiting from rebuilding their households and community in the aftermath of conflict were key to this latter positive outcome. The two overarching conclusions of the chapter are that (1) men's agency and women's agency appear to be tightly interdependent, and together shape prospects for more equitable gender norms and inclusive development at the local level; and (2) conflict periods can provide a window of opportunity for speeding up normative change and gender equality, and policies should be designed to tap into these forces.

STUDY OBJECTIVES AND CONCEPTS

Despite high-profile UN gender summits dating back to 1975, and a stream of women's advocacy, it took the World Bank until 2012 for its flagship annual publication, *World Development Report* (*WDR*), to take on the topic of gender. As background for their report, the *WDR* team commissioned rapid qualitative fieldwork in twenty countries to learn more about trends in gender norms and gender differences in economic decisions, among other issues (Muñoz Boudet, Petesch, and Turk 2012). This chapter presents additional comparative analysis with this data set, focusing on the sample of communities from four countries directly affected by violent political conflict.

Social norms are the rules that guide us on how to behave in our daily lives. The gender dimensions of social norms stem from a society's deepest values about the proper roles and conducts for women and men. Women in many communities in this sample, for instance, may be harshly scolded or physically punished for dressing or speaking inappropriately. Men may face ridicule for not acting tough. These norms are also strongly linked to power, and they structure social interactions in ways that routinely advantage men through processes that are mainly subconscious and hidden, but on occasion more overtly aggressive (Connell 1987; Ridgeway 2011).

Agency refers to men and women conceiving of and acting upon goals for themselves. Increased agency, or empowerment, is loosely defined here as a product of the interaction between agency and local opportunity structures (Petesch, Smulovitz, and Walton 2005; Narayan and Petesch 2007, discussing framework). Of course, not all of women's and men's intended goals are achieved; opportunity structures matter greatly in discussions of agency and empowerment. Local opportunity structures embody a community's normative climate as well as its economic, political, and civic structures and informal associational life. As will be shown in the chapter, these various elements may combine in ways that restrain, enable, or perhaps even motivate agency. Periods of conflict can be moments of rupture for established elites, resource flows, and institutions—and hence moments that potentially allow for more inclusive local opportunity structures to take hold that can create more gender-equitable economic opportunities.

When exploring questions of gender norms and agency, it is helpful to distinguish a relaxation of a gender norm from an actual change in a gender norm (Muñoz Boudet, Petesch, and Turk 2012). A *relaxation* refers to indications that individuals are displaying preferences or practices—or pursuing goals—that deviate from prevailing norms for their gender, but these conducts or beliefs are not registering in local mindsets as the norm. For example, many rural women in this study may be engaging in new livestock activities or additional farm labor to help their households cope with conflict. Yet, local people often do not regard the women's livelihood activities as actual work, and they still identify local women solely as housewives. In a village in Red Sea state, Sudan, where local customs dictate that women generally do not work for pay unless under exceptional circumstances such as widowhood, a woman noted, "Women in our area do not work on farms as farm labor; they help only, in seeding and harvesting." Unpaid farm labor does not violate the cherished household roles for women in this village, while supplying a "costless" supply of helping farmhands. A gender norm *change* indicates that a new behavior or role is openly observed and acknowledged as an acceptable practice for that gender. In Liberia, as discussed later in the chapter, more women than ever are earning independent incomes and are exercising leadership roles under very difficult conditions, and their new roles and influence are openly recognized, although not always favorably.

This study reached a total of twenty-four communities in Afghanistan (two urban, two rural), Liberia (six urban, three rural), Palestine (four urban and two rural), and Sudan (one urban and four rural). The four conflicts in this sample spilled across borders, were widespread and prolonged, and were not contained to specific population groups in peripheral regions, as some wars are. Samples were designed within countries to capture a wide range of gender norms, and encompassed both middle-class and poor neighborhoods of cities and towns, as well as prosperous and poor villages. At the time of the fieldwork, security conditions remained poor in much of Sudan and Palestine, while security had largely been restored for five or more years in the regions sampled from Afghanistan and Liberia.

Field teams applied a standardized package of data collection tools, reaching a total of fifty-nine male and fifty-nine female focus groups of approximately eight participants each, in the conflict sample.[2] In order to assess agency, the adult focus groups reflected on what having power and freedom means, and then each group built its own "ladder," which depicts, at the top step, the characteristics of the most powerful and freest women (or men, if a men's focus group) who live in their neighborhood or village. Focus groups then discussed the characteristics of those of their own gender on the bottom step, or the least powerful and free. The focus group then engaged in a sorting exercise with the ladder steps, positioning one hundred representative women (or men) from their community to indicate the distribution now and ten years ago. This exercise allowed for reflection on the trends in perceived agency for their own gender.

It is important to differentiate this "bottom-up" approach for assessing agency and empowerment from the more conventional survey methods for exploring socioeconomic mobility. It is not possible to compare the different women's and men's ladders and distributions directly because individual ladders differ in the numbers and traits of their steps; but it is possible to undertake rough comparisons of the changes reported on the ladders and the factors perceived to drive these changes. The ladder data frequently captured extensive movements up and down the ladder associated with conflict and recovery experiences; however, the direction of this churning differed significantly by gender.

THE POLARIZING EFFECTS OF CONFLICT ON MEN'S AND WOMEN'S AGENCY

Borrowing measurement tools from the field of socioeconomic mobility, the ladder exercise endeavors to capture men's and women's sense of whether they are gaining or losing power and freedom in their lives. Figure 26.1 compares the average rates of mobility (or movement up or down) on the focus groups' ladders of power and freedom (calculated as the difference between the mean ladder step now and ten years ago, after sorting of one hundred men or women at the two points in time). The figure compares the ratings reported by women's and men's groups from both the conflict and non-conflict samples.[3] Overall, conflict-affected women register the strongest sense of empowerment over the ten-year reference period, while men in these contexts widely report themselves to be falling on their ladders and losing control and authority. Women

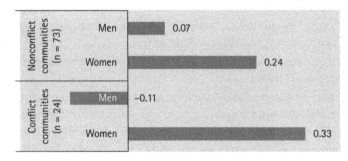

FIGURE 26.1. Average mobility index on women's and men's ladders of power and freedom.

Note: 189 focus groups, 97 communities, 20 countries.

from conflict communities report consistently that many local women are gaining a larger say in their domestic roles, as well as increasing their economic participation.

While about a tenth of the women's ladders feature downward mobility in the conflict sample, more than half of the men's register this. The men's falling was heavily concentrated in the eleven communities reached in Sudan and Palestine, where risks of armed conflict remained high and crippled men's livelihoods.

With great consistency across this sample, men report disruption of their livelihoods and economic inactivity during conflict periods, and wait out the tough times; meanwhile, women can be seen to resist normative dictates and to seize whatever meager opportunities can be found to support their families. The large comparative conflict literature to date, while extensive, historically has been blind to gender or has focused mainly on the experiences of one gender or the other, failing to capture meaningfully the dynamic interplay between men's and women's sharply different coping mechanisms in response to conflict shocks.

WOMEN CLIMBING, MEN FALLING IN A GAZA BORDER TOWN

The contrast between men feeling emasculated and women claiming empowerment was widely on display in a town of Rafah district in Gaza; however, this case also illustrates well why these processes do not necessarily trigger normative change. The town, with a population of 5,500, resides next to the border with Egypt. The community has endured repeated bombings from Israel, and its economy suffered deeply due to tightly restricted cross-border trade and travel. Poverty was estimated by the key informant to affect roughly 35 percent of the community. A male focus group participant explained that it is "no longer a secret" that some local men earn a living by risking their lives digging and conducting trade in underground tunnels to Egypt: "And because people need to be able to provide for their families they no longer fear bombing or dying." With the local economy in shambles and insecurity pervasive, men speak of idleness and hopelessness.

All ten young men in their focus group (ages eighteen to twenty-four) reported themselves out of work, although six had bachelor's degrees, and seven were young fathers. When asked about their goals, a young man replied, "My goal was to get a proper job, but nobody helped me. And what got in my way is the horrible political and economic situation and the fact that I don't have high contacts like other people." The young men talked about too much free time, unemployment, and struggling with "despair and depression." A local woman explained, "In the past, [the men] used to work in Israel, now they play cards. Even those who used to work for the [Palestinian] Authority . . . don't work. Instead of that they fight with us."

For these men, their occupations and economic assets are key determinants of their standing and movements on the ladder; and the health of the local economy greatly shapes their sense of agency (Connell 1987). Accordingly, the "strong men" of the town who are at the top ladder step are said to enjoy stable work with a good income. They are also decision-makers and have freedom to travel. The adult men's focus group indicated three initiatives that can help a local man climb into the top step: "Work in trade and earn a lot of money and become rich. Get promoted. Start a successful [business] project." At the other end of the ladder, their bottom-step men are described as "weak," "uneducated," and relying on an "unstable job," common features of bottom-step men across the sample. Their bottom step has doubled in size to 40 percent of the neighborhood's men, due to business and job losses, dealing drugs, and imprisonment.

Although the women reside in the very same town, their ladder conveys a very different story. Despite the press of conservative norms, religious traditions, poor security, and a weak economy, the share of women on their bottom two steps has plummeted from 60 to 20 percent in the past decade. They have gained power through "marriage, work, a university degree." By way of explanation, the women's focus group reports that many local women are now better educated and have had to develop strong characters to help their families cope with the great insecurity in their lives. For women, both their domestic and economic initiatives are viewed as important for their position on the ladder and in fueling their climb. Few women, in fact, are mentioned as working for pay in this town—and this is consistent with other localities where norms are being forced to relax but have yet to change. Nor do women of the town generally venture out in public unaccompanied by a male due to practices of seclusion, although the female job holders can move about independently.

Conflict has had sharply different effects on men's and women's sense of power and freedom in Rafah. Men report deep unhappiness and question how they alone can meet their household's daily needs, as normative dictates require. Women, for their part, say their harsh circumstances have compelled them to take more initiative, but their community's local opportunity structure provides few outlets for this beyond their domestic role. As is common in the data set more generally, traditional norms continue to be valued despite the women's new conduct. In opportunity structures wracked by conflict and economic devastation, men's and women's agency may well be competing forces, and women's capacities to gain more recognition, status, and normative change constrained because of that competition.

NORMS RELAXING BUT RESISTING CHANGE

Across the global data set—in the peaceful as well as conflict-affected localities—men and women perceived little difference in the factors that fuel their agency and empowerment, but the underlying processes differ greatly due to gender norms.

To climb their ladders, both sexes most often mention their economic initiatives, followed by behaviors and attitudes such as making plans and having a sense of self-efficacy. It is significant that even in traditional communities where few or perhaps no women work for pay, women still mention their own economic activities, more than other factors, as drivers of their agency. In a town in Afghanistan's Kabul province, for instance, gender norms are very restrictive, yet the women's focus group described the most powerful local women as "literate, some of them have a job, can make decisions on expenses." Almost everywhere in this data set, women identify increased agency with beginning or enlarging their economic participation to help support their households through the difficult years of conflict and recovery.

Yet, if men and women report few differences in the factors that drive their agency, the ways that they pursue goals for themselves and perceive empowerment do vary significantly by gender; conflict intensifies these dynamics. What is key to keep in mind is that many behaviors and attitudes attached to exercising agency fit squarely with men's gender-ascribed roles to be providers, to take charge, to be assertive, and to serve as the authority figure for the household. Men fall on their ladders, or become disempowered, when they cannot live up to their expected roles and behaviors. In a town of Greenville, Liberia, where the men's focus group reports disempowerment, their numerous bottom-step men are described as "[n]ot working, no business; they cut palms and give them to their wives to sell before they can get food."

The normative dictates for women stand in opposition to men's, and prescribe submission, modesty, limited physical mobility and social interaction, and strict prioritization of their domestic role and duties. Unlike men, women have to constantly press on the frontiers of expected roles and conduct in order to climb their ladders and gain more voice. Rural women of Red Sea state in Sudan stressed that a woman must be "daring and honest in dealing with men; and the more she can serve women in the village, the higher she ascends the ladder." Yet such leadership qualities are more often deemed to be masculine traits and a clear break with gender norms for women's roles.

Moreover, although economic agency may be central to women's sense of empowerment, the space for this in the difficult local opportunity structures prevalent in this data set is far more constrained than that for men. In most communities in this sample beyond Liberia, seclusion is practiced, and women face strong pressures not to take jobs that require interacting with the opposite sex or to move about in public unaccompanied by an appropriate male escort. These rigorous gender norms are deemed necessary in order to protect their own and their family's honor. The pressures of housework and care, time constraints, religious traditions, poor security, and limited transport add to the hardships of working outside the home. Together, these forces inhibit women from gaining recognition and status for their new economic roles, and this greatly slows down normative change. Even in Liberia, where women have fewer mobility restrictions and a longer tradition of working for pay, their economic outlets are scarce, and they frequently describe expectations to provide sexual favors in exchange for jobs or vending opportunities. Conflict-induced hardships may lighten some normative restrictions on women, but their agency continues to be heavily constrained by significant and pervasive gender inequalities in their access to local institutions, resources, and networks.

Still, despite the strong reputational and physical risks, and despite the additional time burden and unreliable and scant pay on offer, women regularly deem their additional economic roles to be empowering and more desirable than lives with scarcely any choices at all. The normative framework for men's agency, however, differs sharply. Understanding the stressful effects of conflict on local economies and on gender norms and gender relations is necessary for making sense of the polarized agency patterns elicited by the ladder activity.

Many Men and Many Women Climbing in a Liberian Border Town

Liberia stands apart in the sample because gender norms had shifted enough by the time of this study to allow for some women to become powerful leaders, to accumulate and control significant resources, and to enjoy greater freedom of choice and action. In the sampled neighborhood in Monrovia, women on the top step ran big businesses and traveled to "bring goods in from China, Dubai, and Nigeria." The data captured women serving as local elected leaders in six of the nine research communities. Numerous focus group members of both genders mention being inspired by Ellen Sirleaf Johnson's presidency. This was also the sample country that enjoyed the most distance from conflict. Clearly, these macro forces are important, powerfully reinforcing local women's initiatives at the same time as many men were finding pathways to recover.

Significantly, in more than half the Liberian sample, men report climbing their ladders and perceiving empowerment along with the women. And in most of these "twin-climbing" contexts, the normative framework seems to have altered sufficiently to allow for more cooperative and productive gender relations and more inclusive local institutions.

Similarly, in a town of 10,000 that borders Sierra Leone in the Tewor district, both women and men report quite substantial gains in empowerment for their own gender. The men's group from Tewor said that perhaps 40 percent of them have now pulled themselves up out of the bottom step—as farmers, teachers, customs officials, drivers, tradesmen, and businessmen. Similarly, the women report that almost a quarter of them have now moved up out of the bottom step: "After the war, we started making our own businesses." The women largely run the local market, and in the process gained more voice in their households, saying they can now afford to send their children to school.

What is so important about this context where both many women and many men are perceived to be climbing their ladders is that gender norms for women's roles have *changed*. Women not only are active in the town's economy, but also are political and civic leaders. The town's elected leadership is split "50–50" between women and men. The town chief is a man, and they have a "chairlady." There is a commissioner position held by a man, and another township commissioner is a woman, who was pivotal in getting the town's first senior high school. The clan chief is a man, but a woman is the "supervisor for all mosques." In comparison with the Liberian research communities where men reported disempowerment, the men in this community seem at ease and welcoming of women's new roles. One of the adult men suggests that there is "nothing a husband will do without the consent of the wife or vice versa"—although these men make it clear that they remain in control of major household decisions.

This border town offers a hopeful picture of the improved functioning of local market, civic, and political institutions that can accompany a transition to greater gender equality—paradoxically in the wake of conflict. By comparison, the Rafah town in Gaza is populated by economically better off and more educated residents; but there, continued war, high unemployment, and very entrenched gender norms leave few avenues for men and women to find ways to put their own lives and their community on a better path. Rafah's experience with the more static gender norms within a war-ravaged local opportunity structure is unfortunately the more typical one of this data set. Women's sense of agency may be soaring, but that by itself is not enough to usher in normative change.

CONCLUSION

Comparative work with this community data set and others reveals that some, and possibly many, communities can shift rapidly to more inclusive opportunity structures, with periods of violent conflict and recovery propelling this phenomenon (Narayan and Petesch 2010; Petesch 2011). Central to these stories are often complementary trends of rising access to local economic opportunities, combined with supportive public and civic action. Yet, women's significant contributions to these favorable dynamics are only slowly gaining recognition in the policy discourse and literatures about conflict.

Similar to this study, a previous analysis of 125 women's life stories from conflict-affected regions of Colombia, Indonesia, Philippines, and Sri Lanka found exposure to conflict to be empowering for women, although war should certainly never be used as pretext for such a goal (Petesch 2011). Moreover, as in Tewor, the localities where women report greater ability to participate in the economic and political life of their communities are also contexts with more rapid poverty reduction. Empirical work in conflict-affected contexts (Justino et al. 2012; see also Justino, Chapter 6 in this volume) likewise finds that community recovery is stronger where women are more active in the local economy and other public arenas.

Although development interventions were not a focus of this investigation, the findings strongly suggest that decentralized programs with gender and development objectives that aim narrowly at transforming women's lives while disregarding what is happening to men will likely miss their targets. Although men may be reporting disempowerment and great insecurity during and after wartime, they nevertheless remain the dominant authority figures of their households and communities, affecting local women's access to opportunities as well as how the fruits of their labor will be distributed. The forces that fuel men's and women's agency differ but remain interlocked; and gender norms that relax under stressful conditions and enable women to assume new roles are unlikely to hold without reinforcing changes in their local opportunity structures. Interventions are needed within these environments that can support men to recover their breadwinner and authority positions while simultaneously removing diverse barriers for women so that they too can gain strength and recognition in these roles. UN Security Council resolution 1325 (2000), which focuses on advancing women instead of developing strategies aimed at ensuring that both women and men can benefit from recovery programs and participate "in solidarity" in forging more inclusive local-level institutions, also misses the mark (see also El-Bushra 2012).

Innovation is crucially needed in conceptual models and program designs to better account for the powerful drag of slowly changing gender norms on peace and development, as well as the strong gender differences in how conflict affects agency. A great challenge is that conflict pushes women into the economy in large numbers precisely at a time when opportunities are poor and they may face great hazards to their safety and reputations. Simultaneously, men are struggling to cope in an environment where the only jobs on offer are low-paying, dangerous, and possibly illicit, and this is deeply emasculating for them. As documented elsewhere in the *Handbook*, conflict periods also fuel problems of sexual and physical violence, which are generally understood on the ground to be fueled in part by these competing agency dynamics. Local public safety, job creation, and civic engagement strategies are thus needed that are well coordinated and that provide opportunities for economic advancement and civic and political leadership for both genders, but which can account for the reality that women and men in the same localities may often perceive opportunities, constraints, and risks quite differently.

In conclusion, this data set highlights that while conflict experiences push women to adopt new roles and derive a sense of empowerment from this, such processes do not necessarily result in normative change and greater gender equality. Rather, women are far more likely to find effective pathways for challenging and changing restrictive norms in phases when men are also finding pathways to pursue important goals for themselves. These realities point to the need for policies and interventions by governments and donors that are more effective at supporting, simultaneously, both local women's and men's initiatives to recover from conflict and get ahead.

Notes

1. See Muñoz Boudet, Petesch, and Turk (2012) for additional analysis of this data set. The fieldwork was led by Chona Echavez (AREU, Afghanistan), Gwen Heaner (Consultant, Liberia), Khalil Al Medani (SOED, Sudan), and Samia Al-Botmeh (Centre for Development Studies, Birzeit University, Palestine).
2. The focus groups were also separated by generation: with separate male and female focus groups conducted with adults (ages twenty-five to sixty) and with youth (ages eighteen to twenty-four), for a total of four focus groups in every community. In Sudan and Palestine, focus groups were also held with adolescent girls and separately with boys (ages twelve to

sixteen). For a fuller discussion of methodology, see Muñoz Boudet, Petesch, and Turk (2012).

3. The five women's focus groups in Sudan did not carry out the final sorting exercise that provides the mobility index; hence, the conflict sample in Figure 26.1 includes twenty-four focus groups for the men's average mobility index, and nineteen for the women's. The Sudanese women's ladder discussions are very consistent with the women's accounts from the other three countries, and their empowerment trends would have been unlikely to change the general pattern of findings.

References

Bannon, Ian, and Maria C. Correia, eds. 2006. *The Other Half of Gender: Men's Issues in Development.* Washington, DC: The World Bank.

Bouta, Tsjeard, Georg Frerks, and Ian Bannon. 2005. *Gender, Conflict and Development.* Washington, DC: The World Bank.

Connell, R. W. 1987. *Gender and Power.* Oxford: Polity Press.

El-Bushra, Judy. 2012. *Gender in Peacebuilding: Taking Stock.* London: International Alert.

Justino, Patricia, Ivan Cardona, Rebecca Mitchell, and Catherine Müller. 2012. "Quantifying the Impact of Women's Participation in Post-Conflict Recovery." HiCN Working Paper 131, Households in Conflict Network, University of Sussex, Brighton.

Kabeer, Naila. 1999. "Resources, Agency, Achievements: Reflections on the Measurement of Women's Empowerment." *Development and Change* 30, no. 3: 435–464.

Muñoz Boudet, Ana Maria, Patti Petesch, and Carolyn Turk, with Angelica Thumala. 2012. *On Norms and Agency: Conversations on Gender with Men and Women in 20 Countries.* Washington, DC: The World Bank.

Narayan, Deepa, and Patti Petesch. 2007. "Agency, Opportunity Structure, and Poverty Escapes." In *Moving Out of Poverty: Cross-Disciplinary Perspectives on Mobility*, edited by Deepa Narayan and Patti Petesch, 1–44. New York and Washington, DC: Palgrave Macmillan and The World Bank.

Narayan, Deepa, and Patti Petesch, eds. 2010. *Moving Out of Poverty: Rising from the Ashes of Conflict.* New York and Washington, DC: Palgrave Macmillan and The World Bank.

Petesch, Patti. 2011. *Women's Empowerment Arising from Violent Conflict and Recovery: Life Stories from Four Middle-Income Countries.* Washington, DC: USAID.

Petesch, Patti, Catalina Smulovitz, and Michael Walton. 2005. "Evaluating Empowerment: A Framework with Cases from Latin America." In *Measuring Empowerment: Cross-Disciplinary Perspectives*, edited by Deepa Narayan, 39–67. Washington, DC: The World Bank.

Ridgeway, Cecilia L. 2011. *Framed by Gender: How Gender Inequality Persists in the Modern World.* Oxford: Oxford University Press.

....

CHAPTER 27

RISK AND RESILIENCE

The Physical and Mental Health of Female Civilians during War

....

LAUREN C. NG AND THERESA S. BETANCOURT

ARMED conflict jeopardizes the survival of civilians. However, combat itself is not the principal cause of disability and death of civilians during war (Lacina and Gleditsch 2005). Instead, war and armed conflict are so devastating because they disrupt or destroy the fundamental necessities for health and well-being. The more aspects of life that are negatively impacted, the greater the risk to civilian health (Betancourt et al. 2010). For women, these risks are compounded by their frequently lower social status, cultural expectations of motherhood and womanhood, lower access to resources, higher risk of sexual assault and exploitation, and biological differences (such as increased risk to reproductive health). This chapter takes a broad public health view of how female civilians may be impacted during war, surveying a variety of contexts to show these impacts.

A helpful model to recall the overlapping risk and protective factors that impact human security is "SAFE": (1) Safety and security; (2) Access to health care and physiological needs; (3) Family, community, and connection to others; and (4) Education, economic security, and livelihood (Betancourt et al. 2010). Originally applied to child protection during conflict, the SAFE model can be extended to adults. SAFE acknowledges that as war erodes the safety and security of the civilian population, other factors that promote health, such as positive and stable family and community relationships, opportunities for education and economic support, and food, shelter, and health care, are often also compromised, exacerbating poor outcomes. In contrast, if these protective factors can be strengthened, civilian health may be preserved, even in insecure and unsafe environments.

ACCESS TO HEALTH CARE
AND PHYSIOLOGICAL NEEDS:
FOOD, WATER, AND SHELTER

War not only exposes populations to mass violence, it also impacts the availability of natural resources and damages infrastructure. As a result, civilians grapple with declines in their basic needs, drastically increasing the risks to their health. Indeed, the great majority of people, and women in particular, who die during armed conflict perish from infectious disease and malnutrition (both exacerbated during conflict), and from the impacts of displacement (Lacina and Gleditsch 2005).

Housing

Civilian homes and neighborhoods are often destroyed, damaged, or seized during war; alternatively, people may be forcibly evicted from, or prevented from returning to, their homes because their security situation is not assured or is actively threatened. In many armed conflicts, security staff seize homes and property for their own use, and some soldiers remain long after fighting has ceased. For example, in Kathmandu, Nepal, roughly 85 percent of the land seized during the Nepalese civil war was still being held by armed forces six years after the war formally ended (Docherty 2013). As a result of this displacement and disenfranchisement, civilians—the majority of whom are women and children—become homeless during and after war, and are forced to stay outside or in temporary shelters, or to flee to displaced persons or refugee camps (Lindsey 2001). Lack of housing may jeopardize their health through increased exposure to the elements and disease-carrying insects and animals, physical and sexual violence, and increased stress and loss of community and identity.

Water

In addition to having inadequate housing, another major source of health risk during war is reduced access to clean and safe water. Communities that access water through public facilities during peacetime may find that during war, water delivery systems and infrastructure are disrupted, destroyed, inaccessible, or fall into disrepair, with no mechanism for their maintenance (Dodge 1990; Lindsey 2001). For example, by 2012, more than one-third of the water treatment plants in Syria had been destroyed, and the amount of clean water fell by 40 percent compared to pre-war levels (UNICEF 2014). Insufficient access to clean water is exacerbated by disrupted sanitation facilities. Again, using Syria as an example, 66 percent of the country's sewage has gone untreated, as compared to 30 percent before the war (UNICEF 2014). In Iraq in 1993, sewage treatment functioned at only 50 percent of pre–First Gulf War capacity, with solid waste being discharged directly into rivers that were the primary sources of drinking water for many people. As water treatment and sanitation systems break down or become unusable, water-borne infectious diseases spread (Lindsey 2001). The impact of these diseases is usually compounded by weakened immune systems and poor health associated with malnutrition and exposure (Guha-Sapir and van Panhuis 2002). Because women and girls typically gather water, dispose of waste, and wash clothes and household items, they are at increased risk from contaminated water.

Nutrition

In addition to being exposed to infectious disease, armed conflicts are the leading contributor to hunger emergencies; famine and malnutrition have killed thousands of civilians both during and after war (UN Food and Agriculture Organization 2005). War disrupts the availability, quantity, and quality of food, as well as strategies for food collection and provision (Dodge 1990; Plumper and Neumayer 2006). The deliberate or accidental destruction of civilian crops and livestock, or diverting of food supplies to armed groups, is common in areas of armed conflict. Armed groups may be dependent on the civilian population for food, further exacerbating civilian hunger and malnutrition. As security within the community becomes more unstable, the civilian population's ability to farm, fish, and care for livestock becomes increasingly limited. As food availability decreases, prices skyrocket, and formal trading markets are often disrupted, further contributing to food insecurity (Misselhorn 2005; Plumper and Neumayer 2006). Sanctions may further exacerbate the food crisis. In Sierra Leone, UN sanctions reduced food availability, and prices tripled (Solomon 2006). Lack of a well-balanced diet can have serious repercussions. For example, during the war in Mozambique, women and children became afflicted with konzo, a form of paralysis, due to eating insufficiently cooked bitter cassava, as it was the only food available to them (Rehn and Sirleaf 2002).

Women die of food insecurity at disproportionally high rates (Rehn and Sirleaf 2002). This may be due to cultural expectations that men eat first (Gardam and Charlesworth 2000), and to women being more vulnerable to nutrient and protein deficiencies, which can be very serious for women of reproductive age, and may be fatal in pregnant women (Messer and Cohen 2007). During wartime, up to 70 percent of Somali refugee women of reproductive age were anemic (Rehn and Sirleaf 2002), predisposing them to weakness and shortness of breath, and in severe cases to heart failure. Food insufficiency, malnutrition, and stress can also negatively impact pregnancy outcomes.

Complications during pregnancy, amenorrhea, and low quality and quantity of breast milk have also been linked to war-related violence, malnutrition, and stress (Palmer and Zwi 1998). Women who are malnourished may experience amenorrhea, and pregnant and lactating mothers may produce low quality and quantity of breast milk, which can lead to underweight or unhealthy babies and infants (Palmer and Zwi 1998). Women

who are nursing but are unable to feed their babies will often be unable to procure sub-
stitutes, and access to another nursing mother may be limited (Lindsey 2001). The poor
nutritional health of babies and young children can lead to developmental challenges or
delays that can negatively impact entire generations of children, and by extension, the
community at large.

Health care

Health is further compromised during and after armed conflict due to steep declines
in available, accessible, and affordable health services, just as demand is increasing.
Resources may be diverted away from health services to pay for warfare, leading to the
closure of health centers, hospitals, and pharmacies, and loss of funding for medical
staff and medical supplies and equipment (Dodge 1990; Plumper and Neumayer 2006).
While some health facilities remain open, the lack of security for, and the destruction
and disruption of, transportation infrastructure and services that supply and support
health services often lead to inefficient and limited services for the civilian population.
The ability to shift resources between health facilities can fail, resulting in services being
available only to the small percentage of the population who can actually reach the few
functioning health providers. Moreover, because demand is extremely high, and salary
for the remaining medical staff, equipment, and medicines must often be paid solely by
patients, care is unaffordable for most civilians.

Armed groups may also deliberately target medical staff or plunder and damage
health-care facilities for medicine, medical and laboratory equipment, and even patient
records and data. In Afghanistan, between 2012 and 2013, health-care facilities and personnel were attacked or threatened by armed forces fifty-two times. During the Syrian
civil war, 60 percent of hospitals had been destroyed or damaged as of 2014 (UNICEF
2014). These threats and hardships lead to qualified medical staff leaving war-torn areas;
few return, even after the wars have ended. During the war in Côte d'Ivoire, medical staff
was reduced by more than 75 percent, with more than 90 percent of doctors fleeing to
other regions or countries (Betsi et al. 2006). As medical staff flee and supply lines are
cut off, the existing medical equipment goes unused or falls into disrepair. The WHO
estimates that 40 percent of medical equipment in Bosnia, for example, was unused during and after the civil war (Plumper and Neumayer 2006).

Under these circumstances, medical treatment is often unavailable, and public
health services and prevention programs are frequently eliminated. As a result, infectious diseases increase substantially during wars (Ghobarah, Huth, and Russett 2004).
Moreover, influxes of displaced populations may lead to the introduction of new infectious diseases or the exacerbation of existing diseases in the non-displaced civilian population. Diseases that have been successfully eradicated in most countries continue to
infect populations affected by war. During the Syrian civil war, immunization rates fell
from 99 percent pre-war to 52 percent in 2012, and polio re-emerged in the population
after fourteen years of absence (UNICEF 2014). Additionally, as public health systems

shut down and as patients who were being treated prior to the war cannot continue their care, drug-resistant strains of manageable diseases such as tuberculosis and HIV/AIDS can develop (Betsi et al. 2006; Plumper and Neumayer 2006).

The increase in the prevalence and severity of diseases can be especially harmful to women because of their increased social vulnerability and, in many cases, their lack of financial resources to seek the care they require. In cases where health care is available, women are often less likely to have treatment and rehabilitation as compared to men (Rehn and Sirleaf 2002). Additionally, women have unique health-care needs that are often neglected and untreated during wartime. Pregnancy and child-birth continue to be major causes of preventable death and disability in women in low- and middle-income countries, and during war, maternal health problems and mortality increase, often as a result of lack of access to contraceptives and condoms, clean water, obstetric care, and qualified birth attendants, as well as higher rates of maternal malnutrition and unsafe abortions (Ghobarah, Huth, and Russett 2004; Whittington, Salah, and Muhigana 2005). In the Democratic Republic of Congo (DRC), while maternity services at one hospital were comparable to those prior to the war, the pregnancy outcomes (including stillbirths and premature delivery) were worse during the war, likely as a result of increased maternal stress and poor health and nutrition (Ahuka, Chabikuli, and Ogunbanjo 2004). Lack of health-care workers has also been linked to increases in maternal, infant, and under-five child mortality (Anand and Barnighausen 2004).

During war, sexual assault by family, community members, and armed forces increases, and women and girls are the primary targets. The lack of health care, combined with the stigma and shame associated with sexual violence, can prevent victims from seeking care; this can result in devastating physical and mental health complications, which although potentially treatable, may also be deadly. Physical injuries and infections from the assaults are often severe and persist long after conflicts have ended. The abrasions and tearing of tissues that often occur during rape greatly increase the risk of sexually transmitted infection (STI). In some conflicts, intentional infection of the female population was used as a weapon of war (Rehn and Sirleaf 2002). In Sierra Leone it was estimated that 70–90 percent of female rape survivors contracted at least one STI (Whittington, Salah, and Muhigana 2005). Untreated STIs increase the risk of infertility, ectopic pregnancy, inflammatory disease, cervical cancer, and death (Rehn and Sirleaf 2002).

Additional medical complications from sexual assault include miscarriages, hemorrhaging, painful menstruation, sexual dysfunction, trauma and mutilation of genitals and reproductive organs leading to fertility problems, and traumatic fistulas (holes between the vagina, bladder and rectum). Women with a fistula often experience leaking of urine and feces, leading to social rejection. Fistulas require surgical repair, an option that is almost never available to women in areas of armed conflict. High numbers of fistulas have been found in Burundi, Rwanda, Chad, DRC, Sierra Leone, and Sudan, due in part to the large number of women experiencing traumatic rape during the wars in these countries (Bastick, Grimm, and Kunz 2007). Women who become pregnant through rape may have to cope with the mental anguish of the rape as well as subsequent pregnancy, as they are often unable to obtain a safe abortion (see also Theidon, Chapter 11 in this volume); those who have illegal abortions in unsafe facilities may suffer severe medical complications.

The mental suffering that sexual assault survivors endure includes nightmares, nonspecific pain, anxiety, post-traumatic stress disorder (PTSD), and depression (Murthy and Lakshminarayana 2006). This social ostracism increases a women's vulnerability and often leads to further exploitation and to high-risk survival strategies (Rehn and Sirleaf 2002).

Family, Community, and Connection to Others

The breakdown of families and communities contributes to poor mental and physical health. Social support, including positive relationships with community and family members, has been linked with lower rates of mental health problems, even in populations exposed to high rates of violence (Dubow et al. 2012). Positive social support networks can provide emotional and informational support (such as advice giving and sharing of news), and instrumental or material support (such as caring for those who are sick), as well as acting as a buffer to other stressors, insulating individuals from the deleterious effects of violence and conflict.

However, millions of families are torn apart by war through death, abduction, conscription, forced or voluntary displacement or migration, and separation or abandonment due to economic pressures and increased stress (Misselhorn 2005; Palmer and Zwi 1998). Women are usually the ones who remain at home, and often they are left without information about the safety or location of their relatives. While women are the main initiators of requests for news about missing family members, they face a bevy of barriers to accessing information, including a lack of security and financial, cultural, traditional, and social factors that may deny them needed information (Lindsey 2001). It is common for missing people to remain unaccounted for, and the psychological toll of not knowing their fate can result in an inability to heal from, or to address, the traumas of war (Docherty 2013). If a family learns that a loved one has been killed, the body is often not located or returned, and so families cannot organize a proper funeral and burial in accord with cultural or religious practices and are unable to visit their dead relatives' remains. Not being able to participate in these customs can complicate the grieving process (Lindsey 2001). For many survivors, the death or loss of loved ones, or the pain of witnessing or being aware of a loved one's suffering, can lead to severe mental health problems over and above their own exposure to violence (Fazel et al. 2012). With little access to care, many war survivors continue to suffer from complicated grief and depression for years, and even decades.

The insecure environment, increase in poverty, displacement, loss of home and identity, and mental health concerns can strain family relationships. Parents who are unable to protect their children from war and community violence, or to provide for their children's basic needs, may feel hopeless, humiliated, or demoralized. For example, in northern Uganda, both younger and older people reported that relationships between parents and children deteriorated during the armed conflict, with children reporting diminished parental support and parents reporting that children were violent and rebellious (El-Bushra and Sahl 2005; Kelly et al. 2011).

Families under stress also become strained or abusive, which can exacerbate, but also may be caused by, already elevated mental health and substance abuse problems. Rates of reported family and community violence in the civilian population have been found to increase during war (Bastick, Grimm, and Kunz 2007; UNICEF 2014). Beyond the immediate harm to the victims, community violence can also have a devastating long-term social impact, stressing, and even fracturing, the mutual trust that societies depended on before war. As trust decreases, communities previously characterized by strong social networks may become more individualistic, and individuals and families may become increasingly isolated. In Mali, prior to the war, sedentary and nomadic communities shared water and pasture; however, during the war, these ties were severed in many groups, putting both communities at risk (El-Bushra and Sahl 2005). The social protective systems that would have cared for vulnerable family and community members may be weakened, leading to worse mental and physical health within the entire community.

EDUCATION, ECONOMIC SECURITY, AND LIVELIHOOD

During war, as security decreases, civilian educational and employment opportunities plummet, and those that are available are often inconsistent or temporary. Schools and universities are frequently damaged, destroyed, or inaccessible. Teachers flee or stop working because they are not paid, their students stop attending, or they feel unsafe. In Syria, prior to the war, primary school enrollment was nearly universal; however, three years into the war, only half of school-aged children were attending school, and 20 percent of the schools were unusable (UNICEF 2014). Lack of education has long-term negative ramifications for children, families, and communities, as landless and unskilled youth have limited opportunities and become increasingly vulnerable to exploitation and engaging in high-risk survival strategies such as thievery and prostitution. The inability of children to attend school during war has been referred to as an "unnoticed human rights abuse" (Kelly et al. 2011). Indeed, education is strongly associated with the health of children and adults around the world. As indicated in the SAFE model presented earlier, education remains a major element of helping families and communities in low-resource settings move toward a more hopeful future. Thus, access to education should be a matter of immediate concern to organizations working in both emergency and post-conflict settings.

Another critical element of women's security as described in the SAFE model is economic security. As employment opportunities diminish in the context of war, the nature of available jobs also shifts. Many communities that relied on agriculture before the war may be forced off their farms and must subsist on odd jobs during and after the war (El-Bushra and Sahl 2005). Jobs outside of the home or the immediate community, such as salaried jobs and skilled trades, are particularly affected, as they are more likely to be inaccessible or eliminated because employers or customers are unable to pay for services during war. The loss of income, combined with the increase in prices, makes even the most basic needs unaffordable for many. The effects of this overall drop in economic productivity and community wealth can be stark, and the impact compounds as a war drags on. In Nicaragua, per capita income declined an average of 6.5 percent a year during the war, and rose only 2.5 percent a year after the war, resulting in a relative loss of wealth of 10 percent per year (Plumper and Neumayer 2006).

For women, an all-too-common consequence of these conflicts is widowhood. In some war-torn countries, the majority of the adult women are widows (Hynes 2004). In addition to coping with emotional loss and grief, many women are left to support and care for children on their own in societies in which men are traditionally considered the head of household (Kelly et al. 2011). In the context of overall diminished employment and limited social and political change in gender relations, women, particularly female heads of household, are at very high risk for experiencing discrimination and chronic poverty (Docherty 2013). Female heads of household may have few options to provide for their families, particularly when they have been evicted or displaced from their land, which may have provided most of their food. Available jobs are often poorly paid, informal, and temporary (see Justino, Chapter 6 in this volume). These jobs are usually unregulated and unprotected. Women also start small businesses. However, resources to access capital may be redirected to pay for war expenses (Gardam and Charlesworth 2000). In situations where loans are possible, repaying the loan and its interest may seem impossible in conflict-affected settings (Rehn and Sirleaf 2002).

Under these stressful conditions, women, particularly female heads of household, may engage in high-risk survival strategies (such as prostitution, marrying, or having sexual relationships with combatants or other men for protection or resources, and brewing or growing illicit products) to support their families (Hynes 2004; Sideris 2003). Some women may also become involved in the shadow war economies as smugglers of goods (Solomon 2006). Others may join the fighting forces as a way to secure access to food, money, and medical care. Struggling families may push daughters to marry at young ages to relieve their own economic burden or to secure a better life for the daughters (Whittington, Salah, and Muhigana 2005). Women, seeking better opportunities or a way out of the conflict, are also more vulnerable to traffickers, particularly in situations where the political, social, and security structures have been destroyed (Lindsey 2001;

Vandenberg, Chapter 31 in this volume). All of these situations increase the likelihood of exploitation and abuse, and subsequent poor physical and mental health.

MENTAL HEALTH, RESILIENCE, AND HEALING

The more that war erodes the SAFE protective factors, the worse the short- and long-term mental health outcomes of the civilian population are expected to be. Weakening of one protective domain can lead to a cascade of negative impacts on the others, and as result, the mental health of the civilian population plummets (Fazel et al. 2012). War-affected populations have very high rates of depression, anxiety, PTSD, suicidal ideation, and self-harming behavior (Murthy and Lakshminarayana 2006; Ormhaug, Meier, and Hernes 2009). Most studies that have examined gender differences in civilian war survivors have found that women were more likely to develop depression, anxiety, and PTSD than men (Johnson and Thompson 2008). The frustrations with daily hardships suffered during war can also lead to, and exacerbate, aggression, alcoholism, and drug abuse (El-Bushra and Sahl 2005), which in turn can fuel already heightened levels of community and domestic violence. Just as economic stress predicts poor mental health, poor mental health also leads to increases in poverty, perhaps by increasing morbidity and disability, decreasing ability to work, and increasing burden on family members (Lund et al. 2011). Despite extremely high levels of distress common in war zones, in most cases, civilians have little or no access to formal mental health services to help them heal from, and cope with, war experiences and daily hardships.

Resilience is promoted by both formal and informal resources. In the face of lack of assistance and support, war-affected communities activate survival strategies that can maintain or even strengthen aspects of life that promote good health and well-being. Certainly in wartime, critical elements of individual coping, intelligence, and problem-solving matter, as do family, community, and spiritual resources. Many civilians advocate for increased security and justice, form self-help groups to provide social support and psychological care, and cope with their experiences through religion and traditional cultural practices (Kelly et al. 2011; Murthy and Lakshminarayana 2006). In addition, they try to ensure that their homes and communities are safe and free from violence; they band together to provide educational opportunities to children, and to seek out novel solutions for generating income.

By strengthening or counteracting some of the risk factors that war exacerbates, civilians can transform them into protective factors, contributing to the resilience of individuals, families, and communities. In so doing, they are often able to offset some of the negative insults that war inflicts on health. However, while communities and individuals show incredible resilience in coping with devastating circumstances, healing still requires addressing the four SAFE domains of vulnerability holistically, recognizing the ways that they intersect each other.

CONCLUSION

During war, female civilians face unique harms. These harms are often different from those more commonly identified by the international community, which focuses primarily on women who have fought or those who have been sexually abused. The harms that impact women and the fractured households left behind deeply impact families and communities in the short and long term. If the goal of post-conflict reconstruction is to repair societies in the aftermath of conflict, then this particular group, with particular needs, must be identified, heard, and attended to.

REFERENCES

Ahuka, Ona Longombe, Nzapfurundi Chabikuli, and Gboyega A. Ogunbanjo. 2004. "The Effects of Armed Conflict on Pregnancy Outcomes in the Congo." *International Journal of Gynecology & Obstetrics* 84, no. 1: 91–92.

Anand, Sudhir, and Till Barnighausen. 2004. "Human Resources and Health Outcomes: Cross-Country Econometric Study." *The Lancet* 364, no. 9445: 1603–1609.

Bastick, Megan, Karin Grimm, and Rahel Kunz. 2007. *Sexual Violence in Armed Conflict: Global Overview and Implications for the Security Sector.* Geneva: Geneva Centre for the Democratic Control of Armed Forces.

Betancourt, Theresa S., Mary K. S. Fawzi, Claude Bruderlein, Chris Desmond, and Jim Y. Kim. 2010. "Children Affected by HIV/AIDS: SAFE, a Model for Promoting Their Security, Health, and Development." *Psychology, Health & Medicine* 15, no. 3: 243–265.

Betsi, Nicolas Alain, B. G. Koudou, Guéladio Cissé, A. B. Tschannen, A. M. Pignol, Y. Ouattara, Z. Madougou, M. Tanner, and Jürg Utzinger. 2006. "Effect of an Armed Conflict on Human Resources and Health Systems in Côte d'Ivoire: Prevention of and Care for People with HIV/AIDS." *AIDS Care* 18, no. 4: 356–365.

Docherty, Bonnie. 2013. *Assistance Overdue: Ongoing Needs of Civilian Victims of Nepal's Armed Conflict.* Cambridge, MA: International Human Rights Clinic, Harvard Law School.

Dodge, Cole P. 1990. "Health Implications of War in Uganda and Sudan." *Social Science & Medicine* 31, no. 6: 691–698.

Dubow, Eric F., L. Rowell Huesmann, Paul Boxer, Simha Landau, Shira Dvir, Khalil Shikaki, and Jeremy Ginges. 2012. "Exposure to Political Conflict and Violence and Posttraumatic Stress in Middle East Youth: Protective Factors." *Journal of Clinical Child and Adolescent Psychology* 41, no. 4: 402–416.

El-Bushra, Judy, and Ibrahim M. G. Sahl. 2005. *Cycles of Violence: Gender Relations and Armed Conflict.* Nairobi: ACORD and Construction House.

Fazel, Mina, Ruth V. Reed, Catherine Panter-Brick, and Alan Stein. 2012. "Mental Health of Displaced and Refugee Children Resettled in High-Income Countries: Risk and Protective Factors." *The Lancet* 379, no. 9812: 266–282.

Gardam, Judith Gail, and Hilary Charlesworth. 2000. "Protection of Women in Armed Conflict." *Human Rights Quarterly* 22, no. 1: 148–166.

Ghobarah, Hazem Adam, Paul Huth, and Bruce Russett. 2004. "The Post-War Public Health Effects of Civil Conflict." *Social Science & Medicine* 59, no. 4: 869–884.

Guha-Sapir, Debarati, and Willem G. van Panhuis. 2002. *Armed Conflict and Public Health: A Report on Knowledge and Knowledge Gaps*. Brussels: World Health Organisation, Centre for Research on the Epidemiology of Disasters, and Université Catholique de Louvain.

Hynes, H. Patricia. 2004. "On the Battlefield of Women's Bodies: An Overview of the Harm of War to Women." *Women's Studies International Forum* 27: 431–445.

Johnson, Howard, and Andrew Thompson. 2008. "The Development and Maintenance of Post-Traumatic Stress Disorder (PTSD) in Civilian Adult Survivors of War Trauma and Torture: A Review." *Clinical Psychology Review* 28, no. 1: 36–47.

Kelly, Jocelyn, Michael VanRooyen, Justin Kabanga, Beth Maclin, and Colleen Mullen. 2011. *Hope for the Future Again: Tracing the Effects of Sexual Violence and Conflict on Families and Communities in Eastern Democratic Republic of the Congo*. Cambridge, MA: Harvard Humanitarian Initiative.

Lacina, Bethany, and Nils Petter Gleditsch. 2005. "Monitoring Trends in Global Combat: A New Dataset of Battle Deaths." *European Journal of Population/Revue Européenne de Démographie* 21, no. 2-3: 145–166.

Lindsey, Charlotte. 2001. *Women Facing War: ICRC Study on the Impact of Armed Conflict on Women*. Geneva: International Committee of the Red Cross.

Lund, Crick, Mary De Silva, Sophie Plagerson, Sara Cooper, Dan Chisholm, Jishnu Das, Martin Knapp, and Vikram Patel. 2011. "Poverty and Mental Disorders: Breaking the Cycle in Low-Income and Middle-Income Countries." *The Lancet* 378, no. 9801: 1502–1514.

Messer, Ellen, and Marc J. Cohen. 2007. "Conflict, Food Insecurity and Globalization." *Food, Culture and Society: An International Journal of Multidisciplinary Research* 10, no. 2: 297–315.

Misselhorn, Alison A. 2005. "What Drives Food Insecurity in Southern Africa? A Meta-Analysis of Household Economy Studies." *Global Environmental Change* 15, no. 1: 33–43.

Murthy, R. Srinivasa, and Rashmi Lakshminarayana. 2006. "Mental Health Consequences of War: A Brief Review of Research Findings." *World Psychiatry* 5, no. 1: 25–30.

Ormhaug, Christin, Patrick Meier, and Helga Hernes. 2009. *Armed Conflict Deaths Disaggregated by Gender*. Oslo: International Peace Research Institute, Oslo (PRIO).

Palmer, Celia A., and Anthony B. Zwi. 1998. "Women, Health and Humanitarian Aid in Conflict." *Disasters* 22, no. 3: 236–249.

Plumper, Thomas, and Eric Neumayer. 2006. "The Unequal Burden of War: The Effect of Armed Conflict on the Gender Gap in Life Expectancy." *International Organization* 60, no. 3: 723–754.

Rehn, Elisabeth, and Ellen Johnson Sirleaf. 2002. *Women, War, Peace: The Independent Experts' Assessment on the Impact of Armed Conflict on Women and Women's Role in Peace-Building*. New York: UN Development Fund for Women.

Sideris, Tina. 2003. "War, Gender and Culture: Mozambican Women Refugees." *Social Science & Medicine* 56, no. 4: 713–724.

Solomon, Christiana. 2006. "The Role of Women in Economic Transformation: Market Women in Sierra Leone." *Conflict, Security & Development* 6, no. 3: 411–423.

United Nations Children's Fund (UNICEF). 2014. *Under Siege: The Devastating Impact on Children of Three Years of Conflict in Syria*. Amman, Jordan: UNICEF Regional Office for the Middle East and North Africa.

UN Food and Agriculture Organization. 2005. *Armed Conflicts Leading Cause of World Hunger Emergencies*: Rome: UN Food and Agriculture Organization.

Whittington, Sherrill, Rima Salah, and Christine Muhigana. 2005. *The Impact of Conflict on Women and Girls in West and Central Africa and the UNICEF Response*. New York: UNICEF Regional Office for West and Central Africa.

CHAPTER 28

THE GENDER IMPLICATIONS OF SMALL ARMS AND LIGHT WEAPONS IN CONFLICT SITUATIONS

BARBARA A. FREY

SMALL arms and light weapons (SALW), ubiquitous in the world today, are the tools of conflict, whether that conflict is characterized by armed groups fighting over territory, criminal organizations fighting over sites of drug distribution, or mass shootings motivated by gender, race, religion, or ideology. Although SALW were considered strategically unimportant during the Cold War, they moved to the center of the security and development agendas in the 1990s when it became clear that these were the tools of choice in the complex civil wars, insurgencies, terrorism, and criminal violence prolific in the past century (Greene and Marsh 2012). In addition to its role in undermining human rights and humanitarian law, chronic gun violence contributes to the collapse of economic productivity, the erosion of social services, and the disintegration of traditional social bonds in communities. Because of the way firearms are viewed socially and are used as tools of power, protection, abuse, or destruction, these weapons themselves have particular gender implications that merit examination.

Small arms have gendered uses and gendered impacts in all societies. Across the world, men are the primary owners of guns and suffer disproportionate deaths and injuries from their use (Geneva Declaration 2011), as will be detailed in this chapter. The possession and use of guns are shaped by gender ideologies. In general, women play secondary roles with regard to SALW, especially in armed conflict. Women are victimized at the barrel end of the gun, primarily away from the battlefield. Small arms used in conflict exacerbate existing gender differences in societies by increasing the social and physical power of men in both the public and private spheres, while limiting women's opportunities and meaningful participation in decisions over their lives and communities.

Gendered power relations are heightened in armed conflicts. Almost universally, guns are culturally infused with enabling masculinity; armed men are socially constructed either as protectors or—in negative terms—as perpetrators. Gender stereotypes assign feminine qualities to those, including women and less powerful men, who are seen as weak and in need of protection in relation to guns. The real experience is more complex. Both women and men play multiple and sometimes simultaneous roles as victims, perpetrators, and peacemakers. Gender-disaggregated data on proliferation and misuse is lacking, but emerging qualitative research paints a picture of the roles women play in the trade, storage, and use of firearms in conflict situations (Farr, Mryttinen, and Schnabel 2009).

This chapter first surveys the global distribution and ownership of small arms and light weapons, and then turns to definitions. It briefly describes the framework of emerging international law to regulate SALW. The chapter then provides a more in-depth look at the human toll of firearms, and specifically the gendered nature of firearm possession, use, and victimhood. It looks more closely at the experience of women who carry and use small arms, and concludes by considering women's roles in disarmament and policy processes.

Overview of the Availability and Use of Small Arms and Light Weapons

SALW is a category of weapons that is differentiated from other conventional weapons such as battle tanks, armored combat vehicles and aircraft, attack helicopters, warships, missiles, and missile launchers (UN General Assembly 2013, art. 2(1)). "Small arms" is used to describe weapons that can be used by a single person, such as pistols, rifles, assault rifles, and machine guns. "Light weapons" can be used by a small crew, including heavy machine guns, portable anti-tank or anti-aircraft missiles and their launchers, and mortars. The term "firearms" includes small arms and heavy machine guns (UN General Assembly 1997).

There are almost a billion small arms and light weapons in existence, most of which are in the hands of private, non-state actors (Karp 2011). The best estimates suggest that about 3 percent of available firearms are in the hands of law enforcement, 23 percent in the armed forces, and 74 percent in civilian possession. Fewer than 5 percent of the firearms possessed by civilians are carried by gangs, private security companies, and non-state armed groups combined (Karp 2011), but even a small number of firearms can wreak havoc on communities. Firearm stockpiles continue to grow as millions of new guns are produced annually, with far fewer being destroyed.

The global trade in small arms is largely driven by the demand among wealthy nations, but firearms inevitably make their way to poorer societies and situations of armed conflict as recycled goods (De Soysa, Jackson, and Ormhaug 2009). Corruption and porous borders contribute to the ineffectiveness of arms-control regimes. False end-user certificates are commonly used for larger shipments, and the "ant trade"—meaning numerous small-scale transfers—is a regular feature of the transfer of firearms from legal stockpiles to illicit ones. Almost every gun sold on the black market was initially traded legally (Marsh 2012). While women are engaged minimally in the global distribution chains of SALW, they participate regularly in the "ant trade," characterized by concealing, storing, and transporting small numbers of weapons, especially for paramilitaries, insurgencies, or criminal groups (Alison 2009).

A central question in the international discourse on firearms violence is whether the weapons themselves significantly affect the dynamics of armed violence, including its duration and lethality (Greene and Marsh 2012, 251). Firearms have a transformational or multiplier effect because a single weapon could turn a dispute into a massacre, and a flood of small arms could shift the entire balance of power in a community, leading to a lack of personal security that destroys the rule of law (Frey 2003).

The easy availability of firearms alone is problematic. The level of SALW imports per capita in a country correlates positively with higher levels of violations of physical integrity rights; the correlation is even more pronounced in autocracies than in democracies (De Soysa, Jackson, and Ormhaug 2010). While widespread availability of small weapons in communities is associated with higher injury and death rates, general causal relationships are difficult to pin down (Greene and Marsh 2012). Context-specific factors are critical. In unregulated environments, for instance, a few guns in the wrong hands can have devastating results. In other settings, rule of law and responsible traditions of possession, storage, and usage can minimize the impacts of broad availability.

A nascent system of international regulation for SALW has been established in response to the role of these particular weapons in violating human rights and humanitarian law in conflict, post-conflict, and non-conflict situations. Concern about the disproportionate harm imposed by SALW grew out of the new international emphasis on "human security" put forward by human rights and humanitarian organizations. As a result, in 2001, the United Nations adopted the Programme of Action on Small Arms and Light Weapons to take steps to prevent "illicit" weapons transfers, while maintaining sovereign claims to export and import weapons for legitimate government purposes. In 2013, under further pressure from international civil society, states adopted the Arms Trade Treaty to establish universally recognized transfer criteria on both conventional weapons and small arms. The treaty aims to prevent arms-fueled conflicts as well as state-sponsored atrocities.

While small arms have legitimate uses under international law, including law enforcement and national self-defense, they are also the principal tools of international human rights and humanitarian law violations. In research and policy-making, a distinction is therefore made between legal and illicit weapons, and between their use and "misuse." Small arms used by sovereign states and their agents are presumed to be legal. Private actors are entitled to possess and use weapons only in ways that are sanctioned by states. The term "illicit" refers to unsanctioned possession, and "misuse" applies to the unsanctioned operation of weapons.

The legal significance of discharging a weapon depends on the identities of the shooter and the victim(s), and the circumstances and locale in which the weapon is used. Differing domestic and international laws apply in the following situations: misuse of small arms by state agents; misuse of small arms by private persons when the state fails to exercise due diligence; misuse of small arms by state agents in armed conflict; misuse of small arms by non-state actors in armed conflict; and small arms transfer with knowledge that arms are likely to be used to commit serious violations of international human rights and humanitarian law (Frey 2004).

Small arms and light weapons that are used in warfare differ substantially from those used for civilian or criminal purposes. Insurgents typically consist of a few thousand armed combatants who use automatic rifles and light weaponry such as machine guns, mortars, and man-portable missiles and rockets, while criminals typically rely on handguns (Greene and Marsh 2012, 13).

The Human Toll of Small Arms Violence and Its Gendered Impacts

Small arms affect all aspects of the human experience, though the most visible and quantifiable impact is the toll of human carnage. An estimated 508,000 people worldwide died each year in 2007–2012 as a direct result of armed violence—the use or threatened use of weapons. The majority of deaths occurred in "non-conflict" situations (377,000 intentional homicides, 42,000 unintentional homicides, and 19,000 legal interventions), and the remainder, totaling 70,000, are the estimated direct deaths in armed conflict (Geneva Declaration 2015). There were an estimated 60,000 female deaths annually in 2007–2012 from small arms-related violence, most of them outside of direct conflict (Geneva Declaration 2015). A cautious estimate is that three people are injured by guns for every person killed; the lives of those affected are often changed forever due to long-term disability and psychological trauma (Alvazzi 2012).

Eighty percent of homicide victims are men, a ratio that has remained near constant since 2004 (Geneva Declaration 2015). Age is extremely significant: men aged fifteen to twenty-nine represent half of all gun victims, at a rate more than four times higher (22 per 100,000) than that of the general population (5 per 100,000) (Berman, Krause, and McDonald 2006). These patterns are largely replicated in situations of armed conflict (Greene and Marsh 2012). The nature of violence directed at women differs. In conflict situations, female non-combatants are killed in equal numbers as non-combatant men (Greene and Marsh 2012). Women also account for the majority of victims of intimate partner violence worldwide, in conflict and non-conflict situations: worldwide, there are 430 female victims per 100,000 population, while the rate for male victims is 80 per 100,000 (Geneva Declaration 2011).

In addition to deaths and injuries, small arms contribute to a deterioration of economic and social conditions that have strong negative impacts on communities. Firearms-saturated communities suffer from economic as well as physical insecurity, including the deprivation of the right to food, education, and health care, impacting the sectors traditionally managed by women. In many conflict zones, guns and ammunition are more accessible than food and medicine. There are dramatic decreases in food production and, especially in situations of armed violence generated from the "bottom up," armed bands live off the land, causing further shortages, which in turn generate further violence (De Soysa and Gleditsch 1999, 21). Health-care facilities in conflict areas often lack rudimentary medical supplies and personnel, resulting in increased likelihood of infection, disability, and death. Meanwhile, systematic targeting of schools, teachers, and students has become a regular feature of armed conflict, and an estimated 40 percent of out-of-school children in the world today live in conflict-affected countries (Karimova, Giacci, and Casey-Maslen 2014).

Men and women have dramatically different experiences in relation to firearms. With few exceptions, men are in control of guns in their societies from the time they are manufactured until they are destroyed. The victim/perpetrator binary does not always hold: women are also agents of violence, and men are subjected to gender-based violence such as sex-selective killings, forced conscription, and sexual violence (Geneva Declaration 2008). During armed conflict, however, guns are primarily in the possession of men. The number of women who possess and use weapons as soldiers in national armed forces or as part of insurgencies is still very small, though women compose a comparatively larger percentage of national liberation forces worldwide (Geneva Declaration 2008), as will be detailed later in the chapter. Fewer women than men are killed by SALW in close combat, but the presence and misuse of small arms are instrumental in gender-based violence, in the destruction of infrastructure that provides basic human needs, and in limiting the space for women's development and political participation.

A primary obstacle to explaining the relationship between gender and guns, as well as other variables such as race and age, is the absence of disaggregated data due to lack of political will, scarce resources, and the "sheer difficulty of keeping track of firearms-related injuries in places with poor infrastructure and record-keeping capacities" (Farr, Myrttinen, and Schnabel 2009, 5). As information does emerge, it is not surprising that the relationship between gender and guns is as complex and particular as the role of gender in society as a whole. A consistent finding is that the presence of firearms exacerbates the physical and social constraints that particular cultures already place upon women and girls, shoring up the traditional gender roles in societies and increasing the risks for individuals who challenge those roles.

Gender ideologies that dictate the appropriate roles of men and women have a profound relationship to ideas and behaviors about firearms, including who owns them and who uses them, who is killed or harmed by them, and how. The meaning given to firearms in any particular culture is deeply rooted in the social expectations about what is masculine and what is feminine. Guns are unfeminine because they are instruments of power and protection. Globally, SALW are symbols of masculinity, the tools with which young men aspire to gain influence and/or provide protection (Schroeder, Farr, and Schnabel 2005). In traditionally armed societies such as Albania, Afghanistan, Somalia, Uganda, or Yemen, guns are culturally portrayed as an extension, or symbol, of the male identity. Some traditions within Central Europe include the celebration of the birth of a boy with the exclamation, "We have increased by one gun!" (Hillier and Wood 2003, 47). These symbolic constructions evolve depending on the circumstances. In the colonial period of the United States, for instance, guns were regarded merely as utilitarian tools. Later, skill with a gun became "a marker of the man," and in recent years, guns have been elevated to items of fascination bordering on the erotic (Ashkenazi 2012, 242). In most societies with high levels of gun violence, however, guns are not associated with aesthetic values. Instead, they are typically seen as "nothing more than utilitarian tools" (Ashkenazi 2012, 242).

The specific violence inflicted with firearms on women is well documented to include every form of sexual violence. Sexual assaults against women and girls are enabled by firearms, sometimes opportunistic and sometimes as deliberate military and political tactics. In conflict situations, the use of guns as instruments of rape is common; there are similar accounts across many regions of men forced at gunpoint to rape their mothers, sisters, or daughters (Moestue and Leff 2009). The abuse and shaming of women by enemy soldiers can be a highly symbolic way to attack the foundation of a community and to demean males for failure to protect "their" women (Bastick, Grimm, and Kunz 2007; see also Gaca, Chapter 23, and Hadzimesic, Chapter 39, in this volume). Noncompliant men are also subjected to certain forms of sexualized violence as a way of "feminizing" them (Ochieng 2002).

Sexualized violence enforces gender hierarchies that give men power over women, children, and other men, hierarchies that are enhanced further when weapons are introduced. While male-dominated societies often justify small arms possession through the alleged need to protect vulnerable women, firearms in the home actually represent an increased risk to women, as they are more likely to be used to threaten and inflict harm on family members than to protect the home from intruders (Hemenway 2011).

Beyond sexualized forms of violence, small arms play a role in reinforcing a gendered division of labor during wartime. Under a militarized ideology that values armed combat, women are primarily responsible for "unessential" and unpaid responsibilities as caregivers, educators, cooks, and organizers in communities racked by small arms violence (Farr 2002, 21). Where health infrastructures are overburdened or inadequate, the needs of (male) gun victims take precedent over women's health-care needs. Women consequently suffer higher reproductive health problems and maternal mortality, as well as taking on the responsibility for the care of wounded and disabled family members (Farr 2002).

USE OF SMALL ARMS AND LIGHT WEAPONS BY WOMEN

Despite these gendered patterns, case studies show that women do use SALW as aggressors in their roles as soldiers, insurgents, and gang members. Women who possess and use weapons are motivated by many of the same reasons as men: defense of the cause, righting wrongs, and opportunistic gain.

Women have participated actively in armed conflict in at least fifty-seven countries since 1990, though little is known in most cases concerning their percentage as part of military forces (Geneva Declaration 2008). In the 28 NATO countries, the percentage of women rose from 7.4 percent in 1999 to 10.6 percent in 2013 (United Nations 2015). Women comprised 15.1 percent of US active duty forces in 2014, numbering 200,692 (Office of the Deputy Assistant Secretary of Defense 2014). Girls and women have participated in non-state armed forces at a much higher rate; more than 30 percent of the troops were women in the Liberation Tigers of Tamil Eelam (LTTE), the Communist Party of Nepal–Maoists, the Fuerzas Armadas Revolucionarias de Colombia (FARC), and the Sandinista National Liberation Front (Geneva Declaration 2008).

The openings for women to take on close combat roles are increasing at a rapid pace in many organized militaries, especially in Western states, though few yet allow women unrestricted access to all combat roles. Reasons offered for limiting women's combat roles by twenty-seven governments surveyed for the British Ministry of Defence included the "rigorous physical demands of the role, perceived lack of emotional resilience or aggressiveness . . . [and] evidence of enduring negative gender stereotyping from male colleagues, with perceived detrimental effects on team cohesion" (Cawkill et al. 2009, 1). Even when there are no restrictions, women have low levels of participation in direct combat roles. In Canada, for instance, which has had no gender restrictions in its military forces since 1989, 17 percent of troops are women, but women make up only 3.8 percent of close combat troops (Keating 2012).

Female combatants' relationships with weapons are particular to the armed forces in which they participate. Women trained in organized militaries receive similar SALW training as their male counterpoints. The experience of those who are coerced to join insurgencies in civil armed conflicts is evidently quite different. Denov and Maclure (2009) provide a stark profile of the experience of a group of female combatants, ages fourteen to twenty-one, who had been coerced to serve with the Revolutionary United Front (RUF) in the civil war in Sierra Leone between 1991 and 2002. The girls initially carried out domestic duties and later transitioned to the fighting force. They were indoctrinated by enduring routinized violence against themselves and others, in the form of physical assaults and sexual violence, including gang rape. In armed raids, the girls played supporting roles, such as tying people up, and looting and burning homes, before engaging directly in violent acts against people or groups. In arms training, one girl noted that the commander's wife "was encouraging us and each time we practised firing the gun, she would tell us that we could do it. She said that she was a woman, too, and that if she could do it, we could do it" (Denov and Maclure 2009, 59). After training with the guns, the girls were required to shoot a person to prove they were battle ready. "We were told to fire on people above the waist. This would ensure that they would die. If we just wanted to intimidate people and not kill them, we were trained to point the gun in the air" (Denov and Maclure 2009, 63). The girls acknowledged the power of the gun, which gave them status, especially over persons outside their group. Denov and Maclure observed that the girl soldiers' relative power within the group did not change, but, with a gun, they had an opportunity to achieve power in relation to outside groups, especially civilians.

Whether women have access to small arms usually depends on the shortage or abundance of weapons; when there is a scarcity of arms, they are possessed by the powerful members in the group, namely the men. Women in armed conflict more frequently assist with the storage and transfer of weapons in order to make money or to support the military cause. In Somalia, women did not typically sell guns in public, but they transported weapons and ammunition across security checkpoints, stored guns in their homes, and traded in weapons to generate income (Kinzelbach and Hassan 2009). In Northern Ireland, both republican and loyalist paramilitaries relied on women to hide and transport weapons because they were perceived as less dangerous and, thus, much less likely to be searched by the authorities (Alison 2009).

WOMEN IN FIREARMS POLICY AND PEACEMAKING

Women usually play a secondary role in designing policies regarding SALW, including in negotiations to end armed conflicts and in demobilization, disarmament, and reintegration (DDR) programs (see also Bell, Chapter 32, and Mazurana et al., Chapter 34, in this volume). Women's experience regarding small arms is thus regularly overlooked, and their opinions regarding the terms and conditions for restoring security in their communities are habitually undervalued. Despite this, women have been visible occasionally in efforts to disarm combatants and to regulate guns after conflict. In northeastern Uganda, for example, women encouraged men to surrender their arms through discussions at home, and they have educated their communities about the dangers of guns through song and play (Schroeder, Farr, and Schnabel 2005). Somali women have used creative means to attempt to bring peace to their communities, including public recitations of poetry to address misconceptions of masculinity and femininity with regard to firearms (Kinzelbach and Hassan 2009).

DDR programs, designed to construct peace after conflict, often benefit men, as the primary combatants, more than women (see Mazurana et al., Chapter 34 in this volume). If they were not allowed by male leaders to carry guns in combat or were made to surrender their guns to men during the peace process, women cannot access the benefits that accrue from turning in weapons (Schroeder, Farr, and Schnabel 2005, 5). In other situations, though, such as in the disarmament process in northeastern Uganda, male ex-combatants have sent women relatives to surrender their guns because the women are considered to be less likely to face questions about the location of other weapon caches (Schroeder, Farr, and Schnabel 2005). Nonetheless, even when women's participation in DDR is indirect, it can be significant, such as motivating male relatives to surrender their weapons and mobilizing for disarmament.

In an effort to prevent armed conflict, women assume leadership roles in national and transnational activism to regulate the transfer and use of firearms. Women's "peace work" fits within the framework of the feminine, but those women who outspokenly push for disarmament or gun control, unsettling gender hierarchies, are frequently the targets of misogynistic threats above and beyond policy differences. The then-director of Gun Free South Africa observed, "I'm disturbed by the psychological threats often directed at [our] campaigners because we're women rather than because we're anti-guns. I sense that this hostility is roused by the fact that we challenge some men's images of women" (Kirsten 2002, 35). In the international discourse and diplomatic efforts to regulate SALW, activists find that they cannot address issues regarding armed violence without confronting gender ideologies because, in every society, ideas about firearms are inextricably linked to ideas about gender.

CONCLUSION

Small arms have gendered uses and impacts. Easy access to firearms tends to solidify or exacerbate gender hierarchies that give men power over women, children, and other men in their communities. While men are both the primary victims and perpetrators of homicide in the world, women are the primary victims of intimate partner homicide. The call to arms emphasizes physical and military strength, stereotypically the realm of the masculine. In armed conflict, those who are not engaged directly in the battle are often reduced to secondary, feminine, roles such as providing sustenance, care, and sexual services to the fighters. Armed conflict drains resources from communities, destroys social infrastructures that support human security, and reduces the public spaces where women and non-gender-conforming men can participate in public decision-making processes that affect their ways of life.

Despite the international community's emphasis on mainstreaming women in conflict resolution, women are structurally excluded from shaping policies relating to small arms, and few women are engaged in negotiating the content of peace treaties or bilateral treaties that may have disarmament components. Women's absence from—and men's domination of—security sectors and disarmament programs prevents the inclusion of perspectives essential to meaningful arms control and conflict resolution for the broader community. When women are engaged in constructing safe communities and designing global standards, they are able to broaden ideas about human security and reimagine gender-based stereotypes in a way that does not equate masculinity with guns.

REFERENCES

Alison, Miranda. 2009. "'That's Equality for You, Dear': Gender Small Arms and the Northern Ireland Conflict." In *Sexed Pistols: The Gendered Impacts of Small Arms and Light Weapons*, edited by Vanessa Farr, Henri Myrttinen, Albrecht Schnabel, 211–245. Tokyo: UN University Press.

Alvazzi, Anna del Frate. 2012. "A Matter of Survival: Non-Lethal Armed Violence." In *Small Arms Survey 2012: Moving Targets*, edited by Eric Berman et al., 79–105. Cambridge: Cambridge University Press.

Ashkenazi, Michael. 2012. "What Do the Natives Know? Societal Mechanisms for Controlling Small Arms." In *Small Arms, Crime and Conflict*, edited by Owen Greene and Nicholas Marsh, 228–247. New York: Routledge.

Bastick, Megan, Karin Grimm, and Rachel Kunz. 2007. *Sexual Violence in Armed Conflict: Global Overview and Implications for the Security Sector*. Geneva: Geneva Centre for the Democratic Control of Armed Forces.

Berman, Eric, Keith Krause, and Glenn McDonald, eds. 2006. *Small Arms Survey 2006: Unfinished Business*. Oxford: Oxford University Press.

Cawkill, Paul, Alison Rogers, Sarah Knight, and Laura Spear. 2009. *Women in Close Ground Combat Roles: The Experiences of Other Nations and a Review of the Academic Literature*. London: Porton Down.

De Soysa, Indra, and Nils Petter Gleditsch. 1999. *To Cultivate Peace: Agriculture in a World of Conflict*. Washington, DC: Wilson Center.

De Soysa, Indra, Thomas Jackson, and Christin Ormhaug. 2009. "Does Globalization Profit the Small Arms Bazaar?" *International Interactions* 35, no. 1: 86–105.

De Soysa, Indra, Thomas Jackson, and Christin Ormhaug. 2010. "Tools of the Torturer? Small Arms Imports and Repression of Human Rights, 1992–2004." *The International Journal of Human Rights* 14, no. 3: 378–393.

Denov, Myriam, and Richard Maclure. 2009. "Girls and Small Arms in Sierra Leone: Victimization, Participation and Resistance." In *Sexed Pistols: The Gendered Impacts of Small Arms and Light Weapons*, edited by Vanessa Farr, Henri Mryttinen, and Albrecht Schnabel, 51–80. Tokyo: UN University Press.

Farr, Vanessa. 2002. *A Gendered Analysis of International Agreements on Small Arms and Light Weapons*. Bonn: Bonn International Center for Conversion.

Farr, Vanessa, Henri Myrttinen, Albrecht Schnabel, eds. 2009. *Sexed Pistols: The Gendered Impacts of Small Arms and Light Weapons*. Tokyo: UN University Press.

Frey, Barbara. 2003. *Preliminary Report on the Prevention of Human Rights Violations Committed with Small Arms and Light Weapons*. UN Doc. E/CN.4/Sub.2/2003/29 (June 25).

Frey, Barbara. 2004. "Small Arms and Light Weapons: The Tools Used to Violate Human Rights." *Disarmament Forum* 2004, no. 3: 37–46.

Geneva Declaration. 2008. *Global Burden of Armed Violence 2008*. Geneva: Geneva Declaration Secretariat.

Geneva Declaration. 2011. *Global Burden of Armed Violence 2011*. Geneva: Geneva Declaration Secretariat.

Geneva Declaration. 2015. *Global Burden of Armed Violence 2015*. Geneva: Geneva Declaration Secretariat.

Greene, Owen, and Nicholas Marsh, eds. 2012. *Small Arms, Crime and Conflict*. New York: Routledge.

Hemenway, David. 2011. "Risks and Benefits of a Gun in the Home." *American Journal of Lifestyle Medicine* 5, no. 6: 502–511.

Hillier, Debbie, and Brian Wood. 2003. *Shattered Lives: The Case for Tough International Arms Control*. London: Amnesty International and Oxfam.

Karimova, Takhmina, Gilles Giacca, and Stuart Casey-Maslen. 2014. *United Nations Human Rights Mechanisms and the Right to Education in Insecurity and Armed Conflict*. Geneva: Geneva Academy.

Karp, Aaron. 2011. *Estimating Civilian-Owned Firearms*. Geneva: Small Arms Survey.

Keating, Joshua E. 2012. "Where a Woman's Place Is on the Front Lines." *Foreign Policy*, February 10. http://foreignpolicy.com/2012/02/10/where-a-womans-place-is-on-the-front-lines/.

Kinzelbach, Katrin, and Zeinab Hassan. 2009. "The Role of Somali Women in Social Gun Control." In *Sexed Pistols: The Gendered Impacts of Small Arms and Light Weapons*, edited by Vanessa Farr, Henri Mryttinen, and Albrecht Schnabel, 356–389. Tokyo: UN University Press.

Kirsten, Adele. 2002. *White Men with Weapons*. Bonn: Bonn International Center for Conversion.

Marsh, Nicholas. 2012. "The Tools of Insurgency: A Review of the Role of Small Arms and Light Weapons in Warfare." In *Small Arms, Crime and Conflict*, edited by Owen Greene and Nicholas Marsh, 27–32. New York: Routledge.

Moestue, Helen, and Jonah Leff. 2009. "Large and Small: Impacts of Armed Violence on Children and Youth." In *Small Arms Survey 2009: Shadows of War*, edited by Eric Berman et al., 193–217. Cambridge: Cambridge University Press.

Ochieng, Ruth Ojambo. 2002. *A Gendered Reading of the Problems and Dynamics of SALW in Uganda*. Bonn: Bonn International Center for Conversion.

Office of the Deputy Assistant Secretary of Defense. 2014. *2014 Demographics: Profile of the Military Community*. Washington, DC: Department of Defense.

Schroeder, Emily, Vanessa A. Farr, and Albrecht Schnabel. 2005. *Gender Awareness in Research on Small Arms and Light Weapons: A Preliminary Report*. Bern: Swisspeace.

United Nations. 2015. *Preventing Conflict, Securing Justice, Transforming the Peace: A Global Study on the Implementation of United Nations Security Council Resolution 1325*. Geneva: UN Women.

United Nations Conference on the Illicit Trade in Small Arms and Light Weapons in All Its Aspects. 2001. *Report*. UN Doc. A/CONF/192/15 (July 20).

UN General Assembly. 1997. G.A. Res. 52/298, Report of the UN Panel of Governmental Experts on Small Arms (August 27).

UN General Assembly. 2013. G.A. Res. 67/234B, Arms Trade Treaty (April 2).

CHAPTER 29

UNMANNED WEAPONS
Looking for the Gender Dimensions

CHRISTOF HEYNS AND TESS BORDEN

OUR contemporary moment offers a unique opportunity to take stock of where human-ity stands in its relationship to force projection, killing, anonymity, physical presence, displacement, and mortal power. Technological developments allow an increasing move toward greater depersonalization in weapons systems, and what is sometimes called the more "clinical" or "surgical" application of the use of force. It becomes important to examine the gender implications of these shifts in how power is exercised.

The depersonalization of the use of force manifests itself on many fronts—it is not only the axe of the executioner of yesteryear that has largely been replaced over time by the button of the electrical chair; weaponry with out-of-sight strike capability or indeed airpower has in many cases physically removed the person applying force from the target and point of impact. The most dramatic manifestation of this development is the emergence of so-called unmanned weapon systems. The first generation of these weapons is armed drones, which allow their operators from halfway around the world to release force through remote control. The second generation of unmanned systems is autonomous weapons systems (AWS), where the decision to release force is no longer made by a human operator, but by computers. The person on whose behalf force is used is thus not only physically absent from the use of force, but to some extent also psycho-logically absent, in that the decision to kill or injure is made by a machine.

Given the traditionally dominant role of men in the use of force, this process of increased depersonalization amounts in a literal sense to the "unmanning" of weap-ons and their use—it is not only "people" who are being removed from the battlefield and other theaters of armed engagement, it is specifically men who are stepping back. It becomes important to examine the gender implications of these shifts in how power is exercised.

Unmanned systems have a wide range of potential applications. They are primarily presented as new technology, to be used on the battlefield, where the permissive rules on the use of force of international humanitarian law (IHL) primarily apply. However, as the experience with drones has shown, the fact that they are so easy to use and keep one's own forces out of harm's way has often led to them being deployed in situations that do not meet the requirements of an armed conflict, and where the stricter rules of international human rights law should regulate the use of force. Increasingly, however, remote-controlled systems designed to be used during ordinary domestic law enforcement are also available, and in certain cases they are equipped with some levels of autonomy in force release.

Clearly these weapons raise far-reaching legal and ethical questions, which have prompted ongoing debate over the last decade and more. Moreover, they implicate ongoing engagement about the compatibility of these weapons with the international humanitarian law rules on distinction, proportionality, and precaution. However, what has not been investigated is the gender dimensions of the introduction of unmanned systems. This is where we hope to make a contribution.

We believe it is critical that the gender implications—many of them still invisible, yet centrally constitutive—be prominently considered in this move toward weapons autonomy. Many of those implications may be dual (men and women both get killed and caught up in concepts of targeting and collateral damage), but the development and implementation of technology may be distinctly male. Attention to the gendered dimensions of unmanned systems for those who use them and for those on the ground—against whom they are being used—also protects against increased valorization of violence, to ensure respect for the right to life in general and in those cases in which life is taken.

This chapter begins with a brief examination of new weapons systems, how they map onto changes in traditional notions of warfare and other similar conflicts, and the implications for gender rearrangements. The second section investigates how women's roles are affected, both in societies that are targeted and in those that do the targeting. We look at gender tropes and possibilities for reinforcing and upsetting ideas of women's roles. In the third section, we look at men's emasculation in societies targeted by unmanned weapons and at evolving and deflected masculinity narratives in societies that deploy them. In the final section, we engage with feminist critiques and outline concerns about the ethics of care in the context of unmanning. We conclude that the use of unmanned weapons raises concerns about the impact on men and women, as a question of sex, and also reveals interactions of gender identities and dynamics that not only are significant as a matter of theory, sociology, or ethnography, but also have discrete consequences for the protection of human rights.

Many scholars (and numerous chapters in this volume) have pointed out the ways in which conventional war and similar conflicts constitute and are constituted by gender. We expect that with unmanned systems, gender will similarly have both a causative and responsive dimension, shaping the way soldiers engage with and justify their roles and also compensating for deflected masculinity performances that may come with the replacement of fighters with machines. In some ways, traditional gender dynamics and dichotomies may be reinforced and embedded by unmanned systems, but in other ways, they might be crucially distorted. In some cases, these distortions may ultimately bring more equality and less harm, but we caution that in others they may lead to lashing out at women. We problematize this move as a way of recognizing the changes afoot with the withdrawal of boots on the ground—or pilots from the air.

New Weapons, New Conflicts, New Gender Arrangements

As unmanned systems take to the skies (and the ground and the water), the physical as well as psychological distance between the weapon user and the weapon increases. This coincides with a period of what some have called "new wars," under which, as Mary Kaldor describes, "the distinction between state and non-state, public and private, external and internal, economic and political, and even war and peace are breaking down" (Kaldor 2013, 2). Under these paradigm shifts, "warfare" becomes a far cry from the traditional armed conflicts of history (Backstrom and Henderson 2012) and from the picture of war as hand-to-hand combat between men belonging to opposing armies. If wars were once contests over land, power, or a result that would belong to whoever emerged victorious, today's new wars and other conflicts masquerading as wars are arguably composed of sides that want different things. This is especially so in the context of the so-called War on Terror. If the terrorist enemy wants destruction—or so the narrative goes—then the war against it is not ostensibly a contest of who gets to destroy, but rather a kind of targeted self-defense (Department of Justice 2013; Holder 2012).

The ease with which drones and other unmanned systems have already changed the nature of global conflicts is startling. There is no menacing concern about the return of one's own soldiers in body bags, or one's pilots being tortured or put on humiliating display by the enemy after they have been shot down. A button can be pressed to solve a problem in a distant country. The threshold for the use of international force is thus lowered, and the incentives to bring it to an end also lowered. In a world of unmanned systems, the traditional wars that are intense but take place within a limited time span may be replaced by low-intensity but drawn-out conflicts that do not rise, legally at least, to the level of an armed conflict. As we will see, this may affect who the most likely casualties are.

Feminist theory, masculinities theory, and queer theory have been used to interrogate the work done by and on gender in conflict (MacKinnon 2006), terrorism and counterterrorism (Huckerby and Satterthwaite 2013), and post-conflict transition (Ní Aoláin et al. 2012). However, for the most part, these inquiries are based in an assumption of traditional armed conflict. Warfare by way of unmanned weapons systems comprises a fundamental shift in the arrangements of fighters, targets, victims, and damages and justifications. In some senses, this shift may refine historic targeting practices and preferences in ways that sharpen old distinctions and embed them further. In other senses, the shift may confuse the poles of these normative critiques. When only one side is present on the battlefield, what happens to gender relations/dynamics/balances in the country the drone or robot leaves from and that in which it strikes? In this arms race to possess the "unmanned," what becomes exaggerated and what becomes deflected? Who is made a man, and who is emasculated in unmanning?

The new weapons and the new kind of warfare they bring about—counterterrorism 2.0, in the age of autonomy, imminence, and self-defense—are likely to have a new interaction with gender arrangements and tropes, in some areas exaggerating and in others reversing or even obfuscating the framework that was identified in conflict and terrorism studies of the twentieth century.

WOMEN'S ROLES: EQUALITY/INEQUALITY, REMOVAL/ERASURE

Technological developments have specific and still conjectural implications for women and for manifestations of gender. Women are among the civilians that are indiscriminately targeted by "terrorists"; the unmanning of weapons systems gives women new opportunities to participate as "users"; and women suffer—directly or indirectly—much of the damage inflicted by these unmanned systems deep into rural areas in target jurisdictions (Huckerby and Satterthwaite 2013).

Targeted societies

In some essential ways, the gender stratifications and divisions remain. Hilary Charlesworth (1999) has argued that women have been predominately represented in the field of international law as victims "in need of protection" (381). She maintains that even as women's rights have garnered attention in the international law framework, they have been cast in terms of "women's inherent vulnerability" (2009) and somehow tangential to the more important conversations (1994). The relevant law governing the use of force arguably continues to prioritize the public (gendered male) sphere over the private (gendered female) (Charlesworth and Chinkin 1993; Chinkin 1997), and policymakers can be criticized for preoccupation with the individual targeted by the new weapons to the extent of rendering invisible the societal consequences that surround it, most notably those affecting women.

As has historically been true for women and weapons, women on the other side of counterterrorism operations have been erased (Kassem 2013; see also Fink and Davidian, Chapter 12 in this volume), and it is possible that they are indeed rendered invisible and irrelevant by a combination of new weapons, new tactics, and geographic diversity. For example, Amnesty International documents the "particular impact on women" of the US drone program. Men in the Federally Administered Tribal Areas of

Pakistan culturally make the major decisions, including about whether to bring risk into the home and on the family. Testimony collected from women demonstrated that they are scared by the implications of those who might be let into the house by the men, turning their domestic sphere into a potential site of drone attack (Amnesty International 2013). In a society in which men make the critical decisions related to free association, women's right to such association—and to avoid it—is arguably put in the balance. Without any agency in this result, women may be impacted, and even killed, by a drone attack that targets a person their male family members have chosen to invite into the house, or even have chosen to become.

Women's roles in society have been interrupted and attacked by drone strikes. Some women have described the psychological trauma they experience from the sound of drones always buzzing overhead, saying that they fear their families might at any moment be killed by a strike (Stanford and NYU 2012). Children have been kept home from school, because going into the open exposes them to possible attack, putting increasing pressures on the domestic sphere and female caregivers. And women have reported feeling constantly under surveillance, making it harder than otherwise to leave the home (Amnesty International 2013). It is easy to imagine that women also have been left to pick up the pieces, literally and proverbially, after a strike—after a father or son has been killed, a house or livelihood destroyed, land rendered unusable, social services inaccessible, and children traumatized. As the United States expands its definition of who may be legally targeted, there also may be concern that women's "assistance" to targetable men in their roles as wives, sisters, daughters, and community members may come under fire.

Whereas some conventional weapons may not have passed so easily into the domestic sphere (but see Frey, Chapter 28 in this volume), by targeting men wherever they are found, including in proximity to women, drone programs risk magnifying and taking to their full consequences the underlying inequalities of these societies. Wars by such means may entrench and heighten unequal gender roles.

Finally, collateral damage, including in the form of non-lethal disruption of society, will inevitably accumulate as any war is extended further over time. By offering the appeal of "less human cost" to the user state and thus lowering the threshold for going to war, unmanned systems may draw such societies into prolonged but low-intensity conflicts, with no logical end. As war becomes more drawn out, it will affect all aspects of social life in a more pervasive way, especially for the most vulnerable groups, and very likely for women in the circumstances described in the preceding. While international humanitarian law is not concerned with the identity of those whose demise it calls collateral damage, it cannot be ignored when new technologies shift the risks to women.

Thus, although they may not be the primary enemy, women on the ground have experienced substantial harm and have been left to mend holes created by drone strikes, at the same time that they have been erased from the public consciousness of the new weapons users. We cannot help but imagine that the distance of the drone operator from his target must only render the invisibility harder to overcome. The move toward further autonomy, taking the human operator out of the loop entirely with AWS, is likely to continue, if not increase, these erasures.

Targeting societies

The implications for women's roles in societies that develop and deploy new weapons contain more unknowns. As new weapons begin to dominate the national security discourse, it cannot be ignored that this conversation has historically excluded women speakers and women as subjects of concern (Charlesworth and Chinkin 2002). Women remain on the margins of decisions concerning national and international security as a result of limited representation and the masculinity of international security regimes. This layered marginality compounds the exclusion from policy regulation on new weapons.

In other ways, however, new weapons arguably might liberate the woman, or at least remove the stratification of gendered roles by replacing the male warrior with a machine. Unmanned systems to some extent release the soldier from having to deploy to the ground, and so arguments that women do not belong in combat positions or even in troops at all (US Congress 1992) may be deflated, offering emancipation from constricting traditional gender roles for both sexes (Manjikian 2013). There is at least some chance, in theory, that women in a state that possesses unmanned weapons may be free to become more active in militaries when the role of the soldier is increasingly made into a command rather than "shoot and get shot at" function, and that new technologies thus may allow more women to join the military in career positions (Manjikian 2013). If war, as combat, traditionally performed a kind of universal gendering (Goldstein 2003), pushing different profiles into archetypes of masculinities and femininities of soldier, victim, and nurse, the removal of bodies from combat (at least on the side of the new weapons user) has the potential to be gender equalizing. When machines become the soldiers and thereby protectors, the traditional male–female and protector–protected roles are undermined, opening up the possibility of a post-human world (Haraway 1990). As a result, one might think that women's rights and equality advance when traditional male roles are weakened in the society with unmanned weapons systems. Unmanned technology is likely to have far-reaching effects on established—and in many cases macho—military culture. One component of this change is that computer experts ("geeks," not "Top Gun" pilots) are now the ones who make the important decisions. Technically, then, new weapons should allow women to be more involved, because there can be no argument that maleness is needed to operate them. In job description, then, the gender difference clearly disappears. Yet such "hopeful" hypotheses remain vulnerable to multiple attacks. Past experiences of women's incorporation into security frameworks suggest that the disappearance of overt gender difference is often just the assimilation into hegemonic masculinity, and/or the sidelining and distortion of female sexuality and femininities, as at Abu Ghraib.

Of course, removal would occur not only in terms of soldiers from the physical territory of the battlefield. Inasmuch as deployment decisions and technology development remain largely male-dominated, women may still be removed—or erased—from those spaces, undermining any theories of empowerment. Even if computer experts are now the ones who make the important decisions, the relevant fields of science are male-dominated. As examined later in the chapter, the end of the machismo-warrior dynamic could also give rise instead to deflected masculinities, where power is taken out and performed against women in new ways.

An alternative possibility altogether is that traditional male dominance is strengthened in the society using such technology. While the introduction of unmanned systems may in theory empower or at least equalize the role of women, this is not likely to happen in practice (Manjikian 2013). Robot technology is bound to reinforce hegemonic masculinity, rather than eliminate it. The new "super soldiers" are likely to be more male and more lethal and, as adjuncts to war fighters who predominantly make up a world that is run according to male codes, are bound to advance their dominance. Moving the human out into the wider decision-making loop for deployment of autonomous weapons obfuscates the fact that the decisive human players in that loop will remain men.

Finally, if there is eventually a backlash against the increased depersonalization of the use of force, as we think invariably will be the case, and a return to the more personalized use of force, this may strengthen a defense of the old order, including its gender roles.

Emasculation and Narratives of Masculinity

It is also important to ask what the effect of unmanned systems is likely to be on the men in the society that is targeted. Whatever valor may traditionally have been associated with war was largely based on the idea that male combatants proved themselves, when matched against other men under the rules of warfare, to be stronger and more dominant. Such valor was then cogently translated to male citizenship and leadership status in the post-soldiering reality. In contrast, to be subdued by machines with no chance of fighting back is likely to be experienced at some level as particularly shameful (Manjikian 2013). Many would argue that unmanned systems dehumanize everyone targeted, irrespective of sex or age, because machines are given the power of life and death over humans (Human Rights Watch 2012). Thus, as individual men may be targeted and killed, the role and concept of men more generally in targeted societies may undergo both dehumanization and emasculation.

Targeting societies

For those who use them, new weapons obviate the need for boots on the ground for combat purposes. Instead, the fighter is increasingly relegated to the control room—and farther and farther from the controls, as weapons move from drones toward autonomous decision-making. Despite the move, masculinity practice and status may move from the battlefield to the operating station. With boots on the ground becoming increasingly rare, making way instead for *unmanned* systems with little to no risk to the human operator, the traditional soldier who proves (and constitutes) his masculinity by braving fear (Kang 2012) is sidelined. Today's fighting men, then, perform through joysticks rather than the guns of a century ago.

Some work has been done on the effect of distance on the moral capacity to kill. Specifically, Dave Grossman's study on "learning to kill in war and society" (1995) noted the effects of video games on conditioning first-person shooting and applied this analysis to World War II pilots and bombardiers. Grossman's theories are immediately attractive for extrapolation to the issues that will arise with unmanned systems generally: "From a distance I can deny your humanity, and from a distance I cannot hear you scream" (1995, 102), where distances include not only physical distance, but emotional distance and social, cultural, moral, and "mechanical" distance as well (1995, 188–189). On the other hand, Grossman's "screen that separates the gamer from the game" may not accurately describe the drone operator and his target (Gregory 2011, 198). Derek Gregory quotes the commander of the US Air Forces' first dedicated unmanned aerial vehicle (UAV) wing: "You see a lot of detail . . . we feel it, maybe not to the same degree [as] if we were actually there, but it affects us"; "When you let a missile go . . . you know that's real life—there's no reset button" (Gregory 2011, 198). Gregory provides other quotes, for instance of a drone pilot who realizes that "[d]eath observed was still *death*" (Gregory 2011, 198). He suggests, as we hope may be true, that the laws of war and rules of engagement also constrain a video-game mentality about killing. Gregory points, on the one hand, to reports of drone crews experiencing "post-traumatic stress induced by constant exposure to high resolution images of real-time killing and the after-action inventory of body parts" (Gregory 2011, 198). Yet, on the other hand, he notes that the vice chairman of the Joint Chiefs of Staff, under whose authority drone operations fall in the United States, describes "jaded" analysts watching hours of what he and they apparently call "Death TV" (Gregory 2011; Lake 2010). Although this may eventually lead to psychological suffering, it clearly marks a different approach to the humanity of those on the ground.

It will be important, as we continue to use the new weapons, to examine whether and how their human operators are psychologically affected by killing at such distance, and by the easier ability to take off uniforms (both literal and proverbial) and return to homes and families rather than barracks. Will there be a new generation of men who experience post-trauma from drone operations? Or will it, like the executioner with the electric chair, become programmatically easier to separate the self from any individual decision to kill? The long-term implications for the gendered public/private divide, for trauma experience, for masculine identity, and for the "normality" of the exception remain open.

It is easy to imagine that the risk of further obscuring the psychological effect is heightened by the move from drones toward autonomous weapons where the very unidentifiability of the human in control will make it impossible to take off the uniform, both literally and proverbially—but also ever to put it on. And so the role of the man, as much as the soldier's masculinity, is brought into question by his further distancing from the target, enabled and indeed required by the new weapons.

This sidelining of the combat function may be a way of exerting new power, yet also might instead be emasculating as much as it is unmanning. Much has been written, in this volume and elsewhere, on the constitution and performance of masculinity through military culture. John Kang (2012) reminds us of the way that masculinity and femininity—even the vulgarities of naming genitalia—are used in military conversations as stand-ins for bravery and cowardice: to show he is a man, the soldier has to have "balls," lest he be derided as a weak "pussy." Yet Kang deftly points to a central paradox in this context, tracking how manliness is held up as courage in soldiers, but that their testimony often reveals the courage as operating out of fear, the ultimate feminine attribute. In Kang's interrogation of the traditional equation of manliness with bravery, we find soldiers willing to die because they are too afraid of being called afraid (Kang 2012). Still, rooted as it may be in paradoxically feminine instincts, the outward decision to go to the trenches asserts and obtains a certain rewarded masculinity.

It is worth considering, then, how ideas of hyper-masculinity in war will be constructed around new weapons usage. There are a number of possibilities: in the construction of hyper-masculinity in war, is it bravery in the face of physical risk (which might otherwise trigger fear) that is rewarded with the appellation of manliness (Goldstein 2003)? If so, there are real challenges to masculinity construction that will be presented by a so-called riskless war, fought by new weapons that insulate the human from proximity and thus from threat. Can a drone operator—or, more obscured, a military commander who chooses to deploy robots—be afraid for his life when an ocean separates him from the enemy fighter? He may be afraid of many other things, but he is not in imminent and bodily danger; can he be constituted as a hyper-masculine man as such? If this is how manliness in war is ritualized, as Kang's study suggests, then the move to new weapons may not only preclude masculinity construction and performance, but also emasculate those men, castrating them of the manliness they have already donned. And how is masculinity projected in self-defense? Is this potentially the ultimate cowardly move: acting out of fear of threat to self, rather than saving others (Puar 2005)?

Moreover, it is possible that unmanned systems may weaken what is often a "macho military culture." The controversy surrounding the possible introduction of medals for drone operators provides a telling point of reference (Koebler 2013). Ultimately, the Department of Defense chose to issue pins with an "R" that could be affixed to existing medals to denote "remote but direct impact on combat operations." The R pin, for "remote," was to be stylistically similar to the V pin, for "valor" (Tilghman 2016). Likewise, the fact that every move of high-tech weapons such as drones is recorded adds a significant layer of supervision and accountability to its use, and may dampen the "trigger-happy" approach sometimes associated with soldiers who are outside the reach of supervisory structures.

It should likewise not be discounted that the removal of boots on the ground may also remove some of the individual violations that are often perpetrated by those who wear those boots. Unmanned systems, by definition, cannot rape. Nor can they enact other gender-based violence on those women they encounter on the ground. But at the very least, there is the possibility that unmanned systems will allow for a less machismo or hyper-masculine culture in the combat ranks and the territory on which their force is projected.

On the other hand, as we have learned from post-conflict studies (Ní Aoláin et al. 2012) among other disciplines, masculinity does not simply disappear—either after hostilities or, in the scenario we suggest, after emasculating reconfigurations. Instead, it is possible that masculinities, should they "need" to play out, will be deflected elsewhere. This may be as hegemonic masculinities—climbing the professional ladder in an expensive suit—but it may also be in hyper-masculine terms more associated with the military and, ultimately, with aggressive force. One must be very careful, then, that violence, including sexual violence, is not taken out interpersonally in the home, the military ranks, or elsewhere.

Indeed, by contrast to Kang's theory, it is possible that hyper-masculinity is tied not to bravery in the face of physical risk, but rather to pure power, as the proportion of muscle to kill. If this is the case, then the joystick (as a stand-in for new weapons generally) may become the ultimate appendage to that muscle. The new weapons could arguably be seen to allow every energy to be focused on the performance of killing, as human involvement and considerations are distanced and erased. While we hold open that possibility, we also imagine that it is more complicated than just manliness as killing machine: a video-gamer is not hyper-masculine, any more than is the typically queer embodiment of evil who threatens to blow up the world in James Bond films.

In brighter terms, there is also the possibility that the removal from firsthand killing associations will create space for other more positive masculinities to develop, both in the military and in society more broadly. Although women have historically been more involved in calls for peace than men (Peach 1994), the trajectory away from men's conscription last century and from their physical deployment now may offer an alternative to (only) violent conceptions of masculinities.

VACUUMS IN THE ETHICS OF CARE: HEIGHTENED CONCERNS RAISED BY FEMINIST CRITIQUES

Feminist theorists have named important concerns in the performance and impact of militarization and conflict, as illustrated by other chapters in this *Handbook*. We underline the renewed relevance of these concerns and critiques because they are arguably heightened and increasingly urgent in the new weapons paradigm. Despite the allure of targeting "cleanliness," new weapons may in fact cause equal or more societal harm, in new and more endemic ways than past forms of destruction. The possibility of this harm is all the more concerning because of its likelihood of being erased from the view of external publics through narratives of the narrowness and precision of new weapons.

Numerous scholars have called for a reformulation of "just war" theory that adjusts its considerations according to the feminist ethic of care and relational autonomy (Sjoberg 2008). The relative blindness of typical "just war" assessments to human insecurities and long-term social instability that may result from conflict may apply increasingly with new weapons. This is especially so because the determinations of the justness of war are situated evermore in the assertions of (potentially deflected) masculinities.

Laura Sjoberg (2008) argues that there is an increasing political and performative appropriation of just war rhetoric to excuse harm inflicted from faraway locations, which is made easier by the lower thresholds of going to "riskless" war. Feminist theorists rightly critique just war theory for abstracting suffering, which the distance between new weapons operators and their targets is likely only to reinforce. If, as these theorists suggest, military and political leaders instead treated "collateral damage" as central to decision-making, the new weapons users would find themselves significantly hamstrung.

There is also a strong argument to be made for moving from solely a national security approach to what Laura Sjoberg has called "feminist security theory," which would offer "a new way of looking and thinking [about] war-making and targeting decisions that focuses on security and welfare of individual lives" (Nesiah 2013, 137). Targeting injures and kills innocent people, and is not localized to the individual targeted. Feminist theory requires us to focus on these sociological and non-fatal harms and the longer-term and wider-ripple effects of the use of force. From this view also, the purported orderly precision of new weapons may appear highly nebulous. Inasmuch as unmanned weapons kill unnamed individuals and cause emotional trauma of constant fear from the faceless buzzing overhead, we might conclude that we are a far cry from either humane order or an ethic of care, and a commitment to dignity and humane treatment.

Conclusion

The laws of war and international human rights set out to constrain the use of force, but extralegal constraints also play an important role to further limit that death and destruction. It is not a new argument to say that the move toward drones and lethal autonomous robots risks significantly weakening these constraints. In this chapter, we have raised concerns about these effects from a gender perspective, pointing to concerns about the impacts on (1) women on the ground; (2) women in the military; (3) men as soldiers as well as potential enemies; and (4) the potentially deflected masculinities that may arise in this process of "unmanning."

There is also a risk in thinking that because new weapons systems are more depersonalized, and as a result in some respects can remove the traditional divide between the roles played by men and women in the militaries who use them, these new weapons must be welcomed. Even if there are such advantages to be gained, the greater depersonalization of the use of force may create far-reaching problems for the right to life, as well as the right to dignity, of all concerned.

Although we do not seek to offer answers or solutions, we suggest, first, that a gendered consideration of the move toward autonomy in weapons systems—and the new kinds of warfare that come with it—reveals risks to women's bodies and may result in further subordination. It also belies normative assumptions of how femininity, masculinity, and sex are performed in war and counterterrorism—with potential long-term impacts for foreign relations, peace and conflict, and respect for life. In this context, it will be important to query not only where the woman and feminist theory are now and where they may develop, but also what will happen to the men and masculinities when the new conflicts are fought largely without their physical engagement.

REFERENCES

Amnesty International. 2013. "Will I Be Next?" US Drone Strikes in Pakistan. London: Amnesty International Publications.

Backstrom, Alan, and Ian Henderson. 2012. "New Capabilities in Warfare: An Overview of Contemporary Developments and the Associated Legal and Engineering Issues." International Review of the Red Cross 94, no. 886: 483–514.

Charlesworth, Hilary. 1994. "What Are 'Women's International Human Rights?'" In Human Rights of Women: National and International Perspectives, edited by Rebecca Cook, 58–84. Philadelphia: University of Pennsylvania Press.

Charlesworth, Hilary. 1999. "Feminist Methods in International Law." American Journal of International Law 93, no. 1: 379–394.

Charlesworth, Hilary. 2009. "Inside/Outside: Women & International Law." IntLawGrrls (blog). August 20. http://www.intlawgrrls.com/2009/08/insideoutside-women-international-law.html.

Charlesworth, Hilary, and Christine Chinkin. 1993. "The Gender of Jus Cogens." Human Rights Quarterly 15, no. 1: 63–76.

Charlesworth, Hilary, and Christine Chinkin. 2002. "Sex, Gender, and September 11." American Journal of International Law 96, no. 3: 600–605.

Chinkin, Christine. 1997. "Feminist Interventions into International Law." Adelaide Law Review 19: 13–24.

Department of Justice. 2013. "Lawfulness of a Lethal Operation Directed Against a U.S. Citizen Who Is a Senior Operational Leader of Al-Qa'ida or an Associated Force." DOJ white paper. http://msnbcmedia.msn.com/i/msnbc/sections/news/020413_DOJ_White_Paper.pdf.

Gregory, Derek. 2011. "From a View to a Kill: Drones and Late Modern War." Theory, Culture & Society 28, no. 7–8: 188–215.

Goldstein, Joshua. 2003. War and Gender: How Gender Shapes the War System and Vice Versa. Cambridge: Cambridge University Press.

Grossman, Dave. 1995. *On Killing: The Psychological Cost of Learning to Kill in War and Society*. New York: Back Bay Books.

Haraway, D. 1990. "A Manifesto for Cyborgs: Science, Technology and Socialist Feminism in the 1980s." In *Feminism/Postmodernism (Thinking Gender)*, edited by Linda Nicholson, 190–233. New York: Routledge.

Holder, Eric. 2012. Lecture presented at Northwestern University School of Law. March 5. http://www.justice.gov/iso/opa/ag/speeches/2012/ag-speech-1203051.html.

Huckerby, Jayne C., and Margaret L. Satterthwaite. 2013. "Introduction." In *Gender, National Security, and Counter-Terrorism: Human Rights Perspectives*, edited by Margaret L. Satterthwaite and Jayne C. Huckerby, 1–14. New York: Routledge.

Human Rights Watch. 2012. *Losing Humanity: The Case against Killer Robots*. New York: Human Rights Watch.

Kaldor, Mary. 2013. "In Defense of New Wars." *Stability* 2, no. 1: 1–16.

Kang, John M. 2012. "Manliness's Paradox." In *Masculinities and the Law: A Multidimensional Approach*, edited by Frank Rudy Cooper and Ann C. McGinley, 136–145. New York: New York University Press.

Kassem, Ramzi. 2013. "Gendered Erasure in the Global 'War on Terror': An Unmasked Interrogation." In *Gender, National Security, and Counter-Terrorism: Human Rights Perspectives*, edited by Margaret L. Satterthwaite and Jayne C. Huckerby, 15–35. New York: Routledge.

Koebler, Jason. 2013. "Pentagon Says 'Drone Medal' Beats Purple Heart, Bronze Star: DoD Rejects Call by Lawmakers to Demote Distinguished Warfare Medal." *U.S. News & World Report*, March 7. http://www.usnews.com/news/articles/2013/03/07/pentagon-says-drone-medal-beats-purple-heart-bronze-star.

Lake, Eli. 2010. "Drone Footage Overwhelms Analysts." *Washington Times*, November 9. http://www.washingtontimes.com/news/2010/nov/9/drone-footage-overwhelming-analysts/.

MacKinnon, Catharine A. 2006. "Women's September 11th: Rethinking the International Law of Conflict." *Harvard International Law Journal*. 47, no. 1: 1–31.

Manjikian, Mary. 2013. "The Gendering of Lethal Autonomous Warfare Technology." *International Feminist Journal of Politics* 16, no. 1: 48–65.

Nesiah, Vasuki. 2013. "Feminism as Counter-terrorism: The Seduction of Power." In *Gender, National Security, and Counter-Terrorism: Human Rights Perspectives*, edited by Margaret L. Satterthwaite and Jayne C. Huckerby, 127–151. New York: Routledge.

Ní Aoláin, Fionnuala, Naomi Cahn, and Dina Haynes. 2012. "Masculinities and Child Soldiers in Post-Conflict Societies." In *Masculinities and the Law: A Multidimensional Approach*, edited by Frank Rudy Cooper and Ann C. McGinley, 231–251. New York: New York University Press.

Peach, Lucinda J. 1994. "An Alternative to Pacifism? Feminism and Just-War Theory." *Hypatia* 9, no. 2: 152–172.

Puar, Jasbir K. 2005. "Queer Times, Queer Assemblages." *Social Text* 23, no. 3–4: 121–139.

Sjoberg, Laura. 2008. "Why Just War Needs Feminism Now More Than Ever." *International Politics* 45: 1–18.

Stanford Law School and NYU School of Law (Stanford and NYU). 2012. *Living under Drones: Death, Injury, and Trauma to Civilians from US Drone Practices in Pakistan*. Stanford, CA, and New York: International Human Rights and Conflict Resolution Clinic, Stanford Law School and Global Justice Clinic, NYU School of Law.

Andrew Tilghman. 2016. "DoD rejects 'Nintendo Medal' for Drone Pilots and Cyber Warriors." *Military Times*, January 6. http://www.militarytimes.com/story/military/pentagon/2016/01/06/dod-rejects-nintendo-medal-drone-pilots-and-cyber-warriors/78364208/.

US Congress. House. 1992. *Gender Discrimination in the Military: Hearings before the Subcommittee on Military Personnel and Compensation and the Defense Policy Panel.* 102d Cong., 2d sess., July 29 and 30.

CHAPTER 30

GENDER AND PEACEKEEPING

SABRINA KARIM AND MARSHA HENRY

WHAT does gender mean in the context of peacekeeping missions? At first glance, to answer this question, many people think of the increasing proportions of women peace-keepers. While this is a useful statistic, it is also important to remember that gender is not synonymous with women, which means that a gendered understanding of peace-keeping involves more than merely analyzing the numbers of female peacekeepers. In addition to quantifying the number of women in peacekeeping, this chapter looks at two additional manifestations of gender in peacekeeping. First, it examines gendered hierar-chies that exist within peacekeeping missions, which may contribute to a "gendered pro-tection norm" and a potential exacerbation of sexual exploitation and abuse in missions. It then challenges the justificatory rhetoric for including more women in peacekeeping missions. Next, it looks at the gendered context of peacekeeping by analyzing the dis-course used by the United Nations to explain the current rhetoric and practice of the inclusion of women in peacekeeping and by evaluating whether such gender-equality measures are also viewed as beneficial for peacekeeping missions. Finally, it unpacks the gendered hierarchies that exist within peacekeeping missions and the consequences that stem from them.

THE NUMBERS

According to the United Nations, between 1957 and 1989, a total of only twenty women served as UN peacekeepers. With the passing of UN Security Council resolution (SCR) 1325 in 2000, the numbers of women in peacekeeping were to have steadily increased. The percentages continue to remain low.

Indeed, in 2009, in anticipation of the ten-year anniversary of resolution 1325, UN Secretary-General Ban Ki-moon launched a campaign to increase the share of female peacekeepers to 10 percent in military units and 20 percent in police units by 2014. Unfortunately, the United Nations did not meet this objective, but with the passing of

Security Council resolution 2242, the United Nations has set an ambitious new target to double the number of women in peacekeeping in the next five years.

There are three types of security sector personnel in missions. Troop contingents are units from the same country sent to different parts of the host country to enforce or keep the peace. They are called out in emergency situations, provide security to key assets and people, and can sometimes enforce the peace if violence erupts. Second are military observers, individuals typically sent to help coordinate operations or deploy to different parts of the country to report on the peace. In 2015, of the approximately 125,000 peacekeepers, women constituted 3 percent of military personnel. Many missions also include police, the third type of personnel, who might be sent as country contingents (formed police units, or FPUs) or as individuals. The FPUs protect key institutions, provide security to key individuals and assets, and serve as backup in riot situations and during patrols. Individual officers are sent in smaller numbers to monitor, advise, and train local law enforcement. They are not a part of contingents and do not respond to incidents. In 2014, women constituted about 10 percent of police personnel.

Nevertheless, while the overall proportions of women are still quite low, there is a positive trend in the numbers of female peacekeepers for both military and police sectors, and it is becoming rare for missions to not have any female peacekeepers at all (see Figure 30.1). In the post–SCR 1325 period, the United Nations started disaggregating data on peacekeeping deployments in order to gain a better picture of how the composition of peacekeeping has been transformed along gender lines.

Figure 30.2 shows the proportions of women in individual police contingents since late 2009. During this time period, the proportion of women in an individual police role nearly doubled and is at a higher level than the proportions of female military peacekeepers, although the upward trajectory has attenuated. From the end of 2011 to 2013, there was little consistent increase in the proportions of individual female police.

Behind the numbers are gendered stories with consequent implications for peacekeeping. For this reason, rather than focus on overall female peacekeeping trends in what follows, we examine two important aspects: the gendered hierarchies in peacekeeping missions, and the use of gendered discourse in recruiting female peacekeepers.

THE ROLE OF HEGEMONIC MASCULINITY IN PEACEKEEPING

Peacekeeping missions as institutions are not gender neutral. Because peacekeeping missions are composed of national militaries and police, they are highly masculine environments where certain forms of militarized masculinity are valued, and femininity is devalued. This results in two major problems: a male-dominated organization that is not wholly open to women, and an organization that relies on and validates particular ideas of masculinity.

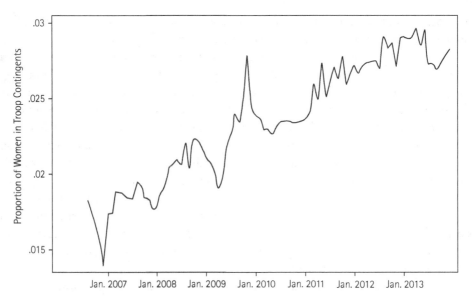

FIGURE 30.1. The rise in the proportions of women in UN peacekeeping troop contingents from late 2006 until the close of 2013.

Source: Many ideas and all figures and tables in this chapter are taken from Karim and Beardsley (2013, 2016, 2017).

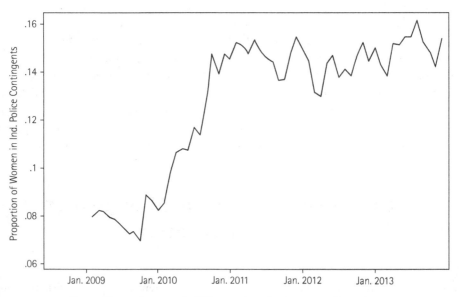

FIGURE 30.2. Proportions of women in UN peacekeeping troop contingents.

Here, the concept of hegemonic masculinity is useful. Hegemonic masculinity represents a successful claim for exercising authority through both formal and informal means and relies on subordinating alternative forms of masculinity (Connell 2005). Multiple types of masculinity can be hegemonic. For example, some privilege physical strength, aggressiveness, and a "machismo attitude," and others privilege rational thought, objectivity, and restraint. Within militaries (and police), hegemonic masculinity is pervasive in a militarized form (Higate 2003). Military institutions rely on a belief that effective combat requires ideals of masculinity—aggressiveness, rationality, and loyalty—over those traditionally associated as feminine behavior, such as passivity/pacificity, emotionality, and partiality. The military also uses physical profiles to stratify its members, with stronger, faster, bigger men rewarded with more privileged positions, usually related to combat (Lomsky-Feder and Rapoport 2003; Titunik 2008). The construction and privileging of masculinities and femininities vary based on time, place, and context. In the case of militaries and police, those masculinities that help combat effectiveness tend to be privileged and thus become hegemonic. In other words, those skills associated with combat and fighting are prioritized over other skills in these institutions. However, militarized masculinity is not the only form of hegemonic masculinity within militaries, as other forms of masculinity, such as protector masculinity, are also privileged. These forms of masculinities are important to understand because the majority of peacekeeping personnel come from militaries and police institutions (see Vandenberg, Chapter 31 in this volume).

Protective masculinity and the gendered protection norm

One type of hegemonic masculinity —"protector masculinity"— manifests itself when males, in the position of power, are expected to help females, in positions of less power. Differential abilities are also implied, where the acts of service flaunt the male's capabilities while hinting that females are often in need of assistance. Protector masculinity is closely linked to the construction of national identities and involves distinct notions of manhood and womanhood: the protector (male soldier) and those to be protected (women and children). Indeed, "the role of the masculine protector puts those protected, paradigmatically women and children, in a subordinate position of dependence and obedience" (Young 2003, 2).

The idea that men are the protectors and women are the protected provides the basis for a gendered "norm of protection" in society at large, and within military and police institutions themselves. The idea of "weak" females appeals to the kind of chivalry and heroism that has been historically associated with the male soldier and the military institution. Women within security forces must negotiate their identity based on this social norm, and even they are often portrayed as weak and in need of defense and protection. Such pervasive social beliefs may contribute to the low numbers of women in military and police institutions, possibly because women themselves hold these beliefs about gender roles and thus opt out of such occupations, or because women are systematically kept out of these institutions because of this stereotype. Those who make it in may be withheld from combat or combat-oriented tasks. Indeed, one common justification to keep women out of combat roles is the fear that men would feel the need to protect their female comrades and consequently jeopardize mission efficacy. Thus, chivalrous masculinity may lead to a "gendered protection norm" that discriminates against female personnel.

Protection masculinity is common not only in military and police institutions, which provide for national defense and security, but also in peacekeeping missions, which consist of military and police personnel. The first challenge that could hinder gender equality in peacekeeping missions is that a norm of protecting women is likely to foster a reluctance (1) to send women to the most dangerous environments; and (2) to allow female peacekeepers to fully use their skills as peacekeepers. Indeed, there is evidence for both these claims (Karim and Beardsley 2013). Female military peacekeepers are more likely to get sent to the "safest" missions, where there are fewer peacekeeping deaths and where the gross domestic product (GDP) of the country is higher. For example, when the United Nations appointed the first female Force Commander of a mission in 2014, she was the Force Commander for one of the most secure missions: UNFICYP in Cyprus.

The norm to protect women can also limit the extent to which female peacekeepers are utilized within missions. Fieldwork in missions has shown that in many troop contingents, women are not allowed to travel alone or without the protection of other peacekeepers, who are most often male. In addition, as many women begin to gain a presence in militaries, they may still hold lower rank positions *en masse*, and as such have less freedom of movement than their male colleagues. In general, the protection norm continues to subject women to an inferior position within the military, police, and peacekeeping missions. Moreover, women are still often confined to traditional roles in peacekeeping missions, such as nurses, doctors, administrators, and logistics, as is the case in some contributing countries where women occupy ancillary or accompanying positions. When they do take on a protection role, such as the all-female formed police units, their contribution is judged based on gender: they are lauded for their access in the community and not for their ability to provide military protection. The norm of protecting women as a goal of peacekeeping makes it even more difficult for the women serving as peacekeepers to be seen—by administrators, colleagues, local populations and even perhaps themselves—as *protectors*.

Militarized masculinity and sexual exploitation and abuse

Across the globe and historically, cultures develop ideas of manhood that motivate men to fight. The ability to carry out violence is sustained by expectations of sexual behavior. Promoting a culture of militarism is done alongside a devaluing of femininity. It is based on the creation of a gendered identity that relies on soldiers to "prove themselves as men," which is often done by questioning their sexual identity (Tickner 1992). Both military culture and society promote this kind of hegemonic masculinity, which rejects all that is "feminine" in order to be a "real man," and "real men" prove themselves on several battlefields. This militarized masculinity is supported by institutional power and has been relied upon in enhancing unit or group cohesion.

In the military, men are socialized to become warriors, and as such, militarized masculinity is instilled through training regiments. The military indoctrination processes and training can sometimes include hazing, which "breaks down the individual and replaces it with a commitment to and dependence on the institution of which they are now a part" (Whitworth 2007, 155). The tactics to socialize recruits into soldiers incorporate rituals to prove one's manhood, encourage warrior qualities such as the suppression of emotions and identity, shame men that behave like "women," and feminize the enemy (see Theidon, Chapter 11 in this volume).

This militarized masculinity and the patriarchy it proclaims have a number of consequences for peacekeeping. Militarized masculinity discriminates against women in traditionally masculine institutions by ensuring that feminine qualities and women in the institution are subdued and excluded, which can lead to discrimination against women, or, at its worst, violence against women (and men). Indeed, one of the more insidious and pervasive consequences is that it can contribute to a culture of widespread sexual harassment and even rape (see Vandenberg, Chapter 31 in this volume, for an overview of crimes committed by peacekeepers and recent UN responses). Despite newer measures to counter sexual abuse, allegations of abuse between peacekeepers and local women continues.

If militarized masculinity is related to sexual exploitation and abuse, changes in a militarized masculine culture may have a positive impact on local populations. It is possible that the deployment of peacekeepers (regardless of sex) that hold more gender-equal views may reduce incidents of sexual exploitation and abuse (SEA). Such men and women may be less likely to be influenced by a culture of militarized masculinity and thus less likely to engage in SEA of local women. Indeed, missions that consist of military personnel from countries with better records of gender equality—more women in the labor force and in primary school, better security for women, and those countries that have adopted an SCR 1325 national action plan—experience fewer counts of SEA allegations (Karim and Beardsley 2016, 2017). This means that troops from countries that hold more egalitarian views about women may be less likely to be abusive toward them; increases in the extent to which these attitudes are held by mission personnel and institutions may reduce some of the pernicious manifestations of militarized masculinity.

Female Peacekeepers

The persistence of gendered inequalities within peacekeeping missions suggests that something must be done to mitigate the harms that come from such a male-dominated institution. One suggestion has been that female peacekeepers themselves help mitigate against the structural inequalities supported by hegemonic and chivalrous militarized masculinities. However, the notion that "adding women and stirring" alone may change the gendered nature of peacekeeping missions is highly problematic.

Peacekeeping operations are not like most traditional military and police activities. The role of peacekeepers, especially in the context of international peace-building mandates, is to monitor peace agreements, provide credible information to all parties, prevent incidents of unrest from escalating, and help rebuild domestic institutions and infrastructure. This is in stark contrast to conventional combat operations, which require militaries to be "fit" and ready to engage. In general, within peacekeeping operations, combat roles are minimized, as the majority of the duties and responsibilities require soldiers to observe the peace, relate to the local population, mediate conflicts, and work with those in the civilian sector and NGOs, as well as personnel from many different national backgrounds. In this sense, peacekeeping does not provide the opportunity to operationalize the combat role to which soldiers within national militaries have been socialized. Peacekeeping missions require a completely different set of skills related to post-conflict peacemaking and post-conflict reconstruction. These skills are generally seen as a more typically "feminine" set of skills; they may challenge the masculine ethos of traditional military culture because they are the very skills that are often devalued in military (and civilian) socialization. In order to "soften" militarized-masculine peacekeeping, the United Nations and others have suggested that integrating more women into peacekeeping missions will enable militaries to modify their soldiering in order to achieve peaceful outcomes.

Since SCR 1325, the international community's main argument for gender balancing in peacekeeping missions has (problematically) rested on claims that women bring an added benefit to peacekeeping missions. Given that there are no current gender restrictions on activities undertaken by peacekeepers (unlike those in combat operations), increasing the number of women may, according to this argument, help to both balance and "equalize" the mission and mitigate against the negative aspects of military masculine cultures. Specifically, the UN Department of Peacekeeping Operations (on its website) makes multiple claims about female peacekeepers, stating that they act as role models in the local environment; inspire women and girls in often male-dominated societies to push for their own rights and for participation in peace processes; empower women in the host community; help make the peacekeeping force approachable for women in the community; and mentor female cadets at police and military academies.[1]

Table 30.1 presents a sampling of some arguments made by the United Nations and others regarding sex-ratio balancing in peacekeeping operations. Many of these arguments are based on "difference"—women's capacities are viewed as different from men's as a result of gender socialization. This means that women are viewed as possessing certain skills, assets, and characteristics distinct from men that make them particularly well-suited to peacekeeping (Bridges and Horsfall 2009; DeGroot 2001). These claims may be manifest in essentialist or biologically based arguments that women inherently possess certain proclivities and sensibilities that make them better equipped to promote peace, or based on more pragmatic issues related to operational effectiveness.

Table 30.1 UN and NGO Justification for Gender Balancing

UN Document	Quote
Francesco Bertolazzi, *Women with a Blue Helmet: The Integration of Women and Gender Issues in U.N. Peacekeeping Missions* (Santo Domingo: UN-INSTRAW, 2010), 18.	"Inside the mission, the female presence can sometimes act as a brake against possible violations of the code of conduct. Where the presence of women in peacekeeping operations was higher, such as in the missions in Guatemala and South Africa, the missions were completed with enormous success and the mandates were completely fulfilled."
DPKO/DFS Guidelines: Integrating a Gender Perspective into the Work of the United Nations Military in Peacekeeping Operations (New York: UN DPKO/DFS, 2010), 13.	"The operational imperative of having a critical mass of female military peacekeepers is widely acknowledged, as it enables better access to women in post-conflict environments to support mandate implementation."
Addressing Conflict-Related Sexual Violence: An Analytical Inventory of Peacekeeping Practice (New York: UN Women, 2010), 14.	"Gender balance in peacekeeping can help the UN to 'lead by example' in relation to women's empowerment as both security providers and beneficiaries. Women may have a comparative operational advantage in sexual violence prevention, having greater proximity to groups at risk."
Ten Year Impact Study in Implementation of UN Security Council resolution 1325 (2000) on Women, Peace, and Security in Peacekeeping (New York: UN DPKO/DFS, 2010), 27.	"The presence of uniformed female peacekeepers has had a positive impact, challenging traditional ideas of gender roles and encouraging many women to enter the security sector."
UN Secretary-General, Letter dated March 24, 2005, from the Secretary-General addressed to the President of the General Assembly, UN Doc. A/59/710, ¶ 43 (March 24, 2005).	"The fifth basic requirement is an increase in the percentage of female peacekeeping personnel. That would facilitate the mission's task of making meaningful contact with vulnerable groups and non-governmental organizations in the local community in its effort to eliminate sexual exploitation and abuse. Victims and their spokespersons tend to be female and the presence of female interlocutors, especially in senior positions, would facilitate efforts to encourage the reporting of abuse, which is the first step in eliminating it. Finally, the presence of more women in a mission, especially at senior levels, will help to promote an environment that discourages sexual exploitation and abuse, particularly of the local population."
SCR 1325 (October 31, 2000).	"Recognizing that an understanding of the impact of armed conflict on women and girls, effective institutional arrangements to guarantee their protection and full participation in the peace process can significantly contribute to the maintenance and promotion of international peace and security."

(Continued)

Table 30.1 Continued

UN Document	Quote
Mainstreaming a Gender Perspective in Multidimensional Peace Operations (New York: UN DPKO, 2000), ¶ 6.	"Women's presence [in peacekeeping missions] improves access and support for local women; it makes male peacekeepers more reflective and responsible; and it broadens the repertoire of skills and styles available within the mission, often with the effect of reducing conflict and confrontation."
Gender Mainstreaming in Peace Support Operations: Moving beyond Rhetoric to Practice (London: International Alert, 2002), 23.	"A more equitable gender balance and the increased presence of female civilian, police and military peacekeepers can have a positive influence on Peace Support Operations and their relations with local populations.
The Role of Women in United Nations Peacekeeping (New York: UN Division for the Advancement of Women, 1995), 8–9.	"Evidence suggests that the increased presence of women helps to create good relations with local communities, since the establishment of trust is an essential element in any peacekeeping operation."
	"It has also been contended that the presence of women contributes to differences in decision-making in terms of content, priorities, management style, organizational culture and group dynamics."

mission rest on the idea that the differences between men and women are significant and salient.

Another area in which the United Nations argues that female peacekeepers are particularly important, especially to increase operational effectiveness, is for addressing sexual and gender-based violence (SGBV). In a 2008 speech, Secretary-General Ban Ki-Moon called for more female peacekeepers to help counter "the abominable practice of sexual violence" resulting from armed conflicts.[2] In practice, according to the United Nations, this assumes that female peacekeepers will be more attentive to SGBV in conducting their daily operations, local women should be more willing to report cases of SGBV to female peacekeepers, and female peacekeepers should be better able to question and offer assistance to survivors of SGBV.

Furthermore, the United Nations has argued that female peacekeepers may improve the mission environment, especially in regard to reducing sexual misconduct. Peacekeeping missions, just like other military settings, create conditions where SEA may develop and/or continue. Such sexual misconduct by peacekeepers is often justified as "normal" masculinity for male soldiers stationed for long periods away from their homes. Including more women has been considered an important policy lever to address such misconduct, such as through using female peacekeepers to monitor the behavior of their male colleagues and deterring unsanctioned behavior by security personnel. Aside from improved accountability, increasing the proportion of women in peace operations is thought to decrease the number of perpetrators of misconduct, assuming that women are less likely to perpetrate SEA.

A critique of the suggested impact of women

There are at least three problems with relying on the preceding arguments to justify increasing the proportions of female peacekeepers to improve so-called mission legitimacy and conduct. First, the arguments made by the United Nations often reduce women to essentialized stereotypes. This perpetuates the perception that women are not well suited to engage in traditional security work, but rather are better suited for activities seen to be stereotypically feminine, such as nursing or administrative work. The success of the all-female Indian Formed Police Unit has been highlighted through its "feminine" work in community engagement, not for the work for which it is deployed: to protect the population. As such, negative stereotypes about women being irrelevant to, or even a liability in, providing physical protection can also be perpetuated when female peacekeeping successes are highlighted based on their performance in doing "feminine" or "feminized" work, such as helping to empower local women. Such stereotyping may have negative downstream effects, such as the marginalization of women from particular "masculine roles" in the post-conflict environment.

Moreover, gender stereotypes often mischaracterize the behavior of many female peacekeepers. Gender is a social construction, and as such, women may be socialized to reproduce masculine norms, especially in militarized work settings. Women also can perpetrate, be accomplices to, and be complicit in acts of violence, challenging the notion of what it means to be a woman (Sjoberg and Gentry 2007). While traditional gender roles have historically recognized men and women as "natural" warriors and homemakers, respectively, women's participation in violence is not a new phenomenon, even if the media has treated it as such, with increased coverage of female suicide bombers and other female rebels as deviant gender examples.

Second, while gender-sensitive issues may sometimes be better handled by women—indeed, we consider in the following how in many cultural contexts, contact with males regarding sensitive issues is prevented—"foreign" women remain potentially limited in helping survivors of SGBV. Gender is not the only relevant axis of identity. Class, race, religion, education, language, ethnicity, nationality, North/South, and so on, all feature heavily in the intersection of peacekeepers and locals (Henry 2012). Cultural sensitivity is not likely undone by gender similarities. Female peacekeepers from outside of the host country region may not be well equipped to judge whether cases involve SGBV, to interview perpetrators, or to attend to the needs of survivors, any more than their male counterparts. In many countries, there are traditional and informal cultural practices to address issues of SGBV, and foreign peacekeepers may not be knowledgeable about them. In fact, peacekeepers may even do harm in advocating for external-centered remedies to SGBV, as such practices may run counter to more culturally appropriate responses. Indeed, international women peacekeepers rarely share the same experiences as local women, making solidarity between women of different cultures, races, ethnicities, religions, and countries elusive.

Third, engaging in such discourse places the onus of missions' success on women, who are likely to remain a minority, and overlooks the potential role that all peacekeepers, including men, can play in carrying out reforms. The expectation that female personnel will be better suited to keep their male counterparts in line displaces the responsibility of individual male peacekeepers onto female personnel, and burdens female peacekeepers disproportionately. Instead of men holding themselves accountable for their behavior, women are expected to be a deterrent and to have a "civilizing" effect on their male colleagues. The resulting burden on women puts them in a bind; the role of monitoring the behavior of their fellow friends, colleagues, and even superiors could disrupt their career advancement and increase undesirable interpersonal conflict. Moreover, to the extent that policy reforms exclude male peacekeepers from playing a significant role, they do not help the largest and most important segment of the peacekeeper population.

Similarly, women may be evaluated as "female peacekeepers" and not as "peacekeepers." As such, only female personnel are evaluated based on instrumental criteria. Male peacekeepers are not; their presence is normalized without evaluating whether masculinity is helpful or harmful to the mission. Men are not evaluated based on their ability to perform caring labor and are often exonerated from misconduct where their behavior is seen as "natural," as in the "boys will be boys" narrative. In this way, relying on particular gender ideas means that women are subjected to a different standard than men in the same occupation. Men are assumed to be naturally competent at providing security in peacekeeping labor, whereas women's presence in the security sector has to be made intelligible through a discourse of effectiveness. Thus, the discourse of "difference" to justify more female personnel consequently singularizes the way in which women are to be evaluated. If the justification for including women in peacekeeping is based on the assumption that women improve mission legitimacy and gender equality by adding a "feminine touch," then they are evaluated based not on the skills they have gained through militarized training, but rather on their ability to conform to specific ideas about femininity and their ability to transform the mission culture.

CONCLUSION

Peacekeeping missions are highly gendered spaces both because of the imbalance of female and male personnel and because of the traditional military cultural practices and ideologies of warriors. The gendering process is evident at the recruitment phase and throughout the discourse that the United Nations uses to increase the proportions of female peacekeepers. It continues into the mission, where the performance of militarized masculinities may contribute to discrimination against women and sexual exploitation and abuse. Nevertheless, gender is a fluid concept and process, which means that power structures that perpetuate such dynamics can be altered. Instead of focusing on numbers—increasing the proportions of women in peacekeeping missions—missions might instead do well to think with a broader understanding of gender and focus on the structures that create and perpetuate gender inequalities. For example, using a discourse of difference to justify women's participation in peacekeeping has dramatic implications for the way women's work in missions is then perceived by other peacekeepers, beneficiaries, and aid workers more generally. Additionally, treating peacekeeping missions as if they are gender-neutral spaces may well facilitate sexual exploitation and abuse, among other gender-based violence.

Instead, promoting gender equality in missions may serve to mitigate some of the pernicious effects mentioned earlier. Policy changes to promote these broader structural changes may include starting formal mentoring programs, or at least workshops for women to discuss problems and expectations about the job during the mission and during pre-deployment; helping train women in domestic military and police forces so that they meet the requirements for peacekeeping deployment; amending requirements for joining missions to account for historically underrepresented groups in peacekeeping operations; basing recruitment criteria for missions and mission leadership positions to include screening based on beliefs about gender equality and not just other skills such as driving, computer skills, and so on; and conducting outreach to local communities, including partnering with NGOs, to make the mission more accessible and SEA reporting easier for locals. Thus, in this sense, it becomes important not only to include more women in peacekeeping missions, but even more so, to make efforts to change policies and structures so that women's equal presence in the mission is not marginal, but part of the very foundation of the mission. Only with a structurally revised gendered vision of peacekeeping will peacekeeping be truly transformative in addressing peace and security globally.

NOTES

1. See "Women in Peacekeeping," accessed September 5, 2016, http://www.un.org/en/peacekeeping/issues/women/womeninpk.shtml.
2. Press Release, Secretary-General, *Far More Must Be Done to Involve Women in Conflict Prevention, Peace Talks*, UN Press Release SG/SM/11647-SC/9365-WOM/1685 (June 19, 2008).

REFERENCES

Bridges, Donna, and Debbie Horsfall. 2009. "Increasing Operational Effectiveness in UN Peacekeeping Toward a Gender-Balanced Force." *Armed Forces & Society* 36, no. 1: 120–130.
Connell, Raewyn. 2005. *Masculinities*. Berkeley: University of California Press.

DeGroot, Gerard J. 2001. "A Few Good Women: Gender Stereotypes, the Military and Peacekeeping." *International Peacekeeping* 8, no. 2: 23–38.

Henry, Marsha. 2012. "Peacexploitation? Interrogating Labor Hierarchies and Global Sisterhood among Indian and Uruguayan Female Peacekeepers." *Globalizations* 9, no. 1: 15–33.

Higate, Paul. 2003. *Military Masculinities: Identity and the State*. Westport, CT: Praeger.

Karim, Sabrina, and Kyle Beardsley. 2013. "Female Peacekeepers and Gender Balancing: Token Gestures or Informed Policymaking?" *International Interactions* 39, no. 4: 461–488.

Karim, Sabrina, and Kyle Beardsley. 2016. "Explaining Sexual Exploitation and Abuse in Peacekeeping Missions: The Role of Female Peacekeepers and Gender Equality in Contributing Countries." *Journal of Peace Research*, vol. 53 no. 1: 100–115.

Karim, Sabrina, and Kyle Beardsley. 2017. *Equal Opportunity Peacekeeping: The Need for Gender Equality in the Search for Qualify Peace*. Oxford: Oxford University Press.

Lomsky-Feder, Edna, and Tamar Rapoport. 2003. "Juggling Models of Masculinity: Russian-Jewish Immigrants in the Israeli Army." *Sociological Inquiry* 73, no 1: 114–137.

Sjoberg, Laura, and Caron E. Gentry. 2007. *Mothers, Monsters, Whores: Women's Violence in Global Politics*. London: Zed Books.

Tickner, J. Ann. 1992. *Gender in International Relations*. New York: Columbia University Press.

Titunik, Regina F. 2008. "The Myth of the Macho Military." *Polity* 40, no. 2: 137–163.

Whitworth, Sandra. 2007. *Men, Militarism, and UN Peacekeeping: A Gendered Analysis*. Boulder, CO: Lynne Rienner.

Young, Iris. 2003. "Logic of Masculinist Protection: Reflections on the Current Security State." *Signs: Journal of Women in Culture & Society* 29, no. 1: 1–25.

CHAPTER 31

PEACEKEEPING, HUMAN TRAFFICKING, AND SEXUAL ABUSE AND EXPLOITATION

MARTINA E. VANDENBERG

In 2016, sexual misconduct by peacekeepers hit the headlines again. In a scathing op-ed titled "I Love the UN, but It Is Failing," Anthony Banbury, then United Nations Assistant Secretary-General for Field Support, announced his resignation. Among the reasons for his departure, he expressed horror that peacekeepers from the Democratic Republic of Congo and the Republic of Congo had "engaged in a persistent pattern of rape and abuse of the people—often young girls—the United Nations was sent there to protect." Banbury criticized the United Nations for cynically deploying these troop contingents, "despite reports of serious human rights violations by these soldiers" (Banbury 2016).

Nearly two decades after allegations emerged that peacekeepers trafficked women and girls into forced prostitution in post-conflict Bosnia and Herzegovina (Human Rights Watch 2002), impunity remains the norm. That is troubling, because much has changed since the NATO-led peacekeeping missions in the Balkans. First, the United Nations adopted a "zero tolerance" policy prohibiting all sexual exploitation and abuse by peacekeeping personnel (UN Secretary-General 2003). In addition, the adoption of the UN Trafficking Protocol in 2000 provided the international community with an agreed-upon definition of human trafficking. The Trafficking Protocol requires states to criminalize human trafficking, defined (in part) under Article 3 as the obtaining of (a) an individual over the age of 18, through force, fraud, or coercion, for the purpose of exploitation; or (b) the obtaining of a child for exploitation, even where force, fraud, or coercion are not used (Protocol 2000, annex II, 53). Third, the United Nations began to discuss—and more important, to report on—these abuses. In 2005, the Secretary-General's Advisor on Sexual Exploitation and Abuse by UN Peacekeeping Personnel, Prince Zeid Ra'ad Zeid Al-Hussein, Permanent Representative of Jordan, issued a groundbreaking report (the Zeid Report). Despite significant fanfare at the time of the report's release, the United Nations implemented very few of Zeid's excellent recommendations. Those that were implemented have largely failed (Askin 2016).

This chapter analyzes human trafficking in the context of peacekeeping operations. More crucially, the chapter addresses sexual abuse committed by peacekeepers and civilians employed within peacekeeping missions. The chapter highlights the persistent lack of accountability for these crimes, years after serious allegations first came to public attention.

PEACEKEEPERS AND SEXUAL MISCONDUCT: A HISTORY OF ABUSE

In recent years, UN officials have condemned sexual abuse, sexual exploitation, and human trafficking by peacekeepers. High-level UN personnel have denounced the perpetrators, published statistics, increased transparency, provided prevention training, convened working groups, and issued reports. But these steps—and international outrage—have not ended the abuse. The headlines alone tell the same story in virtually every peacekeeping mission of the past two decades:

- "Members of a UN Peacekeeping Force in the Central African Republic Allegedly Turned to Sexual Predation, Betraying Their Duty to Protect" (Central African Republic [CAR]; Sleff 2016)
- "Allegations against French Peacekeepers Highlight Obstacles in Addressing Abuse" (CAR; Sengupta 2015a)
- "The UN Let Off Peacekeepers Involved in a Haitian Boy's Rape" (Haiti; Bracken 2014)
- "The UN Confronts Another Sex Scandal: In Haiti, More Than 100 Peacekeepers from Sri Lanka Have Been Deported on Suspicion of Illicit Liaisons" (Haiti; Williams 2007)
- "Report Reveals Shame of UN Peacekeepers" (Haiti, Sierra Leone, Bosnia, Cambodia, East Timor, and the Democratic Republic of the Congo [DRC]; Bowcott 2005)

The Zeid Report responded to allegations against UN peacekeepers, including troops in the Democratic Republic of Congo. In the words of then Under Secretary-General for Peacekeeping, Jean-Marie Guéhenno, the report provided "a candid account of the problem as well as a clear framework for effective action by both the Secretariat and Member States" (Guéhenno 2005). In Secretary General Kofi Annan's cover letter to the Zeid Report, he wrote,

United Nations peacekeeping operations have for decades brought peace and stability to countries emerging from war. The women and men who serve the blue flag do so under arduous and often dangerous conditions. The history of peacekeeping has been one of distinguished collective accomplishment and personal sacrifice.

However, this exemplary record has been clouded by the unconscionable conduct of a few individuals. In particular, the revelations in 2004 of sexual exploitation and abuse by a significant number of United Nations peacekeeping personnel in the Democratic Republic of the Congo have done great harm to the name of peacekeeping. (UN Secretary-General 2005)

Secretary-General Annan's statement included a glaring internal inconsistency. Although he blamed a "few individuals," he conceded in the next sentence that a "significant number of United Nations peacekeeping personnel" committed the abuse. For years, the "few bad apples" thesis has obscured the United Nations' cultural and systemic failures that facilitate impunity for this abuse.

THE EVOLUTION OF ABUSE: FROM TRAFFICKING TO SEXUAL EXPLOITATION AND ABUSE

In Bosnia and Herzegovina, "a few bad apples" were blamed for widespread human trafficking. Traffickers transported girls and women from Eastern Europe and the former Soviet Union to brothels scattered throughout Bosnia and Herzegovina. Indeed, when one analyst wrote about the Bosnian case in 2005, she titled the report, *Barracks and Brothels* (Mendelson 2005). But reports of women trafficked from abroad to fill brothels for forced prostitution within UN mission territories have all but disappeared. The standard operating procedure for traffickers in Bosnia and Herzegovina and Kosovo— trafficking adult women and girls into forced prostitution in nightclubs and brothels— no longer seems to be the norm. The vast majority of sexual abuse and exploitation cases that fill the current UN docket constitute rape or other forms of sexual assault perpetrated against children.

Whether this is an evolution of the abuse or an accident of reporting is unclear. It may be that the cases involving the rape of children, evidenced in the preceding headlines, are simply more likely to be reported to the authorities. Or it may be that trafficking third-country nationals to peacekeeping areas of operation is no longer "necessary" when victims can be found and abused within the country of the peacekeeping mission.

Many of the more recent cases, while horrific and certainly constituting other heinous crimes, do not fall under the legal definition of human trafficking. But whether states classify the crimes as rape or as human trafficking, criminal accountability for the perpetrators is essential. However defined, criminal prosecutions should be brought against the peacekeepers committing these abuses. Instead, we see little—if any—accountability.

To the extent that there has been *any* accountability for these sexual crimes committed by peacekeepers, it has come in the form of adverse employment consequences, such as disciplinary proceedings or repatriation (Guéhenno 2005).

"A Cancer in our System": The UN Response

In 2015, responding to horrifying press reports of peacekeeper sexual misconduct in the Central African Republic (CAR), United Nations Secretary-General Ban Ki-moon compared sexual abuse in UN peacekeeping operations to "a cancer in our system" (Associated Press 2015) and fired his head of peacekeeping in CAR for mishandling the investigations (Sengupta 2015b). He then threatened to "name names"—to publicize the names of national peacekeeping contingents facing allegations of sexual abuse (Sengupta 2015b) He followed through with the publication of the Secretary-General's annual report on sexual exploitation and abuse in March 2016 (Shortell and Roth 2016). Of the reported sixty-nine cases of sexual exploitation and abuse occurring in countries with peacekeeping missions, twenty-three included sex with minors. Fifteen of those incidents ended in paternity (UN News Centre 2016). The report implicated national contingents from twenty-one countries. The largest number of allegations lodged in 2015 focused on personnel from the DRC, Morocco, South Africa, Cameroon, the Republic of the Congo, Rwanda, and Tanzania. Twenty-two of the total sixty-nine cases arose from the peacekeeping operation in CAR (Shortell and Roth 2016).

The following sections explore the United Nations' fitful battle to end sexual exploitation, including human trafficking, by peacekeepers. The next section begins with basic definitions. The following section analyzes the norm of impunity, providing specific case examples. The subsequent section traces new developments, followed by conclusions.

Definitions: What Is Sexual Exploitation and Abuse? What Is Human Trafficking? And Who Are Peacekeepers?

Sexual exploitation and abuse

In 2003, the Secretary-General issued rules prohibiting sexual exploitation and abuse (SEA) by all UN personnel (UN Secretary-General 2003). Section 1 of the Secretary-General's bulletin on special measures for protection from sexual exploitation and sexual abuse defined "sexual exploitation" as "any actual or attempted abuse of a position of vulnerability, differential power, or trust, for sexual purposes, including, but not limited to, profiting monetarily, socially or politically from the sexual exploitation of another." The bulletin further defined "sexual abuse" as "actual or threatened physical intrusion of a sexual nature, whether by force or under unequal or coercive conditions" (UN Secretary-General 2003) According to the UN Conduct and Discipline Unit website, SEA-related offenses include rape, transactional sex, exploitative relationships, and sexual abuse (UN Strategy 2016). These are so-called Category 1 allegations. The Office of Internal Oversight (OIOS) has responsibility to investigate these allegations (UN Secretary-General 2003).

Trafficking in persons

The United Nations Protocol to Suppress, Prevent and Punish Trafficking in Persons, Especially Women and Children (Trafficking Protocol) provides an international legal definition of trafficking in persons:

> "Trafficking in persons" shall mean the recruitment, transportation, transfer, harbouring or receipt of persons, by means of the threat or use of force or other forms of coercion, of abduction, of fraud, of deception, of the abuse of power or of a position of vulnerability or of the giving or receiving of payments or benefits to achieve the consent of a person having control over another person, for the purpose of exploitation. Exploitation shall include, at a minimum, the exploitation of the prostitution of others or other forms of sexual exploitation, forced labour or services, slavery or practices similar to slavery, servitude or the removal of organs. (Protocol 2000, art. 3(a))

The Trafficking Protocol clarifies that where the victim is a child under eighteen, none of the means listed in the definition—such as the threat of use of force—need be satisfied.

The trafficking in persons definition under the Trafficking Protocol does not encompass all sexual contact between a local population and peacekeepers. It is fair to say, however, that some portion of the sexual exploitation and abuse that has plagued the UN peacekeeping operations would also qualify as trafficking under the Trafficking Protocol. In one case, for example, five young Haitian women who followed soldiers back to Sri Lanka were forced into brothels or polygamous households (Williams 2007). Allegations that UN police officers serving with the International Police Task Force (IPTF) in Bosnia purchased women from brothels in Bosnia and Herzegovina provide another example, as do allegations that Romanian IPTF officers trafficked Romanian women to Bosnia for forced prostitution (Human Rights Watch 2002).

In 2004, the UN Department for Peacekeeping Operations (DPKO) developed a draft policy paper that sought to examine the intersection between trafficking and peacekeeping. The policy paper identified peacekeepers as potential "users" of the services of trafficked women, rather than perpetrators of trafficking. Specifically,

> Trafficking is a process which seeks out vulnerable individuals, and then exacerbates their vulnerability (through violence, forced movement, slavery, servitude, coercion, threat and/or deceit) and then subjects them to severe exploitation—often forced prostitution or forced labour—to generate revenue for a third party, often organised crime networks . . . .
>
> The use of trafficking victims by peacekeepers for sexual and other services has been a source of major embarrassment and political damage to UN [Peacekeeping Operations] PKOs. (UN DPKO 2004, paras. 5–7)

Peacekeeping

Peacekeeping missions are sanctioned by the Security Council. Member states that agree to take part in the particular peacekeeping regime send some personnel; other mission staff members are appointed directly (Kanetake 2012). These missions comprise more than just soldiers. Indeed, a given mission may include individual police officers, formed police units, experts on mission, as well as soldiers in national troop contingents (see Peacekeeping Statistics 2016; see also Karim and Henry, Chapter 30 in this volume). As of August 2015, for example, there were sixteen peacekeeping missions, totaling 124,746 personnel. The majority were uniformed personnel (106,245: 90,889 troops, 13,550 police, 1,806 military observers), but civilian personnel made up a significant portion of these missions (18,501 people, comprising 5,315 internationals, 11,476 local staff, and 1,710 UN volunteers) (Peacekeeping Statistics 2016).

Because the United Nations has no standing army, it must rely on troop-contributing countries (TCCs) to provide soldiers. These personnel come from a wide array of countries, with a wide range of social and gender norms. In addition, these countries enforce a broad range of disciplinary mechanisms within their ranks. Unfortunately for the victims in these cases, criminal accountability for sexual misconduct lies with the peacekeepers' sending state.

A Legacy of Impunity: From UN Mission in Bosnia and Herzegovina (UNMIBH) to UN Multidimensional Integrated Stabilization Mission in the Central African Republic (MINUSCA)

The United Nations does not prosecute mission members for trafficking or other forms of sexual misconduct. Instead, the missions can only refer cases back to national authorities and suggest that they prosecute offenders. With very few exceptions, those national authorities do nothing. Allegations from the UN Mission in Bosnia and Herzegovina provide an excellent illustration. And the example of the UN Multidimensional Integrated Stabilization Mission in the Central African Republic (MINUSCA) shows how little has changed over the last decade.

A timeline of impunity

In 1998, Human Rights Watch uncovered allegations of direct involvement in human trafficking by UN Mission in Bosnia and Herzegovina (UNMIBH) personnel. International Police Task Force officers (IPTF) serving with UNMIBH had purchased women (and their passports) from brothel owners, moving the trafficked women into their housing units. In response, UNMIBH (after many denials and much foot-dragging) repatriated eighteen men, sending them back to their home countries for trafficking- and prostitution-related offenses (Human Rights Watch 2002). The legal fiction was that the officers' countries of origin would prosecute them for these alleged crimes. They did not. UN disciplinary action ended with the men's repatriation.

In 2002, a UN official explained why the United Nations could do nothing to prosecute UNMIBH personnel who engaged in criminal activities. In a letter to Human Rights Watch, Andrei Shkourko, the UN Headquarters Bosnia and Herzegovina desk officer, wrote,

> The United Nations does not have the legal authority to take punitive measures against civilian police monitors made available by Member States for United Nations peacekeeping operations, and the *disciplinary follow-up to their misconduct is the responsibility of the contributing countries.* The options available to the United Nations in such cases are limited, therefore, to the administrative action of repatriation with the recommendation to the national authorities concerned to take the appropriate action against the individual in question. (Human Rights Watch 2002, n233; italics added)

Hopes that national authorities would take "appropriate action" against those accused of misconduct soon faded, and it appeared that none of the eighteen repatriated IPTF officers was prosecuted (Human Rights Watch 2002). The allegations in Bosnia exposed the fatal flaw in the United Nations' accountability system: it is not enough for the United Nations to espouse "zero tolerance" for these crimes when the member states that send the troops *do tolerate* the abuse.

Allegations of sexual abuse of children by French peacekeepers in the MINUSCA mission in the Central African Republic hit the headlines in 2015 (Willsher 2015). In addition to the initial allegations that fourteen French soldiers (deployed on a separate French military mission dubbed "Operation Sangaris") had raped minors, five UN peacekeepers from Chad and Equatorial Guinea faced allegations that they had demanded sex acts from "hungry children in return for food" (Willsher 2015). Although France did launch a criminal investigation, critics charged that the authorities in France failed to act on the allegations. French authorities learned of the alleged abuse only after a UN investigation report was leaked by a high-ranking UN official turned whistle-blower (Laville 2016).

In this case, like Bosnia twenty years earlier, the *whistleblower*, Anders Kompass, faced disciplinary action and reprisal. Kompass endured a nine-month investigation of *his* conduct by the Office of Internal Oversight Services (OIOS) for reporting the crimes against children to law enforcement (Patel 2016). Kompass, the whistleblower, was first suspended for leaking documents to the French government, though he was later exonerated.

Sadly, additional allegations emerged in 2016 after the United Nations sent a team to interview children in CAR. A seven-year-old girl told investigators that she had performed "oral sex on French soldiers in exchange for a bottle of water and a sachet of cookies" (*The Guardian* 2016). In a January 2016 press conference, Assistant Secretary-General Anthony Banbury reported four newly discovered child sex abuse cases in CAR. These more recent cases involved UN troops and police from Bangladesh, Congo, Niger and Senegal (*The Guardian* 2016).

Legal and procedural abdication of responsibility

The horrific events in CAR should have raised significant alarm at the United Nations. In a ninety-six-page independent report examining the United Nations' bungling of the child sexual abuse allegations, experts excoriated the organization for allowing the child sexual abuse investigation's findings in CAR to languish, shunted from inbox to inbox (Deschamps, Hassan, and Sooka 2015). And the vicious treatment meted out to whistle-blowers should also raise red flags. In the face of horrific allegations, the first instinct at the United Nations in this case was to punish the whistleblower and take zero action against the perpetrators. These actions send a disturbing message: zero tolerance is actually zero tolerance for whistleblowers.

As in all of the other cases, the United Nations reacted in CAR with one of the only plays in the UN playbook: repatriation (Garrefy 2016). The mission announced that it would send home 120 peacekeepers immediately (Garrefy 2016).

In theory, the UN Headquarters provides investigative reports to the member states, providing the evidence necessary for accountability in the countries of origin. Member states are also required to conduct their own investigations under a revised Memorandum of Understanding (Kanetake 2012). But as a rule, member states are unresponsive. According to December 2015 data on the UN Conduct and Discipline Unit webpage, between 2007 and 2014, the United Nations sent 530 follow-up messages to member states requesting updates on particular cases. States answered just 243 of those *Notes Verbales*, or less than half (Statistics 2016).

To be sure, response rates have improved markedly over recent years. In 2007, the United Nations sent sixty-seven follow-up communications to sending states and received just twenty-three responses. In 2014, the UN sent sixty-one such communications, receiving fifty-two responses.

There is no punishment for failing to answer the mail, just as there is no punishment for failing to hold peacekeepers accountable. These failures to act expose the root of the problem: the United Nations is dependent on member states to offer troops. For that reason, it is reluctant to impose conditions on those troops that might limit states' willingness to commit personnel.

The central flaw in the accountability system designed by the United Nations may be found in paragraph 5 of the Secretary-General's bulletin:

> *Referral to national authorities*
> If, after proper investigation, there is evidence to support allegations of sexual exploitation or sexual abuse, these cases may, upon consultation with the Office of Legal Affairs, be referred to national authorities for criminal prosecution. (UN Secretary-General 2003, para. 5)

Yet, if the United Nations wishes to resolve the ongoing harm, which UN leaders repeatedly claim it wishes to do, it is not enough to repatriate alleged offenders back to sending states that do not prosecute.

There have been a few positive exceptions, in which sending countries have prosecuted offending troops for the crimes they committed, rather than merely repatriating them. In 2009, the United Nations released data indicating that at least fifty peacekeepers had received punishment "ranging from reduction in military rank to eight months imprisonment" for sexual abuse while serving in a UN Mission since 2007 (Klapper 2009). That data, however, could not be independently confirmed. Media reports do indicate that sporadic criminal cases have been brought. In 2001, for example, a Jordanian UN civilian police officer with the UN Transitional Administration in East Timor (UNTAET) faced an indictment in East Timor, the host country, for the alleged rape of a local woman in a hotel (UN News Centre 2001). News outlets reported that South Africa prosecuted two of its soldiers for abuses in Congo; France prosecuted one UN civilian staff member for child rape and creation of pornographic videos of children (Ndulu 2009). A Pakistani military tribunal convened in Haiti convicted Pakistani peacekeepers accused of raping a fourteen-year-old boy in that country (Reuters 2012). However, even where convictions are secured, the sentences are often so light as to compound the injustice. The Pakistani military tribunal in the Haiti case, the first case in which members of the UN Peacekeeping Mission faced criminal charges in Haiti, sentenced the two peacekeepers to just one year in prison and dismissal from the armed forces. Amnesty International, commenting upon the light sentences, called the result a "travesty of justice" (Bhalla 2012).

In another case involving MINUSTAH in Haiti, a grainy cellphone video was alleged to show the rape of a young Haitian by five Uruguayan peacekeepers. The victim, nineteen, traveled to Uruguay to testify in the trial against the Uruguayan marines. The court convicted four of the five defendants, but of "private violence," a far less serious crime than rape (AlterPresse 2013).

Far more common than these exceptional cases, however, are allegations like those made by Haitian NGOs protesting the government of Haiti's renewal of MINUSTAH's mandate. In a shadow report prepared for Haiti's Universal Periodic Review, nongovernmental experts wrote that they had been unable to find any evidence that the 111 soldiers and three officers repatriated by the United Nations back to Sri Lanka for sexual abuse of minors had faced prosecution (Bri Kouri Nouvèl Gaye et al. 2011, para. 22). The NGOs called on the Sri Lankan forces to be prosecuted for war crimes and crimes against humanity "since the victims were subjected to death threats, physical assaults and sexual violence [to force them to engage in] sex with peacekeepers" (Bri Kouri Nouvèl Gaye et al. 2011, para. 20). The most common response remains the same: ignoring the problem until press coverage makes the allegations impossible to ignore, followed by sending the offending troops home.

NEW DEVELOPMENTS AND CONCLUSIONS

UN Secretary-General Ban Ki-moon, responding to global criticism, took several new steps in early 2016 to combat sexual exploitation and abuse in peacekeeping missions. He published the country names of sending states whose troops committed sexual assault. He launched new transparent reporting, and posted those reports on the UN web pages. But, without more, these actions will have little impact.

The United Nations has placed major emphasis on prevention, training, transparency, and "zero tolerance." But the same barriers to accountability exist today as existed in the time of the Bosnia and Herzegovina misconduct allegations: botched investigations, retaliation against whistleblowers, inability to prosecute perpetrators, and entrenched impunity.

Ban Ki-moon's statement on the Conduct and Discipline website page declares categorically, "Let me be clear: the United Nations, and I personally, are profoundly committed to a zero-tolerance policy against sexual exploitation or abuse by our own personnel. This means zero complacency. When we receive credible allegations we ensure that they are looked into fully. It means zero impunity."

But the lofty goal of "zero impunity" glosses over the United Nations' complete reliance on member states to hold perpetrators accountable for these abuses. This effectively renders "zero tolerance" impotent.

A glimmer of possible cultural change emerged in March 2016 with the United Nations' announcement of a raft of policy changes to improve accountability (UN News Centre 2016). But the reforms—many recycled from the 2005 Zeid report—are only as meaningful as the implementation effort that follows.

Advocates in the field welcomed the new accountability initiatives. But for those advocates with long experience in the peacekeeping field, a sense that the community had "seen this movie before" tempered the optimism. For example, Human Rights Watch expressed skepticism, stating that governments should stop paying lip service to zero tolerance and instead "take concrete actions such as improving training for their troops and punishing those responsible for abuses" (Human Rights Watch 2016).

Six radical changes to peacekeeping enforcement policy should be implemented:

- Require states to make *ex gratia* payments to victims. Peacekeepers—and their home states—walk away from the sexual violence they have wrought (not to mention the children they have fathered). States should be forced to make *ex gratia* payments to a victims' fund in any case where an allegation of abuse is substantiated.
- Publish all correspondence on follow-up prosecutions. The United Nations should track not only allegations in theater and updates on the status of the investigation, but also track prosecutions, indictments, and sentencing documents.
- Collect DNA samples from all peacekeepers to assess guilt in cases of sexual exploitation and abuse. Use the DNA database to determine paternity and force peacekeepers to pay child support.
- Suspend countries with significant abuse allegations from participation in peacekeeping operations. Member states that fail to respond to UN requests for data on follow-up to investigations, fail to prosecute, and fail to punish perpetrators should no longer be permitted to contribute troops. Better a shortage of peacekeepers than a surfeit of abuse.
- Waive the immunity of peacekeepers and other UN personnel who commit human trafficking and sexual abuse crimes while deployed.
- Consider the use of civil litigation to hold peacekeepers accountable.

A faint glimmer of change appeared in March 2016 with the Security Council's adoption of resolution 2272, an unprecedented resolution focused solely on addressing sexual abuse by UN peacekeepers (Askin 2016). Security Council resolution 2272 expresses deep concern, but again looks to member states to hold their own personnel accountable. This approach is clearly inadequate.

As Dr. Kelly Askin, a global expert on accountability for rape as a war crime and other gender-based crime, wrote,

> While the Security Council should be lauded for finally making a number of important efforts to redress these crimes, it must go further by ensuring enforcement. To provide real justice, there should be military and civilian trials in the country where the crimes were committed. Troop-contributing countries should consent to having military and civilian courts, ideally staffed by nationals of the peacekeeping troops, deployed with the peacekeepers and UN civilian staff. (Askin 2016, n.p.)

High-ranking UN officials (and former officials) speak of the battle against this abuse in the language of defeat. Sexual abuse by peacekeepers is a "cancer." It is a "losing battle." Many argue that national military contingents' cultures must change. But the culture of the United Nations must also change. The United Nations must engage in radical treatment to defeat this "cancer." Without real enforcement and accountability, abuse—and impunity—will remain the norm.

REFERENCES

AlterPresse. 2013. "Haïti-Minustah/Viol: 4 des 5 agresseurs de Johny Jean condamnés pour violence privée" [Haiti-MINUSTAH/Rape: 4 of 5 Attackers Johny Jean Convicted Private Violence]. March 14. http://www.alterpresse.org/spip.php?article14246#.Vt0i94wrLR0.

Askin, Kelly D. 2016. "Ending Impunity for Crimes Committed by United Nations Peacekeepers." *International Bar Association*. May 25. http://www.ibanet.org/Article/Detail. aspx?ArticleUid=0f942674-16cd-4fd3-92d6-d91fa8a3fa25.

Associated Press. 2015. "Ban Ki-Moon Says Sexual Abuse in UN Peacekeeping Is 'A Cancer in Our System.'" *The Guardian*, August 13. http://www.theguardian.com/world/2015/aug/14/ban-ki-moon-says-sexual-abuse-in-un-peacekeeping-is-a-cancer-in-our-system.

Banbury, Anthony. 2016. "I Love the UN, but It Is Failing." *New York Times*, March 18. www.nytimes.com/2016/03/20/opinion/sunday/i-love-the-un-but-it-is-failing.html.

Bhalla, Nita. 2012. "UN Must Review Policy on Peacekeepers Who Abuse—Amnesty." *Reuters*, March 16. http://in.reuters.com/article/un-must-review-policy-on-peacekeepers-wh-idINDEE82F0IX20120316.

Bowcott, Owen. 2005. "Report Reveals Shame of UN Peacekeepers." *The Guardian*, March 25. http://www.theguardian.com/world/2005/mar/25/unitednations.

Bracken, Amy. 2014. "The UN Let Off Peacekeepers Involved in a Haitian Boy's Rape." *PRI*, October 2. http://www.pri.org/stories/2014-10-02/un-let-peacekeepers-involved-haitian-boys-rape.

Bri Kouri Nouvèl Gaye, Mennonite Central Committee Haiti, Let Haiti Live, UnityAyiti. 2011. *Submission to the UN Universal Periodic Review: Haiti's Renewal of MINUSTAH's Mandate in Violation of the Human Rights of the Haitian People*. Port-au-Prince: Bri Kouri Nouvèl Gaye.

Deschamps, Marie, Hassan B. Jallow, and Yasmin Sooka. 2015. *Taking Action on Sexual Exploitation and Abuse by Peacekeepers: Report of an Independent Review on Sexual Exploitation and Abuse by International Peacekeeping Forces in the Central African Republic*. New York: United Nations.

Garrefy, Conor. 2016. "UN to Send 120 Peacekeepers Home from CAR Amid Fresh Sex Abuse Allegations." *Newsweek*, February 2. http://www.newsweek.com/un-send-120-peacekeepers-home-car-amid-fresh-sex-abuse-allegations-423394.

The Guardian. 2016. "UN Finds More Cases of Child Abuse by European Troops in CAR." January 19. http://www.theguardian.com/world/2016/jan/29/un-finds-more-cases-of-child-abuse-by-european-troops-in-car.

Guéhenno, Jean Marie. 2005. *Presentation by Under-Secretary-General for Peacekeeping Operations to the Security Council*. Statement given to the UN Security Council, New York, May 31.

Human Rights Watch. 2002. *Hopes Betrayed: Trafficking of Women and Girls to Post-Conflict Bosnia and Herzegovina for Forced Prostitution*. New York: Human Rights Watch.

Human Rights Watch. 2016. *UN: Stop Sexual Abuse by Peacekeepers; New Report Reveals Lack of Justice, Protection for Victims*. New York: Human Rights Watch.

Kanetake, Machiko, 2012. "The UN Zero Tolerance Policy's Whereabouts: On the Discordance between Politics and Law on the Internal External Divide." *Amsterdam Law Forum* 4, no. 4: 51–61.

Klapper, Bradley. 2009. "Fifty UN Peacekeepers Punished for Sex Abuses." *Associated Press*, November 5. http://www.independent.co.uk/news/world/politics/fifty-un-peacekeepers-punished-for-sex-abuses-1815403.html.

Laville, Sandra. 2016. "UN Whistleblower Who Exposed Sexual Abuse by Peacekeepers Is Exonerated: Anders Kompass 'Relieved But Sad' after Being Cleared of Wrongdoing for Revealing Abuse in Central African Republic." *The Guardian*, January 18. http://www.theguardian.com/world/2016/jan/18/un-whistleblower-who-exposed-sexual-abuse-by-peacekeepers-is-exonerated.

Mendelson, Sarah E. 2005. *Barracks and Brothels: Peacekeepers and Human Trafficking in the Balkans*. Washington, DC: CSIS Press.

Ndulu, Muna. 2009. "The United Nations Responses to the Sexual Abuse and Exploitation of Women and Girls by Peacekeepers during Peacekeeping Missions." *Berkeley Journal of International Law* 27, no. 1: 127–161.

Patel, Romil. 2016. "Anders Kompass: UN Whistleblower Who Exposed Child Sex Abuse by Peacekeepers in Central African Republic Is Cleared." *International Business Times*, January 18. http://www.ibtimes.co.uk/anders-kompass-un-whistleblower-who-exposed-child-sex-abuse-by-peacekeepers-central-african-1538618.

"Peacekeeping Statistics." 2016. *United Nations Peacekeeping*. Accessed June 2. http://www.un.org/en/peacekeeping/resources/statistics/.

Protocol to Prevent, Suppress and Punish Trafficking in Persons, Especially Women and Children, supplementing the United Nations Convention Against Transnational Organizations (Protocol). 2000. 2237 U.N.T.S. 319 (November).

Reuters. 2012. "Pakistani UN Peacekeepers Sentenced in Haiti Rape Case." March 12. http://www.reuters.com/article/us-haiti-un idUSBRE82C06C20120313.

Sengupta, Somini. 2015a. "Allegations against French Peacekeepers Highlight Obstacles in Addressing Abuse." *New York Times*, May 25.

Sengupta, Somini. 2015b. "3 Peacekeepers Accused of Rape in Central African Republic." *New York Times*, August 19. http://www.nytimes.com/2015/08/20/world/africa/3-peacekeepers-accused-of-rape-in-central-african-republic.html?ref=todayspaper.

Shortell, David, and Richard Roth. 2016. "UN: 69 Allegations of Sexual Abuse against Peacekeepers Last Year, Allegations Most Since 2011." *KSAT*, March 5. http://www.ksat.com/news/national/un-69-allegations-of-sexual-abuse-against-peacekeepers-last-year.

Sleff, Kevin. 2016. "Members of a UN Peacekeeping Force in the Central African Republic Allegedly Turned to Sexual Predation, Betraying Their Duty to Protect." *Washington Post*, February 27. http://www.washingtonpost.com/sf/world/2016/02/27/peacekeepers/.

"Statistics: UN Follow-Up with Member States (Excluding Sexual Exploitation and Abuse)." 2016. *UN Conduct and Discipline Unit*. Accessed June 2. https://cdu.unlb.org/Statistics/UNFollowupwithMemberStatesExcludingSexualExploitationandAbuse.aspx.

UN Department of Peacekeeping Operations (DPKO). 2004. *Human Trafficking and United Nations Peacekeeping*. New York: United Nations.

UN News Centre. 2001. "Jordanian Civilian Police Indicted on Rape Charges." August 24. http://www.un.org/en/peacekeeping/missions/past/etimor/DB/db240801.htm.

UN News Centre. 2016. "'We Must Not Allow Protectors to Become Predators'—UN Field Support Chief." March 5. http://www.un.org/apps/news/story.asp?NewsID=53368#.VtuvHowrLRo.

UN Secretary-General. 2003. *Bulletin: Special Measures for Protection from Sexual Exploitation and Sexual Abuse*. UN Doc. ST/SBG/2003/13 (October 9).

UN Secretary-General. 2005. Letter Dated 24 March 2005 from the Secretary-General Addressed to the President of the General Assembly. UN Doc. A/59/710 (March 24).

"UN Strategy." 2016. *UN Conduct and Discipline Unit*. Accessed June 2. https://cdu.unlb.org/UNStrategy/Enforcement.aspx.

Williams, Carol J. 2007. "The UN Confronts Another Sex Scandal." *Los Angeles Times*, December 15. http://articles.latimes.com/2007/dec/15/world/fg-haitisex15.

Willsher, Kim. 2015. "France Launches Criminal Inquiry into Alleged Sex Abuse by Peacekeepers." *The Guardian*, May 7. http://www.theguardian.com/world/2015/may/07/france-criminal-inquiry-alleged-sex-abuse-french-soldiers-un-central-african-republic.

Zeid, Ra'ad Zeid Al-Hussein (Advisor on Sexual Exploitation and Abuse by UN Peacekeeping Personnel). 2005. *A Comprehensive Strategy to Eliminate Future Sexual Exploitation and Abuse in United Nations Peacekeeping Operations*. UN Doc. A/59/710 (March 24).

CHAPTER 32

WOMEN, PEACE NEGOTIATIONS, AND PEACE AGREEMENTS

Opportunities and Challenges

CHRISTINE BELL

SINCE around 1990, peace processes involving the negotiation of formal peace agreements between the protagonists to conflict have become a predominant way of ending conflict.[1] Since that time, over 800 peace agreements have been negotiated in nearly 100 jurisdictions (Bell 2008). These agreements, which seek to end conflict by setting out a road map for the future, are important documents with significant capacity to affect women's lives. However, a range of obstacles persist for women seeking to influence their design and implementation. These include difficulties gaining access to the talks, as well as achieving material gains for women. This chapter examines these obstacles and the strategies women have used to overcome them, and suggests further ways to build these strategies to advance women's interests and gains from peace processes.

There is no formal definition of a peace process or peace agreement; however, the following definitions operate to define the terms in a broad but coherent way so as to cover agreements produced at different stages of the negotiation process across different conflict types (Bell 2008).

Peace process: an attempt to bring political and/or military elites involved in conflict (defined as having caused more than twenty-five battle-related deaths in one calendar year) to some sort of mutual agreement as to how to end the conflict.[2]

Peace agreement: documents produced after discussion with some or all of the conflict's protagonists that address military violence involving more than twenty-five battle-related deaths with a view to ending it.

Women have been relatively absent from peace processes and agreements. This absence in turn is translated into peace agreement provisions that largely do not address women's perspectives or concerns. Moreover, it can be difficult to trace where and when women have been involved in peace negotiations. Research indicates low numbers of women in the delegations of the parties to the conflict and a very low proportion of female negotiators: negotiating teams drawn from politico-military elites are primarily men. Of thirty-three peace negotiations carried out before 2008, only 4 percent—11 out of 280—of negotiators were women; the average participation of women on government negotiating delegations was, at 7 percent, higher than on the delegations of non-state armed groups (Fisas 2008). Out of a representative sample of thirty-one major peace processes between 1992 and 2011, only 4 percent of signatories, 2.4 percent of chief mediators, 3.7 percent of witnesses, and 9 percent of negotiators were women (UN Women 2012). The United Nations appointed its first female head of peacekeeping operations in 1992 (Margaret Anstee, Angola); however, it only appointed its first female UN Chief Mediator in 2013 (Mary Robinson, UNSG Special Envoy to the Great Lakes Region of Africa), and its first woman commander to head a UN peacekeeping force in 2014 (Major General Kristen Lund, Cyprus).

As regards when and how peace agreements include gender-specific clauses—in the narrow sense of clauses that mention women or sexual violence (for a full discussion of what might comprise "a gender perspective" in a peace agreement, see Bell 2015a) provisions, a review (undertaken by the author) in 2015 indicated that, on average, only 18 percent of peace agreements mention women (Bell 2015a). This figure has risen from around 11 percent pre-2000 (and the passing of UN Security Council resolution 1325) to 27 percent after 2000. However, not all of these references were favorable to women (such as provisions providing blanket bans on abortion), indicating that even where women are mentioned, it does not necessarily connote an attempt to address the equality of women (see generally Bell and O'Rourke 2010).

These deficiencies persist, despite the fact that since 2000 there has been a clear international legal framework underwriting the inclusion of women in peace negotiations and peace agreements. The Convention on the Elimination of All Forms of Discrimination Against Women (CEDAW) provides a broad set of provisions that aim at supporting women's public participation and equality (see Patten, Chapter 13 in this volume). General Recommendation No. 30 (October 18, 2013), on women in conflict prevention and conflict and post-conflict situations, reinforces how CEDAW should impact peace negotiations, the text of peace agreements, and efforts to ensure implementation (CEDAW 2013). resolution 1325 (2000) makes specific provision for a gender perspective to be included in peace negotiations and agreements in paragraph eight, reaffirmed in five subsequent UN Security Council resolutions.[3] As a result, the UN Special Representative for Sexual Violence in Conflict has taken an interest in the presence of women in peace negotiations and whether peace agreements refer to sexual violence, and the UN Department of Political Affairs produced "Guidance for Mediators: Addressing Conflict-Related Sexual Violence in Ceasefire and Peace Agreements" (UN Department of Political Affairs 2012). However, lack of progress in ensuring "women's leadership and participation in conflict resolution and peacebuilding" resulted in UN Security Council resolution 2122 (2013), which committed the UN to "monitoring progress in implementation, and addressing challenges linked to the lack and quality of information and analysis on . . . the role of women in peacebuild-ing and the gender dimensions of peace processes and conflict resolution," and to UN Security Council resolution 2422 (2015), which focuses more generally on the need for better implementation, with repeated calls for support for women's participation in for-mal and informal negotiations processes.

To examine the opportunities and challenges of peace processes for women, it can be useful to consider peace processes as loosely developing in three stages, resulting in three different types of agreement (although these are rarely completely distinct in prac-tice): pre-negotiation stage; framework/substantive stage; and implementation/renego-tiation stage. Women face particular challenges and opportunities of access and capacity to change pre-set agendas at each of these different stages.

PRE-NEGOTIATION PROCESSES, AGREEMENTS, AND WOMEN

The pre-negotiation stage of a peace process typically revolves around how to get the parties into talks, and in particular who is going to negotiate and with what status. Often pre-negotiation processes and agreements are not inclusive of all the parties to the con-flict but involve bilateral agreements between some of the major (usually military) play-ers. For face-to-face or proximity negotiations to take place, each party must be assured that its attempts to engage in dialogue will not be used by the other side to gain mili-tary advantage. In order to get everyone to the negotiating table, agreement needs to be reached on matters such as the following: the return of negotiators from exile or their release from prison; safeguards as to future physical integrity and freedom from impris-onment; and limits on how the war is to be waged while negotiations take place, such as through a form of ceasefire—usually temporary and conditional. Pre-negotiation agree-ments can include mechanisms such as amnesties for negotiators; temporary ceasefire agreements; human rights protections; and monitoring of violations of both ceasefires and of human rights. Pre-negotiation agreements often also typically begin to set the agenda for talks as the parties start to bargain and sound out each other's positions of substantive issues. Often this takes the form of attempts to set preconditions on the negotiating agenda. Where international mediation takes place while conflict is ongo-ing, the pre-negotiation process often involves international attempts to suggest settle-ment terms and gain the parties' consent by setting out a "best guess" as to what they might agree to.

The start of a formal peace process often holds opportunities for women to be involved. A ceasefire can create a space for the mobilization and the activism of women. Women have a strong interest in some sort of ceasefire being achieved: without it, phys-ical integrity, socioeconomic goods, and justice will not be delivered. Further, early agreements create pathway dependencies, and even ceasefire agreements often begin to sketch out preliminary agendas for moving forward: if women can impact on pre-negotiation agreements, they can begin to shape the agenda for the substantive talks, and also the future governance structures.

However, challenges in accessing peace processes remain. Women, and civil society more generally, tend to have a very limited participation in pre-negotiation processes due to secrecy and the fact that politico-military elites pursuing violent conflict are predominantly male. Pre-negotiation talks often culminate in some form of ceasefire, sometimes also establishing international involvement in the form of peacekeeping and international ceasefire monitoring, and setting up processes of demobilization, including temporary or partial amnesties. As these are understood as military matters, they perhaps do not appear to mediators as self-evidently important to women.

Yet, for women it is vital that these mechanisms address particular gender equality issues. If, for example, ceasefire provisions do not specify that sexual violence constitutes a ceasefire violation, it will not be prohibited and monitored as such (Jenkins and Goetz 2010). Research has indicated that even where women are present at talks, issues of ongoing sexual or gender-based violence can be difficult for local women to raise, meaning that if a provision prohibiting sexual violence is to emerge, it must often be suggested and pushed for by the mediator (Jenkins and Goetz 2010). Similarly, processes of demobilization also present women with particular difficulties. Women within state and non-state forces may be left vulnerable by their reduction in status and by the modalities of demobilization, unless attention is paid to this possibility. The separating and quartering of forces to particular areas and the introduction of (mostly male) peacekeepers may also create new problems of violence and trafficking (see Vandenberg, Chapter 31 in this volume), unless anticipated and addressed.

However, it is important to note that the idea of a "gender perspective," as resolution 1325 requires, goes beyond addressing issues of apparent relevance to women. How ceasefire agreements differentiate between civilians and combatants, and the extent to which they make socioeconomic provisions for ex-combatants, while not overtly presenting as "gender" issues, are of particular concern to women, who in all conflicts are overrepresented as "civilians," and tend to bear the brunt of socioeconomic hardship, with further implications for children. The idea of a "gender perspective" should ideally include a women-centered perspective on all aspects of the ceasefire agreement, rather than a few "gender-specific" clauses.

Finally, pre-negotiation talks inevitably begin to set and circumscribe the agenda for substantive peace agreement issues. While these processes focus on how to get the parties into substantive talks, parties often have to be reassured as to how and whether compromising might benefit them. Therefore, pre-negotiation agreements will often begin a larger process of framing the central issues to be resolved, which begins to mark out the road map toward an ultimate settlement. The exclusion of women at this stage reduces their capacity to frame central issues in ways that continue to limit their influence at the framework negotiation stage. In East Timor, for example, while women were included in the formal negotiation process for the constitution, it has been suggested that the final constitution was based on a 1998 draft document that already had been prepared by Fretlin, the dominant political party in the country (Haynes, Ní Aoláin, and Cahn 2011, citing Charlesworth 2003). In other words, while women were admitted to the formal constitution-writing process, the agenda had already been set at an earlier stage in which women's access was more limited.

Despite the importance of women's inclusion and international commitments to it, women still face difficulties in accessing formal processes, and they have often had to use a range of tactics to influence them. Sometimes, women have organized outside of the process to try to influence and penetrate it. Women in Colombia and Liberia, for example, organized outside of formal negotiation processes to try to set their own agenda and influence the talks, and in the most recent peace talks in Colombia, this led to the establishment of a Gender Subcommission, tasked with reviewing all documents issued as part of the peace process and ensuring that they contained gender-sensitive language and provisions (see further Herbolzheimer 2016). Some processes have had a gender advisor appointed: for example, the United Nations Development Fund for Women (UNIFEM) appointed a gender advisor to "support the gender sensitivity of the North Ugandan Peace Talks" (UNIFEM job description), and gender advisors have also been supported in other processes, including the Syria peace talks. In Northern Ireland, women formed a Women's Coalition and used a mechanism designed to ensure the participation of small loyalist political groupings to gain access to the talks. In the Sri Lankan talks between the government and the Liberation Tigers of Tamil Eelam (LTTE), a women's committee made up of women appointed by both sides were appointed within the talks process, along with a human rights advisor. In Guatemala and Sierra Leone, parallel civil society talks and modalities of exchange and endorsement operated to try to open up the peace process to wider civic participation in which women were better represented. In all these processes, women's participation influenced the shape of the agreements produced, whether in terms of specific women's issues or wider issues, or both.

Framework/Substantive Agreements

The second stage of a process is where "framework or substantive" agreements are reached in "the talks proper." These agreements tend to be inclusive of all the main groups involved in waging the war by military means. They set out a framework agreement or "road map" for resolving the substantive issues of the dispute. The agreement usually attempts to provide a constitutional power map for the future of the country, sometimes in the form of actual constitutions, and sometimes in constitution-like provisions embedded in the peace agreement itself. These agreements fundamentally restructure political and legal institutions. They also often reaffirm a commitment to nonviolent means for resolving the conflict; acknowledge the status of the parties in the negotiations; and begin to address some of the consequences of the conflict (such as prisoners, emergency legislation, and ongoing human rights violations).

Given the central focus of peace agreements on some sort of constitutional road map, if women can influence these negotiations, they can influence the structures that can enable or prevent their participation in public life for the indefinite future. Involvement at this stage enables women to engage with the totality of how government is structured and limited, and illustrates what the nation's concept of inclusion will be.

A key difficulty at this stage concerns what to ask for: what a "gender perspective" looks like is not self-evident. In deeply divided societies, the most central issue frequently concerns how parties will participate in government and access power. Peace agreement provisions almost routinely provide for political, territorial, and military forms of power-sharing, which institute a compromise between the different contenders to power by dividing that power between those at the heart of the conflict in complex power-sharing models.

Little has been written or researched as to how women's interests can best be protected with regard to power-sharing arrangements. Traditionally, critics of power-sharing have argued that it can be illiberal in giving groups power in ways that can trammel the rights of individuals, for example to have their vote weighted equally.[4] They have also argued that power-sharing arrangements can reify and entrench the very group identities at the heart of the conflict that the society needs to transcend (O'Leary 2005). Women might be thought to be particularly concerned about these issues (see, e.g., Byrne and McCullagh 2013).

In response, proponents of power-sharing have pointed out that there are different types of power-sharing and that it can include a liberal dimension capable of protecting the rights of groups, such as women, who are outside the main elite "blocs" (O'Leary 2005). Moreover, group rights approaches may have something to offer women. Empirical examination of such arrangements reveals that power-sharing often goes hand in hand with quotas for women, although traditional liberal approaches can find this problematic (Bell 2015b). For example, power-sharing between Hutus and Tutsis in Burundi also included a provision for 30 percent of seats in the legislature to be held by women. Similarly, a peace agreement in Somalia provided that the Transitional National Assembly have at least 12 percent women. In total, six other peace processes between 1990 and 2010 provided for reserved seats or quotas for women in legislative or executive bodies (Bangladesh/Chittagong Hills Tract; Nepal; Papua New Guinea/Bougainville; Philippines/Mindanao; India/Bodoland; Djibouti).

The critical choice for women may therefore be between structures that include "special temporary measures," such as reserve seats and quotas for the inclusion of women in political institutions, and systems that do not. It can be difficult, however, to anticipate how the "technocracy" of a voting system will affect the participation of women in practice. The numbers of women who might be elected, or how quotas for women will be implemented concurrently with other forms of quota, can all be difficult to anticipate without high-level technical advice.

Other dimensions of the governance arrangements may also hold opportunities for gender equality. As part of ensuring equality between identities at the heart of the conflict, peace agreements often provide a new human rights framework, either in the form of specific new rights, or in the form of incorporation of international conventions. Women have often successfully pushed these frameworks to specifically protect women's rights, and sought references to CEDAW and resolution 1325 within the peace agreement. There is also evidence that inclusion of equality for women can, on occasion, be facilitative of agreement between divided politico-military groups. In Northern Ireland, for example, while police reform to ensure Catholic/Protestant equality was a key issue, equality for women was also pressed as important. Reframing equality issues as about more than the "sectarian" dimension was not only important for women, but it usefully helped to reframe zero-sum debates over police reform between divided politico-military elites by reframing Catholic/Protestant inclusion in terms of a broader commitment for the police to be more representative of the society they were to serve. While commitments to equality for women ensued, ironically perhaps, an opt-out of new European Union equality directives in the areas of race and religion (so as to enable 50/50 recruiting policies for Catholics and Protestants to "fast track" a more representative police service) could not be achieved with respect to women, where EU gender-equality law was more established and prevented similar such quotas for women.

Peace agreements often also provide some mechanism for dealing with the past. This can include provisions for international criminal justice, or domestic-based truth commissions. Here, too, there are gender implications, for example, the specific needs of women as soldiers, refugees, and victims in past-focused processes, the inclusion of gender-specific crimes, whether to include socioeconomic violations as well as civil and political ones (a decision with gender implications), and how to make reparations mechanisms women-friendly. A number of the international standards focus on accountability for sexual violence, and also address the permissibility of amnesty.

In summary, while framework/substantive agreements offer a clear opportunity for women to shape the country's constitutional "blueprint" and allocation of power, this requires access, technical expertise, and some common sense of what women want from this deal. All of these are difficult to achieve.

IMPLEMENTATION/RENEGOTIATION AGREEMENTS

The third category of peace agreements is implementation agreements. These begin to develop aspects of earlier framework agreements. By their nature, implementation agreements involve new negotiations and in practice often see a measure of renegotiation as parties test whether they can claw back concessions made at an earlier stage. Sometimes implementation agreements are not documented, and sometimes agreement takes other forms, such as negotiated legislation or constitutions. If successful, these talks will lead to a formal end to the conflict.

Implementation agreements can take place in a more normalized open environment when there is an established ceasefire. This environment can be conducive to broad public consultation. For example, in Northern Ireland the post-agreement process included broad consultations on policing, criminal justice, a bill of rights, and dealing with the past. Agreements in Burundi sketched out a large number of processes for resolving difficult issues, which were then to be taken forward by the society in general. Even where women have been excluded in earlier parts of the peace process, there may be post-agreement opportunities for influence and change.

However, here, too, challenges for women remain. First and foremost, peace agreements are very difficult to implement and seldom move a country from conflict in a completely nonviolent and linear way. Women and other civil society actors who have taken political positions during the peace process may find themselves at the receiving end of renewed threats of violence. These actors may be even more vulnerable to targeting than before because of their increased visibility and because new tactics of war emerge that focus on civil society so as not to be seen as breaching a ceasefire. A peace process will also often formally disband activist networks and means of informal socioeconomic cooperation that operated in the conflict, such as grey or black economies, leaving women vulnerable in the event of an agreement's collapse.

Second, new exclusions can emerge. Implementation talks often focus around bringing in intransigent parties who have operated as "spoilers." Sometimes past agreements in which women made gains can essentially be renegotiated in very exclusive bilateral negotiations to appease the spoilers, even when the initial talks were relatively inclusive.

A final implementation challenge is that of the "answered prayer." When peace agreements are implemented, women are faced with multiple reform processes, social and economic reconstruction, and a range of issues in the home, for example, dealing with returning partners and sons, or relocating as displaced persons. While all these may in a sense be welcome as the problems of "success," they nonetheless present a difficulty in sustaining and building gains for women. It can be difficult to have energy to respond coherently to all these challenges at once. Often, too, external funding sources will view the conflict as "over," and funding will be depleted just at the time the new structures need to bed down. Women's organizations—along with other civil society groups—may also find that they were so successful in arguing for the new institutions to include women that they lose their own leadership capacity as women enter formal institutions. Feminist institutional analysis has also shown that new institutions, while carrying great promise, are often nested in a set of old institutions, which can subvert their promise (Mackay 2009; O'Rourke 2013). Unless a long-term approach to implementation is taken, gains can easily be lost during this phase.

Translating Equality into Action

Progress along three lines is important if women are to be adequately included in peace processes, and their concerns and ideas for change and gender equality are to be integrated into peace agreements and implemented. First, women must be involved in negotiating, reaching, and implementing the peace agreement, and all mediators need to be aware of how the conflict and the peace process affect women. Second, the substance of the peace agreement must take into account the particular needs of women and girls and adopt a gender perspective. Third, feminist advocacy must include a long-term commitment to sustaining the efforts for peace long after the peace agreement is signed. However, for the reasons outlined earlier, achieving these steps is not simple. The following matters are crucial to building strategies for change.

Conceptual gendering of peace processes: Finding "pathways in and pathways out"

The exclusion of women from peace process talks and the limited agendas focused on in these talks point to a need to approach peace processes as gendered from the outset. Despite the fact that peace initiatives will often have been promoted throughout a conflict by civil society and in particular by women, it is often only at the stage where the main protagonists to a conflict—the political and military elites who tend to be primarily and often exclusively men—come together in a formal attempt to mediate an end to the conflict that a formal peace process is considered to exist and attracts sustained international support. To put it strongly, the very idea of a "formal peace process" resulting in a "peace agreement" is one that is defined to occur at the very point at which women are excluded.

Reaching agreement between those at the heart of waging the conflict is clearly essential to achieving peace in practice. However, civic peace initiatives that have preceded it will offer a valuable resource to the process and can put ongoing pressure on the formal peace process. Given the conceptual, structural, and issue-based exclusions of formal peace processes and their excessive fragility, it may be useful to think less of when and how women are included in these formal processes, and to think more broadly about "pathways in and pathways out" of peace processes as a central challenge for the sustainability of these processes themselves. It is beyond the scope of this chapter to provide detail as to how this might work in practice, but there is a strong case for robust international support to be given to parallel processes, which can provide not only a space to generate and incubate creative approaches to conflict, but also an ongoing sense of a peace-process-in-action that can sustain the formal peace process through periods of inevitable collapse. In Colombia, women addressed the gender limitations of the formal peace process head-on by acknowledging the importance of government-guerrilla negotiations, but also articulating fifteen elements of "alternative pathways to peace" that created a wider concept of the "peace process" (see Collective Thought and Action on Women, Peace and Security 2014). The critical issue for women is to find mechanisms for exchange between this type of parallel action and the formal peace process.

Understanding the opportunities and limitations for women(-friendly) mediators

There is considerable evidence of the capacity of mediators to influence what issues are included in negotiations and in the text of peace agreements. Where there is a "gender-friendly" mediator and support for women's participation, it is reflected in better provisions for women as illustrated by the example of Burundi. The peace process in Burundi saw a range of initiatives aimed at the inclusion of women, including UNIFEM convening an All Party Women's Peace Conference with two representatives from each of the warring factions and the seven women observers to the process, and involving an "equality-friendly" mediator in the form of Nelson Mandela. The resultant Arusha Peace and Reconciliation Agreement for Burundi, of August 29, 2008, included more than half the recommendations formulated by the All Party Women's Peace Conference, such as measures on sexual violence and provisions for participation. In the 2005 Constitution, a quota of 30 percent women was provided for the National Assembly. Although ideal, it is very rare to see this level of gender perspective throughout an agreement's text (see Bell and O'Rourke 2010; Bell 2015a).

While organizations such as the United Nations have committed to the importance of women mediators, often international mediators themselves must compromise on what they see as the just and fair solution to the conflict. Justice concerns—including gender justice—face a pressure to give way to an overriding need to stop conflict-related violence at almost any price (cf. Anonymous 2006). Given the fragility of peace negotiations, mediators are often pushed to conservative approaches with regard to advancing equality for women. Sometimes attempting to insert a gender reference in peace agreements can be seen as a distraction from the efforts of achieving a compromise between political and military elites, understood to be essential to any agreement to stop the violence.

There also may be cultural obstacles to parties using women mediators. Where parties to a conflict perceive a cultural clash with the "other side" on the position of women, whereby they believe that their opponents view women as "inferior" or "weak," then they may view key roles for women in peace processes as undermining their negotiation strength from the outset (see, e.g., Aharoni 2011; Francis 2004). In such cases, international appeals to appoint women to negotiation teams may not be enough to overcome local reluctance to include them. Even where conflict protagonists do respond positively to international exhortations to include women, where they do not have women at the top of their internal political and military structures, the women they include will not have the same rank and standing within their grouping as the men, or the culture of the group may not be one in which women have an effective voice. Women's voices may therefore remain marginalized, even when they are formally present: representation does not equate with influence.

Expanding and supporting "gender perspectives" that go beyond "clauses on women"

There is little indication in international standards or in research as to what a "gender perspective" might look like beyond "gender clauses" in a peace agreement. Women often argue for inclusion based not just on capacity to improve awareness of the gendered impact of conflict, but because they feel their experience of conflict brings wider insights into the business of ending it. Women may have an interest in all aspects of peace agreements, and they have multiple identities that put them on different "sides" of the conflict on key issues. Peace agreement frameworks offer a range of choices not ostensibly to do with gender, which nonetheless have critical consequences for women. As already touched on, these include whether liberal or communitarian constitutional frameworks are adopted, how combatant/non-combatant distinctions are drawn, and whether socioeconomic rights provisions are included. Women in the middle of peace processes need information from other similar processes, technical advice and assistance, and capacity to craft alternative drafts, if they are to be effective. They often also need to build effective alliances with other groups and interests. Armed with such resources, however, the capacity to influence outcomes is often significant.

Engaging with "realpolitik"

Finally, there is a tension between more standard setting and leaving room for negotiations to shape outcomes, which requires further scholarly and practical attention. Negotiations are often fraught, and the many international recommendations to guarantee provision for women are replicated in other areas (which also impact on women), for example, on how to deal with refugees, displaced persons, and "return," or "amnesty and dealing with the past," or "non-conflict minorities," or "children." If all international standards were faithfully transcribed into peace agreements, the resulting agreements would be very long and would follow a similar blueprint. The more standard clauses are promoted, the less room negotiations and negotiators will have.

There are several reasons that such an approach may not be ideal for the process and for women. First, a trade-off exists between what an ideal agreement looks like and what is achievable and can be implemented in practice. Women have an interest in the conflict ending, and negotiated agreements with all the gender (and other) inequities of their compromises are often better for women than the other options—namely, to let the war continue indefinitely until someone wins, or to use foreign intervention to assist one side in winning. Often, meaningful change in practice will only be possible when parties to the agreement view implementation as in their self-interest. Peace negotiations are not exercises in ideal-type agreement writing on gender or any other terms. They are rather the product of a complex and fragile negotiations process that may or may not produce results. The stakes are genuinely high and mediators have a difficult task. There are no easy criteria for deciding when an imperfect peace is better than a perfect war, when gender or other justice and equality gains have not been achievable.

Second, standard-setting and "lessons learned" often do not capture the complicated business of grappling with the "realpolitik" of peace negotiations. Sometimes gender deficits may arise because no one has thought to gender-proof the provisions, or to make sure women get a chance to provide input. Here international exhortations and monitoring of their implementation, as provided for in the relevant Security Council resolutions, may help change things. However, often exclusions will happen because of biases such as those discussed earlier: that women are understood to destabilize a party's negotiation strength; that inclusion of any sort of gender or social justice agenda is seen by mediators as belonging to one side in the conflict; or that peace is seen as virtually unobtainable, so that any agenda that is not understood as absolutely vital to obtaining a ceasefire will be excluded. These biases are more likely to be overcome by women engaging with the realpolitik of the situation, than by pushing international mantras. What women lose in ideal-type provisions, they stand to gain in some capacity to achieve implementation of the provisions they do manage to secure. There are, however, few resources to enable women to navigate this terrain. Women must learn from the little documented experiences of women in other peace processes, which, despite different contexts, nonetheless offer a valuable resource to assist in making strategic calculations aimed at creative influence.

Notes

1. This piece builds on an earlier policy paper, Bell (2013). Ideas in it are also significantly developed in Bell (2015a) and Bell (2015b). The piece is an output of the Political Settlement Research Programme (PSRP, www.politicalsettlements.org), funded by the UK Aid, Department of International Development. The funders have had no role or influence in the content of the piece, which does not reflect their views, but those of the author alone.
2. For definition of conflict, see "Definitions," *Uppsala Conflict Data Programme*, accessed May 27, 2016, http://www.pcr.uu.se/research/ucdp/definitions/.
3. UNSC resolution 2242 (2015), while not specifically repeating the resolution 1325 provision on peace agreements, addresses the need for implementation of the resolution, and focuses on women's participation in formal and informal negotiations as part of peace processes.
4. See, for example, Sejdić *and Finci v. Bosnia & Herzegovina*, ECtHR App. Nos. 27996/06 and 34836/06 (2009), in which the ECHR found the disenfranchisement of certain citizens to be a violation of their rights, despite the parties to the Dayton Peace Talks having negotiated this arrangement.

References

Aharoni, Sarai. 2011. "Gender and 'Peace-Work': An Unofficial History of Israeli-Palestinian Formal Peace Negotiations." *Politics & Gender* 7, no. 3: 391–416.

Anonymous. 2006. "Human Rights in Peace Negotiations." *Human Rights Quarterly* 18, no. 2: 249–258.

Bell, Christine. 2008. *On the Law of Peace: Peace Agreements and the Lex Pacificatoria.* Oxford: Oxford University Press.

Bell, Christine. 2013. *Women and Peace Processes, Negotiations, and Agreements: Operational Opportunities and Challenges.* Oslo: Norwegian Peacebuilding Resource Centre.

Bell, Christine. 2015a. *Text and Context: Peace Processes and Peace Agreements: Evaluating their "Gender Perspective."* Edinburgh: Political Settlements Research Programme.

Bell, Christine. 2015b. *Unsettling Bargains: Power-Sharing and the Inclusion of Women in Peace Negotiations.* Edinburgh: Political Settlements Research Programme.

Bell, Christine, and Catherine O'Rourke. 2010. "Peace Agreements or 'Pieces of Paper'? The Impact of UNSC Resolution 1325 on Peace Processes and Their Agreements." *International & Comparative Law Quarterly* 59: no. 4: 941–980.

Byrne, Siohhan, and Allison McCulloch. 2013. "Gender, Representation and Power-Sharing in Post-Conflict Institutions." *International Peacekeeping* 19, no. 5: 565–580.

Committee on the Elimination of Discrimination Against Women (CEDAW). 2013. General Recommendation 30 on Women in Conflict Prevention, Conflict, and Post-Conflict Situations. UN Doc. CEDAW/C/CG/30.

Charlesworth, Hilary. 2003. "The Constitution of East Timor, May 20, 2002." *International Journal of Constitutional Law* 1: 325–334.

Collective Thought and Action on Women, Peace and Security. 2014. *Ethical Pact for a Country in Peace.* London: Conciliation Resources.

Fisas, Vincenç. 2008. *Annuario 2008 de Procesos de Paz.* Barcelona: Icaria Editorial.

Frances, Diana. 2004. *Culture, Power Asymmetries and Gender in Conflict Transformation.* Berlin: Berghof Research Centre for Constructive Conflict Management.

Haynes, Dina Francesca, Fionnuala Ní Aoláin, and Naomi Cahn. 2011. "Gendering Constitutional Design in Post-Conflict Societies." *William & Mary Journal of Women and the Law* 17, no. 3: 509–580.

Herbolzheimer, Kristian. 2016. *Innovations in the Colombian Peace Process.* Oslo: Norwegian Peacebuilding Resource Centre.

Jenkins, Robert, and Anne Marie Goetz. 2010. "Addressing Sexual Violence in Internationally Mediated Peace Negotiations." *International Peacekeeping* 17, no. 2: 261–277.

MacKay, Fiona. 2009. "'Nested Newness' and the Gendered Limits of Change: Institutionalising 'New Politics' in Post Devolution Britain." Paper presented at the Annual Meeting of the Midwest Political Science Association, Chicago, April 2, 2009.

O'Leary, Brendan. 2005. "Debating Consociational Politics: Normative and Explanatory Arguments." In *From Power Sharing to Democracy*, edited by Sid Noel, 3–43. Montreal: McGill/Queen's University Press.

O'Rourke, Catherine. 2013. *Gender Politics in Transitional Justice.* Abington, NY: Routlege Press.

UN Department of Political Affairs. 2012. *Guidance for Mediators: Addressing Conflict-Related Sexual Violence in Ceasefire and Peace Agreements.* New York: UN Department of Political Affairs.

UN Women. 2012. *Women's Participation in Peace Negotiations: Connections between Presence and Influence.* New York: UN Women.

CHAPTER 33

....

WOMEN'S ORGANIZATIONS AND PEACE INITIATIVES

....

AILI MARI TRIPP

WOMEN's mobilization around peace operates at many levels, from the grassroots to the national, regional, and international levels. Many of the issues that have animated women at the local level deal with community reconciliation; access to water, food, and other resources; as well as engagement with the militia toward the goal of disarmament. At the national level, women activists have sought to be included in peace negotiations, and constitution-making processes and elections, often through the adoption of quotas. Women activists have also sought to influence the disarmament and demobilization processes, while being attentive to women's concerns in all aspects of peacemaking, peace-building, and state-building. Coalitions of women's organizations supported by international organizations like the United Nations Development Fund for Women (UNIFEM) and its successor, UN Women, were critical to the success of such initiatives. They have mobilized subregionally in the Horn of Africa, in West Africa's Mano River region, and elsewhere to share strategies and organize collectively. At the international level, they have sought to influence the United Nations in ways that would bring pressure to bear on their governments and other actors involved in peace processes, including advocacy for the passage and monitoring of UN Security Council resolutions calling for measures to increase women's involvement in all aspects of conflict resolution and greater attentiveness to women's concerns in conflict (see Otto, Chapter 8, and Goetz and Jenkins, Chapter 9, in this volume).

A number of key features have characterized women's peace mobilization at all levels in the post–Cold War era. First, although women's organizations have often tried to participate in formal peace negotiations and disarmament processes, they have been largely excluded, with their contributions to peacemaking unrecognized (see Bell, Chapter 32 in this volume). Formal peace processes dominate the scholarship, media reports, and the attention of policymakers and, as a result of these exclusions, women often have been relegated to informal and grassroots peace strategies. These local contributions have not received the recognition they deserve because of their quotidian nature: they are not dramatic, nor do they always directly impact the national-level peace negotiations. Yet they are every bit as important in impacting the daily lives of communities and families.

Second, women's peace efforts have often taken the bridging of difference as a starting point, rather than an end point. In other words, instead of seeing peace as a goal to be reached at the end of talks, they have regarded peace as a process that is achieved by working together across difference around common gender-based and other concerns. For example, in many contexts, women from opposing camps have come together to peace talks or peace conferences, and from the outset worked jointly as a group, rather than sitting at opposite ends of the table with their particular party, faction, or rebel organization (see McWilliams and Kilmurray, Chapter 42 in this volume; Bunting et al. 2001). The bridging of difference occurs among women activists often as a result of the evolution of common women's rights agendas. At the local level, it is often related to the need to find practical solutions to meeting daily needs.

Third, local efforts have been more successful when reinforced by international and regional pressures and support for changes in the status quo when it comes to women's rights. Similarly, international efforts have been bolstered by pressure from below from local women's movements. The interaction between domestic and international pressures and the diffusion of influences from regional and international organizations has often been critical, particularly in demanding greater female political representation, constitutional changes, and changes in legislation.

These characteristics, common to many instances of women's mobilization, are explored here through examples from particular conflicts. The chapter first looks at women's exclusions from formal peace processes and how women's organizations have nevertheless sought to influence those processes, largely through grassroots pressure and informal strategies. It then shows how and why women's organizations have often been oriented toward building bridges across difference. Finally, the chapter concludes by examining the extent to which women activists have engaged in initiatives involving regional and international organizations in order to put pressure on governments through the international arena. Women's multilevel strategies involving institutions at the local, national, regional, and international levels have complemented each other in important ways, while reflecting varied goals and opportunities.

Exclusions from Formal Peace Processes

Scholarship has shown that civil society, including women's organizations, can make a difference in enhancing peace outcomes when they have been included in peace talks. Civil society is often seen as bringing added legitimacy to the negotiation process. Since the Cold War, 34 percent of peace negotiations have included at least one civil society actor. When civil society actors are included in peace agreements, the risk of peace failing is reduced by 64 percent, regardless of regime type (Nilsson 2012). Moreover, when women are brought into the peace processes, the likelihood of their success is enhanced. This was shown to be the case in forty peace processes since the end of the Cold War where women's engagement was positively correlated with greater implementation of the process and had a positive impact on the sustainability of peace (Paffenholz et al. 2016; UN Women 2015).

In spite of the positive benefits of including civil society actors, at the most basic level, women's organizations have found it difficult to get women represented in peace negotiations. While there has been no significant change with respect to women being included as chief mediators, negotiators, or signatories, in recent years there has been an increase in the number and frequency of women's informal representation through consultations between mediation teams and women's organizations. In 2014, mediation teams included at least one woman on all of the peace processes that the United Nations led or co-led, which was a slight increase from 2011. Senior women participated in 75 percent of the processes, compared with 36 percent in 2011. And gender expertise was requested and provided for 67 percent of the processes, compared with 35 percent in 2011 (UN Security Council 2015).

But in spite of these small changes, women are largely excluded from formal peace processes. Not only do women generally not have significant formal roles in the peace talks, they have also experienced difficulty gaining consultative access to the negotiations, which would provide women's organizations with a formal mechanism with which to influence and observe the proceedings (Bell, Chapter 32 in this volume). Overall progress toward increasing women's formal roles has been slow even since 2000, despite passage of UN Security Council resolution 1325.

These exclusions are even more egregious when one considers that often women's organizations have been among the few actors seeking cooperation across political, ethnic, religious, and other differences that had contributed to conflict, yet combatant and government forces were the only ones deemed relevant to bring to the negotiating table. In Sri Lanka, for example, six rounds of peace talks between 2002 and 2003 ended in failure. Women's organizations had worked in the conflict zone for years and had extensive informal networks that had been able to defuse tensions and facilitate inter-community dialogue and cooperation. Moreover, the only committee that truly functioned in the peace process was the Sub-Committee on Gender Issues (SGI), which was made up of members appointed by the Government of Sri Lanka and the Liberation Tigers of Tamil Eelam (LTTE). It worked because the SGI members were "non-political, civil society rights activists, academics and community workers who were not constrained by political considerations, party affiliations or electoral success" (Satkunanathan and Rainford 2009, 123). Nevertheless, the SGI was seen by the Sri Lankan government and the LTTE as a mechanism that existed simply to appease women's and international pressure groups, rather than one that could play a role in the peace process; thus its impact was limited. In spite of the successes of women's organizations in building cooperation across so-called enemy lines, other civil society organizations that were included did little to press for women's participation in peace talks.

Strategies to influence peace negotiations

Women's organizations have sought a variety of strategies to influence talks and advance a women's rights agenda in peace negotiations, often with mixed results. Women's organizations have sought observer status for women when they failed to become negotiators. But being in a non-speaker observer role means that they have limited influence; for this reason, UN Security Council resolution 2242 (2015) calls for women's representation in all peace negotiations, not simply as observers.

Women's organizations and leaders sometimes work behind the scenes through informal initiatives. For example, Betty Bigombe became an unofficial mediator between the Ugandan government and the Lord's Resistance Army (LRA) in northern Uganda, thus paving the way for official talks in Juba in 2006. But in general, apart from those who have held official roles as representatives of their political parties, women's organizations have had to lobby for a role for women through ad hoc pressure as well as collective mobilization. In many cases, UNIFEM, and later UN Women, provided important support for such efforts. More often than not, women's organizations have sought to influence the negotiations from the outside. Some have held parallel peace conferences, rallies, and other events to draw attention to women's demands and exclusions from official peace processes.

From Uganda to Liberia and Nepal, women activists have pressed not only for a role for women representatives in peace talks, constitution making processes, and in the newly constituted political arrangements. They have also at various times advocated for the holding of peace talks (e.g., Nepal in 2004), a rapid conclusion of peace talks when they were lagging (e.g., Liberia in 2003), the holding of elections (e.g., Sierra Leone in 1996), the holding of free and fair elections without interference from militia (e.g., Mozambique in 1994), the delay of elections until soldiers were fully demobilized (e.g., Liberia in 2003), and the demobilization of soldiers with the assistance of civil society and women's organizations (e.g., Liberia in 1996 and 2003).

Women activists' informal peace strategies

While women activists have rarely been part of official peace negotiations, more often they have been engaged in informal efforts to end wars, at times through peace movements, but more often through small collective initiatives, generally outside of or alongside the formal processes established by the United Nations and other governmental actors. Such efforts, which are rarely officially recognized, have, in fact, contributed to both short-term and long-term peace. They often have created the foundation for peace talks and have fostered back channels for negotiation.

Women's collective strategies have ranged from organizing rallies and boycotts to promoting small arms confiscation, organizing reconciliation ceremonies, negotiating with small groups of rebels to disarm, and negotiating with rebels to release abducted children and child soldiers. Peace activists have played a role in preventing the resumption of conflict by monitoring and advocating against the sale of small arms, carrying out conflict resolution workshops, and participating in campaigns for "clean" diamonds. While these initiatives were hardly the sole cause of the decline in conflict, they have increased the pressure for conflict resolution.

The international community, policymakers, media, and scholars have tended to disregard most of the efforts by women peace activists. In part, this is because they are difficult to measure and document; however, it is also because they are considered unimportant since they involve women, whose activities are often seen as relegated to the private sphere. While this may be slowly changing due to efforts by the United Nations and international NGOs, grassroots initiatives still generally receive little attention, since their impacts are localized. Nevertheless, they can be extremely important to the communities affected by conflict. Thus, the lack of research on these activities is more telling of the gaps in the literature than of an absence of women's engagement in informal peace activities.

The case of Somalia

A few examples drawn from Somalia serve to highlight the variety and nature of these types of activities. There was a proliferation of women's NGOs in Somalia after the early 1990s, when feuds between the clans fueled civil war and ultimately state collapse. Women had held positions of power in the Siad Barre government (1969–1991), in the army, as judges, and as ambassadors. With the end of Barre's rule, women became more organized in associations that cut across clan divisions, partly because women did not have the same relationship to clan as men, and unlike men, they married outside of their clan. Women worked on issues of health care, violence against women, food security, education, job training, obtaining housing, and learning about conflict mediation. They persuaded fighters to trade in weapons for career preparation classes (Ingiriis and Hoehne 2013; UNIFEM 1996).

These organizations not only opened up inter-clan dialogue on peace, they also discussed a long-term vision of Somali society and the creation of a national constitution, which was eventually passed in 2012. In 1992 a local women's organization, the Somaliland Women Development Association (SOWDA) in Hargeisa, raised funds and started a police force. Women in Bosaso did the same and managed the police force until a local administration was established in 1998 (Mohamed 2004). One organization in Somalia, the IIDA Women's Development Organization, brought women together from different clan backgrounds. Several networks of women's peace organizations were active during the conflict, including the Nagaad Umbrella Organization and the Somali Coalition of Grassroots Women's Organizations (COGWO), which helped form a broader Peace and Human Rights Network consisting of twenty-two Somali organizations. COGWO has served as a successful mediator between rival faction leaders. Its actions helped diffuse hostilities in the area, so that people no longer feared crossing the Green Line that divided warring clans. Their activities eventually laid the groundwork for more formal peace negotiations (Farah and Lewis 1993; Mohamed 2004; Osman 2000). Today the country is still fragmented and Somalia continues to experience extremist violence, although Somaliland and Puntland have stabilized.

Quotidian informal activities generally do not make it into the headlines, but they are nevertheless essential to both survival and peacemaking. During conflict, because of gendered divisions of labor, some women cared for internally displaced persons, provided trauma counseling, organized basic literacy programs, and ran healing and reconciliation workshops. As best they could, they saw to it that their communities had access to food, fuel, water, and other basic necessities. To obtain these resources, they sometimes have had to work across so-called enemy lines. In individual and collective acts of bravery, women activists have negotiated with fighters and have sought to persuade them to disarm. Thus, the daily practical activities of survival have been at the core of women's mobilization around peacemaking. Rather than being derivative of an essentialized nurturing characteristic of women, these activities are often an extension of the carework roles that women typically adopt (or are forced to adopt) in so many societies.

The example of Nepal

The experience of women in Nepal provides another example of the strategies women have adopted to influence the peace process. Nepal was embroiled in a civil war between the government and Maoist forces from 1996 to 2006, started by the Maoist Communist Party of Nepal, which sought to overthrow the Nepalese monarchy and replace it with a republic under their control. Women had participated for years in many peace rallies in Kathmandu and around the country: in 2004, women rallied to pressure the government and Maoists to resume peace talks, which had collapsed in 2003 after two rounds, and in 2006, millions of women took to the streets to participate in mass demonstrations against King Gyanendra, which led to new talks between the interim government and the Maoists, ending in the signing of a Comprehensive Peace Agreement.

Nepalese women took on leadership roles in their communities and in civil society through grassroots peacebuilding efforts and risked their lives to negotiate with government security forces and Maoist rebels. They provided health and shelter for survivors of the conflict. In order to advance resolution 1325 in Nepal, UNIFEM organized a meeting in 2005 of women from fifty-seven districts together with all political parties, which resulted in a ten-point declaration that contributed to the peace process. UNIFEM and the UN Population Fund (UNFPA) organized workshops, training sessions, and other awareness-raising activities with the police, military, government departments, NGOs, and other stakeholders in promoting the resolution.

Women's organizations held two large national conferences in 2007 to strategize how to bring women into the process. They sought many of the considerations typical of women's rights mobilization during conflict, focusing on women's claims to influence the peace process and political power in a transitional and post-conflict arrangement. Their demands included 33 percent female representation in all decision-making positions and ways to strengthen women's access to policymaking more generally. The Women's Alliance for Peace, Power, Democracy and the Constituent Assembly (WAPPDCA), a coalition of NGOs, sought to be included in peace negotiations every step of the way and used resolution 1325 as a resource to press its demands.

In spite of all these activities, women were not included in the peace talks when the government and the Maoists drew up a twenty-five-point Code of Conduct in 2005, nor were they brought into the Comprehensive Peace Agreement talks. Two women were brought into the constitution-making process consisting of fifteen delegates—but only after most of the drafting had been completed. Moreover, women were initially excluded from the Constituent Assembly committee that reworked the 2006 interim constitution, although later pressure from women's groups expanded the committee to include six Dalit women representatives. The ceasefire monitoring body included twenty-nine men and only two women (Abdela 2011).

Pressure from women's rights activists resulted in an interim constitution mandating a quota for women candidates in the Constituent Assembly (CA), which doubles as a legislative body and an institution tasked with drafting the new constitution. As a result, women won 33 percent of the legislative seats in 2008, a large increase from 17 percent in 2007. In 2009, an umbrella of women's organizations organized a march of over ten thousand rural women in the Kathmandu Valley. They presented 120 demands to the constitution-drafting process. A Women's Caucus within the CA was formed that same year to advance women's rights. It has worked with other CA members, political parties, civil society organizations, marginalized communities, local authorities, the media, and other professionals to develop these recommendations. Partly in response to reticence by parties to support the quota, women activists launched a media and advocacy campaign called 33 Percent Women. They lobbied the president, launched a major media campaign, encouraged women to vote, carried out voter education campaigns, and trained prospective women parliament candidates.

As a result of these lobbying efforts, the Nepalese women made major gains in the new 2015 constitution, including equal rights between spouses in property and family affairs, the right to lineage without discrimination, the right to participate in state structures and bodies based on proportional inclusion, and many other rights regarding reproductive health, education, health, employment, social security, protections against violence, and rights for the LGBTI community. In spite of these positive provisions, women continued major protests after the constitution was promulgated because it included restrictions on a woman's right to pass on citizenship to her child that do not apply to men.

The Nepal case illustrates the enormous challenges that women activists often have faced as a result of exclusions from formal peace processes. It also shows the importance of mass mobilization and pressures by the women's movement in seeking formal representation in the talks and in the new legislature. It highlights the role of international actors like UN agencies and the use of resolution 1325 in achieving their goals of political representation in the aftermath of conflict.

Reasons for Success: Bridging Difference

Many of women's quotidian activities have led women activists to seek to bridge clan, ethnic, and religious difference through peacemaking activities. Peace, thus, is seen as a process, not simply an end point of negotiations. Peacemaking permeates daily life and involves the active building of bridges on a daily basis. This has occurred during conflict as well as in the aftermath of conflict.

Yet women have also participated in and supported conflict and divisive political movements based on nationalism, ethnicity, religion, and other differences. Women have encouraged fighters, have assisted them, and have fanned the flames of conflict. In countries like Liberia and Sierra Leone, women comprised 20–30 percent of the fighters.

Nevertheless, women activists have also engaged in peace-building activities that bridge difference both in communities and in national-level peace talks. Most important, they often share a common agenda regarding women's secondary status. This agenda can cut across differences of all kinds (e.g., class, race, ethnicity, religion) and, unlike other causes, has the *potential* to unite the broadest array of a population because these issues often affect women in every group. Another reason for this unity across difference was mentioned earlier: women are typically relegated to carework roles, which necessitate immediate solutions to problems of survival that cannot wait for the resolution of peace talks.

The example of Burundi

An example from Burundi illustrates how women's organizations have bridged difference. In the 1999 Burundi peace negotiations, the pursuit of commonality was the foundation for women's engagement in the talks, not an end point, as is commonly the practice. Formal peace talks were initiated in 1999 in Arusha, Tanzania, to lay the basis for a new constitutional arrangement and, in 2000, seventeen parties signed peace accords in Pretoria, South Africa. Women in the Burundi peace talks sat together, rather than with their ethnically based political parties. One of the participants in the 1999 Arusha talks, Alice Ntwarante, explained,

> We [the women] were united in purpose, despite our ethnic split—three Hutus and three Tutsis. The various political parties to which we women belonged tried to split us up, but we resisted them. We said, "No! We stand together with our sisters. We are here to represent women, not as members of such-and-such a political party." Our unity spoke for us. We said to all Burundian women: "Come and join us! There is a place for you!" This was the big success of Arusha for women—that we remained united.

She contrasted the stance of the women to that of the male party negotiators:

> I told myself, here are the men, the key players, who are going to negotiate, but right at the start of the conference they can't communicate with one another. Each was turning his back on his adversary. Each had brought his ideas to the peace table. They were partisan, even extremist. (Bunting et al. 2001)

This is not to say that the women did not have differing views or disagreements, but they started from the point of unity, sharing a common women's rights agenda. This was a considerable accomplishment given the general weakness of civil society, which at the time was riven by political and ethnic divisions. While a few organizations like the human rights group Ligue Iteka and the development organization Organisation d'Appui à l'Autopromotion played similar peace-building roles, there were not many that could bridge differences across such a wide swath of the population as key women's organizations (De Reu 2005).

Burundian women's peace efforts began in 1993 when the organization Women for Peace was formed with the support of African Women in Crisis (AFWIC) and UNIFEM. The following year, the Collectif des Associations et ONGs Féminines du Burundi (CAFOB) was formed as an umbrella for seven organizations; it quickly grew to fifteen organizations by 1996. CAFOB insisted during the peace talks that women be represented in all aspects of the peace process and that all issues raised be looked at from a gender perspective. They also demanded a 30 percent quota for women in the legislature, the judiciary, and the executive branches of government, as well as in all bodies created by the peace accord. They argued that the final agreement include rights to property, land, and inheritance, along with a formal recognition that Burundi girls and women suffer discrimination because of culture and policies that are not sensitive to women's particular needs. The demands highlighted the need for (1) equal access to education for girls; (2) an end to impunity when it comes to rape, sexual violence, prostitution, and domestic violence; (3) attention to the needs of women refugees and in particular female- and child-headed families; and (4) many other crucial concerns. Twenty-three of these recommendations were ultimately included in the final peace accord as a result of the group's lobbying efforts and ability to remain united in purpose.

The second explanation for efforts to bridge difference has to do with the ways in which women have often cooperated around meeting daily needs across ethnic divides. During the civil war in Burundi, such cooperation between the Tutsi and Hutu groups served as a balm for women. The Centre for Women in Burundi worked with Hutu women from Busoro and Tutsi women from Musaga villages and reported stories of women who in the worst of the fighting in 1999 came to organize an exchange of humanitarian aid as a gesture of solidarity between them. Women from Musaga collected what food and clothing they could find for the women in Busoro, who had been previously attacked. As they heard gunshots in the surrounding hills, they gathered at an administrator's office, gave speeches pledging support to one another, and chanted and sang and danced for hours, "We are the women of Busoro, we are the women of Musaga, give us peace, give us peace now!" until the gunshots subsided (FAS 2001).

In Burundi, as in so many conflicts, the nature of women's demands reflected the ongoing and multifaceted nature of women's struggles. It shows how peace is not something that is attained in one event or agreement, but rather, through an ongoing series of concrete actions and activities involving people on all sides of a conflict.

INTERNATIONAL PRESSURE

Women's movements and women's activism around peace have been supported to a certain degree by international initiatives from regional and international organizations. They also have been supported by changes in international norms, which influence the actions of donor, diplomatic, United Nations, and regional bodies, and international NGOs. The Fourth UN Conference on Women in Beijing in 1995 played an important role in changing some of the norms and practices regarding women's leadership. resolution 1325 did the same for women's involvement in peace-building activities. Numerous commentators, however, have observed how the lack of support from the international women's movement has frayed these capacities and linkages, with serious implications for local mobilization.

Tangible technical and financial support from UNIFEM/UN Women, UN peacekeeping forces, and other UN agencies has often been critical in helping women's rights organizations gain access to peace talks and other transitional processes. Organizations like the NGO Working Group on Women, Peace and Security serve as a link between women's human rights activists in countries affected by conflict and policymakers at the UN Headquarters. Similarly, regional organizations like the Federation of African Women's Peace Networks (FERFAP), Mano River Union Women Peace Network (MARWOPNET), and Femmes Afrique Solidarité (FAS) were instrumental in facilitating local women's peace initiatives in countries like Liberia and Sierra Leone.

Thus, even though peace movements have been driven by local-level dynamics, they have benefited from critical international support and pressure on their governments in terms of changes in international norms regarding women's rights and representation, interventions by the United Nations and other multilateral actors, and financial aid from bilateral and other donors, in addition to the adoption of key UN treaties regarding the role of women in peacemaking.

CONCLUSION

Women's movements have pressed their demands for peace, for a greater role for women in peacemaking and in politics, and for gender equality. Women's exclusions from formal peace-building processes and negotiations have relegated their activities to more informal and localized arenas that all too often go unacknowledged by scholars, journalists, and policymakers. Peacemaking for them goes well beyond peace negotiations and disarmament exercises: it includes informal strategies and permeates everyday life.

The practical everyday nature of women's peace-building has meant that women activists have tended to pursue peace *as a process* during conflict. In conventional peace negotiations, the signing of a peace agreement, holding of elections, and demobilization of militia are generally seen as the end point. In contrast, peace is often seen by women's organizations as an ongoing process that involves working together to solve common problems and meet important everyday needs.

The ability of women's organizations to build bridges across ethnic, religious, clan, and other differences that have contributed to conflict stem from (1) the common concerns they often share to improve women's status as citizens and political actors, and (2) the quotidian nature of women's concerns in running households and communities, which require the kind of cooperation that cannot wait for the resolution of peace talks.

Finally, international and regional pressures and support have bolstered local and national initiatives of women peace activists through the passage of resolution 1325, direct support by women's organizations, and the diffusion of international norms regarding women's rights and participation in peace processes.

REFERENCES

Abdela, Lesley. 2011. "Nepal and the Implementation of UNSCR 1325." In *Women, Peace and Security: Translating Policy into Practice*, edited by Funmi Olonisakin, Karen Barnes, and Eka Ikpe, 66–86. New York: Routledge.

Bunting, Ikaweba, Enid de Silva Burke, and Jennifer Klot. 2001. *Engendering Peace: Reflections on the Burundi Peace Process*. Nairobi: UNIFEM.

De Reu, Stijn. 2005. "The Impact of International NGOs and Civil Society Organisations on the Peace Process In Burundi." *Journal of Humanitarian Assistance*, April 2005: 1–21.

Farah, Ahmed Yusuf, and I. M. Lewis. 1993. *Somalia, The Roots of Reconciliation—Peace Making Endeavors of Contemporary Lineage Leaders: A Survey of Grassroots Peace Conferences in Somaliland*. Hargeisa, Somaliland: ActionAid.

"Femmes Africa Solidarité (FAS)—What's New?" 2001. http://www.fasngo.org/en/activities/bestpract/linx/glakes/busoro_and_musaga.htm.

Ingiriis, Mohamed H., and Markus V. Hoehne. 2013. "The Impact of Civil War and State Collapse on the Roles of Somali Women: A Blessing in Disguise." *Journal of Eastern African Studies* 7, no. 2: 314–333.

Mohamed, Faiza Jama. 2004. "Somali Women's Role in Building Peace and Security." Speech given at the UN Security Council ARRIA Formula Meeting on Women, Peace and Security, New York, October 23.

Nilsson, Desirée. 2012. "Anchoring the Peace: Civil Society Actors in Peace Accords and Durable Peace." *International Interactions* 38, no. 2: 243–266.

Osman, Hibaaq. 2000. "Women's Work Is Peace: Lessons from Training Projects in the Horn of Africa." In *Training to Promote Conflict Management*, edited by David Smock, 28–31. Washington, DC: US Institute of Peace.

Paffenholz, Thania, Nick Ross, Steven Dixon, Anna-Lena Schluchter, and Jacqui True. 2016. *Making Women Count—Not Just Counting Women: Assessing Women's Inclusion and Influence on Peace Negotiations*. Geneva and New York: Inclusive Peace and Transition Initiative and UN Women.

Satkunanathan, Ambika, and Charan Rainford. 2009. "Inclusivity, Participation and the Politics of Exclusion." In *Mistaking Politics for Governance: The Politics of Interim Arrangements in Sri Lanka 2002–2005*, 118–130. Colombo, Sri Lanka: International Centre for Ethnic Studies.

UNIFEM. 1996. *Annual Report: Celebrating 20 Years of Commitment to the World's Women*. New York: UNIFEM.

UN Security Council. 2015. *Report of the Secretary-General on Women and Peace and Security*. UN Doc S/2015/716 (September 16).

UN Women. 2015. *Preventing Conflict, Transforming Justice, Securing Peace: A Global Study on the Implementation of United Nations Security Council Resolution 1325*. New York: UN Women.

CHAPTER 34

....

GENDER AND DISARMAMENT, DEMOBILIZATION, AND REINTEGRATION

Reviewing and Advancing the Field

....

DYAN MAZURANA, ROXANNE KRYSTALLI, AND ANTON BAARÉ

DISARMAMENT, demobilization, and reintegration (DDR) is a process that seeks to enhance security, stability, and post-conflict recovery "by removing weapons from the hands of combatants, taking the combatants out of military structures and helping them to integrate socially and economically into society by finding civilian livelihoods" (UN DDRRC 2006, 6). The three discrete, but interrelated, stages of DDR involve:

- *Disarmament*: collection, documentation, control, and disposal of small arms, ammunition, explosives, and light and heavy weapons from combatants and the civilian population;
- *Demobilization*: formal and controlled discharge of active combatants from armed forces and groups, including a phase of reinsertion that provides short-term assistance to ex-combatants;
- *Reintegration*: a political, social, and economic process with an open time frame in which ex-combatants acquire civilian status and gain sustainable employment and income. This process primarily takes place in communities at the local level (UN DPKO 2014).

DDR has received much scholarly and policy attention, culminating in a number of important large-scale DDR initiatives, including the UN Integrated Strategy on DDR (IDDRS) (2004–2006), the Stockholm Initiative on DDR (2004, 2006), and the Multi-Country Demobilization and Reintegration Program (MDRP) (2002–2009), as well as numerous studies of DDR in nearly every country where it has been carried out in the past twenty years.

It is important to note that there have been broad shifts within the debates on DDR writ large, within which an increased focus on women, gender, and DDR have formed a part. A recent review of the academic and policy DDR literature finds that DDR has evolved over the years from minimalist security-focused interventions privileging the military and police to maximalist interventions that span into development, transitional justice, and state-building. This shift is coupled with increased professionalization and standardization within the national to international agencies seeking to manage DDR processes (Muggah 2010).

A gender-focused approach to DDR is three-pronged: it involves using gender analyses to improve the standards of support for women in DDR programs, prioritizes parallel programs and funding for women, and involves demilitarizing masculinity and femininity among ex-combatants. In this chapter, we explore why, despite increasing attention to gender and DDR, institutions and policymakers still find it so difficult to align DDR conceptually, logistically, and programmatically with the needs of women. We argue that this is due to four challenges in the conceptions of women, gender, and DDR.

First, despite extensive advocacy for a rights-based approach that would emphasize women's right to participate in DDR, these programs often remain inaccessible to female combatants and females associated with fighting forces due to conceptual and implementation barriers. Second, for the women who are able to access them, the content of DDR often does not reflect their wartime experiences or post-demobilization needs. Third, it is important to consider alternatives to current forms of DDR, as well as look outside and beyond the traditional DDR framework to address the reality that a formal DDR program may not be suitable or desirable for many women who have been combatants. Finally, DDR programs fall short in confronting the violent, militarized masculinities of male combatants, which contribute to continued violence in public and private spaces post-conflict.

Importantly, these four points reflect the ways in which debates, scholarship, and policy about women, gender, and DDR have evolved over the last decade. The first international approach to women and DDR began most visibly in 2000 and is best exemplified by UN Security Council resolution 1325 on Women, Peace and Security and various engagements by the United Nations Development Fund for Women (UNIFEM), which focused on getting women into DDR programs. This approach was then subject to a number of studies and initiatives looking closely at the exclusion of women and girls, as well as male youth, from DDR programs, and their experiences within the fighting forces and DDR (Douglas et al. 2004; McKay and Mazurana 2004). The research found that many DDR programs failed to enable women, girls, and boys associated with fighting forces to enter the process. If they did get in, the programs failed to adequately take into account their experiences of the war or anticipate the challenges they would face in reintegration into their communities and, hence, failed to meet their needs. These critiques helped to shape the second approach to DDR policy and programs, which attempted to make them more accessible to and relevant for women and girls, and (to a lesser extent) boys (Brooks 2005). The third approach began around 2008 and has applied the most explicitly gendered focus in beginning to look at how DDR processes intersect with, shape, and are shaped by masculinities and femininities. This approach also explored the ways in which DDR can contribute to more transformative gender relations in the post-conflict period, as for example in World Bank–funded DDR programs in Uganda (Universalia Management Group 2012).

While scholarship and policy on women, girls, gender, and DDR have evolved rather rapidly since 2005, the programmatic responses have not. Hence, the gender-informed demands and expectations now being placed on DDR programs do not align with how most DDR programs are negotiated, funded, and embedded nationally, and how they operate.

State of Knowledge: Four Main Gendered Critiques of Disarmament, Demobilization, and Reintegration

This section presents the gendered shortcomings of existing conceptions of DDR throughout the cycle of conflict and peace-making. We contend that gender analyses enable a sharper focus not only on people's gendered identities and power dynamics, but also on how institutions are gendered and produce gendered meanings and outcomes.

Peace accords and national DDR legislation

DDR protocols and standards increasingly require that institutions incorporate a gender perspective into the design of DDR programs (UN DDRRC 2007). This is a crucial development and invites questions about temporality: When are DDR programs framed and designed? Are they part of the peace process? What are the political dynamics of those conflicts and peace processes, and how do they shape negotiations around DDR? Who participates in the process, and whose interests are reflected within and whose are not?[1] The reality is that DDR is often flagged early in closed negotiations, when women and civil society members are almost always absent, and hence their voices and priorities are not heard (see Bell, Chapter 32 in this volume). The staff of the Multi-National Demobilization and Reintegration Program (MDRP), a seven-country multi-donor trust fund to assist in the DDR of over 300,000 fighters in Africa, emphasized that more often than not, determination of the categories of women who were eligible to benefit from DDR were primarily influenced by criteria anchored in peace accords, or national legal instruments such as Letters of Demobilization Policies, as in Rwanda (MDRP and UNIFEM 2005).

Exclusion of women from these negotiations and political-legal processes framing DDR thus often results in their exclusion from or marginalization within technical DDR programs.

Excluding and marginalizing women combatants

One of the greatest challenges for women's and girls' inclusion into DDR programs is the lack of common agreement on what makes an eligible "combatant" (i.e., an eligible participant). To try to address this constraint, the international community, including the IDDRS, has broadened the concept of female ex-combatants to include females in their different roles related to armed groups, referred to as "females associated with armed groups." Yet debates exist on whether determinations of eligibility should be made on a universal or country-by-country basis. Developing a comprehensive DDR program is challenging, given limitations in their time frame for implementation and the recognition that such programs are not comprehensive postwar recovery efforts (MDRP 2010).

Caramés and Sanz's (2009, 10) fifteen-country comparative study of DDR programs found great variation in eligibility criteria for DDR programs (Table 34.1). A gender analysis shows that determining DDR eligibility based on the possession of a weapon (a common criteria) can exclude women and girls who may not have carried guns or who had them taken away by male commanders during cantonment and registration processes. Similarly, assessing one's status in an armed group based on whether she or he fulfilled a combat role can lead to the exclusion of women and girls from DDR. Male commanders often participate in drawing up lists or gathering their fighters. They may deliberately leave women and girls out, whether to enable their fighters to keep them as "prizes," or because they are using the females' weapons to reward other male fighters or family members, or to downplay females' role in the conflict. Additionally, male commanders may view women's and girls' role differently from how they themselves self-identify (Mazurana and Cole 2013). The definition and determination of eligibility matter not only because they may affect women's and girls' access to resources through DDR programs, but also because reframing and marginalizing women's and girls' wartime roles can be an instrument for their depoliticization after conflict (MacKenzie 2009).

Furthermore, where women have been instrumental to the success of insurgent forces and those insurgents have succeeded in becoming or incorporating into new national armies, there is often a deliberate strategy to use DDR to move women combatants out of the composition of those forces, to secure positions for men (new clients often without old patronage systems) in the new national armed forces, and to push women back into traditional gender roles. In such cases, women are disproportionately targeted for DDR in efforts to firmly masculinize the new armies and gain the patronage of male fighters for military and political leaders. This was the case in Eritrea upon winning independence, and most recently in South Sudan when it was women combatants who were disproportionality targeted by the Sudan People's Liberation Army/Movement for DDR (Barth 2002; Hale 2001; Mazurana 2005). Therefore, questions of eligibility are

Table 34.1 Eligiblity Criteria in DDR Programming

Country and Program	Arms Surrender*	Membership in a Group (External or Objective Evaluation)	Membership in a Group (List or Other Internal or Subjective Evalution)	Nationality	Commitment to the Peace Process or DDR (Individual)	Commitment to the Peace Process or DDR (Group)	Free from Prosecution
Afghanistan (DDR)	YES	YES	YES	YES	NO	YES	NO
Afghanistan (CIP)	NO	YES	NO	YES	YES	NO	YES
Angola (GPDR)	NO	YES	NO	YES	NO	NO	NO
Burundi (NCDDR)	NO	YES	NO	NO	NO	NO	NO
Chad (PNRD)	NO	YES	YES	NO	NO	YES	NO
CAR (PRAC)	NO	YES	YES	NO	NO	YES	NO
Colombia (AUC)	NO	YES	NO	YES	NO	NO	NO
Côte d'Ivoire (NPRRC)	N.A	YES	NO	N.A	NO	NO	NO
Eritrea (EPDR)	NO	NO	YES	NO	NO	NO	NO
Indonesia (Aceh)	YES	YES	NO	NO	NO	NO	NO
Liberia (DDRR)	NO	YES	YES	NO	NO	NO	NO
Nepal (AMMAA)	NO	YES	YES	YES	YES	YES	YES
DRC (NPDDR)	NO	NO	YES	NO	NO	NO	NO
Rwanda (RDRP)	NO	YES	YES	YES	NO	NO	NO
Sudan (DDRP)	NO	NO	YES	NO	NO	NO	NO
Uganda (Amenesty)	NO	YES	YES	YES	YES	NO	NO
YES TOTAL	2	13	12	7	3	4	2
NO TOTAL	13	3	5	8	13	12	14

* At a ratio of one weapon per combatant.

questions not only of definition, but also of who makes the determination, on which basis, at which time, and what are the long-term gendered implications of inclusion or exclusion from DDR for the ex-combatant.

Finally, in cases in which a gender-aware approach to DDR is incorporated, desired impact requires consistent application from design through implementation and monitoring, as well as dedicated funding and staff. Gender-aware DDR therefore transcends the identities of the participants and requires a scrutiny of the institutions and their processes, as well as the mechanisms of gendered inclusion and exclusion throughout the cycle of conflict, peace negotiations, peace accords, and peacemaking (Basini 2013).

DDR fails to address gender transformation for equality

The third gendered critique of DDR relates to the ways in which DDR programs acknowledge and imagine men's and women's wartime experiences and post-demobilization roles. In order to disarm, demobilize, and reintegrate former combatants, institutions and DDR managers need to understand female combatants' diverse wartime roles and experiences, including why they joined armed groups in the first place (Theidon 2007); whether they joined voluntarily or by force (Mazurana and Cole 2013); their roles and responsibilities within the group (Tabak 2011); their vulnerability to sexual violence or other abuses within the group (McKay et al. 2006); the likely challenges they will face during reintegration; whether the armed forces they were part of were "winners" or "losers" in the conflict (Farr 2002); how long they have been away from the community (Veale 2003); if they entered the fighting forces as children (Hobson 2005; Veale and Stavrou 2003); and levels of community acceptance when fighters have broken societal norms and taboos (Brooks 2005; Hobson 2005).

Failures to create programs that are aware of and meet women combatants' needs are often due to common gendered assumptions, including the following. Narratives of victimhood are deeply feminized, conjuring images of women as passive participants in war. These tropes, which emphasize women's identity as victims of violence, often overshadow the narratives of women as agents of violence within armed groups (Helms 2013; MacKenzie 2009). Relatedly, to the extent that women's and girls' participation within armed groups is discussed, the emphasis is often on their forced recruitment, forced marriage with combatants, sexual slavery, sexual abuse, and other types of victimization and vulnerability within the group. While this is an essential perspective in a comprehensive gender analysis, it fails to reflect women's and girls' full range of roles and activities in armed groups. Further, when women's and girls' activities and roles in armed groups are discussed, they are often cast in the light of two extremes: either traditional gender roles, such as women's/girls' involvement as cooks, porters, nurses, communication and intelligence personnel, caretakers, or domestic workers within armed group settings are emphasized over their identity as combatants, or their actions as combatants are scrutinized as extraordinary (in ways that men's are not) because they deviate from expectations of traditional peaceful femininity (MacKenzie 2009; Meertens and

Zambrano 2010; Phipps 2010). These gendered assumptions obscure a fuller under-standing of women's and girls' wartime experiences and needs during the DDR process and into the post-conflict period.

DDR fails to acknowledged the militarization of masculinity and feminity

The fourth and final main critique is that DDR should acknowledge how masculinity and femininity are militarized and reconfigured prior to and during wartime (Enloe 2000) and are reshuffled again during demobilization and the post-conflict period. In this way, DDR managers would realize that DDR may be unappealing to or challenging for women and girls who experienced emancipation within the armed group and found a mode of empowerment within it that they could not access in their family or commun-ity. Females who experienced and/or perpetrated violence within armed groups and forces challenge the binary identities of being either a "victim" or an "agent of violence," which can render their social reception challenging.

The Revolutionary Armed Forces of Colombia (FARC) serve as an example of eman-cipatory experiences within armed groups inhibiting women's and girls' demobiliza-tion. The group enticed women and girls to join by, among other factors, emphasizing its "emancipatory ideal" within its statute (Herrera and Porch 2013, 627). For women and girls whose gender severely limits their opportunities in patriarchal settings in Colombia—especially in rural areas where the FARC exerted control—the FARC rep-resented a space for autonomy and sexual freedom, and opened an opportunity to prove their worth (Herrera and Porch 2013). Similar expectations of gender equality in guerrilla life underpinned women's motivations to join the national liberation wars in El Salvador, Eritrea, Mozambique, Nepal, Nicaragua, and Sri Lanka (Mazurana and Cole 2013). While there are limits to the power of women and girls within the groups, and variations to the influence they hold within these groups, any perceived or actual emancipation or gender equality that women and girls experience in wartime can render their demobilization undesirable or difficult—particularly when they are, all too often, expected to return to more restrictive traditional gender roles (Coulter 2009; Luciak 2001).

Additionally, the reconstruction of femininity in DDR programs requires acknowl-edging that the labels "perpetrator" and "victim" are insufficient for capturing the full texture of women's and girls' experiences within armed groups and forces. To illustrate, female ex-combatants in the Democratic Republic of Congo (DRC) face the assump-tion that they have been sexually abused and carry sexually transmitted diseases, even when that is not the case, leading to their stigmatization and marginalization (MDRP 2010).

In certain contexts, the violence that women and girls commit as members of armed groups and forces is seen as more transgressive than that of males and as a violation of all that it means to be feminine, significantly complicating women's and girls' reintegration into post-conflict communities. Female combatants who participated in the Maoist military wing in Nepal "were treated as equals in the PLA and bore arms, and are now encountering rejection from their communities and struggling with traditional female roles" (IRIN 2010). In this respect, gendered ideas about women and girls being more peaceful and less violent than men can, in the eyes of their fighting force, add both an element of surprise and tactical effectiveness to women's and girls' wielding of violence (Bloom 2011; Mazurana 2013). At the same time, it makes the reintegration of these women and girls into post-conflict communities challenging because of the violation of expectations of hegemonic femininity.

Reconstructing Masculinities, Femininities, and Relationships after War

Despite the growing literature on gender, non-state armed groups, conflict, and DDR, to some stakeholders adding gender still only means "adding" women. Males are often the default when gendered assumptions are made in DDR programs, yet masculinity itself is insufficiently examined in DDR processes. An examination of militarized masculinity within armed groups sheds light on the parameters to consider during and after the DDR process.

In addition to ideological, political, economic, and sociocultural factors that prompted men to join an armed group, livelihood concerns are a significant motivating factor. Participation in an armed group provides men with food and a gun, and, at times, with wages, thus offering a modicum of protection, livelihood security, and masculine status. Furthermore, in heavily militarized societies, participation in an armed group is not an aberration, but a rite of passage for men and an exercise of sanctioned masculinity (Theidon 2009; see also Theidon, Chapter 11 in this volume). Masculinity is not an inherent status; rather, it has to be constantly conferred and recognized by self and others (Kimmel 2010). The factors that served men as combatants do not serve as well in civilian life (Theidon 2009). Reconfiguring wartime masculinity in transitional times during DDR requires satisfying a number of needs otherwise addressed by the armed group, including securing livelihoods and protection and providing social services outside the context of an armed group. A 2006 evaluation of DDR programs in Colombia found that "31% of the demobilized had not received any financial support, 55% did not have access to state healthcare, 66% had not received any psychosocial support, 55.7% were not enrolled for schooling, and 59.8% did not have any employment or work" (Derks et al. 2011, 23). Unmet livelihood and protection needs can make men more open to recruitment by armed groups, gangs, and criminal groups, as studies on recidivism show (FIP 2014). Reconfiguring masculinities necessitates a discussion of how these men can become loving, nonviolent partners and fathers who can interact with their families without reinforcing patriarchal, gendered divisions of labor and responsibilities and without the threat and use of violence (Theidon 2009).

The reorientation of masculinities and femininities in wartime and their reconfiguration in times of transition have significant implications for marriage and families. In a number of countries, women and girls were forcibly or voluntarily married within armed groups (Mazurana and Cole 2013). When these women seek to reintegrate—particularly into societies in which divorce and/or prior marriages are not legally or socially sanctioned—they may face significant stigmatization (Hale 2001; Mehreteab 2002). Women who were married prior to joining the armed group may have been separated from their husbands and family (Tabak 2011), and reunification may be either logistically or socially impossible. Children born of forced relationships within armed groups or forces are often heavily stigmatized and are at risk of further abuse from family and community in the future (McKay et al. 2010). Women and girls who emerge single also face difficult partnership prospects upon their demobilization because they are viewed as undesirable partners—even for male ex-combatants. "All the male ex-combatants [in Colombia] said they would not be interested in having a female ex-combatant as a partner now because *la mujer guerillera es muy puta* [the female guerrilla is a real whore or slut]" (Theidon 2009, 29). Therefore, a gender-aware approach to DDR transcends getting women into DDR programs and requires examining how these programs imagine, address, and reconstruct masculinity, femininity, and relationships in the aftermath of conflict.

WHEN WOMEN DO NOT WANT TO ENTER DDR PROGRAMS

For some women, DDR may not be a desired or suitable transition after conflict. Women's lack of participation in DDR also results from (a) real or perceived stigmatization, threat, and abuse by family and community if their ex-combatant status is known; (b) safety concerns regarding the demobilization centers; and (c) inability or lack of desire to demobilize due to ongoing armed conflict (Mazurana and Cole 2013). They may fear that their entry into formal DDR programs will exacerbate the stigma against their wartime participation. Some studies found that women prefer anonymizing themselves after demobilization, often by moving to an urban center, as opposed to joining a formal program (Schwitalla and Dietrich 2007).

Logistical challenges can also hinder women ex-combatants' participation in DDR. These obstacles include the distance from the site of the program, lack of transportation or funds to reach the site, lack of child-care options, and difficulty balancing the demands of DDR participation against the immediate need to secure one's livelihood (Stark et al. 2009). The accessibility of the programs may also depend on other demands on participants' time, such as the need to take care of the family and other dependents in the aftermath of war, with much of the caregiving falling to women (see Justino, Chapter 6 in this volume).

Reimagining DDR as a Portfolio
of Options

This chapter has highlighted the limits of contemporary approaches to women's and girls' inclusion in DDR. To date, approaches assume that DDR programs actually are more beneficial to the women and girls who could qualify to participate in them than possible alternatives that would *not* require them to come forward and possibly face stigmatization as combatants or being associated with (ir)regular forces.

Applying a "where rights meet needs" approach often (grudgingly) acknowledges that programming involves necessary trade-offs between rights and needs (Goldewijk and de Gaay Fortman 1999). Nevertheless, questions have been raised about the limitations of exclusively arguing that the best interest of women and girls is in terms of fulfillment of rights to enter DDR, perhaps at the expense of more comprehensively responding to the women's and girls' more pressing needs through parallel processes that might actually better address both overall rights and needs. At the same time, DDR planners ultimately need to be accountable to program beneficiaries. As a first step, this involves national programs and international institutions assisting in DDR to acknowledge "duty-bearing" responsibility for the consequences of the political and operational trade-offs, in which women's and girls' priorities and rights were not and or could not adequately be considered or acted upon (Baaré 2006). It should be noted that this responsibility would also cover other often-underserved groups, including young men often excluded from, or opting out of, formal DDR (Annan et al. 2008; Utas 2003). Such responsibilities would include ensuring timely and adequate alternative programming for the categories of persons under discussion.

The fundamental questions that should be raised, therefore, are how best to provide women and girls in armed forces and armed groups during the disarmament and reintegration period with assistance that is (a) in fulfillment of their fundamental civil, political, economic, and social rights; (b) accessible and applied in a way that they can actually participate in the programs that provide services; (c) made up of the services that they themselves prioritize; (d) delivered in ways that do not stigmatize them as participants, and; (e) delivered in a way that meets their interests.

We contend that what is needed is a *portfolio view* (a range of coherent projects) rather than a *project view* on how to best serve the needs and rights of women and girls. The critical difference between these views is that whereas a project view typically necessitates that beneficiaries participate in a series of predetermined and limited activities (and often must do so sequentially), a portfolio view is more focused on creating a menu of options from which participants can choose based on what best meets their interests and needs. Ultimately, improving DDR outcomes for women and girls needs to start with a rethink of the individual trajectories that the target group needs to undergo. The accountant's view that this trajectory must be through a linear progression is outdated and should be made obsolete as a basis for planning. As the northern Uganda case illustrates (Annan et al. 2008), female and male ex-combatants constantly (re)evaluate their choices about which services they can access, which are useful to them, and where benefits outweigh potential harms and stigmas in the formal process; based on this always incomplete knowledge, they then make decisions about whether to participate and access services, and if so, when and how.

Additionally, improving reintegration outcomes for women and girls associated with fighting forces requires specialized reintegration support. Where donors support joint funding mechanisms, such as UN or World Bank trust funds, such arrangements should from the outset have a "window" to fund specific evidence-based activities that women and girls need and want, and these should be managed by specialized agencies (MDRP 2010). It is important that these agencies not specifically associate their services with persons associated with fighting forces in order to help reduce stigma, which seems to be a significant factor in both males and females choosing to stay away from DDR processes. For example, responding to the psychological, health, and social needs of those who were abused by armed groups and those who perpetrated abuse in times of transition and DDR programs requires nuancing an understanding of conflict to transcend the labels "victim" and "perpetrator" toward a more layered approach to wartime identities, roles, experiences, and harms. Under this conception of DDR, the women and girls would be able to enter the process at different stages and have a portfolio of choices from which to manage their transition out of armed forces and groups and into civilian life. DDR remains an integral part of post-conflict transition, and its capacity to be fully relevant to the experiences of both women and men requires sustained rethinking and remaking of existing programs with a view to ensuring the full and meaningful participation of all those who have engaged in armed conflict.

NOTE

1. Peace processes and DDR program design are significant not only because they delineate access to resources, but also because they have significant implications for transitional justice, accountability, the conferring of identities of "victim" or "perpetrator" upon conflict-affected individuals, and for demarcating their access to reparations, political power, and peace dividends in the transitional period.

REFERENCES

Annan, Jeannie, Christopher Blattman, Khristopher Carlson, and Dyan Mazurana. 2008. *The State of Female Youth in Northern Uganda: Findings from the Survey of War-Affected Youth (SWAY), Phase II.* Uganda: SWAY.

Baaré, Anton. 2006. "An Analysis of Transitional Economic Integration." In *Stockholm Initiative on Disarmament Demobilisation Reintegration: Background Studies,* edited by Lena Sundh and Jens Samuelsson Schjølien, 17–54. Stockholm: Swedish Ministry of Foreign Affairs.

Barth, Elise. 2002. *Peace as Disappointment: The Reintegration of Female Soldiers in Post-Conflict Societies. A Comparative Study from Africa.* Oslo: International Peace Research Institute (PRIO).

Basini, Helen S.A. 2013. "Gender Mainstreaming Unraveled: The Case of DDRR in Liberia." *International Interactions* 39, no. 4: 535–557.

Bloom, Mia. 2011. *Bombshell: The Many Faces of Women Terrorists.* Toronto: Viking Canada.

Brooks, Andy. 2005. *The Disarmament, Demobilization and Reintegration of Children Associated with the Fighting Forces: Lessons Learned from Sierra Leone.* Dakar: United Nations Children's Fund.

Caramés, Albert, and Eneko Sanz. 2009. *DDR 2009: Analysis of Disarmament, Demobilisation and Reintegration (DDR) Programmes in the World during 2008.* Bellaterra: School for a Culture of Peace.

Coulter, Chris. 2009. *Bush Wives and Girl Soldiers: Women's Lives through War and Peace in Sierra Leone.* Ithaca, NY: Cornell University Press.

Derks, Maria, Hans Rouw, and Ivan Briscoe. 2011. "A Community Dilemma: DDR and the Changing Face of Violence in Colombia." Peace and Security Development Network Paper No. 00030, Netherlands.

Douglas, Sarah, Vanessa Farr, Felicity Hill, and Wenny Kasuma. 2004. *Getting It Right, Doing It Right: Gender and Disarmament, Demobilization and Reintegration.* New York: UNIFEM.

Enloe, Cynthia. 2000. *Maneuvers: The International Politics of Militarizing Women's Lives.* Berkeley: University of California Press.

Farr, Vanessa. 2002. "Gendering Demilitarization as a Peacebuilding Tool." Bonn International Center for Conversion, Paper 20, Bonn, Germany.

Fundacion Ideas Para la Paz (FIP). 2014. "Return to Legality or Recidvisim of Excombatants in Colombia: Dimension of the Phenomenon and Risk Factors." FIP, Serie Informes No. 22, Bogotá, Colombia.

Goldewijk, Berma Klein, and Bas de Gaay Fortman. 1999. *Where Needs Meet Rights: Economic, Social and Cultural Rights in a New Perspective.* Geneva: World Council of Churches.

Hale, Sondra. 2001. "Liberated, But Not Free: Women in Post-War Eritrea." In *The Aftermath: Women in Post-Conflict Transformation,* edited by Sheila Meintjes, Anu Pillay, and Meredith Turshen, 122–141. London: Zed Books.

Helms, Elissa. 2013. *Innocence and Victimhood: Gender, Nation, and Women's Activism in Post-War Bosnia-Herzegovina.* Madison: University of Wisconsin Press.

Herrera, Natalia, and Douglas Porch. 2013. "'Like Going to a Fiesta': The Role of Female Fighters in Colombia's FARC-EP." *Small Wars & Insurgencies* 19, no. 4: 609–634.

Hobson, Matt. 2005. *Forgotten Casualties of War: Girls in Armed Conflict.* London: Save the Children.

IRIN. 2010. "Nepal: Reintegration Challenges for Maoist Female Ex-Combatants." April 14. http://www.irinnews.org/report/88806/nepal-reintegration-challenges-for-maoist-female-ex-combatants.

Kimmel, Michael. 2010. *Misframing Men: The Politics of Contemporary Masculinities.* New Brunswick, NJ: Rutgers University Press.

Luciak, Ilja. 2001. *After the Revolution: Gender and Democracy in El Salvador, Nicaragua and Guatemala.* Baltimore, MD: Johns Hopkins University Press.

MacKenzie, Megan. 2009. "Securitization and Desecuritization: Female Soldiers and the Reconstruction of Women in Post-Conflict Sierra Leone." *Security Studies* 18, no. 2: 241–61.

Mazurana, Dyan. 2005. *Women in Armed Opposition Groups in Africa and the Promotion of International Humanitarian Law and Human Rights.* Report of a workshop organized in Addis Ababa by Geneva Call and the Program for the Study of International Organization(s), November 23–26, 2005.

Mazurana, Dyan. 2013. "Women, Girls, and Non-State Armed Opposition Groups." In *Women and Wars*, edited by Carol Cohn, 146–168. Cambridge: Polity Press.

Mazurana, Dyan, and Linda Eckerborn Cole. 2013. "Women, Girls, and Disarmament, Demobilization, and Reintegration (DDR)." In *Women and Wars*, edited by Carol Cohn, 194–214. Cambridge: Polity Press.

McKay, Susan, and Dyan Mazurana. 2004. *Where Are the Girls? Girls in Fighting Forces in Northern Uganda, Sierra Leone and Mozambique: Their Lives during and after War.* Montreal: Rights & Democracy.

McKay, Susan, Malia Robinson, Maria Gonsalves, and Miranda Worthen. 2006. *Girls Formerly Associated with Fighting Forces and Their Children: Returned and Neglected.* London: Coalition to Stop the Use of Child Soldiers.

McKay, Susan, Angela Veale, Miranda Worthen, and Mike Wessells. 2010. *Community-Based Reintegration of War-Affected Young Mothers: Participatory Action Research (PAR) in Liberia, Sierra Leone and Northern Uganda.* Laramie: University of Wyoming Gender & Women's Studies Program.

Meertens, Donny, and Margarita Zambrano. 2010. "Citizenship Deferred: The Politics of Victimhood, Land Restitution and Gender Justice in the Colombian Post (?) Conflict." *International Journal of Transitional Justice* 4, no. 2: 189–206.

Mehreteab, Amanuel. 2002. *Veteran Combatants Do Not Fade Away: A Comparative Study on Two Demobilization and Reintegration Exercises in Eritrea.* Bonn: Bonn International Center for Conversion.

Muggah, Robert. 2010. "Innovations in Disarmament, Demobilization and Reintegration Policy and Research: Reflections on the Last Decade." Norwegian Institute of International Affairs, NUPI Working Paper 774, Oslo, Norway.

Multi-National Demobilization and Reintegration Program (MDRP). 2010. *The Multi-Country Demobilitzation and Integration Program Final Report: Overview of Program Achievements.* Washington, DC: The International Bank for Reconstruction and Development/The World Bank.

MDRP and UNIFEM. 2005. "Taking a Gender-Perspective to Strengthen the Multi-Country Demobilization and Reintegration (MDRP) in the Greater Great Lakes Region." Workshop Report, October 31–November 2, Kigali, Rwanda.

Phipps, Alison. 2010. "Violence and Victimized Bodies: Sexual Violence Policy in England and Wales." *Critical Social Policy* 30, no. 3: 359–383.

Schwitalla, Gunhild, and Luisa Maria Dietrich. 2007. "Demobilisation of Female Ex-Combatants in Colombia." *Forced Migration Review* 27: 58–59.

Stark, Lindsay, Neil Boothby, and Alastair Ager. 2009. "Children and Fighting Forces: 10 Years on from Cape Town." *Disasters* 33, no. 4: 522–547.

Tabak, Shana. 2011. "False Dichotomies of Transitional Justice: Gender, Conflict and Combatants in Colombia." *New York University Journal of International Law & Politics* 44, no. 1: 104–156.

Theidon, Kimberly. 2007. "Transitional Subjects: The Disarmament, Demobilization and Reintegration of Former Combatants in Colombia." *International Journal of Transitional Justice* 1, no. 1: 66–90.

Theidon, Kimberly. 2009. "Reconstructing Masculinities: The Disarmament, Demobilization, and Reintegration of Former Combatants in Colombia." *Human Rights Quarterly* 31, no. 1: 1–34.

UN Department of Peacekeeping Operations (DPKO). 2014. "Disarmament, Demobilization and Reintegration." Accessed June 8. http://www.un.org/en/peacekeeping/issues/ddr.shtml.

UN Disarmament, Demobilization, and Reintegration Resource Center (DDRRC). 2006. *Integrated Disarmament, Demobilization, and Reintegration Standards Module 1.20: Glossary: Terms and Definitions.* New York: UN DDRRC.

UN Disarmament, Demobilization, and Reintegration Resource Center (DDRRC). 2007. *Integrated Disarmament, Demobilization, and Reintegration Standards.* New York: UN DDRRC.

Universalia Management Group. 2012. *Evaluation of the Transitional Demobilization and Reintegration Program (TRDP).* Montreal: Universalia.

Utas, Mats. 2003. "Sweet Battlefields: Youth and the Liberian Civil War." PhD diss., Uppsala University.

Veale, Angela. 2003. "From Child Soldier to Ex-Fighter: Female Fighters' Demobilization and Reintegration in Ethiopia." Institute for Security Studies, ISS Monograph No. 85, Pretoria.

Veale, Angela, and Aki Stavrou. 2003. "Violence, Reconciliation and Identity: The Reintegration of the Lord's Resistance Army Child Abductees in Northern Uganda." Institute for Security Studies, ISS Monograph No. 92, Pretoria.

CHAPTER 35

DECOLONIAL FEMINISM, GENDER, AND TRANSITIONAL JUSTICE IN LATIN AMERICA

PASCHA BUENO-HANSEN

DURING the last few decades, feminist practitioners, activists, and policymakers have achieved major gains in addressing gender-based violence during internal armed conflict in legal frameworks and international policy. According to the 1993 UN Declaration of the Elimination of Violence Against Women, gender-based violence identifies any act "that results in, or is likely to result in, physical, sexual or psychological harm or suffering to women, including threats of such acts, coercion or arbitrary deprivation of liberty, whether occurring in public or in private life."[1] UN Security Council resolution 1325 on Women, Peace and Security, adopted in 2000, along with its seven follow-up resolutions, offers a key example of the advances made in this realm. Yet, given pervasive levels of gender-based violence during internal armed conflict, it would appear that it remains difficult to stop in practice, with few legal cases moving through judicial systems and ongoing impunity. Uncovering the reasons for this difficulty demands a reflection upon the roots of gender-based violence in hetero-patriarchal social structures, where there is a structural privileging of males over females in a binary sex/gender system that assumes heterosexuality.

This chapter addresses the heteronormativity of gender-based violence in Latin America, tracing this back to the legacy of Spanish colonialism, and using Peru as a lens.[2] Specifically, it illustrates the contributions of decolonial feminisms to the study of gender, conflict, and transitional justice in Latin America through an examination of the Peruvian experience. Latin American–based decolonial theory assists in this endeavor of demystifying the entanglements of economic exploitation and the naturalization of racial categories. This decolonial feminist analysis examines the Peruvian internal armed conflict (1980–2000) and transitional justice process (2001 to the present), with a focus on cases of sexual violence in the Andean department of Huancavelica. Rethinking gender and conflict from a decolonial feminist perspective illustrates and emphasizes a continuity of gender-based violence from the colonial encounter to the contemporary moment. This approach, linking the historical colonial experience in Peru to the modern transitional justice experience, challenges assumptions regarding the role of the state, temporal relations, and victimhood that undergird programmatic and policy work in the gender and conflict context.

The field of transitional justice has gained ground over the past decades in response to the needs of post-conflict societies, which have typically fallen beyond the reach of criminal law and formal justice mechanisms. The term "transitional justice" marks a shift toward engaging political transition and the problems encountered by human rights advocates and activists to foster social reconciliation and peace in the aftermath of collective violence. After two decades of global advocacy and activism, transitional justice theory and practice have evolved to the point of including gender as an analytical component. Yet, operationalizing gender means that it is usually reduced to focus on a homogenous grouping called "women" and superficially added on to the transitional justice project at hand.

A DECOLONIAL FEMINISM READING OF THE PERUVIAN CONTEXT

Gender essentialism is "the notion that a unitary, 'essential' women's experience can be isolated and described independently of race, class, sexual orientation and other realities of experience" (Harris 1990, 585). Gender-essentialist methods that add on "women" to a preexisting project assume a certain type of woman as normative, while marginalizing differences among women. In the case of Peru, differences based on race, ethnicity, indigeneity, sexual orientation, class, literacy, language, religion, and ability, for example, mark significant sociopolitical power dynamics that find their roots in the colonial encounter between Spaniards and the indigenous peoples that populated the territory now called Peru. Glossing over the enduring quality of these complex relations undermines the possibility of reaching transitional justice goals of justice and reconciliation, as well as potentially contributing to repeating cycles of violence and ongoing discrimination.

A disproportionate focus on sexual violence, particularly rape, constitutes another troubling aspect of the incorporation of gender in transitional justice processes and mechanisms. While decades of feminist advocacy and activism made it possible to bring sexual violence to light as a crime against humanity and a war crime, a singular focus on the juridical category feeds into a weak conceptualization of gender analysis in its own right. Although the Peruvian Truth and Reconciliation Commission (PTRC) was not mandated to investigate sexual violence, it included the violation under the umbrella of torture and other grave violations in compliance with international human rights law. According to the Rome Statute of the International Criminal Court, which Peru ratified

November 10, 2001, sexual violence includes "rape, sexual slavery, enforced prostitution, forced pregnancy, enforced sterilization, or any other form of sexual violence of comparable gravity," further defined as "crimes against humanity."

After the internal armed conflict (1980–2000) and the authoritarian regime of President Alberto Fujimori (self-coup in 1992–2000), the state held very little legitimacy on both domestic and international fronts. After the Peruvian internal armed conflict ended, President Alejandro Toledo adopted a transitional justice agenda by mandating the PTRC (2001–2003) to investigate the causes and consequences of the violence. The PTRC hired a gender consultant six months into its mandated investigation (Bueno-Hansen 2015). The gender consultant's initial attempts to integrate gender as a transversal axis of analysis throughout the investigation gave way to the "add-on" model that reinforces gender essentialism. Transitional justice mechanisms, such as truth and reconciliation commissions, develop a national narrative of what happened, offering a break from the past and a promise of non-repetition. Transitional justice offers the possibility of state rehabilitation in important and underappreciated ways. Thus, the Peruvian nation-state in crisis reconfigured itself through a transitional justice process. This process simultaneously included historically marginalized populations of the Andes and the Amazon to legitimate itself, while also entrenching social hierarchies, through multiple tactics including gender essentialism. An inherent contradiction exists in that stabilizing the nation-state leads to dependence on established social hierarchies, while changing deep-rooted conditions of injustice requires questioning and further destabilizing the same hierarchies. To make sense of that contradiction, the assertion that the transitional justice process risks re-legitimatizing the Peruvian nation-state must be viewed with an eye also cast on the afterlife of Spanish colonialism.

In relation to gender-based violence, the state is directly implicated through both the generalized practice of sexual violence perpetrated by the armed forces and the state reconsolidation based on hetero-patriarchal logics that reduce women to their experience of victimhood. Intractable hetero-patriarchal social structures maintain and perpetuate gender-based violence. Legal scholar Rhonda Copelon (2011) asserts, "The recovery of the state" by utilizing international criminal law "obscures the violence of the state-based order. The state may, for example, have been instrumental in perpetuating the systemic gender inequality that influenced the conditions for large-scale rape in the first place" (422). Discussions of gender and conflict must address the nexus of violence that constitutes the state and its disciplining practices regulating and constraining women's lives.

In what follows, this chapter uses a decolonial feminist approach to highlight an analysis of colonialism and gender, thereby addressing the limitations of gender essentialism. The next section explains the conceptual and historical context of such an analysis. The decolonial feminist approach then yields to an exploration of rural community perspectives on sexual violence during the internal armed conflict. This section utilizes a southern Andean theory/metaphor of *el patrón* to underscore the continuity of gender-based violence across various historical moments. In other words, sexual violence during the internal armed conflict manifests in the continuation of historical colonial violence, but with a new perpetrator. Linking the historical to the modern conflict weakens assumptions of linear temporal relations that disassociate the violence of differing historical moments such as the colonial encounter, feudalism, and the internal armed conflict. Finally, to broaden thinking about gender-based violence, victimhood, and the benevolence of the state, this chapter concludes by bringing two complex issues to the fore: (1) women who exchange sex for release of a detained family member under the coercive context of military occupation during internal armed conflict, and (2) the vital role of systematic sexual violence in the construction of military masculinities.

DECOLONIAL FEMINISM

References to the legacy of colonialism in contexts of conflict and post-conflict are typically framed under the rubric of post-colonial theory. Indeed, post-colonial theory, born from African and Asian independence struggles, offers a foundation for the study of conflict. In comparison to African and Asian independence struggles that took place throughout the 1900s with a concentration in the 1960s and 1970s, Latin American independence struggles took place in the early part of the 1800s. The Latin American context initiated a different trajectory for theorizing five hundred years of Spanish and Portuguese colonialism. The contributions that feminist Latin American decolonial theory offer to the study of gender and conflict (Martinez Salazar 2012) are related to those of feminist postcolonial theory (Ponzanesi 2014), yet maintain distinct differences in historical and regional context.

Furthermore, a growing body of feminist theorizing that centrally engages decolonial theory elucidates the historic power relations in which gender and sexuality are embedded (Mendoza 2016). Specifically, feminist decolonial theorizing foregrounds the interwoven dynamics of labor and economic exploitation, racialization, and heteropatriarchy. This section explains the significance of gender-based violence within the colonial encounter. The historical and conceptual reference points offered here contextualize how this violence is understood at the rural community level. In addition, these reference points assist in the re-evaluation of common assumptions regarding the role of the state, temporal relations, and victimhood that undergird programmatic and policy work on gender and conflict.

The narrative of modernity, originating in Europe and commonly identified with progress and development, has a hidden flipside (Mignolo 2011). The other side of modernity is coloniality, which encompasses the modes of control used by Europeans to manage their American and Caribbean colonies from the 1500s on (Tlostanova and Mignolo 2012, 38). These modes of social, political, and economic control perpetuate injustice, commodification, and disregard for human life (Mignolo 2011, xviii). Therefore, modernity/coloniality refers to the project of colonization of the Américas, the epistemic system entrenched by this process, and its contemporary manifestations within the modern nation-state (Mignolo and Schiwy 2003, 20).

In terms of social relations, colonization established "intersubjective relations of domination," trapping the colonized population in the past along a linear temporal trajectory that glorifies Europe as modern (Quijano 2000). To exploit resources, colonial actors exacerbated preexisting differences and fueled conflict among indigenous peoples. A system of racial categorization dictated the spaces inhabited by and the interrelations between Spanish and indigenous peoples. European control of knowledge production, subjectivity, and culture established social relations that function through to the present day and continue to serve Euro-centered capitalism and the European descendents in Peru (Quijano 2000, 540). A decolonial approach confronts and counteracts the manifestations of the multiple social hierarchies of colonialism in the contemporary nation-building context.

Modern hetero-patriarchy in Latin America can be understood only by holding the two analytical elements together, that of gender and coloniality. The representative of Peruvian modern hetero-patriarchy, the literate urban able-bodied light-skinned heterosexual male of colonial descent, can exist only in opposition to the abject subject of the nation-state, the indianized woman (de la Cadena 1995, 202). One of the generally recognized modes of domination within modernity/coloniality is the "control of gender and sexuality: nuclear family, binary, normative sexuality, patriarchal superiority."[3] This system aims to dismantle precolonial, communal, and sociopolitical organizations and knowledge production based on multiple and dynamic genders and sexualities.

During the colonial period, European/white women did not commonly travel to Peru. When they did, these colonizer women were prized for their purity and embodied the "light" side of the gender system. Sexual relations with such women would occur only in the context of marriage with a European/white man, recognized by the Church and only for reproductive purposes. The flip side of this rigid sexual morality was the utter permissibility for European/white men to access, use, rape, and abuse women of lower classes and darker complexions. The indigenous and African colonialized women experienced dehumanization through labor exploitation, as well as "forced sex with white colonizers" (Lugones 2007, 206). The "dark" side of the gender system is construed as intrinsically violent and animalistic. Rigid sexual morality enforced by the Catholic Church legitimated these inequalities in Peru.

Race, class, and gender intertwine in a braid of domination, creating "a single structure running through all social relations, institutional and personal, public and private, production and reproduction, in the process of daily life and in the historical development of Latin America" (Francke 1990, 85). Sexual violence during internal armed conflict and the impunity surrounding it should be understood in relation to this panorama of social relations based on coloniality and gender.

EL PATRÓN THEORY/METAPHOR: RURAL COMMUNITY PERSPECTIVES

A decolonial feminist approach establishes the groundwork to explore rural community perspectives on sexual violence during the more recent internal armed conflict. The

Peruvian internal armed conflict of 1980–2000 started when the Shining Path ("Sendero Luminoso," the Communist Party of Peru) rejected formal incorporation as a political party into the political system. During the 1980 elections, the Shining Path burned ballot boxes in the rural Andean community of Chucchi, Ayacucho, and took up arms with the goal of overthrowing the government through a Maoist revolution. Other armed actors included the Tupac Amaru Revolutionary Movement (MRTA) and the armed forces. Caught in the crossfire, civilians, mostly Quechua-speaking peasants, suffered greatly, losing their lives, families, homes, livestock, agricultural lands, and livelihoods. The conflict strongly impacted the poorest areas of the southern Andes, including the regions of Ayacucho, Huancavelica, and Apurimac.

This section analyzes the case of sexual violence during internal armed conflict in the department of Huancavelica. The districts of Manta and Vilca are in Huancavelica, the poorest region of Peru, with 88 percent of the population living in poverty and 74 percent in extreme poverty. At 3,532 meters above sea level, the communities are largely composed of subsistence farmers and herders who supplement their livelihood with seasonal labor migration to cities. In the early years of the conflict, Shining Path began to have a presence in the northern cone of Huancavelica, where Manta and Vilca are located. In 1984, the Political Military Command established a counter-guerrilla military base in the district of Manta to crush subversive activity. The officers forced the community to build the military base with materials from their own homes, and the military dominated the community for eleven years, during which time the entire region was under a state of emergency (between 1983 and 1999) (PTRC Juridical Unit 2003, 11). The Manta and Vilca case exemplifies how the military perpetrated the majority of sexual violence against women from Andean Quechua-speaking or Amazonian ethno-linguistic communities in and around military installations.

The population of Manta maintains that with the establishment of the military base came the beginning of a "permanent practice of detentions, abuse and executions against men and women assumed to be collaborating with the Shining Path. In the case of women, torture commonly included sexual violence, which was regularly perpetrated by groups of military" (PTRC Juridical Unit 2003, 7). The victims of sexual violence occupy the bottom ranks of the social hierarchy. The profile of the victims of sexual violence reflect 75 percent Quechua-speaking women, 83 percent from rural areas, the majority with primary education or less and between the ages of ten and twenty-nine (PTRC 2003, vol. 6, chap. 1.5). As shown in earlier work, the pattern of sexual violence perpetrated during the internal armed conflict reproduces gender and racial hierarchies (Bueno-Hansen 2015).

From a historical perspective, Manta has long experienced a chain of vertical relations, which included abusive *patrones*, or powerful regional landowners that profited from indigenous labor. Like much of Latin America, this brutal semi-feudal system dominated social, political, and economic relations for centuries. Peru began to dismantle this system in the 1950s. Accounts of *patrónes* in the collective memory of Manta include unbridled exploitation of peasants, forced recruitment of young men for military service, theft of animals, and sexual abuse of women. Acting with complete impunity as a result of tight ties with the regional elite, *patrónes* kept the labor in place through a feudal ideology based on racial hierarchies and hetero-patriarchy. The theory/metaphor *el patrón* as developed by communities in the southern Andes critically identifies patterns of illegitimate authority, economic exploitation, and cultural domination. These patterns of social relations connect historical moments that modernity posits as distinct through a naturalized order of progression.

Quechua-speaking peasants from the Andean highlands find themselves in a precarious position of vulnerability to sexual abuse and humiliation with no recourse. "*El patrón* was the owner of both the land and the people that inhabited it. In the case of women, they were obligated to submit themselves to sexual practices against their will as a form of 'pleasing' the owner" (Ruiz Bravo, Neira, and Rosales 2007, 265). For generation upon generation, ruling elites have imposed multiple social exclusions upon rural Quechua-speaking women, and the practice of sexual violence epitomizes this dehumanizing logic. *El patrón*, as a metaphor used within southern Andean communities, elucidates the way class, race, ethnicity, and gender function within the local social imaginary to map a paternalist system, "marked by power, domination and coloniality" (Ruiz Bravo, Neira, and Rosales 2007, 260).

Sexual violence during the internal armed conflict can be understood as a continuation of violence with a new *patrón*. Communities in the southern Andes affected by the internal armed conflict understand sexual violence in relation to its perpetration in other historical moments. Ruiz Bravo, Neira, and Rosales (2007) assert that within the rural communities of the southern Andes, *el patrón* theory/metaphor "politicizes illegitimate situations that take an emotional toll, that coerce desire and impede the consolidation of citizenship and democracy" (280–281). The sexual violence during the internal armed conflict that took place in the 1980s and 1990s in Manta and Vilca exemplifies such illegitimate situations. The pattern of sexual violence echoes colonial legacies as manifested during the system of semi-feudalism and throughout the recent internal armed conflict. Critical attention to the colonial legacy implies a rethinking of history that challenges basic assumptions such as linear progression and the separation of historical moments. This approach looks at the specificity of each set of social relations while attending to continuities and discontinuities. In addition to questioning assumptions regarding linear temporality, the following sections challenge assumptions regarding the nature of victimhood and the benevolence of the state.

EXCHANGING SEX FOR FREEDOM

Generally speaking, a sexual act under coercive circumstances qualifies as sexual violence, thereby producing a victim and a perpetrator. Long-term military occupation, as well as the system of semi-feudalism and the resulting contexts of multiple power imbalances, renders the nature of victimhood quite complex. For example, women during internal armed conflict may exchange sex for release of a detained family member and understand what they did as an act of resistance.

This complex issue of exchanging sex for freedom further expands the conceptual parameters for thinking about gender-based violence. With regard to the binary of consent/coercion, the PTRC draws its understanding of sexual violence from the Rome Statute article 7(1) as "an act of a sexual nature by force, or by threat of force or coercion, such as that caused by fear of violence, duress, detention, psychological oppression or abuse of power, against such person or persons or another person, or by taking advantage of a coercive environment or such person's or persons' incapacity to give genuine consent."

In conversations with women in Manta during my visits to the community,[4] they were divided on this issue of women who traded sex, or access to their bodies, for the freedom of their family member (Bueno-Hansen 2015). Some said that women were forced into doing this as the only way to save their family member. Others argued that the women chose to do this and that choice was a sign of courage, family loyalty, and bravery. By allowing sexual access to one's body, one could potentially save a husband, brother, or son. Some women saw themselves as protagonists in the decision to utilize this sexual currency as a means to an end. Historically, women's bodies have been objects of exchange. In feudal times, "women were given to the [land]owner by their parents as a way to avoid retribution or fines for lost livestock" (Ruiz Bravo, Neira, and Rosales 2007, 265). This relation repeats itself in the context of the internal armed conflict with different actors. By listening to the women's debates on the issue, the multiple subject positions of women come to the surface. They do not understand their experiences under the singular rubric of victimhood.

This issue of exchanging sex for the freedom of their loved ones was not isolated to Manta: it was a generalized practice in which military actors took advantage of their power to set the rules and the modes of currency. It is clear that the military presence in rural communities altered the power relations to the point of establishing a generalized environment of terror, coercion, and intimidation. Under these conditions, is consent possible? This question has animated major contestation in multiple post-conflict contexts. The legal framework of establishing individual consent or coercion makes it difficult to holistically assess this environment and the historic patterns that underlie it. By exploring the question of how women engage the state, or how they respond when engaged by the state, the two most often postulated faces of the state appear more clearly: that of paternalistic protector or hyper-aggressive rapist-soldier.

Taking the analysis of *el patrón*, or patterns of hierarchical relations, seriously forces a conceptual opening to make space for simultaneous and incongruous readings of sex acts under the coercive context of military occupation during internal armed conflict. Through the practice of conceptual capaciousness, one can value the legal tools to end impunity, acknowledge historic power relations, and honor the subjectivities of women maneuvering within such contexts. These women are protagonists, witnesses, survivors, victims, and at times perpetrators, but by no means are they reduced to any of these as a singular identity. By focusing on the patterns, women's multiple and seemingly contradictory responses become intelligible.

MILITARY MASCULINITIES

Sexual violence during the internal armed conflict in Manta and Vilca is also emblematic of the multipurpose function of sexual violence. This practice is not just a method of torture to gain information, a weapon of war, a human rights violation, and a crime against humanity. It also serves an important purpose *within* the military. Systematic sexual violence, especially in its collective form of gang rape, establishes and reinforces internal hierarchies as well as a highly aggressive form of masculine expression (see also Gaca, Chapter 23, and Eriksson Baaz and Stern, Chapter 41, in this volume). As feminist international relations scholar Laura Sjoberg (2013) explains, militarized masculinity refers to "war's reliance on militarism and militarism's reliance on commanding and transforming masculinity/ies in times of war" (171). Examining the construction of military masculinities in the context of coloniality and hetero-patriarchy exposes the nexus of violence that constitutes the state.

The Peruvian practice of giving/gifting women to the troops, called *pichana*, during searches or incursions and the order by which the gang rape would occur demand a nuanced analysis of the gendered and racialized dynamics of the military (Instituto de Defensa Legal 2010). As political scientist Elizabeth Wood (2008) indicates, paying attention to the leadership, the hierarchy, the units of combatants, and individual combatants allows for such an analysis. In general, hegemonic and subordinate masculinities are reinforced through military indoctrination (Sjoberg 2013). The practice of gang rape buttresses social hierarchies. The perpetrator's social position determines his access to the women being violated. In addition, women are valued more or less for their social position. Depending on where women were situated along the gender and racial hierarchy, some "were less dehumanized than others, some women deserved more respect and also some soldiers deserved 'better versions of women' than others" (Boesten 2008, 201).

These military rituals of domination and submission reproduce racial and gender hierarchies. The experience of Peru is no different: the more "desirable" lighter-skinned, higher-class women were reserved for the officers, reinforcing hegemonic masculinity. The soldiers in Peru were given the "less desirable" peasants, reinforcing subordinate masculinity. Most soldiers, being young men from rural areas, were obligated to participate in the abuse of rural young women. The racial insults they spoke while raping were similar to those insults that they had themselves received at other moments in their own lives. Soldiers distanced themselves from the discrimination they received by displacing it onto women, thereby reinforcing racialized and gendered hierarchies as the basis of social cohesion and an expression of militarized masculinity. Anthropologist Kimberly Theidon explains how this shared experience of brutalizing women unites soldiers through a collective sense of guilt that also shifts the social norm around shame (Theidon 2013). Collectively eliminating a sense of shame in soldiers results in a heightened capacity for brutality. Such training in hyper-aggressive masculinity serves the primary goals of degrading, humiliating, and controlling the population to gain compliance through domination.

CONCLUSION

Decolonial feminisms demystify the blueprint of historic power relations foundational to the nation-state. The state's intrinsic gender and racial hierarchies make addressing gender-based violence through the legal system quite difficult. A decolonial feminist approach questions the assumed benevolence of the state, the separation of historical moments into discrete and unrelated realities, and a totalizing conception of victimhood.

Rural community members in the southern Andes speak about themselves and their struggles through *el patrón* theory/metaphor, which in turn reflects the ongoing experience, affect, and sentiment of resistance. Mobilizing the theory/metaphor of *el patrón* to analyze the racial and gender dynamics of the internal armed conflict uncovers historic power asymmetries and the effects of long-term occupation. Focusing on patterns of violence, rather than the individual cases, illuminates women victims' understandings of their experiences, makes visible the blurred line between consent and coercion, and allows for an exploration of how community members navigate such situations.

The inquiry into the multipurpose use of sexual violence by the military highlights the hetero-patriarchal structure underpinning the expressions of military masculinities in the case of Peru and its direct link to the systematic perpetration of sexual violence. At both levels, the practice reinforces racial and gender hierarchies. A decolonial feminist approach brings the contradictory facets of the state into view—the benevolent state promising justice and reconciliation, and the violent state that perpetuates gender-based violence by reinforcing racial and gender hierarchies. This contradiction undermines transitional justice processes, which depend on the assumption of the benevolence of the state.

The analysis of patterns of hierarchical relations brings seemingly separate moments into conversation, specifically the experiences of the colonial encounter, the semi-feudal system, and the internal armed conflict. Furthermore, a decolonial feminist approach invites a conceptual opening to make space for simultaneous and incongruous readings of what constitutes violation and harm. Through the critical practice of conceptual capaciousness, one can value the legal tools to end impunity, acknowledge patterns of power relations, scrutinize the nexus of violence that constitutes the state, and honor the subaltern subjectivities maneuvering within such contexts.

NOTES

1. United Nations General Assembly Res. 48/104, *Declaration on the Elimination of Violence Against Women*, at art. 1, December 20, 1993.
2. For a comparative Latin American analysis, see Bueno-Hansen (2016).
3. The four spheres of the colonial matrix of power include: (1) economic control: appropriation of land, exploitation of resources, and human labor; (2) control of authority: political,

military, legal, financial systems; (3) control of gender and sexuality: nuclear family, binary, normative sexuality, patriarchal superiority; and (4) control of knowledge and subjectivity through education and colonizing existing knowledge (Tlostanova and Mignolo, 2012, 44).
4. I conducted ethnographic research in Manta (2006 and 2007).

References

Boesten, Jelke. 2008. "Narrativas de sexo, violencia y disponibilidad: Raza, género y jerarquías de la violación en Perú." In *Raza, etnicidad y sexualidades: Ciuidadanía y multiculturalismo en América Latina*, edited by Peter Wade, Fernando Urrea Giraldo, and Mara Viveros Vigoya, 199–220. Bogotá: Universidad Nacional de Colombia.

Bueno-Hansen, Pascha. 2015. *Feminist and Human Rights Struggles in Peru: Decolonizing Transitional Justice.* Urbana: University of Illinois Press.

Bueno-Hansen, Pascha. 2016. "Ending the Colonial/Modern Occupation of Indigenous Women's Bodies in Guatemala and Perú." *The Feminist Wire*, May 10. http://www.thefeministwire.com/2016/05/ending-occupation/.

Copelon, Rhonda. 2011. "Toward Accountability for Violence against Women in War: Progress and Challenges." In *Sexual Violence in Conflict Zones: From the Ancient World to the Era of Human Rights*, edited by Elizabeth D. Heinaman, 232–256. Philadelphia: University of Pennsylvania Press.

de la Cadena, Marisol. 1995. "Women Are More Indian: Gender and Ethnicity in a Community in Cuzco." In *Ethnicity, Markets and Migration in the Andes*, edited by Brooke Larson, Olivia Harris, and Enrique Tandeter, 329–348. Durham, NC: Duke University Press.

Francke, Marfil. 1990. "Género, clase y etnía: la trenza de la dominación." In *Tiempos de ira y amor: Nuevos actores para viejos problemas*, edited by Carlos Iván Degregori, Nelson Manrique, Gonzalo Portocarrero, and Antonio Zapata, 79–103. Lima: DESCO.

Harris, Angela P. 1990. "Race and Essentialism in Feminist Legal Theory." *Stanford Law Review* 42, no. 3: 581–616.

Instituto de Defensa Legal. 2010. *Protocolo para la investigación de casos de violación sexual en el conflicto armado interno.* Lima: Instituto de Defensa Legal.

Lugones, Maria. 2007. "Heterosexualism and the Colonial/Modern Gender System." *Hypatia* 22, no. 1: 186–209.

Martinez Salazar, Elga. 2012. *Global Coloniality of Power in Guatemala: Racism, Genocide, Citizenship.* Lanham, MD: Lexington Books.

Mendoza, Breny. 2016. "Coloniality of Gender and Power: From Postcoloniality to Decoloniality." In *The Oxford Handbook of Feminist Theory*, edited by Lisa Disch and Mary Hawkesworth, 100–121. Oxford: Oxford University Press.

Mignolo, Walter. 2011. *The Darker Side of Western Modernity: Global Futures, Decolonial Options.* Durham, NC: Duke University Press.

Mignolo, Walter, and Freya Schiwy. 2003. "Double Translation: Transculturation and the Colonial Difference." In *Translations and Ethnography: The Anthropological Challenge of Intercultural Understanding*, edited by Tullio Maranhãs and Bernard Streck, 3–29. Tucson: University of Arizona Press.

Peruvian Truth and Reconciliation Commission. 2003. *Final Report.* Lima: Truth and Reconciliation Commission.

Peruvian Truth and Reconciliation Commission Juridical Unit. 2003. *Violencia sexual en Huancavelica: Las bases militares de Manta y Vilca*. Lima: Peruvian Truth and Reconciliation Commission.

Ponzanesi, Sandra. 2014. *Gender, Globalization and Violence: Postcolonial Conflict Zones*. New York: Routledge.

Quijano, Aníbal. 2000. "Coloniality of Power, Eurocentrism, and Latin America." *Napantla: Views from the South* 1, no. 3: 533–580.

Ruiz Bravo, Patricia, Eloy Neira, and José Luis Rosales. 2007. "El orden patronal y su subversion." In *Clases sociales en el Peru: Visions y trayectorias*, edited by Orlando Plaza, 259–282. Lima: PUCP, CISEPA.

Sjoberg, Laura. 2013. *Gendering Global Conflict: Toward a Feminist Theory of War*. New York: Columbia University Press.

Theidon, Kimberly. 2013. *Intimate Enemies*. Philadelphia: Pennsylvania University Press.

Tlostanova, M. V., and Walter Mignolo. 2012. *Learning to Unlearn: Decolonial Reflections from Eurasia and the Americas*. Columbus: Ohio State University Press.

Wood, Elisabeth Jean. 2008. "Sexual Violence during War: Toward an Understanding of Variation." In *Order, Conflict and Violence*, edited by Stathis N. Kalyvus, Ian Shapiro, and Tarek Masoud, 321–351. Cambridge: Cambridge University Press.

CHAPTER 36

....

GENDER AND GOVERNANCE IN POST-CONFLICT AND DEMOCRATIZING SETTINGS

....

LISA KINDERVATER AND SHEILA MEINTJES

THIS chapter focuses on women and post-conflict governance, in effect the first pillar of the United Nations Security Council resolution 1325, with particular emphasis on women's experiences of political participation and representation in post-conflict settings. It explains that although transitions to peace and democracy provide unique opportunities for women to gain access to governing processes and influence gender-equality policy outcomes, this window does not remain open for long. Comparative political studies analysis has demonstrated that women can make significant economic, political, and sociocultural gains during transitions to peace and democracy, but that many of these gains tend to be lost when competitive electoral politics resume (Meintjes 2002). Drawing mainly on examples from sub-Saharan Africa, this chapter identifies the primary mechanisms behind this type of democratic reversal.

Women's political participation and representation in long-term post-conflict governance are hindered by a number of factors. These factors have much in common with those that render states fragile or weak, and include institutional constraints; historical political conditions; donor-driven agendas and state-building packages; prevailing cultural norms; and the nature of the women's movement and civil society more generally. The chapter explores the conditions under which women's movements and policy agencies sustain their activism and influence after the transition to peace and democracy. For those few cases where organized women have been able to sustain representational gains won in transition, a similar set of minimal conditions appear to be present.

Success comes with constituency building, the formation of alliances between parliamentarians (or other legislative) and advocacy bodies outside parliament, and inside, between gender advocacy parliamentarians and influential and sympathetic male politicians and bureaucrats (Waylen 2007). In many respects, these processes are short-lived, and while laws and policies may have been put in place, they tend to remain as monuments to active agency, rather than reflecting ongoing alliances. While arguments for more women's representation in decision-making are often made—whether for more women at the peace table or in leadership roles in politics—simply adding women does not ensure that they will represent a constituency of women, or promote women's interests. Thus, the post-Beijing Plan of Action, which promoted gender mainstreaming as a means to transform male-centered power, needs to be critically revisited.

Advances in women's rights in sub-Saharan Africa have been, in many respects, the most far-reaching of post-conflict states (Tripp et al. 2009; Tripp 2015). Despite the tremendous suffering brought on by war and armed conflict, prolonged conflict disrupts gender relations and provides opportunities for those relations to be reshaped (see Justino, Chapter 6 in this volume). Several authors in this *Handbook* suggest that the timing of the end of conflict is crucial for strategic action, as negotiations for peace and new constitutional dispensations present opportunities for more inclusive processes(see Bell, Chapter 32 in this volume). Moreover, organized women have had significant political resources and leverage due to their active role in the conflict, demanding peace and a place at the peacemaking table (see Tripp, Chapter 33 in this volume). These organized formations have often received support from international and regional organizations. Organized women may also have an advantage when traditional political actors, whether political parties or particular members of the political elite, are forced to rely on this constituency for votes. At the same time, women may be afforded greater legitimacy precisely because of their conventional treatment as outsiders and their exclusion from the patronage and crony relations that led to the conflict in the first place. In the aftermath of the genocide in Rwanda, for example, more than any other type of local organization, women's organizations had the greatest political space to advocate for their rights because the government typically viewed them as apolitical (Burnet 2008). Perhaps more than anything else, struggles for rights during conflict or in authoritarian situations produce politically experienced women capable of running for political office.

Many of the activists in transitional situations are part of movements that transform into political parties, where they participate in constitutional processes and later are part of processes drawing up new legislative programs (see McWilliams and Kilmurray, Chapter 42 in this volume). Often it is these women politicians who promote gender policy and the development of more gender-responsive or women-friendly institutions devoted to implementing a "woman's agenda" in the state (Geisler 2004; Tripp et al. 2009). In South Africa it was the combination of women activists in social movements and civil society, students, and exiled South Africans who brought a new discourse of feminism into the framework of government policy that influenced the gender dynamics of the new democratic state (Seidman 1999). Women who challenge traditional gender roles during war or revolution are likely to spearhead feminist struggles in the new regime. These women represent a large pool of experienced activists and potential candidates, and they are part of an established network that includes both national and international political allies (Viterna and Fallon 2008).

But what happens once the peace settlement is signed, a new negotiated constitution is in place, and the transitional government has been replaced by an elected one? What form does the "new" state take? And what effects do the new institutional arrangements have on the possibilities for gender equality? How are gender equality institutions integrated into governments? In other words, how does governance—the traditions and institutions of effecting power and authority—integrate gender equality, gender equity, and gender justice? How do the formal structures of engendering the state promote gender equality or protect the gender equality won?

LOSING GROUND: THE TROUBLE WITH CONSOLIDATION

Institutional constraints

Transitional processes offer opportunities for building states and institutions that are more responsive and accountable to women. However, in post-conflict contexts, women who mobilized for peace and democracy are often largely excluded from transitional negotiations for peace and a new political settlement. This has certainly been the case in Sierra Leone and Liberia, where it was women who made up the majority of peace activists. In spite of their exclusion from negotiated settlements, women in transitional democracies have often been successful in influencing governance reform "from without" and have been able to win formal inclusion in new constitutions, as well as access to governing institutions. Unfortunately, "technical" reforms are rarely matched with political reforms that reallocate resources and challenge gender hierarchies. Thus, rather than gender ministries and quotas resulting in more gender-sensitive policies, they tend to be filled with socially conservative women or women co-opted by party patronage structures. While instruments such as quotas have been seen as a necessary means to further the presence of women in politics and policy agendas, they are susceptible to manipulation and party patronage, and can yield "token women," whereby wives and relatives of traditional male power holders occupy these seats (Rai 2003). Critical attention must therefore be paid to the state's motivations for adopting such instruments.

In Uganda, reserve seats are used to benefit the ruling elite, and through a system of patronage, women in top positions are kept silent on women's issues; they must serve the regime or be penalized (Tamale 1999). In Rwanda's post-genocide political system, women parliamentarians have been present in remarkable numbers. At around 64 percent, the percentage of women in Rwanda's Chamber of Deputies is the highest in the world. However, it is very difficult to discuss substantive representation (women's, men's, or otherwise) in an authoritarian context, given Rwanda's slide in this direction (see Buss and Ali, Chapter 44 in this volume). Longman (2006) argues that as the government has become more authoritarian, so debate has been severely restricted, and parliament increasingly functions to legitimize government policies through the appearance of democratic procedure. He contends that women are *invited* into the National Assembly because they are not perceived as a threat. Because of women's high numbers, women-friendly legislation may be easier to adopt, but only when it supports the government's agenda. Moreover, women's rights are largely inhibited under a regime that generally refuses to recognize human rights.

In addition to the problem of "token women," another unintended outcome of institutional mechanisms for the advancement of women is the demobilization of women activists and decreased male support as a result of women's ostensible inclusion in new governing structures. In South Africa, partly because of the governing party's elite bias, "women's politics in the democratic period has been reduced to the strategy of proportional quotas for women in government" (Hassim 2006, 260). Such measures can also be problematic when they are perceived as gender equality *outcomes* in and of themselves. Rather than being viewed as an instrument for achieving greater gender equality, they are held up as evidence of having already achieved gender equality. Similarly, the presence of a few highly visible women in power is often problematic. The symbolic power of Ellen Johnson Sirleaf's presidency is palpable, though paradoxical. Though having a female in the country's highest office sends a message to girls and women that they, too, can aspire to and hold elected office, antifeminists use Johnson Sirleaf's presidency to claim (absurdly, of course) that gender inequality in Liberia has been overcome (Kindervater 2017). Perhaps more problematic, some opponents of the President and the ruling party claim the President has "failed," which has somehow become generalized to women as having failed, leading too many to claim that they will never again vote for a woman.

Many of the explanations for the ineffectiveness of women's policy agencies are linked to the lack of central government commitment and capacity. Although national machineries to advance the status of women have been established in sub-Saharan Africa since World Conferences on Women in Nairobi (1985) and Beijing (1994), these agencies are often tasked with greater roles and responsibilities in post-conflict settings (Geisler 2004). However, they remain underfunded, and while ministries in African governments generally are chronically under-resourced, spending decisions remain in the hands of leading male politicians. The low priority given to women's specific needs and interests in societies facing post-conflict reconstruction means little redistribution of resources into the developmental needs of women—health, education, and community development seem less important than getting the economy on track. The creation of women's ministries to monitor gender-equality advancement becomes a means for government to point to commitment, yet at the same time sideline women's issues (Kwesiga 2003; Rai 2003). While gender desks and focal points may be established in many ministries, the lowly position of the femocrats means they have no authority to intervene in policymaking. Budgetary allocations are made on the basis of national priorities that do not single out gender-equality outcomes.

Thus femocrats continue to be denied access to planning and policymaking processes, and there remains significant resistance to the implementation of gender-sensitive policy. Moreover, gender ministries tend to have too broad or poorly defined mandates, are often badly coordinated, and suffer from a lack of information, as well as weak monitoring and evaluation mechanisms (Rai 2003). These ministries rarely have the jurisdiction to integrate objectives into other departments, which lack incentives to implement and comply with gender policies. Institutionalized male bias manifests in other ways throughout the state and bureaucracy. Women customarily occupy the lowest paid and least influential positions; they may not receive the same skills-building opportunities as male counterparts; and they often face discrimination and sexual harassment from male colleagues (Bauer and Britton 2006).

Political parties and patronage

While post-conflict settlements require a degree of compromise and are often followed by processes of reckoning with the excesses of war, governance in the post-transition period tends to support, at least initially, a return to political party contestation for state power. Political parties thus play a central role in establishing modes of govern-ance, including who should run for political office and who should be appointed to the bureaucracy. Political parties remain the primary gatekeepers for all political can-didates. Parties control candidate selection and the appointment to decision-making roles in party and government. Political aspirants from a number of the major politi-cal parties in Liberia complain that they receive little support from their parties. There were Temporary Special Measures in place in 2005, in the "Guidelines Relating to the Registration of Political Parties and Independent Candidates" that stated each party "shall ensure" that 30 percent of its candidates be women (Section 15.2). Although the data from 2005 is not publicly available, anecdotal evidence from interviews suggests that only a few parties met the threshold (Kindervater 2017). The "Act to Amend Certain Provisions of the 1986 election Law" (Republic of Liberia 2014) included amendments to Section 4.5 of the New Elections Law. Specifically, the added subsections 1b and 1c state that a coalition or party "should *endeavour* to ensure" it has no less than 30% of either gender on its candidate lists and within its leadership. Clearly the language is such that the National Elections Commission has no practical or legal recourse to force parties to comply so it is little wonder that only one of the 24 registered parties in 2017 met the 30% threshold (National Elections Commission 2017). Despite having a female presi-dent, the percentage of women in Liberia's Senate and House of Representatives remains incredibly low—in no small part because of the party system (Kindervater 2017).

The nature of political competition and the electoral system have a significant impact on women's political participation and leadership. In response to local, national, and international demands and struggles for gender justice and gender rights since the 1990s, post-conflict states have implemented gender mainstreaming. The post-Beijing landscape has led political actors, at least putatively, to promote the adoption of party quotas. However, this has been instrumentalized in ways that have mainly benefited women political elites. Even then, those women politicians remain hostage to mascu-linist political patronage systems and elite politics. While party contestation is at the heart of electoral systems, a key factor in post-conflict countries is that in the transition period, ideology plays less of a role than the competition for power and authority. This promotes a highly personalized form of politics, where party patronage plays a leading role in determining who becomes a political candidate.

Moreover, women candidates seldom receive the same support from voters as men do. Indeed, even women voters tend to vote for men at the polls. What this means is that women are dependent upon political parties for entry into politics. Political parties tend to recruit women known to be compliant to the political elite. Although proportional representation systems are more supportive of women's representation, in these systems women are dependent upon the commitment of the political parties to gender equity in placing women on the lists (Meintjes and Simons 2002). There is little evidence to suggest that political parties in post-conflict states are committed to gender equity.

In African contexts, as well as in many political systems, candidates have to fund their own campaigns. Women are less able to garner sufficient funds to wage their electoral campaigns because they lack sources of patronage and find it more difficult to build constituencies outside of the party. It is difficult for women to become candidates for office in their own right. In situations where political parties recognize the importance of women voters, and women's and youth wings have formed to mobilize support, they tend to have a symbolic role. They are used to build support among *women*, but have little actual power or influence. Indeed, the role of political parties is in some respects to demobilize and depoliticize women's independent activism by appropriating their agendas. In contexts where there is well-organized and regular cooperation with "society-based feminists," there is often a long-term challenge for governments to meet gender needs and interests. Equally, though, women officeholders' professional and political constraints—namely the party system—often thwart collaboration (Hassim 2003, 2006).

Historical political conditions

Perhaps the most obvious problem with a sustained, democratic peace following conflict is that the instigators and perpetrators of war are so often part of the negotiated settlement and the new political dispensation (see Bell, Chapter 32, and Hadzimesic, Chapter 39, in this volume). Warlords and mercenaries become ministers and senators. Thus the integration of women into politics remains dependent upon the patronage of these political and military elites.

Maintaining associational autonomy has thus been particularly difficult where organized women are perceived as a threat to the state. Despite the critical roles women played in struggles for independence, nationalist discourse has frequently sidelined gender issues (Ní Aoláin, Haynes, and Cahn 2011). Generally, organized women tended to make significant gains because their political support was necessary for the newly elected ruling party to consolidate power, but women's organizations and associations faced a backlash in the aftermath. Numerous strategies were employed to control these organizations. The creation or exacerbation of tensions among civil society organizations by the gender machinery appropriating campaigns and treating them as short-term events was one effect. Another was through establishing women's wings in political parties. A further strategy was to demobilize any form of "movement" politics by mandating registration in state-run umbrella organizations. Co-option, particularly through state-centered clientelism and patronage networks, was particularly effective in demobilizing civil society.

In many African countries, for example, post-independence and post-conflict women's politics has been characterized by elite women serving the aspirations of their own families and political parties. This particular phenomenon has been referred to as the "first lady syndrome." First ladies, high-ranking military officers, and a small group of elite women (who derived their authority from their husbands) commandeered the national machinery, which was used to integrate women into development projects and promote women's traditional roles (Geisler 2004; Mama 2005). The consequence of this tendency has been to hold back a transformative feminist participation in national politics. Where feminists have ventured to stand for office, there has been a backlash against them by both women and men politicians and a real cynicism toward the establishment of state gender machinery. The gender machinery has been seen as yet another institution to be used by the political elite. Amina Mama captures the instrumentalism embedded in the gender machinery: "eight years of femocracy . . . generated promises to appoint token women, and made the parading of expensively attired wives into a political tradition" (Mama 1995, 56). Even in an ostensibly democratic context such as South Africa, it has been suggested that the African National Congress Women's League ceased to be a progressive institution with the election of Winnie Mandela, becoming "as moribund and ineffectual as most post-independence women's party organizations have become elsewhere" (Geisler 2004, 86).

Donor-driven agendas and state-building packages

After the Nairobi UN World Women's Conference in 1985, and especially since the Beijing conference in 1995, gender mainstreaming has been incorporated into the agenda of many international organizations that have pressured states to establish gender-equity policies. Many indebted states established gender ministries and other gender-equality instruments as part of loan conditionality with bilateral donors and the International Monetary Fund (IMF) and the World Bank. However, evidence has shown that while governments had developed legislative and public policies, these made little substantive improvement or change to women's lives. If anything, they have led to further impoverishment (Dennis and Zuckerman 2006). Because national machineries and women's advocacy organizations are chronically under-resourced, they are dependent on donor funding and are susceptible to trends in international development and humanitarian interventions. Although this point is relevant to most, if not all, countries in the Global South, regardless of transition politics, it is worth mentioning here because of its potentially demobilizing effect on feminist action. To be sure, the availability of donor funds for NGOs under structural adjustment policies (SAPs, beginning in the 1980s) and the World Bank's "good governance" agenda (1990s to the present) is partly responsible for the proliferation of civil society (including women's) organizations in the same period, though the important distinction between presence and influence must be kept in mind.

Donors in post-conflict settings have established development agendas that have taken two major turns. One, the Women in Development (WID) framework, largely ignores women's undervalued productive contributions and merely adds women to preconceived development plans that emphasize income-generating projects and micro-credit, particularly those related to women's traditional activities. Gains in gender equity tend to remain limited to women's reproductive roles. The other, Gender and Development (GAD), constitutes a shift in focus and offers a more relational approach in integrating a gender focus into all areas of policy and law. It also promotes the idea of "gender budgets" that mandate specific gender-equality outcomes in the national budget (Kabeer 1994). The former approach tends to dominate in post-conflict countries because rebuilding the economy and meeting basic needs are prioritized. Even where GAD approaches exist in post-conflict countries, there is often a lack of expertise to mainstream gender. States have had to rely on UN gender experts for assistance. This does not translate into long-term gender expertise.

The processes of post-conflict development and reconstruction have not necessarily extended transformative possibilities for women, particularly for those who do not have access to education, jobs, land, and other economic resources. Humanitarian aid during conflict tends to deal with refugee crises, and in the early transition focuses on immediate needs for food and shelter. Longer-term development aid from international organizations has come with different objectives, to rebuild states. The World Bank and multilateral state interventions have been more concerned with stabilizing the state system and have provided aid for reconstruction, rather than to promote social transformation.

International institutions including the World Bank have, however, adopted gender prescriptions within their funding models. But their focus has tended to be on short-term technical projects, driven by quantifiable targets, which do not probe their gendered effects. Good governance, the mantra of international aid conditionality, has thus had a limited impact on gender-equality outcomes. Donors have been influenced by this agenda as well, so that funding has increasingly also been geared toward short-term projects, and driven by quantifiable targets, meaning that broader strategic transformation goals often lack support. Moreover, the professionalization of NGOs—resulting from donor demands for complex reporting and accountability mechanisms—moves many organizations further away from the grassroots, reducing their influence on social change.

The lack of discursive and political space to address the root causes of women's subordination in these transitional contexts means that real transformation is constantly deferred. While gender machinery has been established in many post-conflict states, including in one-party states, the outcomes for gender equality and gender equity are limited. In Zimbabwe, for instance, despite some early progressive achievements in the 1980s following the end of the white supremacist regime of Ian Smith, the women's machinery failed to follow up on the legal reforms. Instead, the co-option of leading political activists into the power elite, with their lack of focus on women's needs and interests, saw a retreat from policy gains. The Women's Ministry, once a model for gender equity, fell "from prominent test case to obscurity in the space of the decade" (Geisler 2004, 118). In South Africa, in the 1990s, the machinery was designed to strengthen ties with women's organizations, but their demobilization meant that the role of the women's movement was reduced to nothing more than a development partner as the African National Congress (ANC) centralized power in the twenty-first century. Indeed, South Africa has jettisoned its broad-based gender institutions in the bureaucracy, the Offices on the Status of Women at national and provincial levels, which have successively been replaced by an ineffectual Ministry for Women, Children and Persons with Disability (2007–2014) and a Ministry of Women based in the Presidency from 2014, stringently criticized for its antifeminist rhetoric by feminist civil society organizations (Tugwana, Nsibande, Bollbach, and Msezane 2014).

Ideological conditions: Prevailing cultural norms and prohibitions

While formal institutions at least nominally embrace gender equality, customary law prevails over constitutional and common or civil law, and men continue to dominate in informal institutional arenas. In many post-conflict societies, deeply entrenched male biases often reassert images and standards of idealized femininity that prevent women from being politically active, from seeking public office, or from gaining public support. In many African contexts, even if women were active in the civil conflict, the post-transition context sees women still largely subordinate in the home and often prohibited from certain activities, such as speaking in public and traveling. Although women activists may attempt to redefine political roles for themselves, many reject them altogether as politics is often synonymous with corruption and violence, and signifies a realm culturally marked as masculine (Tripp et al. 2009).

So while the international norms and practices promoted by UN Women and other international organizations emphasize women's human rights, the rhetoric of gender equality and women's rights masks the active reassertion of patriarchal power and authority in many post-conflict regimes. When human rights discourses are not radicalized, they often fail to promote gender rights and equality. State-reinforced gender ideologies that emphasize women's social roles have not been effectively challenged. Indeed, in many post-conflict societies the maternal discourse of "mothers of the nation," which is often invoked by women themselves to gain entry into negotiations, can, in the long run, deter a more progressive discourse of social and gender transformation.

Much of the literature on women's political gains in post-conflict societies argues for real transformative politics to grow and sustain itself and for an ideology and practice grounded in feminist philosophy and consciousness-raising to ensure long-term gains.

Constructed as part of Western cultural imperialism, the terms "feminist" and "feminism" are much maligned and misunderstood in many post-conflict situations. Instead, a focus on women's empowerment has become the main trajectory of gender-policy processes. Yet while this has enabled a strong focus on women's needs and interests, it has tended to exclude a more relational gendered approach that would have allowed for a more critical perspective to question masculinist power. The problem is that "empowerment" is almost exclusively discussed as something given or bestowed on women, and it is almost always limited to economic empowerment.

The terms "gender," "gender equity," and "gender equality" also appear to be misunderstood and poorly communicated to those populations and groups from whom women's advocates are seeking support. For example, in Liberia, women's advocates frequently emphasize women's equality with men, and in the same breath state that women can, as a matter of fact, do *better* than men. Such beliefs, that women can and should do better than men, are built on essentialized assumptions of difference between men and women. Although the trope "women make peace, men make war" may provide organized women with some legitimacy to be included in transitional processes, these gendered ideologies pose significant barriers to long-term feminist success.

First, to present women *as a group* as being better leaders, more peace-loving, more honest, is essentialist and discriminates against men. Second, it is an adversarial position that may provoke men, rather than recruit them as allies in promoting the idea of gender equality and gender equity. And finally, it sets women up for failure because the standard is not for women to perform *as well as* men, but to perform *better than men*. If and when the performance of individual women in positions of authority falls below this standard, opponents use that as a justification to deny *all* women positions of authority.

The nature of the women's movement and "civil" society

Women's organizations have a number of intra-organizational problems related to lack of funding and qualified staff. Such problems are compounded during transitions, where there may be a significant loss of women leaders from civil society following the establishment of national machinery. In South Africa, the movement of key women activists into the state created a "vacuum of women activists," which had a profound effect on the capacity and direction of the women's movement and gender activism (Britton 2006; Hassim 2006). Elite bias and ethnic, religious, or other types of cleavages also threaten the strength and stability of women's organizations and movements (Tripp et al. 2009). Support networks are an integral variable affecting the consolidation of women's wartime gains, as women who organized as soldiers, in refugee camps, for national liberation, or for peace are often unable to sustain these linkages after the conflict is over. During the anti-apartheid struggle, for example, the women's movement in South Africa was a broad church, but in the years after the ANC victory, poor and rural women were increasingly unable to identify with the movement and its leadership. Further divisions became apparent between feminists in civil society and those in the state, showing that sustained cooperation between them is a long-term challenge (Bauer and Britton 2006).

Of course, civil society is not unified but fragmented and full of conservative actors that often hinder socially progressive action (Goetz and Hassim 2003). Constitutionally guaranteed equality can be overridden by culture and customary practice; for instance, opposition to access to governing institutions mediated by elites, as well as by family, community members, religious, and informal or customary authorities, hinders those who are not part of these networks, and even where they are, women may face stigma, harassment, or intimidation, and even physical violence. Thus, the state-building project needs to include the expansion of the state's jurisdiction over areas that have typically been viewed as being under the purview of tradition and culture, and thus under the authority of traditional leaders and customary law. The reification of "culture" and "tradition" is something that requires a substantial and sustained public critique in these contexts. At the same time, progressive women's organizations and women's movements need to be mobilized to ensure that the state itself acts in the interests of women.

CONCLUSION

Despite these cautionary remarks, and the observation that national gender machinery and gender mainstreaming in governance processes have been captured by party elites, these mechanisms have made some important gains for women in post-conflict societies. These include the adoption of women's budgets, targeting outcomes for women, women's freedom of choice in marriage, rights to bodily integrity, as well as substantive rights to inheritance, to land, and, in some countries, to social grants. None of these gains would have been possible without paper rights—constitutions, laws, and policies. But if we do not turn our attention to the pervasive patriarchal cultures and practices that dominate all over the globe, we will never transform gender power relations that subordinate and oppress women in many parts of the world. This is where feminist agendas for transformation should focus in post-conflict settlements. Interventions must involve leadership, negotiation, and decision-making training and support for women involved in peace-building and governance processes.

Although we have noted some of the problems with quotas and reserved seats for women, these may be highly effective when they operate in conjunction with other mechanisms, particularly a politically active, relatively autonomous women's movement. Although the extent to which numerical or descriptive representation translates into substantive representation is hotly debated, the high numbers of women in Rwanda's lower house, for example, is by no means a small or inconsequential feat. Thus, strengthening partnerships between grassroots women and politically elite women in government and the bureaucracy can bring ongoing policy benefits.

Globally, the structures of governance in the postwar settlements of the 1980s and 1990s have been the outcome of negotiations that saw countries forced into making democratic concessions. However, international norms tended to be adopted without real commitment, as a means for countries to acquire donor support. Instead, politics has acquired a strongly patrimonial form in which clientelism and patriarchal patronage has become dominant. In those contexts, the form and content of democratic politics become conservative rather than transformational. A key factor is the way that bureaucratic elites have themselves become significant actors in aggregating interests through processes of governance. These are highly gendered processes—dominated by androcentrisim.

In the aftermath of conflict or after years of dictatorship or authoritarian rule, it is the confluence of the material conditions—international, regional, and national (that is, the socioeconomic resources and the political conjuncture)—that determines the form of state and governance. The balance of political forces, the extent of state and popular power, militarization, the mobilization of civil society, including women and youth formations, and the positioning of religious bodies all shape the form of the new political and constitutional dispensation. Equally important, is not simply the power and authority wielded by different groups in the process of establishing a new political order, but the ideological perspectives of the different players. A problem in the aftermath of conflict has been how the political elites that are involved in negotiating new dispensations navigate their way toward creating institutions and frameworks that are able to withstand patronage and personal interests.

Constitutions are probably easier to make than the institutions established to ensure the implementation of their values. It is in this arena that technical expertise and political ideals come together. It matters who is writing the law and who is creating new institutions. It is intensely political, but it is also highly technical and bureaucratic. Thus the presence of women, especially those with a progressive, feminist agenda, is vital in promoting ideas that can be absorbed into the policy and practices of governance. It is at the intersection of government and civil society where these ideas are negotiated and translate into policies. This is a dynamic space, one that requires women's organizations and women's movements to constantly intercede and to make significant demands of both politicians and femocrats.

References

Bauer, Gretchen, and Hannah Britton. 2006. "Women in African Parliaments: A Continental Shift?" In *Women in African Parliaments*, edited by Gretchen Bauer and Hannah E. Britton, 1–30. Boulder, CO: Lynne Rienner.

Britton, Hannah. 2006. "South Africa: Mainstreaming Gender in a New Democracy." In *Women in African Parliaments*, edited by Gretchen Bauer and Hannah E. Britton, 59–84. Boulder, CO: Lynne Rienner.

Burnet, Jennie E. 2008. "Gender Balance and the Meanings of Women in Governance in Post-Genocide Rwanda." *African Affairs* 107, no. 428: 361–386.

Dennis, Suzanne, and Elaine Zuckerman. 2006. *Gender Guide to World Bank and IMF Policy-Based Lending*. Washington, DC: Gender Action.

Geisler, Gisela. 2004. *Women and the Remaking of Politics in Southern Africa: Negotiating Autonomy, Incorporation, and Representation.* Uppsala: Nordiska Afrikainstitutet.

Goetz, Anne Marie, and Shireen Hassim. 2003. "Introduction: Women in Power in Uganda and South Africa." In *No Shortcuts to Power: African Women in Politics and Policy Making,* edited by Anne Marie Goetz and Shireen Hassim, 1–28. London: Zed Books.

Hassim, Shireen. 2003. "Representation, Participation and Democratic Effectiveness: Feminist Challenges to Representative Democracy in South Africa." In *No Shortcuts to Power: African Women in Politics and Policy Making,* edited by Anne Marie Goetz and Shireen Hassim, 81–109. London: Zed Books.

Hassim, Shireen. 2006. *Women's Organizations and Democracy in South Africa: Contesting Authority.* Madison: University of Wisconsin Press.

Kabeer, Naila. 1994. *Reversed Realities: Gender Hierarchies in Development Thought.* London: Verso.

Kindervater, Lisa. 2017. "After a Critical Juncture and Before a Critical Mass: Women's Political Effectiveness in Post-Conflict Liberia." PhD diss., Wits University.

Kwesiga, Joyce. 2003. "The National Machinery for Gender Equality in Uganda: Institutionalized Gesture Politics?" In *Mainstreaming Gender, Democratizing the State? Institutional Mechanisms for the Advancement of Women,* edited by Shirin Rai, 203–221. Manchester: Manchester University Press.

Longman, Timothy. 2006. "Rwanda: Achieving Equality or Serving an Authoritarian State?" In *Women in African Parliaments,* edited by Gretchen Bauer and Hannah E. Britton, 133–150. Boulder, CO: Lynne Rienner.

Mama, Amina. 1995. "Feminism or Femocracy? State Feminism and Democratization in Nigeria." *Africa Development* 20, no. 2: 37–58.

Mama, Amina. 2005. "Women Mobilised—Editorial." *Feminist Africa,* no. 4. http://agi.ac.za/journal/feminist-africa-issue-4-2005-women-mobilised.

Meintjes, Sheila. 2002. "War and Post-War Shifts in Gender Relations." In *The Aftermath: Women in Post-Conflict Transformation,* edited by Sheila Meintjes, Anu Pillay, and Meredeth Turshen, 63–77. London: Zed Books.

Meintjes, Sheila, and Mary Simons. 2002. "Why Electoral Systems Matter to Women." In *One Woman, One Vote: The Gender Politics of South African Elections,* edited by Glenda Fick, Sheila Meintjes, Mary Simons, 162–175. Johannesburg: Electoral Institute of Southern Africa.

National Elections Commission. 2005. *Guidelines Relating to the Registration of Political Parties and Independent Candidates.* Monrovia: Republic of Liberia. http://www.necliberia.org/content/legaldocs/guidelinesandreg/regofpoliticalparties.pdf.

National Elections Commission. 2017. *Final Candidate Listing.* Monrovia: Liberia. http://www.necliberia.org/pg_img/Final%20Candidates%20listing.pdf.

Ní Aoláin, Fionnuala, Haynes, Dina Francesca, and Naomi Cahn. 2011. *On the Frontlines: Gender, War, and the Post-Conflict Process.* Oxford: Oxford University Press.

Rai, Shirin. 2003. "Institutional Mechanisms for the Advancement of Women: Mainstreaming Gender, Democratizing the State?" In *Mainstreaming Gender, Democratizing the State? Institutional Mechanisms for the Advancement of Women,* edited by Shirin Rai, 15–39. Manchester: Manchester University Press.

Republic of Liberia. 2014. "An Act to Amend Certain Provisions of the 1986 Elections Law." [New Elections Law]. Monrovia: Liberia. http://www.necliberia.org/doc_download/New%20Elections%20law%20Amendments.pdf.

Seidman, Gay. 1999. "Gendered Citizenship: South Africa's Democratic Transition and the Construction of a Gendered State." *Gender and Society* 13, no. 3: 287–307.

Tamale, Sylvia. 1999. *When Hens Begin to Crow: Gender and Parliamentary Politics in Uganda.* Boulder, CO: Westview Press.

Tripp, Aili Mari. 2015. *Women and Power in Post-Conflict Africa.* Cambridge: Cambridge Studies in Gender and Politics.

Tripp, Aili Mari, Isabel Casimiro, Joyce Kwesiga, and Alice Mungwa. 2009. *African Women's Movements: Transforming Political Landscapes.* Cambridge: Cambridge University Press.

Tugwana, Jabu, Nondumiso Nsibande, Katie Bollbach, and Nandi Msezane, 2014. "Shabangu Sprouts Antifeminist Rhetoric." *BDLive*, November 11. http://www.bdlive.co.za/opinion/2014/11/11/shabangu-spouts-antifeminist-rhetoric.

Viterna, Jocelyn, and Kathleen Fallon. 2008. "Democratization, Women's Movements, and Gender-Equitable States: A Framework for Comparison." *American Sociological Review* 73, no. 4: 668–689.

Waylen, Georgina. 2007. "Women's Mobilization and Gender Outcomes in Transitions to Democracy: The Case of South Africa." *Comparative Political Studies* 40, no. 5: 521–546.

PART V

CASE STUDIES

CHAPTER 37

....

WHO DEFINES THE
RED LINES?

*The Prospects for Safeguarding Women's Rights and
Securing Their Future in Post-Transition Afghanistan*

....

SARI KOUVO AND COREY LEVINE

> To be honest: We Afghan women are just a little football for our govern-
> ment and the international community.[1]

DURING the 2004 presidential election, the Kandahar provincial *Ulema*, a religious
advisory body composed of "learned men" from the community,[2] issued a *fatwah*.[3] In it,
the *Ulema* stated that it was the religious duty of the men of Kandahar province, which is
one of the more conservative provinces in the country, to let their wives, daughters, and
mothers vote.

The election took place in an atmosphere of optimism. Women all over the country
lined up to exercise their constitutional right to vote, many of them for the first time in
their lives. The elections were far from perfect, but after three decades of war, in one of
the world's poorest countries, nobody expected perfect. There was a sense that this was
the beginning of change for the country, especially for women, who had a few months
before been guaranteed equality in Afghanistan's new Constitution.[4]

Fast forward to 2012. Just a few days before International Women's Day on March 8,
the national *Ulema* issued a statement that focused on reconciliation with the Taliban.
The statement also provided the *Ulema*'s vision for women's rights. While affirming such
issues as women's rights to inheritance, it also claimed that "men are fundamental and
women are secondary" and condoned the "harassment and beating" of women as long
as there is a "Shariah-compliant reason" (Afghanistan Analysis 2012).[5]

Such a statement from the national *Ulema* was not surprising. It is known for its conservative stance. What was surprising, however, was that the statement was endorsed

by then President Karzai, who came out publicly in support of the opinions expressed by the national *Ulema*. The statement was further promoted through its appearance on the president's official website.[6] There was also a lack of publicly expressed outrage from the international community. The US Embassy, the European Union, the United Nations, and Canada all issued statements congratulating Afghan women on International Women's Day, but none of the statements made any reference to the *Ulema* statement.

The *fatwah* by the Kandahar *Ulema* that encouraged women's active participation was not necessarily representative for either Afghanistan or Kandahar in 2004, but official Afghan discourse has changed since then, as has the international diplomatic responses to it. This begs the question: What happened in the intervening years to the groundwork that was previously laid toward Afghan women's rights?

Since the emergence of the Taliban movement and their rise to power in the mid-1990s, the situation of Afghan women has been a headline-making issue for the international media and a study in contrast for international policymakers. In the early days of the intervention, women's rights were viewed as an issue that demanded attention and action, as there was broad recognition—from Afghans and the international community alike—that change from the Taliban years was needed.

From the enthusiasm of the early years, there was the slow evolution of understanding that "saving Afghan women" was not such an easy task, especially as the Afghan government and the international community looked to reconciliation with the Taliban, and women's rights were quietly shelved from fiscal priorities. As such, Afghanistan is a very instructive—albeit disheartening—case study for a handbook on gender and conflict.

In this chapter, we analyze the complex and contested role that women's rights have played, and continue to play, in the post–9/11 intervention in Afghanistan. While the rhetoric of "women's rights" has become a policy issue in Afghanistan that is not easily brushed away, the reality is much different. Yet, how Afghans and international actors view this, as well as what role Afghan women themselves have in defining what is relevant for them, varies.

The outline of this chapter is as follows: first, we provide an overview of some of the changes in the struggle for equality for Afghan women and girls subsequent to, and as a consequence of, the intervention. We then analyze how these newfound freedoms, as well as access to public space, are slipping away as conservative voices once again gain ascendency in the country, aided and abetted by the international community, which prioritizes "peace" over women's rights. In conclusion, we show how the women and girls of Afghanistan have ultimately been abandoned by the same forces that promised to "liberate" them.

It is important to point out, however, that Afghanistan is merely the latest in a long line of post-conflict countries in which women's rights have been traded away or pushed back during the "settling in" period as the geopolitical interests of stakeholders, both domestic and international, jockey for position. It serves as a useful reminder, not only of the necessity to hold fast to "red lines" in the struggle for equality, but also of the importance of ensuring that they are defined by the women and girls who have lived through, and been impacted by, the conflict.

THE UPS, THEN DOWNS, OF WOMEN'S RIGHTS FOLLOWING INTERNATIONAL ENGAGEMENT IN AFGHANISTAN POST–9/11

> When the international community came to Afghanistan in 2001, they were looking for women who fitted [sic] their idea of "liberated women." They did not engage with religiously educated or conservative women. This was a lost opportunity: women's rights were made foreign to Afghanistan.[7]

Afghanistan has endured war for more than thirty years now. The conflict has left no Afghan life untouched: massive human rights violations have been the norm throughout the different phases of the conflict, and Afghanistan's low human development index is, in large part, a consequence of the conflict.

The Taliban's rule in the 1990s was the most infamous in terms of its cruelty and brutal oppression of women and girls. However, discriminatory decrees comparable to those adopted by the Taliban, demanding that women cover and not go outside without a *mahram* (male guardian), were adopted by the Mujahedeen government that preceded it. Ultimately, the Taliban did not *invent* gender discrimination in Afghanistan; they merely brought customs that have existed for centuries to the fore as an integral part of their governance.

The US-led military campaign that toppled the Taliban was done as retaliation for the 9/11 terror attacks on US soil, but the campaign was also partly justified by linking it to the liberation of Afghan women. In the words of First Lady Laura Bush, the intervention was equivalent to "a fight for the rights and dignity of women" (Wilkens 2012). However, had the 9/11 terror attacks not occurred, it is unlikely that a forceful intervention—humanitarian, political, or military—would have been undertaken to protect Afghan women. After all, the Taliban brutally ruled the country for almost five years before the events of September 11, 2001, created the interest in intervention.

The international engagement in Afghanistan resulted in what has become one of the costliest stabilization and reconstruction exercises in history. At the height of the intervention, more than 130,000 foreign troops were stationed in the country as part of the NATO-led International Security Assistance Force (ISAF). By 2012, Afghanistan had also become the single largest recipient of aid in the world (Paris 2013).

According to a 2012 World Bank report, international civilian assistance to Afghanistan amounted to approximately six billion dollars a year, which represented nearly 40 percent of the country's gross domestic product (GDP). Integral to this assistance have been efforts to promote the rights, and improve the lives, of Afghan women and girls. Initiatives to "gender mainstream" development in the country have resulted in the re-drafting of laws, integrating gender components into development and aid policy frameworks, and highlighting the participation of women within Afghan structures and institutions and at international conferences where Afghanistan's future has been decided.

Some of the oft-cited successes of the intervention's focus on women's rights include items in the 2004 Constitution, which guarantees the equal rights of women and men, provides education for all, and sets a minimum quota for women in the Afghan parliament (Articles 22, 43, 83 and 84, respectively). There also has been a significant increase of women in public life. We now see women as educators, journalists, and civil servants, including appointments of female ministers, deputy ministers, heads of public commissions, and heads of departments. Public commitments to women continued with the 2004 ratification of the UN Convention on the Elimination of All Forms of Discrimination Against Women (CEDAW) without any reservations; the adoption of the National Action Plan for the Women of Afghanistan (NAPWA), the government's main vehicle for implementing policies and commitments to advance the status of women, which sets out in detail how this will be achieved through 2017; the emphasis on gender mainstreaming in the Afghanistan National Development Strategy; the adoption of the Elimination of Violence Against Women Law (EVAW law) by presidential decree in 2009, and the adoption of the National Action Plan (NAP) for UN Security Council resolution 1325 on Women, Peace and Security in 2015.

These formal advancements are significant, as they provide tools for Afghan women and women's rights defenders to lobby for social and political change. They also ensure that the Afghan government and international donors are forced to continue their attention to the situation of Afghan women and girls. However, these legal and policy developments do not necessarily constitute sustainable change. They are rather, as we have argued elsewhere, placeholders for change, offering well-intentioned hope without necessarily the ability to deliver on that hope (Kouvo and Levine 2016).

The Afghan government's "commitment" to women's rights has largely been a response to international demands. This does not mean that the Afghan government is "against" women's rights; rather, it means that women's rights are not its main priorities, and that the changes in laws, policies, and women's participation have been internationally driven. The Afghan government complied as long as the international community was seen as powerful and willing to provide funds or transfer power in exchange for compliance. Similarly, international donors have allowed themselves to be steered by what could be called "strategic naïveté" in their efforts to promote women's rights. Initiatives were designed with the idea that because the Taliban were now banished, promoting women's rights would be easy. There was little appreciation of how deeply rooted conservative and traditional ideas of women's and men's roles are in Afghan society.

Ultimately, both the Afghan government and its international partners failed to fundamentally alter the discriminatory attitudes and the oppression that women face in Afghanistan. Laws and policies have been adopted with little attention to whether

Afghan society was ready, or would even welcome, these changes. During the early years of the intervention, it was relatively easy to have laws drafted and formalized since there were no legislative processes in place; they were simply adopted by presidential decree. The process neither reflected a consensus opinion of Afghan society nor was supported by a functioning system of rule of law and state institutions. As such, there has been a growing tension between the progressive laws and policies that were adopted in the early days of the intervention and the norms and values of the more conservative elements of Afghan society, which can be seen in the Afghan Parliament's response to many of these laws and policies.

The EVAW law is a perfect example of this. In May 2013, attempts to have EVAW ratified by the Lower House of Parliament were thwarted by conservatives claiming that it was "un-Islamic."[8] An abolition of the law was only narrowly avoided, and the debate resulted in public demonstrations in Kabul against the EVAW law and against "democracy" (Kouvo and Roehrs 2013; Osman 2013). The EVAW debacle illustrates that laws are blunt tools for social change. When "progressive" laws are pushed in a society where there is no consensus about the norms underlying the legal text, there will be resistance. Thus, in a context like Afghanistan, new legislation can have a boomerang effect: resistance to the social changes being proposed through legal methods will end up adversely affecting the very population for whom the laws and policies are meant to benefit.

As a result, after more than a decade of intervention with concerted efforts on the part of the international community to improve the lot of the country's women and girls, Afghanistan remains a country where the barometers for gender equality and female social inclusion remain near the bottom: little has changed with regard to female literacy, health, or employment indicators. In other words, Afghan women have very little to show for the years of international engagement in their country.

Even worse is the boomerang effect. There has been a growing backlash against Afghan women's rights, indicating that the clock is turning back. As a result of the furor in Parliament over EVAW, then President Karzai backed away from his own signature, telling a group of women's rights activists that the law ran counter to Islam and they should stop campaigning for it (Sethna 2013). At the same time, the Afghanistan Independent Human Rights Commission showed an increase of 25 percent of *reported* cases of violence against women between 2012 and 2013 (Habib 2013). What these statistics indicate is a rise in Afghan women's willingness to report extreme cases of violence, though the extreme nature of the violence also exemplifies a society in flux.

There has been a significant increase in intimidation, threats, attacks, and assassinations on women who are active in public life. In the latter half of 2013, at least four policewomen were killed, targeted for being women working in the public domain (Rubin 2013); and two elected female representatives were attacked—one wounded and one killed—within a few months of each other in November 2014 and February 2015 (Amnesty International 2015). While the backlash is often directed at women's participation in public life, the brutal mob murder of a twenty-seven-year-old religious teacher, Farkhunda, in Kabul in March 2015 is a tragic illustration of how the backlash has inserted itself into everyday life in Afghanistan.

Backing this up is the Asia Foundation's annual "Survey of the Afghan People," which shows the impact of the backlash in terms of an overall trend toward more conservative thinking with regard to gender equality. For example, fewer people than in previous years agreed that women should have the right to work, decide for themselves whom to vote for, have equal representation in political leadership, or have equal opportunity in education (Shawe et al. 2013).

The survey also indicates that Afghans feel that the promises of the international community have turned out to be hollow and meaningless for the most part. In the following section, we examine more closely how Afghan women's rights began to be traded away in the process of the transition, as well as the search for peace and reconciliation in Afghanistan.

The Transition Process, or How Women's Rights Became Negotiable in the Elusive Search for Peace and "Security"

> There is no political will to build on initial achievements for women's rights.[9]

In 2011, a few months after it was revealed that the United States had entered into secret direct negotiations with the Taliban for a settlement to the ongoing conflict, then-US Secretary of State Hillary Clinton spoke about the possibility of negotiating with the Taliban. Quoting Richard Holbrooke, the former US Special Representative to Afghanistan and Pakistan for the Obama administration, Clinton noted, " 'In every war of this sort, there is always a window for people who want to come in from the cold . . . . If they are willing to accept the red lines and come in . . . there has to be a place for them.' And, that is the policy of the United States." (Coll 2011). She went on to identify those "red lines," observing that "the potential for sustainable peace will be subverted if women are silenced or marginalized . . . . They have an important role to play at the provincial and local levels if genuine reconciliation is going to take root" (Asia Society 2011).

Just a few years before the *Ulema* statement controversy, then President Karzai was also drawing "red lines" when it came to women's rights. Mirroring similar sentiments to those of Hillary Clinton, he assured women that "our constitutional achievements, our gains towards promotion and our gains in terms of Afghan women will not be hurt or blunted, but these gains will be even strengthened to bring peace to Afghanistan" (Nabizada 2011).

Yet, the "red lines" indicated by Clinton and Karzai have proven to be temporary, transmutable, and easily erased. As the insurgency began to heat up, so did the backlash against women's rights. This is nothing new—while truth may be the first casualty in war, gender equality is often the second. The backlash also neatly dovetailed with the repercussions that had been gaining momentum from the push—through policy and legal changes—toward women's rights and gender mainstreaming.

These two events together created a "perfect storm" for both sides—the international community and the Afghan government—to walk away from their stated intentions of the goal of gender equality. Although the rhetoric of women's rights remained in place, the real reason for intervention in the first place, the "War on Terror," began to take overt precedence. And as the insurgency grew, so did the international community's insistence on "Afghan ownership."

When the cracks began appearing in the "nation-building" aspects of the intervention, Afghan ownership provided a convenient "out" for the international community in terms of their commitments, especially with regard to the more troublesome aspects of the engagement, particularly with regard to women's rights.

This can be clearly seen in the muted response of the international community to Karzai's unqualified endorsement of the 2012 *Ulema* statement. As Afghan women's activists pointed out, the president's endorsement was a signal to the Taliban that women's rights could serve as a bargaining chip in any future peace talks. They also viewed the lack of a strong public reaction by the international community as an indication that the international community was unlikely to kick up a fuss as the so-called red lines of women's rights became more lines drawn in the sand—easily erased in the ever-changing tide of global geopolitics, as illustrated by the structures and institutions of the official peace process.

The High Peace Council (or should it be known as the "War Council"?)

The Consultative Peace *Jirga* (assembly), which took place in July 2010, laid out the framework for a peace process, including the establishment of the High Peace Council (HPC), the body responsible for providing overall "political and strategic leadership" to the reconciliation process. The final number of women at the *jirga* was just over 20 percent of approximately 1,600 participants. However, it was only after months of lobbying that women were granted these seats. Women's rights activists claimed that they had been deliberately excluded from the *jirga* because they were seen to be too outspoken about women's rights, and at the assembly itself very few women were given the opportunity to speak (Reid 2010). In fact, the final resolution coming out of the assembly did not provide for any guarantees for women's continued participation in the implementing bodies of the peace process.

When Karzai unveiled his seventy-member High Peace Council later that year, only ten of the appointees were women. Although some of them have a women's rights background, they have been unable to have an impact on the Council.

The official reconciliation tool, the Afghanistan Peace and Reconciliation Program (APRP), did not address how the program would deliver a peace dividend for women based on their gender. Rather, women were seen to benefit simply because their husbands, fathers, or other male family members benefited from the program.

Although the HPC and other official organs of the peace process have been marginalized in the broader political arena toward ending the conflict, serving more as forums for discussions than platforms for negotiations, there are still areas of the official process that can have a deleterious effect on women's rights. One of the strategies currently used to reintegrate former combatants under the APRP has been to include them in the Afghan Local Police (ALP). This community police initiative sounds good on paper: an initiative that will allow Afghans themselves to protect their communities against insurgents. The reality is, however, much more complex. Because of a lack of vetting and accountability mechanisms, the ALP has, in many communities, become a program that provides thugs beholden to the local strongman with weapons and guns. Afghan women activists claim that ALP commanders have been responsible for rape and other acts of gender-based violence (Levine 2011).[10] The uniforms provide the ALP with government legitimacy and enable them to act with a fair bit of impunity.

However, the High Peace Council and the APRP are only the "poster boys" for reconciliation. The real work is being done behind the scenes by senior Afghan and international diplomats—and by the parties positioning themselves, with their negotiables and non-negotiables, in policy debates and the media, none of which has included women. A 2014 study that tracked twenty-three known peace talks between the Taliban, the Afghan government, and the international community since 2005 found that in talks between the Taliban and the Afghan government women were present on only two occasions, and in talks with the international community, not one Afghan woman had been involved. (Oxfam 2014). Although Afghanistan's current president, Ashraf Ghani, promised to include women in peace talks, he has qualified his statements, saying he will only "bother" women to participate at "the right time," which suggests that their involvement in peace talks are ultimately irrelevant to achieving a settlement with the Taliban (Human Rights Watch 2016).

Although women's groups continue to demand that peace talks include female participants in the talks, as well as a clear commitment to women's rights by all parties, the reality on the ground is that these rights are slowly being dismantled piece by piece. And as illustrated above, as the transition process has moved forward, it has become obvious that despite, or perhaps because of, the international community's "best intentions" in the early years of the intervention, women's rights now have taken on a symbolic role, rather than a representation of any meaningful change in the country.

CONCLUSION

We do not oppose reconciliation, but we do not tolerate deals which ignore the Constitution, the value of human rights, and women's achievements.[11]

The international community used women's rights to help justify its presence in Afghanistan, but as donors exit the country, claiming that their work is done, Afghan women should not have to worry that the promises made to them will be negotiated away. Although Western diplomats have tried to put forth arguments suggesting that the Taliban have altered their position on women's rights, there is little real evidence of this. Instead, members of the Taliban continue to attack girls' schools and kill women working in the public arena. Most alarming is not that the Taliban continues to be misogynistic in their policies and brutal in their practices, but that the Afghan government has shown little interest in defending women's rights in their dealings with the Taliban. Yet for meaningful sustainable peace to happen, women must be included in every step of the process. Instead, over the past several years, the government has become a participant in a backlash against women's rights in which international reactions have been muted, as the story with the national *Ulema* at the beginning of this chapter illustrates. The Western diplomatic presence in Afghanistan chooses its battles, and women's rights is not an issue for which political capital is likely to be expended.

As the war has heated up in Afghanistan, we can see the change in rhetoric—away from the dulcet tones of promoting gender equality toward a more patronizing and antagonistic view of women's rights and their full participation in Afghan society.

The international intervention gave Afghan women the opportunity to expand their space, mostly through legislation and policy. But because laws are blunt tools for social change, they are not the most effective tools, and as a result can bring about a backlash, which Afghan women and girls have experienced firsthand. Added to this are the geopolitical dynamics of a male-centric world. This all but guaranteed that the protection of female rights and the push for gender equality would disappear once the international community came face to face with the realities of intervention and the "War on Terror."

As the country transitions into the "decade of transformation" (2015–2024), there is a risk that the baby of women's rights will be thrown out with the bathwater of international intervention now that NATO troops have (for the most part) pulled out and Western influence declines even further as aid priorities shift to other "hot spots." While there are still gains in women's rights that have yet to be eroded, time is running out for the women and girls of Afghanistan. The loud, clear, and consistent voices of female activists, Parliamentarians, and other female leaders are being lost to the winds of political and military disengagement. What is needed is visionary leadership on the part of political leaders, but that seems to be in short supply.

Although many Afghan women are calling for change, the picture of what that change looks like differs depending on the individual woman and her location within Afghan society—her family situation and how much support she has from the males within it, where she lives, what ethnic group she is from, her level of education, and her access to the "outside" world.

Given the current security climate, as well as the conservative, patriarchal nature of Afghan society, Afghan women face many challenges in determining, let alone articulating, what rights should be a fundamental and intrinsic part of their lives. Many Afghan women are also as deeply skeptical as their male counterparts regarding what they see as "Western-imported" norms and values, although most acknowledge the desire for improvement in the lives of women and girls. And, like other feminist movements around the world, Afghan women are divided regarding not only what kind of change there should be, but what road needs to be taken in order to get there.

The following can be considered a baseline for change on women's rights in other transition countries as determined by the lessons drawn from the case study of Afghanistan:

- Securing equality between women and men in national constitutions is a fundamental and necessary foundation for equality and rights struggles. Beyond formal equality, legal strategies for change must be carefully designed to take into account the local social, cultural, and political context. This does not mean that *any* cultural excuse should be accepted; rather, it means that there needs to be a *real* commitment to supporting women's own priorities and work toward rebuilding their society. How this translates on the ground can be as varied as working within Shariah law and traditional mechanisms of justice.
- Allow time for consultation, and for ideas to develop and process to settle. Change comes slowly. International interventions today are notorious for coming in with "guns blazing," setting up structures and institutions with time pressure and little consideration for realities on the ground. This strategy only works for appearances, as the international community will have pulled out before the house of cards that was built by their experts and with their funds comes tumbling down.
- For change to continue and to be sustainable, support and pressure needs to be even and not, as one Afghan women's rights activist called the international engagement, "seasonal." Ultimately, if Afghan women are to gain anything from twelve years of international intervention in their country, the pressure for their full partnership must continue, not only in the current peace and reconciliation process, but in all aspects of the slow and onerous road to rebuilding the country. It is the only way to help guarantee that women's current hard-won rights are not traded for the political opportunism and deal-making of a "rented peace." It is a lesson that the global community must learn to apply as its gaze turns to other conflict-ridden places so that the rhetoric of gender equality has the chance to become the reality of women's rights.

Notes

1. Author's interview of director, Afghan Women's NGO, 2012.
2. There are *ulemas* at all three levels of government—community, provincial, and national. Although an *ulema* is formally a nongovernmental organization, all members, whether local, provincial, or national, receive a government salary.
3. This, and other statements noted in this chapter, were made to the authors during on-site interviews.
4. The Constitution was adopted in 2004 by the *Constitutional Loya Jirga* after an extensive drafting process that included consultations with civil society and other elements of Afghan society, which produced local buy-in to the document.

5. It should be noted that there are inherent tensions in the Afghan Constitution between Shariah law (Article 3: *No law shall contravene the tenets and provisions of the holy religion of Islam in Afghanistan*) and international human rights law (Article 7: *The state shall observe the United Nations Charter, inter-state agreements, as well as international treaties to which Afghanistan has joined, and the Universal Declaration of Human Rights*).

6. As the National *Ulema* lacks its own website, the Karzai government publishes some of its statements. Some of the "Jihadi leaders" who are members of the national *Ulema* act as key, although unofficial, advisors to the president. They also overlap with the country's judiciary, which gives the *Ulema* an influential, quasi-governmental position with regard to Afghanistan's state institutions. Although the statement has no legal effect per se, in a deeply religious and conservative country with little rule of law and where challenging Islam is very dangerous, this kind of political posturing—especially when religion is involved—carries a significant amount of weight.

7. Author's interview of director, Afghan Women's NGO, 2012.

8. The law must be passed by Parliament in order to become binding law, even though it has already been signed by the president.

9. Author's interview of director, Afghan Women's NGO, 2012.

10. The most famous case is that of Lal Bibi, an eighteen-year-old girl who was raped and tortured by four ALP members in Kunduz province in 2012 (BBC 2012; Kouvo and Samandary 2014).

11. Soraya Sobrang, Afghanistan Independent Human Rights Commissioner for Women's Rights; as quoted in Levine (2011).

References

Afghanistan Analysis. 2012. "English Translation of Ulema's Declaration on Women." March 5. http://afghanistananalysis.wordpress.com/2012/03/04/english-translation-of-ulema-councils-declaration-about-women/.

Amnesty International. 2015. *Their Lives on the Line: Women Human Rights Defenders under Attack in Afghanistan.* London: Amnesty International.

Asia Society. 2011. "Clinton to Taliban: Dump al-Qaida or 'Face Consequences.'" February 18. http://asiasociety.org/policy-politics/strategic-challenges/us-asia/clinton-taliban-dump-al-qaida-or-face-consequences.

BBC. 2012. "Lal Bibi Rape: Afghan Policemen Sentenced to 16 Years." November 7. http://www.bbc.com/news/world-asia-20239567.

Coll, Steve. 2011. "U.S.-Taliban Talks." *The New Yorker*, February 28. http://www.newyorker.com/magazine/2011/02/28/u-s-taliban-talks.

Habib, Mina. 2013. "Human Rights Impetus 'Waning' in Afghanistan." *Institute for War and Peace Reporting.* December 10. http://iwpr.net/report-news/arr-issue-471.

Human Rights Watch. 2016. "Afghanistan: Include Women in New Peace Talks." January 4. https://www.hrw.org/news/2016/01/04/afghanistan-include-women-new-peace-talks.

Kouvo, Sari, and Corey Levine. 2016. "Law as a Placeholder for Change? Women's Rights and Realities in Afghanistan." In *The Public Law of Gender: From the Local to the Global*, edited by Kim Rubenstein and Katharine G. Young, 195–216. Cambridge: Cambridge University Press.

Kouvo, Sari, and Christine Roehrs. 2013. "On a Knife's Edge: The Looming Parliamentary Debate about the Elimination of Violence against Women Law." *Afghanistan Analysts Network.* May 16. http://www.afghanistan-analysts.org/

on-a-knifes-edge-the-looming-parliamentary-debate-about-the-elimination-of-violence-against-women-law.

Kouvo, Sari, and Wazhma Samandary. 2014. "A War with No End in Sight: The Backlashes Regarding Afghan Women's Rights." *Afghanistan Analysts Network*. February 17. http://www.afghanistan-analysts.org/a-war-with-no-end-in-sight-the-backlashes-regarding-afghan-womens-rights.

Levine, Corey. 2011. *"A Woman's Place Is at the Peace Table:" An Analysis of Women's Participation in the Afghan Peace Process*. Ottawa: Peacebuild.

Nabizada, Khushnood. 2011. "Women's Rights Will Never Be Sacrificed in Peace Talks: Karzai." *Khaama Press*, March 8. http://www.khaama.com/womens-rights-will-never-be-sacrificed-in-peace-talks-karzai.

Osman, Borhan. 2013. "The EVAW Law—an Evil Law? The Backlash at Kabul University." *Afghanistan Analysts Network*. May 26. https://www.afghanistan-analysts.org/the-evaw-law-an-evil-law-the-backlash-at-kabul-university/.

Oxfam. 2014. *Behind Closed Doors: The Risk of Denying Women a Voice in Determining Afghanistan's Future*. Oxford: Oxfam GB.

Paris, Roland. 2013. "Afghanistan: What Went Wrong?" *Perspectives on Politics* 11, no. 2: 538–548.

Reid, Rachel. 2010. *The "Ten-Dollar Talib" and Women's Rights: Afghan Women and the Risks of Reintegration and Reconciliation*. New York: Human Rights Watch.

Rubin, Alissa J. 2013. "Afghan Policewoman Is Killed, Fourth in Last Six Months." *New York Times*, December 5. http://www.nytimes.com/2013/12/06/world/asia/gunmen-kill-afghan-policewoman.html?_r=1&.

Sethna, Razeshta. 2013. "Afghan Women's Rights under Threats." *The Guardian*, June 20. http://www.guardian.co.uk/global-development/2013/jun/20/afghan-womens-rights-under-threat.

Shawe, Keith, Shahim Ahmad Kabuli, Shamim Sarabi, Palwasha Kakar, and Zach Warren. 2013. *Afghanistan in 2013: A Survey of the Afghan People*. Kabul: The Asia Foundation.

Wilkens, Ann. 2012. *Missing the Target: A Report on the Swedish Commitment to Women, Peace and Security in Afghanistan*. Stockholm: Kvinna till Kvinna, Operation 1325, and Swedish Committee for Afghanistan.

The World Bank. 2012. *Afghanistan in Transition: Looking Beyond 2014*, Vol. 1: *Overview*. Washington, DC: The World Bank.

CHAPTER 38

"THAT'S NOT MY DAUGHTER"

The Paradoxes of Documenting Jihadist Mass Rape in 1990s Algeria and Beyond

KARIMA BENNOUNE

> The violence that ripped Algeria apart during the entire decade of the
> 1990s . . . "authorized" rape "that expression of hate toward all women"
> which destroyed so many of them—mothers, young girls, children, in
> their very beings and in their relationships with others and the world.
> (Réseau Wassila 2005)

FEMINIST international lawyers have long sought to explain sexual abuse of women in conflict situations in the context of underlying gender subordination, which both promotes the abuses and discourages victims from reporting them.[1] They have also sought to relate such violations in conflict to "peacetime" violence against women, and to ongoing discrimination. However, international law and mainstream human rights practice have paid less attention to combating ideologies that promote and normalize such rape, to overcoming the social attitudes that permit it to go on in a collectively imposed silence, or to grappling with how international lawyers can circumvent that silence and document these abuses. While it is often difficult to prove crimes committed during conflict, rape remains one of the only international crimes for which victims are routinely blamed and judged by their own societies and families (see Theidon, Chapter 11, and Sellers, Chapter 16, in this volume). It is perhaps the only offense whose performance is understood to affect the honor of the victim herself.

Taken together, all of this means that much more attention must be paid to those many forgotten country situations in which virtually no accounting has been made for widespread rape committed during conflict due to such factors. International human rights lawyers must grapple with faults in how we document and investigate such abuse and the ways our methodology may compound this reality. This chapter offers a case study from Algeria toward those ends.

Between 1993 and 1997, during the first years of Algeria's "dark decade" (Bennoune 2013), 5,000 rapes of women by non-state fundamentalist[2] armed groups battling the Algerian state were officially reported. The actual figure is assumed by experts to be considerably higher. However, due *inter alia* to the shame that attaches to rape in Algeria, very few victims have spoken publicly about their experiences. Moreover (and in part as a result), virtually no documentary record of these crimes against humanity exists in English. Except for the efforts of some Algerian women's human rights defenders, and a few Algerian journalists, no one has documented this part of the 1990s atrocities. No major international human rights group ever published a single dedicated report in English on this topic.

This chapter aims to fill this lacuna in the Anglophone historical record, a particularly urgent task given that similar practices are today being used by jihadist groups from Nigeria to Iraq. Given the need to tackle past and current patterns of jihadist rape, the chapter also asks if international human rights law is helpful in resurfacing such atrocities in contexts where the topic itself is taboo, or if there are doctrinal and methodological difficulties in international human rights theory and practice that make it even more difficult to document such abuses, whose name cannot even be spoken.

Sexual Violence by Fundamentalist Armed Groups in 1990s Algeria: Reconstructing the Documentary Record

During the 1990s, Algeria was beset by the violence of fundamentalist armed groups that terrorized the civilian population in their effort to take power and impose their version of an "Islamic state." In so doing, the jihadists violated virtually every single norm of human rights law, international humanitarian law, and also of Islamic humanitarian law, and may have killed as many as 100,000 to 200,000 people. The UN Special Rapporteur on Violence Against Women asserted in January 1998 that the situation in Algeria then represented "the most violent conflict in the world."

The jihadists themselves made little effort to hide their crimes. The Algerian state responded with its own abuses, which included as many as 8,000 forced disappearances. Nevertheless, the atrocities of the armed jihadists constituted the bulk of the violence in the country during the "dark decade," and were distinct in the way they so often targeted women *as* women. In the words of the Coalition of Associations of Victims of the 1990s, which includes victims of both state and non-state actors, the 1990s was a period in which Algeria

experienced a bloody war fought by the Islamist armed groups against society which caused hundreds of thousands of victims. Unarmed citizens, who were not protected by the state, were the principal targets of assassinations, torture, disappearances, mass rapes and massacres. In its fight against terrorism, the state engaged in massive and indiscriminate repression of the population, including ... extrajudicial executions, torture and forced disappearances .... No investigations have ever been carried out to determine the fate of these disappeared persons, or those who were kidnapped by the Islamist armed groups.[3]

With regard to the mass rapes cited by the Coalition, women victims of those rapes who had been kidnapped by Algeria's armed fundamentalist groups during the "dark decade" were most often subsequently found dead. Those victims were, of course, never able to tell their stories. For other women, the ordeal—and their lives—continued, but sometimes the social silencing was almost as complete.

Those abducted women who survived their kidnappings by jihadists were considered *sabayas*, part of the spoils of war (see Gaca, Chapter 23, this volume), and were reduced to slaves—domestic and sexual. *Sabayas* were divided up like the rest of the spoils of war, with those considered the most attractive raped first by the commander of the armed group, and then passed on to other men. Such practices were no accident—but rather the result of an ordered and explicit strategy. The rapes were "systematic, planned and [explicitly] justified" (Rachda 2004, 13). For example, the Armed Islamic Group's commander Antar Zouabri was reported to have ordered his men to "capture the supporters of the tyrants in their villages, eradicate them .... *capture their women* and confiscate their belongings" (Collectif 95 Maghreb Egalité 1997, 57; italics added). All this was considered an "offering to God." Algeria's fundamentalists relied on an archaic practice largely unknown in Sunni Islam known as *zaouj el muta*, or temporary marriage, to justify the rapes. The victims became, however briefly and involuntarily, their wives, a practice meant to render their crimes licit and their rapes mere marital sex. As in the current praxis of Boko Haram and Islamic State (ISIS), forced marriage was imposed by 1990s Algerian jihadists as a kind of customary law, becoming the "juridico-religious" justification of mass rape. This line of argument was ultimately rejected by the mainstream of Algerian society in the 1990s. Indeed, one victims' rights activist, Cherifa Kheddar, notes that the rapes became a way of punishing the entire population for refusing the jihadists' version of Islamization. In her words, the jihadists' view was "you refused and you will pay for it in our attack on the honor of Algerian society through Algerian women."[4]

The documentary record of these events that does exist is largely found inside Algeria, and consists of some official statistics that have been made public, the work of Algerian women's human rights defenders, and journalistic accounts. I interviewed the Algerian journalist pseudonymed Salima Tlemcani at length about the rapes perpetrated by members of the fundamentalist armed groups. She had undertaken extensive research at the time and has classified the stages of these atrocities.

At the beginning of the 90s, it was not kidnappings, but fathers who "marry" their daughters to terrorists. They call them "moujahideen" (holy warriors). The women do the domestic work. They are submitted to sexual slavery. They have no right to say no. In the second phase, people did not let their daughters marry terrorists. So, they kidnapped girls. It was collective rape. When a girl gets pregnant, they kill her. The third level was rapes committed at the time of massacres. They rape on the spot and then they kill.[5]

Some women journalists, like Tlemcani, tried to chronicle these unthinkable stories. In January 1995, women's rights activist Zazi Sadou wrote on the front page of the Algerian newspaper *El Watan* about those (she estimated then in the hundreds) who were "kidnapped in a street, at a schoolhouse door . . . abducted in front of the their parents . . . held captive by terrorist armed groups to offer a 'warrior's comfort' to pseudo-moujahidines" (Sadou 1995). In her article, a seventeen-year-old pseudonymed Ouarda tells of being abducted off an Algiers street, threatened with a knife, driven far outside the capital, kept with more than a dozen other women, raped by multiple members of a jihadist armed group (despite her protestation that "God condemns this") to the point where she bled nearly continuously, subjected to domestic and sexual slavery, and forced to watch the killing of girls who tried to escape, until she was later rescued by watchful villagers when being moved from one camp to another. The Algerian journalist Amel Boumediene (1995) wrote at about the same time as Sadou of "The Martyrdom of Kheira," describing the kidnapping of a young woman who recited verses from the Qur'an during her captivity to cope with her ordeal, but was raped "in the name of God" nonetheless, repeatedly and by many armed men, and was forced to work all day (30–31). The women journalists like Sadou, Boumediene, and Tlemcani who recorded and publicized these testimonies risked their lives to do so.

Collectif 95, a group of prominent women's rights advocates from across the Maghreb who came together to prepare for the UN Fourth World Conference on Women, published a heavily documented report in 1999 suggesting that by then, 5,000 women had been subjected to the practice (Collectif 95 Maghreb Egalité 1999, 101). Salima Tlemcani told me in 2010 that she now believed "the number is much higher" (Bennoune, 2013, 139). The Rachda Association, after citing figures including an official claim of 2,000 such rapes, and a figure of 8,000 put forward by groups of victims of terrorism, concluded that "what is certain is that we are talking about a phenomenon about which it is extremely difficult to be precise because of the reticence of officials to provide information and the refusal or the fear of victims and their families to openly declare rape" (Rachda 2004, 35). Taken together, these reports suggest that at least 8,000 women, and perhaps as many as 10,000—or even many more—may have been raped by the Algerian fundamentalist armed groups in just a few years.

The psychologist Cherifa Bouatta, who has long worked with women victims of fundamentalist violence in Algeria, compares these sexual assaults in her country to the mass rapes in the armed conflict in Bosnia in the same time frame, and recounts the testimony of an eighteen-year-old named Lila:

> They arrived, I don't know how many there were, whoever had money they took his money, whoever had daughters, they took his daughters. They knocked me out. When I came to, I was in a sort of hole. They wanted to come near me.
>   I don't know how many there were . . . .
>   I knew I was pregnant. I didn't get my period anymore. I didn't say anything.

The army rescued me. They looked for my family. My parents thought I was dead. I went to my aunt's, then to my sisters. I was ashamed in front of everyone. I couldn't go home pregnant. In our region, that is shameful. I came here to hide.

Now, I don't expect anything . . . . I wait for death. An individual tortured me and abandoned me and the society is merciless . . . . In the beginning I said to myself, I will give birth and it will be over, but after nine months . . . you remember that there is a child . . . I try to forget. *I do not wish to recount.* (cited in Bouatta 2000, 66–67; italics added)

The Response of Family, Society, and State to Non-State Actor Rape

Lila's desire not to recount what happened to her is entirely understandable. The women survivors were assaulted again when they returned to families, many of whom disowned them, to a society that often shamed them, and to a state that sometimes refused to recognize them (see Theidon, Chapter 11, this volume). The shame expressed itself in moral ways, but also in logistical and administrative ways that were just as debilitating. Those who became pregnant bore the obvious evidence of their "dishonor" and were often hidden, and sometimes struggled to obtain an abortion either because they were not at liberty until too late in their pregnancy for an abortion to be performed, or because of the status of abortion under Algerian law. Moreover, rape victims were not recognized as victims of terrorism, which would have entitled the women in question to compensation from the state.[6] Salima Tlemcani explained that one government official told her that if the women received compensation, just like victims of terrorist bombings did, that it would have been tantamount to prostitution, giving the women a salary for what they endured. Some individual local officials tried to help particular women victims by granting them an exceptional status, but even this was a rarity.

The refusal of family, society, and state to respond to the rapes appropriately formed concentric circles of denial and deprivation around the victims (see also Hadzemesic, Chapter 39 in this volume). In Zazi Sadou's foundational article in the newspaper *El Watan*, one of the young victims was confronted, after her release,

> with the total indifference of her father. For him, I am no longer his daughter, but rather she-with-whom-shame-had-arrived. When I said I wanted to go and live at my Aunt's house, he simply asked me not to report what had happened to the authorities. (Sadou 1995)

The theme of disowning daughters recurs. Salima Tlemcani recalls,

> There was an adolescent girl of 17 who was recovered by the military in a forest, seven months pregnant . . . . She stayed in the psychiatric hospital of Blida. They found her

father and called him. He says, "no I have a daughter but she is married and she left." They bring in the daughter. She is frail, even half crazy. As soon as she sees him, she says, "papa." The man turns his head to the army officer who rescued her and says, "No, that's not my daughter."

Subsequently, the hospital personnel were afraid the father would kill the daughter because she was pregnant, so they separated them. Tlemcani continues,

> There are horrible things, girls who didn't want to go back to the house, who ended up in prostitution, others went crazy. Rare are those who survived the rapes. Some live their grief because it remains a taboo subject. Even if she comes back from far away, she will never say to her parents that she was raped and her parents will never accept that she says she was raped because it is seen as a harm of which you must never speak. (Bennoune, 2013, 139)

The Silence

What then do we do with a human rights methodology so often based on testimonies when some things cannot be spoken? I myself rely greatly on testimonies in my recent work on fundamentalist violence, because it is compelling and specific. Giving space for victims to speak remains a vital task. But focusing solely on testimonies risks being an approach based on a male presumption of freedom of expression.

In fact, international human rights methodology has come to rely too much on victim testimony, including in armed conflict situations. To provide just one piece of empirical support for this claim, consider Human Rights Watch's online note about research methodology. The emphasis on storytelling is noticeable. "All [our personnel] . . . regularly . . . conduct field investigations, interviewing victims . . . to put the human story front and center of our reporting and advocacy" (Human Rights Watch 2016). Much of this document is about interview methodology, and presumes that interviews are possible. Particularly striking is the following statement: "Human Rights Watch interviews victims and witnesses in order to give them an opportunity for their voices and stories to reach a wider audience." This sentence puts forth both a laudable goal and a set of gendered assumptions about what victims want and what may be socially possible for them. Given the current constraints, this is exactly the opposite of what some of these Algerian survivors currently seek.

This problematic aspect of centering victim narratives has been recognized in both the psychological and human rights literature by a few scholars such as Kay Schaffer and Sidonie Smith (Schaffer and Smith 2004; see also De Ridder 1997). Yet, while this reality has led experts to call for a shift away from victim testimony in prosecutions in international criminal contexts, the practice has not yet been substantially revisited in the context of documentation. Experiences that cannot be testified about often cannot be documented in the field of human rights either. This creates significant methodolog- ical obstacles, and risks revictimizing women with a second erasure of their experience in light of the social pressure under which they live, or alternatively subjecting them to what Shaffer and Smith have criticized as the "indignity of public exposure."

Over the course of four years, between 2010 and 2014, I attempted numerous times to interview victims of rape by the Algerian fundamentalist armed groups, with the assistance of prominent local women's rights defenders. In all that time, I was never able to interview one woman, who openly told me she herself had been sexually assaulted. One psychologist who has long treated women victims of the fundamentalist violence of the 1990s said that in one instance, it took two years of meetings for one woman to tell her that she had been raped. Many of the women journalists who wrote about this themselves described the great difficulty they had in convincing the survivors to grant interviews.

Herein lie terrible and particular methodological difficulties. Few victims of other forms of torture are likely to ever refuse to say, later on when safe from the conflict, that they were tortured. For many women who have been political prisoners or have been caught up in armed conflict, this gendered revision of their history and rendering invis- ible of what was done to them recurs. Hence, documenting these rapes will require reli- ance on multiple forms of sources, including official statistics, medical records, forensic information, scholarly work, journalistic accounts, and perpetrator confessions, and cannot simply depend on victims being able to speak or at least to speak again later.[7]

However, the narratives of the mainstream human rights movement assume that vic- timhood is an honorable status and that victims will wish to be recognized as such. This is a gendered assumption that reflects Catharine MacKinnon's assertion that "[m]ale reality has become human rights principle, or at least the principle governing human rights practice" (MacKinnon 1993, 59, 70). For women victims of rape and other forms of sexual violence, including women in many Muslim-majority contexts like Algeria, precisely the opposite of this human rights assumption about the desirability of own- ing victimhood may often be true. The only "honorable" choice for those whose honor has been attacked is silence and obscurity. Herein lies a major conundrum for lawyers and other documenters of human rights abuse. It is a truism that it is impossible to prove anything without evidence. Rigorous methodology is important to substantiate one's findings and to avoid error, especially about a topic as contentious as abuses in armed conflict. But what do you do when vast sectors of society—and pervasive social attitudes—conspire to make the evidence impossible to obtain?

Security Council resolution 2106 stresses "that effective investigation and documen- tation of sexual violence in armed conflict is instrumental both in bringing perpetrators to justice and ensuring access to justice for survivors." In light of the social silencing about rape in contexts like 1990s Algeria, how then must we reconfigure the project of documentation and of accountability?

One approach is to broaden human rights documentation methodology beyond its current focus on the use of testimonies, as outlined earlier. Another is to think about ways in which to create an environment in which testimonies will be forthcoming. For example, an Algerian woman social worker who works with women victims of the 1990s violence asserts that we should not give up on testimonies which she views as necessary, even if currently unavailable. Her view is that practical assistance offered to these women if they were to come forward, even now, "might get them to speak."[8] This could be in the form of material, medical, and legal assistance, for them, their families, and their children, and other forms of reparation, compensation, and recognition of their suffering. In fact, it is long past time to try all these approaches and break the silence.

THE SOUND OF SILENCE

One of the interesting questions that arises out of this history concerns the politics of the production of knowledge and of the writing of history in the field of human rights. These processes are shaped by relations between international and domestic NGOs, and between those who work in a "mainstream" human rights paradigm versus those who work in a gender-specific way. While Algerian women's human rights NGOs and NGOs comprised of victims of terrorism were documenting these systematic rapes by the fundamentalist armed groups during and immediately after the time frame in which they occurred, the major international human rights groups only referred to the issue in passing, often downplaying it and never issuing a single dedicated report on the topic. In 1996, Human Rights Watch suggested that "common criminals" might be responsible (Human Rights Watch 1996). Amnesty International regularly referred to "claims" about these rapes, while asserting government abuses as "confirmed."

These discrepancies were further reflected in the strong criticism made by many local human rights defenders—women human rights defenders in particular—of the way the international human rights groups often described what occurred in Algeria in the 1990s within the narrow parameters of their traditional methods. Mirroring the classical bias against working on "private" violations (with all of its gendered implications), the mainstream international human rights groups focused on abuses committed by the Algerian state, and said much less about the far more widespread abuses by non-state armed groups (see Amnesty International 1994).

International human rights NGOs have both the financial and logistical means to occupy the documentary and historical field, whether by being cited in UN reports that their own documents often help to shape, being quoted in the international media, being able to produce their documents in English, or circulating them on the Internet. Their local counterparts—local NGOs, including women's NGOs—simply cannot compete.

Nearly every document cited in this article was obtained only after extensive field research, including five visits to Algeria during the 1990s, and eight between 2010 and 2014. Some of them represented the last available copy of a particular source, which may be entirely unavailable in English and nonexistent in cyber-space. There is a gendered aspect to this. Abuses of women's rights are most likely to get left out of the official human rights record, at least in the early phases of documentation, as the story of Algeria's mass rapes makes clear. Methodology writes history, so the long-term cost for this can be very high.

The gaps in the documentation are further reflected in international efforts for accountability. Note that in the 1990s—the decade that saw the advent of the ad hoc International Tribunals, and of the Pinochet case—there were virtually no official attempts at the international level to hold accountable Algeria's fundamentalist armed groups, the most deadly perpetrators during Algeria's 1990s nightmare. The only two accountability processes for Algerian women victims internationally—both organized by feminists—were laudable efforts, but neither was able to deliver concrete justice for victims beyond the important possibility of being heard.[9] These included (1) the symbolic Global Tribunal for Accountability of Violations of Women's Human Rights, organized by women's NGOs at the Fourth World Conference on Women at which Zazi Sadou testified about women rape victims; and (2) the noteworthy but unsuccessful litigation in the United States against the Islamic Salvation Front and spokesman Anwar Haddam under the Alien Tort Claims Act in *Doe v. Haddam* (Bennoune 2011). The dearth of accountability processes beyond these mirrors and magnifies the rape victims' own socially enforced silence.

CONCLUSION: BEYOND SILENCE

In light of the failure to prosecute perpetrators inside Algeria or internationally, alternative means are being sought to construct the historical record and to record victim experiences. The Coalition of Associations of Victims of the 90s is pushing for a truth commission about the violence of the 1990s, which is unfortunately unlikely to occur any time soon. If it does take place, such a mechanism must include the issue of rape, and must be constructed in a manner likely to facilitate the gathering of testimonies and other evidence. As with the "comfort women" of World War II, truth and justice may be a long time in coming. However, women's human rights defenders on the ground take the long view. As Cherifa Kheddar insists, "What is certain is that other women who did not testify at that time will someday be capable of overcoming the social pressure and the psychological effects to testify. The women who have already testified might even testify again. But, we cannot decide when that will be. It is up to them."[10]

Given that rape by jihadist armed groups is also a contemporary phenomenon in places like Northern Mali, Iraq, and Syria, the need to expose this history of abuse in Algeria is now transnational. Human rights law and practice have a significant role to play in this process. The first step is to help break the silence in every way possible. In a work on Algeria's "collective trauma" of the 1990s, based on extensive field research, feminist psychologist Cherifa Bouatta concludes that "[v]ictims need social recognition .... The law must speak to put everything back in order and specify the identity of each person: the victim and her victimizer" (Bouatta 2007, 186). International human rights law and practice can only contribute to this process if they heed voices like hers, and find ways to speak to and of these victims, and if they recognize the experiences of those who, for now, cannot speak.

Notes

1. The author would like to thank Anita Barooni, Laurance Lee, and Anna von Herrmann for research assistance. She would also like to acknowledge Cherifa Kheddar, Cherifa Bouatta, Malika Mahdi, le Centre pour l'information et documentation sur les droits des enfants et de la femme (CIDDEF), and l'Association pour l'Aide, la Recherche et le Perfectionnement en Psychologie (SARP) for making her field research possible. All non-English-language sources cited were translated by the author.

2. Algerian sociologist Marieme Hélie-Lucas defined fundamentalisms as "political movements of the extreme right, which in a context of globalization ... manipulate religion ... in order to achieve their political aims" (Hélie-Lucas 2001, 49, 54). In Algeria, "fundamentalist armed groups" were most often simply called "terrorists."

3. Petition: "Together against impunity in Algeria," Coalition of Associations of the Victims of the 1990s, on file with the author.

4. Cherifa Kheddar (president, Djazairouna), interview by Karima Bennoune, July 18, 2014, on file with the author.

5. Salima Tlemcani (Journalist, El Watan), interview by Karima Bennoune, November 24, 2010, on file with the author.

6. Raped women were omitted from "L'instruction relative à l'indemnisation des victimes du terrorisme complétant celles du 10 avril 1994 (94/91 and 94/86)," procedures for compensation that were adopted by the government council on February 5, 1997 (see Collectif 95 Maghreb Egalité 1997, 57). This failure has only just been corrected by Executive Order on February 4, 2014. See Hadjer Guenanfa, *Les femmes violées par des terroristes reconnues comme victimes*, TSA, February 4, 2014, http://www.algeria-watch.org/fr/article/pol/amnistie/femmes_violees_reconnues.htm.

7. Many of these kinds of sources may also require victims to speak, at least initially. However, in the Algerian context, some did speak at the time, to local women's human rights defenders, and even to Algerian government and military personnel who found them. One Algerian social worker's assessment is that their testimonies are unavailable today because many of the surviving women "have tried to hide themselves." Interview with Anonymous, by Karima Bennoune, June 27, 2013, on file with the author.

8. Interview with Anonymous, by Karima Bennoune, June 27, 2013, on file with the author. Her suggestion is supported by the fact that immediately following the Executive Order recognizing women who had been raped as victims of terrorism entitled to benefits, fifteen women came forward to declare their rapes to government officials. Guenanfa, *supra* note v. Of course, in documentation terms, this also raises ethical questions about creating incentives to recount abuse.

9. There was also very little accounting under municipal law because Algeria's Charter for Peace and National Reconciliation of 2005 codified impunity for state and non-state

perpetrators. Charter for Peace and National Reconciliation (Presidential Decree 05-278, enacted on February 28, 2006); see Joffé (2008). Rape was not a crime for which perpetrators were supposed to benefit from amnesty, according to article 10 of the Charter. In practice, the "reconciliation" foreclosed almost all accountability processes.

10. Interview by Karima Bennoune with Cherifa Kheddar in Algiers, July 2014.

REFERENCES

Amnesty International. 1994. *Algeria: Repression and Violence Must End*. London: Amnesty International.

Bennoune, Karima. 2011. "The Paradoxical Feminist Quest for Remedy: A Case Study of Jane Doe v. Islamic Salvation Front and Anwar Haddam." *International Criminal Law Review* 11: 579–587.

Bennoune, Karima. 2013. *Your Fatwa Does Not Apply Here: Untold Stories from the Fight against Muslim Fundamentalism*. New York: W. W. Norton.

Bouatta, Chérifa. 2000. "Le viol: un polytraumatisme." *Revue Psychologie* 8: 75–88.

Bouatta, Chérifa. 2007. *Les traumatismes collectifs en Algérie*. Algiers: Casbah.

Boumediene, Amel. 1995. "Vivre en Algérie: Le martyre de Kheira." *Le Nouvel Observateur*, January 19–25.

Collectif 95 Maghreb Egalité. 1997. *Violences à l'égard des femmes et violations de leurs droits (Algérie-Maroc-Tunisie)*. Algiers: Collectif 95 Maghreb Egalité.

Collectif 95 Maghreb Egalité. 1999. "Al Unf dad al nisa bilJazair: Istimal al ilightisab kasilah filharb [Violence against Women in Algeria: The Use of Rape as a Weapon of War]." In *Maghrebin Women between Symbolic Violence and Physical Violence*. Rabat: Collectif 95 Maghreb Egalité.

De Ridder, Trudy. 1997. "The Trauma of Testifying: Deponent's Difficult Healing Process." *Track Two* 6, no. 3–4.

Hélie-Lucas, Marieme. 2001. "What Is Your Tribe? Women's Struggles and the Construction of Muslimness." In *WLUML (Women Living Under Muslim Laws) Dossier*, 23–24. London: WLUML.

Human Rights Watch. 1996. *World Report 1996: Algeria*. New York: Human Rights Watch.

Human Rights Watch. 2016. "About Our Research." Accessed May 23. http://www.hrw.org/node/75141.

Joffé, George. 2008. "National Reconciliation and General Amnesty in Algeria." *Mediterranean Politics* 2, no. 13: 213–228.

MacKinnon, Catharine. 1993. "Crimes of War, Crimes of Peace." *UCLA Women's Law Journal* 4, no. 1: 59–86.

Rachda. 2004. *Temps de viols et de terrorisme*. Algiers: Rachda Association.

Réseau, Wassila. 2005. *Algérie: Le Viol des femmes par les terroristes: Un crime contre l'humanité: Actes de la journée d'étude du 8 mars 2004*. Algiers: Réseau Wassila.

Sadou, Zazi. 1995. "Le martyre des femmes violées." *El Watan*, January 11.

Schaffer, Kay, and Sidonie Smith. 2004. *Human Rights and Narrated Lives: The Ethics of Recognition*. New York: Palgrave Macmillan.

CHAPTER 39

....

CONSEQUENCES OF CONFLICT-RELATED SEXUAL VIOLENCE ON POST-CONFLICT SOCIETY

Case Study of Reparations in Bosnia and Herzegovina

....

LEJLA HADZIMESIC

ATROCITIES unimaginable for post–World War II Europe were committed during the 1992–1995 war in Bosnia and Herzegovina (BiH). The international judicial bodies convened to prosecute these war crimes, the International Criminal Tribunal for Yugoslavia (ICTY) and the International Court of Justice (ICJ), each ultimately determined that a number of war crimes and crimes against humanity had been committed, and characterized some as genocide.

Approximately 100,000 people were killed in BiH alone (ICTY 2016a), and out of 31,000 persons registered as missing during the conflict, 8,000 remain missing twenty years after the formal conclusion of hostilities (Sarkin et al. 2015). A further approximately 1.2 million people became refugees, and around one million persons were internally displaced within BiH (Nenadić and Džepar-Ganibegović 2010, 9) as a result.

The aspect of this conflict that had the greatest impact on the evolution of international law was the widespread use of rape by one ethnicity to humiliate another ethnicity. In effect, this was the first time in the history of international law where rape was legally recognized by an international judicial body as potentially constituting genocide, a crime against humanity, and a war crime. The case against Dragoljub Kunarac, Radomir Kovač, and Zoran Vuković (the "*Foča*" case) was the first at the ICTY in which the accused were convicted of rape as a crime against humanity. This decision also set a legal standard for sexual enslavement as a crime against humanity. The ICTY held that in the context of a widespread and systematic attack on civilians, rape was used to implement a strategy of "expulsion through terror" (ICTY 2016b). Despite these landmark legal findings, the post-conflict response to this crime has been inadequate, and has been further compounded by traditional cultural values.

This chapter focuses on the obfuscation and obstruction that can undermine one aspect of transitional justice—reparations. The first part of this chapter discusses the conflict in BiH, identifying how the world's attention was captured by the realization that women were being raped on a horrifying scale. It then turns to analyze BiH's post-conflict obligations under international law. The second part of the chapter explores how women were treated as symbols of community honor in BiH, a perspective that undermined the already too limited support for women who had been raped. This enduring view of women as objects of abuse, rather than subjects of war, is evident in the post-conflict treatment of survivors and the lack of initiatives offered by political elites to prioritize rehabilitation or other support for women who survived sexual violence during the conflict. The third section describes the difficulties in discharging the legal and human rights obligations concerning reparations to women, given the complex and fragmented post-conflict government structure, and elucidates persistent issues with transposing international legal obligations into domestic law and rights, particularly with respect to women survivors of conflict-related sexual violence. This section also analyzes the existing transitional justice initiatives on the ground, identifying many of their flaws and unpacking the common misconception of social welfare as reparation. The chapter concludes that the current failures to respect women's basic rights twenty years after the conclusion of the conflict amount to a violation of the basic rights of women.

This case study argues that it is crucial to unpack the situation of survivors in post-conflict societies such as BiH, and analyze it through a human rights framework, looking at the current BiH authorities as duty bearers, and women survivors of sexual violence as rights holders. The running thread through this chapter is that the government's ongoing marginalization of survivors after the conflict, which perpetuates their stigmatization, is a breach of their human rights, and directly contributes to the survival of heteromasculinity as one of the dominant ideologies in the society.

THE CONFLICT IN BiH AND ITS ROLE IN CLARIFYING THE INTERNATIONAL LEGAL STATUS OF CONFLICT-RELATED SEXUAL VIOLENCE

BiH declared independence from the Socialist Federal Republic of Yugoslavia in late 1991, followed by a referendum affirming this decision in early 1992. While the referendum was mostly boycotted by the Serbian segment of the population, of those who voted (only 63 percent turnout), 92.7 percent were in favor of independence. Tensions escalated, resulting in a devastating four-year conflict, which formally ended at the signing of the Dayton Peace Accords in 1995 (Amnesty International 2009).

Certain parts of BiH were hit especially hard. For example, as both the ICTY and the ICJ recognized, genocide was committed in Srebrenica, where approximately 7,000 men and boys were killed in July 1995. While only the atrocities in Srebrenica were technically deemed genocide, the ultimate discovery of mass graves all over the country established that "ethnic cleansing" and mass atrocities were carried out pervasively.

The widespread use of rape was reported relatively early in the war, and while there were survivors of rape and other forms of sexual violence among all ethnic groups, the majority of them were Muslim women (Amnesty International 1993; Bassiouni et al. 1994). The exact number of survivors is unknown, and suggested figures range from a disputed early estimate of 50,000 (Amnesty International 2009; Vranić 1996), to later estimates of 20,000 (Parliamentary Assembly of the Council of Europe 2009), to denials that wide-scale rape ever happened (Amnesty International 2012). During the conflict, there were no institutional structures for reporting, and the perpetrators were often those in power, so many victims stayed silent out of fear of retribution (Mazowiecki 1993). The importance of estimating the total numbers of women who were raped is twofold: first, estimates provide a basis for a meaningful reparation plan; and, second, it would counter political manipulation of victims' suffering and prevent politicians from using victims' stories for their own political purposes.[1]

What Sexual Violence Represents during Conflict

The crime of sexual violence, including rape committed during the BiH conflict, is used not only to reinforce heteromasculinity (see also Gaca, Chapter 23 in this volume), but also to reinforce a singular kind of hetero-nationality (Hague 1997, 53–60), in which the victims are not only subordinate to the perpetrators because of their gender, but also because of their ethnicity. MacKinnon cut to the root of the matter when she characterized this as particular men raping particular women for particular reasons (2006). Though survivors of conflict-related sexual violence are not only women,[2] and perpetrators are not only men, in a patriarchal society in which heteromasculinity is the norm, masculinity is attributed to perpetrators, while femininity is attributed to victims (Allen 1996).

Inherent but largely unexamined is the traditional idea of honor in BiH society, in which woman's chastity, a particular feminine trait, is a reflection of male, and therefore collective, honor (Olujic 1998). Without this notion deeply engrained in society, the policy of collective rapes as a tool of warfare would never have been as effective as a way of harming the collective.

Traditionally, women have not been seen as equal to men in BiH society. Yugoslavia under Tito was arranged so that men and women had equal education and employment opportunities. However, traditional family and societal values remained strong, particularly in rural areas (where most of these crimes were committed during the conflict). Examples of these traditional values in rural areas include the following practices: after receiving minimum education, women would marry relatively young; would bear children and stay at home looking after the household; were expected to be obedient in their homes toward their husbands, brothers, fathers, and other male relatives; and any attack on a woman's "honor" (i.e., sexual intercourse outside marriage, with or without her consent) would be seen as the woman's fault.

This gender hierarchy helped make the use of mass rape so effective in BiH. Many women interviewed after the conflict admitted that they were coping with the trauma on their own, as they were afraid to share their stories with their husbands, brothers, fathers, and other male relatives. Because these traditional values survived the conflict, and are still present in BiH society, they continue to impact the lives of the survivors and to shape the community. Efforts to follow up on the *gender* aspect of the aftermath have been fairly limited. Even more uncommon are attempts to address the trauma at the intersection of gender and ethnicity.

DOMESTIC RESPONSES TO INTERNATIONAL POST-CONFLICT LEGAL HUMAN RIGHTS OBLIGATIONS

Rape is a crime under international law, and as such, it entitles victims to reparation. In December 2005, the UN General Assembly adopted a resolution, *Basic Principles and Guidelines on the Right to a Remedy and Reparation for Victims of Gross Violations of International Human Rights Law and Serious Violations of International Humanitarian Law* ("The Basic Principles") (UN General Assembly 2005). The Basic Principles request that states ensure that domestic law provide at least the same level of protection to victims as international law. The Nairobi Declaration on Women's and Girls' Right to Remedy and Reparation tried to remedy the gender deficits of the Basic Principles by pointing out that reparation programs must specifically address the needs of victims by emphasizing the importance of empowerment and transformation, and by addressing the political and structural inequalities that allow these violations to occur in the first place (Nairobi Declaration 2007). In order for the reparation programs to be effective in the long term, sociocultural injustices and structural inequalities must be addressed. These documents have no enforcement mechanism and, accordingly, there is a certain level of skepticism regarding the degree of obligation they create. On the other hand, the documents reference a number of legally binding instruments to which BiH is a signatory. These obligations stem from the BiH ratification of all nine core international human rights treaties, strengthened by the fact that international human rights obligations are reiterated in the Dayton Agreement (Dayton Agreement 1995), which formulated the Constitution of post-conflict BiH.

These instruments require states to either provide an effective remedy or to ensure the provision of appropriate compensation to the victims. General Comment No. 3 of the International Covenant on the Economic, Social and Cultural Rights emphasizes that when it comes to progressive realization, although the state does not have to immediately effectuate its obligations, it does have to take certain steps toward the goal of implementing them within a reasonable period of time.

Given the foregoing, the first step that authorities in BiH should have taken was to conduct a sensitive assessment of the estimated number of women who could benefit from these concrete measures. Although establishing the number of victims is not an obligation per se, it is clear that no such reparation initiative could be regarded as meaningful unless it is based on needs and cost assessments, as described in General Comment 3. Such an assessment could help both to determine the potential number of beneficiaries, allowing the state to determine the amount of compensation it might need, and the types of services the beneficiaries need. Ideally, it would also acknowledge that these needs may change over time.

THE POST-CONFLICT GOVERNMENT STRUCTURE OF BiH

Because of the peculiar state structure devised as a part of the Dayton Agreement, it has remained unclear which level of government in which entity is bound by obligations to make reparation to the victims of wartime crimes. Indeed, this peculiar political structure has made it possible for local political figures to dodge any number of obligations, claiming lack of clarity with regard to who is responsible for the undertaking. This is one of the evident fault lines that have emerged from internationally brokered peace agreements like the one in BiH, where the international community has goals of its own (in this case, reversing ethnic cleansing and liberalizing the economy).

The Dayton Agreement set out an entirely new government structure, aimed theoretically at undoing the ethnic cleansing that had been carried out during the war. Post-conflict BiH consists of two semi-autonomous entities: Federacija (FBiH) and Republika Srpska (RS). All three major ethnicities are supposed to be represented within all public institutions, in proportion to their presence in the area, the proportions set according to the 1991 pre-war census.[3] This, it was believed, would help "undo" ethnic cleansing.

Postwar, both entities have their own governments, parliaments, and judiciaries. The FBiH is further split into ten cantons, each of which has its own judiciary and is individually responsible for the provision of social welfare to its residents. In the RS, the system is fairly centralized, with municipalities acting only as service providers. This means that depending on their residence, citizens have access to very different types of social services (Amnesty International 2009).

Transitional Justice and Other Initiatives

Taking into account the transitional justice framework and the relevant international human rights instruments applicable to victims of conflict, it is important to note the legal distinction between *social benefits* and *reparations for* crimes under international law. This is particularly important in BiH, where presently most initiatives to address the needs and rights of victims (including victims of conflict-related sexual violence) are introduced as social welfare measures. In BiH, social benefits, such as monthly pensions for citizens with disabilities, are available to some victims of conflict-related sexual violence because of the bodily harm inflicted on them during the conflict. Yet the state also views this universally available benefit as a form of compensation or reparation for harms suffered due to conflict. This view is not in line with international law.

Indeed, very little has been done in terms of providing actual reparations for victims of conflict in BiH. Further, the limited engagement by the BiH authorities toward the victims of massive and horrific crimes committed during the conflict does not appear to be an oversight. In order for victims to be granted any form of compensation for crimes committed against them, the relevant authorities, under the international standards, should ensure acknowledgment and apology to the victims. Because BiH society has not gone through a healing process of dealing with the past, political elites tend to avoid such acknowledgment and apology for fear that both will be seen as an admission that "their side" committed crimes during the conflict. Instead, they opt for an easier, and institutionally neutral, solution of treating victims of conflict as mere beneficiaries of the social welfare system, like any other person in need.

The next section describes both the social benefits available in BiH, with a particular focus on victims of conflict-related sexual violence, and attempts by the state to address transitional justice issues, such as reparation for victims of conflict-related sexual violence.

Status and Treatment of Victims of Conflict-Related Sexual Violence and the Social Benefits Linked to This Status

Because social welfare is the responsibility of the entities (FBiH and the RS), survivors are identified and handled differently between the entities, according to either where they currently live or where the crime transpired. The fact that benefits might be linked with the current place of residence, and not the place where the crime was committed, suggests that the system in place represents social welfare benefits and not a form of reparation. While discrimination against the victims of sexual violence is present in both entities, and generally both entities treat their victims poorly, the virtual nonexistence in the RS of both victim status designation and consequent treatment of victims of conflict-related sexual violence, regardless of their ethnicity, is deeply troubling.

Before going into the relevant legislation at the entity levels, it is worth mentioning that there is also the theoretical possibility of a compensation option through civil lawsuits; in practice, these are virtually unenforceable and consequently are not frequently used by survivors.[4]

In FBiH, the laws that govern welfare[5] treat war veterans (largely men) and the victims of sexual violence that fall under the category of civilian victims of war (largely women) very differently. While both groups are given social benefits (mainly monthly pensions) on the basis of disability, the level of physical injury required to qualify for compensation differs. War veterans are eligible for the status of disabled veterans if they have at least a 20 percent disability rating, while the level required for civilian victims of war is at least 60 percent. Further, civilian victims of conflict are entitled to only 70 percent of the amount of monthly pension that a war veteran with the same disability level would receive.

Treating civilians and war veterans differently implies that civilian casualties are somehow less important and deserve less protection. Both the UN Human Rights Committee and the UN Committee on Economic, Social and Cultural Rights criticized this discrepancy between the treatment of civilians and combatants and urged BiH to coordinate the entity provisions and address the discrimination in their treatment of survivors (UN Human Rights Committee 2006, para. 15; UN Committee on Economic, Social and Cultural Rights 2006, paras. 18, 39). The CEDAW Committee particularly highlighted discrimination against women survivors of sexual violence as one of the major issues that BiH needs to address in its implementation of the Convention (UN Committee on the Elimination of Discrimination Against Women 2013). The Committee Against Torture also expressed concern over the lack of adoption of the Law on Victims of Torture, and especially the lack of psycho-social and legal support available to the victims of sexual violence.

There are further inter-entity legislative inconsistencies, which impact the internally displaced persons (IDPs) who return to their homes in the RS from FBiH (primarily Bosniaks returning to a now-Bosnian Serb-dominated region). For example, Amendments to the RS Law on the Protection of Civilian Victims of War imposes a limitation: persons who had acquired rights as civilian victims of conflict in FBiH or in other countries in the region are excluded from the RS program. In practice, this meant that returnees would lose their benefits upon return to their pre-war homes. The issue was resolved when FBiH decided to allow the claimants to continue to receive compensation from FBiH upon their return to the RS.

Creating further obstacles for victims, the RS Law on Protection of Civilian Victims of War (art. 33) set a five-year deadline within which a victim had to apply for the certificate indicating that he or she is a civilian victim of war. The deadline expired on December

31, 2007, effectively excluding all potential claimants who, for whatever reason, could not start the procedure by then. As has been discussed and will be discussed further, many victims of sexual violence have missed that deadline.

TRANSITIONAL JUSTICE RESPONSES TO CONFLICT-RELATED SEXUAL VIOLENCE IN BiH

As mandated by international law, BiH has developed its own, quite complicated, transitional justice standards. Obviously, none of the standards creates an obligation on victims of conflict-related sexual violence to speak out; quite the contrary, the standards assert an obligation on the authorities to provide adequate services based on the needs of those who are to benefit from them. The following text discusses the existing initiatives in BiH.

Criminal justice

Very few cases that involve sexual violence[6] have been prosecuted since the conflict. The jurisdictional overlap (between the thirteen jurisdictions) over war crimes cases was somewhat resolved through the adoption of the National Strategy for War Crimes Processing in 2008 and the Structured Dialogue on Justice, launched in 2011 by the European Commission (Amnesty International 2012). Unfortunately, neither of the two documents has ensured in practice the desired victim-centered approach. Still lacking are victim-witness support and protection, crucial in rape cases considering that the key evidence is victims' testimonies. Very often, victims have been intimidated by their perpetrators during trials at the local courts, so victims end up either retraumatized or simply giving up to avoid further traumatization, or in many cases, both. Additionally, the definition of rape in domestic legislation is not in line with the international standards (the concept of coercive circumstances is often neglected by national courts). In practice, this means that the prosecutor follows the procedure of an ordinary rape trial, making women prove that they did not consent and were afraid for their lives, which further retraumatizes them during the trial.

Reparation

The Draft Strategy on Transitional Justice (the Strategy), which was finalized in 2011 and presented to Parliament in 2012, has still not been adopted, and neither has the draft Law on the Rights of Victims of Torture (UN in Bosnia and Herzegovina 2015). The Strategy envisioned a range of measures addressing reparation, institutional reform, and truth-telling.

While the drafting of a program for improving the status of women victims of sexual violence has been completed, the document has encountered political opposition and has not yet been adopted either (UN Office of the Special Representative of the Secretary-General for Sexual Violence in Conflict 2015). This latter document was endorsed largely by victims themselves, because it covers a range of rehabilitation measures sensitive to the needs of victims of sexual violence, such as special medical and psychological needs in the existing local community health-care centers.

Rehabilitation

Rehabilitation is seen as a separate form of reparation in BiH, with a focus on medical and psychological care, as well as legal and social services, in accordance with the UN Basic Principles. However, most of the services available, which tend to be sporadic and scattered, are provided by NGOs. The state is perceived to be absent and unreliable. Nevertheless, the predictability of NGOs as service providers is also rather limited because their funding depends on (mainly foreign) donors. It is difficult to expect from them consistent service provision, particularly given the intermittent and often short-term focus of donors. Additionally, only a handful of NGOs operate at the local community level as service providers for women victims of sexual violence, so it is difficult to talk about NGOs replacing the role of the state in the case of BiH. The focus of their work with victims is to assist them with individual development, with the aim of social reintegration.

In international human rights law, rape also has been recognized as a breach of the right to health (Hunt 2004; UN Committee on the Elimination of Discrimination Against Women 1992), and in order to satisfy the requirement of restoration, there must be available, accessible, and good quality health care provided by the relevant public service entities (Hunt 2004). However, the main issue in devising a long-term, large-scale policy in BiH is that the prevalence of trauma is still unknown. The Ministry for Health and Social Welfare of Republika Srpska conducted a survey in 2008, in which 45.4 percent of the sample of 533 veterans suffered from post-traumatic stress disorder (PTSD). However, civilians, including rape victims, were not included in the survey. The WHO estimates the number of persons suffering from PTSD to be at 10 percent of the entire population of BiH, based on a larger-sample study, but that is an estimate of the number of those who have been *diagnosed*, rather than the number of those who *are* suffering from war-related psychological trauma (Milić 2011). Despite these figures, there is only one mental health-care center per 40,000–50,000 people in BiH (Amnesty International 2009). In many places, there are no resident psychiatrists, so survivors depend on visiting physicians, who often do not have enough time to see or develop a relationship with everyone who requires treatment. The needs of wartime sexual violence survivors are therefore not met.

Finally, the mental care centers that do exist are far from sensitive to rape victims: they are usually located in the center of small communities where people know each other and where there is a tremendous stigma about being marked as "crazy" when seen visiting. If a woman visits the center, her community assumes she has been raped, and that therefore something is wrong with her (and something is wrong with her male family members who let her walk around these centers showering dishonor on themselves and their families). Even if a victim disregards all of this likely stigma and still seeks assistance in the center, she is not likely to be adequately treated, because most of the psychologists and psychiatrists working there are not trained to treat war trauma, and especially not rape as war trauma.[7]

THE ADDED COMPLEXITIES
OF MASSIVE DISPLACEMENT

Another difficulty arising out of the Dayton Peace Agreement is the provision in Annex VII, which requires the return of refugees and IDPs to their pre-war homes (the goal of the international community being to undo ethnic cleansing). The focus in implementation of Annex VII has been on repossession of property, which, while essential, is not sufficient to accomplish a sustainable return. For example, if a returnee repossesses her property, but does not get a job or access to adequate health care or social benefits, or still fears being mocked or that her children will be taunted, her return to the place where she was harmed is not going to be sustainable. Ultimately, she will sell her property and move permanently to the place of her wartime displacement.

Uniformity of legislation for provision of social welfare benefits is essential for returnees. Yet the discrepancies between entities mean that in some cases, returning IDPs are discriminated against. Further, in addition to these discrepancies, there are also discrepancies in acknowledgment, public apologies, and memorialization—crucial aspects of helping victims restore their lives. In RS especially, where the bulk of the rapes took place, there is a lack of acknowledgment that sexual crimes even occurred, and a culture of impunity prevails—denial by the political leaders of the crimes committed by their ethnic group leads to denial of the crimes by local communities.

Further, due to the very slow pace of war crime prosecutions (Amnesty International 2012), victims often return to areas in which their assailants still reside, where they hold the positions of power, and where they are often still hailed as local heroes (Amnesty International 2009). Without public acknowledgment and acceptance, survivors are returning to areas in which they are marginalized and stigmatized, in addition to not receiving social benefits. Due to the mentioned climate of fear and impunity, coupled with benefits discrimination, they simply do not return, which furthers the project of ethnic cleansing, though now through different means. It is even harder for women, because most of the places of potential return are rural areas. Life for women is difficult in rural areas, where the level of both security and support is generally much lower. As a consequence, women fear returning to their pre-war properties on their own, as they fear intimidation.

Conclusion

The conflict in BiH, with the huge number of human losses and the devastating fates of thousands of its citizens, was also characterized by massive rape and other forms of sexual violence. The lack of uniformity and strong political opposition to acknowledging and making reparation for crimes committed during the war are apparent in the weak measures undertaken. In addition to the general denial and culture of impunity for crimes committed during the conflict by some political elites in the country, the lack of adequate reparation measures and the violations of economic and social rights of women survivors of conflict-related sexual violence appear interrelated with the patriarchal values that are re-emerging postwar. While there are certainly emancipated women in BiH who have made successful careers and have addressed their wartime suffering by themselves, rural, vulnerable, and marginalized women are being shamed back into the shadows. A reparations framework that provides a comprehensive approach to recognizing and surmounting cultural norms, economic realities, and psychological trauma would help these women, their families, and their communities move forward.

Notes

1. For the past two decades, particularly during election campaigns, nationalist parties give statements exaggerating the number of victims from their ethnicity, attempting to engender fear among voters. Such statements raise hope and expectations in victims, which then, once the elections are over and their expectations are unmet, leads them to increased distress and anguish.
2. For example, the Bessouni report, *Bosnia Herzegovina v. Yugoslavia (Serbia and Montenegro) Application of the Convention on the Prevention and Punishment of the Crime of Genocide*, ICJ, General List No. 91, 20 March 1993, § 44D (d) (h), substantiates sexual violence committed against men, yet the Češić case, *Prosecutor v. Ranko Češić* (Sentencing Judgement), IT-95-10/1-S, International Criminal Tribunal for the former Yugoslavia (ICTY) is the only one in which a conviction was made based in part on the allegations of sexual violence against men.
3. The new census took place in October 2013, but the final results and its implications on the government representation were not published at the time of writing this article.
4. Compensation through a civil lawsuit is recognized in international standards (UN General Assembly 2005, paras. 6–7). However, this standard has never been recognized in domestic legislation.
5. In FBiH, the *1999 Law on Principles of Social Welfare, Protection of Civilian Victims of War and Protection of Families with Children* and the *2004 Law on Rights of War Veterans and Their Family Members* regulate the provision of social benefits. The corresponding laws in RS are the *1993 Law on Protection of Civilian Victims of War* and the *2007 Law on the Rights of War Veterans, Disabled War Veterans and Families of the War Veterans Who Died in the Homeland War*.

6. Out of the tens of thousands of allegations, only around forty cases involving sexual violence have been prosecuted either by the ICTY or the entity courts since 1995.

7. Information obtained through several visits to the centers in the period 2013–2014 and direct interviews with seven victims.

REFERENCES

Allen, Beverly. 1996. *Rape Warfare: The Hidden Genocide in Bosnia-Herzegovina and Croatia.* Minneapolis: University of Minnesota Press.

Amnesty International. 1993. *Bosnia-Herzegovina: Rape and Sexual Abuse by Armed Forces.* London: Amnesty International.

Amnesty International. 2009. *"Whose Justice?" The Women of Bosnie and Herzegovina Are Still Waiting.* London: Amnesty International.

Amnesty International. 2012. *When Everyone Is Silent: Reparation for Survivors of Wartime Rape in Republika Srpska in Bosnia and Herzegovina.* London: Amnesty International.

Bassiouni, M. Cherif, William J. Fenrick, Keba M'baye, Christine Cleiren, and Hanne Sophie Greve. 1994. *Final Rep. of the Comm'n of Experts Established Pursuant to Sec. Council Resolution 780 (1992).* UN Doc. S/1994/674 Annex (May 27).

Dayton Agreement on Implementing the Federation of Bosnia and Herzegovina, with Attached Agreed Principles for the Interim Statute for the City of Mostar. 1995. 35 I.L.M. 170 (November 10).

Hague, Euan. 1997. "Rape, Power, and Masculinity: The Construction of Gender and National Identities in the War in Bosnia-Herzegovina." In *Gender and Catastrophe,* edited by Ronit Lentin, 50–63. London: Zed Books.

Hunt, Paul. 2004. *Rep. of the Special Rapporteur on the Right of Everyone to the Enjoyment of the Highest Attainable Standard of Physical and Mental Health to the Commission on Human Rights,* UN Doc. E/CN.4/2004/49 (February 16).

International Criminal Tribunal for the Former Yugoslavia (ICTY). 2016a. "The Conflicts." Accessed May 24, 2016. http://www.icty.org/sid/322.

International Criminal Tribunal for the Former Yugoslavia (ICTY). 2016b. "Landmark Cases." Accessed May 25, 2016. http://www.icty.org/sid/10314.

MacKinnon, Catharine A. 2006. *Are Women Human?* Cambridge, MA: The Belknap Press of Harvard University Press.

Mazowiecki, Tadeusz (Special Rapporteur on the Situation of Human Rights in the Territory of the Former Yugoslavia). 1993. *Rep. on the Situation of Human Rights in the Territory of the Former Yugoslavia.* UN Doc. E/CN.4/1993/50 (February 10).

Milić, Amina. 2011. "Bosnians Still Traumatised by War." Institute of War and Peace Reporting. April 11. https://iwpr.net/global-voices/bosnians-still-traumatised-war-0.

"Nairobi Declaration on Women's and Girls' Right to a Remedy and Reparation." 2007. International Meeting on Women's and Girls' Right to a Remedy and Reparation, Nairobi, Kenya.

Nenadić, Mario, and Nermina Džepar-Ganibegović. 2010. *Revised Strategy of Bosnia and Herzegovina for the Implementation of Annex VII of the Dayton Peace Agreement.* Sarajevo: Ministry of Human Rights and Refugees of Bosnia and Herzegovina.

Olujic, Maria B. 1998. "Embodiment of Terror: Gendered Violence in Peacetime and Wartime in Croatia and Bosnia-Herzegovina." *Medical Anthropology Quarterly* 12, no. 1: 31–50.

Parliamentary Assembly of the Council of Europe. 2009. "Resolution 1670: Sexual Violence against Women in Armed Conflict." Council of Europe. Adopted May 29.

Sarkin, Jeremy, Lara Nettelfield, Max Matthews, and Renee Kosalka. 2015. *Bosnia i Herzegovina—Missing Persons from the Armed Conflicts of the 1990s: A Stocktaking.* Sarajevo: International Commission on Missing Persons.

UN Committee on Economic, Social and Cultural Rights, 35th Sess. 2006. *Consideration of Reports Submitted by States Parties under Articles 16 and 17 of the Covenant: Bosnia and Herzegovina: Concluding Observations of the Committee on Economic, Social and Cultural Rights.* UN Doc. E/C.12/BIH/CO/1 (January 24).

UN Committee on the Elimination of Discrimination Against Women, 11th Sess. 1992. *General Recommendation 19.* UN Doc. A/47/38 (January 29).

UN Committee on the Elimination of Discrimination Against Women. 2013. *Concluding Observations on the Combined Fourth and Fifth Periodic Reports of Bosnia and Herzegovina.* UN Doc. CEDAW/C/BIH/CO/4-5 (July 30).

UN General Assembly. 2005. G.A. Res. 60/147. *Basic Principles and Guidelines on the Right to a Remedy and Reparation for Victims of Gross Violations of International Human Rights Law and Serious Violations of International Humanitarian Law* (December 16).

UN Human Rights Committee, 88th sess. 2006. *Consideration of Reports Submitted by States Parties under Article 40 of the Covenant: Concluding Observations of the Human Rights Committee: Bosnia and Herzegovina.* UN Doc. CCPR/C/BIH/CO/1 (November 22).

UN in Bosnia and Herzegovina. 2015. "BiH Parliamentary Assembly's Joint Committee for Human Rights Hosted Thematic Session on the Occasion of the Occasion of the International Day in Support of Victims of Torture." June 26. http://ba.one.un.org/content/unct/bosnia_and_herzegovina/en/home/presscenter/bih-parliamentary-assemblys-joint-commission-for-human-rights-ho.html.

UN Office of the Special Representative of the Secretary-General for Sexual Violence in Conflict. 2015. "Bosnia and Herzegovina." http://www.un.org/sexualviolenceinconflict/countries/bosnia-and-herzegovina/.

Vranić, Seada. 1996. *Breaking the Wall of Silence: The Voices of Raped Bosnia.* Zagreb: Izdanja Antibarbarus.

CHAPTER 40

COLOMBIA

Gender and Land Restitution

DONNY MEERTENS

TRANSITIONAL JUSTICE, GENDER, AND LAND

THIS chapter focuses on women and land rights in the aftermath of armed conflict. The Colombian case study provides an example of how gendered hierarchies in peasant society and male bias in rural policies configure a particular set of obstacles that prevent women from fully enjoying redress and citizenship rights after conflict. Gendered impacts of violent conflict have mostly been analyzed in terms of victims and perpetrators, sexual violence, forced displacement, and human security. Notwithstanding the rise of the "transitional justice" movement and its expansion as a field of policy in post-conflict societies, the interconnectedness of land, gender, and conflict issues remains a rarely explored subject of research,[1] and is particularly relevant in Colombia, where uneven land distribution is considered a contributing factor to the long-standing conflict.

This Colombian case study focuses on the history of land rights for women, culminating in the 2011 Law on Victims and Land Restitution (the Law). This law is considered an innovative transitional justice effort that could ultimately serve as a model for its ability to counteract land grabs during violent conflict, in Colombia as well as in other transitional societies. The Law provides a series of special measures to enhance women's rights in land restitution, but faces many obstacles to its effective implementation.

To understand the challenges women face in realizing their land rights, the chapter undertakes a journey in two directions: setting out a brief history of women's access to land in Colombia, and exploring the "agrarian question" (a shorthand for unequal land distribution and peasant exploitation) that was at the origins of Colombia's protracted armed conflict—a conflict that lasted five decades and came to its end in November 2016 with the signature of the Peace Accords between the government and the Fuerzas Armadas Revolucionarias de Colombia (FARC) guerilla movement. Prior to this historical overview is a brief reference to the core concepts of transitional justice, gender justice, access to land, and property rights.

With the rise and expansion of transitional justice theory during the last decade, its intersections with gender and gender justice have also become a sub-field of inquiry. However, transitional justice (particularly reparations) *mechanisms* have proved more resistant to a gender-sensitive approach. Women's economic and social rights are still frequently overlooked in both literature and practice (Oré Aguilar 2011, 125), as "justice" is predominantly oriented toward accountability for violations of civil and political rights (Rubio-Marín 2009). One of the problems with transitional justice mechanisms for victims of forced displacement is the lack of gender justice *generally*, which requires linking gender not just to return policies, but also to policies that guarantee *equal rights* in the restitution of housing, land, and property (Hovil 2012; Hovil, Chapter 21 in this volume; Williams 2012). The Colombian case study underscores the need to include land issues in transitional justice, showing the obstacles that need to be overcome for a gender-sensitive restitution process.

Family, Women, and Land Rights

What questions arise when examining gender and land in general? Gender *in*equity in land issues is strongly tied to the male-biased concept of the "family" in law, public policy, and social practice. Deconstruction of this traditional family concept allows us to focus on the inequities that women experience as part of their historically constructed subject position in this context. Therefore, when using the terms "women's rights" and "women's access," I refer to them as defined by the *gendered nature* of formal law, cultural entitlements, or social practices that create particular obstacles for women under a specific formal or customary system of land rights. Further, it is necessary to distinguish between *land rights*—a legally and socially recognized claim endorsed by a legitimate external authority—and *access to land*, a much more diffuse term that may include a variety of formal and informal tenancy or exploitation arrangements (Deere and León 2001, 3).

In gender and land studies, the concept of *effective rights* was introduced to describe women's rights to land that are both legally supported and socially acknowledged (Agarwal 1994). A more radical notion followed, that of *independent rights* for women, to be distinguished from the land rights tied to the male-headed family concept that is so common in Latin America (Deere and León 2001). Independent land rights for peasant women are those not tied to a male-owned or male-controlled property. A more practical notion is that of *joint ownership* for spouses, implemented under agrarian reform policy since the 1990s in Colombia and other Latin American countries. Although considered a progressive step toward gender equality in land rights by providing a legal base for peasant women's bargaining power, joint ownership in a formal or informal marital relationship may hamper women's independent land claims in cases of divorce, abandonment, domestic violence, or disappearance of men in the midst of war. Judicial or policy decisions may favor a conservative vision of family unity and endorse the right of a male head of family to keep the family—and the land—together against women's will.[2] Moreover, joint ownership does not automatically transform male-dominated decision-making on production, credit assignments, or inheritance practices (Deere and León 2001).

These basic conceptual entry points connect in three ways to the history of land, gender, and conflict in Colombia. First, an enormous gap exists between formal equality for women and men as guaranteed in the 1991 Constitution, and the persistence of gender inequalities in society, particularly rural society. Property rights, as well as agricultural and livestock activities, remain closely associated with male labor, making existing land rights for women ineffective. Second, the poorly developed rural land registration system (*cadaster*) fosters high levels of informal land tenure for smallholders, particularly women. Unregistered properties easily fall into the hands of armed actors or are usurped by unscrupulous local power holders. The absence of a land deed or any other document that might validate possession also hampers a war widow trying to prove her relationship with the land.

Third, rural policy is family-centered. Although independent land rights are sometimes granted to women, this only occurs when they are officially considered *female heads of household*. In practice, this means the absence of men. If an adult male forms part of her household, a woman will not be considered the "head" and thus cannot qualify for the recognition of independent rights. Women's property rights become invisible under this patriarchal bias. Men remain socially entitled as rights-bearers who represent the whole family, in spite of marital regime reforms and the legal capacity given to married women in most of the Latin American countries over the course of the twentieth century (Deere and León 2001). Thus, assessing the gendered impact of armed conflict on land rights and designing its redress need to be done against the backdrop of this so-called historical debt to women.

Struggles over Land (and Gender Equity) in Colombia

Agrarian struggles have been recurrent in Colombia since the 1930s, when an agrarian reform law was counteracted by large estate holders who feared property claims by the peasants, organized in combative *Ligas Campesinas* (peasant leagues). Women played no *visible* role in these agrarian struggles (Meertens 2000), and female participation in peasant organizations was unknown, with one outstanding exception on the Caribbean coast, where an anarchist-inspired woman, Juana Julia Guzman, became an originator of the peasant movement and rural women's empowerment in the 1970s (Comisión Nacional de Reparación y Reconciliación 2010; Meertens 2000, 2006). In those years, rural women's subjugated positions remained unquestioned. They were supposed to contribute with unpaid labor to the agricultural and livestock production undertaken by men. Moreover, as a classic study of early twentieth-century coffee *haciendas* revealed (Jiménez 1989), tenant wives and daughters suffered a double subjugation: to their husbands or fathers, and to the sexual privileges of the *hacendados*, who were entitled to choose young peasant women as their concubines. This tradition of combined sexual and class domination, also common in the Caribbean coast, was revived in the 1990s by one of the paramilitary warlords (Comisión Nacional de Reparación y Reconciliación, 2011).

The 1960s and 1970s inaugurated an era of redistributive land reforms in Latin America, in which the unequal position of women remained nevertheless unchanged. The 1961 Agrarian Reform Law in Colombia was the first attempt at land redistribution and the creation of family-sized, agrarian units.[3] It relied on the dominant family-based policy design. With the family as the basic production unit, the "logical" beneficiaries of agrarian reform were the male heads of household, considered the only true producers. This was in accordance with the *social practices* in rural society, in which men represented the family and administered their common goods, in spite of the 1932 changes to the Civil Code that formally gave independent property and inheritance rights to married women. In land reform policy and practice, women head of households did not qualify for land assignment. Not even widows were considered legitimate successors of their deceased husbands. They were not seen as possessing productive or management capabilities and therefore were not eligible for the right to landed property, unless they had adult sons who could carry out agricultural tasks. Thus, agrarian reform policy reproduced the prevailing patriarchal social norms, rather than the official equality-based civil code. The male-headed family model remained unchallenged, and its consequences reach into the current thinking and policymaking on peace and transitional justice.

The failure of agrarian reform set the stage for the rise of a strong and combative peasant movement in the 1970s that carried out hundreds of land occupations, in order to force redistribution of mostly unproductive large estates. Women played a visible yet simultaneously subordinate role in these actions. They were on the front lines during occupations, confronting the police, but never participated in the planning or political decision-making (Comisión Nacional de Reparación y Reconciliación 2010). Women were seen as rural housekeepers providing economic support for the peasant activists and national leaders, carrying out small fundraising initiatives in local *comités femeninos* (Meertens 2000; Zamosc 1987).

In the 1980s and 1990s, women's access to land and social participation occurred against the background of profound institutional changes. Policies of redistributive land reform were abandoned and replaced by the key words of "modernization," "efficiency," and "productivity." On the one hand, the *Integrated Rural Development* policy included a renewed preoccupation with food production and the recognition of women as agricultural producers in national development policy, which improved their social status in rural society. On the other hand, a new, *market-led agrarian reform law* (1994), oriented toward land acquisition by underprivileged groups, included female beneficiaries in highly competitive production goals, without sufficient capacity building or domestic workload alleviation, leading to women's economic marginalization. In spite of these flaws, the Law constituted a landmark for women's rights, as joint land ownership for spouses was made mandatory for government-sponsored land adjudication. Priority arrangements were also made for women heads of household and for a new category of *unprotected women*, which was applied to the forcibly displaced. However, slow progress in land acquisition, the economic marginalization of women's collective enterprises, and resistance by male civil servants and spouses rendered the law's good intentions hollow.

Moreover, individual peasant women still experienced legal and social limitations to property rights, as access to land was generally mediated by a *twofold informal* relationship: an unregistered marriage with a man holding an unofficial tenure. Indeed, in the 1980s only 20 percent of rural households held land deeds, and over 40 percent of heads of rural households had not formalized their marital relationships (FAO 1996).

While a new progressive National Constitution (1991), still current, recognized formal equality between men and women and defined the Colombian nation as multicultural and ethnically diverse—giving more room for positive actions for women and endorsing collective territorial rights and semi-autonomous justice systems for indigenous and afro-Colombian groups—increasing violence in the countryside rendered this positive development practically ineffective. As armed conflict dominated rural society, the only national peasant women organization, ANMUCIC,[4] suffered severe persecution and became fragmented (Meertens 2006). In public policy, questions of agrarian reform, rural development, food production, or women's participation became overshadowed by combating insurgency, peace talks, and rehabilitation plans alternatively undertaken by the successive governments.

In conclusion, the increasingly market-oriented agrarian reform policies of this period have had little positive impact on structural injustices—including gender inequality—in rural society. The "historical debt to peasant women" can still be summed up as the persistence of four key processes of patriarchal denial of citizen's rights for women: (1) male-biased family-oriented agrarian reform policies; (2) underenforcement of positive actions provided for in the law to enhance women's rights; (3) male-biased rural society's social practices concerning inheritance, rural production, and estate management, and (4) cultural obstacles for women to assume leadership in rural organizations beyond the community level. These patriarchal elements of discrimination interplayed with the political economy of armed conflict and its impact on women's security (Meertens 2006; Meertens and Zambrano 2010).

ARMED CONFLICT, VIOLENT LAND DISPOSSESSION, AND GENDER

The unequal distribution of land[5] has been considered one of the root causes of Colombia's protracted conflict (Grupo de Memoria Histórica 2013). Nevertheless, since the 1960s, a decade in which the current main guerrilla groups were founded, the "land question" progressively lost its initial meaning as an aim of social justice and became an asset for coca cultivation and a source of financing for the war. Above all, land acquired a strategic meaning of territory, both in its traditional sense of political domination, and as corridors for moving people, arms, and drugs. During the 1980s and 1990s, guerrillas and paramilitary groups disputed territorial control, engaging in an endless chain of massacres and violent attacks to the civil population in order to establish their local bastions of power. During the first decade of the twentieth century, the number of forcibly displaced people from the rural areas had risen to nearly five million and their abandoned lands to six million hectares (Comisión de Seguimiento a la Política Pública Sobre Desplazamiento Forzado 2009). The abandoned lands—small peasant farms—then fell in the hands of the armed actors themselves (mostly paramilitary), or were grabbed and accumulated by local elites or agro-industrial enterprises, leading to a new concentration of landholdings known as the "counter agrarian reform" (Comisión Nacional de Reparación y Reconciliación 2010). The land grabs served twofold elite interests: punishing peasant communities for their supposed guerrilla support, and recovering once parceled land to the benefit of their former owners or new large-scale commercial exploitations.

The land grabs also involved gender issues with respect to human and legal security. Young adult women are overrepresented in the displaced population and constitute nearly half of the heads of displaced households. They have suffered a disproportionate impact by the forced displacement and violent dispossessions, particularly as victims of sexual violence.[6] Seventeen percent of them reported physical aggression and sexual violence as an impetus for displacement (Defensoría del Pueblo 2008). Rape and other forms of sexual abuse have been used to intimidate local communities in order to grab their land. For example, in the Magdalena department (a stronghold of one of the cruelest paramilitary warlords), rape cases were directly related to land abandonment and dispossession, as whole peasant communities fled the region. Even after returning home, following paramilitary demobilization in 2006,[7] peasant women still faced insecurity as former perpetrators remained in the community (Comisión Nacional de Reparación y Reconciliación 2010; 2011, 212, 252, 255, 267).

All these experiences demand reconsideration of transitional justice mechanisms in practice, as well as consideration of these questions: How can restitution be provided for rights that never existed? And should the transformations in society needed for the recognition of women's rights come from the transitional justice mechanisms or from other processes? The next section considers these questions through the detailed examination of the flaws and potentials of the Victims and Land Restitution Law.

LAND RESTITUTION AND GENDER HIERARCHIES

The Victims and Land Restitution Law (2011) has several special features to be highlighted. It was issued *during* conflict (more than a year before peace talks began in 2012), as a means of comprehensive reparations for all war victims, including those of assassinations, massacres, forced disappearance, sexual violence, and forced displacement. It thus turned the balance to the *victim* side of conflict, and introduced a *civil* transitional justice procedure for land restitution as an integral part of reparations. It pursues land restitution through a combined administrative-judicial process re-establishing victims' rights in cases of conflict-related dispossession. The Law's scope is limited to *restoring* the situation that existed before human rights violations were committed, except for formalizing land tenure. Victim and peasant organizations have criticized this limited potential for more structural agrarian reform, but women's organizations advocating for *short-run* gender-transformative measures achieved a special resolution on positive actions for women claimants (Ministerio de Agricultura 2013). These include special protection; flexibility of proof; prioritization of women heads of households in procedures; and *mandatory joint ownership* for partners. In spite of its (already discussed) limitations, joint ownership may have a positive effect for rural women, although it is still limited to victims and not to the peasant population in general.

During the law's first four years of implementation, over 60,000 victims filed claims, 40 percent of them women. As of the end of 2015, about 1,800 court rulings for restitution had been issued and more than 3,600 claims resolved, most of them involving women only as partners or dependents.[8] It is unclear how many women heads of household received an independent land deed over this period. However, according to my research data in the Montes de Maria region, for example, a percentage as low as 15 percent of the local court rulings granted independent land deeds to women heads of household. The law's implementation and its affirmative measures, in particular, have met with a set of serious obstacles. These are first of all related to security and local governance, second to the high levels of informality in land tenure, and third to the patriarchal culture and practices in rural society. In all three aspects, gender hierarchies work against women claimants.

In many localities, violence related to guerrillas, criminal bands, and drug-trafficking continues, and "anti-restitution armies" have been formed by those trying to uphold their illegally acquired landholdings. Perpetrators may still exercise control over women's lives, watching over victims'—particularly women's—visits to government and prosecutor's offices. Also, former perpetrators who had demobilized and confessed under the Justice and Peace Law (2005) are being released from jail and returning to their communities. Many testimonies of women also refer to re-victimizations by civil servants who do not take their claims seriously. So threats, fear, and prejudice hamper access to justice at the local level, and governmental protection measures remain inadequate, as they rely more on mechanical devices than on restoring social cohesion or enhancing women's organizations. The extremely high levels of impunity in all these situations make security an ongoing and in practice unattended problem, and affect decisions to file a claim, to return to the land, to seek compensation, or to stay in the cities.

Informality of tenure, conflated with instability in marital and family relationships, also hampers the land restitution process. Although women benefit from the shift in the burden of proof[9] (concerning land possession before violence and displacement), obstacles to evidence-collection remain, both in cases of conflicts with powerful new occupants of the land as well as in cases of "horizontal" conflicts with new smallholders or family members. Peasant women were supposed to know how to work the land, but *not* to administrate property. Consequently, their knowledge of formal aspects of extension, boundaries, and legal registration happened to be more limited, acting against them in the establishment of judicial proof. In the case of widows, the land might have been owned or possessed by the relatives of their deceased or disappeared husbands and returned to them instead, leaving the widow and orphans without compensation. Furthermore, family ruptures and recompositions, as well as unregistered successive and simultaneous marital relationships, contribute to complexity. Marital relationships frequently break up during displacement, and the male partner may now claim the land with a newly constituted family. The originally victimized family members, although also rights-bearers, may not be aware of these claims, and thus are left without recourse.

In all these cases, women's former legal relationship with the land had been mediated by a male partner. Now that they claim restitution as independent women, extra-judicial mechanisms are needed to prove their rights of possession. The Law allows new figures, like the collection of community testimonies or women's own memories of working on the land, to be used as proof of former possession. These procedures, currently prepared during the administrative process and then handed over to the judge and validated, constitute one of the most innovative, gender-sensitive aspects of the law to be taken into account for further post-transitional jurisprudence.

Several big questions remain. We will never know how many women refrained from reclaiming land out of fear, lack of information, or lack of rights-consciousness. But we may ask how many women entering the restitution process receive independent land rights and how many joint ownership. Or how many got stuck during the process in conflicting demands embedded in patriarchal traditions. Or—perhaps the most crucial question—what happened after the land has been given back to them. The case-by-case rulings in traditional jurisprudence make it difficult to follow the process once the land is handed over. Judges order physical protection by police forces for this handover—a militarized notion of protection highly criticized by women's organizations—as well as prioritization of the female beneficiaries for productive projects and affiliation to health services. These are all standardized orders, for which no explicit follow-up procedure is established. It will therefore be crucial to promote some sort of collectivization of women's experiences after land restitution in order to share the problems, safeguard the gains, and link them critically to development efforts in their region. Women owners of the restituted lands may play an important role in rebuilding communities and in the consolidation of the so-called peasant-reserve zones[10] meant to blind their economies from unbridled capitalist accumulation.

For the gender-sensitive post-restitution scenarios to work, other conditions need to be fulfilled. Thus far, lessons learned refer to the technical-administrative and judicial process. Beyond this, the improvement of local democratic governance will be a *sine qua non* for women's human security. The broader recognition of women's effective and independent rights to landed property will enhance their enjoyment of legal security. This last issue may require the extension of the special solutions set forth in the judiciary process, to become valid alternatives generally, to what agrarian and family law pre-scribe in normal times. The extent to which these concepts and alternative solutions become concrete tools for the transformation of gender relations in the implementation of the Victim's Law may set crucial examples not only for Colombia, but for other transitional processes in the world.

CONCLUSION

The Colombian case forces consideration of the basic question of what conflict, displacement, and dispossession of land do to structural gender hierarchies, and how these might be transformed by post-conflict transitional measures. Most gender justice literature has focused backward, seeking redress for past human rights violations, particularly sexual violence. Land restitution in Colombia provides a different focus.

Now that awareness has increased among rural women, and long-forgotten issues of gender-skewed land rights are being taken up, victims and women's organizations should help create a new, forward-oriented framework of both redress *and development* that might be applicable in other post-conflict scenarios. The broader involvement of civil society organizations is crucial to overcome the limitations of victim-oriented policies and to make the community at large the stakeholders of gender-sensitive development (UN Women and UNDP 2012). The transformative capacity of a restitution law, as a mechanism of transitional justice, can only be effective when firmly tied to the subsequent stages of a gender-sensitive rural development process. In the Colombian case, this should imply linking women's participation in land restitution to their effective participation in agrarian reform measures after a peace agreement is reached —a huge task given the invisibility of gender issues in the current government–guerrilla peace talks (2013).

In this long-term perspective, one of the most persistent problems is how to tackle the male bias in both public policy and private practice. Making non-state actors accountable for discrimination is difficult to achieve (Goetz 2007), particularly in the private sphere. Transitional justice measures may help. In spite of their obvious limitations in scope and time, as exceptional measures they may create new judicial and policy precedents for wider democratic development efforts in the future.

NOTES

1. Except a few studies on gender, land, and housing issues in postwar Bosnia, Guatemala, and Sri Lanka, including Mohan (2011) and UN Women and United Nations Office of the High Commissioner for Human Rights (2013), 59–66.
2. In Brazil, these negative effects of joint ownership have been partly counteracted by legal provisions allowing women victims of violence to stay in the house independently of who owns it (UN Women and United Nations Office of the High Commissioner of Human Rights 2013), 25.

3. Political opposition by big landowners made this law, as well as successive attempts, a nearly complete failure (Machado 2009; Meertens 2006).
4. *Asociación Nacional de Mujeres Campesinas e Indígenas de Colombia* (National Association of Peasant and Indigenous Women of Colombia).
5. None of the usual terms in English (land grabbing, land seizures, land dispossession) constitutes an adequate definition of the Spanish term *despojo* used in Colombia. Throughout this chapter I use all three, according to context.
6. Corte Constitucional [C.C.] [Constitutional Court], abril 14, 2008, Auto 092/08 (Colom.).
7. Under the Justice and Peace Law (2005), the paramilitary leaders were supposed to confess all their crimes for the sake of reduction in punishment. They confessed thousands of homicides, but remained silent on land dispossession and on sexual violence; see also O'Rourke (2012).
8. Official national statistics only produce gender-disaggregated data in terms of women and men "associated" with restitution results, that is, those who conform to the claimants' family groups.
9. Not the claimants but the perpetrators and/or supposed usurpers of the land now must prove the legitimacy of their holding.
10. *Zonas de reserva campesina.*

References

Agarwal, Bina. 1994. *A Field of One's Own: Gender and Land Rights in South Asia.* Cambridge: Cambrige University Press.

Comisión de Seguimiento a la Política Pública Sobre Desplazamiento Forzado. 2009. *El Reto ante la tragedia humanitaria del desplazamiento forzado: Reparar de manera integral el despojo de tierras y bienes,* vol. 5. Bogotá: Consultoría para los Derechos Humanos.

Comisión Nacional de Reparación y Reconciliación, Grupo de Memoria Histórica. 2010. *La Tierra en disputa: Memorias del despojo y resistencias campesinas en la Costa Caribe 1960–2010.* Bogotá: Fundación Semana and Taurus.

Comisión Nacional de Reparación y Reconciliación, Grupo de Memoria Histórica. 2011. *Mujeres y guerra: Víctimas y resistentes en el Caribe Colombiano.* Bogotá: Fundación Semana and Taurus.

Deere, Carmen Diana, and Magdalena León de Leal. 2001. *Empowering Women: Land and Property Rights in Latin America.* Pittsburgh: University of Pittsburgh Press.

Defensoría del Pueblo. 2008. *Promoción y monitoreo de los derechos sexuales y reproductivos de mujeres víctimas de desplazamiento forzado con énfasis en violencias intrafamiliar y sexual.* Bogotá: Defensoría del Pueblo.

Food and Agricultural Organization of the United Nations (FAO). 1996. *Women in Agricultural and Rural Development.* Rome: FAO.

Goetz, Anne Marie. 2007. "Gender Justice, Citizenship and Entitlements: Core Concepts, Central Debates and New Directions for Research." In *Gender Justice, Citizenship and Development,* edited by Maitrayee Mukhopadhyay and Navsharan Singh, 15–57. Ottawa: International Development Research Center.

Grupo de Memoria Histórica. 2013. *Basta ya! Colombia: Memorias de guerra y dignidad.* Bogotá: Centro Nacional de Memoria Histórica.

Hovil, Lucy. 2012. "The Nexus between Displacement and Transitional Justice: A Gender-Justice Dimension." In *Transitional Justice and Displacement,* edited by Roger Duthie, 329–359. New York: Social Science Research Council.

Jiménez, Michael. 1989. "Gender, Class and the Roots of Peasant Resistance in Central Colombia 1900–1930." In *Everyday Forms of Peasant Resistance*, edited by Forrest D. Colburn, 120–150. Armonk, NY: M. E. Sharp.

Machado C., Absalón. 2009. *La reforma rural, una deuda social y política*. Bogotá: Universidad Nacional de Colombia, Centro de Investigaciones para el Desarrollo.

Meertens, Donny. 2000. *Ensayos sobre tierra, violencia y género: Hombres y mujeres en la historia rural de Colombia, 1930–1990*. Bogotá: Universidad Nacional de Colombia, Centro de Estudios Sociales.

Meertens, Donny. 2006. *Tierra, derechos y género: Leyes, políticas y prácticas en contextos de guerra y paz*. Bogotá: UNIFEM.

Meertens, Donny, and Margarita Zambrano. 2010."Citizenship Deferred: The Politics of Victimhood, Land Restitution and Gender Justice in the Colombian (Post?) Conflict." *International Journal of Transitional Justice* 4, no. 2: 189–206.

Ministerio de Agricultura y Desarrollo Rural, Unidad de Restitución de Tierras 2013. *Resolución no. 80. Por la cual se adopta el Programa de Acceso Especial para las Mujeres, Niñas y Adolescentes en la Etapa administrativa del procesos de Restitucion de Tierras Despojadas*. Bogotá: Ministerio de Agricultura y Desarrollo Rural.

Mohan, Sharanya Sai. 2011. "The Battle after the War: Gender Discrimination in Property Rights and Post-Conflict Property Restitution." *Yale Journal of International Law* 36, no. 2: 461–495.

Oré Aguilar, Gaby. 2011. "Asserting Women's Economic and Social Rights in Transitions." In *Rethinking Transitions: Equality and Social Justice in Societies Emerging from Conflict*, edited by Gaby Oré Aguilar and Felipe Gómez Isa, 123–170. Cambridge: Intersentia.

O'Rourke, Catherine. 2012. "Transitioning to What? Transitional Justice and Gendered Citizenship in Chile and Colombia." In *Gender in Transitional Justice*, edited by Susanne Buckley-Zistel and Ruth Stanley, 136–162. Houndmills, UK: Palgrave MacMillan.

Rubio-Marín, Ruth. 2009. "Gender and Collective Reparations in the Aftermath of Conflict and Political Repression." In *The Gender of Reparations: Unsettling Gender Hierarchies While Redressing Human Rights Violations*, edited by Ruth Rubio-Marín, 381–402. Cambridge and New York: Cambridge University Press.

UN Women and UNDP. 2012. *Reparation, Development and Gender*. Kampala, Uganda: UN Women and UNDP.

UN Women and United Nations Office of the High Commissioner for Human Rights. 2013. *Realizing Women's Rights to Land and Other Productive Resources*. New York: United Nations.

Williams, Rhodri. 2012. "Protection in the Past Tense: Restitution at the Juncture of Humanitarian Response to Displacement and Transitional Justice." In *Transitional Justice and Displacement*, edited by Roger Duthie, 85–138. New York: Social Science Research Council.

Zamosc, León. 1986. *The Agrarian Question and the Peasant Movement in Colombia: Struggles of the National Peasant Association, 1967–1981*. Cambridge and New York: Cambridge University Press.

CHAPTER 41

....

KNOWING MASCULINITIES IN ARMED CONFLICT?

Reflections from Research in the Democratic Republic of Congo

....

MARIA ERIKSSON BAAZ AND MARIA STERN

IT has become increasingly clear that an understanding of the dynamics of violent conflict, including why and how it occurs, as well as why and how it abates, requires paying attention to gender. Gendered analysis allows us to see how notions of masculinity and femininity (as well as the drawing of lines of distinction between the two as distinct and oppositional categories) inform the workings of violence, and how articulations of masculinity and femininity are shaped by violence. It also allows us to see—and claim space for attending to—those who have been subject to the harmful workings of gender in myriad ways. The ways in which women and girls are impacted by violent conflict, as well as how women and girls act (for example, as agents of violence as well as peacemakers), have finally been recognized as vitally and integrally important to peace and security on a global scale. So too have masculinity and the masculine subjects produced through gendered structures—the military being at the forefront—and discourses.[1] Based on our research on gender in the armed forces in the Democratic Republic of Congo (DRC), and in particular on conflict-related sexual violence in this context, this chapter critically reflects on how we can make claims more generally about what masculinity is and does.

By being attuned to, and asking questions about, the interrelationship between gender and violence, we are able to interrogate how the workings of gender have silenced, harmed, rendered invisible, and embedded harmful relations of power, as well as circumscribed political imaginaries so that we find it hard not only to act otherwise, but to think and dream otherwise. Additionally, we create space for recognizing the ways in which many work toward peace and security (as processes, promises, and practices) in ways we would not otherwise see and recognize. Indeed, gendered analysis provides us with tools for interrogating the very distinctions between peace and war, "domestic" violence and political violence, structural violence and direct violence, and much more (Shepherd 2010; True 2012).

Yet, despite its progressive appeal, political purchase, and success in bringing attention to the workings of gender, the ways in which "gender" is referred to and analyzed have led us to query what might be at stake in the firm arrival of "gender" in academic and policy responses to redressing violent conflict and "gendered" harms (see also Kirby 2013). But *gender* is rarely posed as a question (see Zalewski 2010). Instead, assumptions about "what gender is and does" tend to lead us down narrow avenues of analysis and render certain "solutions" not only possible, but even seemingly necessary. Military masculinity, for instance, has become a shorthand for a host of often universalizing understandings about the workings of gender (and heterosexuality), the interrelationships between gender and violence, and the foundations of conflict-related sexual violence, as well as militarized violence more generally (compare Dietrich Ortega 2012; Higate 2012; Hutchings 2008). To be clear, we do not pretend that posing gender *as a question* instead of something known is a simple or easy endeavor (Zalewski 2010). As practiced (post-structural and postcolonial) feminist scholars of global politics, we have strived to explore how gender intersects with violent conflict in a particular context as an open inquiry, yet we nonetheless remain confined by our understandings of what "gender" means and does (Stern and Zalewski 2009). The conundrum that the limits of our conceptual and political imaginaries, coupled with our quest for open inquiry, presents is not intended as a signal for refusing research on gender and violent conflict on the grounds that it is impossible or too restricted—on the contrary. We raise this conundrum so that we can better explore how we pay attention to gender in/and violent conflicts, and importantly, how we can learn from the limitations that doing so necessarily entails.

This chapter critically reflects on how we can make knowledge claims about militarized masculinity in the violent conflict in the DRC. The DRC has been the site of protracted and bloody conflict, involving several foreign armies and a plethora of armed groups. Importantly, the country (and the Great Lakes region more generally) has seen and continues to see vast amounts of violence against the civilian population, including sexual violence, committed by both the national armed forces (FARDC) and different armed groups (see, e.g., UN Secretary-General 2015). The effects of conflict-related sexual violence, as well as the fear of it, are devastating. Lives, bodies, and livelihoods are destroyed, as is social cohesion in communities affected by it. The destructive consequences impact also upon the lives of perpetrators who continue to live with the psychological ramifications of their violent acts.[2] Effectively redressing and even preventing (or diminishing) conflict-related sexual violence depends upon a better understanding of the ways in which gender works in forming the conditions of possibility for such violence.

This chapter draws on research conducted between 2005 and 2013, which has focused on exploring the workings of gender in the FARDC through several interrelated research projects.[3] The research projects were based on interviews and ethnographic

fieldwork with soldiers and officers, and we enjoyed access though both informal channels (contacts with particular commanders who granted access) and formal channels
(permit from the Ministry of Defense). We chose to focus our inquiry on the government forces[4] since much of the violence committed during this period against civilians,
including sexual violence, was committed by these forces. One particular aim was getting a better understanding of sexual violence committed by the army through attending to gendered discourses among military staff. Direct questions about involvement
in rape were not posed. Nonetheless, the way the soldiers we interviewed spoke about
specific instances of rape indicated that many were speaking from personal experience.
Our positions as white women researchers from Sweden did, of course, shape both our
access and the soldiers' narratives. Contrary to what we anticipated, we experienced
that our positionality actually facilitated our access in the military sphere. Women
are often seen as harmless and less threatening than men are in this context (we have
compared notes with male colleagues who have tried to conduct research within the
FARDC). Being seen as relatively innocuous, we believe, enabled us to gain easy access
to conversations with military staff. Our status as "harmless" also likely influenced their
readiness to share (certain) stories with us. Clearly, however, our positionality also
shaped the stories they told us (and, undoubtedly, how we heard them). For instance,
we were surely not allowed entry into the kinds of discussions that occur in the inner
circle of closed masculine spaces. However, given one author's status as an "outsider
within" and through "hanging out" with military staff in everyday settings (workplace,
private homes, bars, etc.), we were privy to conversations that, we expect, most outside observers—be they men or women—rarely access. Furthermore, we suspect that
in their conversations with us—as white, educated women from Europe, presumably
with access to important people who could concretely influence their situation—the
soldiers might have emphasized their vulnerabilities as fathers and men (see Eriksson
Baaz and Stern 2015, 2016).

In this chapter, we revisit some key insights suggested by our research. In particular, we highlight how our ways of seeing, thinking, and analyzing gender were heavily
shaped by dominant understandings, and how these often fitted poorly with what our
interviews told us. Framed differently, the stories we collected did not easily fit into the
available imaginaries of gender conflict and violence, led to unlikely places, and challenged some dearly held truths (see Eriksson Baaz and Stern 2016). Clearly, research
"results"—especially in qualitative research—do not "speak for themselves"; rather, we
imbue meaning on our "findings" through the lens available to us (Higate 2006). The
point is not simply that "we learned new things" about gender and conflict that we did
not expect. Instead, we highlight and explore some of the subtle limits of the analytical tools and imaginaries circumscribing our efforts to understand the interworkings
of gender and violent conflict in particular, and militarized masculinity more specifically. We start by reflecting the frames through which we sought to understand militarized masculinity, which (given their firm grounding in feminist research and policy)
surely are quite familiar to most readers. We then turn to a discussion of how the stories
of soldiers in the Congolese national army resonated with our preconceived notions,

followed by how their stories troubled our understandings. We conclude with some further reflections about "thinking otherwise."

ANTICIPATIONS RESONATING WITH THE DOMINANT GENDER STORY: MACHO-VIOLENT FORM OF MASCULINITY

As noted earlier, there is a wealth of excellent feminist research on the connections between gender, militarization, and warring. In direct contrast to essentialist arguments that militarized violence emerges from the "natural" (heterosexual) makeup of men/boys, the bulk of feminist research on militarization has departed from the notion that gender is *produced* though intersecting power relations and structures (Stern and Zalewski 2009). (That gender is *lived* differently by different people does not necessarily undermine the notion that "hegemonic" masculinities prevail and condition both the ways that gender is experienced and reproduced; compare Connell 1995; see also Bergren 2014.) Such research has convincingly shown how military institutions tend to foster a particular, often "macho-violent," form of masculinity—a masculinity that poses problems for civil military relations, especially in post-conflict societies (see, e.g., Enloe 1990, 2000; Goldstein 2001; Higate and Hopton 2005, Price 2001). As we have argued eslewhere (Eriksson Baaz and Stern 2008, 2009, 2011), this research emphasizes how men (and women) "learn" to be violent in the military, as soldiering requires a willingness to kill the enemy to protect the state/nation. Through militarization, an ideal type of masculinity becomes linked to the ability and willingness to commit violence. Women's (and "femininity's") association with a need for protection, peacefulness, and life-giving acts as the counterpart to the supposed "masculinity" of protecting, warring, and killing (compare Enloe 1990; Goldstein 2001). The feminine serves as the opposing entity in the binary pair of masculine–feminine, thus working as the "constitutive outside" to the seemingly inherent masculinity of the military (Pin-Fat and Stern 2005).

Such understandings have enabled the notion of rape as a weapon of war to gain both explanatory and political currency (Eriksson Baaz and Stern 2013a). According to such reasoning, certain gender ideologies serve as the condition of possibility for rape as an effective weapon to be wielded in conflict settings. Simply put, rape can act as an effective tool of humiliation and intimidation, and is used strategically by warring parties. Rape can be symbolically conceptualized as a way to punish, humiliate, and torture seemingly "subversive" women for threatening national security (and identity) through their perceived challenges to strictly defined notions of femininity and masculinity. As women often are cast as the symbolic bearers of ethno/national identity through their roles as biological, cultural, and social reproducers of the community, rape of "enemy" women can also aim at destroying the very fabric of society (e.g., Enloe 2000; Goldstein 2001; Yuval-Davis 1997). Moreover and importantly, rape in wartime can be seen as a particularly effective means to humiliate (feminize) enemy men by defiling "his" women/nation/homeland, and proving him to be an inadequate protector (see Gaca, Chapter 23 in this volume).

It would make good sense if this reasoning could be a starting point for understanding the particularities of how gender and military masculinity work in the Congolese context. Resonating with such frameworks, one might expect interviews with army staff to reiterate "macho-violent" forms of masculinity, which are articulated in opposition to the feminine Other. While we did not expect access to the kinds of discussions around these issues that occur in the inner circle of closed masculine spaces, we nonetheless anticipated that we would pick up on hints of a certain celebration of sexual violence as part of hyper-masculine performance. At the least, we expected to hear stories about rape as ordered from "above," or at least implicitly encouraged. These expectations were shaped in part by the prevailing discourse of rape as a weapon of war.

To a certain extent, we did certainly find what we were looking for. The soldiers and officers whom we spoke to firmly located and negotiated their military gendered identities by referring to a global military ethos and by comparing themselves to other armed forces worldwide (see Eriksson Baaz and Stern 2008, 2011). Their notions of what it means to be a good military male in the DRC bore many resemblances to the dominant and generalized notion of military masculinity. Yet, the notion of "heroic masculine violent achievement" central to militarized narratives (see Higate 2001) occupied a rather limited space in soldiers' responses, as we will further discuss later. Nonetheless, representations of soldiering as necessitating physical strength and capacity for violence were certainly present in the interview texts—in the context of discussions about women's participation in the armed forces. In such discursive contexts, in which the soldiers negotiated their identities as military males in relation to women's (potentially increasing) participation in the armed forces, their voices did indeed often echo military (traditionalist) discourses and identities articulated elsewhere (compare Gutmann 2000; Mitchell 1998, 1989; van Creveld 2000). For instance, when arguing against women's inclusion in the armed forces, many male soldiers referred to the familiar military traditionalist argument of women's supposedly physical and psychological weakness (van Creveld 2000). Hence, in relation to the question of women's capacities as soldiers, they portrayed masculinity as embodying physical strength, willingness to endure extreme physical danger, and readiness to take lives, while women, they explained, are less aggressive, less daring, and less able to suppress minor personal harms. In short, female soldiers, the male soldiers told us, were simply just not up to the job of combat.

Moreover, other aspects of familiar militarized discourses on masculinity resonated in the soldiers' narratives. Similar to many other military contexts, the (male) soldier's libido was often represented as a natural (biological) force, which ultimately demands sexual satisfaction from women. Even if members of the armed forces did not celebrate rape in their conversations with us, they nevertheless presented it as a somewhat unavoidable consequence of men being deprived of sex, due to the lack of financial means and leave/R&R. During fieldwork we often encountered comments alluding to such notions of the power of the male heterosexual libido (which also posed a host of difficult ethical dilemmas in terms of how we could respond to such statements) (see Eriksson Baaz and Stern 2016). Importantly, such comments that tightly link (militarized) masculinity to virility and sexual potency and that portray sexual violence as a substitution for "normal" sexual encounters resonate with militarized discourses elsewhere, and is not specific to the Congolese armed forces.[5]

In short, to a certain extent the interview texts did fit quite neatly into our already formed framings. Yet, as we address in the next section, on the whole, when we probed the meaning of masculinity in different discursive contexts with the members of the armed forces, it was clear how the workings of gender refused to be pinned down and how identities shifted and slided (see Eriksson Baaz and Stern 2013b; Dietrich Ortega 2012). The elegant frames for making sense of, and providing solutions to, gendered violence were revealed to be paltry indeed.

TROUBLING ENCOUNTERS AND VOICES: DISSONANCE

Violent heroes?

While "heroic masculine violent achievement" did feature in the army staff's narratives, it did so almost exclusively in relation to discussions about women's place in the army. Surprisingly (for us), these values did not figure centrally in definitions of what makes a "good" or "successful" soldier for the majority of those interviewed. Instead, in the more general conversations around "what makes a good soldier," courage, strength, and the capacity for violence occupied a quite marginal role, even when explicitly mentioned or asked about. Rather, the soldiers lauded the military code and identified discipline, rationality, order, and education as the features of a good soldier. They explained that discipline not only signifies the capacity to follow orders, but also being a good protector of civilian men and women. Moreover, and importantly, the soldiers overwhelmingly spoke of administration—working behind a desk—as the ultimately desirable position. Hence, the celebrated successful soldier in their accounts was an educated soldier (preferably an officer), who does administrative work (e.g., works in military courts, or at the ministry of defense), not the tough, brave soldier, fighting at the front. In addition to citing such work as what they desired, they often complained that it was unfair that the women (who in the Congolese army predominantly are found within administration) were "getting all the good jobs." The value placed on "desk work" as signifying the high status that comes from being a "good provider" must be understood in relation to the ways in which masculinity is imbued with different meanings in different military contexts (cf. Dietrich Ortega 2012), the challenging socioeconomic situation that military staff face, and the prevailing discourses on desirable masculinity as inherently connected to resources and power (further explained below).

Moreover (and in contrast to our expectations, which were shaped by dominant understandings of militarized masculinity), the stories were punctuated with recurrent articulations of vulnerability and failure. The ideal militarized masculinity that emerged in these stories was not steeped in the heroism (or even the longing for heroism) of combat. Rather than representing themselves as (aspiring to be) heroic and brave military men, they told stories of the horrors of combat, of their fears, and how they would not engage in combat without drinking or taking drugs to calm their anxieties (Eriksson Baaz and Stern 2013a). While such accounts are surely familiar to scholars of psychology and military sociology and history (see Collins 2008; Goldstein 2001; Wilk et al. 2010), they rarely figure in dominant accounts of the militarized masculinity that is thought to underpin the kind of (sexual) violence against civilians that many of the soldiers we talked to and their colleagues committed. Moreover, their stories featured memories of physical violence to which they had been subjected:, before they willingly or unwillingly had entered the armed forces (many claimed to have been forcibly recruited) and of abuse suffered at the hands of commanders once they joined the army. The stories were also marked by a deep-seated feeling of neglect, as well as a frustration and dissatisfaction with superiors. Commanders were portrayed as unfair and as benefiting themselves at the expense of subordinates (e.g., by embezzling soldiers' salaries and rations and by an unfair distribution of the unofficial resources). It was the neglect and greed of the superiors, the soldiers explained, that destroyed the army/discipline and that forced soldiers to act in ways that are ultimately foreign to both the army and to their own sense of self (e.g., theft, rape, and other violence against civilians). In this sense, they abdicated responsibility for their actions, and blamed both their superiors and their situation for the violence they committed. Yet such abdication also coexisted with instances of self-criticism, guilt, and responsibility, as well as difficult ethical self-reflection (Eriksson Baaz and Stern 2009).

While we (given the focus of the research) mainly aimed to "talk to them as soldiers" (to call upon their identity as soldiers), the army staff we talked to often steered the conversation away from this subject, and instead, talked about themselves as fathers and husbands. Their representations of themselves as family members, like those as soldiers, were marked by a strong sense of vulnerability and failure; they portrayed themselves as failed husbands and fathers since poor salaries and social conditions did not enable them to provide for their families. (Heterosexual) manhood, they conveyed, was intimately connected to being a provider; the impossibility of providing for their families and the sense of hopelessness and failure this created occupied a central place in their narratives. Stories of hungry, unschooled, sick, and sometimes dying children and comments that "my wife does not love me anymore" (since I cannot provide for her) were recurrent in the interview material. This suffering was also presented as a main explanation for various forms of (ill-)discipline, in particular "illegal taxation," theft, fraud, selling of weapons and uniforms, but also other forms of violence against civilians (including sexual violence). In short, in contrast to dominant notions attached to militarized masculinity as embodying control and (appearances of) unassailability, the stories were strongly marked by articulations of vulnerability and failure, in ways that we had not anticipated, and that disrupted (and rendered visible) our limited frames of understanding. Indeed, the interview material we collected not only disrupted our expectations of soldiers' subject positions as soldiers (and fathers and husbands), it also troubled our previous notions of the logics of sexual violence (Eriksson Baaz and Stern 2016).

Further, and as noted earlier, we expected to hear stories of ordered, or at least implicitly encouraged, rape (e.g., statements by soldiers that commanders don't really care if they rape and/or do not explicitly forbid them from raping), in line with the concept of rape as a weapon of war discourse. Yet, such accounts were largely absent in the conversations. The soldiers were always asked whether they had ever received explicit orders or felt they were encouraged to rape. Their answer was always no. Given the openness with which the soldiers talked about their commanders generally (accusing them of stealing salaries and food rations, being incompetent, etc.), itself a manifestation of the breakdown of command and discipline so characteristic of the FARDC at that time, there is no reason to doubt that they would be forthcoming if they had ever received such orders or felt they were encouraged to rape (Eriksson Baaz and Stern 2013a). Moreover, while in many testimonies violence against civilians was clearly expressed as a manifestation of a "need to put them in their place," "show them a lesson," and "punish" them, which resonated with the basic logic of rape as a weapon of war discourse, these acts of punishments were not discursively linked to (i.e., not described as following from) strategic goals or orders by commanders. Instead, they were described as linked to sentiments of humiliation and mistreatment, stemming from civilians' lack of respect and perceptions of soldiers as losers and useless people. In short, the accounts of rape as a weapon of war encouraged by commanders was glaringly absent.

In addition, the soldiers' testimonies showed no hint of rape as an expression of successful masculine performance. (Indeed, it became clear to us that we were indeed "expecting" to notice, if not explicit celebrations, at least hints of such an attitude. What might we have missed, we wonder, as we tuned our ears to the frequencies we anticipated; Eriksson Baaz and Stern 2016.) As explained earlier, virility and maintaining multiple sexual relations were celebrated and indeed presented as a way to perform and live up to the ideals of masculinity. Yet, the soldiers never spoke of rape in this way. While they may have explained or even excused rape, they nonetheless presented it as an expression of failed masculinity. In referring to instances of rape, almost all of their accounts included a statement that rape is bad and forbidden, both in military and civilian life. A successful, celebrated man, they explained, is a man with the financial and material resources to "keep"/"support"/"pay for" many women (Eriksson Baaz and Stern 2008). In the soldiers' testimonies, the man who rapes was, rather, portrayed as an emasculated man, who, deprived of the resources needed to perform hegemonic masculinity, is "forced" to rape (Heberle and Grace 2011). In short, rape was not linked to "successful" masculinity, nor was it presented as morally excusable for the purposes of warring.

The other of victimhood?

Thus far we have revisited how the "data" we collected did not easily fit into the available imaginaries provided by the dominant framings of the interrelationship between gender, armed conflict, and violence. However, perhaps the most surprising discord between what we unwittingly anticipated and what we experienced was the recognition and empathy we felt in our meetings with the army staff (see Eriksson Baaz and Stern 2016). Without realizing it, we were prepared to meet with the sorts of violent subjects scripted through dominant discourses (immoral beasts; violent macho wannabe *Rambo* types; "rational" soldiers well-indoctrinated with the necessity/utility of Othering their enemy though sexual violence, etc.). While prevalent in general literature on post-conflict reconstruction (see Baines 2009; Moser and Clark 2001), recognition of the blurring of lines of distinction between victims and perpetrators remains remarkably absent in accounts of conflict-related rape. However, on the whole we encountered subjects, who themselves, as demonstrated earlier, were subjected to various forms of violence and suffering (e.g., as fathers of hungry, sick, and sometimes dying children due to extreme poverty; being forcibly recruited/kept in the army against their wish and suffering abuse from within the military organization). Additionally, they clearly engaged in ethical and moral reflection about the violence committed.

Yet, the dominant stories we were tuned to hear rendered our listening and empathy with perpetrators of violent acts (including sexual violence) both uneasy and difficult, and raised further questions about research ethics and the politics of knowledge production—especially in post-colonial contexts. We were asked a recurring question when talking to people (mostly people from the "international" community)—a haunting question: "How is it? It must be very difficult to conduct such interviews and to speak to those people?" (read: awful/bestial rapists) (Eriksson Baaz and Stern 2013a). Most of the time we braced ourselves and responded: yes, it was (and is), but also that our sympathies were called forth through listening to the soldiers' own stories, not only—as one would expect—through listening to the acts that some of them had committed and/or were defending. Questions about who should be "given a voice" (the perpetrators of violent acts?) and whose suffering matters (Butler 2004), as well as what our interpretations of the soldiers' stories *do* politically and ethically, came to the fore.

Noting our surprise and unease enabled us to query the gap between the often extreme dehumanization of the rapist/soldier in the story of rape in the DRC, and the encounter with these soldiers as a site of knowledge. It led to further interrogating how dominant grids of intelligibility for understanding gender and (sexual) violence draw lines of distinctions between the human and the somehow non-human, between victims and perpetrators, as well as between different forms of violence.

CONCLUSIONS: THINKING OTHERWISE?

The dissonance between our imaginaries of the constellation of gender-armed conflict-violence and the soldiers' actual stories prompted us (to some extent) to notice and interrogate our previous understandings and strive to "think otherwise." Thinking otherwise involved both noting and exploring the limits of our grids of intelligibility, as well as seeking new explanatory frameworks for making sense of the knowledge we gained.

For instance, our analysis of the gendered workings of the Congolese army made us venture into military sociology, a field that seldom features in feminist texts (where citing military sociology implies that one is associated with militaristic goals) (for some exceptions, see Basham 2009; Higate 2013; Wood 2009, 2010, 2012). Yet, military sociology (which in contrast to the dominant story of wartime rape explores the failings and effects of military organizations to work according to the ideals of discipline, hierarchy, and control) helped us to make better sense of the workings of the Congolese military and the manifestations in terms of violence against civilians. We came to see the ways in which the widespread occurrence of sexual violence by the Congolese army was largely a reflection of low levels of unit cohesion (in particular, vertical cohesion) and the breakdown of the chain of command. Instead of reflecting control and the tidy workings of the military (i.e., the enforcement of orders down the chain of command), instances of sexual violence reflected dysfunctional chains of command, high levels of frustration, and (non-strategic) spirals of violence (Eriksson Baaz and Stern 2013a; Wood 2012). Recognition of this, in addition to the ways in which the soldiers themselves were subjected to various forms of violence and suffering, also cast doubt on the ethics, as well as the effectiveness, of the main remedy proposed by the international community: "deterrence through severe punishments." This recognition suggests the need for measures other than deterrence that are designed to attend to both the traumas and the working conditions of the soldiers (cf. Baines 2009).

Moreover, while our analysis also came to emphasize the workings of militarized masculinities that are tightly linked to virility and sexual potency (a familiar account), we came to highlight how militarized (and mythologized) masculinities (and the attendant promises and entitlements associated with inhabiting these masculinities) rarely resonate with soldiers' sense of self, lived experiences, or with the actual conditions of militarized men's lives (Higate and Henry 2004; Whitworth 2004). Building upon a notion of identity as a continual process, which can never be fully realized,[6] we argued that the fragility and indeed impossibility of militarized masculinity requires continual concealment through military institutional practices, and in the individual expressions of such masculinity. Hence, while inhabiting any subject position (such as that of masculine heterosexual soldier), feelings of "failed masculinity" can be seen to contribute to sexual violence in that it becomes a way to try to perform and try to regain masculinity and power (see Alison 2007; Eriksson Baaz and Stern 2009; Niehaus 2005). While this is certainly not a new insight in feminist theory or masculinity studies more generally, it tends to be forgotten in relation to our expectations of militarized masculinities in the prevailing rape as a weapon of war discourse (Alison 2007; Eriksson Baaz and Stern 2009; Niehaus 2005). Importantly, militarized masculinities cannot be ascribed various attributes that are assumed to be shared by military males globally (in contrast to civilian males, and both military and civilian women). While shaped in a global landscape, military masculinities are constructed in national and local contexts and are also often articulated in various ways, depending on the sections or parts of the same military institution. By paying close attention to the meanings attached to "gender" and "the military" by military staff in various settings, we learn how gender and the military are open questions that are constantly renegotiated and reconfigured, rather than fixed entities (Eriksson Baaz and Stern 2013b).

This line of reasoning is surely familiar to many critical feminist scholars. Nonetheless, in light of experience from researching the connections between masculinity and violence in a specific warscape, it bears repeating that any pre-decided notion of how gender (as a known entity) works and what it does in particular contexts must be both limited and limiting. Exploring and querying these limits allows us to begin to pose gender as a question and to think otherwise. Certainly, posing gender as an open question is not easy, or even really possible. Importantly, we do not suggest that we were successful in doing so. While the dissonance we experienced after many and long conversations with army staff in the DRC forced us "to think otherwise" in some respects, our thinking and analysis is certainly still limited by the available imaginaries, in ways in which we are not, and perhaps cannot, be aware.

Notes

1. Men and boys *as gendered subjects* who act and are acted upon in violent conflict, as a category distinct from "the military," have received far less attention; a growing number of studies, however, are addressing this under-researched field (see Carpenter 2006; Dolan, Chapter 7 in this volume). Additionally, the global policy community has recognized, for example, the need to address men and boys as victims/survivors of sexual violence (see Sivakumaran 2010; Thiedon, Chapter 11 in this volume).
2. As our research shows, the assumption that perpetrators acknowledge that this is a wrong act and that this has psychological consequences is not always the case (see also Hadzimesic, Chapter 39 in this volume)
3. This text is based on research results that have appeared elsewhere (see Eriksson Baaz and Stern 2008, 2009, 2011, 2013a, 2013b, 2016). Some of the phrasing occurs verbatim in these other works. We have referenced these sources, although we have not cited directly for the sake of readability.
4. This included soldiers and officers of different ranks from various previous armed group affiliations before integration into the government forces, and both men and women (although we interviewed more men than women).
5. For example, men's sexual needs are often presented as the reason for R & R (also to reduce the risk of supposedly unhealthy homosexual acts). Army brothels have also frequently

been used, not the least during World War II. The prostitution rings that notoriously surround army bases, including current UN forces worldwide such as MONUC, are another
example of this phenomenon.

6. The fulfillment of any identity position is therefore impossible and bound to "fail" (see
Butler 1990; Hall 1996).

References

Alison, Miranda. 2007. "Wartime Sexual Violence: Women's Human Rights and Questions of
Masculinity." *Review of International Studies* 33, no. 1: 75–90.

Baines, Erin K. 2009. "Complex Political Perpetrators: Reflections on Dominic Ongwen." *The
Journal of Modern African Studies* 47, no. 2: 163–191.

Basham, Victoria. 2009. "Effecting Discrimination: Operational Effectiveness and Harassment
in the British Armed Forces." *Armed Forces & Society* 35, no. 4: 728–744.

Bergren, Kalle. 2014. "Sticky Masculinity: Post-Structuralism, Phenomenology and Subjectivity."
Critical Studies on Men, Men and Masculinities 17, no. 3: 231–252.

Butler, Judith. 1990. *Gender Trouble: Feminism and the Subversion of Identity*. London:
Routledge.

Butler, Judith. 2004. *Precarious Life: The Powers of Mourning and Violence*. London/New
York:Verso.

Carpenter, Charli R. 2006. "Recognizing Gender-Based Violence Against Civilian Men and
Boys in Conflict Situations." *Security Dialogue* 37: 83–103.

Collins, Randall. 2008. *Violence: A Micro-Sociological Theory*. Princeton, NJ: Princeton
University Press.

Connell, R. W. 1995. *Masculinities*. Los Angeles: University of California Press.

Dietrich Ortega, Luisa Maria. 2012. "Looking Beyond Violent Militarized Masculinities."
International Journal of Feminist Politics 14, no. 4: 489–507.

Enloe, Cynthia. 1990. *Bananas, Beaches and Bases: Making Feminist Sense of International
Politics*. Berkeley: University of California Press.

Enloe, Cynthia. 2000. *Maneuvers: The International Politics of Militarizing Women's Lives*.
Berkeley: University of California Press.

Eriksson Baaz, Maria, and Maria Stern. 2008. "Making Sense of Violence: Voices of Soldiers in
the Congo (DRC)." *The Journal of Modern African Studies* 46, no. 1: 57–86.

Eriksson Baaz, Maria, and Maria Stern. 2009. "Why Do Soldiers Rape? Masculinity, Violence,
and Sexuality in the Armed Forces in the Congo (DRC)." *International Studies Quarterly* 53,
no. 2: 495–518.

Eriksson Baaz, Maria, and Maria Stern. 2011. "Whores, Men and Other Misfits: Undoing the
'Feminization' of the Armed Forces in the DR Congo." *African Affairs* 110, no. 441: 563–585.

Eriksson Baaz, Maria, and Maria Stern. 2013a. *Sexual Violence as a Weapon of War? Perceptions,
Prescriptions, Problems in the Congo and Beyond*. London: Zed Books.

Eriksson Baaz, Maria, and Maria Stern. 2013b. "Fearless Fighters and Submissive Wives:
Negotiating Identity among Women Soldiers in the Congo (DRC)." *Armed Forces and
Society* 39, no. 4: 711–739.

Eriksson Baaz, Maria, and Maria Stern. 2015. "Research in the Rape Capital of the World:
Fame and Shame." In *Masqueredes of War*, edited by Christine Sylvester, 197–206. London:
Routledge.

Eriksson Baaz, Maria, and Maria Stern. 2016. "Researching War Time Rape in the Democratic Republic of Congo: A Methodology of Unease." In *Researching War: Feminist Methods, Ethics and Politics*, edited by A. T. Wibben, 197–206. London: Routledge.

Goldstein, Joshua S. 2001. *War and Gender: How Gender Shapes the War System and Vice Versa*. Cambridge: Cambridge University Press.

Gutmann, Stephanie. 2000. *The Kinder, Gentler Military*. New York: Scribner.

Hall, Stuart. 1996. "Introduction: Who Needs 'Identity?'" In *Questions of Cultural Identity*, edited by Stuart Hall and Paul du Gay, 15–30. London: Sage Publications.

Heberle, Renée, and Victoria Grace, eds. 2011. *Theorizing Sexual Violence*. New York: Routledge.

Higate, Paul. 2001. *Military Masculinities: Identity and the State*. London: Praeger.

Higate, Paul. 2001. 2006. "Reflexivity and Researching the Military." *Armed Forces & Society* 32, no. 2: 219–233.

Higate, Paul. 2001. 2012. "Foregrounding the In/Visibility of Military and Militarized Masculinities." In *Beyond "Gender and Stir:" Reflections on Gender and SSR in the Aftermath of African Conflicts*, edited by Maria Eriksson Baaz and Mats Utas, 31–37. Uppsala: The Nordic Africa Institute.

Higate, Paul. 2001. 2013. "Mercenary Killer or Embodied Vetran? The Case of Paul Slough and the Nisour Square Massacre." In *Corporeality: The Body and Society*, edited by Cassandra A. Ogden and Stephen Wakeman, 99–120. Chester: University of Chester Press.

Higate, Paul, and Marsha Henry. 2004. "Engendering (In)Security in Peace Support Operations." *Security Dialogue* 35, no. 4: 481–498.

Higate, Paul, and J. Hopton. 2005. "War, Militarism, and Masculinities." In *Handbook of Studies on Men's Masculinities*, edited by Michael S. Kimmel, Jeff Hearn, and Robert W. Connell, 389–404. Thousand Oaks, CA: Sage.

Hutchings, Kimberly. 2008. "Making Sense of Masculinity and War." *Men and Masculinities* 10, no. 4: 389–404.

Kirby, Paul. 2013. "Refusing to Be a Man? Men's Responsibility for War Rape and the Problem of Social Structures in Feminist and Gender Theory." *Men and Masculinities* 16, no. 1: 93–114.

Mitchell, Brian. 1989. *Weak Link*. Washington, DC: Regnery Publishing.

Mitchell, Brian. 1998. *Women in the Military*. Washington, DC: Regnery.

Moser, Caroline O. N., and Fiona C. Clark. 2001. *Victims, Perpetrators or Actors: Gender, Armed Conflict and Political Violence*. London: Zed Books.

Niehaus, Isak. 2005. "Masculine Domination in Sexual Violence: Interpreting Accounts of Three Cases of Rape in the South African Lowveld." In *Men Behaving Differently: South African Men since 1994*, edited by Graeme Reid and Liz Walker, 65–87. Capetown: Double Storey Books.

Pin-Fat, Véronique, and Maria Stern. 2005. "The Scripting of Private Jessica Lynch: Biopolitics, Gender, and the 'Feminization' of the U.S. Military." *Alternatives* 30: 25–53.

Price, Lisa S. 2001. "Finding the Man in the Soldier-Rapist: Some Reflections on Comprehension and Accountability." *Women's Studies International Forum* 24, no. 2: 211–227.

Shepherd, Laura J. 2010. *Gender Matters in Global Politics*. London: Routledge.

Sivakumaran, Sandesh. 2010. "Lost in Translation: UN Responses to Sexual Violence against Men and Boys in Situations of Armed Conflict." *International Review of the Red Cross* 92, no. 877: 259–277.

Stern, Maria, and Marysia Zalewski. 2009. "Feminist Fatigue(s): Reflections on Feminism and Familiar Fables of Militarisation." *Review of International Studies* 35, no. 3: 611–630.

True, Jacqui. 2012. *The Political Economy of Violence against Women*. Oxford: Oxford University Press.

UN Secretary-General. 2015. *Report of the Secretary General on the United Nations Organization Stabilization Mission in the Democratic Republic of the Congo*. UN Doc. S/2015/486.

van Creveld, Martin. 2000. "The Great Illusion: Women in the Military." *Millennium* 29, no. 2: 429–442.

Whitworth, Sandra. 2004. *Men, Militarism, and UN Peacekeeping: A Gendered Analysis*. Boulder, CO: Lynne Rienner.

Wood, Elisabeth J. 2009. "Armed Groups and Sexual Violence: When Is Wartime Rape Rare?" *Politics Society* 37, no. 1: 131–162.

Wood, Elisabeth J. 2010. "Sexual Violence during War: Variation and Accountability." In *Collective Violence and International Criminal Justice*, edited by Alette Smeulers, 295–322. Antwerp: Intersentia.

Wood, Elisabeth J. 2012. "Rape during War Is Not Inevitable: Variation in Wartime Sexual Violence." In *Understanding and Proving International Crimes*, edited by Morten Bergsmo, Alf Butenschoen Skre, and Elisabeth J. Wood, 389–419. Beijing: Torkel Opsahl Academic E-Publisher.

Wilk, Joshua E., Paul D. Bliese, Paul Y. Kim, Jeffrey L. Thomas, Dennis McGurk, and Charles W. Hoge. 2010. "Relationship of Combat Experiences to Alcohol Misues among U.S. Soldiers Returning from the Iraq War." *Drug and Alcohol Dependence* 108, no. 1–2: 115–121.

Yuval-Davis, Nira. 1997. *Gender and Nation*. London: Sage Publications.

Zalewski, Marysia. 2010. "'I Don't Even Know What Gender Is:' A Discussion of the Connections between Gender, Gender Mainstreaming and Feminist Theory." *Review of International Studies* 36, no. 1: 3–27.

CHAPTER 42

NORTHERN IRELAND

The Significance of a Bottom-Up Women's Movement in a Politically Contested Society

MONICA MCWILLIAMS AND AVILA KILMURRAY

LIKE all political processes, conflicts and transitions are gendered, with men and women often playing different roles and delivering different outcomes for both. The involvement of women activists in conflict and post-conflict societies shows how women have struggled to have these gender differences addressed as part of conflict transformation. Women's contribution to peace-building also tends to occur through their mobilization across ethnic/political divides, in diverse social movements, rather than in established political processes, as is more typical with men. Northern Ireland provides an example of these multiple dynamics.

This chapter addresses the contributions made to conflict transformation by women's activism in Northern Ireland (1968–1994) and shows how this seeded the formation of the Northern Ireland Women's Coalition political party (1996–2006). It traces the various stages of activism, from "civil rights" activism to the "accidental activism" arising out of the crisis; from the women's peace movement to the more aligned "conflictual activism"; and from women's community activism to feminist change agents. The trajectory shows that faced with exclusion from formal institutions, the women's movement/sector became an alternative means to confront institutions, achieve access, and bring about change.

The chapter highlights how women activists built broad alliances in civil society, enabling them to enter a new "transitional space." This space, which opened prior to peace negotiations in 1996, provided the possibility for a new women's political party (Northern Ireland Women's Coalition) to be elected to the negotiations that resulted in the Belfast/Good Friday Agreement. The chapter notes how women activists framed their gender-specific interests to relate to the new constitutional framework, building on skills honed through women's activism. This tracks a comparative practice, seen in at least two other societies, Iceland and Israel, as women's parties drew public attention to women's marginalization and inserted gender politics onto the political map by pressuring other parties to adapt their behavior and policy commitments to include women's issues. The extent to which this happened successfully in Northern Ireland will be examined.

The chapter also shows how movements and parties can interact creatively in the context of new institutional opportunities, especially where innovative electoral rules are crafted to ensure the inclusion of unusual political forces. While some features are necessarily unique to the historical/political context of Northern Ireland, the approaches adopted may apply to other situations where innovation in political mechanics may alter the institutional dynamics and may present opportunities. The possibilities that this can present are examined, as well as the lessons learned.

CHARTING THE CONTEXT

For decades, the strife in Northern Ireland was viewed as ingrained conflict, beyond reason and rationality and ultimately insoluble within an internal, localized frame of reference.[1] Rooted in the sixteenth-century colonial conquest of Ireland by Britain, followed by population settlement to stabilize and control the territory, Northern Ireland was the last part of the Island territory to remain contested following independence for the Irish Republic in 1922. In Northern Ireland, respective mandates for Irish and British political/cultural identities were mutually exclusive and were resistant to political accommodation from the formation of Northern Ireland in 1921. However, the 1998 peace agreement negotiated an accommodation, establishing power-sharing arrangements between the "two sides" and recognizing the legitimacy and ethos of both identities. The contested explanatory narrative still has resonance, however; the UK government characterized the internal strife experienced from the late 1960s as criminal disorder, rather than considering that the legal threshold of armed conflict had been met. Consequently, the Geneva Conventions were never formally recognized as applicable to the conflict—a lack of recognition that continues, given the consistent refusal of the United Kingdom to acknowledge the applicability of Security Council resolution 1325 (2000) and successor resolutions on women, peace, and security to the protection of women's interests in the jurisdiction (CEDAW 2013).

Alongside the political circumstances, local religious institutions exerted a conservative influence on social policy, impacting negatively on the position of women. The primacy of the family and the home were asserted by both church and state, and employment opportunities were restricted for married women until EU membership in the mid 1970s. Men dominated public decision-making at every level.

During this period, the women's movement built on a combination of factors. There was the preexisting network of women activists from previous civil rights protests from the late 1960s to mid-1970s. Following from this "civil rights activism," a second category emerged, identified by McWilliams (1995) as "accidental activism." This occurred where women were left to maintain family and community when relatives were imprisoned following internment without trial and subsequent judicial measures. The ongoing conflict gave rise to two additional categories: "peace activism" involved organizations such as Women Together (established in 1970), Women for Peace (1972), and the Peace Women (1976), and "conflictual activism" referred to women actively involved in the conflict. The largest group of women political prisoners took part in protests, including hunger strikes, in solidarity with their male comrades' demand for the reinstatement of Special (Political) Category Status. Outside the prisons, women also mobilized in "Relatives Action Committees" and "Women against Imperialism" (Loughran 1986). The vocal, and often antagonistic, nature of "conflictual activism" questioned assumptions of women as intrinsic peacemakers.

The fifth category of activism—the feminist agenda as agents for change—saw the emergence of the Northern Ireland Women's Rights Movement in 1975. The organizational movement developed a charter of demands on domestic violence (with Women's Aid), legal reform (with Women's Law & Research Group), and societal change. This was a period in which reforms were instituted as a direct result of campaigning—such as legislation on sex discrimination, divorce, and domestic violence. (The issue of reproductive rights was, however, viewed as too radical for Northern Ireland's policymakers.)

COMMUNITY-BASED WOMEN'S ACTIVISM: DIFFERENCES IN THE PEACE-BUILDING AGENDA

The formation of local women's groups and the opening of numerous women's centers across Northern Ireland in the 1970s and 1980s showed how women activists in Northern Ireland responded to "the politics of location" and how women's communal activism was "a situated politics of everyday life" (Porter 1998, 36). Most of the local groups and centers operated in largely single-identity community areas, predominantly Protestant or Catholic, and responded to the political complexion of their location. The latter was moderated to a degree by the emergence of a number of support and networking structures that provided a focus of solidarity between individual groups and centers. While women had always been active in local communities, women-specific community action flourished in the 1980s and 1990s.

An early initiative connected to cross-community peace-building was the Women's Information Group (WIG). Empowering women in working-class areas on both sides of the sectarian divide through accessible information on issues, such as housing and finances, had the secondary aim of building contact between otherwise divided communities. Monthly meetings rotated between venues in single-identity Catholic and Protestant communities, enabling participants to see how people lived in "the other" community, on the other side of dividing "Peace Walls," and to question preexisting stereotypes. While these benefits were explicit, any suggestion that the initiative was a basis for political mobilization was played down. The Women's Information Group meetings required the very different political affiliations to be carefully mediated, largely by focusing on issues with which women self-identified—poverty, health care, domestic violence, and education. Many women in these cross-community settings were more comfortable with nomenclature such as "family feminists," since their immediate concerns revolved around keeping their families safe.[2] The emphasis was in grounding women's issues and participation in approaches that they felt comfortable with, rather than the more ideologically framed feminist demands.

The declaration of Republican and Loyalist ceasefires in 1994 opened up new transitional spaces for women to meet and to re-envision politics and political participation. The introduction of an "EU PEACE Programme," to help embed the peace process, assisted in the delivery of much needed resources for women's groups in disadvantaged communities. Networks expanded in rural and urban areas, as well as across the community divide, highlighting the potential complementarity between the (formal) peace process and (informal) peace-building. In a separate initiative, the Northern Ireland Women's Coalition was established as a women-directed political party in 1996, highlighting the distinction between small "p" politics and large "P" politics as the latter increasingly became an option. In contrast, women community activists, while aware that many priorities were political in nature, emphasized their involvement in informal/local community action (the small "p") rather than the large "P" politics of the more formal political process. This distinction threw up quandaries as the Women's Coalition was challenged by the more orthodox political parties about its representativeness. Political positioning and identification were to become a disputed discourse as mainstream political engagement followed.

PRIORITIZING POLITICAL PRESENCE

Although praised for their peace-building efforts on a cross-community basis, women remained on the margins of the peace process in the pre-negotiation phase (Bell 2004). Countering this marginality by coming into the political mainstream was an entrée not only into political negotiations, but also to political representation and ultimately constitutional influence. To enable this, contact was established between the Northern Ireland Women's European Platform (NIWEP) and the Women's Political Association in the Republic of Ireland (an all-party initiative to promote women's political participation). US Ambassador to Ireland (Jean Kennedy Smith) invited women activists to her residence, which resulted in calls for a bill of rights, quotas, and an inclusive peace process (Hinds 1999). The following year (1995), a conference attended by over 200 women from all sides of the community was organized by McWilliams to discuss the potential for participation in the process following the Downing Street Declaration.[3] The conference report, "Women, Politics and the Way Forward," strengthened recommendations already emerging from a range of initiatives (including women who attended the 1994 Beijing Women's conference) to address likely marginalization in the talks process.

The proposals for "All Party Talks" tabled by the British and Irish governments (Spring 1996) included the listing of named parties that would contest the election and a designated electoral system to facilitate the representation of the smaller political parties with links to Loyalist paramilitary organizations. [4] In response, a group of women activists lobbied for the inclusion of other political parties not on the list. Anderson (2010) terms this a form of "procedural grafting" and outlines how women in Northern Ireland and Burundi made use of this mechanism to enter formal peace negotiations. Both the successful representation and the proposed electoral system encouraged women to form the Northern Ireland Women's Coalition in order to contest the election. The Coalition's platform, "Bringing Beijing Back Home," stood on the three principles—human rights, inclusion, and equality—and instigated a call for a "New Voice for New Times." The title "Coalition" was intentionally chosen over that of "Party" in order to open membership to women irrespective of preexisting political or community background, provided they subscribed to the three principles. The Women's Coalition was deliberately structured in a bi-communal manner, with two leaders, one drawn from the Catholic/Nationalist identity and the other from Protestant/Unionist. Refusing to adopt a position on the constitutional question, the Coalition strategized a politics that promoted the greater presence of women, as well as a forum for active citizenship during the political transition. An energetic six-week election campaign saw the Coalition garnering enough votes to return two delegates to the Peace Talks. Out of nine parties and twenty-three delegates, they were the only women at the negotiating table when the talks commenced in 1996.

The formation of the Northern Ireland Women's Coalition was not without controversy or opposition. It was condemned, patronized, or ridiculed by various political parties (Kilmurray and McWilliams 2011). It became the norm for some male representatives to be verbally abusive to the Women's Coalition delegates and their advisors. There was also, however, a renewed interest in asserting a woman-friendly face of mainstream politics with established parties fronting women to counter the Coalition, where previously there had been general agreement that women were disinterested in politics. This was seen as a benchmark of success by the Coalition, encouraging an inclusive and more female face of politics as a necessary part of the political transformation.

Women in the community-based sector continued to hold political allegiances that spanned the spectrum of political options. Many Coalition activists had come from this sector alongside trade unionists, feminist academics, and the issue-based women's organizations. There was a clear heterogeneity of women's interests and identities. It required the type of "transversal politics" that Yuval-Davis (1998) has conceptualized— a shift that does not require individuals to abandon their identity but rather to leave themselves open to both the identity of others and to dialogue. A particular concern expressed by organizations in the women's sector was whether perceived political alignment with the Coalition would put donor and statutory/public funding at risk.[5] As a result, some Coalition supporters had to adopt tactics such as being "sleeper" members so that their involvement remained below the party political radar.

Rebouche and Fearon (2005) argue that what the Women's Coalition achieved was extensive in terms of process, although more limited with regard to outcomes. The Coalition's goals were both policy and process oriented; its strategy was to aim for inclusion, so as to increase the political representation of women, and to gain policy influence. In relation to outcomes, it built on the experience of gender activists in South Africa, strategizing to frame its demands within the framework of constitutional change and equality. The Coalition was successful in having "the right of women to full and equal participation in political life" inserted into the Belfast/Good Friday Agreement while also ensuring that the final accord acknowledged issues of gender equality and non-discrimination independently of the issue of national identity. The Coalition consistently argued that women needed to have a designated "place" in the Agreement to better identify with it. The more challenging issue was enforcing these commitments, as the outcomes of agreements "are not determined by words, but by power relations that impose their interpretations" (Chomsky 1998, 26).

The Coalition also supported the introduction of a new human rights body, a Bill of Rights, and a stronger mandate for the Equality Commission. Affirmative action, such as temporary special measures and quotas, were subsequently supported to enable more Catholics to be recruited as part of the policing reforms.[6] In addition, it argued for the rights of victims and survivors of the conflict to be recognized; for community development to be sustained and resourced; and for integrated education and mixed housing to increase the provision of services on a non-sectarian basis. Had the Coalition not been present at the peace talks, it is doubtful that these proposals would have made their way into the final agreement. As Cahn, Haynes, and Ní Aoláin (2010) note, if women are absent from peace negotiations, these much-needed social services, such as justice, care for victims, education, health, and well-being, are more likely to be absent in post-conflict societies.

The Coalition's proposal for a civic forum was accepted as part of the new governance arrangements. This envisaged a citizens' assembly that would act in an advisory role to the directly elected Northern Ireland Assembly, providing formal recognition of the contribution of participatory democracy in the new dispensation. Although established, the civic forum was stood down in the wake of the subsequent collapse of the Legislative Assembly; unlike the latter, it was not reinstated. Another notable failure was the inability to achieve an electoral system that would be supportive of more equal gender representation. The ethos of the existing "constitutional" parties in Northern Ireland did not lend itself to the promotion of collective, more deliberative forms of decision-making such as the civic forum, to women's inclusion, or to the diversity of political opinion through an alternative election system. The established parties did not see these proposals as relevant to either conflict transformation or as a necessary part of the reconstruction of the political system that Wolff (2005) posits as central to women's participation.

The instability of the post-Agreement period resulted in a continuing emphasis on the predominantly male preserves of demilitarization, decommissioning of weaponry, and reconfiguring of policing and security—shot through with arguments over the allocation of political power. The "command and control" approach to politics by the two parties that were to edge their way into prime electoral position left less room for innovative forms of participatory democracy.[7] In short, despite the Coalition almost doubling its vote in the 1998 Northern Ireland Assembly election, it was to lose both its Assembly members in the election of 2003. It made the decision to dissolve itself and reintegrate its activists into civil society in May 2006—a decade after its launch. Although essential for the implementation of the peace agreement in Northern Ireland, the power-sharing consociational arrangements put in place for the governance of a contested society did not suit smaller non-single identity parties that sought to frame politics in a different manner.

A POLITICS OF PRESENCE AND VOICE

The plurality of women's voices has been celebrated in feminist analysis (Benhabib 1996). This plurality was reflected in the diversity of the women's sector in Northern Ireland, where women played a crucial role in conflict-related areas such as supporting victims/survivors of the conflict. However, despite being very active, women were all too often "hidden" in the various theorizations and public narratives of competing nationalisms (Ní Aoláin, Haynes, and Cahn 2011).

Community-based women's groups could steer their small "p" priorities and interests through the shoals of specific and competing identities, although they will be mindful of what may be politically accepted to the very different parties represented in government in Northern Ireland. In short, they will be affected by what Hobson (2003) terms the "discursive opportunity"—what it is politically possible to say—that impacts on the mis/non-recognition of women. To counter this, Fraser (2003) holds that redressing misrecognition means replacing institutionalized values that impede parity of participation with values that enable or foster participation, particularly of marginalized women.[8] The Northern Ireland Women's Coalition did strive to ensure that the Belfast/Good Friday Agreement took note of discursive opportunity, as well as fostering participation for women at all levels of decision-making.

Women activists also struggled to ensure that the narrative and ongoing legacy of the conflict surfaced the issue of gender-specific harms. Addressing human rights violations is crucial to conflict transformation, as the "Families of the Disappeared" have shown. This group, founded by women who were silenced throughout the conflict, managed to raise their profile and mobilize to have a Commission for the Location of Victims Remains established. They also provided much needed solidarity for other families to come forward. Equally, it was former women prisoners who established the first Republican ex-prisoners' self-help group (Tar Anall), although support work with political ex-prisoners became increasingly male dominated.[9]

Despite the contribution of women activists to conflict transformation, the promise of increased participation and recognition for women failed to materializes, other than a small number of elected politicians. Women's groups provided detailed critiques of the

lack of attention to women's voices in relevant policies agreed by the devolved government following the implementation of the peace agreement (Hegarty 2010). In short, the
"situated politics of everyday life does not automatically translate into electoral representation and decision-making" (Porter 1998, 50). This is particularly true in a contested
society, where a range of conflict-related challenges have yet to be addressed and which
lacks a dedicated feminist perspective at the heart of decision-making. In the hierarchy
of political risk management, the "women's dimension" is easily overlooked since it does
not threaten the distribution of power that underpins the calculus of violence.

Women's Activism: A Sector, a Movement, or a Political Presence?

Social movements have been variously described as "conscious, concerted and sustained
efforts by ordinary people to change some aspects of their society by using extra institutional means" (Goodwin and Jasper 2009). Molyneaux (1988) sees women's movements
as a form of female collective action in pursuit of social and political goals, demonstrating a level of participation and agreement that distinguishes the collective action from
small-scale women's organizations or networks. Women activists in Northern Ireland
attempted to combine elements of both by strategizing in innovative ways to design collective action to advance the emancipation, empowerment, and public participation of
women within their divided society. This started with self-conscious movement building in the 1970s, variously influenced by issues of national identity and the ongoing
armed conflict. What McAdam et al. (2001) refer to as "the politics of everyday life" was
not strong enough to avert the politics of the conflict, although a range of the extra-
institutional approaches adopted did in fact deliver policy change. It is questionable
whether the women's movement survived into the late 1980s, when a publicly funded
women's sector became more prevalent given the increased availability of both philan-
thropic and government program resources. The latter, in particular, placed an emphasis on service delivery, which the more advocacy-oriented women's groups and centers
translated into learning to inform policy demands. The relationship with funders meant
that groups, in the main, became more comfortable with "institutional means" to ensure
that gender interests were reflected in policymaking. Although there was a shared baseline of promoting women's interests, the lack of a shared alternative macro-analysis or
narrative became clear when the chillier climate of decreasing resources became apparent in recent years. Feminist solidarity became increasingly strained when competition
for scarce resources trumped the primacy of reinforcing women's activism that was necessary to realize the commitments inserted in the Good Friday Agreement.

   Whatever the limitations of the women's sector in Northern Ireland in terms of clarity of narrative and demands, the contribution to peace-building and conflict transformation remained substantial. Cross-community women's activism served to challenge

uni-communal stereotypes, while the women's networks provided space for inclusive self-reflection and cross-community engagement. Similarly, the focus on thematic issues, such as violence against women, women's health, women's human rights, and equality raised concerns that impacted women, irrespective of their national/ethnic identity. Both the validity of raising such issues and the experience of relationship building through working together remained important amidst so much division.

What the Northern Ireland Women's Coalition offered was an innovative platform to draw on the experience of women who had cut their teeth in the women's movement, and also a sensitivity to the issues and relationship-building identified by the women's sector, in order to develop a new macro-narrative for a post-conflict society. All too often, social movements and party/political formations are viewed as mutually exclusive options; however, the movement-party may be an effective mechanism for changing the patterns of democratic representation of marginalized groups. It also brings in its wake the ability to have a contagion effect on other political parties in terms of gender-specific policies and representation, while insisting on the centrality of women's issues more generally. To have an impact on sustainable conflict transformation, it also needs the ability to last beyond the transitional spaces that the early phase of a peace process allows.

CONCLUSION: LESSONS LEARNED

There have been lessons learned in engaging in this process. First is the need to sharpen the framing of women's issues as injustices in order to ensure attention on the agenda for political change. A second lesson is the importance of deconstructing political systems and processes to effectively achieve a greater electoral presence of women given that there is nothing set about democratic mechanisms. When the nature of formal negotiations was outlined in Northern Ireland, women activists moved quickly to strategize to prevent further exclusion. In trans/forming into a political grouping, the Women's Coalition used the new electoral provisions to increase women's participation in the political process in a cross-community manner. Similarly, the Coalition questioned assumptions during the crafting of the Belfast/Good Friday Agreement by posing new questions of old problems. Senator Mitchell (1999), the chairperson of the peace talks, concluded that "the emergence of women as a political force was a significant factor in achieving the Agreement."

The third learning point is the need to ensure that clauses in a peace agreement are enforceable, with implementation plans and measurement indicators. There is a need for institutional guarantees rather than simply "party political will." The optimistic rhetoric of peace can all too soon give way to the real politik of exclusive deals. In Northern Ireland, the sharing of power among the political elites failed to translate into inclusive power sharing with civic society, within which women are more often active. The fate of the civic forum and clauses concerning women's participation in political life are cases in point.

Finally, there is the need to rupture the zero-sum determination of politics in a contested society since it leaves little room for complexity, compromise, or change narratives.[10] In the post-conflict context, the unreformed default electoral system favored the predominance of larger, more established parties. The movement-party approach requires the investment of time and energy in articulating and messaging a new political culture, rather than remaining caught in the meshes of political system building. In this context, we agree with Goldstone (2003) that both social movement and conventional political activities can become parallel approaches to influencing political outcomes. When a society is transitioning from conflict, women's activism is crucial to both.

NOTES

1. The division of Ireland in 1921 resulted from an agreement to provide independence to twenty-six of the thirty-two counties of Ireland.
2. When First Lady Hillary Clinton visited members of this group in 1995, she commented on the application of the term "family feminists." Her experience in Northern Ireland was reflected in the organization that she subsequently founded (Vital Voices).
3. The Downing Street Declaration in 1993 opened the door to paramilitary-related parties to participate in negotiations for a constitutional settlement if they abandoned violence. This was followed by a Framework Agreement, published by the Irish and British governments in February 1995, advocating a power-sharing government in Northern Ireland, accompanied by cross-border cooperation.
4. The Ulster Democratic Party and Progressive Unionist Party were successfully elected to the peace talks as a result of these provisions.
5. Initiatives such as Women into Politics adopted a stance of political party neutrality, emphasizing the importance of political activism for women per se, rather than any preference for the Coalition.
6. The quotas were not extended to women recruits despite the under-representation of women in the police.
7. Sinn Fein and the Democratic Unionist Party, with opposite political ideologies, entered a coalition power-sharing executive.
8. Fraser (2003) differentiates this from "identity politics," which effectively valorizes group specificity—arguably as demonstrated through the power-sharing system of government instituted in Northern Ireland.
9. A number of these women later entered politics through Sinn Fein and held government positions in the Northern Ireland Executive.
10. The delay in delivering on the peace agreement's proposal for a Bill of Rights is a telling example of how human rights also became the subject of an antagonistic and adversarial discourse in Northern Ireland.

REFERENCES

Anderson, Miriam J. 2010. "Transnational Feminism and Norm Diffusion in Peace Processes: The Cases of Burundi and Northern Ireland." *Journal of Intervention and Statebuilding* 4, no. 1: 1–27.

Bell, Christine. 2004. "Women Address the Problems of Peace Agreements." In *Peace Work: Women, Armed Conflict and Negotiation*, edited by Radhika Coomeraswamy and Dilrukshi Fonseka, 96–126. Delhi: Women Unlimited.

Benhabib, Seyla, ed. 1996. *Democracy and Difference: Contesting the Boundaries of the Political*. Princeton, NJ: Princeton University Press.

Cahn, Naomi, Dina Francesca Haynes, and Fionnuala Ní Aoláin. 2010. "Returning Home: Women in Post Conflict Societies." *University of Baltimore Law Review* 39: 339–369.

Committee on the Elimination of Discrimination Against Women (CEDAW). 2013. *Committee Concluding Observations on the United Kingdom's Treaty Reporting Obligations*. UN Doc. CEDAW/C/GBR/CO/7 (July 30).

Chomsky, Noam. 1998. "Power in the Global Arena." *New Left Review* 230: 3–27.

Fraser, Nancy. 2003. "Rethinking Recognition: Overcoming Displacement and Reification in Cultural Politics." In *Recognition Struggles and Social Movements: Contested Identities, Agency and Power*, edited by Barbara Hobson, 21–34. Cambridge: Cambridge University Press.

Goldstone, Jack. 2003. "Bridging Institutionalized and Non-Institutionalized Politics." In *States, Parties, and Social Movements*, edited by Jack Goldstone, 1–24. Cambridge: Cambridge University Press.

Goodwin, Jeff, and James Jasper, eds. 2009. *The Social Movements Reader: Cases and Concepts*. Malden, MA: Wiley-Blackwell.

Hegarty, Angela. 2010. *A Gender Critique of the Draft Consultation on Cohesion, Sharing and Integration Strategy*. Belfast: Women's Resource & Development Agency.

Hinds, Bronagh. 1999. "Women Working for Peace in Northern Ireland." In *Contesting Politics: Women in Ireland, North and South*, edited by Yvonne Galligan, Eilis Ward, and Rick Wilford, 109–129. Boulder, CO: Westview Press and PSAI Press.

Hobson, Barbara, ed. 2003. *Recognition Struggles and Social Movements: Contested Identities, Agency and Power*. Cambridge: Cambridge University Press

Kilmurray, Avila, and Monica McWilliams. 2011. "Struggling for Peace: How Women in Northern Ireland Challenged the Status Quo." *Solutions* 2, no. 2. https://www.thesolutionsjournal.com/article/struggling-for-peace-how-women-in-northern-ireland-challenged-the-status-quo/.

Loughran, Christina. 1986. "Armagh and the Feminist Strategy." *Feminist Review* 23, 59–79.

McAdam, Doug, Sidney Tarrow, and Charles Tilly. 2001. *Dynamics of Contention*. Cambridge: Cambridge University Press.

McWilliams, Monica. 1995. "Struggling for Peace and Justice: Reflections on Women's Activism in Northern Ireland." *Journal of Women's History* 7, no. 1: 13–39.

Mitchell, George. 1999. *Making Peace*. Toronto: Random House.

Molyneaux, Maxine. 1988. *Women's Movements in International Perspectives*. Basingstoke, UK: Palgrave Press.

Ní Aoláin, Fionnuala, Dina Francesca Haynes, and Naomi Cahn. 2011. *On the Frontlines: Gender, War and the Post Conflict Process*. Oxford: Oxford University Press.

Porter, Elisabeth. 1998. "Identity, Location, Plurality in Women, Nationalism and Northern Ireland." In *Women, Ethnicity, and Nationalism: The Politics of Transition*, edited by Rick Wilford and Robert Miller, 32–53. London: Routledge.

Rebouché, Rachel, and Kate Fearon. 2005. "Below and Beyond Power Sharing: Relational Structures across Institutions and Civil Society." In *Power Sharing: New Challenges in Divided Societies*, edited by Ian O'Flynn and David Russell, 172–188. London: Pluto Press.

Wolff, Stefan. 2005. "Electoral Systems Design and Power Sharing Regimes." In *Power Sharing: New Challenges in Divided Societies*, edited by Ian O'Flynn and David Russell, 172–188. London: Pluto Press.

Yuval-Davis, Nira. 1998. "Gender and Nation." In *Women, Ethnicity, and Nationalism: The Politics of Transition*, edited by Rick Wilford and Robert L. Miller, 23–35. New York and London: Routledge.

CHAPTER 43

GENDERED SUFFERING AND THE EVICTION OF THE NATIVE

The Politics of Birth in Occupied East Jerusalem

NADERA SHALHOUB-KEVORKIAN

> Why this torture, why can't I be treated as a human being, why can't I have my baby under normal conditions and not under such horror, why am I perceived to be a criminal? A terrorist? (Ghaida, twenty-one years old)[1]

IN the context of settler colonialism in East Jerusalem, the inscription of colonial power over women's pregnant and birthing bodies is marked by painful dispossession, and results in distinct suffering.[2] The dispossession of land, home, livelihood, and protection, and the targeting of pregnant women in Palestine are particularly poignant representations of the interlocking power of gender and race. Yet the gendered violence that pregnant women experience and the accompanying condition of suffering remain mostly invisible from analysis on sexual violence.

On the struggle of Palestinian women, Sayigh notes,

> we must begin by recognizing that the silence and distortion that surround Palestinian women are not a true reflection of their passivity—far from it—but are the signs of an exclusion from history that they share with women generally, and also with peasants as a class. Their problem is not primarily a problem of oppression by their own society, but of colonialism, and to put the two problems on equal footing is to make a false start. (Sayigh 1983, 880)

Indeed, Israeli settler colonialism shapes and defines the pregnancies and birthing realities of Palestinian women in East Jerusalem. In order to better understand how women experience gendered violence and suffering in conflict zones, specifically in a militarized and occupied homeland, this chapter draws from the voices of pregnant Palestinians navigating that terrain. Their stories articulate how suffering is tied to being a colonized body, while also revealing how this suffering constitutes resistance and opens up spaces for female agency.

Following Andrea Smith's reflection that "putting native women at the center of analysis compels us to look at the role of the state in perpetrating both race-based and gender-based violence" (Smith 2005, 8), the voices shared in this chapter enable an interrogation of how Israel, as a settler colonial state (Masalha 2012; Wolfe 2006), invades and attempts to control the private, intimate spheres of Palestinian life—pregnancy and birth. This invasion, as Patrick Wolfe has argued, is a "structure and not an event"; in other words, "elimination is an organizing principle of settler colonialism" (Wolfe 2006, 388). Wolfe's claim that settler colonialism performs this "logic of elimination" assists us in locating Palestinian women's experiences of pregnancy and birth within a framework of racial and gendered targeting, rooted in the relationship indigenous peoples have with the land—the "territoriality" that is "settler colonialism's specific, irreducible element" (Wolfe 2006, 388).

Elimination is accompanied by a constant process of erasure of the indigenous society and its history—perhaps even *structural erasure*, to mirror Wolfe's term "structural genocide"—captured by Smith's explanation of a "logic of genocide," one of the defining elements of a white supremacist settler state. Smith (2010, 59) explains, "[t]his logic holds that indigenous peoples must disappear. In fact, they must always be disappearing, in order to enable non-indigenous peoples' rightful claim to land." In this way, the pregnant indigenous body directly confronts the logic of genocide, as it represents the opposite of disappearance. Because the pregnant body carries this power (willingly or not) to challenge the settler colonial society, pregnant women are faced with constant harassment and intimidation—their bodies are, quite literally, sites of struggle. This chapter will start by sharing Palestinian birthing women's voices and by explaining the political work of the Israeli legal regime when marking birthing women's bodies. It will then move into revealing women birthing resistance. The chapter will conclude in problematizing the targeting of women's bodies and lives.

TARGETING THE BODY, TARGETING THE NATION

I have argued elsewhere that since the *Nakba*, Palestinian women's memories and narratives have identified how their bodies have been turned into political weapons to be used both by the colonizing power, against them, and by themselves and their own society, as sites of defense against continuing colonization. This weaponization of women's bodies is not peripheral to the struggle to eliminate and erase Palestinian society; rather, it is central to the project's success (Shalhoub-Kevorkian 2009). Simply put, "control over women's reproductive abilities and destruction of women and children is [*sic*] necessary to destroy a people" (Smith 2005, 80; see also Gaca, Chapter 23 in this volume). Because of this, women's pregnant bodies are particularly vulnerable to becoming targets of the colonizer. Smith (2005) explains the motivation behind the gendered targeting of indigenous women in North America: "It is because of a Native American woman's sex that she is hunted down and slaughtered, in fact, singled out, because she has the potential through childbirth to assure the continuance of the people" (79). Hiam's and Rawda's experiences in East Jerusalem reveal this targeting:

> I was walking with my sister-in-law; both of us were pregnant, barely managing to climb the hill, when the border patrol passed in their jeep. The moment they noticed us, they circled back and threw three tear gas bombs on us. When we both started running and screaming, "Why, why did you asphyxiate us, why tear gas!?" they started laughing and kept on driving. (Hiam, twenty years old)
>
> I could tell you that the moment my pregnancy was showing, I started facing more hardships and attacks while walking to my college. They used to delay buses, just because they know, that as a pregnant woman, I need to reach the bathroom, or need to be warm and not sitting in a bus for three hours, freezing to death. My two friends that study law with me in the college were also pregnant, and we could all tell you that we can't even say that one week passed without being delayed, attacked, threatened, screamed at, and much more. (Rawda, twenty years old)

Because women's bodies are often conflated with the nation/land (Shalhoub-Kevorkian 2009), Hiam's story holds a double meaning: at once her immediate, daily reality is disrupted, terrorized, and threatened because of her pregnant body. But Hiam and her sister-in-law also embody the nation, and thus the Israeli border patrol must extend its power over them—humiliating and endangering the women is a performance of the settlers' eliminatory power and intention over all of Palestinian society. Rawda's experience, too, illustrates how the settler state inflicts a specific suffering on pregnant women, intervening in the routine of their daily lives to impose further discomfort and harm. When pregnant, these seemingly ordinary moments—traveling to school, taking the bus, taking a walk with a family member—become moments of gendered suffering, whereby women articulate the intensified control over their lives performed by the forces of colonization. These are, indeed, moments when women's bodies are weaponized against them. Ghaida's story illustrates how, under military occupation, seeking basic prenatal care is marked by fear and panic:

> Because I was pregnant, I felt that the soldiers at the checkpoints wanted to humiliate and torture me more. My story with the soldiers at the checkpoint is a long story, but during my pregnancy they behaved more aggressive and [in a] nasty manner . . . . While I was trying to reach my doctor after I discovered some blood spots,

and was worried that I was about to have the baby before time, I was delayed for two hours at the checkpoint . . . in the heat, with all the people in the crowd.

They decided that I couldn't cross the checkpoint because my passing permit was not "an original"—as they claimed. I got very upset, very hurt, and had tears in my eyes, but had no time to cry; I just sat for three minutes and thought about a way out . . . they delayed me, made me so anxious and tired, and treated me like a criminal; they prevented me from reaching the hospital . . . . I ended up sneaking in like a thief, and had no other choice but to take a taxi to help me reach the hospital without any delay. (Ghaida, twenty-one years old)

Not only did Ghaida suffer from the anxiety of not reaching the hospital, her experience also shows how colonial laws—legally classifying who can travel where, and at what time—are manifested as on-the-ground domination during what should have been a simple trip to the doctor. Here, spatial control and legal policies meet to aggressively shape Ghaida's pregnancy as *criminal*—as she notes, she was forced to "sneak [to the hospital] like a thief." Suffering, then, is not only temporal and tangibly felt, but carried into Ghaida's awareness of her imposed criminality.

Mary's experience of pregnancy was also confined by the system of identification cards, to the point where she was too afraid to leave her home:

I do not have an ID, and my eldest son is also without an ID, so, when I was pregnant, I feared moving from my neighborhood in Wadi al-Joz to my parents' [home] in Sheikh Jarrah [that is about 20 minutes away by foot], because I would be caught while out walking, and if so [as a person without an ID], they [the authorities] would have the power to prevent me from having my baby girl in the hospital here in Jerusalem, right here [she showed me the hospital from her window]. So, I sat in my house all day and felt totally suffocated. (Mary, twenty-six years old)

Like Ghaida, Mary's indigeneity positions her as a criminal who does not belong in her home/land, and because of this, her mobility while pregnant is severely restricted. In their study on childbirth in Palestine, Giacaman et al. (2005) observed the shift from home birth to hospital birth as not simply representing an advance in medicine and technology. Rather,

this policy of shifting childbirth to government hospitals was also motivated by political concerns related to population enumeration, an issue that cannot be underestimated in the context of the Palestinian-Israel conflict where demography plays a significant role. Promoting hospital births meant that the Palestinian population could be more easily counted, registered, identified and thus controlled. It would appear that the promotion of hospital births was not merely a strategy derived from biomedicine, but also a political strategy related to the imperatives of military occupation. (133)

Thus sites of birth are sites in which the colonial power can gather information on the colonized. Not only are hospital births locations for reinforcing colonial rule, but women's access to these hospitals become opportunities for the colonizer to remind pregnant women of the lack of control they have over their lives. In this way, surveillance over the birthing female body is embedded within the framework of the logic of elimination and structural erasure.

This surveillance and its accompanying legal categorization prevented Mary from moving freely during her pregnancy, causing her to carry a heavy emotional burden. She was forced to endure this suffering isolated and trapped within her home, magnifying her stress. Hiam shares a story that further uncovers how lack of access to the hospital can reshape a moment of excitement—going into labor—into a condition of suffering:

> I was on my way to the hospital, alone, for my husband was at work. I called him, and he said he would meet me on the road. I needed to walk four minutes [to the arranged meeting point], but one of them [a Jewish settler] saw me, and started saying, "*Rooh moot* (go die), *rooh moot*," and I started walking faster from fear, hoping to meet my husband, but he pushed me, and I fell to the ground, with my pain, in the middle of the street. People came to help me, but my water broke, and I was embarrassed to get up. I needed a woman driver, to pick me up from the ground and take me to the hospital, I needed an ambulance, but here, you could die before an ambulance arrives. (Hiam, twenty years old)

A private, intimate moment—Hiam's water breaking—was thus turned into a moment of shame and powerlessness. Her urgency was met with the reality that "here, you could die before an ambulance arrives." Her powerlessness is also found in Iman's story, whose pregnancy was interrupted by the loss of her home. She recalls,

> I was in my seventh month, when we received a demolition order, asking us to demolish our house with our own hands, otherwise, they would bring their bulldozers and demolish it. I received the court order, and felt suffocated—how could we demolish our house? How can they do this to us after [we] abided by all their rules, paying a lawyer to represent us in the court, paying all the taxes, giving all the needed money and papers to the municipality. How can I, now, when about to give birth to my daughter, lose my home? But, we both did demolish the house, together, keeping one room with the hope they will leave us alone. It was on that day when Mahmoud and I finished demolishing the house, when I was still in my seventh month that I gave birth to Nour. Mahmoud first wanted to call her Nakba (referring to the Palestinian loss of homeland and expulsion in 1948), because we had her when we lost our house, when we demolished it with our own hands to prevent them from doing so, and then charging us 70,000 shekels (about $19,000) for their bulldozers. His cry when telling his brother he wants to call our baby Nakba deeply saddened me, made me realize that even giving birth in Jerusalem is a continuous Nakba. We both were in the lowest mood ever, crying, depressed, and heavily sad. I stayed in this crying mood, so depressed for over a month, but Mahmood took care of both of us, and was in love with the baby. We actually decided to name her Nour—that means light—hoping she will bring some light to our life. But, their court system, their regulations, their laws did not leave us alone. Even Nour, a baby who is now eleven months old, is still

without a birth certificate, because she is our daughter, not the daughter of a Jewish settler. Nour brightened our lives, but the demolition of our house turned my husband into a sick man, suffering from a very high blood pressure, constantly sleeping. If we did not have Nour in our lives, I think that Mahmoud would have committed suicide, and I think I would have done the same. (Iman, twenty-eight years old)

Iman faces the reality of a demolished home and an undocumented child, simply because she is an indigenous woman living in a "conflict zone." Israeli colonial policies in East Jerusalem have attempted to cast her, her husband, and their child outside of their homeland—to render them homeless and invisible. The legality of home demolitions and the refusal to provide Palestinian children with Jerusalem ID cards are called into question by Iman's narration of her experience of pregnancy and motherhood. Her story embodies the Palestinian past—she and her husband considered naming the child after the 1948 dispossession of the Palestinian people—and perhaps, a Palestinian future, in the hope represented by resolving to call the child Nour, or "light."

Stoler has remarked, "racism is not an effect but a tactic in the internal fission of society into binary opposition, a means of creating 'biologized' internal enemies against whom society must defend itself" (Smith 2005, 8). As "biologized internal enemies," pregnant Palestinian women confront a legal system built to erase them. Because, as noted earlier, indigenous women "[have] the potential through childbirth to assure the continuance of the people" (Smith 2005, 79), and the settler colonial project must eliminate the *people*, Palestinian women's bodies are conflict zones themselves. Palestinian women are aware that their birthing bodies, as racialized bodies, constitute threats to the colonizing Jewish state, and this awareness both limits their mobility and engenders their consciousness of resistance.

BIRTHING RESISTANCE, STANDING IN THE WAY OF SETTLER COLONIALISM

I made it. I wanted to have Eiman in Jerusalem. I promised I would never deny my children this privilege . . . . I told myself that I could not let them inherit suffering . . . . I can't see my kids suffer more from being alone, away from their cousins, family, grandparents, land, home, and schools.

You might think I am crazy . . . but, it is better to take the bus, wait at the checkpoints, be humiliated on the way, be threatened by their rifles, be worried and scared . . . it is better to go through all this than to end up having a child who is undocumented, unrecognized, and most of all deprived of his family, his support, his *eizwi* [extended community's support] . . . . What do I feel? I feel tired, happy, sad, terrorized by their policies and threats . . . but I also feel like I did it. (Aida, twenty-three years old).

While all of the women who narrated this chapter were targeted throughout their pregnancies and experienced a distinct gendered suffering as pregnant Palestinian women under a settler colonial regime, they also found ways to exercise agency and make meaning of their suffering. While they experienced a particular victimhood as pregnant women, their stories of birth are also stories of resistance. Smith conceptualizes "the ability to reproduce" as "stand[ing] in the way of the continuing conquest of Native lands, endangering the continuous success of colonization" (Smith 2005). Aida, Mary, Hiam, Iman, Ghaida, and Rawda's narrations of their pregnancies echo the knowledge of this power. For example, Hiam's experience of humiliation motivated her to acquire a driver's license:

> I will do all I can to prevent incidents like mine from happening. I will drive women to schools, to hospitals, and will never allow them to humiliate us the way they did to me. (Hiam, twenty years old)

Mary, whose undocumented status prevented her from leaving her home during her pregnancy, found a way to document abuse and cruelty perpetuated by the Israeli Defense Forces. She took photographs from her windows:

> One day, I will use it [the photographic evidence] to expose them. The day will come, and I will go back to school, get my BA in Media Studies, and publish a book about their violence. You will be surprised, but I have photos that are unique, with many details. The day will come. (Mary, twenty-six years old)

Despite the severe suffering endured by pregnant Palestinian women, the stories in this chapter are not stories of defeat. In fact, their voices signify resilience and continuity. Acquiring a driver's license, collecting proof of Israeli human rights violations, or simply refusing to be displaced by Israeli laws are all methods of resistance the women chose to engage in. Thus, while it is not their choice that their bodies are sites of colonial conflict, they do choose to persist against the structural erasure they experience daily.

CONCLUSION

The suffering articulated across the corpus of women's narrations of pregnancy and birth uncovers and challenges the violent economy of settler colonialism. Inscribing suffering on Palestinian bodies has been a normative practice of the Zionist settler colonial regime before, during, and after the creation of the state of Israel. This regime uses both legal and extralegal means to achieve its inscription of colonial power. Because of this, the use and abuse of women's bodies and (re)productivity have been embedded in the Israeli legal system, which works to render its violent operation invisible. The voices of women shared throughout this chapter attempted to unveil this state violence, and link the experiences of suffering and conflict to the settler colonial framework.

The infliction of pain and suffering, as the women's voices reveal, has been justified through the law, and legitimized through the language and politics of the settler colonial state's perpetual "conflict." The rule of law—or, to be more precise, the rule by law that denies Palestinians the right to movement, the right to maintain stability in their homes and on their lands, the right to being a legal entity—legitimates exterminatory and eliminatory violence to enable the maintenance of the settler state's monopoly over geography and history. The Israeli legal system and its accompanying regulatory bureaucracies place Palestinian society—embodied by pregnant women's bodies—as outside the law.

The legal privileging and sanctification of the Jewish Israeli body and life, and the illegality and profanity of the Palestinian body and life, results in the Israeli state situating Palestinian women's birthing bodies in a condition of justified suffering. Israeli colonial legal discourse that dictates which women have the right of movement, which ones can hold an ID and give birth in a safe space, and which ones should be evicted to a zone of exile and criminality works to exonerate Israeli society from the culpability of its actions. Creating a judiciary system that endorses suffering constructs a culture that legalizes Palestinian suffering. This culture that endorses Palestinian suffering has a long and complex genealogy that can be traced back to the pre-nation-state Zionist colonial conflict against the native Palestinians.

The unique condition of suffering experienced by birthing Palestinian women manipulates the body and the soul. It is inscribed within a political economy that does not end with the birth of the newborn. Women's voices of suffering indicate how their bodies, their land and homes they inhabit, and their lives always already signify violence (see the analysis suggested by Da Silva 2009). The embodiment of violence situates Palestinian women not only beyond due process of law, but also even beyond humanity. Surveillance over women's birthing bodies adds to the discretionary power of the Jewish state and intensifies the machinery of a well-calculated regime of racial profiling that renders Palestinian suffering as expendable—and perhaps even necessary—in light of preserving and securing the settler colonial society. The architecture and bureaucracy of security—be it judicial, military, punitive, or technological—works to ensure a necropolitical regime of violence that maintains women's suffering as invisible in the face of what we experience as "Zionist racial logic." Unless the racialized and gendered structures of the settler state are discontinued, Palestinian birthing women's bodies and lives, and their newborns, will continue to be weaponized by the settler colonial conflict.

NOTES

1. Data collection was conducted in three Palestinian hospitals that are located in occupied East Jerusalem. For more details on the methodology, see Shalhoub-Kevorkian (2015).
2. This study would not have been possible without the heartfelt contributions of many individuals. In particular, I would like to thank all the birthing Palestinian women who agreed to be interviewed for this study and who shared very personal and intimate details; the hospitals' administrations and their staffs for allowing me to collect the data and consult with them at various stages of the study; my very insightful field workers, attorney Riham Abu Jaber, feminist activist Aida Isawi, and social worker Layal Souri. I am also very grateful for

all the work and support of the YWCA staff, mainly Mrs. May Amireh, Ms. Hanan Kamar, Ms. Mira Rizek, and Ms. Sandrine Amer, for enabling me to carry out this study with all its complexity. A special thank you goes to Kate Rouhana and Sarah Ihmoud for their editorial counsel and insightful comments.

REFERENCES

Da Silva, Denise Ferreira. 2009. "No-Bodies: Law, Raciality and Violence." *Griffith Law Review* 18, no. 2: 212–236.

Giacaman, Rita, Laura Wick, Hanan Abdul-Rahim, and Livia Wick. 2005. "The Politics of Childbirth in the Context of Conflict: Policies or de Facto Practices?." *Health Policy* 72, no 2: 129–39.

Masalha, Nur. 2012. *The Palestinian Nakba: Decolonising History, Narrating the Subaltern, Reclaiming Memory.* London: Zed Books.

Sayigh, Rosemary. 1983. "Women in Struggle: Palestine." *Third World Quarterly* 5, no. 4: 880–886.

Shalhoub-Kevorkian, Nadera. 2009. *Militarization and Violence against Women in Conflict Zones in the Middle East: The Palestinian Case-Study.* Cambridge: Cambridge University Press.

Shalhoub-Kevorkian, Nadera. 2015. "The Politics of Birth and the Intimacies of Violence against Palestinian Women in Occupied East Jerusalem." *British Journal of Criminology* 55, no. 6: 1187–1206.

Smith, Andrea. 2005. *Conquest: Sexual Violence and the American Indian Genocide.* Brooklyn: South End Press.

Smith, Andrea. 2010. "Queer Theory and Native Studies: The Heteronormativity of Settler Colonialism." *GLQ: A Journal of Lesbian and Gay Studies* 16, no. 1-2,: 42–68.

Wolfe, Patrick. 2006. "Settler Colonialism and the Elimination of the Native." *Journal of Genocide Research* 8, no. 4: 387–409.

....

CHAPTER 44

RWANDA

*Women's Political Participation
in Post-Conflict State-Building*

....

DORIS BUSS AND JERUSA ALI

RWANDA provides a rich context in which to examine women's participation in post-conflict transitional justice and reconstruction processes. Since 1994 and the end of the genocide and civil war, an array of measures have been implemented to facilitate women's participation in political life, including election quotas and women-specific political institutions, as well as legal changes to formalize women's rights. These measures appear to have made a significant impact, with women elected to political office in unprecedented numbers in the 2013 elections, when they were elected to fifty-one—almost 64 percent—of Rwanda's parliamentary seats.

Increasing women's participation in public life is a much-vaunted goal of post-conflict peace- and state-building. A growing number of international policies and programming are aimed at including women in peace negotiations, transitional justice mechanisms, and—our interest here—post-conflict reforms to political processes and public administration. Rwanda exhibits some of the best practices on gender-equality reforms recommended by international organizations, while offering a cautionary tale about how success is understood and measured. Researchers have sounded alarms about the increasingly authoritarian nature of the Rwandan government, where the de facto one-party state (Longman 2011) is accused of human rights abuses, forging war in the neighboring Democratic Republic of Congo (DRC), instituting heavy-handed "social engineering" policies (Ansoms and Marysse 2011), and deepening inequality (Samset 2011). Rwanda's remarkable achievements in the areas of women's political representation are offset by other developments that appear to undermine meaningful democracy (Burnet 2008).

As a case study, Rwanda highlights the difficulties in measuring success in "including women" as a post-conflict peace- and state-building strategy. This chapter draws on the Rwandan example to explore the emerging international normative framework on women's participation as a post-conflict peace- and state-building goal. Missing from this framework, we suggest, is a clear vision of how and in what ways women's participation is linked to other peace-building and transitional justice goals, such as gender equality, or a democratic, inclusive state.

We begin with a discussion of Rwanda and its significance as a case study on women's increased participation in public life. The first section provides an overview of the civil war and genocide and the array of measures instituted in the 1990s and early 2000s promoting women's equality. The second section considers some feminist analysis of women's increased public participation as a component of gender equality to explore the significance of the emerging normative framework on women's participation in post-conflict contexts. The remaining sections of the chapter then consider the Rwandan example, and its mixed outcomes on equality and peace-building, to explore some of the challenges in pursuing changes to the gender order in post-conflict peace- and state-building.

The Rwanda Genocide and Its Aftermath

The Rwanda genocide unfolded over a 100-day period starting April 6, 1994, when the plane carrying Rwandan president Habyarimina was shot down returning from peace negotiations with the Rwandan Patriotic Front (RPF), an army of exiled Rwandans, which had initiated an on-again, off-again civil war. An estimated 500,000–800,000[1] Tutsi and politically moderate Hutu Rwandans were killed during the genocide, and another nearly two million fled the country in a mass exodus said to have been "masterminded by the ideologues of the genocide" (Prunier 1995, 314). Meanwhile, thousands of diaspora Rwandans who had been living in exile returned to Rwanda—they or their parents having left in the 1950s, 1960s, or early 1970s.

The patterns of violence and victimization during the 1994 genocide are complex, varying in scale and intensity in different regions and time periods of the genocide (Des Forges 1999). The forms of violence and the means of participation also had gendered variations. Men tended to police the blockades and engage directly in killing, while women provided support to the men, while also looting (African Rights 1995b). The genocide leaders prosecuted by the International Criminal Tribunal for Rwanda have been all men, except for one woman (Drumbl 2013). While all Tutsi were the targets of violence, men were killed in higher numbers, with women subjected to rape and sexual violence, including in captive or forced-marriage situations (African Rights 1995a, chap. 10).

In the post-genocide period, Rwandan women, constituting 70 percent of the population, became heads of households, taking on the tasks normally done by men, such as running the farms and repairing damaged houses, all while feeding and providing for multiple dependents (Burnet 2012). Women performed these multiple roles even as they suffered severe health complications and extreme poverty.

In the first nine years following the genocide (1994–2003), the transitional government introduced various changes to elevate women's legal and social status. These changes, too numerous to fully list here, were focused on formal legal recognition of women as citizens with certain rights, and innovations to political and administrative institutions. The Matrimonial Regimes, Liberalities and Successions Act,[2] for example, passed in November 1999 (the "Inheritance Law"), enabled Rwandan women to contract, hold jobs and bank accounts, and own and inherit property (Burnet 2008, 376–377; Katengwa 2010, 75). The Ministry of Gender, Family, and Social Affairs (MIGEGASO, later renamed Ministry of Gender and Women in Development [MIGEPROF]) was introduced with a mandate to, among other things, "integrate gender analytical frameworks into all policies and legislation," and to educate and promote those frameworks at all levels of government (Burnet 2008, 367–368). But it was the new 2003 Rwandan Constitution and the introduction of electoral quotas that has become the symbol of Rwanda's commitment to women's rights.

The preamble to the 2003 Constitution formally recognizes the equal rights of women and men and reserves 30 percent of all elected posts in official bodies, such as the Cabinet, Parliament, and District Councils, for women, and twenty-four seats in indirectly elected posts in Parliament (or, the Chamber of Deputies) (Abbott and Rucogoza 2011). Article 185 of the Constitution also establishes a Gender Monitoring Office to ensure "gender equality and complementarity" through independent monitoring of public policy and administration.[3] Capacity for women in public office is supported in various ways, such as through "women's councils," whose wide-ranging purposes include to "promote women's interests in development, to advise local governance structures on women's issues, and to teach women how to participate in politics" (Burnet 2008, 368), and the Forum for Women Parliamentarians, which supports women in elected office (Katengwa 2010). Politically, Paul Kagame, RPF leader and Rwanda's president, is also seen as personally backing the promotion of women's status in Rwanda, bringing political heft to women's rights.

These and other policy changes were mostly introduced during the post-genocide transitional period, with an active women's movement (Burnet 2008, 2012), as well as the RPF, providing important momentum. The RPF, for example, appointed a number of high-ranking women to the transitional government, including Rose Kabuye, a lieutenant colonel in the RPF (Longman 2006), and Aloisea Inyumba, lead RPF fundraiser, who was appointed minister of Gender and Social Affairs in 1994 (All Africa 2012). Both these women (and others) are credited with helping to advance women's rights, including the rights of genocide widows and orphans (Burnet 2008, 377; Longman 2006).

The explanations given for the RPF's commitment to women's status in Rwanda are varied. Supporters of the regime highlight the role of Paul Kagame and the significance of his upbringing in exile in Uganda in a female-headed household (Powely 2005). The influence of Uganda's Museveni government (Burnet 2008: 366–367; Longman 2006, 140; Powely 2005) is also important, as is the role of international donors and actors

(Oomen 2005). The reforms initiated in post-genocide Rwanda coincided with an international commitment to gender equality that took shape through various UN conferences, including the 1994 Beijing World Conference on Women (Mageza-Barthel 2012, 169), leading in turn to the growth of transnational feminist activism and the diffusion of women's rights as global and regional norms (Tripp 2006). Finally, the RPF and President Kagame won international "accolades" (Burnet 2008, 366, 370–371) and the support of international leaders for their gender-equality policies at a time when the government's authoritarian policies and role in the Congo wars should have been attracting more international critique.

Rwanda's large numbers of women elected to office, as well as its efforts to advance women's equality, has positioned this "tiny East African" country (Bauer and Britton 2006) as an international success story on women's rights. Reports about Rwanda routinely highlight the fact that women occupy a majority—just under 64 percent—of the seats in Parliament. The numbers, as we explore in the following, tell only part of the story. The research on Rwanda suggests that the impacts of women's increased participation are mixed, with notable gains made in some areas (such as women elected to national office), and significant challenges in others (highly centralized decision-making and increased insecurity). To better understand the uneven results in Rwanda, the following section provides an overview of women's public participation as a peace- and state-building goal that is intended to produce positive governance and peace effects.

WOMEN'S POLITICAL PARTICIPATION AS A PEACE- AND STATE-BUILDING GOAL

Increasing the numbers of women in elected office, for many feminists, is not an end in itself, but is embraced as good feminist public policy when it results in other, more substantive outcomes. The question of increasing women's public participation is one of effect: Will the inclusion of women in the political arena—potentially only a "symbolic" gain for gender equality—have a multiplier effect, so that other positive changes to the gendered political, economic, and social order might result?

Shirin Hassim (2006, 2010), writing on gender quotas on the African continent, refers to this as the "virtuous circle of representation" in which increases in women's political participation are hoped to have aspirational, knock-on effects. These effects, according to Hassim (2006, 172), are usually laid out as follows: by increasing the numbers of women in decision-making office, it is hoped, women will have "influence" over budgetary, policy, or government decision-making; this influence will ultimately impact these decision-making venues "in ways that would redress inequalities," with better gender equality the result. Increases in gender equality will, in turn, help to spur increased political involvement, improved gender policy, and so on.

In international policy, the "virtuous effects" hoped for by increasing women's public participation as a peace- and state-building goal are not clearly articulated. In the realm of peace-making, the UN Security Council (UNSC) resolutions on women, peace, and security have been the primary driver for the institution of gender-specific initiatives in post-conflict and transitional contexts, with resolution 1325 (2000) laying a foundational requirement that women be included in peace-building. Inclusion in this context means that women must be "represented" and "participate" (para. 1). This is a form of "descriptive" representation (Pitkin 1967), in which the aim is numeric inclusion of women *qua* women.

The various UNSC resolutions on the topic, using minimalist language, suggest a direct, rather than circular effect. For the UNSC, women's participation as decision-makers, peacekeepers, negotiators, and experts is linked to the "maintenance and promotion of international peace and security" (see SCR 1889 [2009] and 1960 [2010]); that is, women's participation in decision-making is necessary for peace.[4]

The field of transitional justice provides more conceptual thinking on the need for women's participation. Women's inclusion in transitional justice institutions is seen fundamentally as a claim for justice (O'Rourke 2012, 42; Phillips 1998, 2012), that is, a claim about the significance of gendered differences in the experience of conflict and the need to recognize and address these through post-conflict transitional justice (Ní Aoláin, Haynes, and Cahn 2011). Inclusion in this sense has both symbolic and material dimensions. Including women in post-conflict transitional and state building processes is an important first step in signaling that women are full members of the (new) polity (Rubio-Marin 2012). Substantively, an inclusive approach to post-conflict accounting is thus thought to bring about a more sustainable transition.

Within the emerging international aid apparatus on state-building, women's participation also features as a tool of development, resulting in the adoption of gender quotas and the introduction of "women's political machineries" (Goetz 2009). A report by UN Women (Lukatela 2012) provides an attempt to explicate the rationales for these policy developments, linking, in turn, what are otherwise disconnected policy realms.

The report, *Gender and Post-Conflict Governance: Understanding the Challenges,* outlines the available research on the relationship between women's political participation and the conditions for good peace- and state-building. The reporting, noting that the research in this area is limited, identifies three main rationales for women's political participation and the pursuit of "gender responsive governance": women's participation (1) "is a fundamental human right" (2) that produces "economic, political and social outcomes" (3) impacting "stability and success of peace-building efforts and governance reforms" (Lukatela 2012, 22). The report suggests that countries with proportional-representation electoral systems combined with quotas "have experienced more stability" than other post-conflict countries; women in countries with quotas "tend to build on their electoral success" to exceed quota levels; women in public office become role models, stimulating, in turn, improved educational achievement for children and youth; and employing women in public service delivery results in better quality and improved access, with more equal employment "improving the wellbeing" of households (10).

Collectively, these three sources—the UNSC, transitional justice scholarship, and UN Women's work on gender governance—suggest a number of post-conflict-specific "virtuous effects" that are hoped to result from women's increased public participation: increasing women's participation will lead, it is hoped, to the symbolic inclusion of women in the polity, generating positive economic, political, and social outcomes, such as a strong, inclusive state, which, in turn, will help bring about stability and improved state-society relations, public services, and collective well-being, thus strengthening the prospects for peace.

In the following section, we consider the results of Rwanda's commitment to women's inclusion in terms of these hoped-for effects. The Rwandan example highlights some troubling difficulties in advancing women's participation as a post-conflict peace- and state-building goal. Some of these difficulties are particular to the Rwandan situation, with its authoritarian government and involvement in the wars in DRC, but others speak to challenges more generally in seeking to change the gender order in post-conflict contexts.

BEYOND COUNTING: RWANDA AND WOMEN'S POLITICAL PARTICIPATION

The extensive changes to women's legal and political status in post-genocide Rwanda, outlined earlier, appear to have made symbolic and material impacts on the inclusion of women as equal members of Rwandan society. In her extensive study of women in Rwanda, anthropologist Jennie Burnet (2011, 311) identifies a marked change in gender roles in Rwanda beginning in the late 1980s, and developing significantly after the 1994 genocide. In a series of interviews and focus groups conducted from 1997 to 2009, Rwandans "consistently reported that women felt freer to speak out in public, had increased access to education, and had become 'entrepreneurs' in every arena, including politics" (316). In the words of Burnet's research participants, Rwandan "women have found respect" (320). This "respect" was felt in public, and to a lesser degree in private spheres, with women also sharing more often in decisions about domestic resources (319).

Women's increased participation is found also in the economic sphere, with a growing number of women in paid employment or owning small businesses. Women's experiences during the 1994 genocide have also been given a high profile, which positively signals a formal recognition of women and their suffering. The transitional government and its elected successor took a number of steps to officially recognize harms experienced by women, particularly the use of sexual violence during the genocide. The 1996 Genocide Law, for example, included "sexual torture" in the Category One list of offenses, comparable with planning and instigating the genocide (Burnet 2012, 195). Imagery of sexual violence victims is also included in public memorials and government statements (Burnet 2012, 107–08).

Collectively, these developments suggest that increasing women's public participation has produced some positive economic, political, and social outcomes. But the extent to which those outcomes will endure, and/or lead to stability, a fair and more inclusive society, and the conditions for a durable peace is much less clear.

While women are represented in Parliament in high numbers, women parliamentarians do not appear to have had a significant impact on the legislative agenda (Burnet 2008, 2011; Longman 2006). Initiatives specifically linked to women parliamentarians are few in number and primarily include the 1999 Inheritance Law (see earlier in this chapter), the inclusion of gender quotas in the 2003 Constitution, and the 2008 Gender Based Violence (GBV) act (Burnet 2011; Powely 2006). The legislative agenda comes from the executive branch, with Parliament "forced into a 'largely reactive mode'" (Powely 2006, 11). To the extent that women parliamentarians advance any legislative initiatives, these are successful only when "consistent with the agenda of the RPF leadership" (Longman 2006, 149).

In the context of Rwanda's centralized political system dominated by the executive, women's political participation may simply buttress a regime with limited commitment to equality and democracy. The allegiance of women political officeholders, for example, is likely oriented toward the RPF governing regime, to which elected officials owe their political seats, rather than to a constituency of voters. In Rwanda's single-party system, "women elected to seats reserved for women [are] nominated, or at least vetted, by the RPF" (Burnet 2011, 310). In this context, women parliamentarians may have limited options in resisting legislation detrimental to equality generally or to women's rights specifically. For example, while the 2008 GBV act was a positive development, making domestic violence illegal, it was followed a year later by a new labor code, which significantly rolled back employment protections for women, reducing "paid maternity leave from eight to two weeks and [increasing] the work week from five to six days and from 40 to 45 hours" (Burnet 2011, 314).

This change to labor conditions is consistent with the RPF government's neoliberal-inflected re-engineering of Rwanda's economy and society (Ansoms 2009). Women's increased participation in the economic arena, while important, may also constitute a reworking of women's roles to serve a particular model of economic growth (Sjoberg 2010). Equally, for some rural women, the impact of "empowerment" has had the effect of increasing their workload while undermining their "economic security" (Burnet 2011, 5). And while relative poverty has decreased in Rwanda, absolute poverty is on the rise, and so is inequality (Samset 2011). The United Nations Development Programme (UNDP), for example, found "large and growing inequalities between social classes, geographic regions and gender . . . placing Rwanda among the top 15% most unequal societies in the world" (Samset 2011, 272).

Just as economic growth is tied to a limited and potentially problematic form of economic liberalism, state and civil society relations are also constrained and a source of emerging insecurity. Women's empowerment comes at a time when the space for open political engagement is narrowing. The possibility for meaningful grassroots or civil society participation is limited. Local NGOs are harassed and intimidated by the state

(Human Rights Watch 2013), and recent killings and suspicious deaths of opposition members have led to growing international concern about the government's human rights record (Weiner 2014). Even within government, spaces for participation are limited, with a small ruling elite dominating decision-making (Debusscher and Ansoms 2013; Gready 2011, 89; Reyntjens 2004). The overall result of these factors—centralized, controlling government, the increasing dominance of sections of the community in public life, together with the reduction in size and space of civil society activism—makes a thicker version of representation highly unlikely in Rwanda, with implications for long-term stability and peace.

The recognition of women's experiences of the genocide also has been uneven. While Tutsi women survivors of sexual violence have secured recognition as genocide victims, other categories of victims are excluded from both state recognition and assistance. In the constrained account of the genocide allowed by the RPF government (Waldorf 2011), atrocities committed alongside the genocide, for example by the RPF, are not admitted, Hutu victims are not recognized, and even some Tutsi victims—such as Tutsi wives of prisoners and Hutu widows—are not officially embraced (Burnet 2012, chap. 4; Hintjens 2008).

The overall peace-building effects of women's political participation in post-genocide Rwanda are similarly uneven. Not only has Rwanda been implicated in regional conflicts, the RPF's heavy-handed governance and social engineering have ominous implications for both state viability and long-term peace. Some scholars note parallels between the authoritarianism of the RPF and its predecessor—the Habyarimana regime—that governed prior to the genocide, suggesting that future conflict may result (Ansoms 2009; Cassimon, Engelen, and Reyntjens 2013). Against this backdrop, the high profile given to women's political participation raises the worrying prospect that gender equality may be used as a convenient foil for otherwise troubling government policies.

CONCLUSION: RWANDA AND WOMEN'S PARTICIPATION AS A PEACE- AND STATE-BUILDING GOAL

Rwanda is a popular case study in scholarly research on transitional contexts, in large part because it offers a neat contradiction. The country has adopted, formally at least, many internationally sanctioned best practices on transitional justice and post-conflict, and yet Rwanda has an authoritarian government, with a troubling human rights record and complicity in regional conflicts. It is a pariah in some circles and a celebrated success story in others.

Rwanda's contradictions crystallize some of the fault lines in international law and policy on women's inclusion as a peace- and state-building goal and the difficulty in changing the gender order post-conflict. The first difficulty, we suggest, is that changes brought about through increased women's participation are more likely to be uneven, contradictory, and nonlinear than is often recognized. Gains in one area can be accompanied by losses in another. The reasons for this unevenness are important. Efforts to improve women's status in a post-conflict society implicitly engage ideas about gender, equality, and the good society. And yet, the various policies and best practices on enhancing women's equality post-conflict are largely silent about the vision of change that underpins these goals. The uneven results on women's political participation, we suggest, point to multiple levels at which the meanings of gender, equality, and the state are being negotiated and contested. The uptake of gender-equality policies needs to be studied in more detail, and not simply in terms of the formal indicators of their effects (numbers of women in elected office, for example). More attention is needed on how key principles or norms of gender equality and state-building—"equality," "participation," and "inclusion"—take on certain meanings or force, underpinning dominant conceptions of "good governance" or "stability" that do little to contest oppressive social dynamics or inequalities (Cooper 2004, chap. 5; True 2011).

A second and related difficulty arises in relation to the "opportunity structures" for effecting change to the gender order post-conflict. The case of Rwanda raises the uncomfortable prospect that women's newfound political voice may be co-opted by an authoritarian or highly unequal political process. Further, even substantial numbers of women active in political life may not open spaces for political contestation, despite indicators of political support for gender equality. These results highlight, again, the need for a more nuanced gender lens to analyze how and in what terms political openings become available.

NOTES

1. Estimates of the numbers killed vary significantly, with the figure of 500,000 preferred by some scholars (Des Forges 1999; Straus 2006), and 800,000 used by some international institutions, including the International Criminal Tribunal for Rwanda.
2. Law no. 22/99 of 12/11/1999 to Supplement Book I of the Civil Code and to Institute Part Five Regarding Matrimonial Regimes, Liberalities and Successions (Rwanda).
3. See also Law no. 51/2007 of 20/09/2007 Determining the Responsibilities, Organisation and Functioning of the Gender Monitoring Office in Rwanda.
4. For a critical discussion of this idea, see Charlesworth (2008).

REFERENCES

Abbott, Pamela, and Marklin Rucogoza. 2011. *Legal and Policy Framework for Gender Equality and the Empowerment of Women in Rwanda*. Kigali: Institute for Policy Analysis and Research—Rwanda.

African Rights. 1995a. *Rwanda: Death, Despair and Defiance*. London: African Rights.

African Rights. 1995b. *Rwanda Not So Innocent: When Women Become Killers*. London: African Rights.

All Africa. 2012. "Rwanda: Aloisea Inyumba, a Life of Dedication to Rwanda." December 10. http://allafrica.com/stories/201212100133.html.

Ansoms, An. 2009. "Re-Engineering Rural Society: The Visions and Ambitions of the Rwandan Elite." *African Affairs* 108, no. 431: 289–309.

Ansoms, An, and Stefaan Marysse, eds. 2011. *Natural Resources and Local Livelihoods in the Great Lakes Region of Africa: A Political Economy Perspective*. New York: Palgrave.

Bauer, Gretchen, and Hannah E. Britton. 2006. "Women in African Parliaments: A Continental Shift?" In *Women in African Parliaments*, edited by Gretchen Bauer and Hannah E. Britton, 1–44. Boulder, CO: Lynne Rienner.

Burnet, Jennie E. 2008. "Gender Balance and the Meanings of Women in Governance in Post-Genocide Rwanda." *African Affairs* 107, no. 428: 361–86.

Burnet, Jennie E. 2011. "Women Have Found Respect: Gender Quotas, Symbolic Representation, and Female Empowerment in Rwanda." *Politics & Gender* 7, no. 3: 303–334.

Burnet, Jennie E. 2012. *Genocide Lives in Us: Women, Memory, and Silence in Rwanda*. Madison: University of Wisconsin Press.

Cassimon, Danny, Peter-Jan Engelen, and Filip Reyntjens. 2013. "Rwanda's Involvement in Eastern DRC: A Criminal Real Options Approach." *Crime, Law and Social Change* 59, no. 1: 39–62.

Charlesworth, Hilary. 2008. "Are Women Peaceful? Reflections on the Role of Women in Peacebuilding." *Feminist Legal Studies* 16, no. 3: 347–361.

Cooper, Davina. 2004. *Challenge Diversity: Rethinking Equality and the Value of Difference*. Cambridge: Cambridge University Press.

Debusscher, Petra, and An Ansoms. 2013. "Gender Equality Policies in Rwanda: Public Relations or Real Transformations?" *Development and Change* 44, no. 5: 1111–1134.

Des Forges, Alison. 1999. *Leave None to Tell the Story: Genocide in Rwanda*. New York: Human Rights Watch.

Drumbl, Mark. 2013. "'She Makes Me Ashamed to Be a Woman': The Genocide Conviction of Pauline Nyiramasuhuko." *Michigan Journal of International Law* 34, no. 3: 559–603.

Goetz, Anne Marie. 2009. "Governing Women or Enabling Women to Govern: Gender the Good Governance Agenda." In *Governing Women: Women's Political Effectiveness in Contexts of Democratization and Governance Reform*, edited by Anne Marie Goetz, 239–256. New York: Routledge.

Gready, Paul. 2011. "Beyond 'You're with Us or Against Us': Civil Society and Policymaking in Post-Genocide Rwanda." In *Remaking Rwanda: State Building and Human Rights after Mass Violence*, edited by Scott Straus and Lars Waldorf, 87–100. Madison: University of Wisconsin Press.

Hassim, Shireen. 2006. "The Virtuous Circle of Representation: Women in African Parliaments." In *Women in African Parliaments*, edited by Gretchen Bauer and Hannah E. Britton, 246–266. Boulder, CO: Lynne Rienner.

Hassim, Shireen. 2010. "Perverse Consequences: The Impact of Quotas on Democratization in Africa." In *Political Representation*, edited by Ian Shapiro, Susan C. Stokes, Elisabeth J. Wood, and Alexander Kirshner, 200–235. Cambridge: Cambridge University Press.

Hintjens, Helen. 2008. "Post-Genocide Identity Politics in Rwanda." *Ethnicities* 8, no. 1: 5–41.

Human Rights Watch. 2013. "Rwanda: Takeover of Rights Group." August 14. http://www.hrw.org/news/2013/08/14/rwanda-takeover-rights-group.

Katengwa, M. Juliana. 2010. "The Will to Political Power: Rwandan Women in Leadership." *Institute of Development Studies Bulletin* 41, no. 5: 72–80.

Longman, Timothy. 2006. "Rwanda: Achieving Equality or Serving an Authoritarian State?' In *Women in African Parliaments*, edited by Gretchen Bauer and Hannah E. Britton, 133–150. Boulder, CO: Lynne Rienner.

Longman, Timothy. 2011. "Limitations to Political Reform: The Undemocratic Nature of Transition in Rwanda." In *Remaking Rwanda: State Building and Human Rights after Mass Violence*, edited by Scott Straus and Lars Waldorf, 25–47. Madison: University of Wisconsin Press.

Lukatela, Ana. 2012. *Gender and Post-Conflict Governance: Understanding the Challenges*. New York: UN Women.

Mageza-Barthel, Rirhandu. 2012. "Asserting Their Presence! Women's Quest for Transitional Justice in Post-Genocide Rwanda." In *Gender in Transitional Justice*, edited by Susanne Buckley-Zistel and Ruth Stanley, 163–190. New York: Palgrave Macmillan.

Ní Aoláin, Fionnuala, Dina F. Haynes, and Naomi Cahn. 2011. *On the Frontlines: Gender, War, and the Post-Conflict Process*. Oxford: Oxford University Press.

O'Rourke, Catherine. 2012. "Dealing with the Past in a Post-Conflict Society: Does the Participation of Women Matter? Insights from Northern Ireland." *William & Mary Journal of Women and the Law* 19, no. 1: 35–68.

Oomen, Barbara. 2005. "Donor-Driven Justice and Its Discontents: The Case of Rwanda." *Development and Change* 36, no. 5: 887–910.

Phillips, Anne. 1998. *The Politics of Presence*. New York: Oxford University Press.

Phillips, Anne. 2012. "Representation and Inclusion." *Politics & Gender* 8, no. 4: 512–518.

Pitkin, Hanna F. 1967. *The Concept of Representation*. Berkeley: University of California Press.

Powely, Elizabeth. 2005. "Rwanda: Women Hold Up Half the Parliament." In *Women in Parliament: Beyond the Numbers*, edited by Julie Ballington and Azza Karam, 154–163. Stockholm: International Instituted for Democracy and Electoral Assistance.

Powely, Elizabeth. 2006. "Rwanda: The Impact of Women Legislators on Policy Outcomes Affecting Children and Families." The State of the World's Children 2007 Background Paper, UNICEF.

Prunier, Gérard. 1995. *The Rwanda Crisis: History of a Genocide*. New York: Columbia University Press.

Reyntjens, Filip. 2004. "Rwanda, Ten Years On: From Genocide to Dictatorship." *African Affairs* 103, no. 411: 177–210.

Rubio-Marin, Ruth. 2012. "Reparations for Conflict-Related Sexual and Reproductive Violence: A Decalogue." *William & Mary Journal of Women and the Law* 19, no. 1: 69–104.

Samset, Ingrid. 2011. "Building a Repressive Peace: The Case of Post-Genocide Rwanda." *Journal of Intervention and Statebuilding* 5, no. 3: 265–283.

Sjoberg, Laura. 2010. "Reconstructing Womanhood in Post-Conflict Rwanda." In *Women, War, and Violence: Personal Perspectives and Global Activism*, edited by Robin M. Chandler, Lihua Wang, and Linda K. Fuller, 171–186. New York: Palgrave MacMillan.

Straus, Scott. 2006. *The Order of Genocide: Race, Power, and War in Rwanda*. Ithaca, NY: Cornell University Press.

Tripp, Aili Mari. 2006. "The Evolution of Transnational Feminisms: Consensus, Conflict, and New Dynamics." In *Global Feminism: Transnational Women's Activism, Organizing, and Human Rights*, edited by Myra Marx Ferree and Aili Mari Tripp, 51–75. New York: New York University Press.

True, Jacqui. 2011. "Feminist Problems with International Norms: Gender Mainstreaming in Global Governance." In *Feminism and International Relations: Conversations about the Past, Present and Future*, edited by J. Ann Tickner and Laura Sjoberg, 73–89. New York: Routledge.

Waldorf, Lars. 2011. "Instrumentalizing Genocide: The RPF's Campaign against 'Genocide Ideology.'" In *Remaking Rwanda: State Building and Human Rights after Mass Violence*, edited by Scott Straus and Lars Waldorf, 48–66. Madison: University of Wisconsin Press.

Weiner, Joann. 2014. "Does Rwanda's Economic Prosperity Justice President Kagame's Political Repression?" *Washington Post*, August 13. http://www.washingtonpost.com/blogs/she-the-people/wp/2014/08/13/does-rwandas-economic-prosperity-justify-president-kagames-political-repressin.

CHAPTER 45

....

SRI LANKA

The Impact of Militarization on Women

....

AMBIKA SATKUNANATHAN

THIS chapter examines the impact of militarization on women in the north of Sri Lanka after the end of the armed conflict, drawing on primary data collected in northern Sri Lanka from December 2010 to January 2014.[1] The chapter focuses on how militarization was entrenched through a process of normalization, the different ways in which militarization shapes daily life, and its specific impacts on women. It concludes with an analysis of the complex strategies used by women to cope with and challenge this militarization.

BACKGROUND TO THE CONFLICT

....

Following Sri Lanka's independence from Britain in 1948, the country enacted laws that discriminated against minority communities, including against the Tamils of Indian origin whose ancestors had been brought to the island to work on the plantations in the 1800s. In 1972, Sri Lanka severed all legal ties with Britain and became a republic with a new constitution which enshrined a "Sinhala only" policy, gave primacy to Buddhism as a state religion by making it a "duty of the state to protect and foster Buddhism," and removed provisions that prevented the enactment of legislation detrimental to minorities. Incidents of collective violence, to which Tamils were repeatedly subjected in 1958, 1977, 1981, and 1983, exacerbated existing ethnic tensions. This, along with several failed attempts by moderate Tamil political parties to find a resolution through negotiation, led some Tamil youth to take up arms. The Liberation Tigers of Tamil Eelam (LTTE), which emerged as the strongest armed group after internecine violence, perpetrated gross violations of human rights over the next decades, including suicide bombings targeting civilians, assassination of politicians, extrajudicial killings, and the use of child soldiers. Simultaneously, the country experienced a youth insurrection in the Sinhala-dominated southern part of the country during the late 1980s, which was crushed through state-sponsored violence and violations such as extrajudicial killings and disappearances. These insurgencies led to the imposition of states of emergency (SOE) and the promulgation of Emergency Regulations (ERs), which conferred wide powers on many officials—including the president, ministers (through delegation by the president), and members of the armed forces and the police. Although these powers were used against the youth of the majority community during uprisings in the South, for the large part, the laws were targeted at the Tamil community of the North.

The armed conflict between the government of Sri Lanka and the LTTE came to an end in May 2009 with the defeat of the LTTE. Both parties to the conflict stand accused of gross violations of international humanitarian and human rights law, particularly during the last stages of the war. This has been affirmed by the 2011 Report of the Secretary-General's Panel of Experts on Accountability in Sri Lanka and the 2015 Report of the "Investigation on Sri Lanka" by the UN Office of the High Commissioner on Human Rights. Until January 2015, when Maithripala Sirisena won the presidential election and brought about regime change, the government of the time continued to use national security concerns to legitimize serious human rights violations, and failed to put in place a genuine reconciliation or truth-seeking process or to address accountability issues, which, in turn, facilitated ongoing violations, including sexual violence, as well as scaled-up militarization in the North, leading to widespread insecurity. Following the presidential election in January 2015 and parliamentary election in August 2015, the new government announced that it would establish mechanisms to deal with issues of transitional justice. As of July 2017, while the only legislation that has been enacted to establish an Office of Missing Persons has not yet been operationalized, members of civil society have raised concerns about what they perceive as attempts to backtrack on commitments made by the government to the Human Rights Council and about lack of transparency and inclusiveness in the transitional justice process.

STATUS OF WOMEN IN POSTWAR SRI LANKA

In the past five decades, the progress of women in the socioeconomic and legal spheres has been considerable. They enjoy 90 percent literacy and good health indicators and are more visible in the public sphere, including in the commercial sector, bureaucracy, and universities. Some progress also has been made in reforming discriminatory laws, and there are efforts, particularly by NGOs, to increase awareness of women's rights. Yet, patriarchal values and discriminatory practices exist, and women continue to face exclusion in politics, social marginalization, and gender-based violence. The gendered division of labor remains unchanged, despite women's increasing entry into the job market, with women bearing the bulk of responsibility for housework and child care. Women in conflict-affected areas and the plantation sector face challenges accessing basic services such as education and health care, and are subject to economic exploitation.

As a result of the conflict, nearly 80 percent of the displaced population was female, and more than 23 percent of households in Sri Lanka are now female-headed. The vast majority of these households are in the North, where female-headed households face physical, economic, and social insecurity. The vulnerability of women to violence and harassment restricts their freedom of movement; this, in turn, adversely impacts other aspects of their lives, including their livelihood opportunities and the access of girls and young women to education. The prevailing sense of insecurity and lack of income generation opportunities, coupled with a perceived breakdown in moral standards, has resulted in a high incidence of underage marriages in the hope of ensuring the physical and economic security of young women.[2]

A study of the gendered impact of militarization needs to take into account issues of preexisting and structural gender inequality within the Tamil community. In the conservative and traditional Tamil community, the Tamil nationalist struggle, like other nationalist movements (see Yuval-Davis 1997), was instrumental in bringing women into the public sphere. This sometimes blurred the boundaries between the public and private spheres, and politicized the private sphere, through which women were mobilized to support the nationalist struggle. In the 1980s, prior to the emergence of the LTTE as the largest Tamil militant group, women members of various militant movements were able to exercise limited and sometimes even transgressive agency. However, even this agency depended on, and differed, according to the ideology of each movement. Generally, the space given to women seems to have been determined by the strategic needs of the organization, rather than a commitment to women's empowerment. Women created alternate spaces, which sometimes unwittingly or indirectly challenged gender stereotypes and social restrictions on the behavior and rights of women. Despite this, women were not always able to challenge systemic inequalities or exercise agency and create space for their voices to be heard (Satkunanathan 2012). The failure to effect fundamental change within the Tamil community on issues of gender equality, coupled with fears about the decimation of Tamil culture due to rapid postwar social change, has resulted in the re-emergence of patriarchal and discriminatory practices against women in the North.

BANAL MILITARIZATION: CREATING A NARRATIVE OF NORMALCY

Given the thirty-year armed conflict and youth insurrections in the South, militarization has been a feature of daily life in Sri Lanka for decades. Yet, despite this, a distinction should be made between the process and form of militarization that existed before May 2009 and the militarization that has become an entrenched and normalized part of life after May 2009. Cynthia Enloe (2000) defines militarization as a "step-by-step process by which something becomes controlled by, dependent on, or derives its value from the military as an institution or militaristic criteria" (291). Her warning that "militarization is such a pervasive process, and thus so hard to uproot, precisely because in its everyday form it scarcely looks life threatening" provides a useful framework; it enables us to identify and understand strategies used to entrench militarization by looking beyond the visible and most obvious to understand the insidious and rapid militarization that has taken place since the end of the armed conflict.

Prior to the end of the war, the impact of militarization was felt mainly in the North and East, where military action and (unofficial) rules shaped and dictated daily civilian life. Although following the end of the war, systematic militarization has occurred throughout the country (Satkunanathan 2014), this chapter focuses on the North.

Militarization in the North took place in complex ways at multiple levels. The statement by the Northern Security Forces Commander following the end of the war that "security forces in the North will be engaged in a new role of developing the region" (Palakidner 2009) signaled that the military would play an active public role. The capture of civilian space was supported by the ever-growing number of entities that became part of the defense complex, such as the Civil Security Department (CSD) and the Civil Affairs Office (CAO). This structure was bolstered by the more public and interventionist role played by military officials in a manner unseen in the past, such as military commanders making public statements on a number of issues ranging from the laws under which civilians will be prosecuted for certain offenses to the behavior expected of university students (Satkunanathan 2013). Following regime change in January 2015, although the military no longer played an overt role in public affairs in the North, the military infrastructure (i.e., the business ventures and multiple defense entities) is yet to be dismantled.

Beyond the noticeable physical presence of the military camp[3] or Civil Affairs Office, it is the military's involvement in civil administration, development activities, and commercial activities that have played a key role in normalizing militarization. Including the general public in "the projects and imperatives of the state" blurs the lines between the military and non-military sectors of society, whereby the public becomes an active participant in the militarization process (Laswell, quoted in Bernazzoli and Flint 2010, 160). As early as 2009, the military began to play an active role in development activities;[4] for instance, authorization to NGOs to implement projects was given by the military, permission to travel into the Vanni for official purposes was refused to certain individuals deemed to be a threat to national security, and local development committee meetings have been held at army camps and chaired by the commander of the area.

The army's keen understanding of the effectiveness of using education to construct the belief that adulation of the military is an integral part of being patriotic (Bernazzoli and Flint 2010) led to its involvement in the education sector in the North. The military provided scholarships and distributed books to students, cadet corps were established in schools, and leadership training programs for students were held with the involvement of the army, which also organized school tours. Youth were encouraged to join the CSD, which began to pay the salaries of preschool teachers in the Vanni and to monitor the administration of these schools in 2013. Engaging with youth and the educational sector is one of the ways in which the military changes the "meanings and uses of people, things and ideas" (Enloe 2000, 289). Even following regime change, some of these activities, such as the CSD running preschools and the military's charitable educational activities, continue.

The armed forces in Sri Lanka also began to undertake commercial activities. Since the army is subsidized by the state, it is able to offer goods and services for cheaper rates, thereby forcing small farmers and retailers, particularly in the North, out of business. This impacts women who, as unskilled workers, engage in day labor in the agricultural or commercial sector.

The militarization occurs with no legal framework to address it. The law of armed conflict does not regulate such rapid postwar militarization, since the presumption that ending armed conflict ousts these norms also assumes the end of the application of the laws of war. Equally, human rights law, which should apply in these contexts, remains underdeveloped and is ill-equipped to address the de facto militarization of the ordinary.

GENDERED IMPACT OF MILITARIZATION

In the postwar context, militarization and patriarchy function in tandem, resulting in women being faced with multilayered forms of oppression. As the rest of the chapter illustrates, structural inequalities within the Tamil community exacerbate the impact of militarization on women and, by extension, the community, and thereby facilitate the entrenchment and normalization of militarization. At the same time, militarization enables patriarchal practices to re-emerge in the guise of protecting Tamil women and culture from the military.

Military engagement in the North that impacts the lives of women takes numerous forms. In addition to the physical presence of the military, which causes women to fear, and makes them vulnerable to, sexual violence and harassment, the military carries out surveillance and monitoring, creating fear and suspicion among people, which leads to self-censorship and a breakdown of intra-community trust and relations. This results in the isolation of women-headed households and reduces their access to traditional community support mechanisms such as extended family or neighbors. Further, military involvement in everyday life through development and charitable activities, including education and social events and engagement in commercial activities, impacts adversely on women's lives. The most insidious and harmful form of military action is the enforcement of extralegal rules and practices that cause physical, economic, and social insecurities for women.

Militarization has created the belief among both men and women that an extensive and deep-seated surveillance mechanism exists in the North and would result in punitive measures being taken against those who are perceived to contravene the dictates of the military. This has enabled the military to control the behavior of the population, even in the absence of a visible physical uniformed military presence. Women—particularly those in the Vanni who have previously not been exposed to the Sri Lankan armed forces and who view them as strangers and aggressors—appear to experience more fear than men, due to apprehension that increased scrutiny could lead to sexual violence or harassment. Since many communities in the Vanni tend to have women-headed households due to the death, disappearance, or detention of male family member(s), the lack of male presence in homes only serves to increase this sense. Further, since many women are the sole providers for their families, they are afraid that any disruption could prevent them from meeting the basic needs of their families.

Becoming the subject of military scrutiny and the resulting punitive measures to which they could be subjected is foremost on the minds of women attending meetings and workshops. Women therefore sometimes expressed reluctance to participate for fear that military intelligence is monitoring their activities. This played out in the research for this chapter, where arranging interviews with respondents often required considerable discussion about a safe venue that would not place the interviewer or respondent in danger. Often, in the course of such meetings and interviews, close attention had to be paid to the movement of people in the surroundings. It could take something as innocuous as a man on a motorcycle passing by and looking toward the building to create anxiety that the meeting was being monitored. Further, many would not discuss issues even remotely related to human rights violations and the actions of the military on the phone since they believe all phone calls are being monitored. Feelings of insecurity and fear are heightened due to the Sri Lankan armed forces being perceived as an occupying army that is ethno-culturally and linguistically different and that is determined to subjugate the population. Although after regime change in 2015 there are virtually no fetters on freedom of expression and association, civil society organizations in the North and East continue to report surveillance, and at times intimidation by state security agencies.

In the North, "militarization operating through capillaries of power blurs the boundaries between military and civilian activities and institutions, producing patterns of impunity for state violence" (Duschinski 2009, 708). Militarism becomes natural and taken for granted through activities of people in everyday settings. This can be better understood by studying the process through which the population is convinced that the military is of "critical importance to their own well-being" (Bernazzoli and Flint, 2009, 397).

In the narrative of the government of the time, the LTTE was positioned as the main source of insecurity to the Tamil community, while the army was portrayed as the rescuer that was ensuring security by preventing a resurrection of the armed group. Following regime change, the need to prevent future insurrections is still used to justify the continued existence of the military complex. Women appear very aware of the strategy used by the government to control the population in the guise of providing security. For instance, a woman referring to the presence of the army said, "We have no security but they (the government) say this (the presence of the army) is security." Statements of Tamil women in the North that "security means a place without the army" and "there is no security as long as the army is present" demonstrate that paternalistic definitions of security constructed by the state increase the insecurity of those who sup-posedly are being protected (Laliberte 2013, 2). The complicated reality for these women is illustrated by narratives of women who, even while critiquing certain acts of the LTTE such as forced recruitment, unequivocally stated that women felt more secure when the LTTE was in control pre-2009. One increasingly heard that "a woman could walk unac-companied even at midnight" at that time, which points to women's primary fear, that of sexual violence, particularly by the military, which in turn restricted their freedom of movement (Satkunanathan 2012).

Women spoke of many unofficial processes made possible through the sweeping powers given to the military and law enforcement officials by national security laws, and the resultant climate and culture of impunity as factors that increased their insecurity. These processes, which came into being during the lifetime of the conflict, remained unchallenged and continued after the end of the war. During 2006–2008, for instance, residents of Jaffna in the North, which was under the control of government forces, had to obtain a pass, much like a visa, from the army to travel to the South. The army would often state the reason for refusing to give travel passes as suspicion of involvement in anti-state activities and would ask the person to present himself at the camp, either weekly or daily, and sign in. Hence, the refusal of a travel pass often led people to change their residence or to surrender to the Human Rights Commission or the courts to be placed in protective custody for fear of being disappeared or killed by the army. This marked the individual as a person under threat. It also impacted adversely on women who had been left behind at home with no livelihood options, and who then also had to regularly cope with visits, interrogation, and harassment by the armed forces and intel-ligence officers and to find means to protect their male children. These unofficial forms of surveillance and monitoring that came into being during the period of emergency exacerbated the insecurity experienced by women since it also rendered their ability to seek remedies virtually nonexistent.

Militarization also creates forms of exclusion and inclusion (Stern 2006), whereby certain populations such as former combatants (men and women), families of miss-ing combatants (mostly women), and families of the disappeared who are engaged in campaigning for answers (mostly women) were viewed with suspicion by the state. Following regime change, although key figures within the government do not appear to hold this position, generally this continues to be the perception. At the same time, these populations were encouraged to become part of the militarization project. Hence, they formulated parameters for inclusion and exclusion within the communities to increase their security (Stern 2006), and to resist and cope with violence and the impact of militarization and unofficial norms and rules that came into being during the per-iod of emergency. For instance, former combatants and families of missing combatants who were often harassed and interrogated became military informants, or used their links with the military to intimidate or gain an advantage within the community. For instance, since they were in the employ of the military, there were reports of such per-sons using their contacts in the army to intimidate others in cases of disputes, most com-monly property disputes. The community, well aware of this possibility, distances itself from these persons. Particularly during the war, the community did not engage with families of those who were killed or disappeared by the state, mostly women-headed households, due to fear that these families were under the surveillance of the army, and hence anyone who had contact with them would likewise be subject to state scrutiny, and would be targeted by the state as a family that supported the LTTE. Following the end of the war, people who were displaced from the Vanni to Jaffna, once again mostly women-headed households, experienced the same fate. Their suffering, which has been produced by deeply entrenched patterns of militarization, was therefore rendered invisible by the fear created by the national security rhetoric (Duschinski 2009). For example, during focus group meetings and interviews, the author asked women whose male family members were in rehabilitation centers for former combatants, were in detention, or had disappeared whether they had the support of their families. Most women said that other than immediate family members, others did not associate with them due to fear they would be targeted by state actors. This forced women to seek the support of those who had experienced the same kinds of loss, and hence themselves had limited social, economic, and emotional resources, thereby placing great strain on these fragile social networks.

Since even civil society activities were subject to military scrutiny, the space for women activists to advocate their needs and rights was limited. In the North, women's rights activists were often labeled as anti-national or as terrorists. These women became doubly deviant—a terrorist and a woman who has transgressed socially acceptable female behavior (Pickering and Third 2003)—particularly due to their ability to reproduce political dissidence through socialization and education in the domestic sphere (Pickering and Third 2003). That is what happened to "S," a woman from Mullaitivu in the North, who was one of the first to file legal action in 2013 against military acquisition of her land. S was not only subjected to harassment, surveillance, and death threats, but her activism and activities to reclaim her land were equated by the military to engaging in terrorist activity.

In addition to existing barriers to reporting sexual and gender-based violence, military presence constitutes an additional obstacle that prevents women from seeking assistance due to fear that the perpetrator could be a military officer. For example, women reported an increase in sexual harassment, particularly in public transport, but said that since they don't know whether the person is an intelligence officer or affiliated or linked to the military in some way, they do not report it for fear of reprisals.

VICTIMHOOD, AGENCY, OR VICTIMCY?

The dominant narrative constructed by the government in postwar Sri Lanka posits Tamil women as persons without agency, either as misguided and misled terrorists who had to be rescued and shown the "correct" path, or impoverished and exploited women in need of assistance. I borrow the term "victimcy" to describe the complex lived realities, which defy efforts to neatly box women's experiences and strategies.[5] Yet women find alternatives, options, and survival strategies, even within the restrictive environment they inhabit. These strategies constitute "unlikely forms of resistance, subversions rather than large scale collective insurrections, small or local resistances not tied to the overthrow of systems or even to ideologies of emancipation" (Abu-Lughod 1990, 41).

Due to their experience of living in a militarized society, women in the Vanni in particular, who are quite adept at navigating military controls, have become participants in normalizing and entrenching militarization as a survival strategy due to lack of other viable options. The complexity and fluidity of lived realities and the inherent danger of increased militarization in the context of a weak civil administration are illustrated by instances of women complaining to the army about various concerns, including domestic violence, which only serve to increase their vulnerability. Further, due to a lack of other economic opportunities,[6] female-headed households were forced to find employment mainly in different sections of the military machinery. For instance, in addition to the over two hundred women who have been recruited to the army since November 2012, thousands of women work in eight agricultural farms run by the military in the Vanni. As a survival strategy, some women enter into sexual relationships with members of the military in which they are often powerless, but which provide them security and sometimes an elevated position within the social setting they occupy (Utas 2005).

Even under significant conditions of oppression, women have exercised more positive forms of agency, for instance by forming collectives, such as savings groups and community networks to provide mutual economic, social, and emotional support in cases of sexual and gender-based violence, despite restrictions on freedom of association. Though the women had no political motivation in doing so, in a context where the notion of security is highly militarized and civic activism is forcefully discouraged and immediately viewed as anti-state, their act becomes extremely and inadvertently political. These collectives, which are neither perfect nor always fully functional, nevertheless continue to serve as networks and a means of group negotiation with the state, the military, and often even society. If an act of violence is perpetrated against a woman, the member of the collective who lives in the village contacts others for advice and receives support in lodging a complaint and accessing remedies and services. These collectives have links with NGOs and rights activists, which enable them to be in a better position than the average villager to access remedies. Although many of these collectives existed in the Vanni during the LTTE era, at the time they functioned solely as savings groups, whereas postwar they have become more engaged in rights issues and even in local advocacy.

In a context in which they have very little access to information, women piece together bits of information they gather through conversations with family, friends, acquaintances, and neighbors in an effort to understand what is taking place within their environment and, before January 2015, to predict potential danger. For instance, when the army visited houses with registration lists, women tried to ascertain whose names were on the list in order to share this information with others. During 2006–2008, the army instituted a process that entailed confiscating the national identity cards (NIC) of individuals, either at a checkpoint or during a search operation, and instructing these persons to show up at the army office or checkpoint to collect the NIC. When persons turned up at the designated office, they were instructed to report to the army office on a weekly or fortnightly basis and sign in. Based on patterns they observed in this process, women realized that when a person who was signing in regularly was asked not to return, this meant the person would be abducted or killed soon thereafter. As a result of learning this pattern, women were able to send men in their households to LTTE-controlled areas and thereby ensure their safety.

In the context of continuing structural inequalities within the Tamil community, the activism of women has, however, led to community backlash, with many women complaining that they face questions, ridicule, and even animosity from family members and the community by engaging in civic activism. For instance, women said they were scolded by family members who grumbled that the women received little by way of assistance toward livelihoods, despite contributing hours to the collective. When women were single, their status, women said, caused people in their communities to remark that they were constantly attending meetings and returning home with "things," implying that they were engaging in questionable activities in order to obtain said "things." Implicit here is the undermining of the status and integrity of women who engage in civic action by casting aspersions on their "honor" and integrity. At the same time, the community approaches these women for assistance and advice due to their links with NGOs, local government officials, and their knowledge of administrative processes. These various forms of reaction and interaction underscore the complexity of the space occupied by women in conflict and post-conflict settings.

Conclusion

Since the end of the armed conflict in May 2009, the process of militarization in Sri Lanka has accelerated and has become normalized and entrenched. Until January 2015, unofficial rules and processes that were put in place in 2009 continued to be used to control the northern population and to create insecurity among women. Although the situation has vastly improved, as of late July 2017 the vast military complex remained mostly in place, with the northern population continuing to complain of surveillance and harassment of certain sections of the community, such as rights activists. While Tamil women in the North are struggling to cope with the aftermath of the armed conflict, militarization has added an extra layer of complexity and complications that restrict their life choices. Despite attempts by various actors, including the state, to portray women and their experiences in essentialized ways, women challenge these notions by using creative and simple strategies, which rely on collective support and action for their success. Most important, the experiences of women illustrate that in reality women are not just victims or agents, but inhabit a space in which sometimes in the same instance they lay claim to victimhood and also exercise agency. Sri Lanka is a useful case study of postwar militarization that offers lessons in identifying the complex and insidious strategies utilized by the state to entrench militarization. Additionally, it increases understanding of the impact of militarization on the lives and life choices of women and the ways in which they live with and counter it.

NOTES

1. This chapter is based on primary data collected through individual interviews and focus group meetings with women chosen through purposive sampling in Jaffna, Vavuniya, Kilinochchi, Mullaitivu, and Mannar in the Northern Province. Thirty-four individual interviews were conducted, with each interview lasting 60–90 minutes. Fourteen focus groups were convened, with each discussion lasting 90–120 minutes. Interviews were also conducted with thirty-one community activists and development workers. All interviews and focus group meetings were conducted in the Tamil language and the recordings translated into English by the author. The identities and specific locations of the interviewees have been withheld on their request.
2. This is due to the opening of the North to rest of the country and the world from which it was previously cut off, and the postwar breakdown of social norms and networks, coupled with the re-emergence of conservative and patriarchal practices.
3. A June 2013 UNHCR report conducted a survey of 917 households, which found that 82 percent of respondents in Mullaitivu, 58 percent in Kilinochchi, and 57 percent in Jaffna said that the nearest army/navy/air force camp was less than one mile from their residence, while 63 percent in Trincomalee in the East said it was one to five miles from their residence (UNHCR 2013).
4. According to the UNHCR, 36 percent of respondents in Jaffna, 30 percent in Mannar and Mullaitivu, and 25 percent in Kilinochchi stated that the military was engaged in activities such as building houses for returnees; 24 percent of respondents in Kilinochchi, 21 percent in Mullaitivu, and 19 percent in Jaffna stated that the military was involved in development activities in their villages (UNHCR 2013).
5. "Victimcy" is the term constructed by Mats Utas to problematize the oppositional way in which victimhood and agency are positioned. He argues that the new term describes the agency of women who use victimhood as one of many survival strategies when navigating the social landscape in war zones (Utas 2005).
6. Since 2012, the food security situation in the North worsened. A comprehensive assessment by the World Food Programme (WFP) conducted in late March 2012 in the Northern and Eastern Provinces found that 44 percent of the population could not get adequate, nutritious food (WFP 2012). According to an August 2013 WFP study of 300 households interviewed over two days in Vavuniya and Mullaitivu districts, half reported selling assets, such as jewelry, to cope with diminishing income and rising debt (WFP 2013).

REFERENCES

Abu-Lughod, Lila. 1990. "The Romance of Resistance: Tracing Transformations of Power through Bedouin Women." *American Ethnologist* 17, no. 1: 41–55.
Bernazzoli, Richelle M., and Colin Flint. 2009. "Power, Place and Militarism: Toward a Comparative Geographic Analysis of Militarization." *Geography Compass* 3, no. 1: 393–411.

Bernazzoli, Richelle M., and Colin Flint. 2010. "Embodying the Garrison State? Everyday Geographies of Militarization in American Society." *Political Geography* 29, no. 3: 157–166.

Duschinski, Haley. 2009. "Destiny Effects: Militarization, State Power, and Punitive Containment in Kashmir Valley." *Anthropolitical Quarterly* 82, no. 3: 691–717.

Enloe, Cynthia. 2000. *Maneuvers: The International Politics of Militarizing Women's Lives.* Berkeley: University of California Press.

Laliberte, Nicole. 2013. "In Pursuit of a Monster: Militarization and (In)Security in Northern Uganda." *Geopolitics* 18, no. 4: 1–20.

Palakidner, Ananth. 2009. "Security Forces to Assist Rehabilitation and Reconstruction- Maj Gen Marl." *Sunday Observer* 30 (August).

Pickering, Sharon, and Amanda Third. 2003. "Castrating Conflict: Gender(ed) Terrorists and Terrorism Domesticated." *Social Alternatives* 22, no. 2: 8–15.

Satkunanathan, Ambika. 2012. "Whose Nation? Power, Agency, Gender and Tamil Nationalism." In *Sri Lankan Republic at 40: Reflections on Constitutional History, Theory and Practice*, edited by Asanga Welikala, 612–660. Colombo: Centre for Policy Alternatives.

Satkunanathan, Ambika. 2013. "Militarisation as Panacea: Development and Reconciliation in Post-war Sri Lanka." *Open Democracy*, March 19, 2013. https://www.opendemocracy.net/opensecurity/ambika-satkunanathan/militarisation-as-panacea-development-and-reconciliation-in-post-w.

Satkunanathan, Ambika. 2014. "The Executive and the Shadow State in Sri Lanka." In *Sri Lankan Presidentialism 35 Years On: Provenance, Problems, Prospects*, edited by Asanga Welikala, 370–398. Colombo: Centre for Policy Alternatives.

Stern, Maria. 2006. "'We' the Subject: The Power and Failure of (In) Security." *Security Dialogue* 37, no. 2: 187–205.

United Nations High Commissioner for Refugees (UNHCR). 2013. *Durable Solutions? A Protection Assessment of Sri Lankan Internally Displaced Persons Who Have Returned, Relocated or Are Locally Integrating ("Tool Three"): Data and Analysis.* Sri Lanka: UNHCR.

Utas, Mats. 2005. "West-African Warscapes: Victimcy, Girlfriending, Soldiering: Tactic Agency in a Young Woman's Social Navigation of the Liberian War Zone." *Anthropological Quarterly* 78, no. 2: 403–430.

World Food Programme (WFP). 2012. *Food Security in the Northern and Eastern Provinces of Sri Lanka: A Comprehensive Food Security Assessment Report.* Sri Lanka: World Food Programme.

World Food Programme (WFP). 2013. "Food Security, Nutrition Situation." Presentation in Sri Lanka, on file with author.

Yuval-Davis, Nira. 1997. *Gender and Nation.* London: Sage Publications.

INDEX

....

Tables, figures, and boxes are indicated by an italic *t*, *f*, and *b* following the page/paragraph number.

Colombia
  agrarian reform in, 524, 527
  agrarian struggles in, 523–26
  anti-restitution armies in, 527
  ANMUCIC (Asociación Nacional de Mujeres
    Campesinas e Indígenas de Colombia), 525
  armed conflict in, 521, 526
  children in, born of sexual violence, 152
  Civil Code in, 524
  Constitution of, 523, 525
  CRSV data from, 320, 323
  DDR process in, 448
  DDR programming in, 446t, 449
  displaced persons in, 526
  Fuerzas Armadas Revolucionarias de
    Colombia (Revolutionary Armed Forces
    of Colombia), 371, 448, 521
  gender equality in, 525
  gender inequalities in, 523
  impunity in, 527
  Integrated Rural Development policy, 524
  Justice and Peace Law in, 527, 530n7
  land grabs in, 526
  land restitution in, 521–29
  land rights in, 522–25
  Law on Victims and Land Restitution (2011), 521
  Ligas Campesinas (peasant leagues, 523
  market-led agrarian reform law in, 524–25
  Peace Accords in, 521
  peace process in, 421, 425
  peasant movement in, 524
  peasant-reserve zones in, 528
  reparations in, 256, 527–29
  Revolutionary Armed Forces of Colombia
    (see Fuerzas Armadas Revolucionarias de
    Colombia)
  rural policies in, family-centered, 523
  sexual and class domination in, 524
  sexual violence in, 234–37, 526
  transitional justice in, 521–29
  unprotected women in, 525
  Victims and Land Restitution Law in, 526–29
  women in combat roles in, 371
  women's employment in, 79–80
  women's empowerment in, 351
  women's property rights in, 523
  women's rights in, patriarchal denial of, 525

colonialism, 63, 66, 456, 459–60
  administrative aspects of, 271
  armies under, 268, 269
  capitalism and, 270
  citizenship and, 63
  colonies under, pacification of, 267–73
  in East Jerusalem, 558–65
  economies of, women in, 270–71
  European women's involvement in, 271–72
  gender analysis of, 25, 265, 268
  masculinity and, 268–69
  militaristic nature of, 272–73
  political status and, 66
  Portugal, colonialism of, 459
  post-colonial theory and, 459
  power matrix of, 465–66n3
  sex and gender coercion and, 265–66
  social relations and, 459–60
  violence of, 267
Columbus, Christopher, 305, 309
combatants, gender significations of, 12
command responsibility, 97
Commission on the Status of Women (UN), 123
Committee on the Elimination of All
    Forms of Discrimination Against
    Women, 171, 172, 174, 176, 178–82.
    See also conventions: Convention
    on the Elimination of All Forms of
    Discrimination Against Women
Committee Against Torture, 514
communities, breakdown of, during
    conflict, 359–60, 362
community stigma, xxxix
complementarity, 172–73
  effects of, 231–34, 236
  facets of, 226–28
  gender-sensitive approach to, 226
  narrow construction of, 227
  positive, 227, 231
  success of, 229, 232–33
concentration camps, 270
conflict
  aftermath of, and LOAC, 39
  alternative mappings of, 288
  assessment of, 49, 53
  CEDAW applied to, 173–77
  civilian health risks during, 354